WONDER WOMAN BLACK and GOLD

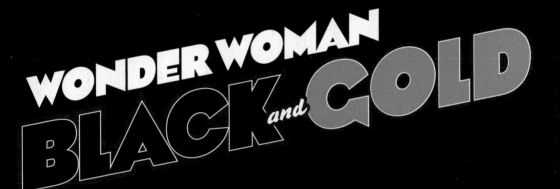

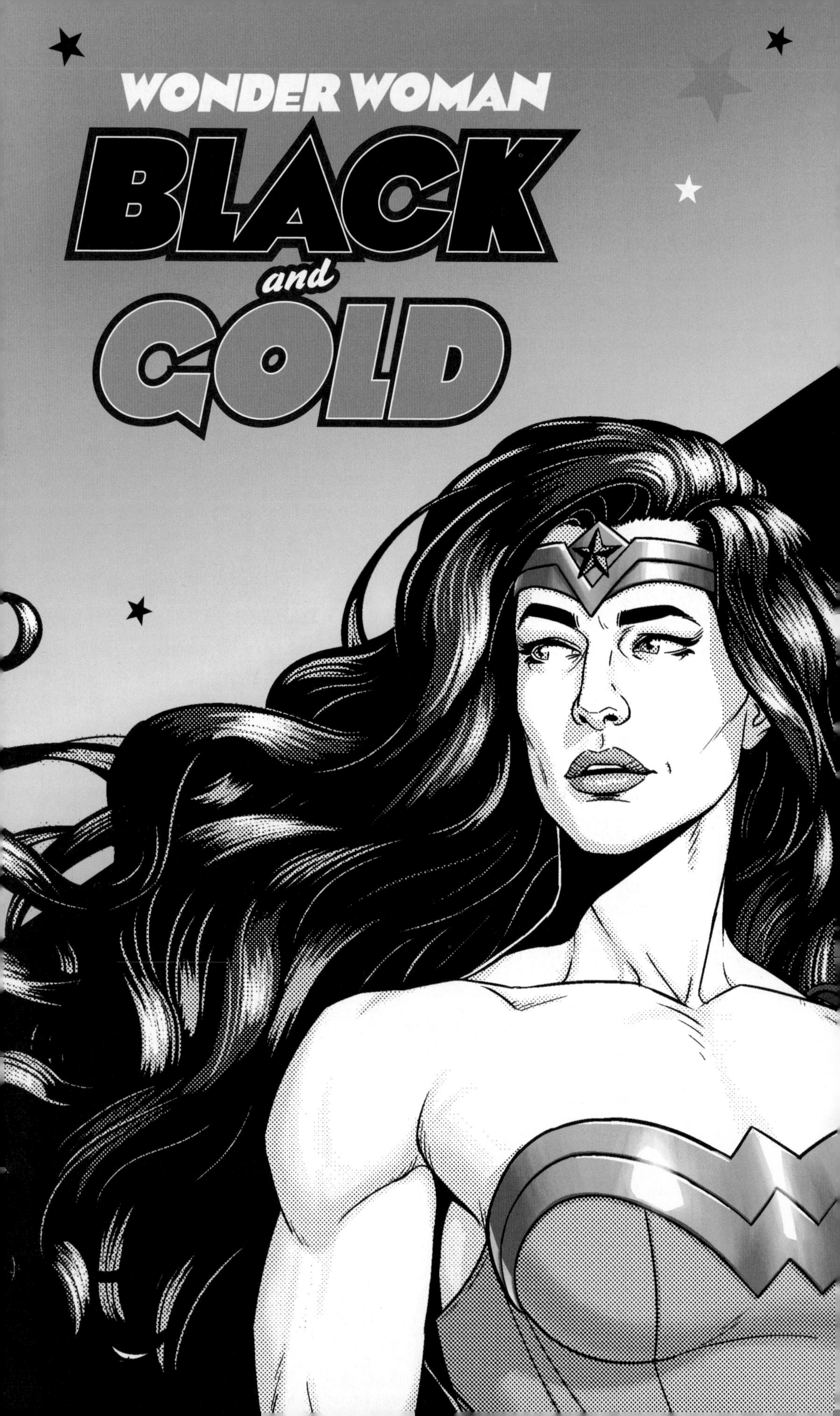
WONDER WOMAN
BLACK
and
GOLD

AJ Mendez
Nadia Shammas
John Arcudi
Amy Reeder
Becky Cloonan
Mariko Tamaki
Che Grayson,
Tillie Walden
Stephanie Williams
Rachel Smythe
Janet Harvey Nevala
Robert Venditti
Paula Sevenbergen
Nnedi Okorafor
Aimee Garcia
Andrew Constant
Paul Azaceta
Sina Grace
Andrew MacLean
Sherri L. Smith
Peter J. Tomasi
Sanya Anwar
Kurt Busiek
Josie Campbell
Trung Le Nguyen
Marguerite Sauvage
Liam Sharp
Michael W. Conrad
Christos Gage
Dr. Sheena C. Howard

writers

Ming Doyle
Morgan Beem
Ryan Sook
Amy Reeder
Becky Cloonan
Jamie McKelvie
Corin Howell
Tillie Walden
Ashley A. Woods
Rachel Smythe
Megan Levens
Steve Epting
Inaki Miranda
Jack T. Cole
Sebastian Fiumara
Nicola Scott

Paul Azaceta
Leonardo Romero
Andrew MacLean
Colleen Doran
Christian Alamy
Sanya Anwar
Benjamin Dewey
Carlos D'Anda
Trung Le Nguyen
Marguerite Sauvage
Liam Sharp
Noah Bailey
Kevin Maguire
Jamal Campbell

artists

Jordie Bellaire
Eva De La Cruz
Annette Kwok
John Kalisz
Adriano Lucas

colorists

Becca Carey
Ariana Maher
Mike Heisler
Gabriela Downie
Pat Brosseau
Simon Bowland
AndWorld Design
Rob Leigh
Dave Sharpe
Wes Abbott
Richard Starkings
Comicraft's Tyler Smith
Clayton Cowles

letterers

Jen Bartel

collection cover artist

Wonder Woman created by
William Moulton Marston

Superman created by
Jerry Siegel and Joe Shuster
By Special Arrangement with
the Jerry Siegel Family

BRITTANY HOLZHERR
Editor – Original Series & Collected Edition

JAMIE S. RICH
DIEGO LOPEZ
BIXIE MATHIEU
Editors – Original Series

STEVE COOK
Design Director – Books

MEGEN BELLERSEN
Publication Design

ERIN VANOVER
Publication Production

RYANE LYNN HILL
Production Editor

MARIE JAVINS
Editor-in-Chief, DC Comics

ANNE DEPIES
Senior VP – General Manager

JIM LEE
Publisher & Chief Creative Officer

DON FALLETTI
VP – Manufacturing Operations & Workflow Management

LAWRENCE GANEM
VP – Talent Services

ALISON GILL
Senior VP – Manufacturing & Operations

JEFFREY KAUFMAN
VP – Editorial Strategy & Programming

NICK J. NAPOLITANO
VP – Manufacturing Administration & Design

NANCY SPEARS
VP – Revenue

WONDER WOMAN BLACK & GOLD

DC Comics, 4000 Warner Blvd., Bldg. 700, 2nd Floor, Burbank, CA 91522
Printed by Transcontinental Printing Interweb Montreal, a division of Transcontinental Printing Inc., Boucherville, QC, Canada. 7/7/23. First Printing.
ISBN: 978-1-77952-044-9

Library of Congress Cataloging-in-Publication Data is available.

Cover by Jen Bartel

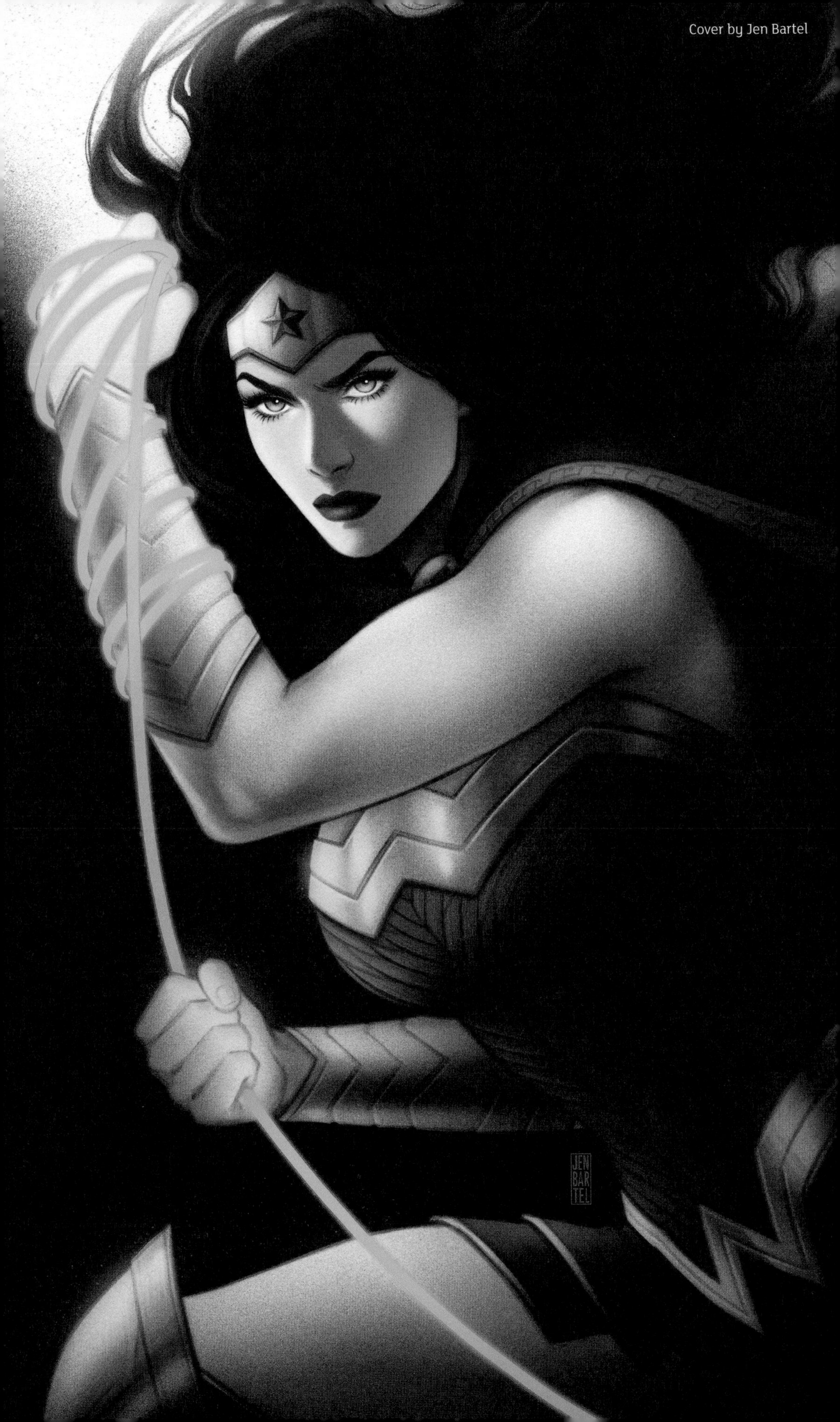
JEN BARTEL

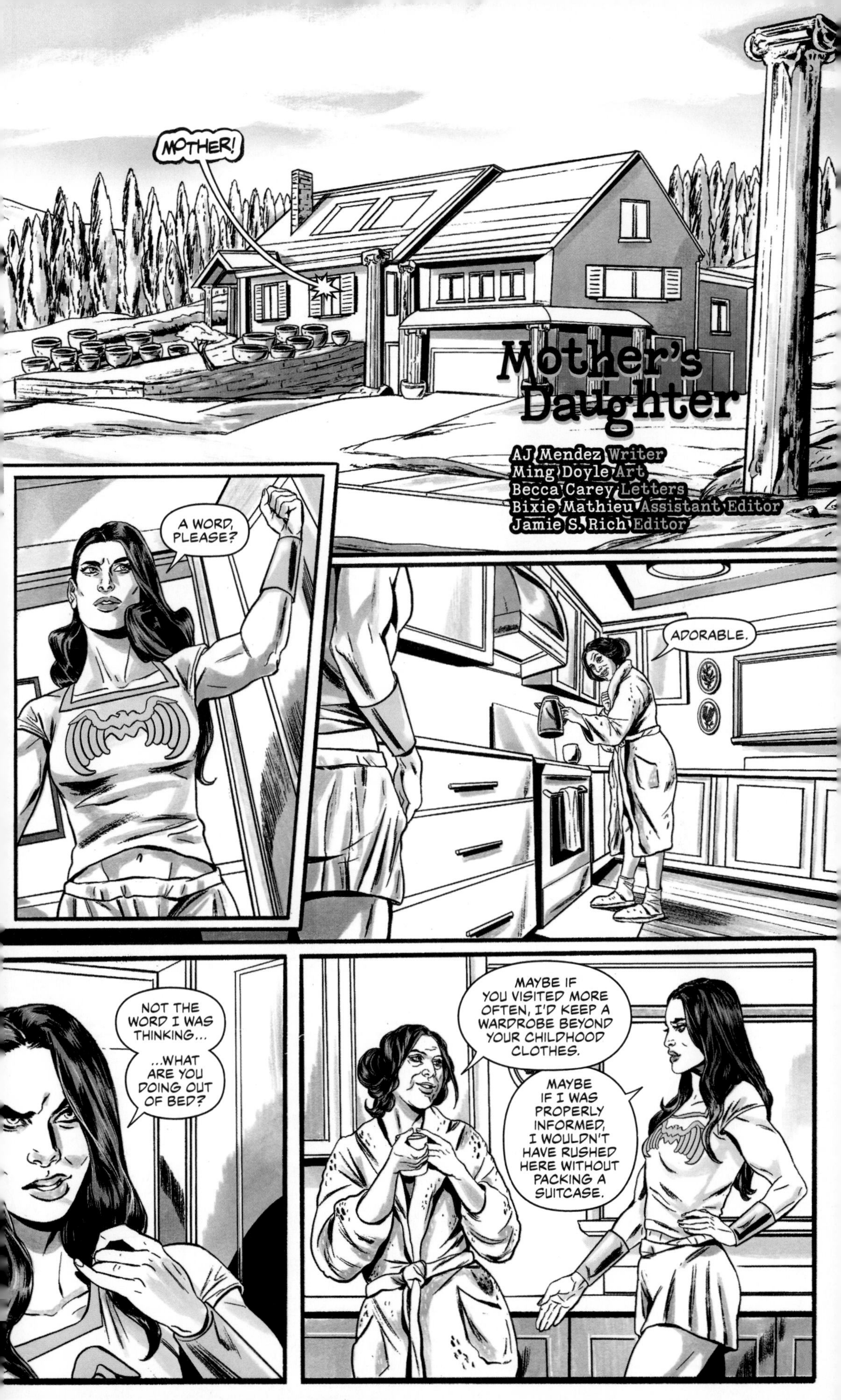

MOTHER!
Mother's Daughter
AJ Mendez Writer
Ming Doyle Art
Becca Carey Letters
Bixie Mathieu Assistant Editor
Jamie S. Rich Editor
A WORD, PLEASE?
ADORABLE.
NOT THE WORD I WAS THINKING...
...WHAT ARE YOU DOING OUT OF BED?
MAYBE IF YOU VISITED MORE OFTEN, I'D KEEP A WARDROBE BEYOND YOUR CHILDHOOD CLOTHES.
MAYBE IF I WAS PROPERLY INFORMED, I WOULDN'T HAVE RUSHED HERE WITHOUT PACKING A SUITCASE.

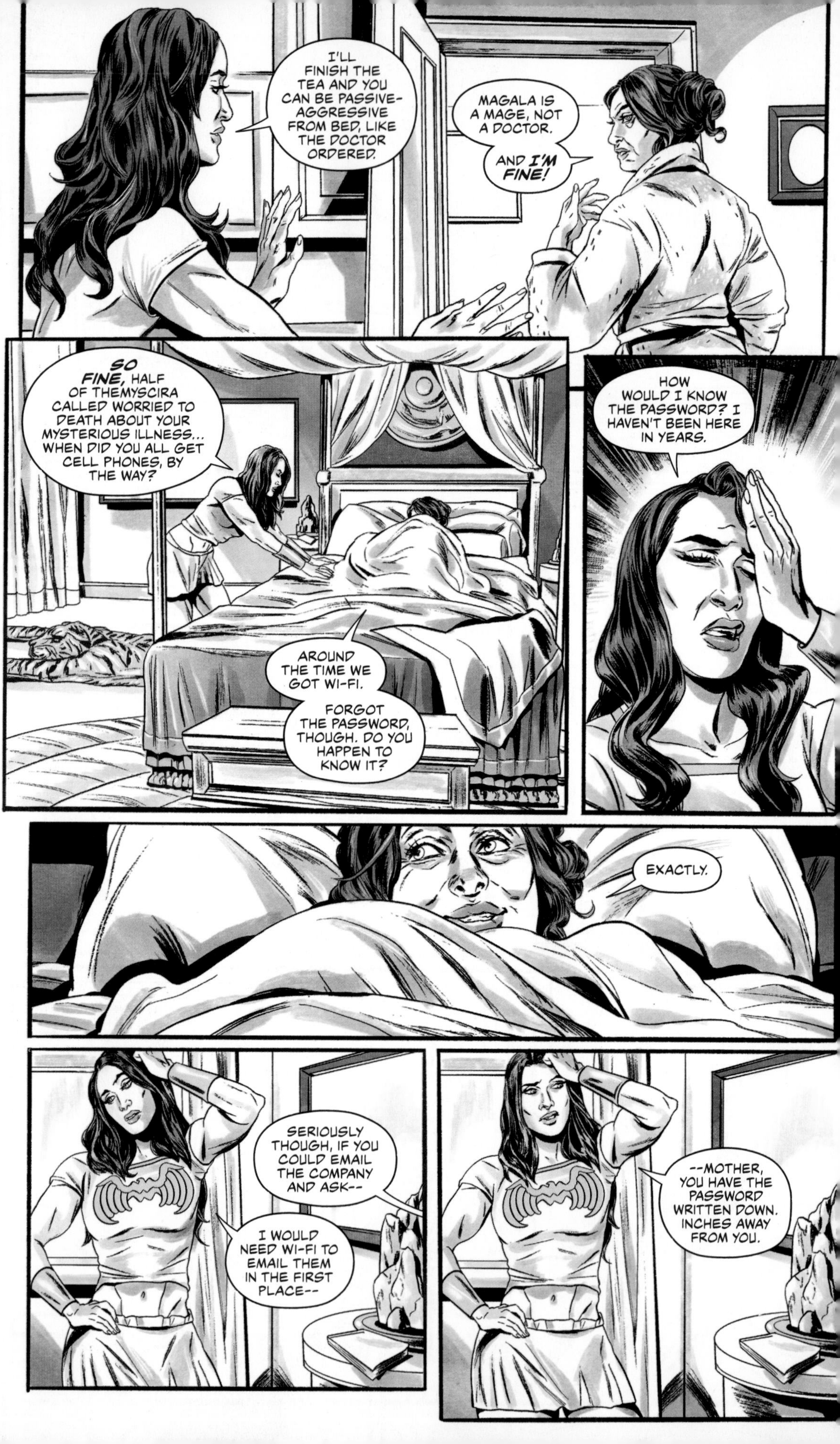
I'LL FINISH THE TEA AND YOU CAN BE PASSIVE-AGGRESSIVE FROM BED, LIKE THE DOCTOR ORDERED.
MAGALA IS A MAGE, NOT A DOCTOR.
AND *I'M FINE!*
SO FINE, HALF OF THEMYSCIRA CALLED WORRIED TO DEATH ABOUT YOUR MYSTERIOUS ILLNESS... WHEN DID YOU ALL GET CELL PHONES, BY THE WAY?
AROUND THE TIME WE GOT WI-FI.
FORGOT THE PASSWORD, THOUGH. DO YOU HAPPEN TO KNOW IT?
HOW WOULD I KNOW THE PASSWORD? I HAVEN'T BEEN HERE IN YEARS.
EXACTLY.
SERIOUSLY THOUGH, IF YOU COULD EMAIL THE COMPANY AND ASK--
I WOULD NEED WI-FI TO EMAIL THEM IN THE FIRST PLACE--
--MOTHER, YOU HAVE THE PASSWORD WRITTEN DOWN. INCHES AWAY FROM YOU.

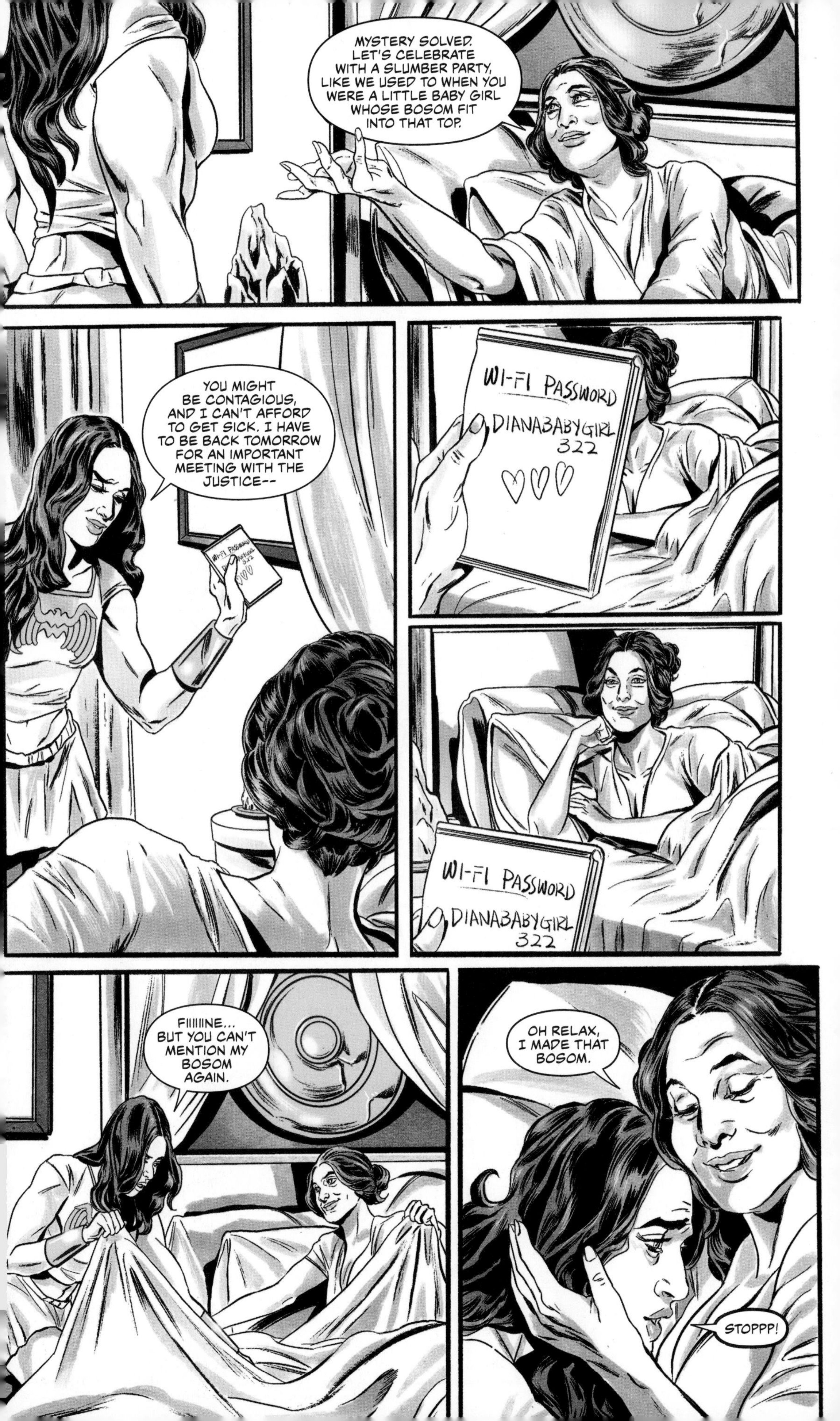
MYSTERY SOLVED. LET'S CELEBRATE WITH A SLUMBER PARTY, LIKE WE USED TO WHEN YOU WERE A LITTLE BABY GIRL WHOSE BOSOM FIT INTO THAT TOP.
YOU MIGHT BE CONTAGIOUS, AND I CAN'T AFFORD TO GET SICK. I HAVE TO BE BACK TOMORROW FOR AN IMPORTANT MEETING WITH THE JUSTICE--
WI-FI PASSWORD
DIANABABYGIRL 322
WI-FI PASSWORD
DIANABABYGIRL 322
FIIIIINE... BUT YOU CAN'T MENTION MY BOSOM AGAIN.
OH RELAX, I MADE THAT BOSOM.
STOPPP!

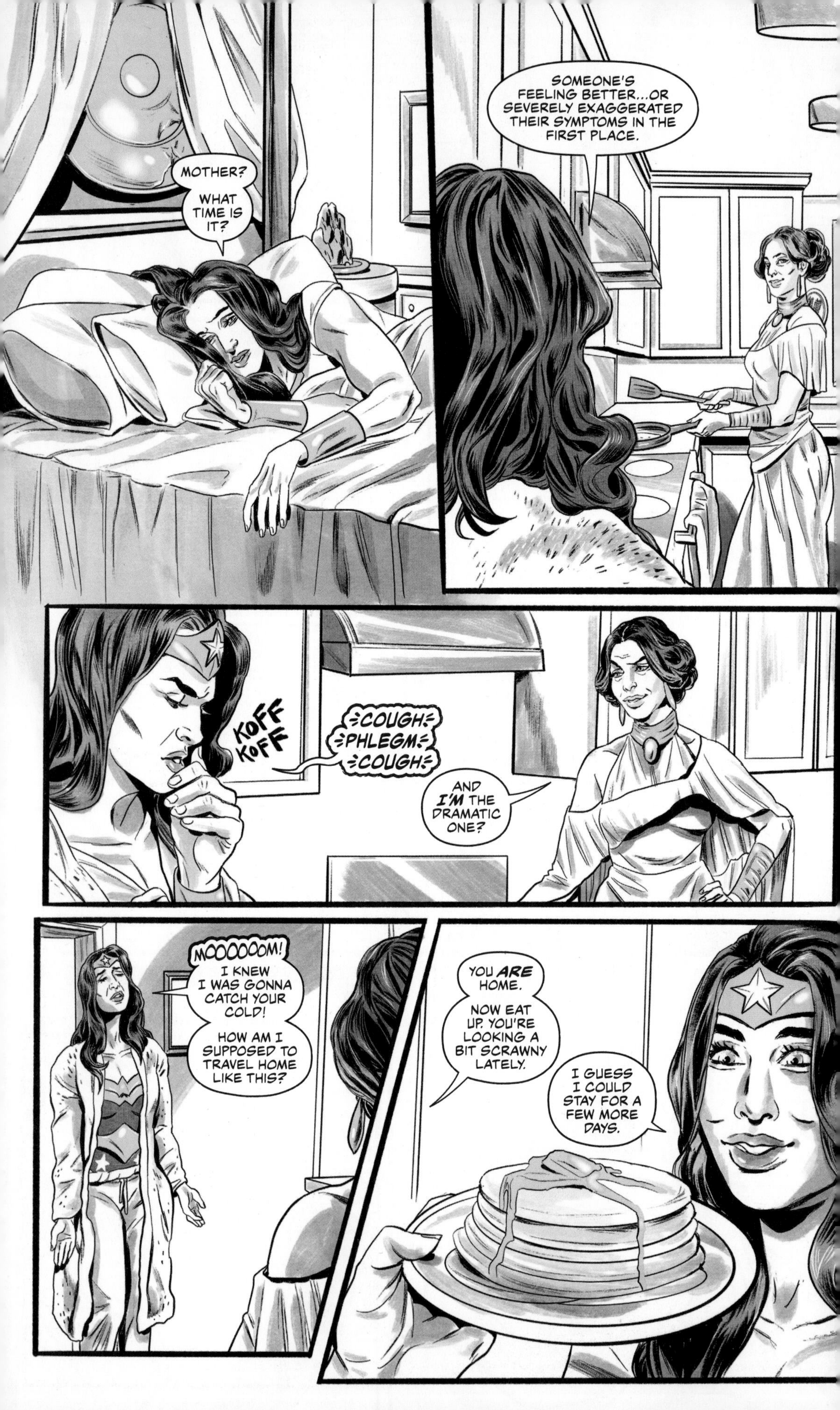
MOTHER?
WHAT TIME IS IT?
SOMEONE'S FEELING BETTER...OR SEVERELY EXAGGERATED THEIR SYMPTOMS IN THE FIRST PLACE.
KOFF KOFF
COUGH PHLEGM COUGH
AND I'M THE DRAMATIC ONE?
MOOOOOOM!
I KNEW I WAS GONNA CATCH YOUR COLD!
HOW AM I SUPPOSED TO TRAVEL HOME LIKE THIS?
YOU ARE HOME.
NOW EAT UP. YOU'RE LOOKING A BIT SCRAWNY LATELY.
I GUESS I COULD STAY FOR A FEW MORE DAYS.

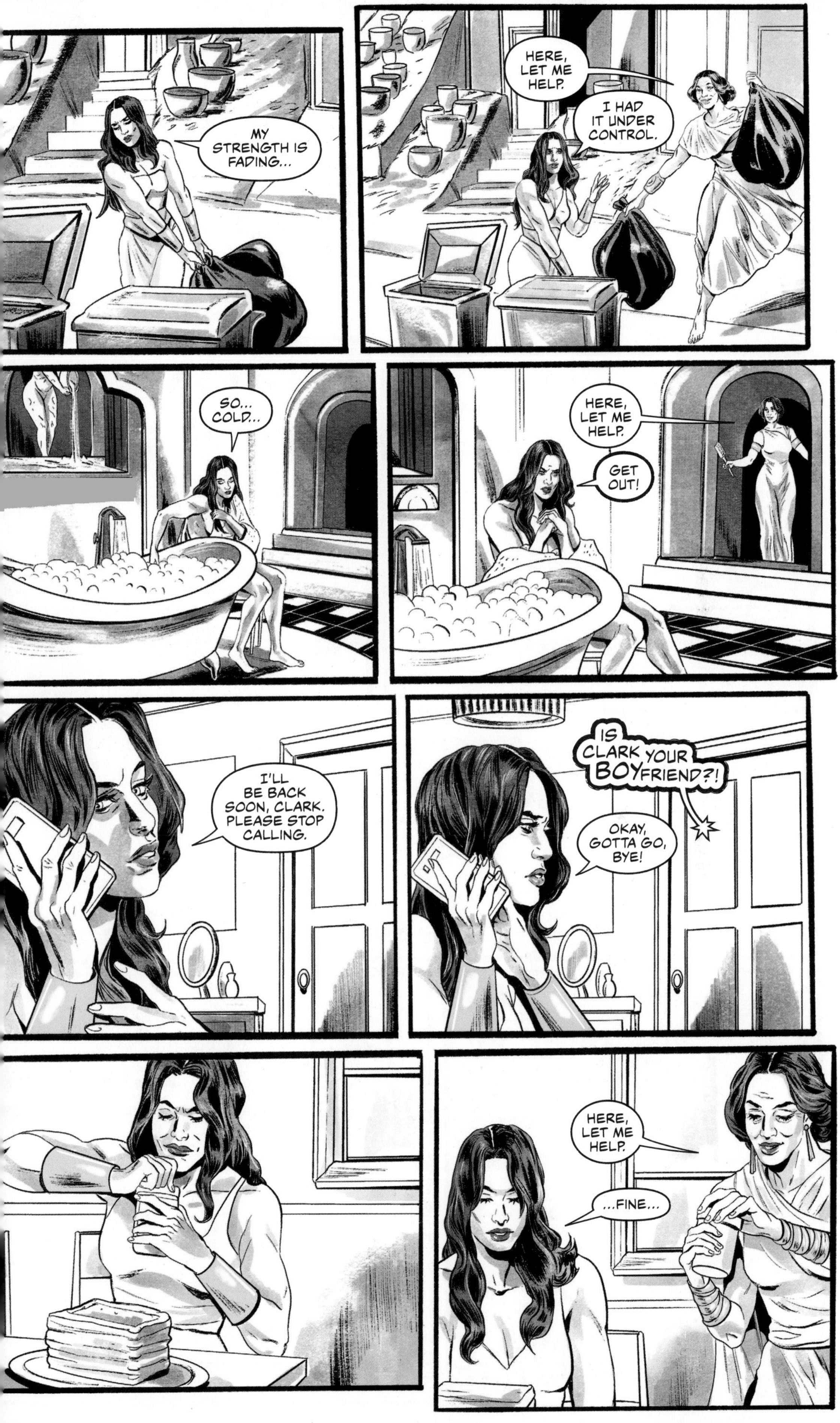
MY STRENGTH IS FADING...
HERE, LET ME HELP.
I HAD IT UNDER CONTROL.
SO... COLD...
HERE, LET ME HELP.
GET OUT!
I'LL BE BACK SOON, CLARK. PLEASE STOP CALLING.
IS CLARK YOUR BOYFRIEND?!
OKAY, GOTTA GO, BYE!
HERE, LET ME HELP.
...FINE...

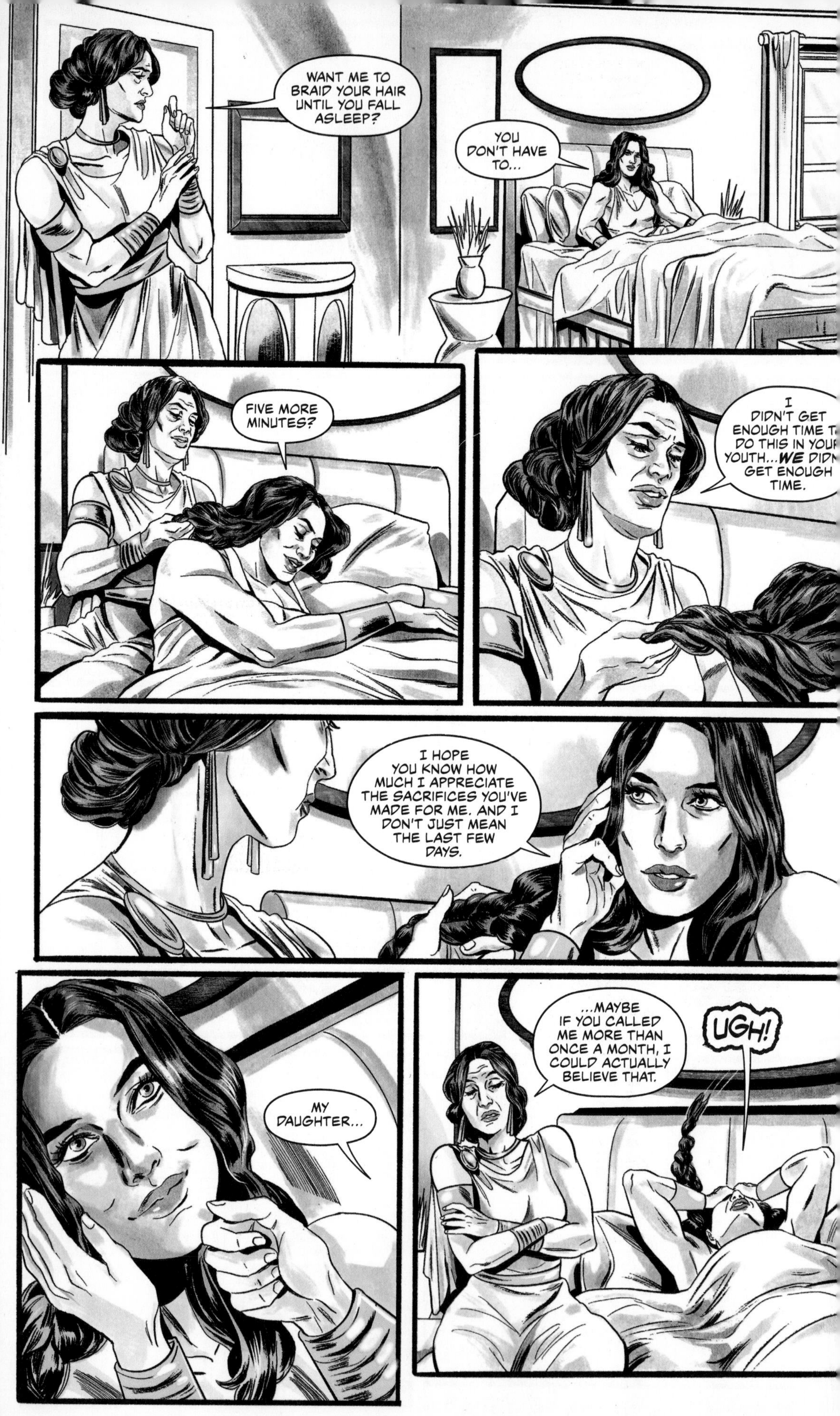
WANT ME TO BRAID YOUR HAIR UNTIL YOU FALL ASLEEP?
YOU DON'T HAVE TO...
FIVE MORE MINUTES?
I DIDN'T GET ENOUGH TIME T DO THIS IN YOUR YOUTH...WE DIDN GET ENOUGH TIME.
I HOPE YOU KNOW HOW MUCH I APPRECIATE THE SACRIFICES YOU'VE MADE FOR ME. AND I DON'T JUST MEAN THE LAST FEW DAYS.
MY DAUGHTER...
...MAYBE IF YOU CALLED ME MORE THAN ONCE A MONTH, I COULD ACTUALLY BELIEVE THAT.
UGH!

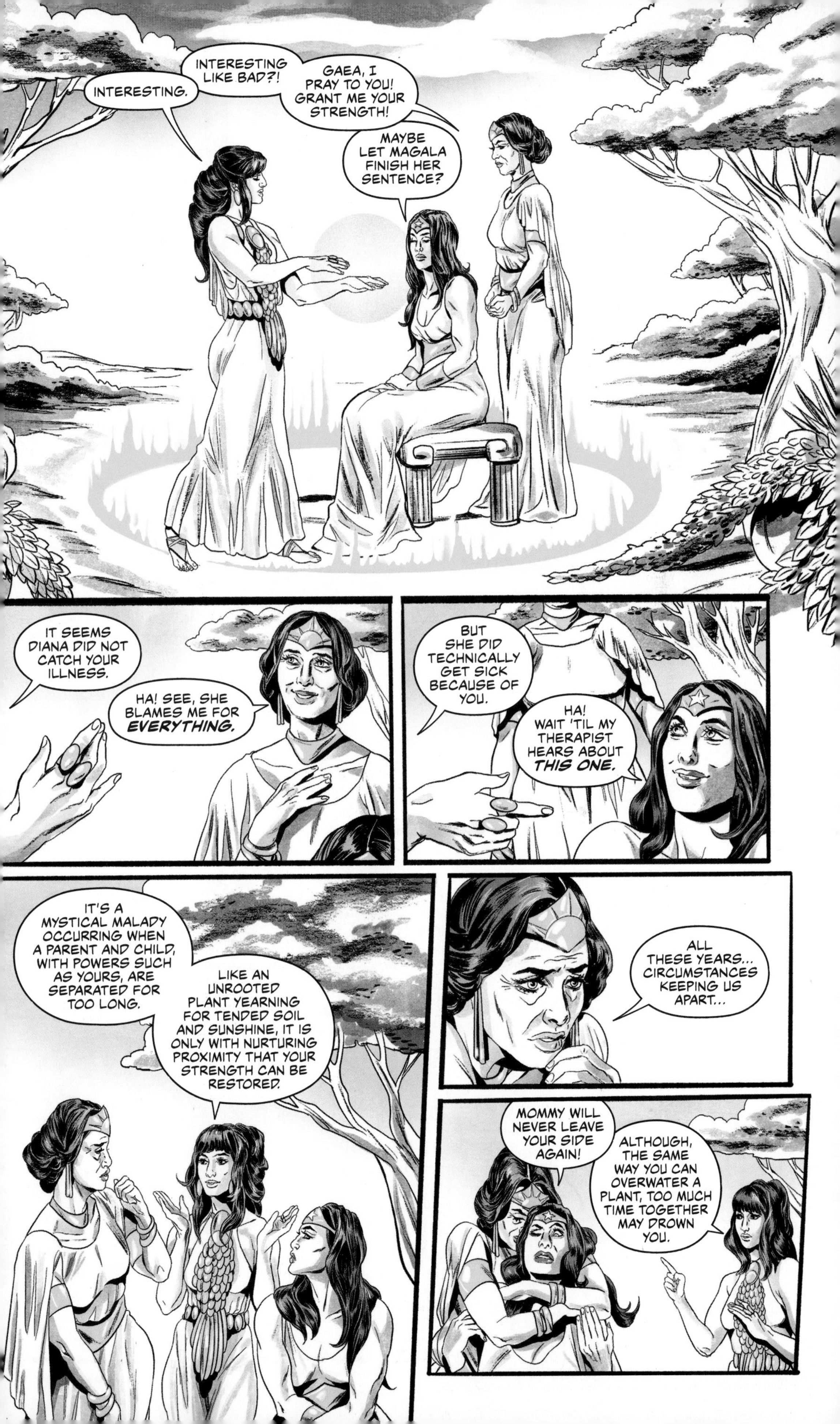

INTERESTING.
INTERESTING LIKE BAD?!
GAEA, I PRAY TO YOU! GRANT ME YOUR STRENGTH!
MAYBE LET MAGALA FINISH HER SENTENCE?
IT SEEMS DIANA DID NOT CATCH YOUR ILLNESS.
HA! SEE, SHE BLAMES ME FOR *EVERYTHING.*
BUT SHE DID TECHNICALLY GET SICK BECAUSE OF YOU.
HA! WAIT 'TIL MY THERAPIST HEARS ABOUT *THIS ONE.*
IT'S A MYSTICAL MALADY OCCURRING WHEN A PARENT AND CHILD, WITH POWERS SUCH AS YOURS, ARE SEPARATED FOR TOO LONG.
LIKE AN UNROOTED PLANT YEARNING FOR TENDED SOIL AND SUNSHINE, IT IS ONLY WITH NURTURING PROXIMITY THAT YOUR STRENGTH CAN BE RESTORED.
ALL THESE YEARS... CIRCUMSTANCES KEEPING US APART...
MOMMY WILL NEVER LEAVE YOUR SIDE AGAIN!
ALTHOUGH, THE SAME WAY YOU CAN OVERWATER A PLANT, TOO MUCH TIME TOGETHER MAY DROWN YOU.

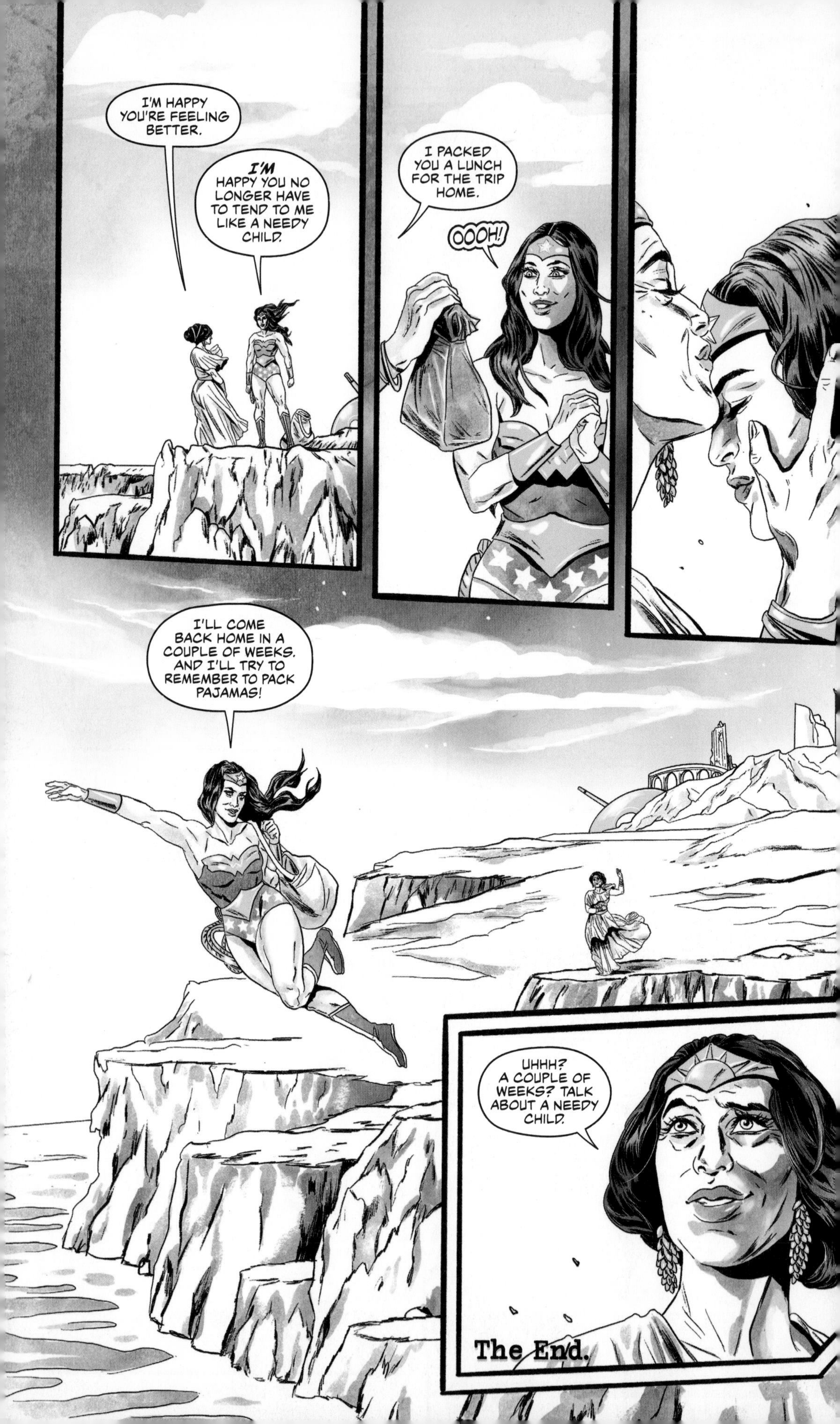
I'M HAPPY YOU'RE FEELING BETTER.
I'M HAPPY YOU NO LONGER HAVE TO TEND TO ME LIKE A NEEDY CHILD.
I PACKED YOU A LUNCH FOR THE TRIP HOME.
OOOH!
I'LL COME BACK HOME IN A COUPLE OF WEEKS. AND I'LL TRY TO REMEMBER TO PACK PAJAMAS!
UHHH? A COUPLE OF WEEKS? TALK ABOUT A NEEDY CHILD.
The End.

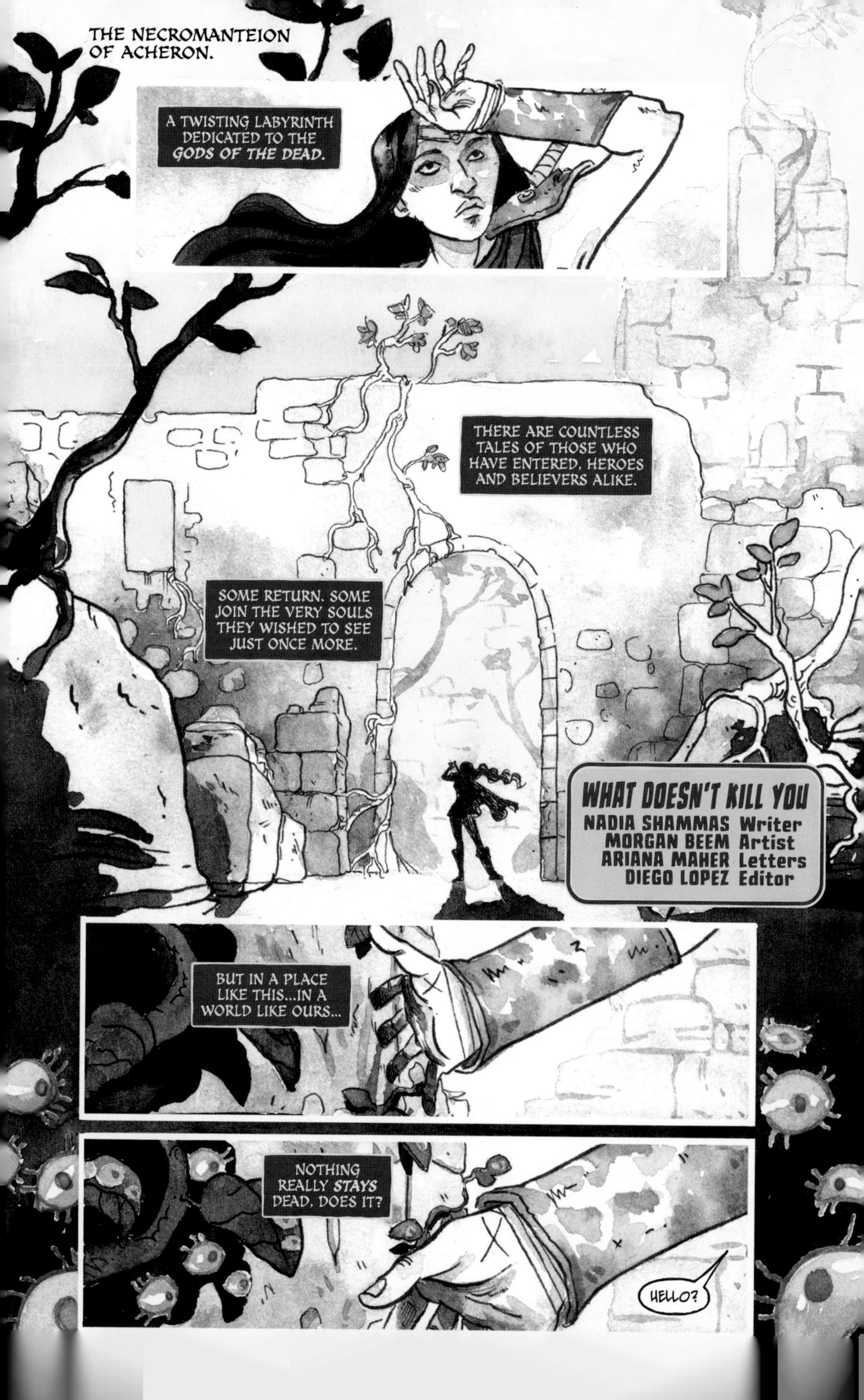

THE NECROMANTEION OF ACHERON.
A TWISTING LABYRINTH DEDICATED TO THE GODS OF THE DEAD.
THERE ARE COUNTLESS TALES OF THOSE WHO HAVE ENTERED, HEROES AND BELIEVERS ALIKE.
SOME RETURN. SOME JOIN THE VERY SOULS THEY WISHED TO SEE JUST ONCE MORE.
WHAT DOESN'T KILL YOU
NADIA SHAMMAS Writer
MORGAN BEEM Artist
ARIANA MAHER Letters
DIEGO LOPEZ Editor
BUT IN A PLACE LIKE THIS...IN A WORLD LIKE OURS...
NOTHING REALLY STAYS DEAD, DOES IT?
HELLO?

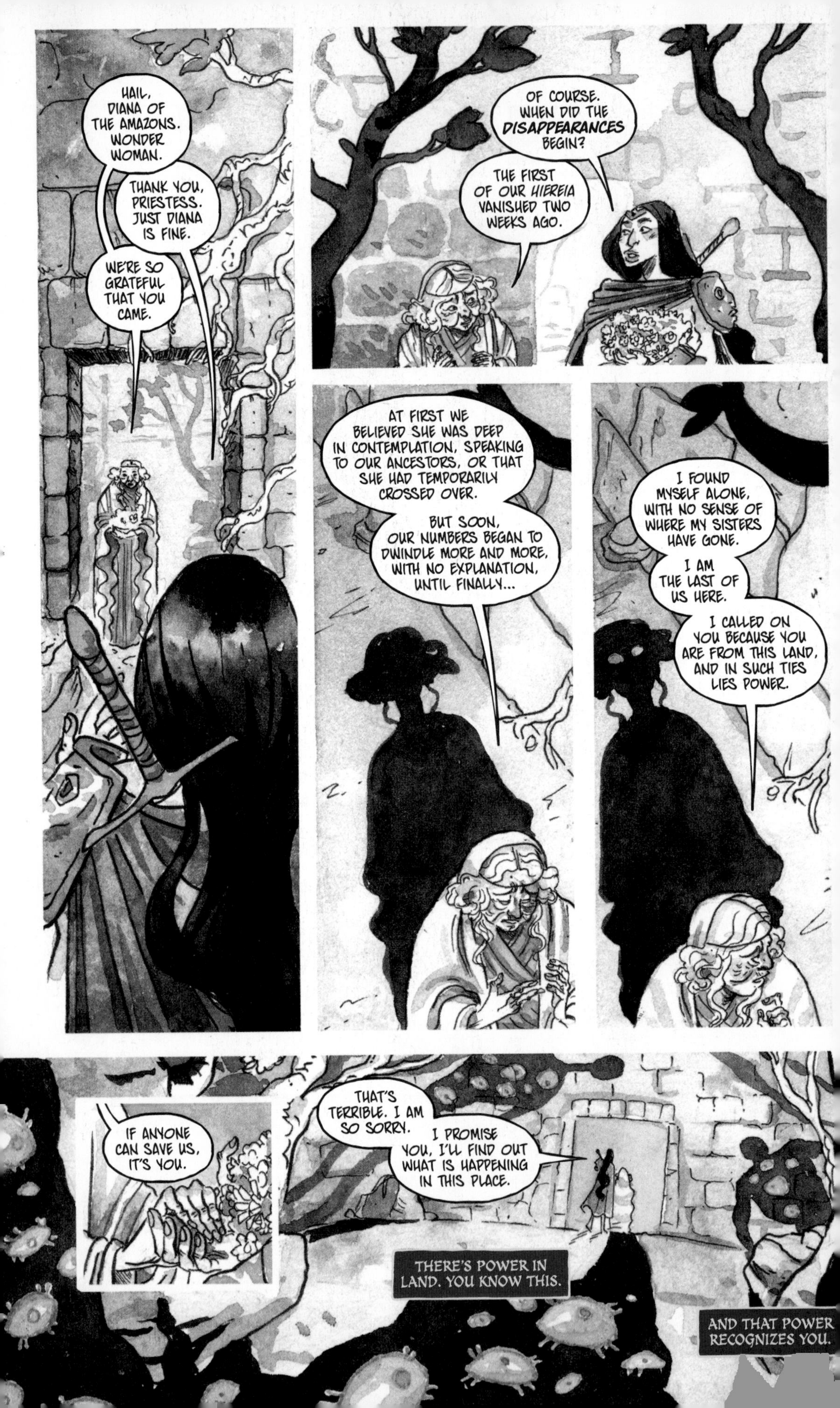

HAIL, DIANA OF THE AMAZONS. WONDER WOMAN.
THANK YOU, PRIESTESS. JUST DIANA IS FINE.
WE'RE SO GRATEFUL THAT YOU CAME.
OF COURSE. WHEN DID THE DISAPPEARANCES BEGIN?
THE FIRST OF OUR HIEREIA VANISHED TWO WEEKS AGO.
AT FIRST WE BELIEVED SHE WAS DEEP IN CONTEMPLATION, SPEAKING TO OUR ANCESTORS, OR THAT SHE HAD TEMPORARILY CROSSED OVER.
BUT SOON, OUR NUMBERS BEGAN TO DWINDLE MORE AND MORE, WITH NO EXPLANATION, UNTIL FINALLY...
I FOUND MYSELF ALONE, WITH NO SENSE OF WHERE MY SISTERS HAVE GONE.
I AM THE LAST OF US HERE.
I CALLED ON YOU BECAUSE YOU ARE FROM THIS LAND, AND IN SUCH TIES LIES POWER.
IF ANYONE CAN SAVE US, IT'S YOU.
THAT'S TERRIBLE. I AM SO SORRY.
I PROMISE YOU, I'LL FIND OUT WHAT IS HAPPENING IN THIS PLACE.
THERE'S POWER IN LAND. YOU KNOW THIS.
AND THAT POWER RECOGNIZES YOU.

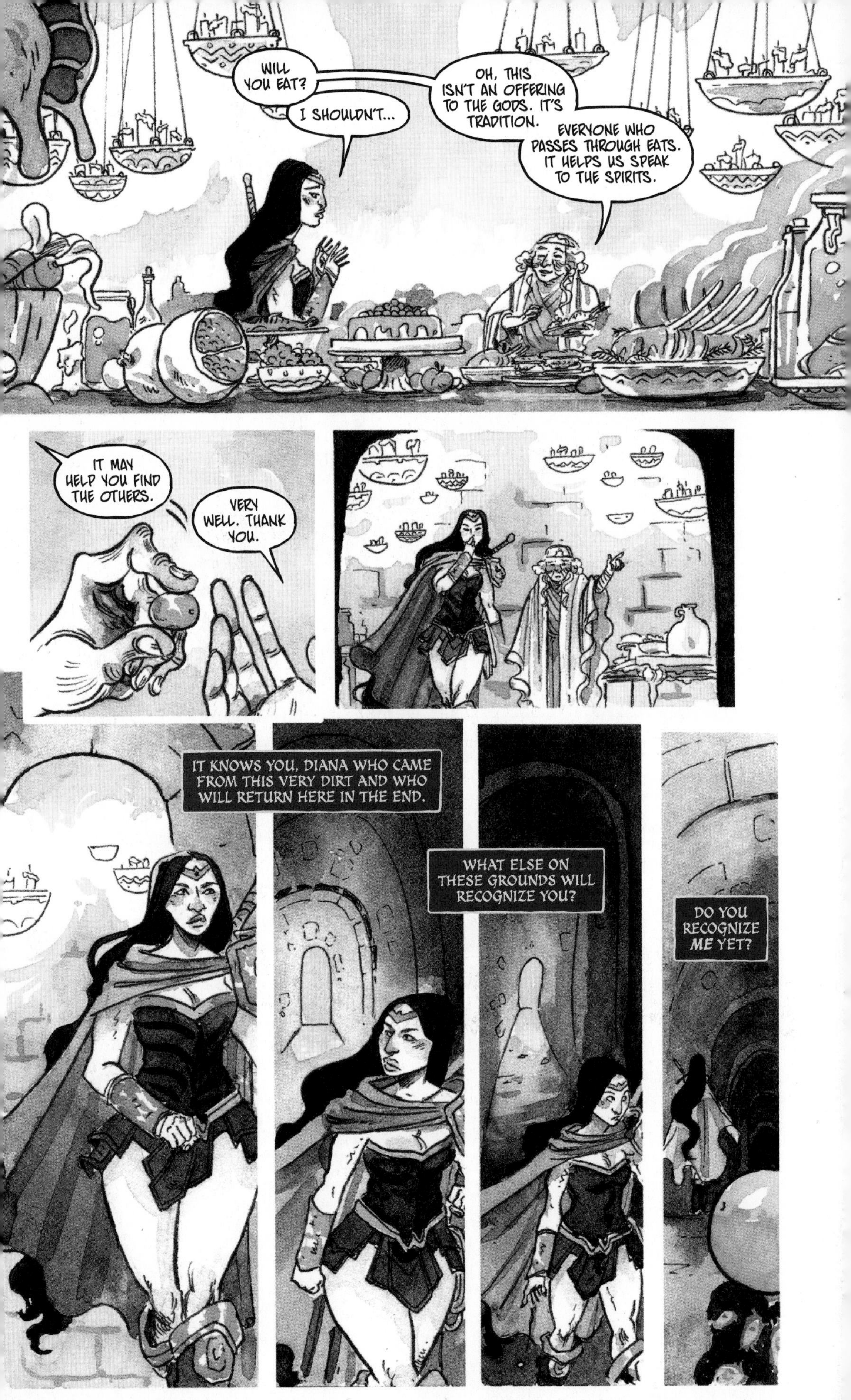
WILL YOU EAT?
I SHOULDN'T...
OH, THIS ISN'T AN OFFERING TO THE GODS. IT'S TRADITION.
EVERYONE WHO PASSES THROUGH EATS. IT HELPS US SPEAK TO THE SPIRITS.
IT MAY HELP YOU FIND THE OTHERS.
VERY WELL. THANK YOU.
IT KNOWS YOU, DIANA WHO CAME FROM THIS VERY DIRT AND WHO WILL RETURN HERE IN THE END.
WHAT ELSE ON THESE GROUNDS WILL RECOGNIZE YOU?
DO YOU RECOGNIZE *ME* YET?

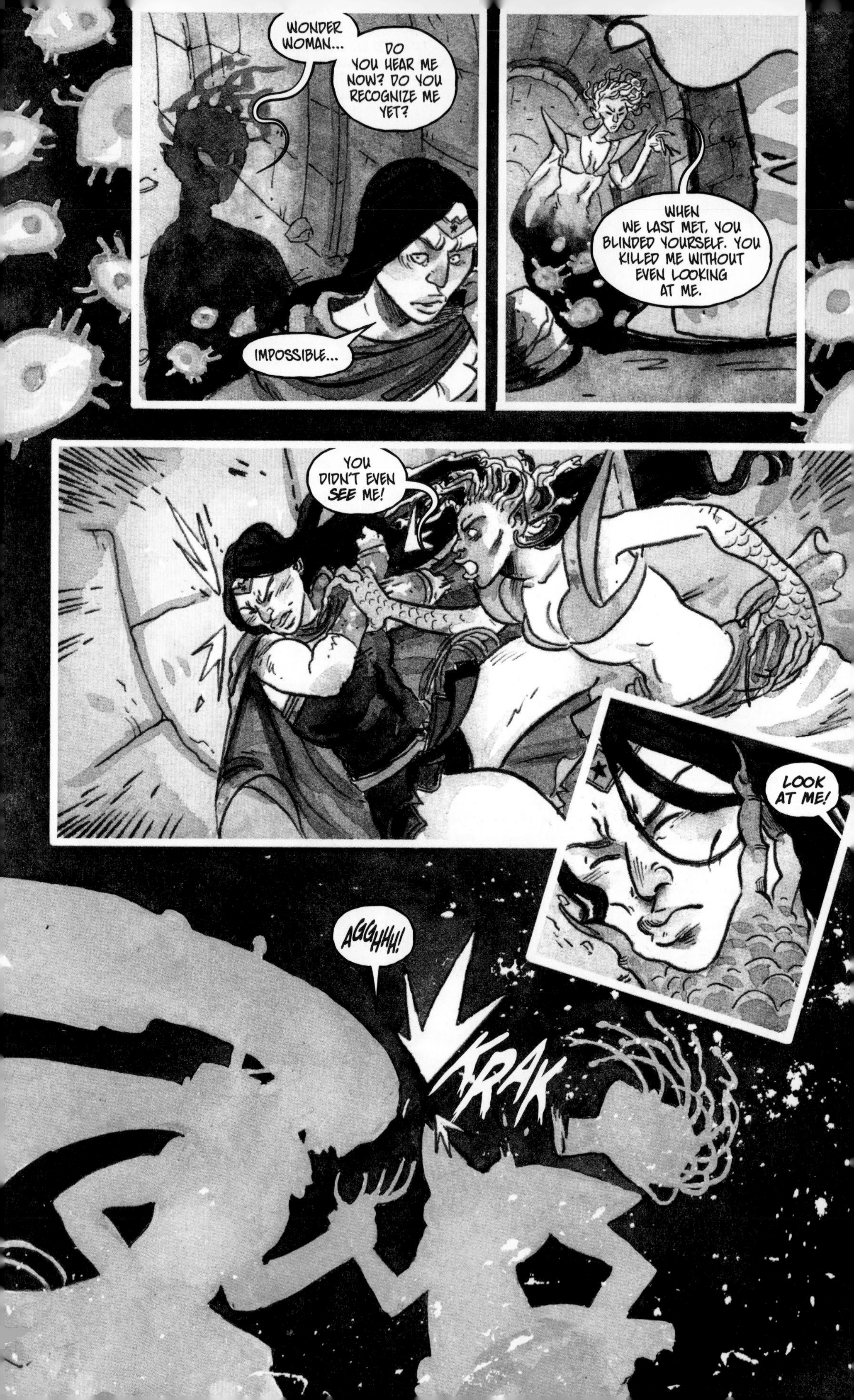
WONDER WOMAN...
DO YOU HEAR ME NOW? DO YOU RECOGNIZE ME YET?
IMPOSSIBLE...
WHEN WE LAST MET, YOU BLINDED YOURSELF. YOU KILLED ME WITHOUT EVEN LOOKING AT ME.
YOU DIDN'T EVEN SEE ME!
LOOK AT ME!
AGGHHH!
KRAK

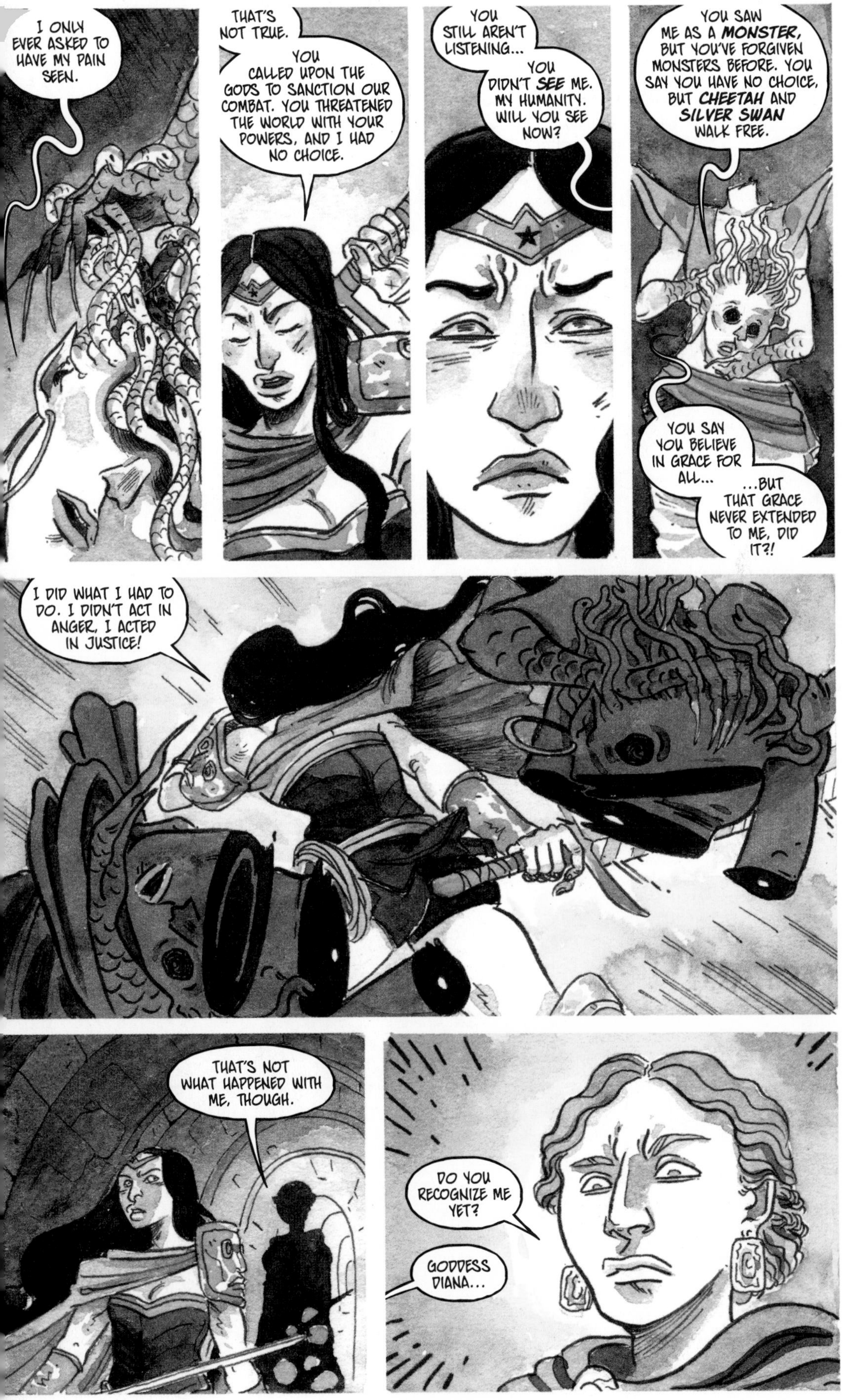
I ONLY EVER ASKED TO HAVE MY PAIN SEEN.
THAT'S NOT TRUE.
YOU CALLED UPON THE GODS TO SANCTION OUR COMBAT. YOU THREATENED THE WORLD WITH YOUR POWERS, AND I HAD NO CHOICE.
YOU STILL AREN'T LISTENING...
YOU DIDN'T **SEE** ME. MY HUMANITY. WILL YOU SEE NOW?
YOU SAW ME AS A **MONSTER**, BUT YOU'VE FORGIVEN MONSTERS BEFORE. YOU SAY YOU HAVE NO CHOICE, BUT **CHEETAH** AND **SILVER SWAN** WALK FREE.
YOU SAY YOU BELIEVE IN GRACE FOR ALL...
...BUT THAT GRACE NEVER EXTENDED TO ME, DID IT?!
I DID WHAT I HAD TO DO. I DIDN'T ACT IN ANGER, I ACTED IN JUSTICE!
THAT'S NOT WHAT HAPPENED WITH ME, THOUGH.
DO YOU RECOGNIZE ME YET?
GODDESS DIANA...

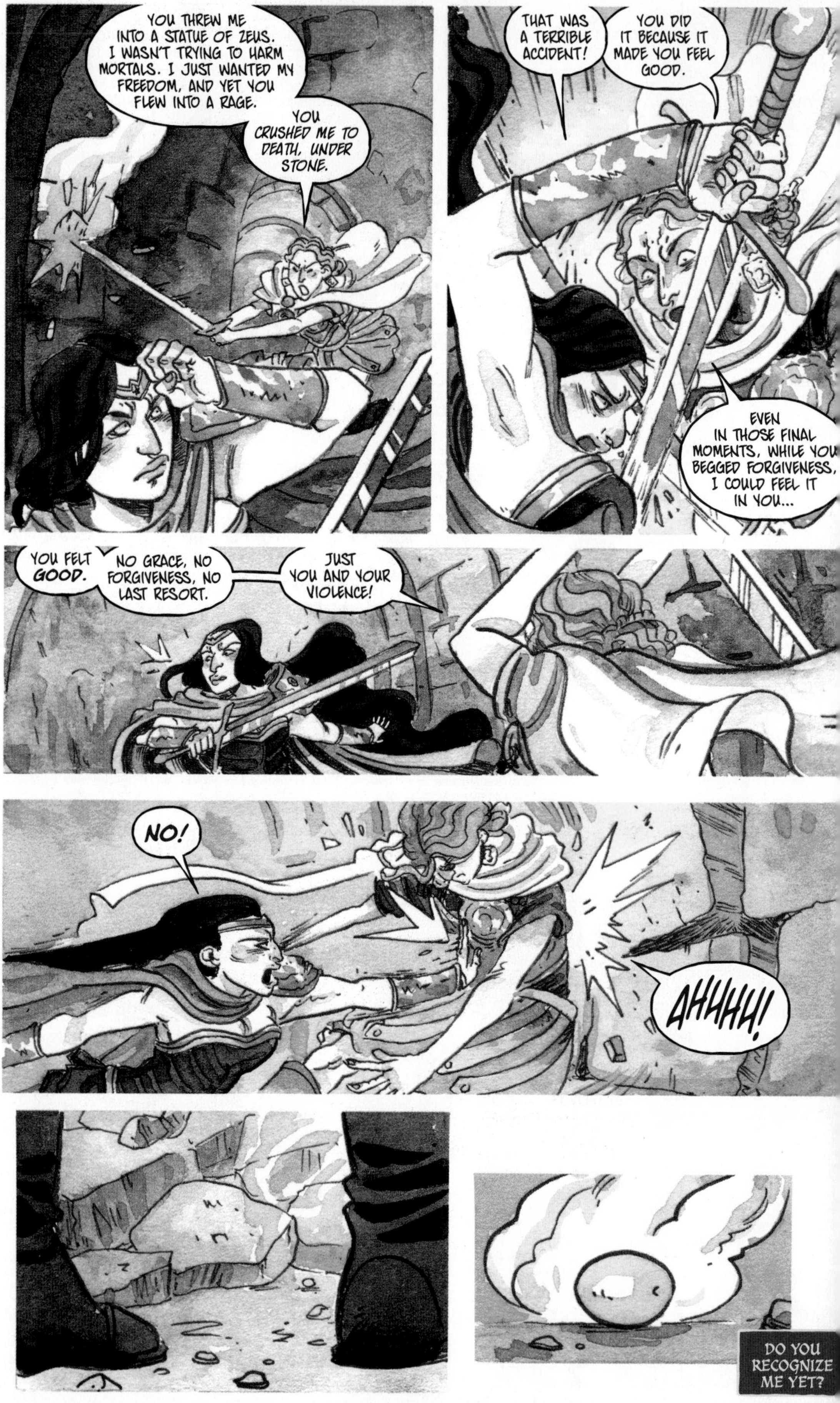

YOU THREW ME INTO A STATUE OF ZEUS. I WASN'T TRYING TO HARM MORTALS. I JUST WANTED MY FREEDOM, AND YET YOU FLEW INTO A RAGE.
YOU CRUSHED ME TO DEATH, UNDER STONE.
THAT WAS A TERRIBLE ACCIDENT!
YOU DID IT BECAUSE IT MADE YOU FEEL GOOD.
EVEN IN THOSE FINAL MOMENTS, WHILE YOU BEGGED FORGIVENESS, I COULD FEEL IT IN YOU...
YOU FELT **GOOD.**
NO GRACE, NO FORGIVENESS, NO LAST RESORT.
JUST YOU AND YOUR VIOLENCE!
NO!
AHHHH!
DO YOU RECOGNIZE ME YET?

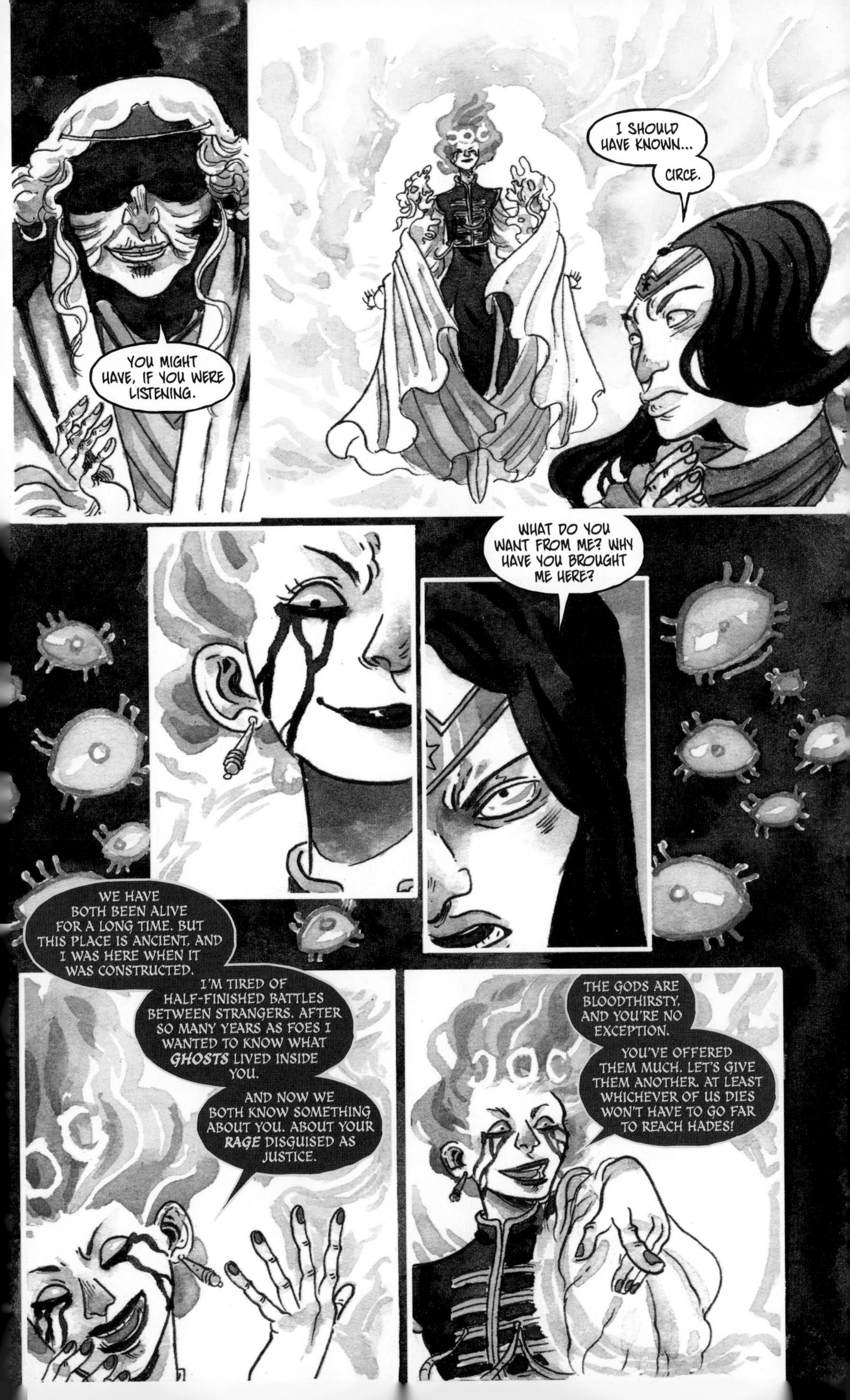
YOU MIGHT HAVE, IF YOU WERE LISTENING.
I SHOULD HAVE KNOWN...
CIRCE.
WHAT DO YOU WANT FROM ME? WHY HAVE YOU BROUGHT ME HERE?
WE HAVE BOTH BEEN ALIVE FOR A LONG TIME. BUT THIS PLACE IS ANCIENT, AND I WAS HERE WHEN IT WAS CONSTRUCTED.
I'M TIRED OF HALF-FINISHED BATTLES BETWEEN STRANGERS. AFTER SO MANY YEARS AS FOES I WANTED TO KNOW WHAT GHOSTS LIVED INSIDE YOU.
AND NOW WE BOTH KNOW SOMETHING ABOUT YOU. ABOUT YOUR RAGE DISGUISED AS JUSTICE.
THE GODS ARE BLOODTHIRSTY, AND YOU'RE NO EXCEPTION.
YOU'VE OFFERED THEM MUCH. LET'S GIVE THEM ANOTHER. AT LEAST WHICHEVER OF US DIES WON'T HAVE TO GO FAR TO REACH HADES!

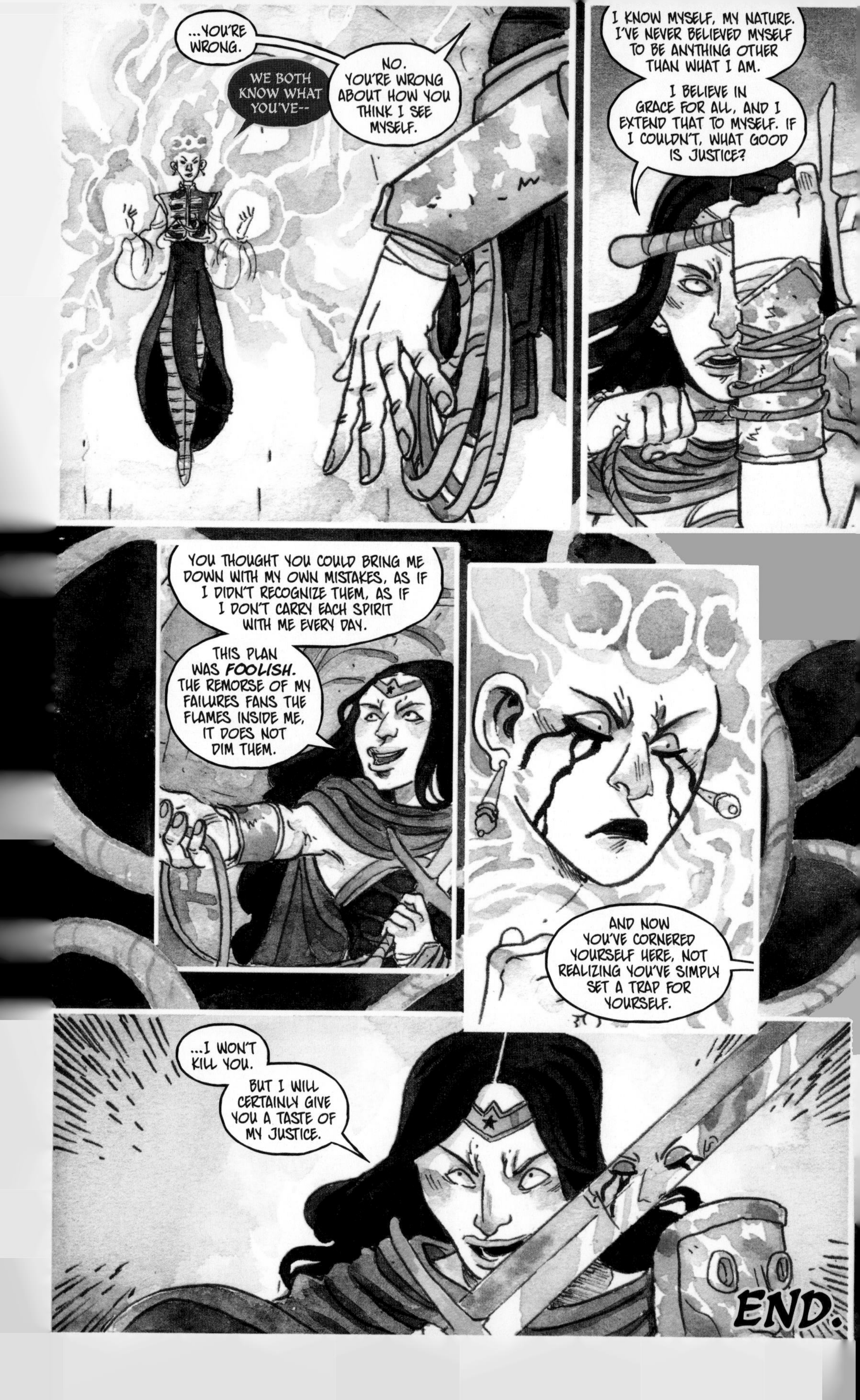
...YOU'RE WRONG.
WE BOTH KNOW WHAT YOU'VE--
NO. YOU'RE WRONG ABOUT HOW YOU THINK I SEE MYSELF.
I KNOW MYSELF, MY NATURE. I'VE NEVER BELIEVED MYSELF TO BE ANYTHING OTHER THAN WHAT I AM.
I BELIEVE IN GRACE FOR ALL, AND I EXTEND THAT TO MYSELF. IF I COULDN'T, WHAT GOOD IS JUSTICE?
YOU THOUGHT YOU COULD BRING ME DOWN WITH MY OWN MISTAKES, AS IF I DIDN'T RECOGNIZE THEM, AS IF I DON'T CARRY EACH SPIRIT WITH ME EVERY DAY.
THIS PLAN WAS **FOOLISH.** THE REMORSE OF MY FAILURES FANS THE FLAMES INSIDE ME, IT DOES NOT DIM THEM.
AND NOW YOU'VE CORNERED YOURSELF HERE, NOT REALIZING YOU'VE SIMPLY SET A TRAP FOR YOURSELF.
...I WON'T KILL YOU.
BUT I WILL CERTAINLY GIVE YOU A TASTE OF MY JUSTICE.
END.

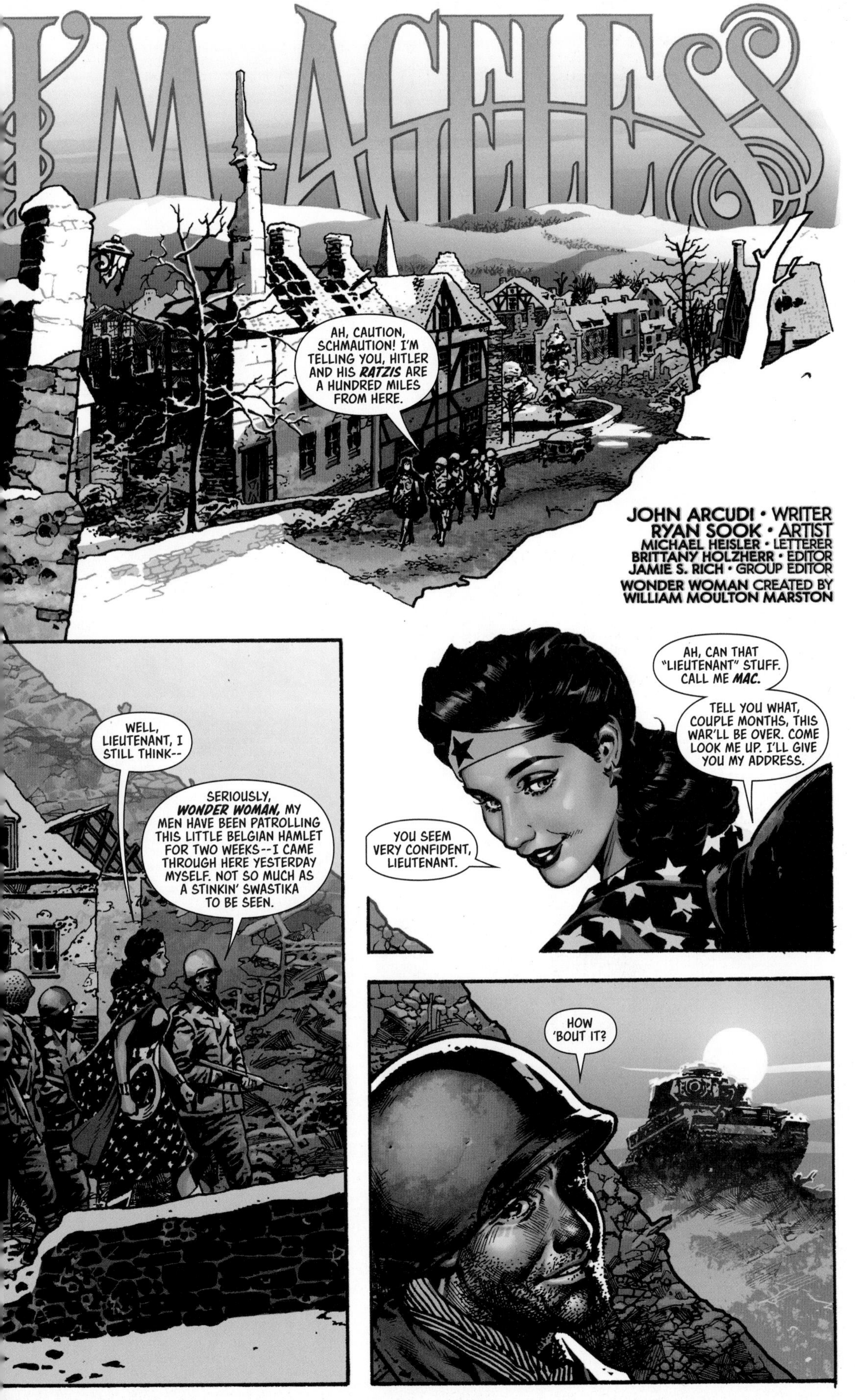
I'M AGELESS
AH, CAUTION, SCHMAUTION! I'M TELLING YOU, HITLER AND HIS *RATZIS* ARE A HUNDRED MILES FROM HERE.
JOHN ARCUDI • WRITER
RYAN SOOK • ARTIST
MICHAEL HEISLER • LETTERER
BRITTANY HOLZHERR • EDITOR
JAMIE S. RICH • GROUP EDITOR
WONDER WOMAN CREATED BY WILLIAM MOULTON MARSTON
WELL, LIEUTENANT, I STILL THINK--
SERIOUSLY, **WONDER WOMAN,** MY MEN HAVE BEEN PATROLLING THIS LITTLE BELGIAN HAMLET FOR TWO WEEKS--I CAME THROUGH HERE YESTERDAY MYSELF. NOT SO MUCH AS A STINKIN' SWASTIKA TO BE SEEN.
YOU SEEM VERY CONFIDENT, LIEUTENANT.
AH, CAN THAT "LIEUTENANT" STUFF. CALL ME ***MAC.***
TELL YOU WHAT, COUPLE MONTHS, THIS WAR'LL BE OVER. COME LOOK ME UP. I'LL GIVE YOU MY ADDRESS.
HOW 'BOUT IT?

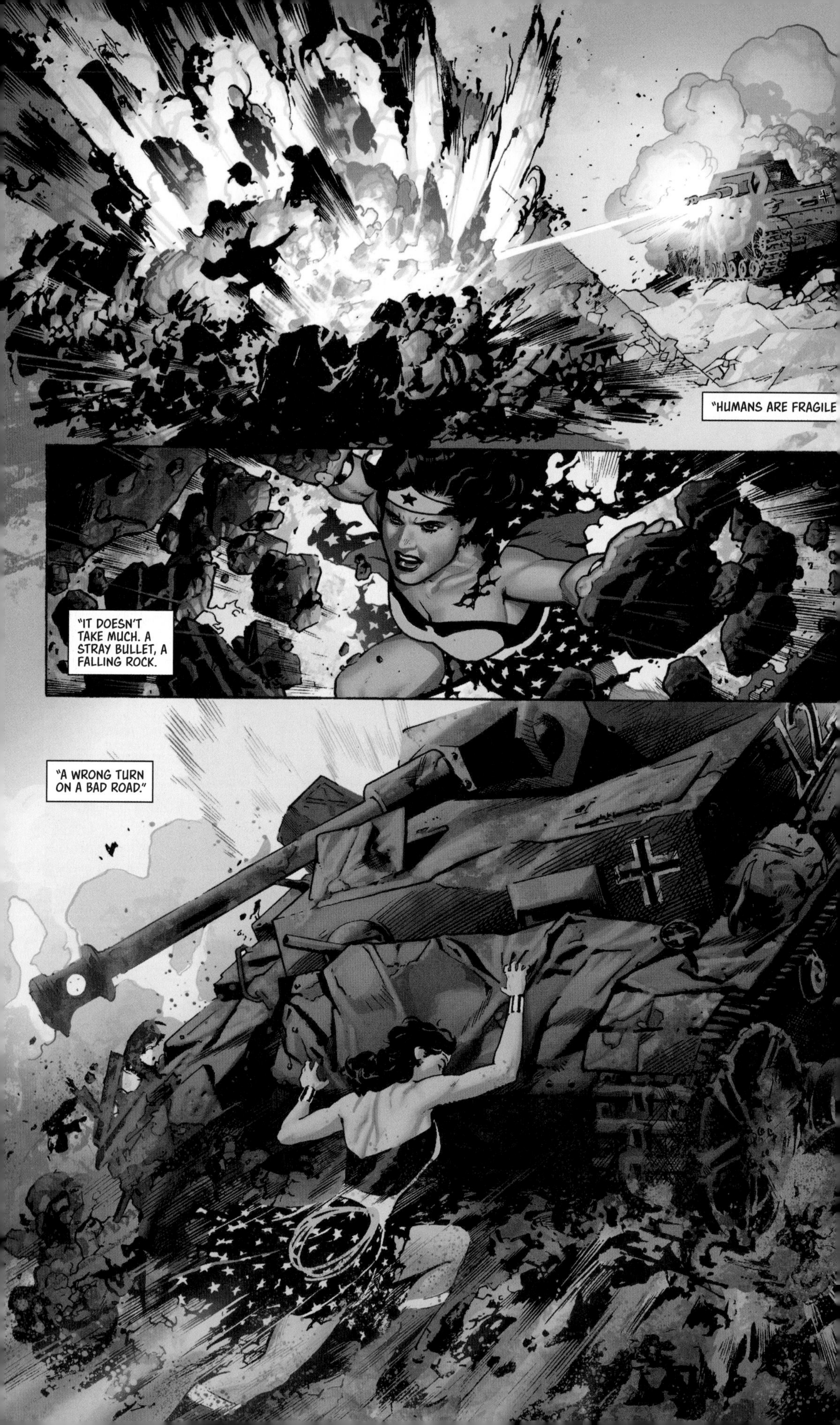
"HUMANS ARE FRAGILE
"IT DOESN'T TAKE MUCH. A STRAY BULLET, A FALLING ROCK.
"A WRONG TURN ON A BAD ROAD."

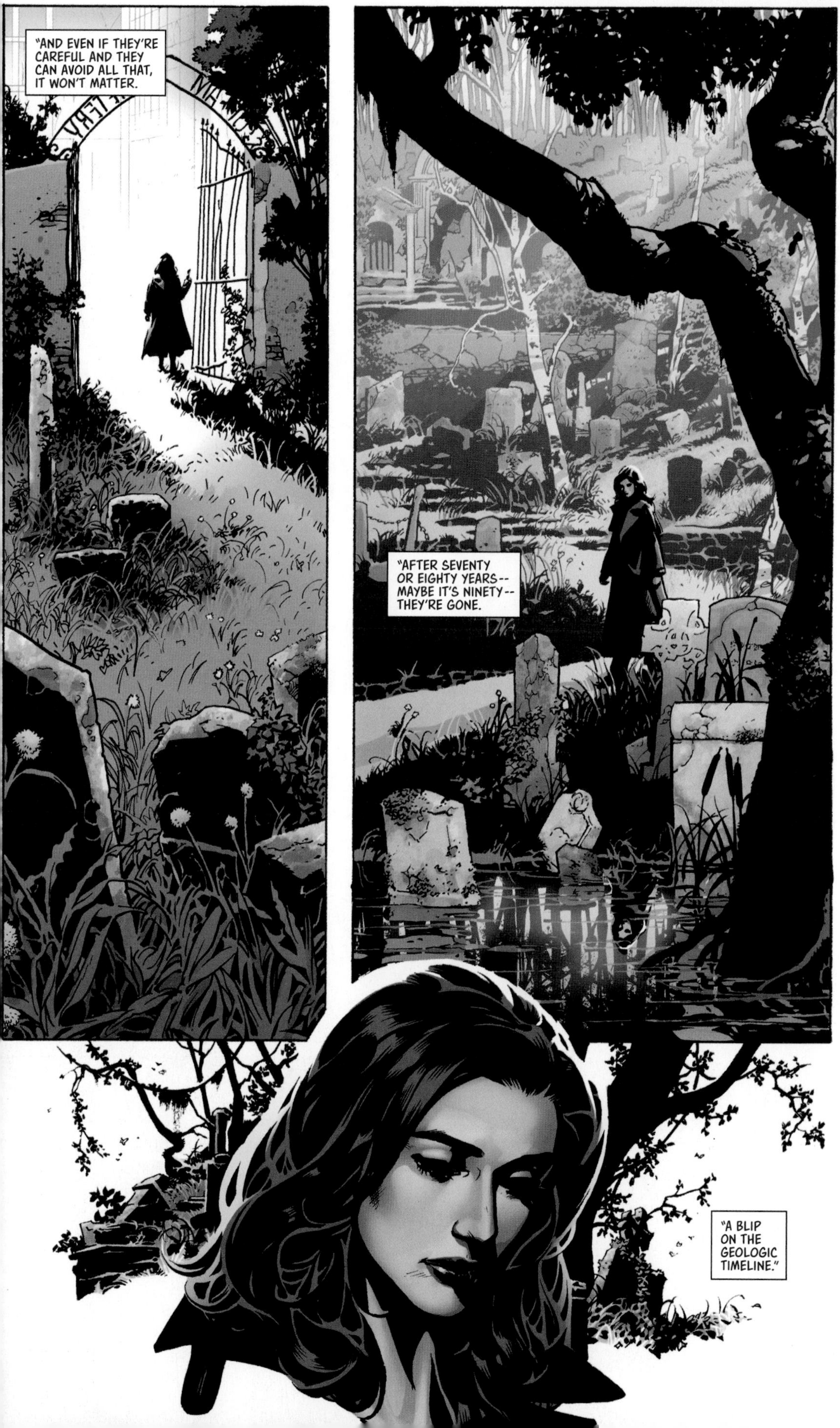
"AND EVEN IF THEY'RE CAREFUL AND THEY CAN AVOID ALL THAT, IT WON'T MATTER.
"AFTER SEVENTY OR EIGHTY YEARS-- MAYBE IT'S NINETY-- THEY'RE GONE.
"A BLIP ON THE GEOLOGIC TIMELINE."

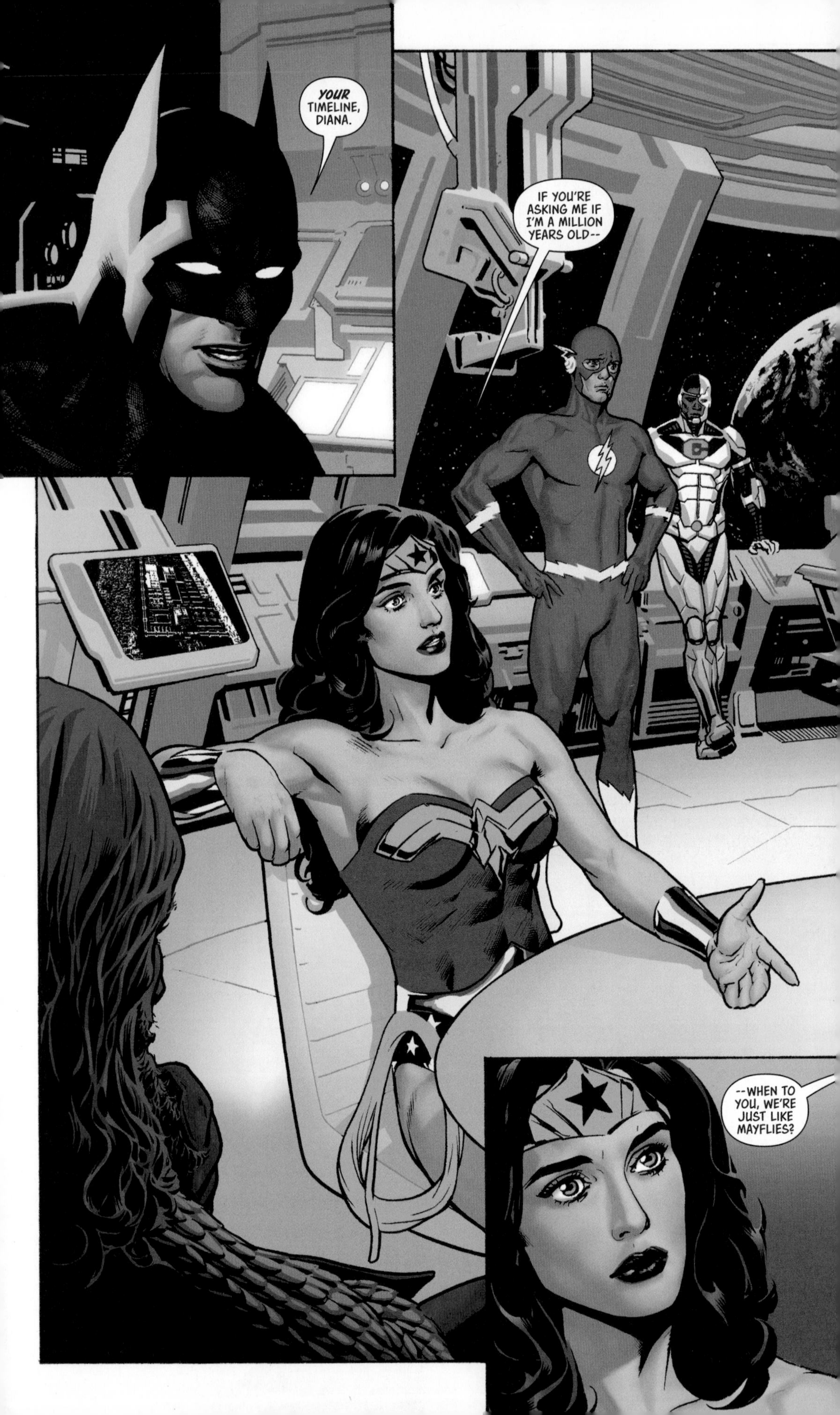

YOUR TIMELINE, DIANA.
IF YOU'RE ASKING ME IF I'M A MILLION YEARS OLD--
--WHEN TO YOU, WE'RE JUST LIKE MAYFLIES?

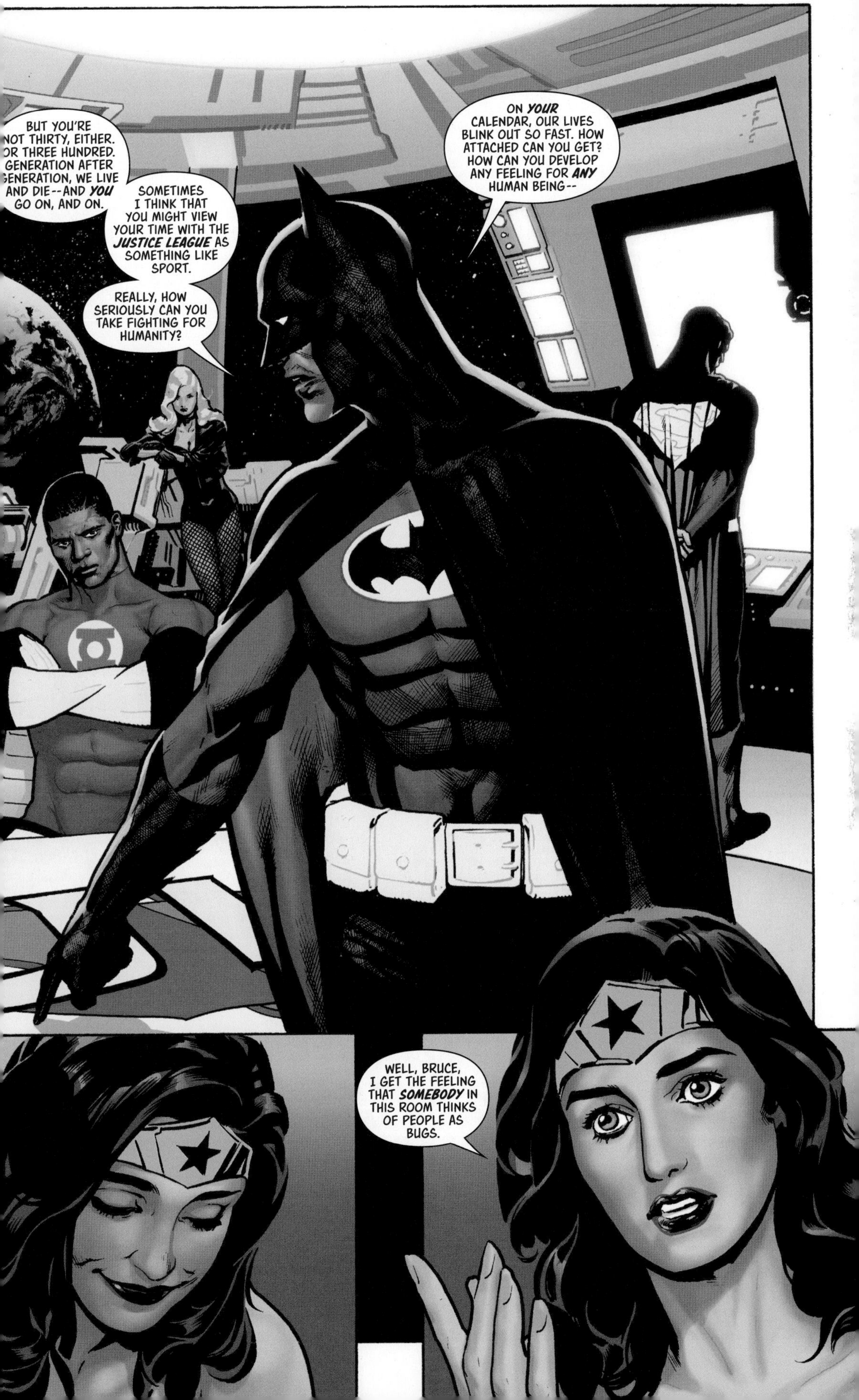
BUT YOU'RE NOT THIRTY, EITHER. OR THREE HUNDRED. GENERATION AFTER GENERATION, WE LIVE AND DIE--AND YOU GO ON, AND ON.
SOMETIMES I THINK THAT YOU MIGHT VIEW YOUR TIME WITH THE JUSTICE LEAGUE AS SOMETHING LIKE SPORT.
REALLY, HOW SERIOUSLY CAN YOU TAKE FIGHTING FOR HUMANITY?
ON YOUR CALENDAR, OUR LIVES BLINK OUT SO FAST. HOW ATTACHED CAN YOU GET? HOW CAN YOU DEVELOP ANY FEELING FOR ANY HUMAN BEING--
WELL, BRUCE, I GET THE FEELING THAT SOMEBODY IN THIS ROOM THINKS OF PEOPLE AS BUGS.

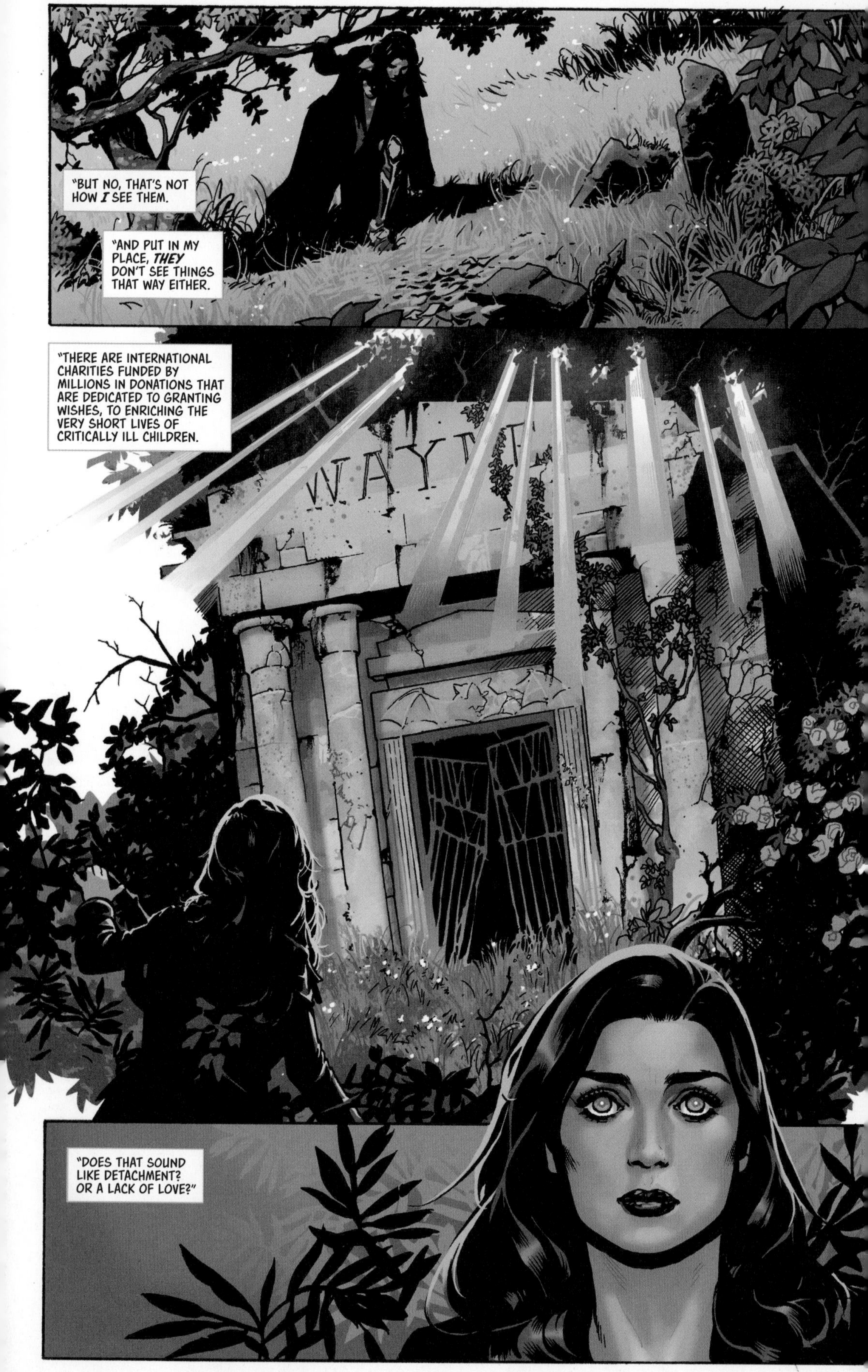
"BUT NO, THAT'S NOT HOW *I* SEE THEM.
"AND PUT IN MY PLACE, *THEY* DON'T SEE THINGS THAT WAY EITHER.
"THERE ARE INTERNATIONAL CHARITIES FUNDED BY MILLIONS IN DONATIONS THAT ARE DEDICATED TO GRANTING WISHES, TO ENRICHING THE VERY SHORT LIVES OF CRITICALLY ILL CHILDREN.
"DOES THAT SOUND LIKE DETACHMENT? OR A LACK OF LOVE?"

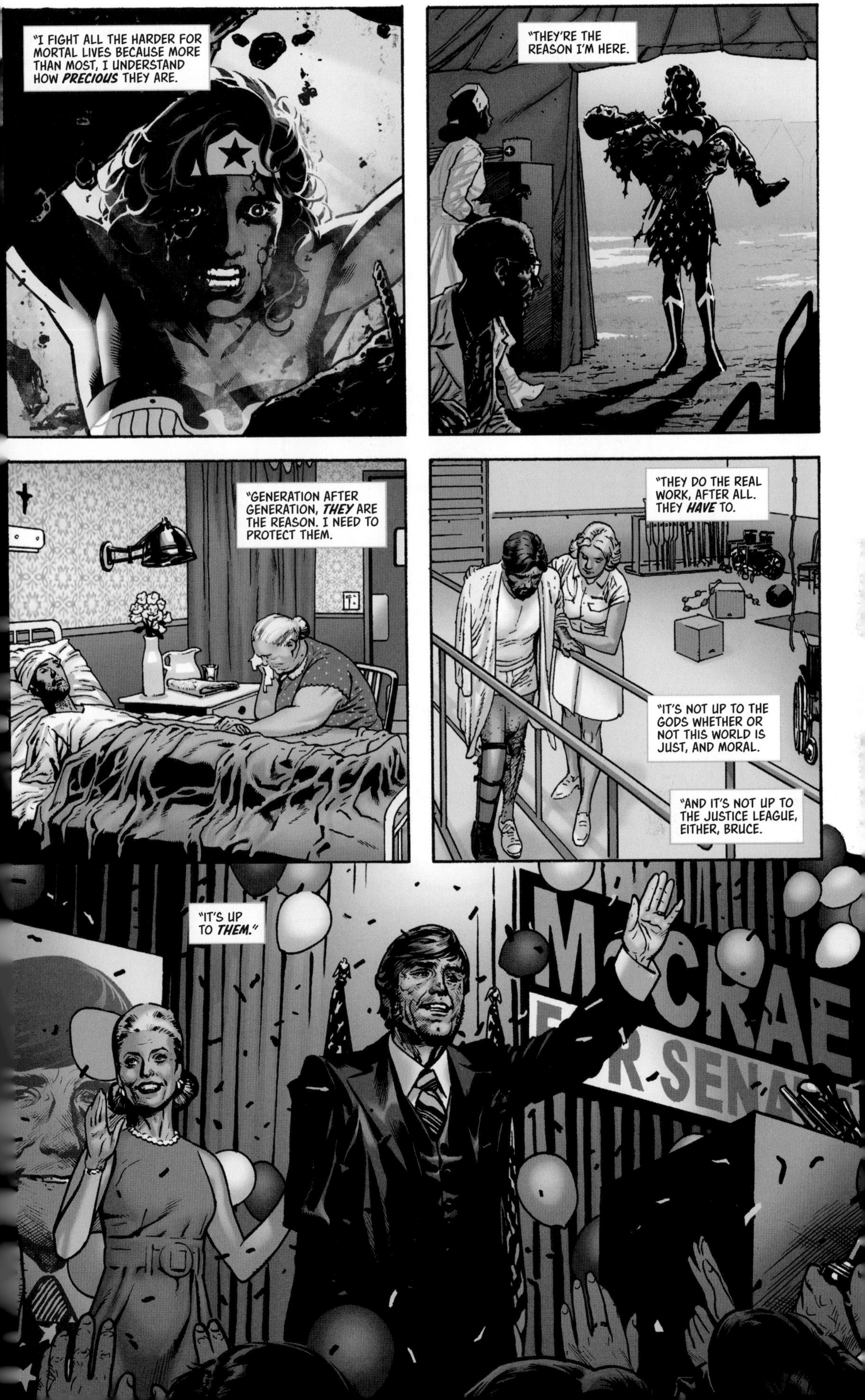
"I FIGHT ALL THE HARDER FOR MORTAL LIVES BECAUSE MORE THAN MOST, I UNDERSTAND HOW *PRECIOUS* THEY ARE.
"THEY'RE THE REASON I'M HERE.
"GENERATION AFTER GENERATION, *THEY* ARE THE REASON. I NEED TO PROTECT THEM.
"THEY DO THE REAL WORK, AFTER ALL. THEY *HAVE* TO.
"IT'S NOT UP TO THE GODS WHETHER OR NOT THIS WORLD IS JUST, AND MORAL.
"AND IT'S NOT UP TO THE JUSTICE LEAGUE, EITHER, BRUCE.
"IT'S UP TO *THEM*."

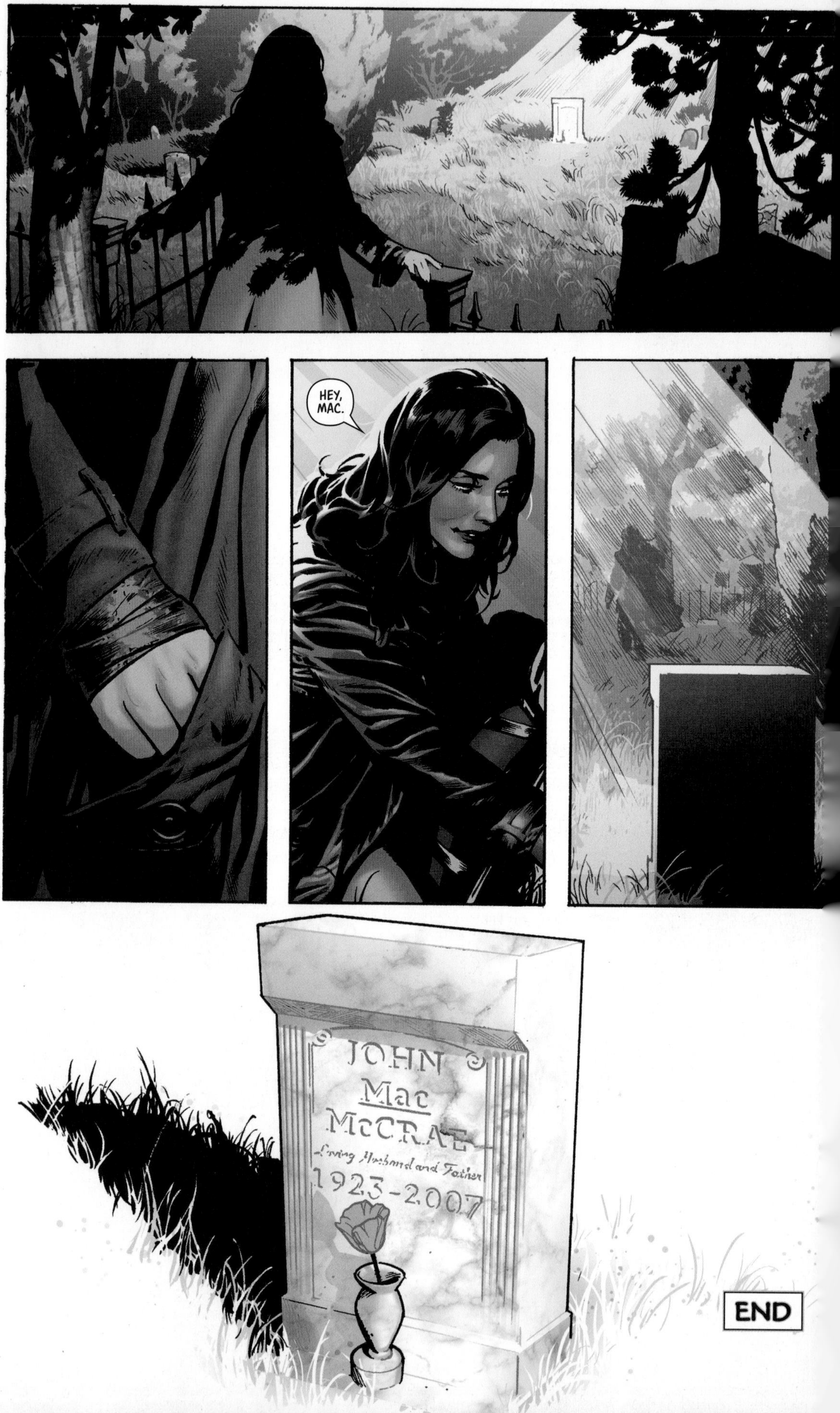
HEY, MAC.
JOHN
Mac
McCRAE
Loving Husband and Father
1923-2007
END

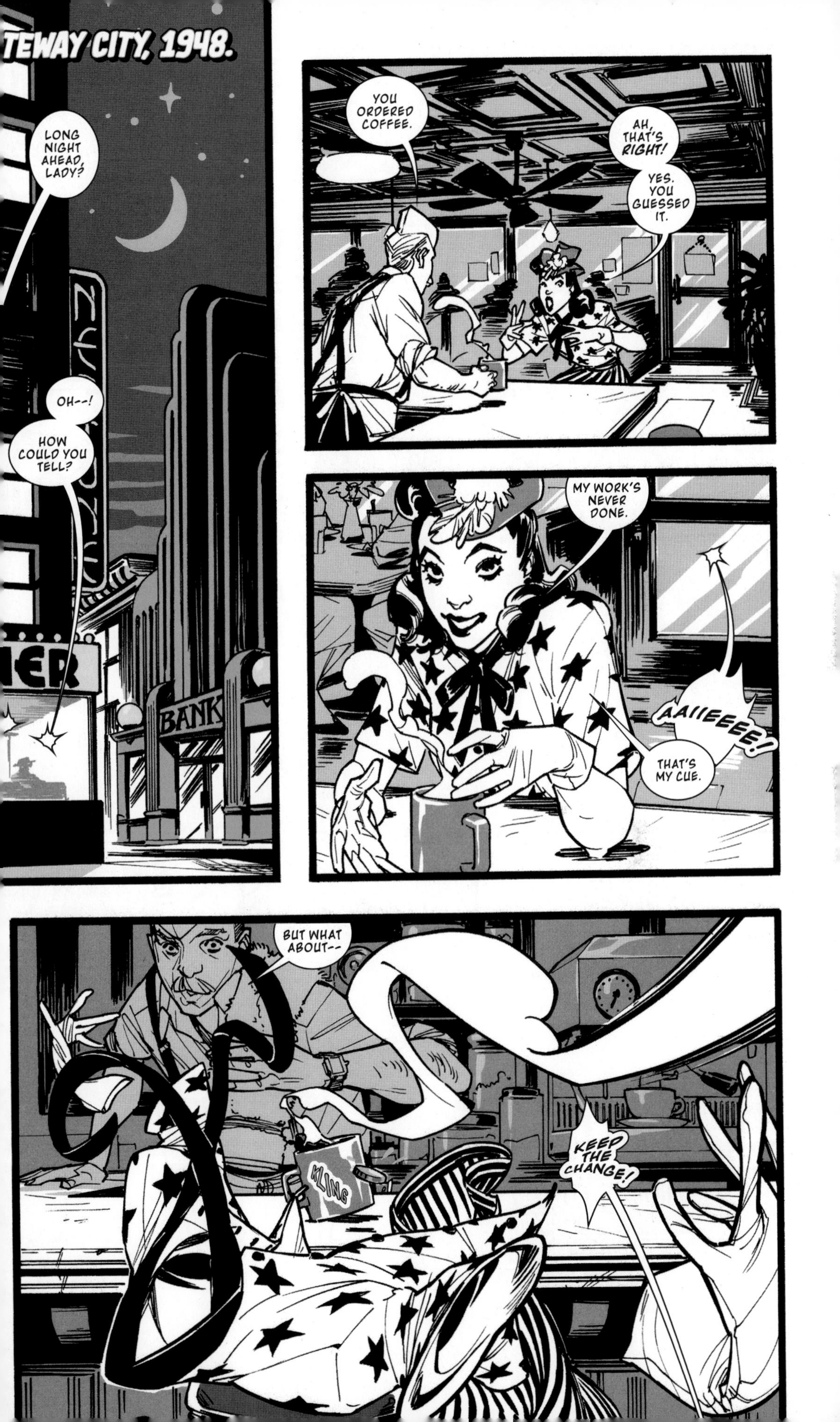

TEWAY CITY, 1948.
LONG NIGHT AHEAD, LADY?
OH--!
HOW COULD YOU TELL?
YOU ORDERED COFFEE.
AH, THAT'S RIGHT!
YES. YOU GUESSED IT.
MY WORK'S NEVER DONE.
AAIIEEEE!
THAT'S MY CUE.
BUT WHAT ABOUT--
KLING
KEEP THE CHANGE!
BANK
IER

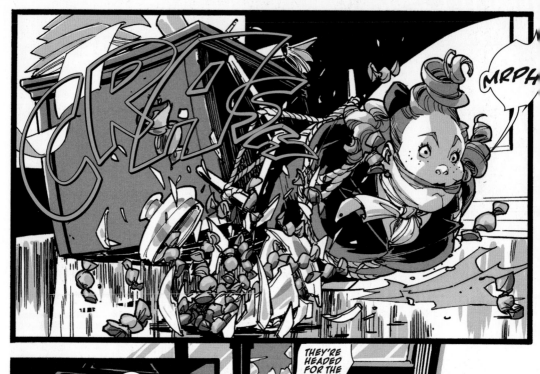

MRPH

ARE YOU ALL RIGHT? LOOKS LIKE THEY DID THEIR WORST!

NEVER YOU MIND ME!

THEY'RE HEADED FOR THE VAULT!

THEN THEY'RE PLAYING WITH FIRE.

GOLDEN AGE
AMY REEDER WRITER/ARTIST
GABRIELA DOWNIE LETTERER
BRITTANY HOLZHERR EDITOR
JAMIE S. RICH GROUP EDITOR
WONDER WOMAN CREATED BY WILLIAM MOULTON MARSTON.

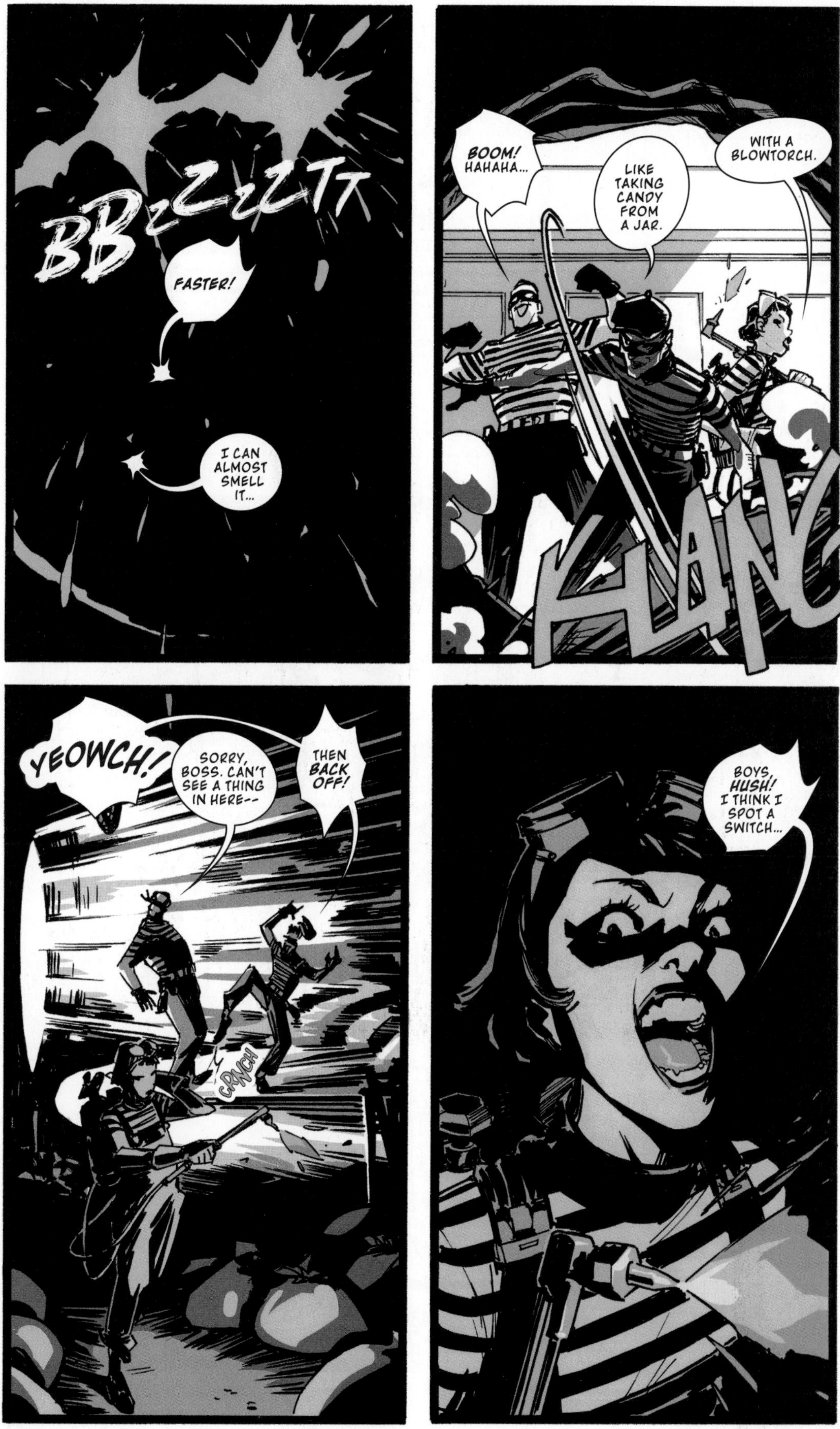
BBzZzZTT
FASTER!
I CAN ALMOST SMELL IT...
BOOM! HAHAHA...
LIKE TAKING CANDY FROM A JAR.
WITH A BLOWTORCH.
KLANG
YEOWCH!
SORRY, BOSS. CAN'T SEE A THING IN HERE--
THEN BACK OFF!
CRUNCH
BOYS, HUSH! I THINK I SPOT A SWITCH...

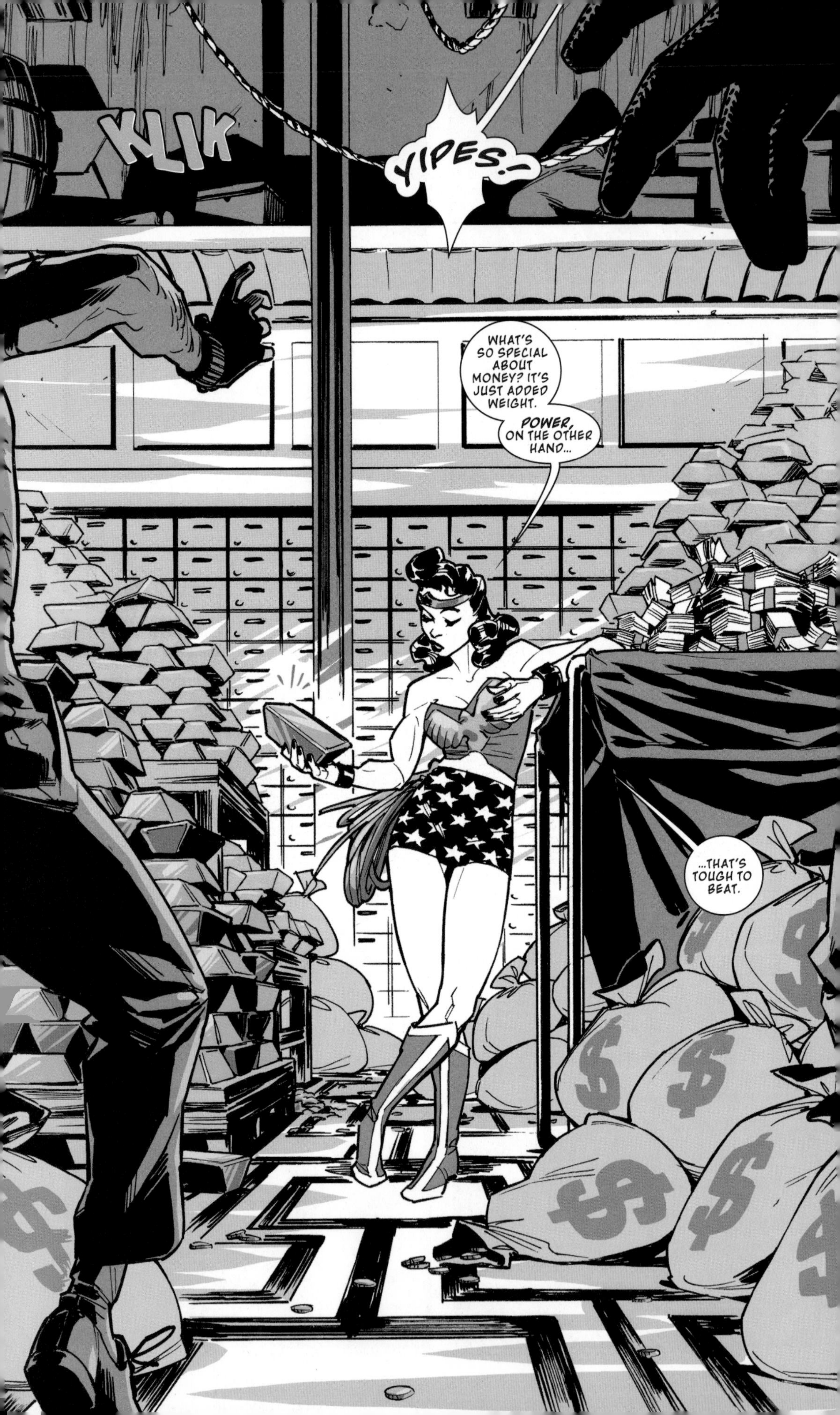
KLIK
YIPES!
WHAT'S SO SPECIAL ABOUT MONEY? IT'S JUST ADDED WEIGHT.
POWER, ON THE OTHER HAND...
...THAT'S TOUGH TO BEAT.

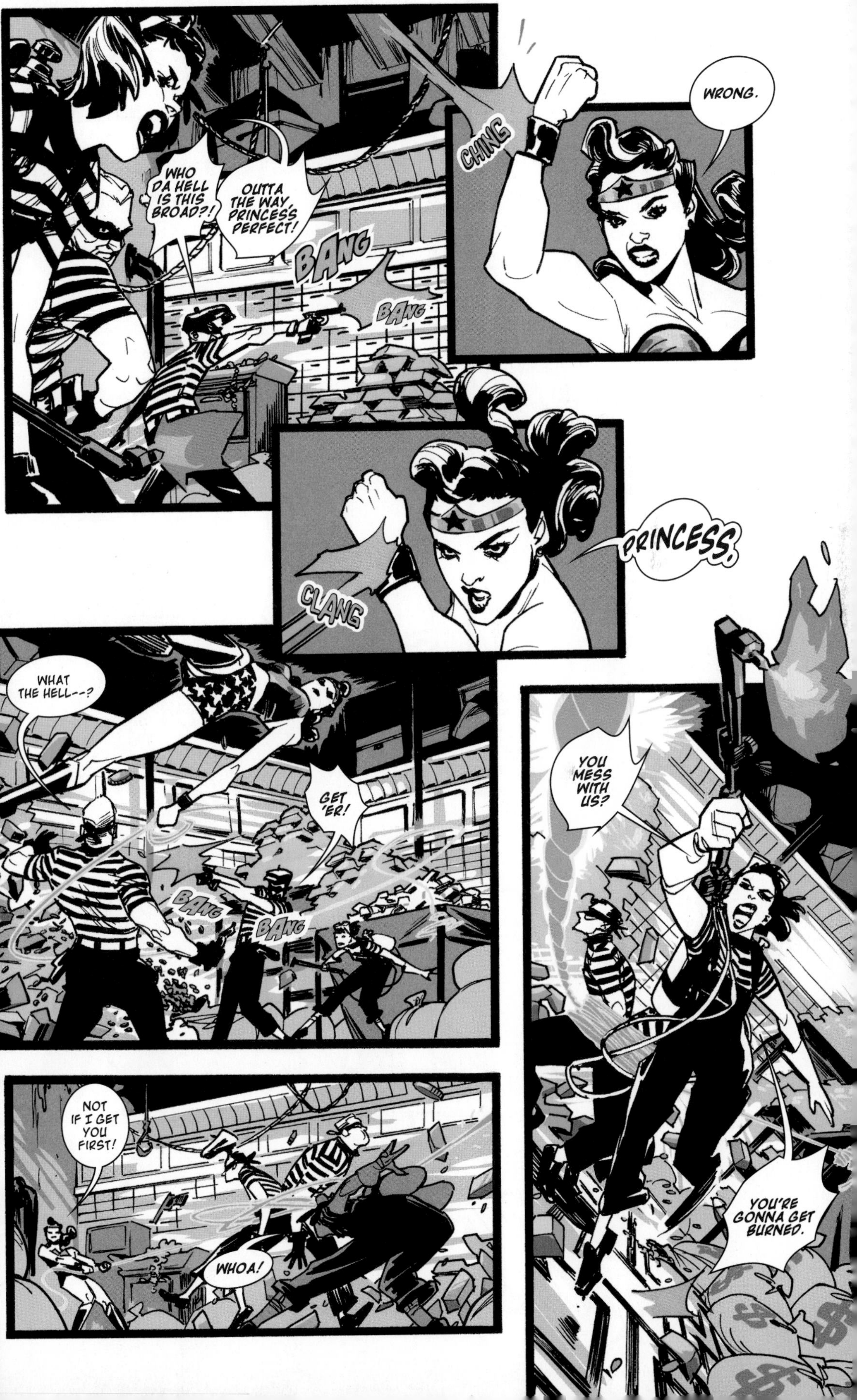
WHO DA HELL IS THIS BROAD?!
OUTTA THE WAY, PRINCESS PERFECT!
BANG
BANG
CHING
WRONG.
CLANG
PRINCESS.
WHAT THE HELL--?
GET 'ER!
BANG
BANG
YOU MESS WITH US?
YOU'RE GONNA GET BURNED.
NOT IF I GET YOU FIRST!
WHOA!

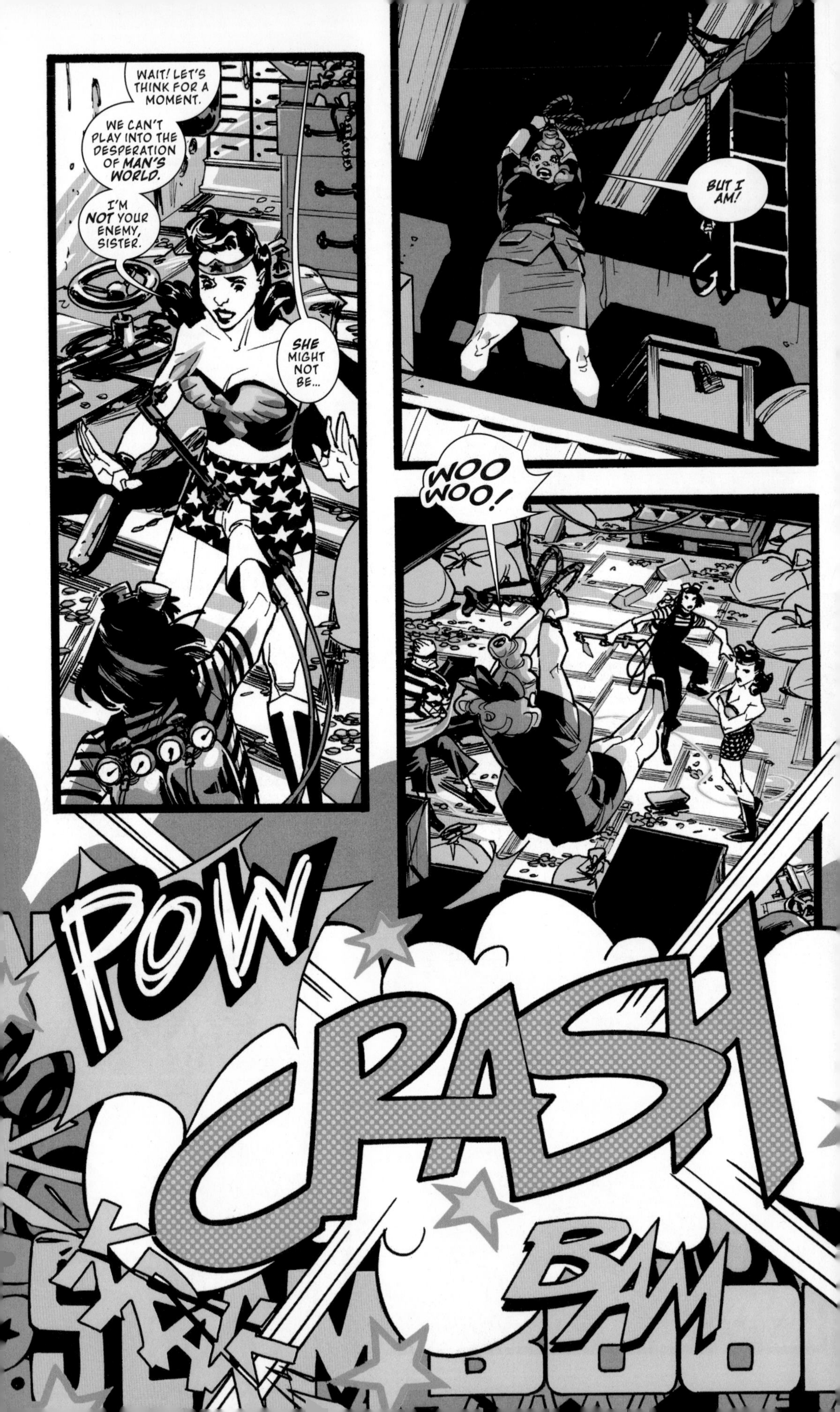
WAIT! LET'S THINK FOR A MOMENT.
WE CAN'T PLAY INTO THE DESPERATION OF MAN'S WORLD.
I'M NOT YOUR ENEMY, SISTER.
SHE MIGHT NOT BE...
BUT I AM!
WOO WOO!
POW
CRASH
BAM

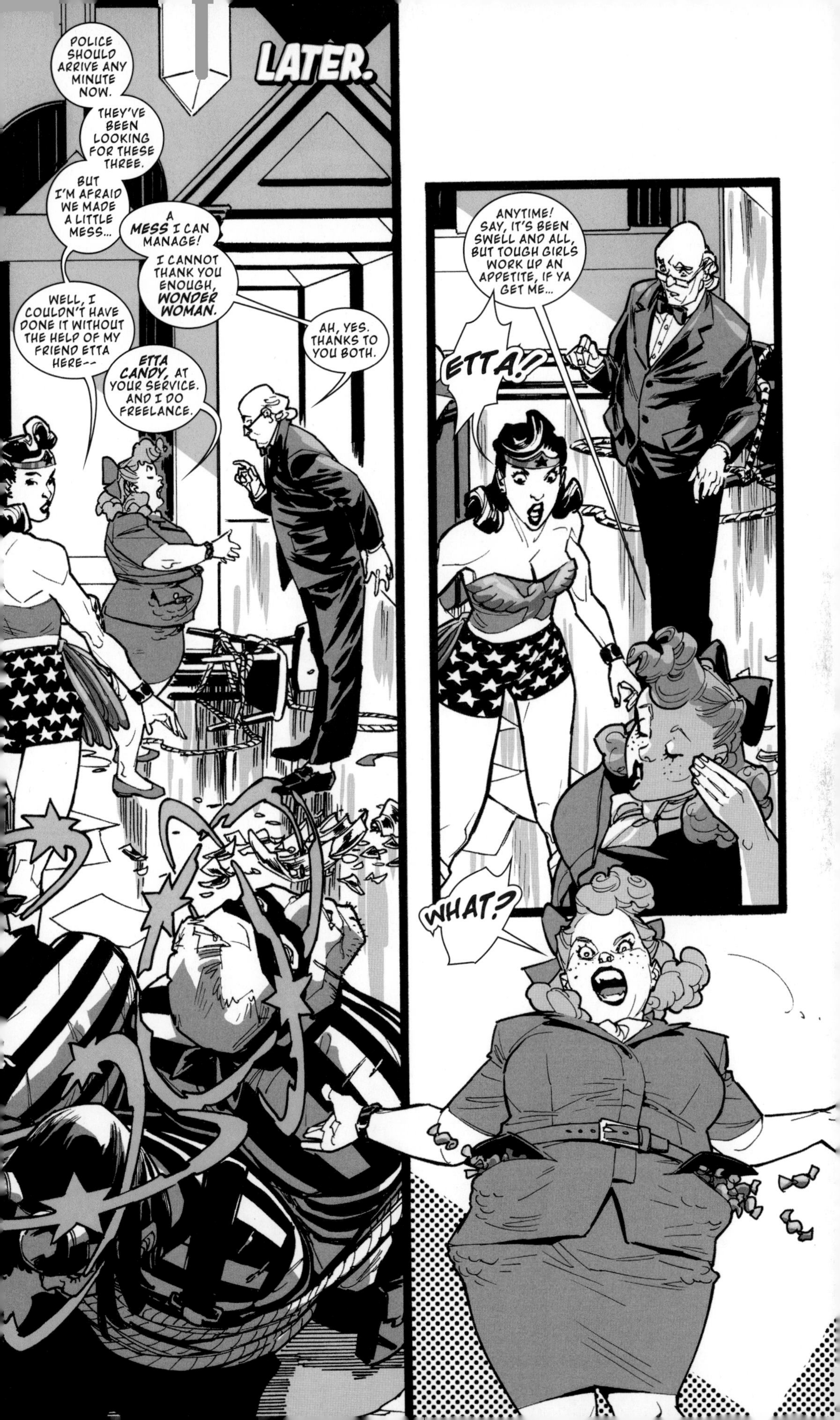
LATER.
POLICE SHOULD ARRIVE ANY MINUTE NOW.
THEY'VE BEEN LOOKING FOR THESE THREE.
BUT I'M AFRAID WE MADE A LITTLE MESS...
A MESS I CAN MANAGE!
I CANNOT THANK YOU ENOUGH, WONDER WOMAN.
WELL, I COULDN'T HAVE DONE IT WITHOUT THE HELP OF MY FRIEND ETTA HERE--
ETTA CANDY, AT YOUR SERVICE. AND I DO FREELANCE.
AH, YES. THANKS TO YOU BOTH.
ANYTIME! SAY, IT'S BEEN SWELL AND ALL, BUT TOUGH GIRLS WORK UP AN APPETITE, IF YA GET ME...
ETTA!
WHAT?

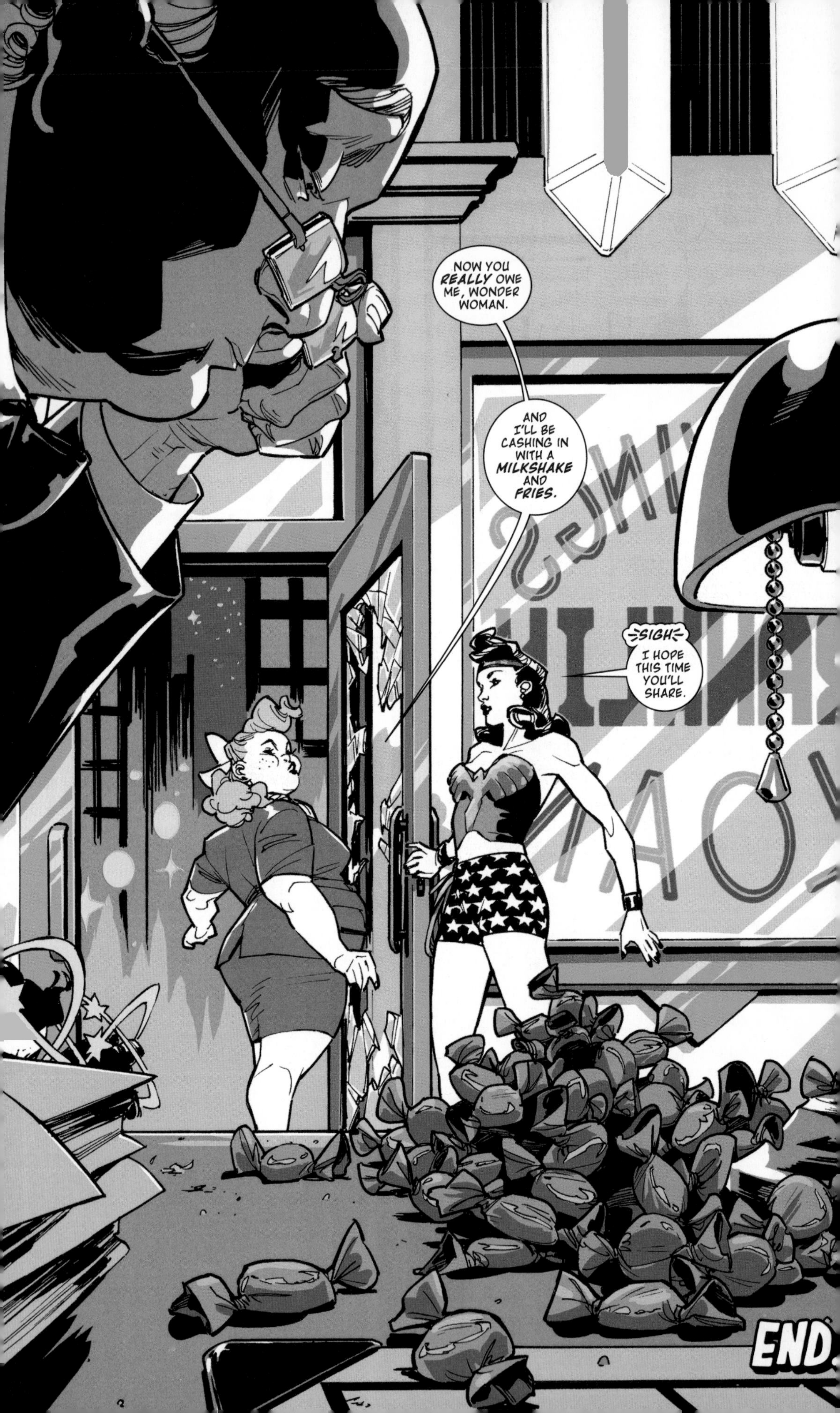
NOW YOU REALLY OWE ME, WONDER WOMAN.
AND I'LL BE CASHING IN WITH A MILKSHAKE AND FRIES.
SIGH
I HOPE THIS TIME YOU'LL SHARE.
END.

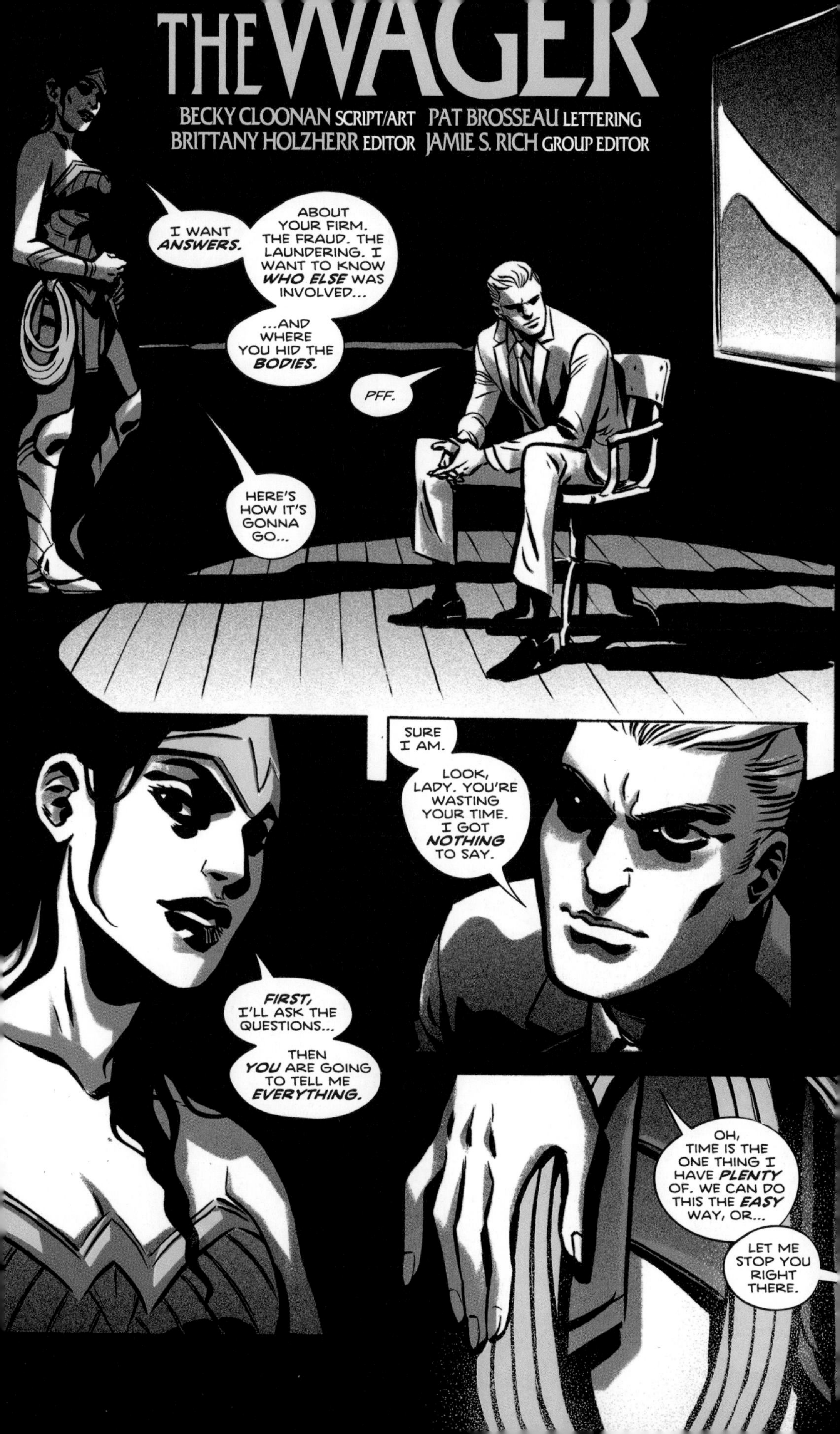
THE WAGER
BECKY CLOONAN SCRIPT/ART PAT BROSSEAU LETTERING
BRITTANY HOLZHERR EDITOR JAMIE S. RICH GROUP EDITOR
I WANT ANSWERS.
ABOUT YOUR FIRM. THE FRAUD. THE LAUNDERING. I WANT TO KNOW WHO ELSE WAS INVOLVED...
...AND WHERE YOU HID THE BODIES.
PFF.
HERE'S HOW IT'S GONNA GO...
FIRST, I'LL ASK THE QUESTIONS...
THEN YOU ARE GOING TO TELL ME EVERYTHING.
SURE I AM.
LOOK, LADY. YOU'RE WASTING YOUR TIME. I GOT NOTHING TO SAY.
OH, TIME IS THE ONE THING I HAVE PLENTY OF. WE CAN DO THIS THE EASY WAY, OR...
LET ME STOP YOU RIGHT THERE.

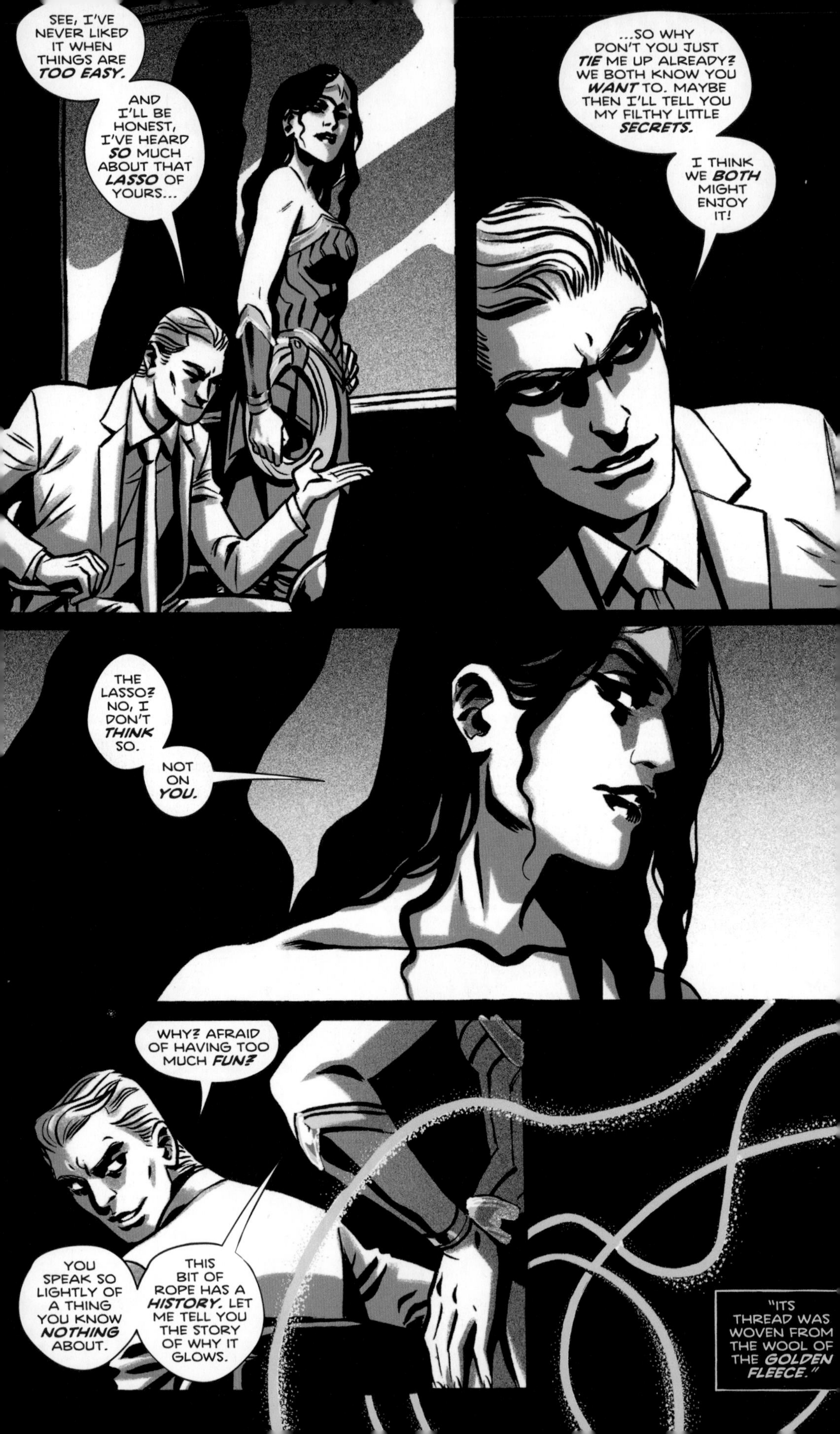

SEE, I'VE NEVER LIKED IT WHEN THINGS ARE TOO EASY.
AND I'LL BE HONEST, I'VE HEARD SO MUCH ABOUT THAT LASSO OF YOURS...
...SO WHY DON'T YOU JUST TIE ME UP ALREADY? WE BOTH KNOW YOU WANT TO. MAYBE THEN I'LL TELL YOU MY FILTHY LITTLE SECRETS.
I THINK WE BOTH MIGHT ENJOY IT!
THE LASSO? NO, I DON'T THINK SO.
NOT ON YOU.
WHY? AFRAID OF HAVING TOO MUCH FUN?
YOU SPEAK SO LIGHTLY OF A THING YOU KNOW NOTHING ABOUT.
THIS BIT OF ROPE HAS A HISTORY. LET ME TELL YOU THE STORY OF WHY IT GLOWS.
"ITS THREAD WAS WOVEN FROM THE WOOL OF THE GOLDEN FLEECE."

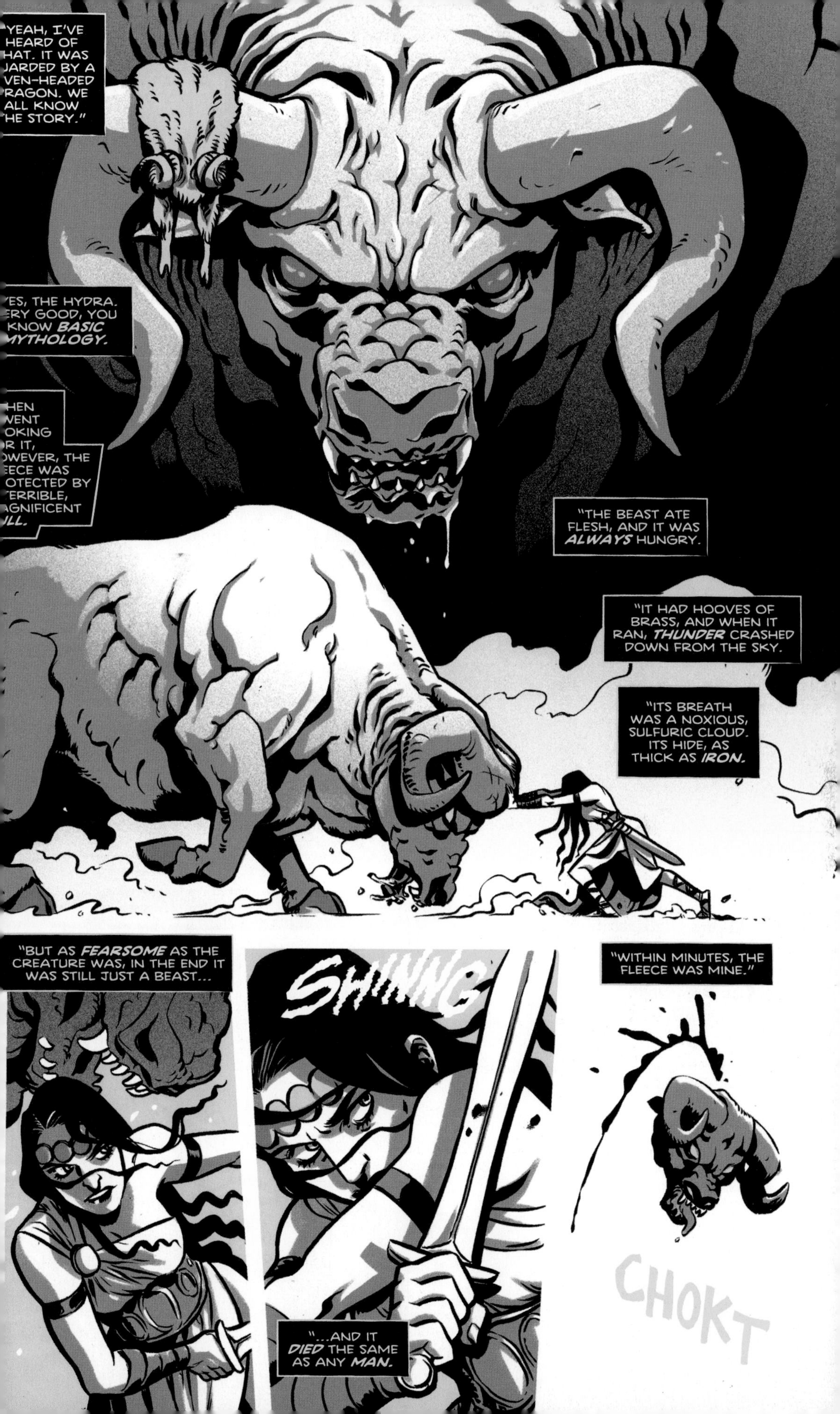
"YEAH, I'VE HEARD OF HAT. IT WAS JARDED BY A VEN-HEADED RAGON. WE ALL KNOW HE STORY."
ES, THE HYDRA. ERY GOOD, YOU KNOW BASIC MYTHOLOGY.
HEN WENT OKING R IT, OWEVER, THE EECE WAS OTECTED BY TERRIBLE, AGNIFICENT ILL.
"THE BEAST ATE FLESH, AND IT WAS ALWAYS HUNGRY.
"IT HAD HOOVES OF BRASS, AND WHEN IT RAN, THUNDER CRASHED DOWN FROM THE SKY.
"ITS BREATH WAS A NOXIOUS, SULFURIC CLOUD. ITS HIDE, AS THICK AS IRON.
"BUT AS FEARSOME AS THE CREATURE WAS, IN THE END IT WAS STILL JUST A BEAST...
SHING
"...AND IT DIED THE SAME AS ANY MAN.
"WITHIN MINUTES, THE FLEECE WAS MINE."
CHOKT

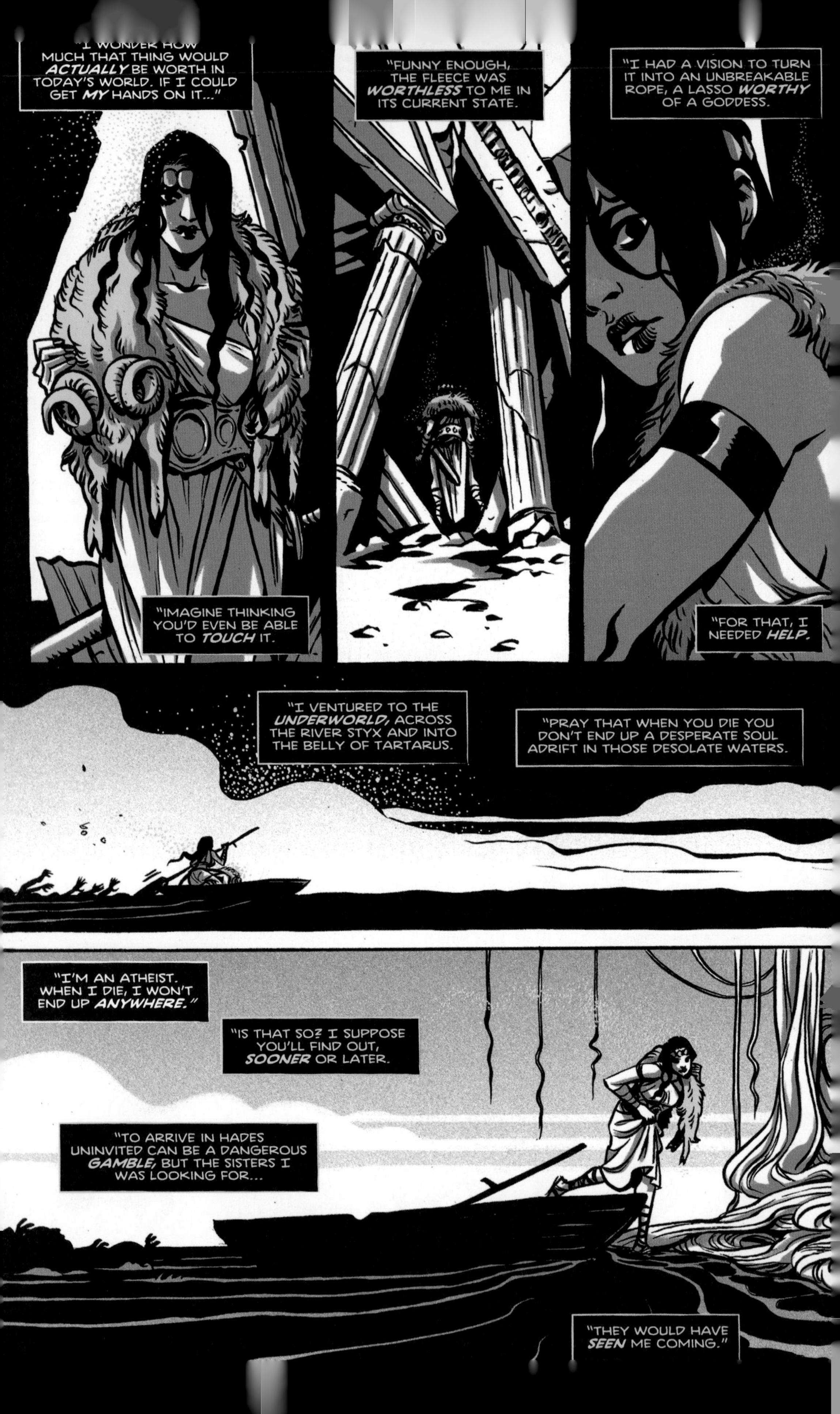
"I WONDER HOW MUCH THAT THING WOULD ACTUALLY BE WORTH IN TODAY'S WORLD. IF I COULD GET MY HANDS ON IT..."
"IMAGINE THINKING YOU'D EVEN BE ABLE TO TOUCH IT.
"FUNNY ENOUGH, THE FLEECE WAS WORTHLESS TO ME IN ITS CURRENT STATE.
"I HAD A VISION TO TURN IT INTO AN UNBREAKABLE ROPE, A LASSO WORTHY OF A GODDESS.
"FOR THAT, I NEEDED HELP.
"I VENTURED TO THE UNDERWORLD, ACROSS THE RIVER STYX AND INTO THE BELLY OF TARTARUS.
"PRAY THAT WHEN YOU DIE YOU DON'T END UP A DESPERATE SOUL ADRIFT IN THOSE DESOLATE WATERS.
"I'M AN ATHEIST. WHEN I DIE, I WON'T END UP ANYWHERE."
"IS THAT SO? I SUPPOSE YOU'LL FIND OUT, SOONER OR LATER.
"TO ARRIVE IN HADES UNINVITED CAN BE A DANGEROUS GAMBLE, BUT THE SISTERS I WAS LOOKING FOR...
"THEY WOULD HAVE SEEN ME COMING."

THE FATES.

"CLOTHO, THE **SPINNER.** SHE TWISTS AND SHAPES THE THREAD OF EACH LIFE.

"LACHESIS, THE ALLOTTER, WHO **DRAWS** EACH ONE OUT...

"...AND **ATROPOS.** THE UNTURNABLE, THE INFLEXIBLE. THE **INEVITABLE.**

"EVERY HUMAN LIFE IS CONNECTED TO A THREAD YOU SEE HERE. SPUN, MEASURED...

"...AND **CUT.**"

SNIK

AH. THIS WOOL YOU BRING US WILL MAKE FOR A **FINE** THREAD. UNBREAKABLE, **INCORRUPTIBLE.**

GREAT STORY. LET'S SAY FOR ARGUMENT'S SAKE THAT I **BUY** ALL THIS. THERE'VE BEEN OVER ONE HUNDRED BILLION PEOPLE ON EARTH.

"IT'S A MATTER OF PRACTICALITY. WHERE THE HELL DOES ALL THAT STRING **GO?**"

"WHAT DO YOU THINK THE UNDERWORLD IS MADE OUT OF? EVERY CUT THREAD **EXPANDS** ITS DOMAIN.

"THEY HAVE TO **MAKE ROOM.**"

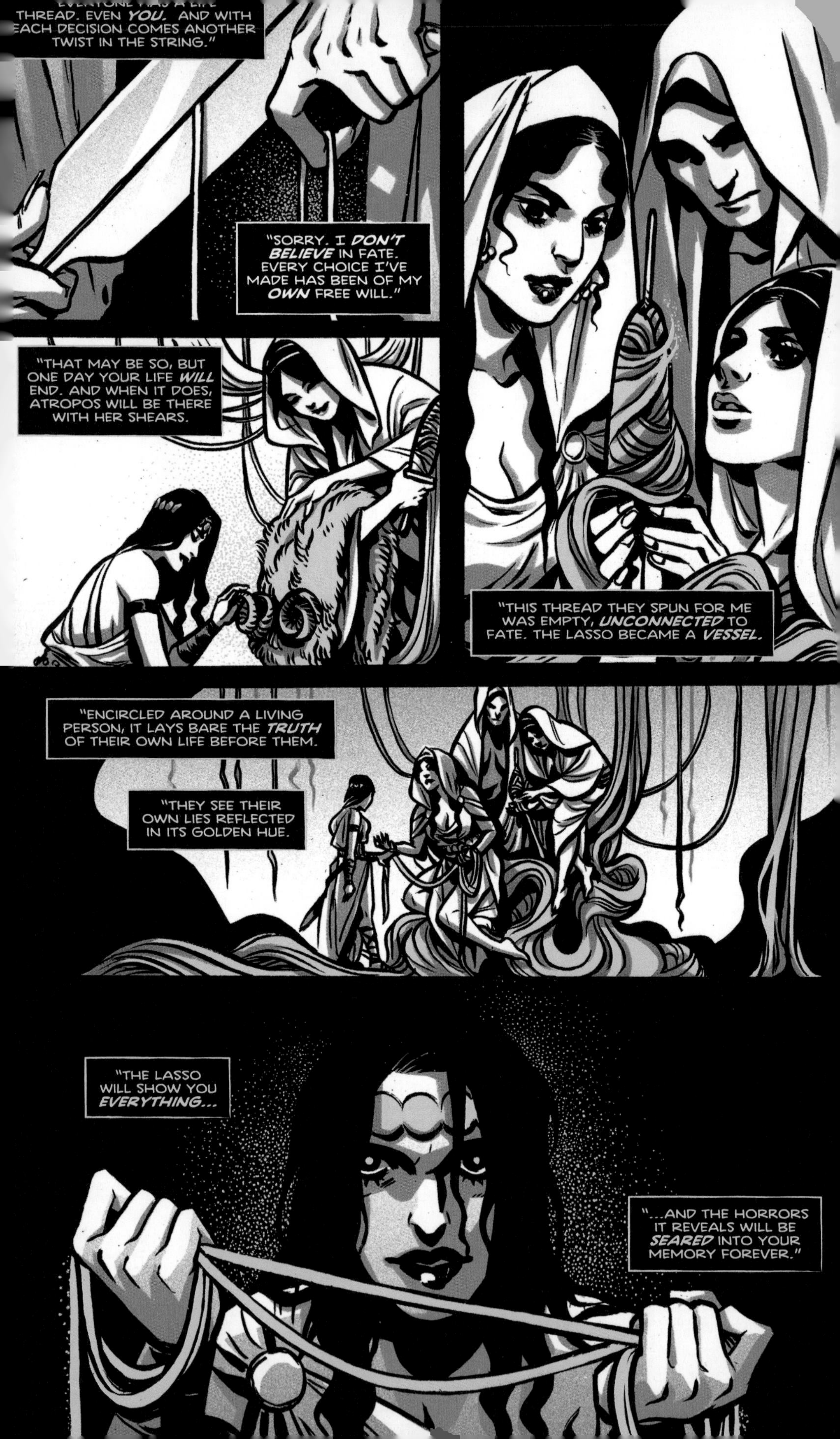
THREAD. EVEN *YOU.* AND WITH EACH DECISION COMES ANOTHER TWIST IN THE STRING."
"SORRY. I *DON'T BELIEVE* IN FATE. EVERY CHOICE I'VE MADE HAS BEEN OF MY *OWN* FREE WILL."
"THAT MAY BE SO, BUT ONE DAY YOUR LIFE *WILL* END. AND WHEN IT DOES, ATROPOS WILL BE THERE WITH HER SHEARS.
"THIS THREAD THEY SPUN FOR ME WAS EMPTY, *UNCONNECTED* TO FATE. THE LASSO BECAME A *VESSEL.*
"ENCIRCLED AROUND A LIVING PERSON, IT LAYS BARE THE *TRUTH* OF THEIR OWN LIFE BEFORE THEM.
"THEY SEE THEIR OWN LIES REFLECTED IN ITS GOLDEN HUE.
"THE LASSO WILL SHOW YOU *EVERYTHING...*
"...AND THE HORRORS IT REVEALS WILL BE *SEARED* INTO YOUR MEMORY FOREVER."

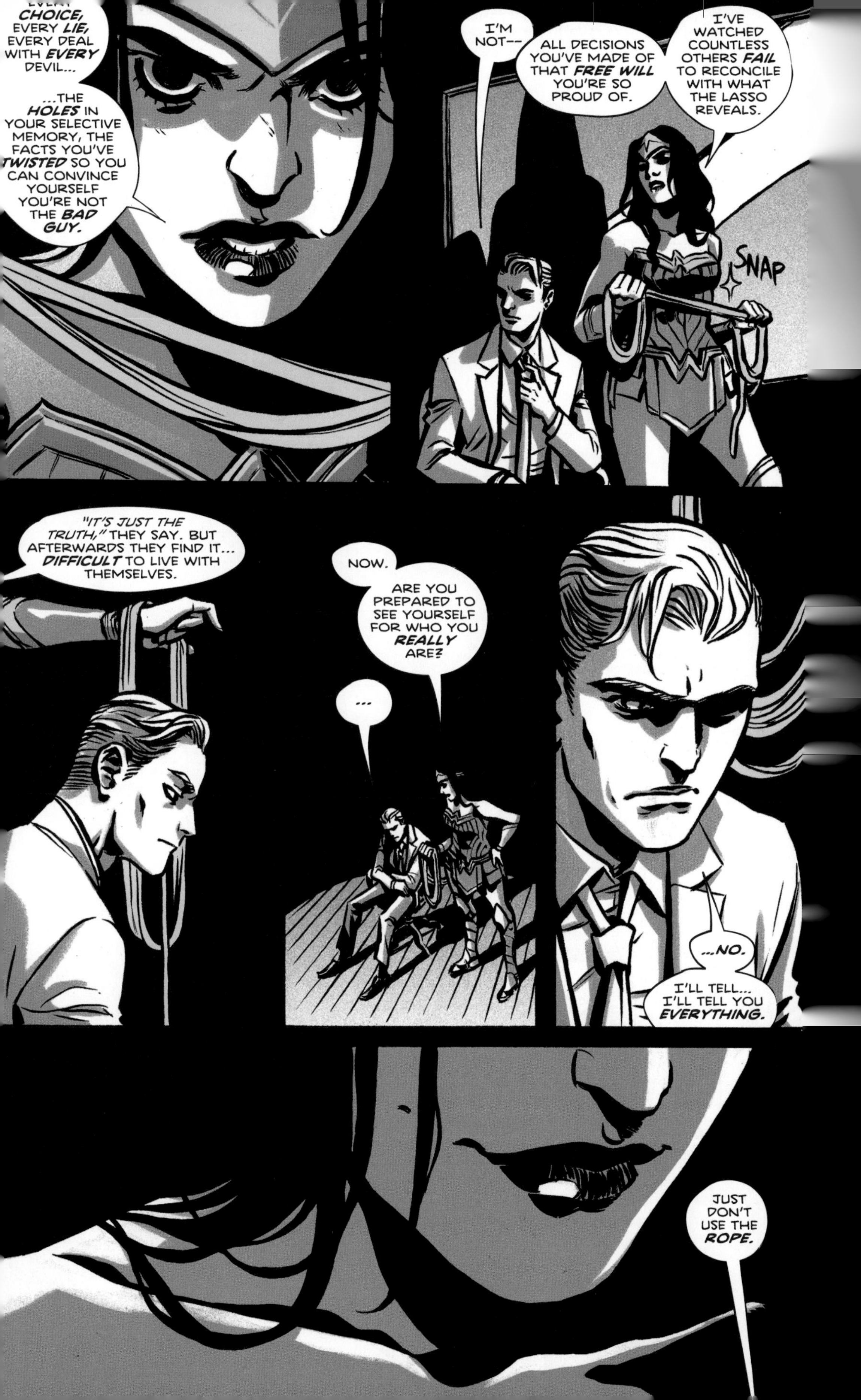
CHOICE, EVERY LIE, EVERY DEAL WITH EVERY DEVIL...
...THE HOLES IN YOUR SELECTIVE MEMORY, THE FACTS YOU'VE TWISTED SO YOU CAN CONVINCE YOURSELF YOU'RE NOT THE BAD GUY.
I'M NOT--
ALL DECISIONS YOU'VE MADE OF THAT FREE WILL YOU'RE SO PROUD OF.
I'VE WATCHED COUNTLESS OTHERS FAIL TO RECONCILE WITH WHAT THE LASSO REVEALS.
SNAP
"IT'S JUST THE TRUTH," THEY SAY. BUT AFTERWARDS THEY FIND IT... DIFFICULT TO LIVE WITH THEMSELVES.
NOW.
ARE YOU PREPARED TO SEE YOURSELF FOR WHO YOU REALLY ARE?
...
...NO.
I'LL TELL... I'LL TELL YOU EVERYTHING.
JUST DON'T USE THE ROPE.

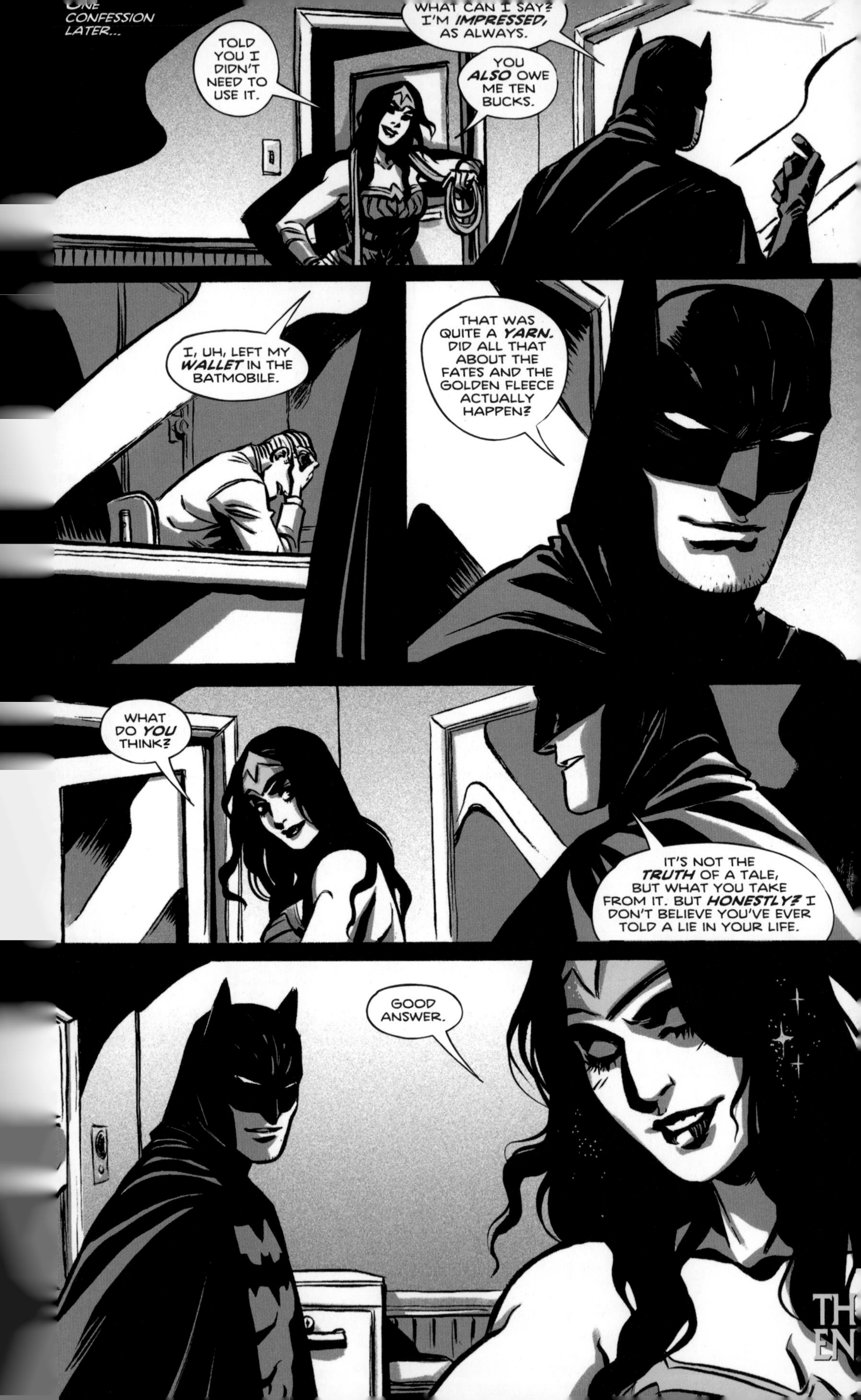
ONE CONFESSION LATER...
TOLD YOU I DIDN'T NEED TO USE IT.
WHAT CAN I SAY? I'M IMPRESSED, AS ALWAYS.
YOU ALSO OWE ME TEN BUCKS.
I, UH, LEFT MY WALLET IN THE BATMOBILE.
THAT WAS QUITE A YARN. DID ALL THAT ABOUT THE FATES AND THE GOLDEN FLEECE ACTUALLY HAPPEN?
WHAT DO YOU THINK?
IT'S NOT THE TRUTH OF A TALE, BUT WHAT YOU TAKE FROM IT. BUT HONESTLY? I DON'T BELIEVE YOU'VE EVER TOLD A LIE IN YOUR LIFE.
GOOD ANSWER.

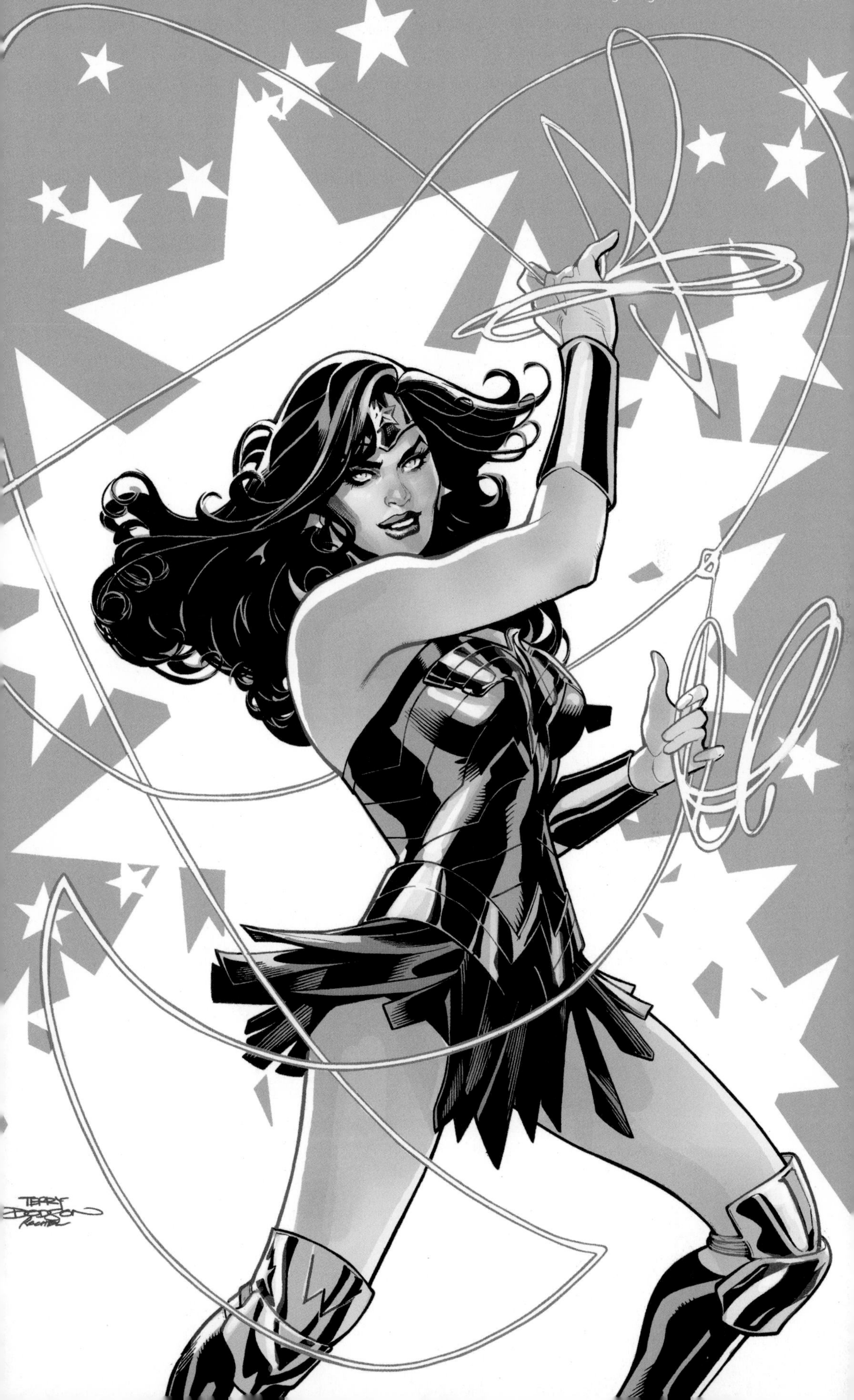
TERRY DODSON

Cover by Terry Dodson and Rachel Dodson

MUSIC WAS THE FIRST THING TO GO.

FIRST, LOVE SONGS. WHICH, OBVIOUSLY NOT EVERYONE LIKES LOVE SONGS.

BUT SUDDENLY, NO ONE DID.

SUDDENLY EVERYONE HATED LOVE SONGS. NOT BECAUSE THEY WERE BAD.

BUT BECAUSE THEY WERE **PAINFUL** TO LISTEN TO.

AFTER THAT IT WAS JUST THE SOUND OF PEOPLE'S VOICES.

EVERYONE WISHED EVERYONE WOULD STOP TALKING.

AND THEY DID.

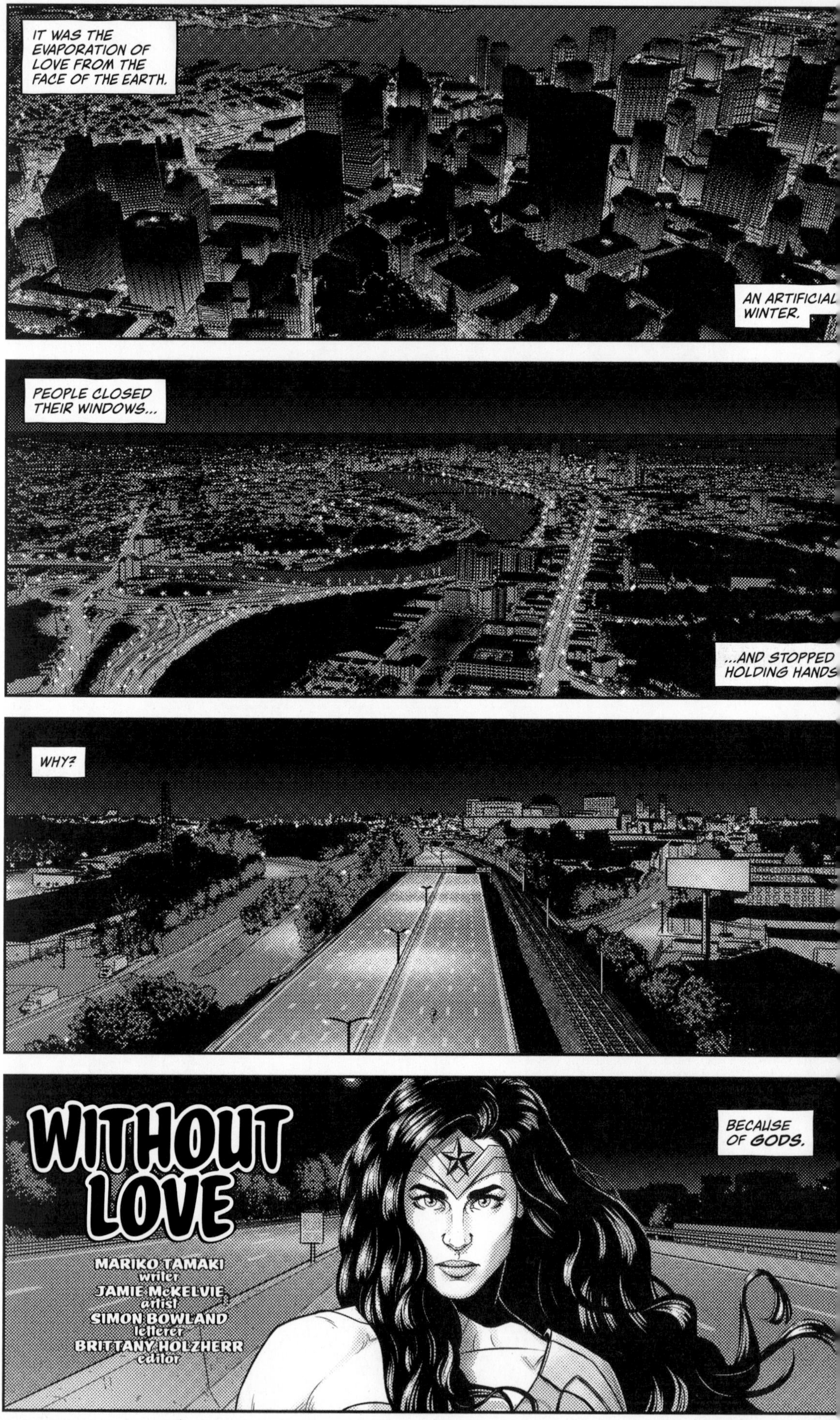
IT WAS THE EVAPORATION OF LOVE FROM THE FACE OF THE EARTH.
AN ARTIFICIAL WINTER.
PEOPLE CLOSED THEIR WINDOWS...
...AND STOPPED HOLDING HANDS
WHY?
BECAUSE OF GODS.
WITHOUT LOVE
MARIKO TAMAKI writer
JAMIE McKELVIE artist
SIMON BOWLAND letterer
BRITTANY HOLZHERR editor

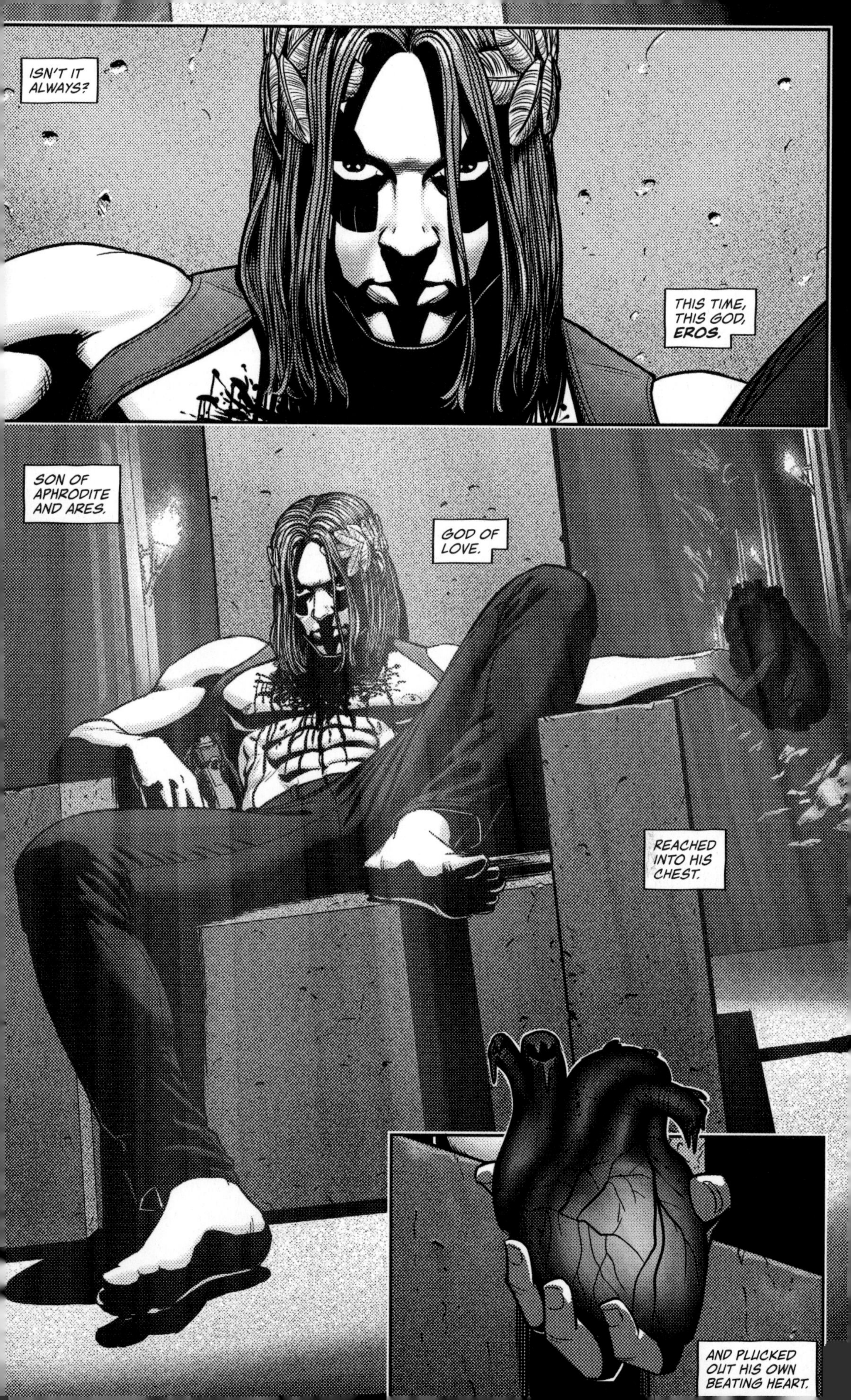
ISN'T IT ALWAYS?
THIS TIME, THIS GOD, **EROS.**
SON OF APHRODITE AND ARES.
GOD OF LOVE.
REACHED INTO HIS CHEST.
AND PLUCKED OUT HIS OWN BEATING HEART.

KNOWING IT
WOULD STOP
THE WORLD.

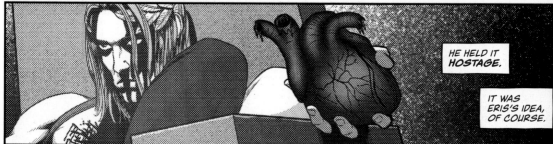

HE HELD IT
HOSTAGE.

IT WAS
ERIS'S IDEA,
OF COURSE.

ERIS.

BORED.
RECKLESS.

WHISPERER
OF CHAOS.

BRING
HER TO YOU.
CALL HER TO
YOU.

"BREAK THEIR
HEARTS...AND
SHE'LL HAVE
NO CHOICE."

YOU'RE
HERE.

YES.

FOR
ME.

NO.

FOR
THEM.

NO.

ERIS.

SISTER.

YOU ARE
HERE BY MY
DEVICES. NOT
FOR LOVE.

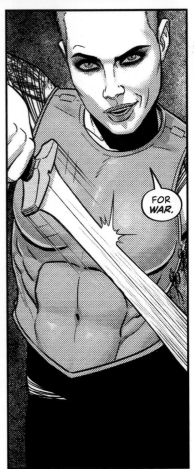

FOR
WAR.

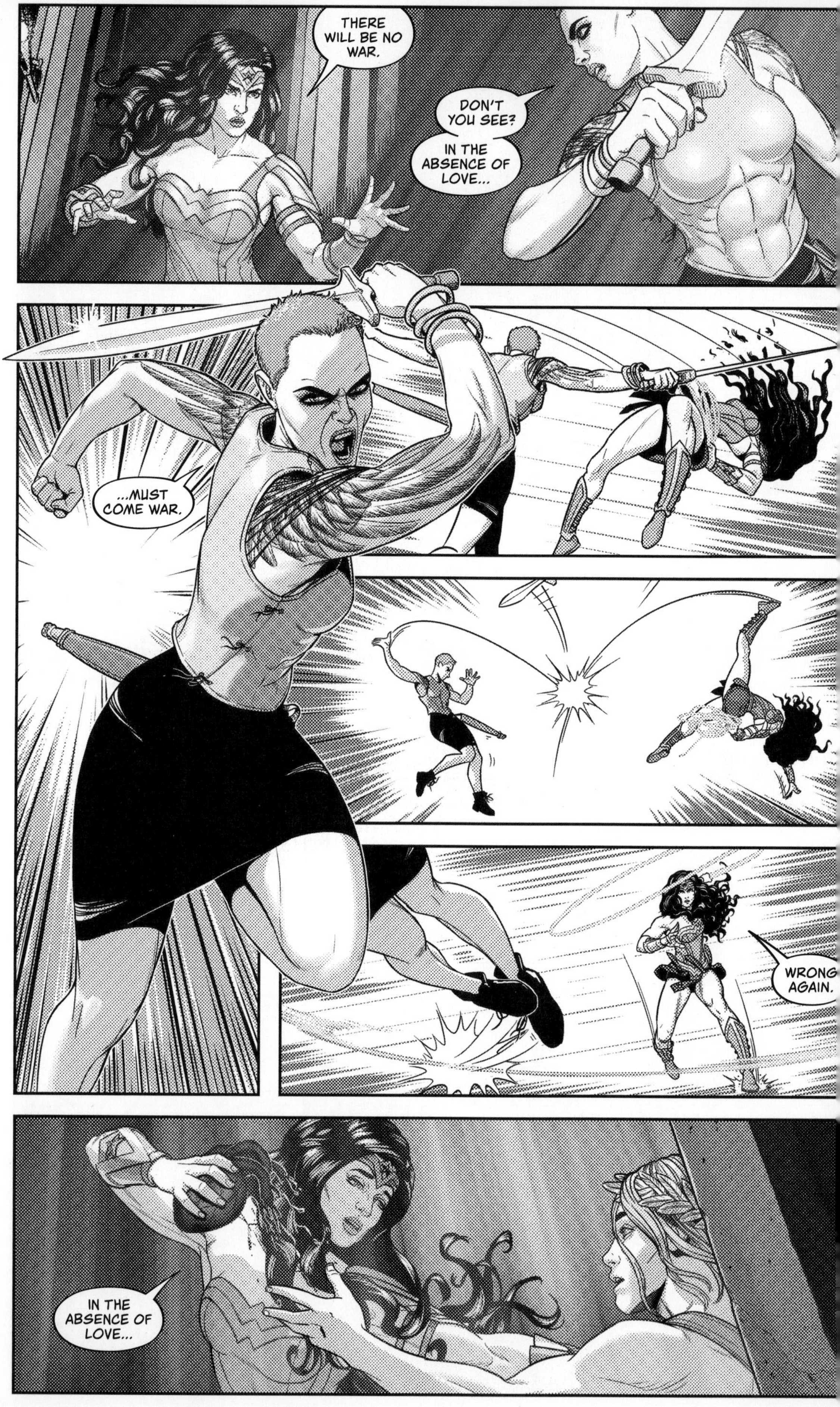
THERE WILL BE NO WAR.
DON'T YOU SEE?
IN THE ABSENCE OF LOVE...
...MUST COME WAR.
WRONG AGAIN.
IN THE ABSENCE OF LOVE...

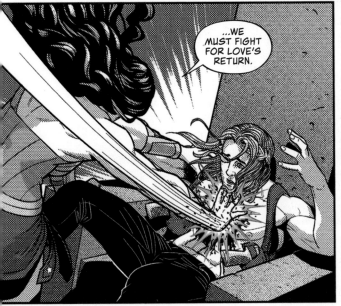

...WE MUST FIGHT FOR LOVE'S RETURN.

RAH!

I WILL FIGHT FOR LOVE'S RETURN.

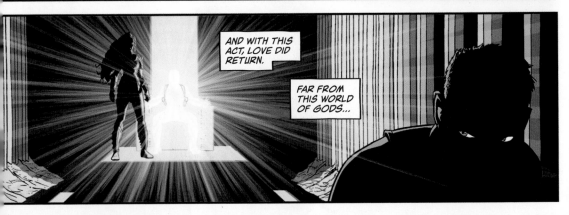

AND WITH THIS ACT, LOVE DID RETURN.

FAR FROM THIS WORLD OF GODS...

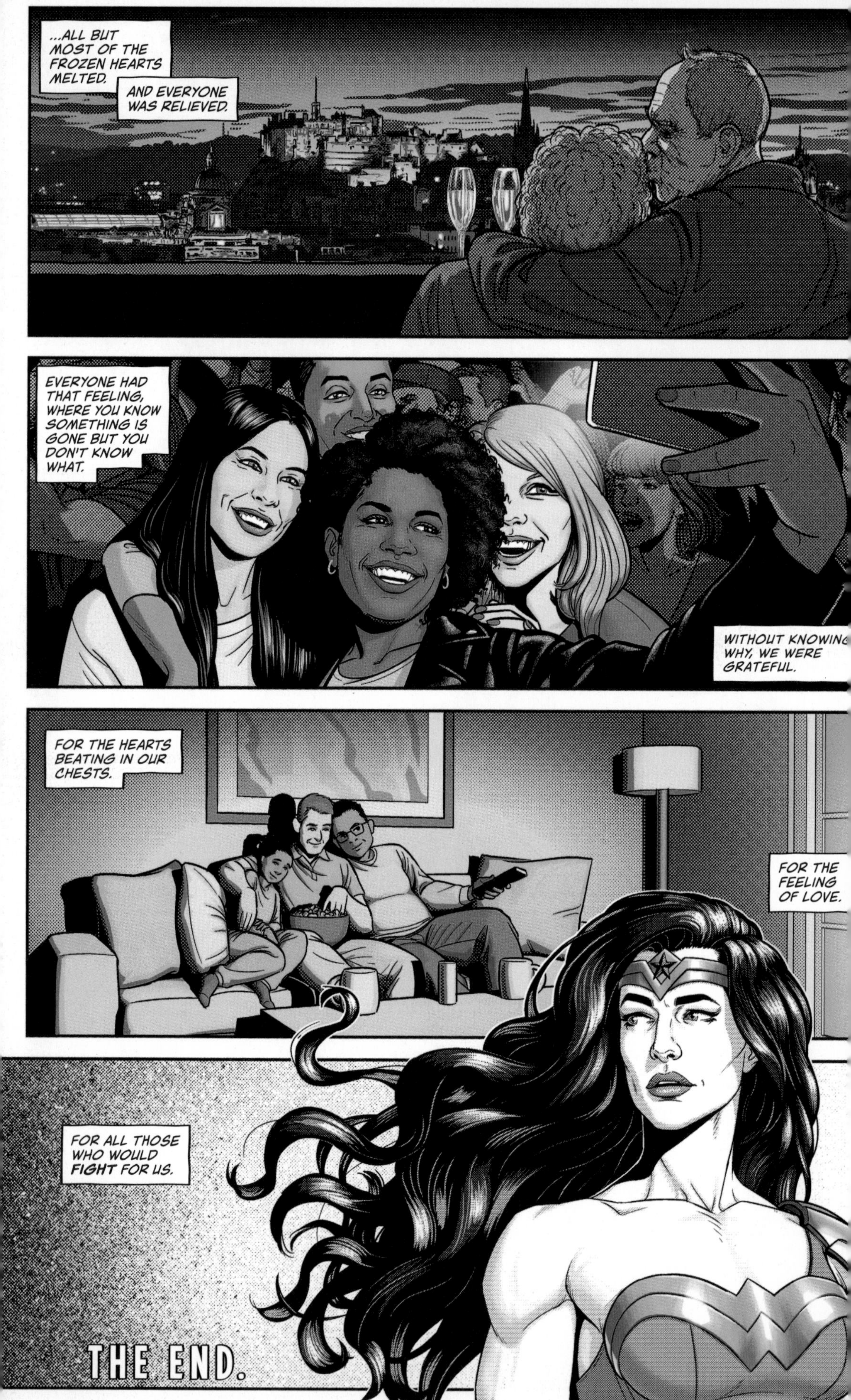
...ALL BUT MOST OF THE FROZEN HEARTS MELTED.
AND EVERYONE WAS RELIEVED.
EVERYONE HAD THAT FEELING, WHERE YOU KNOW SOMETHING IS GONE BUT YOU DON'T KNOW WHAT.
WITHOUT KNOWING WHY, WE WERE GRATEFUL.
FOR THE HEARTS BEATING IN OUR CHESTS.
FOR THE FEELING OF LOVE.
FOR ALL THOSE WHO WOULD FIGHT FOR US.
THE END.

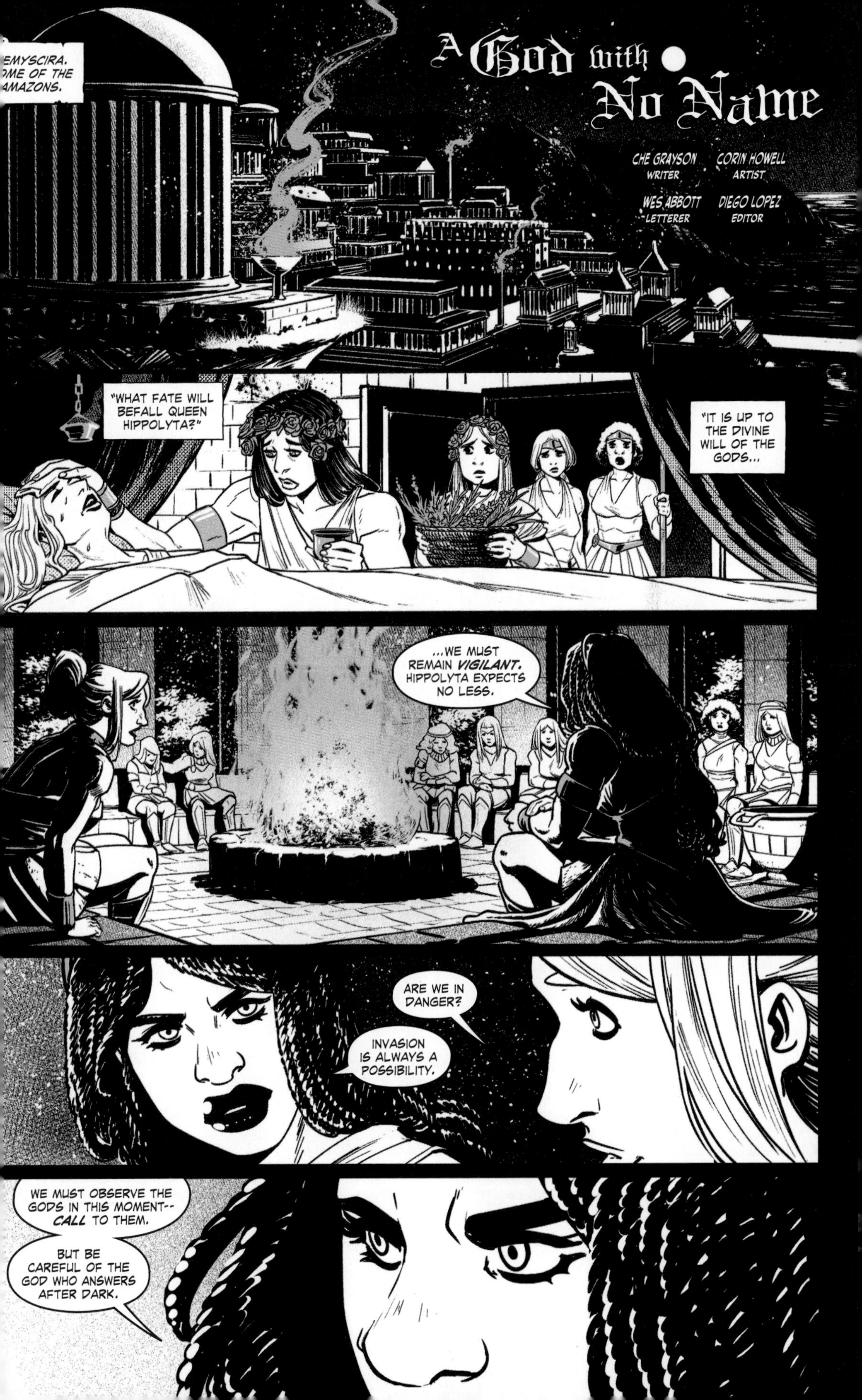

EMYSCIRA. OME OF THE AMAZONS.
A God with No Name
CHE GRAYSON WRITER
CORIN HOWELL ARTIST
WES ABBOTT LETTERER
DIEGO LOPEZ EDITOR
"WHAT FATE WILL BEFALL QUEEN HIPPOLYTA?"
"IT IS UP TO THE DIVINE WILL OF THE GODS...
...WE MUST REMAIN VIGILANT. HIPPOLYTA EXPECTS NO LESS.
ARE WE IN DANGER?
INVASION IS ALWAYS A POSSIBILITY.
WE MUST OBSERVE THE GODS IN THIS MOMENT-- CALL TO THEM.
BUT BE CAREFUL OF THE GOD WHO ANSWERS AFTER DARK.

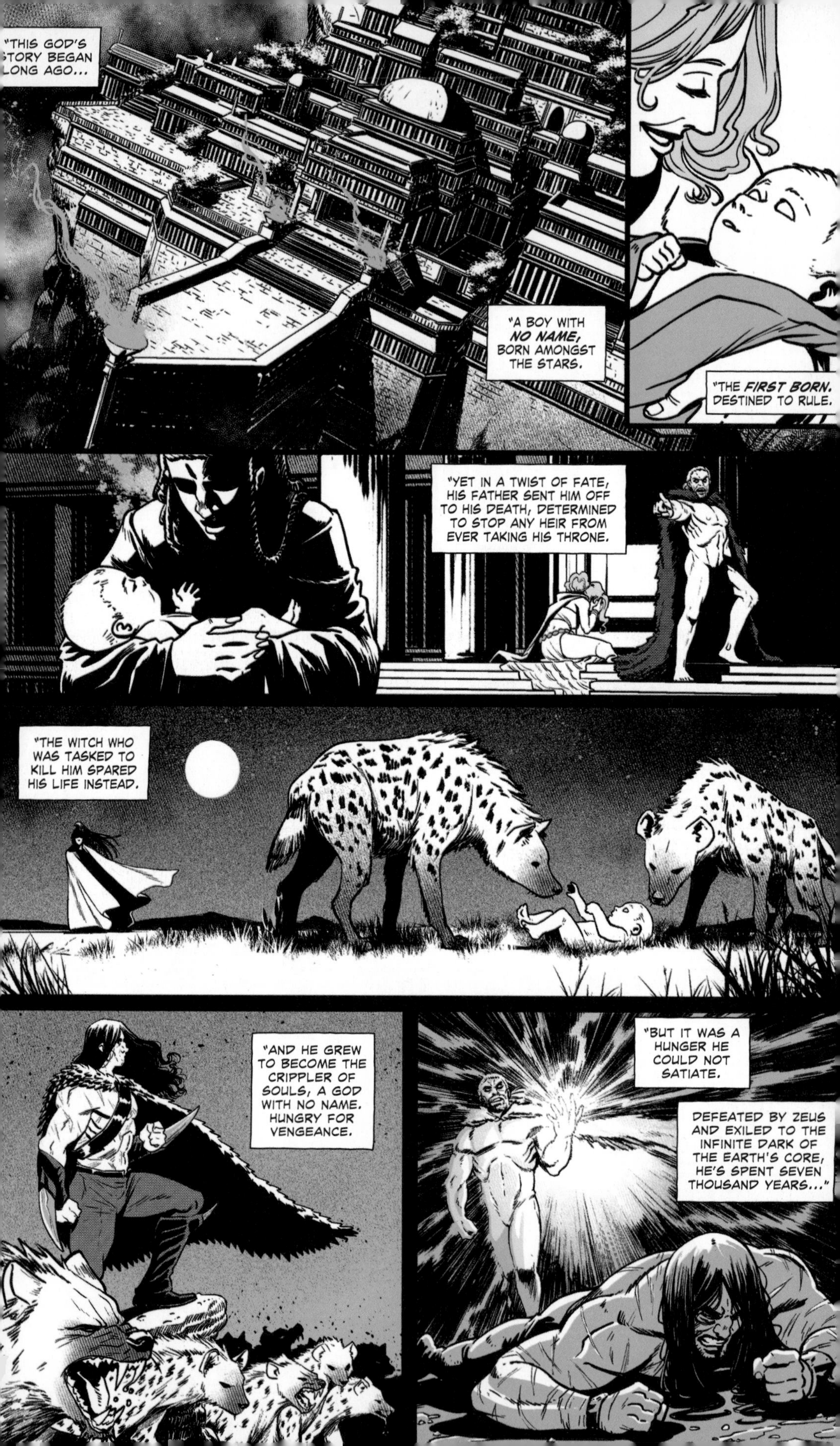

"THIS GOD'S STORY BEGAN LONG AGO...
"A BOY WITH NO NAME, BORN AMONGST THE STARS.
"THE FIRST BORN. DESTINED TO RULE.
"YET IN A TWIST OF FATE, HIS FATHER SENT HIM OFF TO HIS DEATH, DETERMINED TO STOP ANY HEIR FROM EVER TAKING HIS THRONE.
"THE WITCH WHO WAS TASKED TO KILL HIM SPARED HIS LIFE INSTEAD.
"AND HE GREW TO BECOME THE CRIPPLER OF SOULS, A GOD WITH NO NAME. HUNGRY FOR VENGEANCE.
"BUT IT WAS A HUNGER HE COULD NOT SATIATE.
DEFEATED BY ZEUS AND EXILED TO THE INFINITE DARK OF THE EARTH'S CORE, HE'S SPENT SEVEN THOUSAND YEARS..."

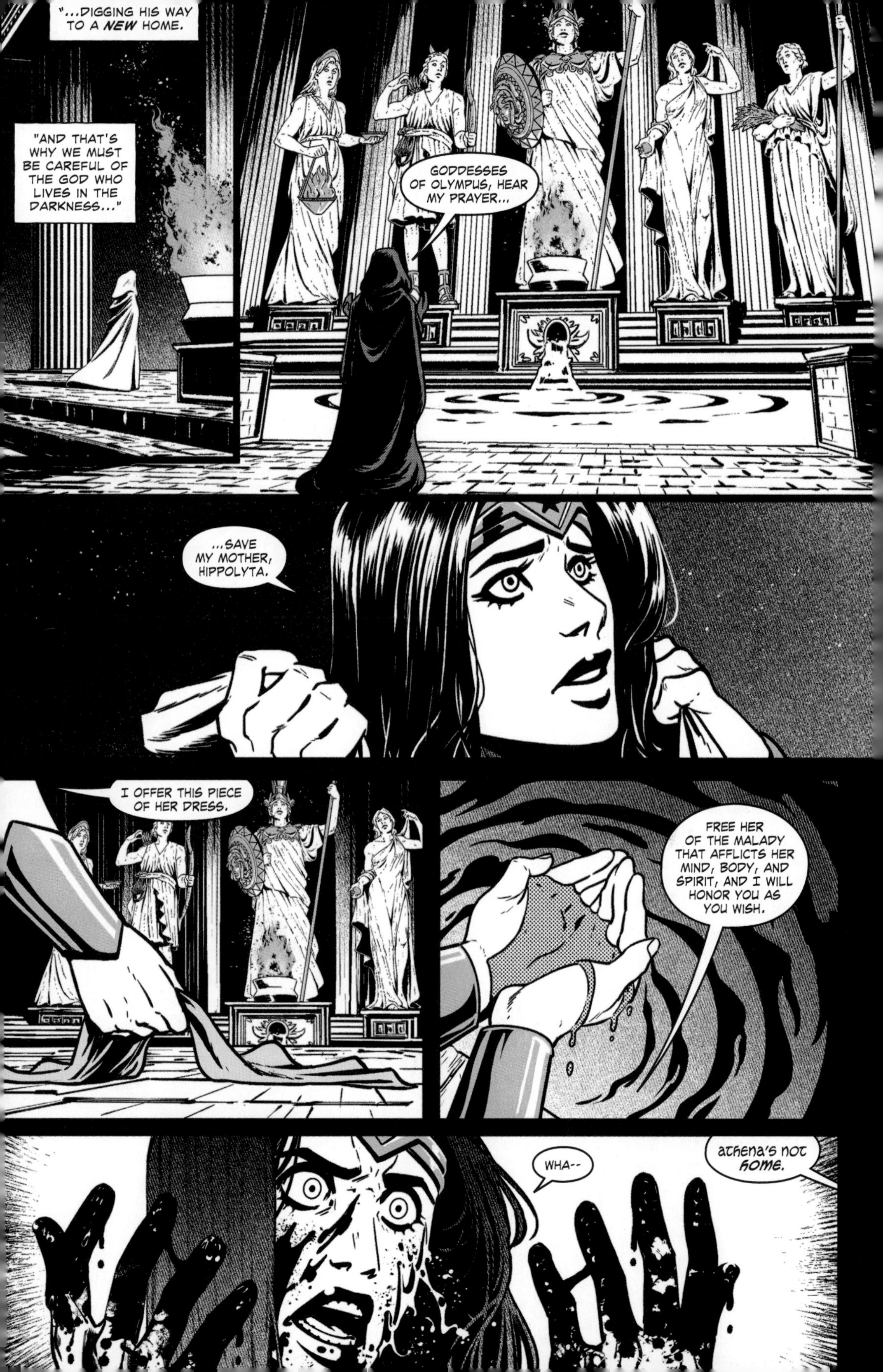
"...DIGGING HIS WAY TO A *NEW* HOME.
"AND THAT'S WHY WE MUST BE CAREFUL OF THE GOD WHO LIVES IN THE DARKNESS..."
GODDESSES OF OLYMPUS, HEAR MY PRAYER...
...SAVE MY MOTHER, HIPPOLYTA.
I OFFER THIS PIECE OF HER DRESS.
FREE HER OF THE MALADY THAT AFFLICTS HER MIND, BODY, AND SPIRIT, AND I WILL HONOR YOU AS YOU WISH.
WHA--
athena's not *home*.

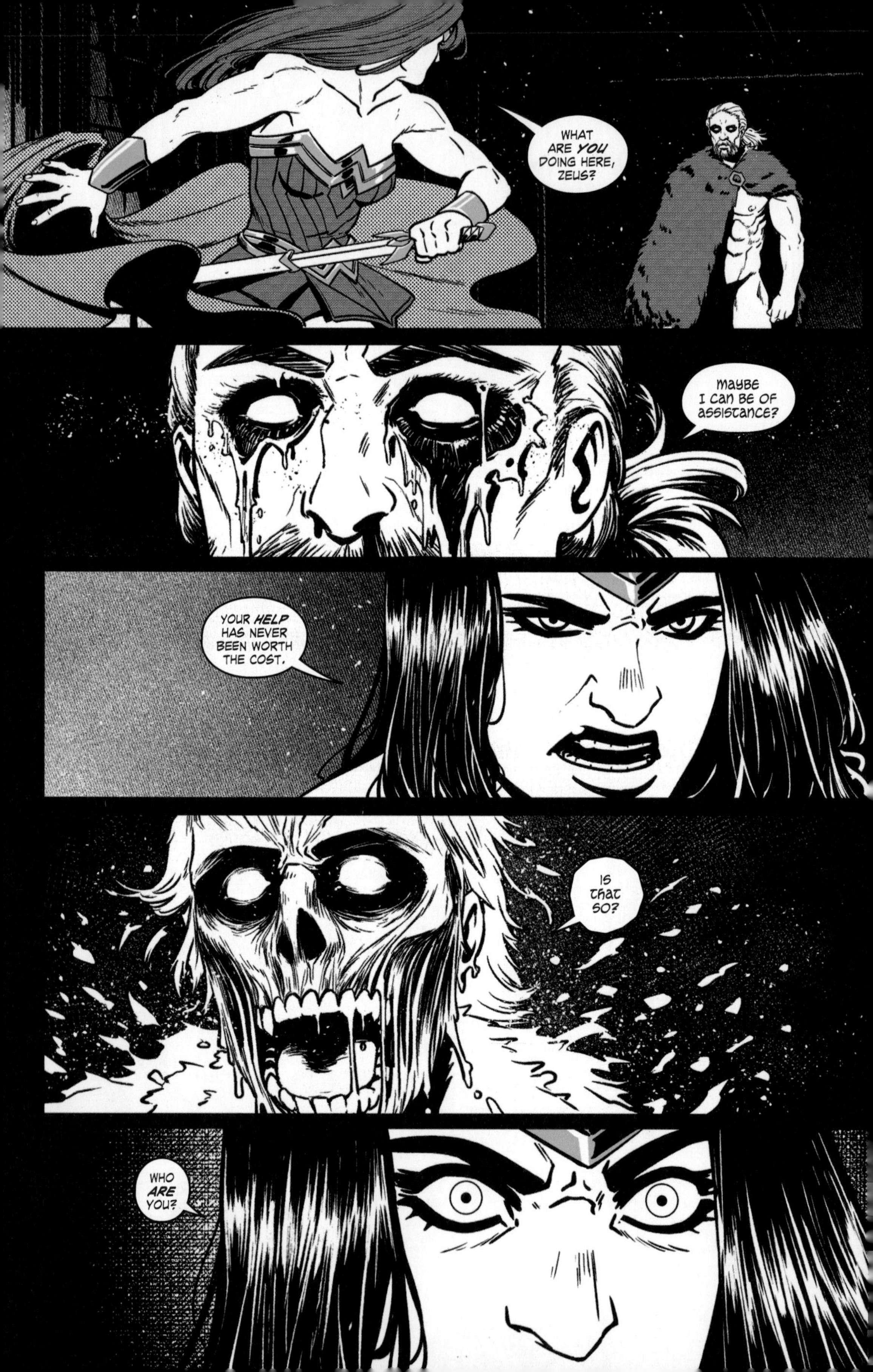
WHAT ARE YOU DOING HERE, ZEUS?
MAYBE I CAN BE OF ASSISTANCE?
YOUR HELP HAS NEVER BEEN WORTH THE COST.
IS THAT SO?
WHO ARE YOU?

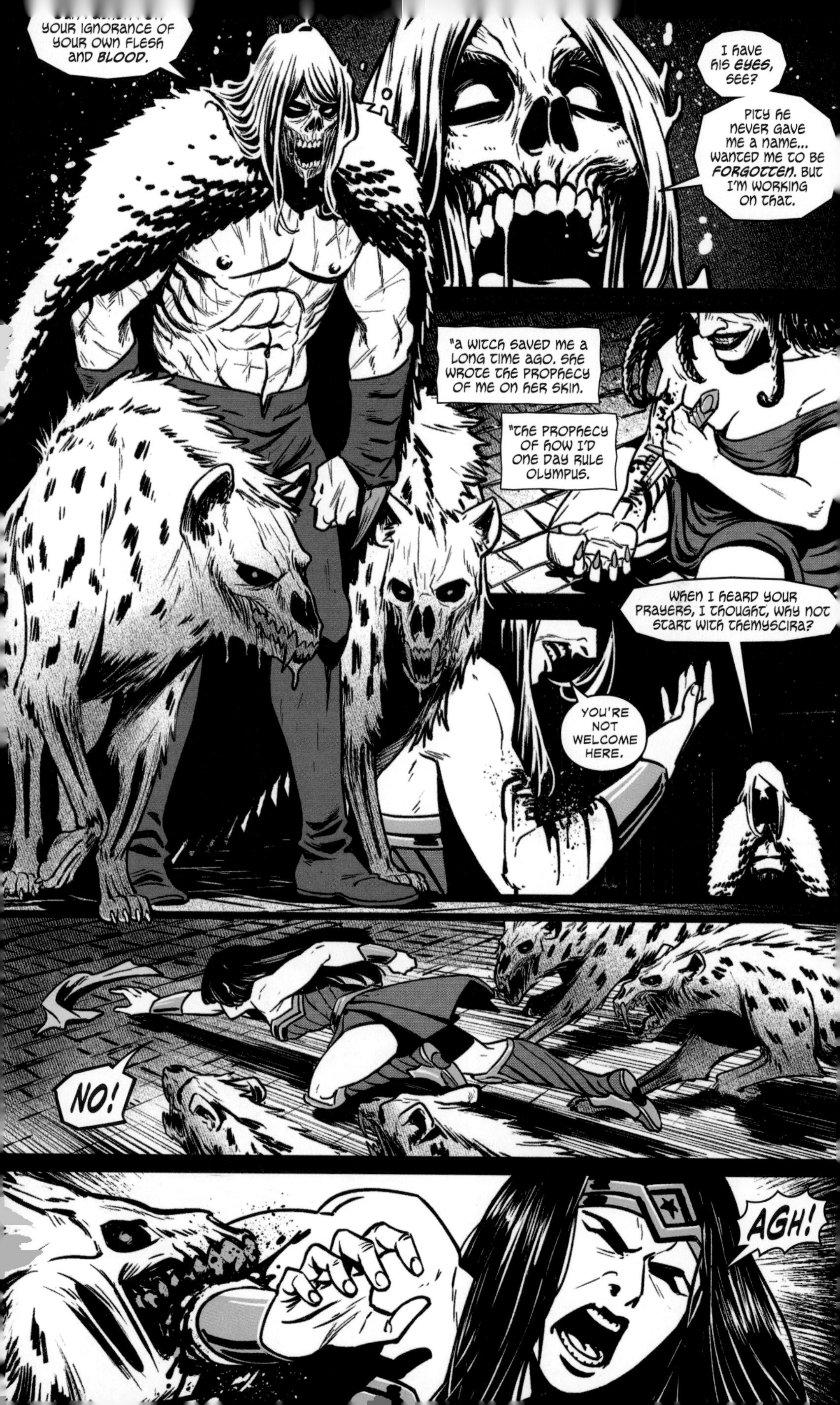
YOUR IGNORANCE OF YOUR OWN FLESH AND BLOOD.
I HAVE HIS EYES, SEE?
PITY HE NEVER GAVE ME A NAME... WANTED ME TO BE FORGOTTEN. BUT I'M WORKING ON THAT.
"A WITCH SAVED ME A LONG TIME AGO. SHE WROTE THE PROPHECY OF ME ON HER SKIN.
"THE PROPHECY OF HOW I'D ONE DAY RULE OLYMPUS.
WHEN I HEARD YOUR PRAYERS, I THOUGHT, WHY NOT START WITH THEMYSCIRA?
YOU'RE NOT WELCOME HERE.
NO!
AGH!

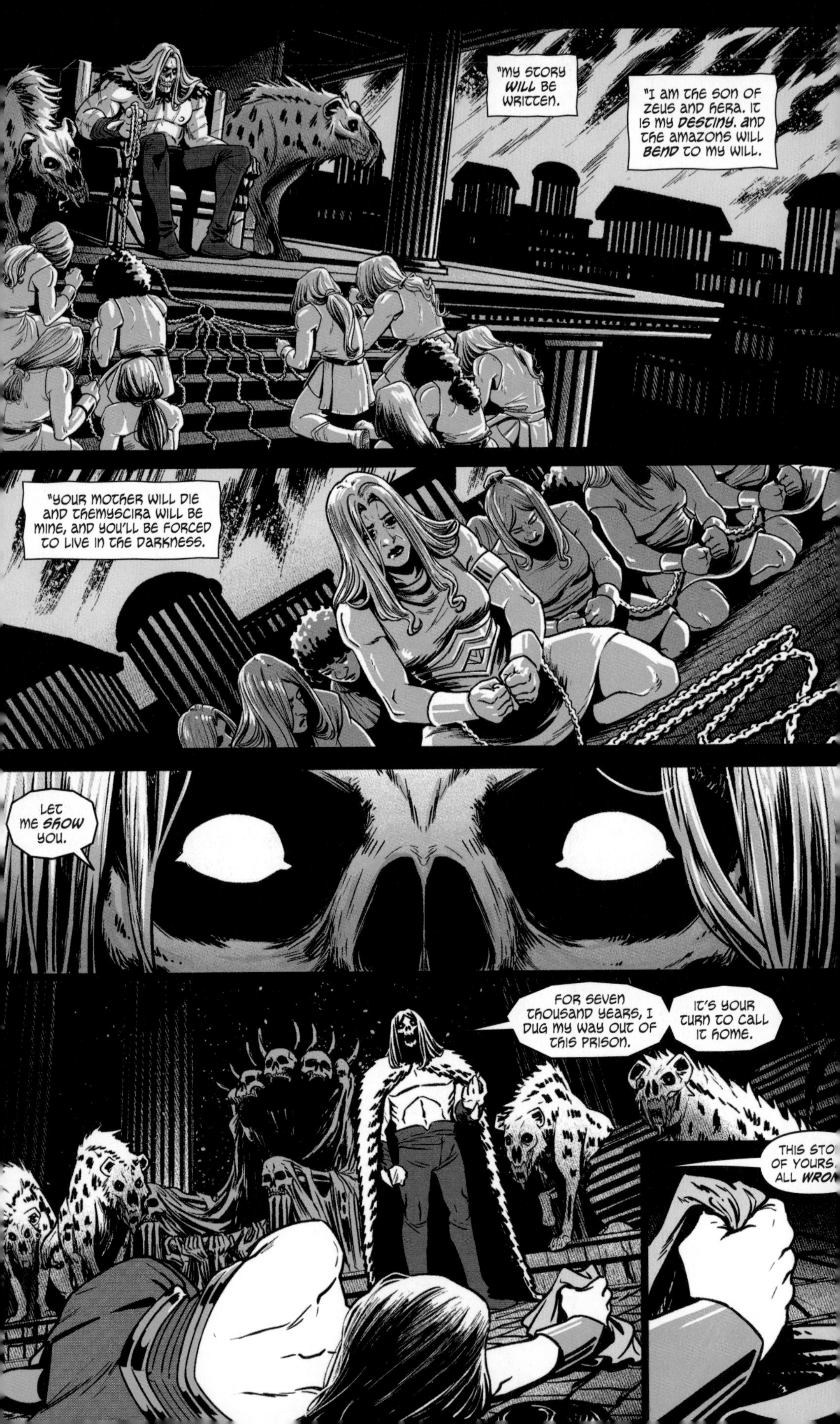
"MY STORY WILL BE WRITTEN.
"I AM THE SON OF ZEUS AND HERA. IT IS MY DESTINY. AND THE AMAZONS WILL BEND TO MY WILL.
"YOUR MOTHER WILL DIE AND THEMYSCIRA WILL BE MINE, AND YOU'LL BE FORCED TO LIVE IN THE DARKNESS.
LET ME SHOW YOU.
FOR SEVEN THOUSAND YEARS, I DUG MY WAY OUT OF THIS PRISON.
IT'S YOUR TURN TO CALL IT HOME.
THIS STO
OF YOURS
ALL WRON

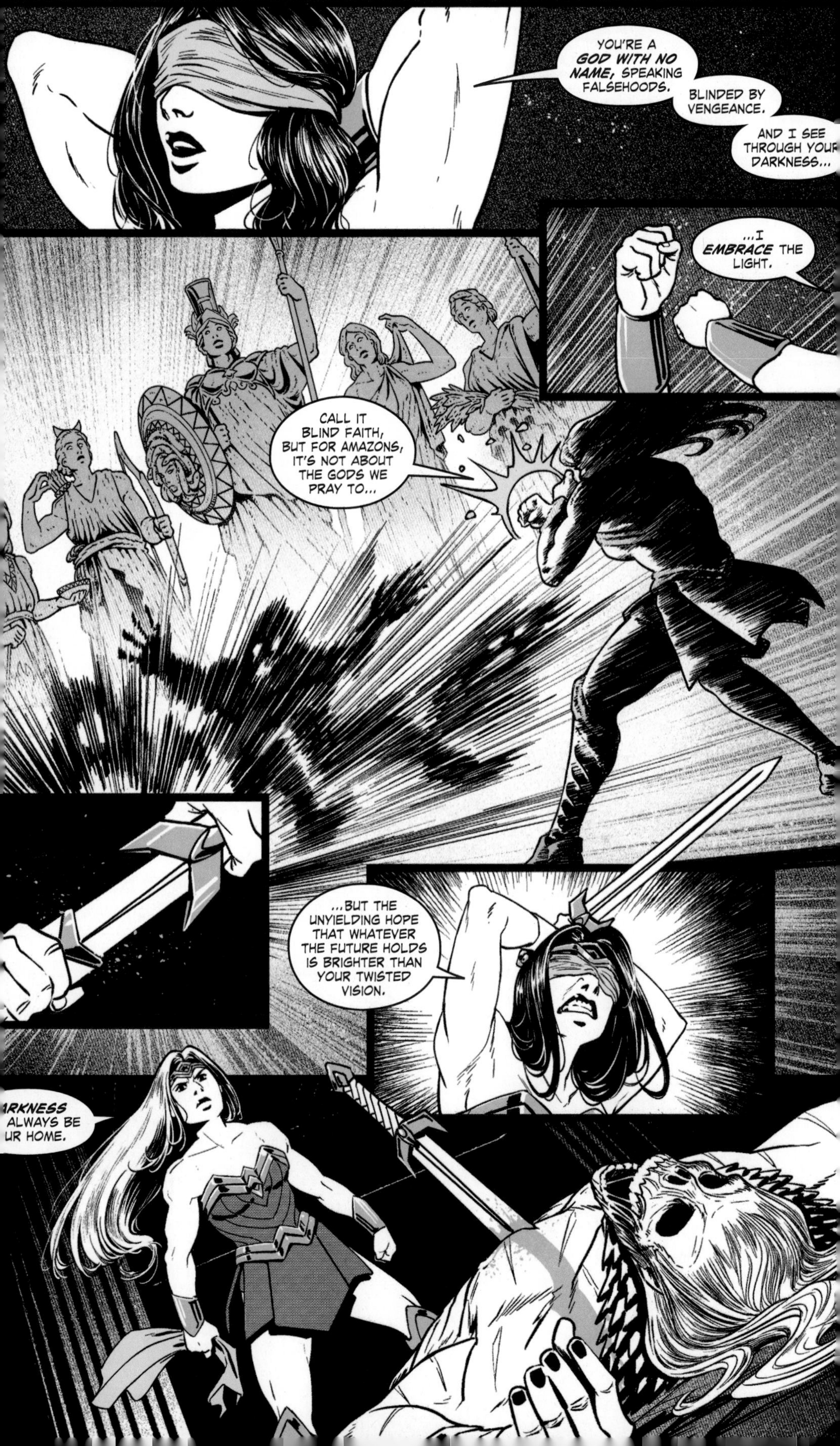
YOU'RE A *GOD WITH NO NAME,* SPEAKING FALSEHOODS.
BLINDED BY VENGEANCE.
AND I SEE THROUGH YOUR DARKNESS...
...I *EMBRACE* THE LIGHT.
CALL IT BLIND FAITH, BUT FOR AMAZONS, IT'S NOT ABOUT THE GODS WE PRAY TO...
...BUT THE UNYIELDING HOPE THAT WHATEVER THE FUTURE HOLDS IS BRIGHTER THAN YOUR TWISTED VISION.
ARKNESS ALWAYS BE UR HOME.

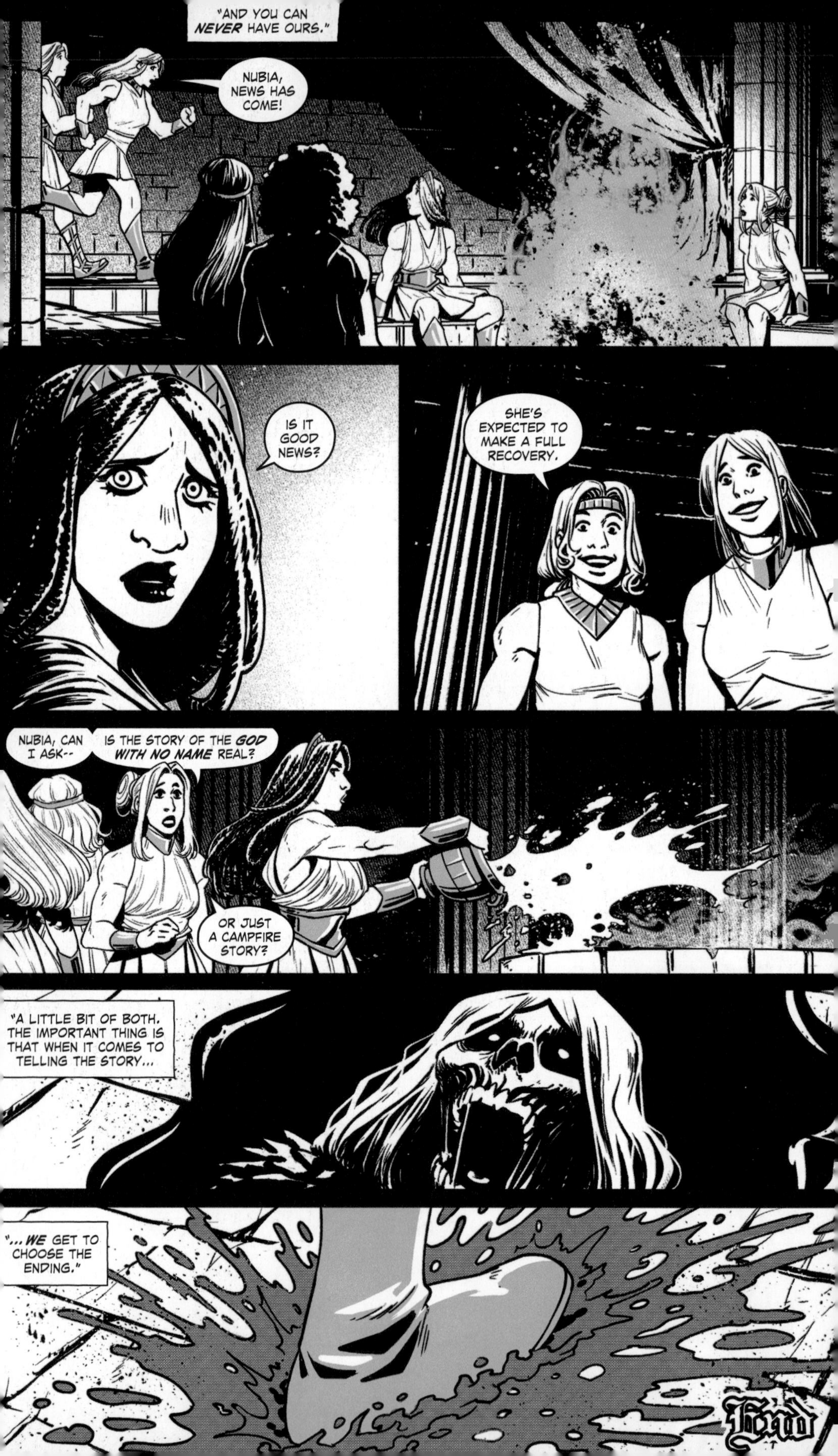
"AND YOU CAN NEVER HAVE OURS."
NUBIA, NEWS HAS COME!
IS IT GOOD NEWS?
SHE'S EXPECTED TO MAKE A FULL RECOVERY.
NUBIA, CAN I ASK--
IS THE STORY OF THE GOD WITH NO NAME REAL?
OR JUST A CAMPFIRE STORY?
"A LITTLE BIT OF BOTH. THE IMPORTANT THING IS THAT WHEN IT COMES TO TELLING THE STORY...
"...WE GET TO CHOOSE THE ENDING."
End

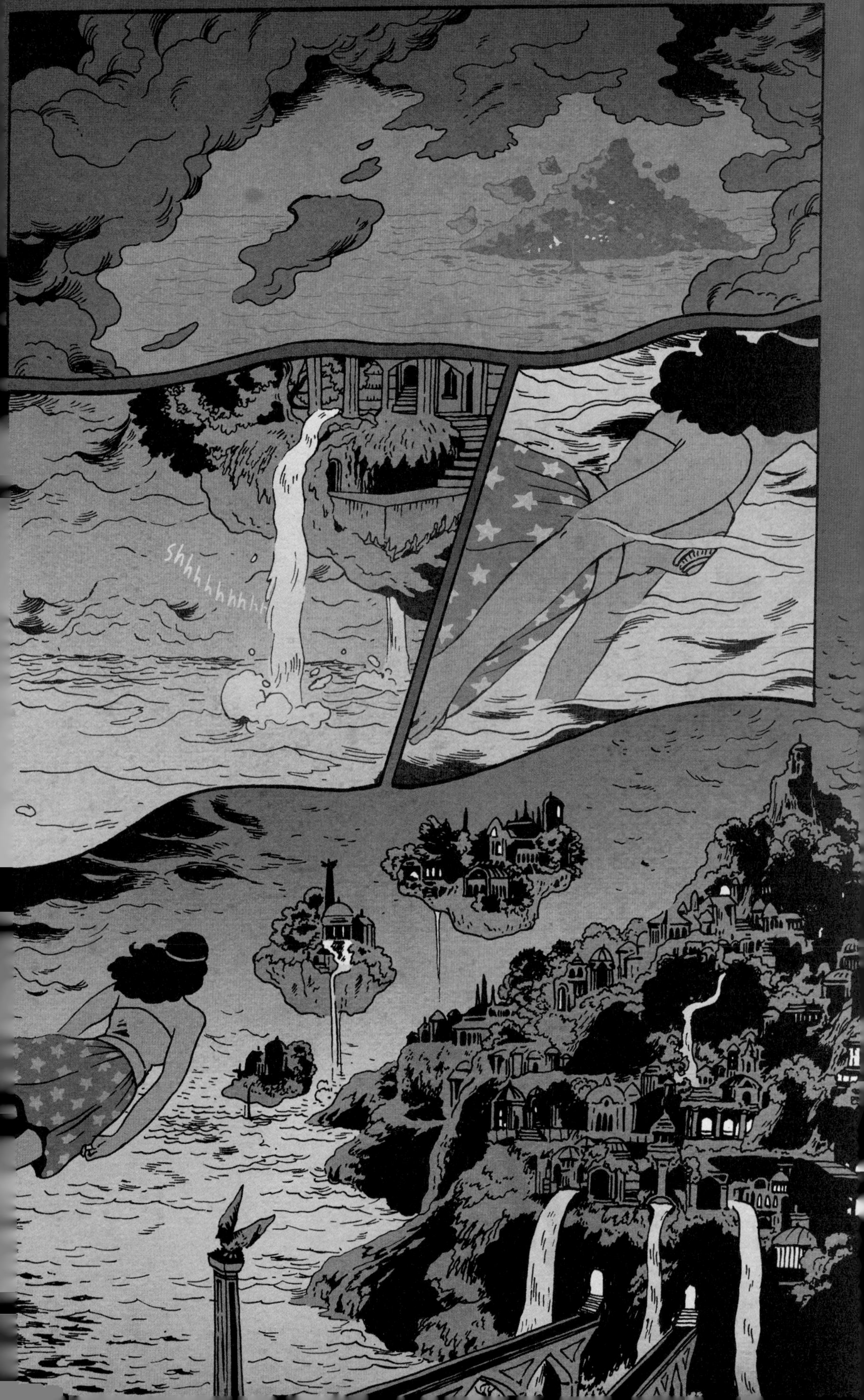
Shhhhhhhhh

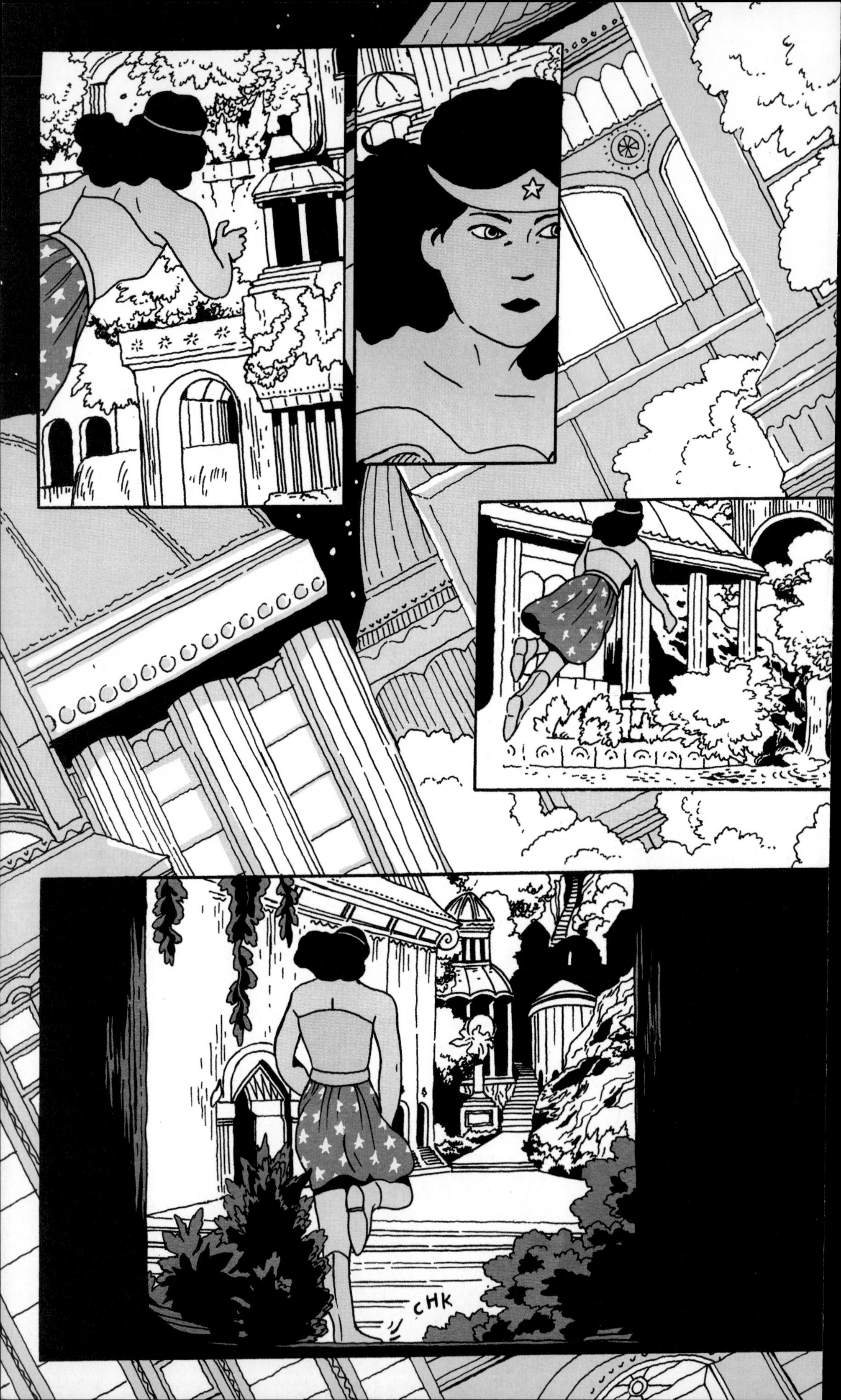
CHK

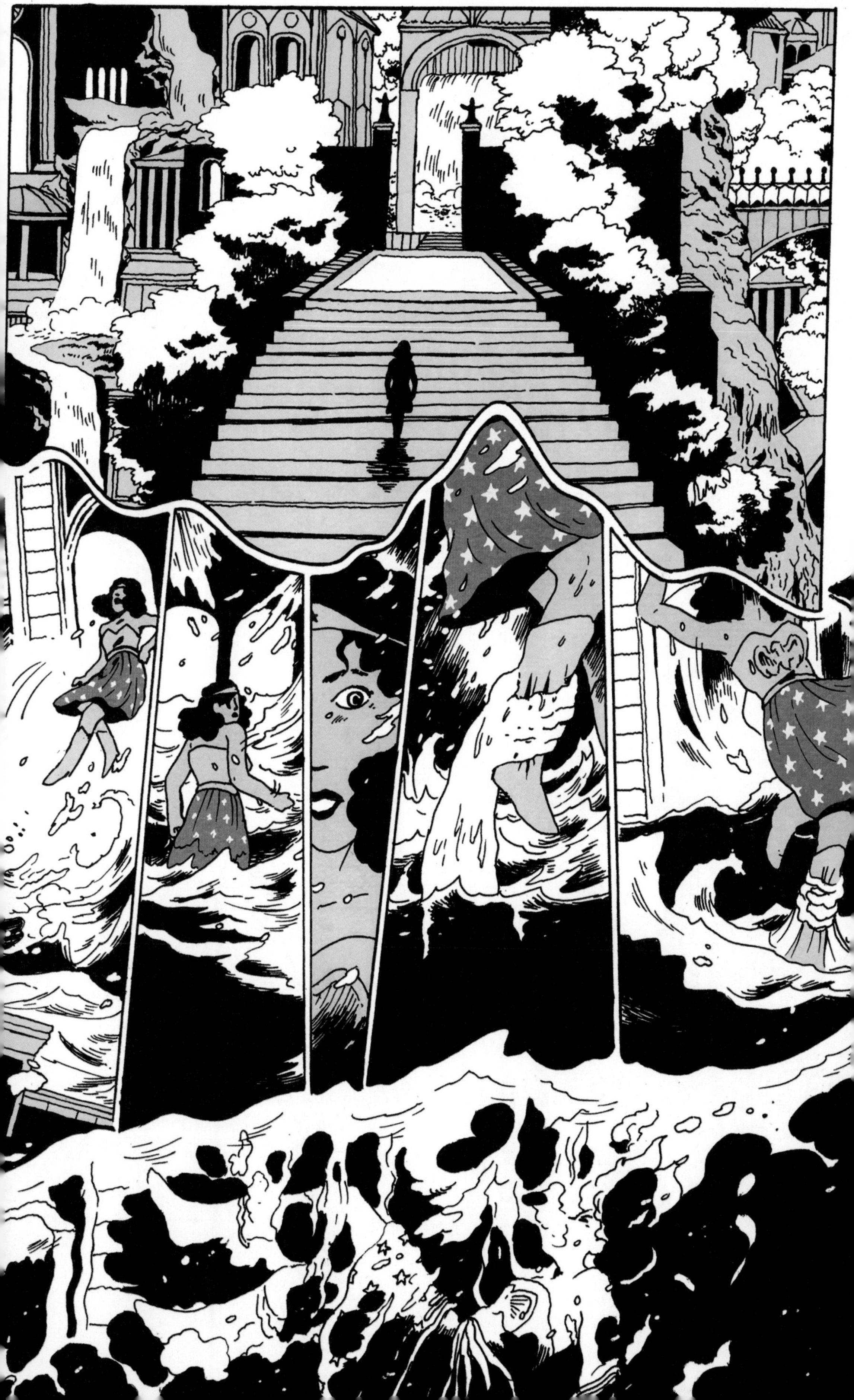

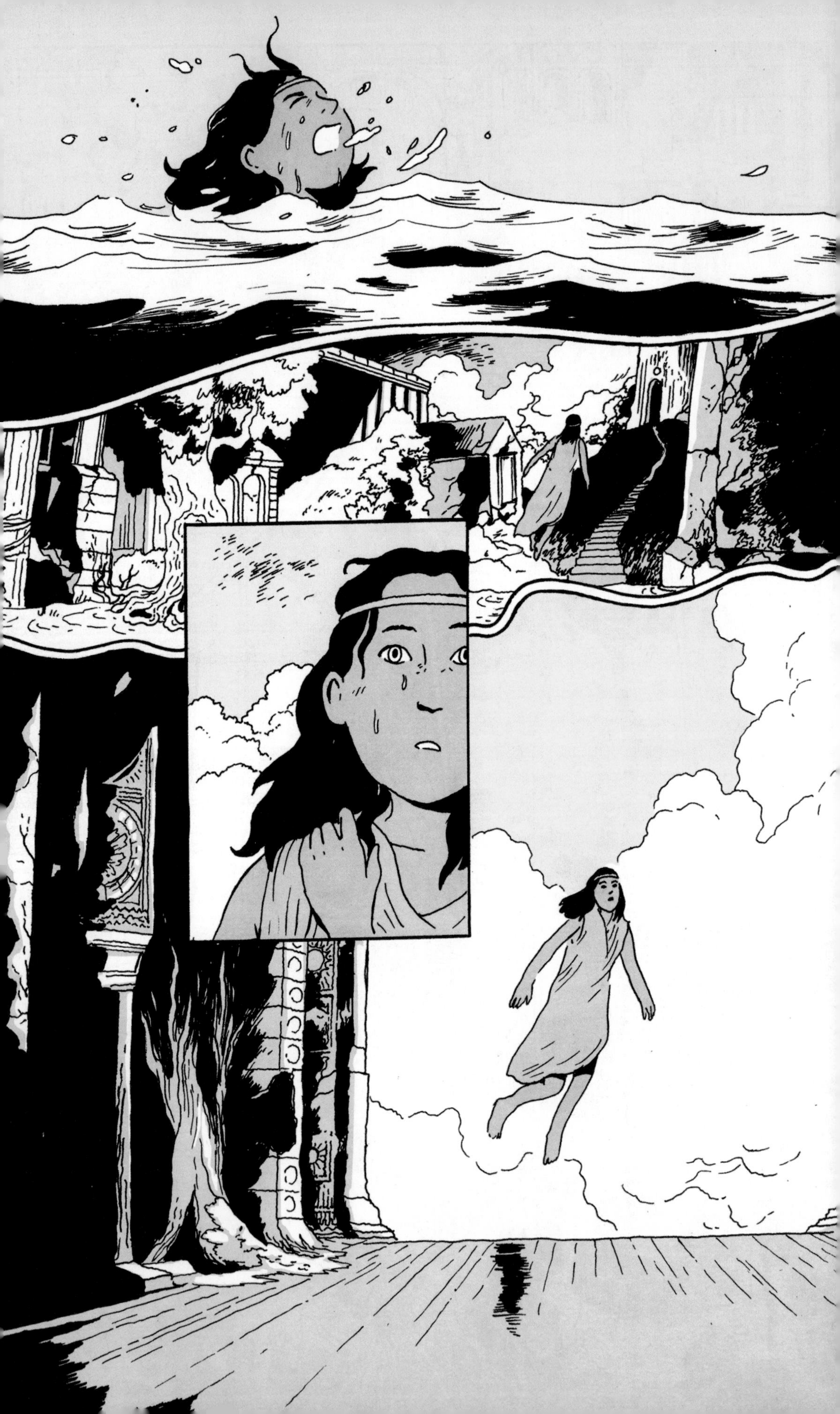

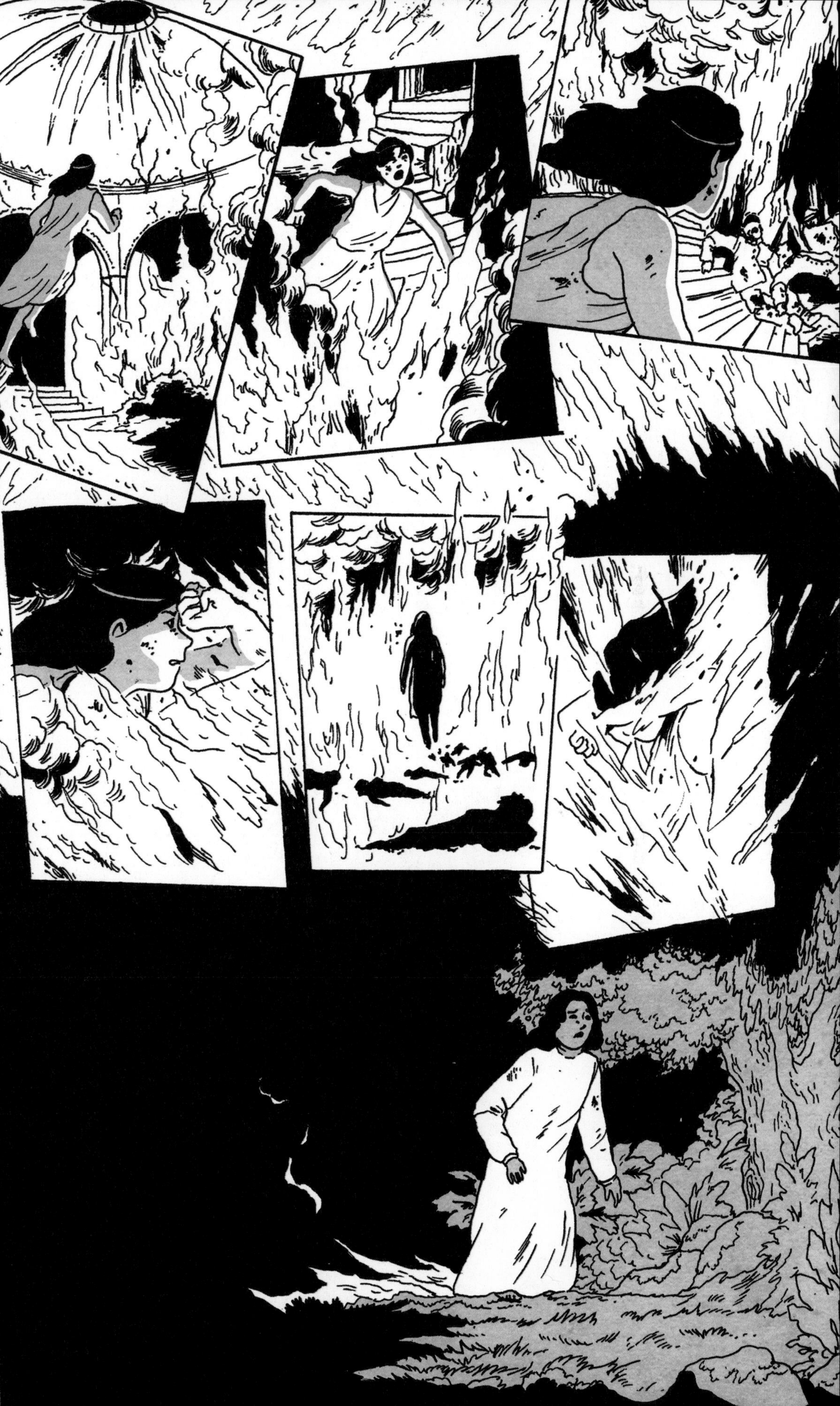

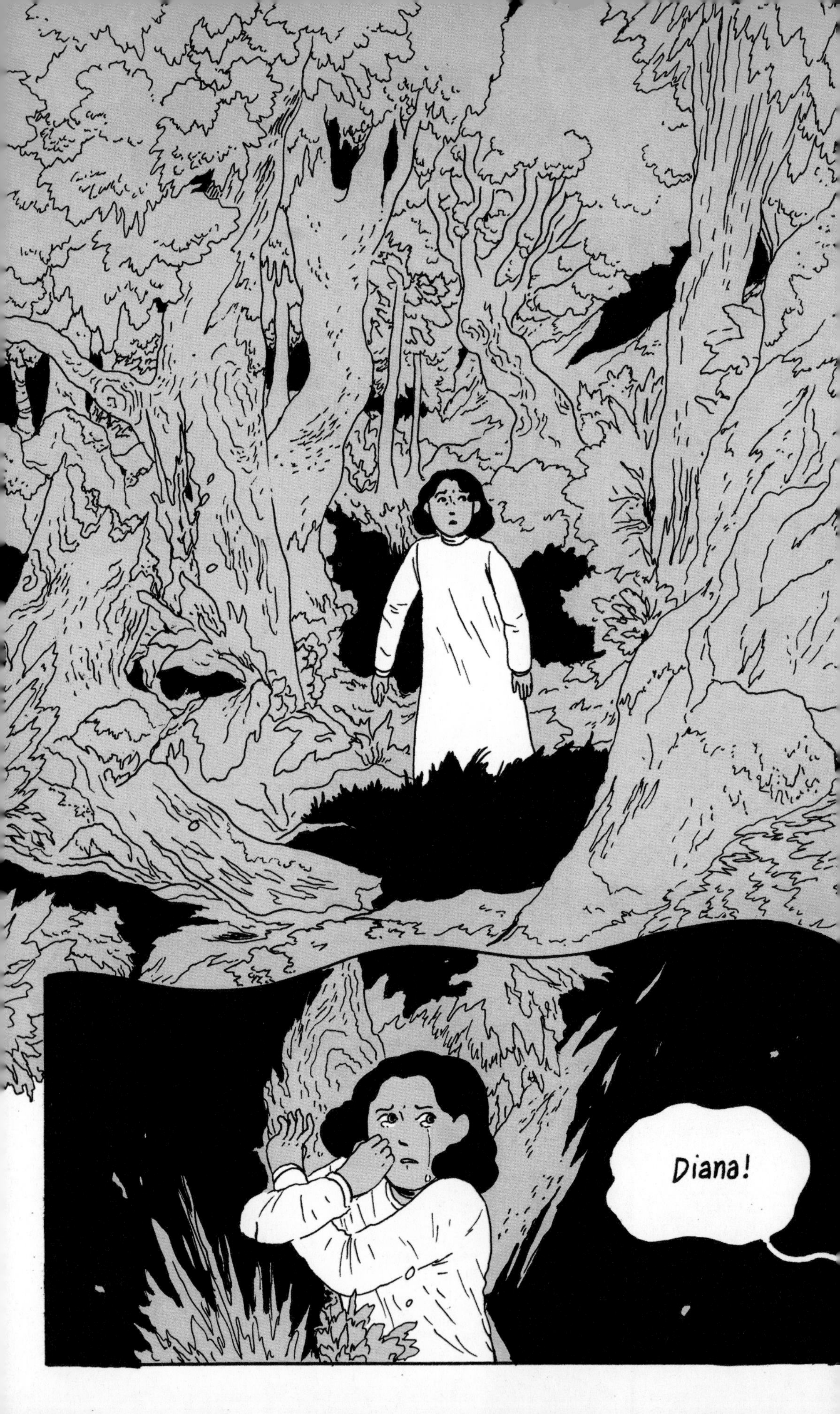
Diana!

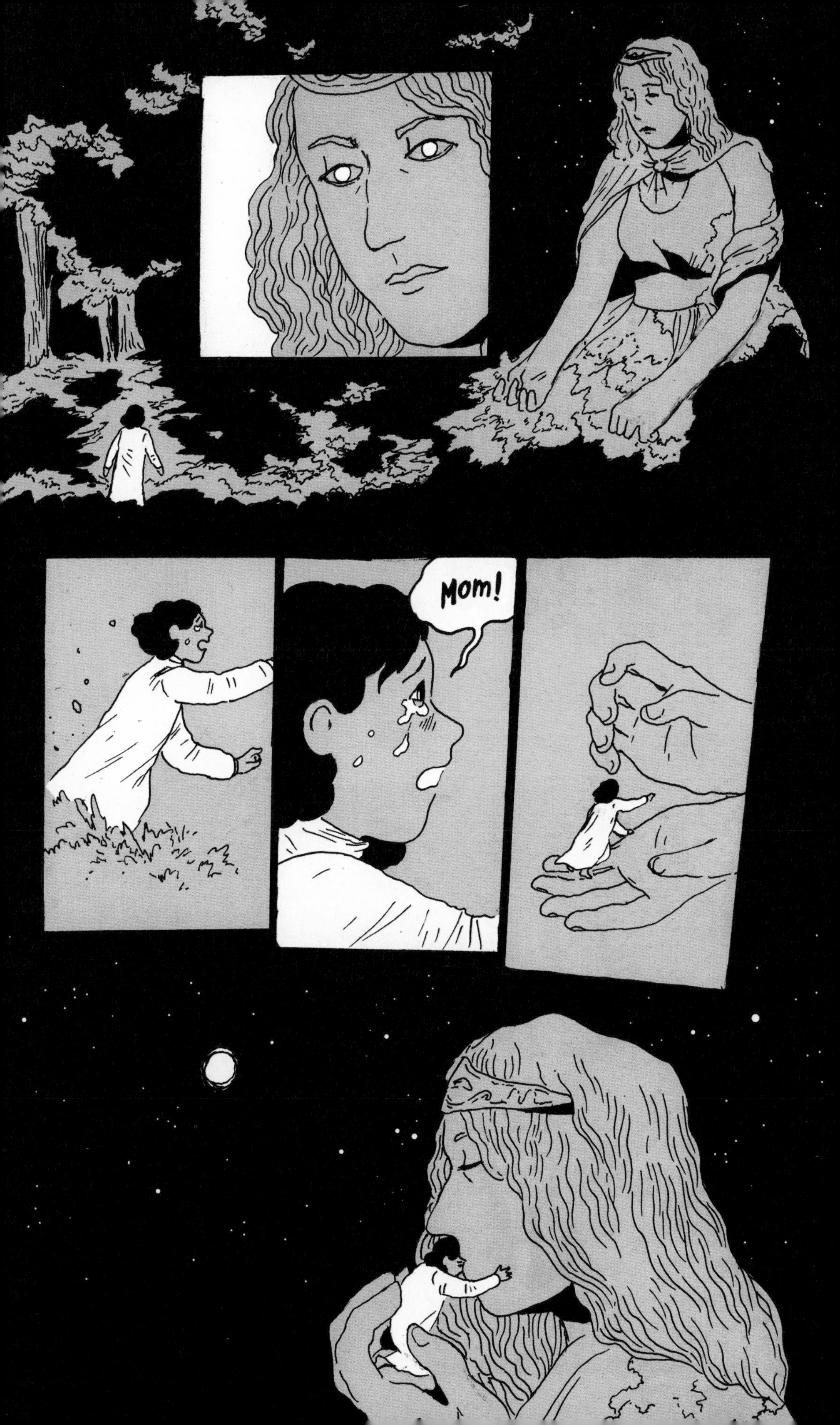
Mom!

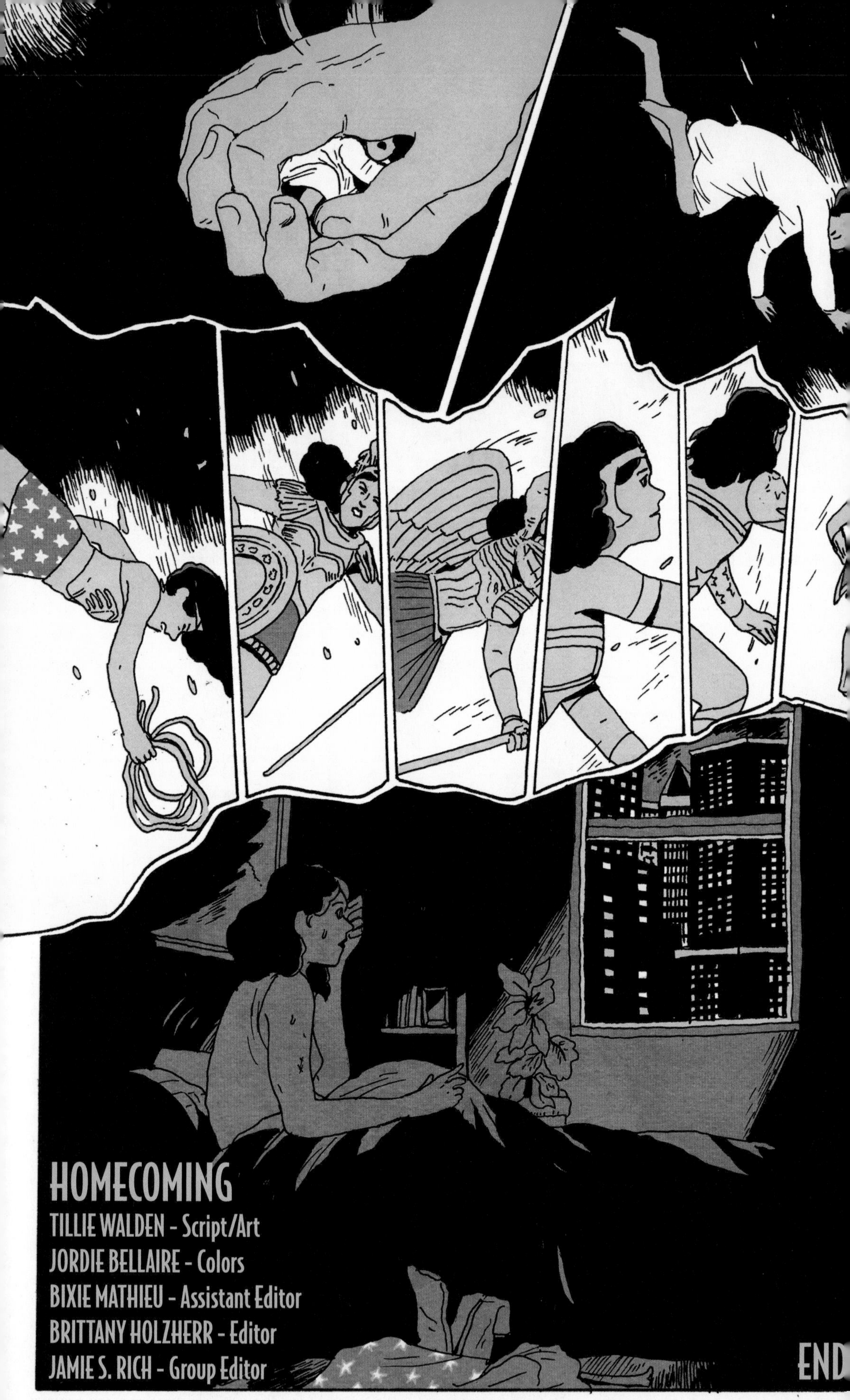

HOMECOMING
TILLIE WALDEN - Script/Art
JORDIE BELLAIRE - Colors
BIXIE MATHIEU - Assistant Editor
BRITTANY HOLZHERR - Editor
JAMIE S. RICH - Group Editor
END

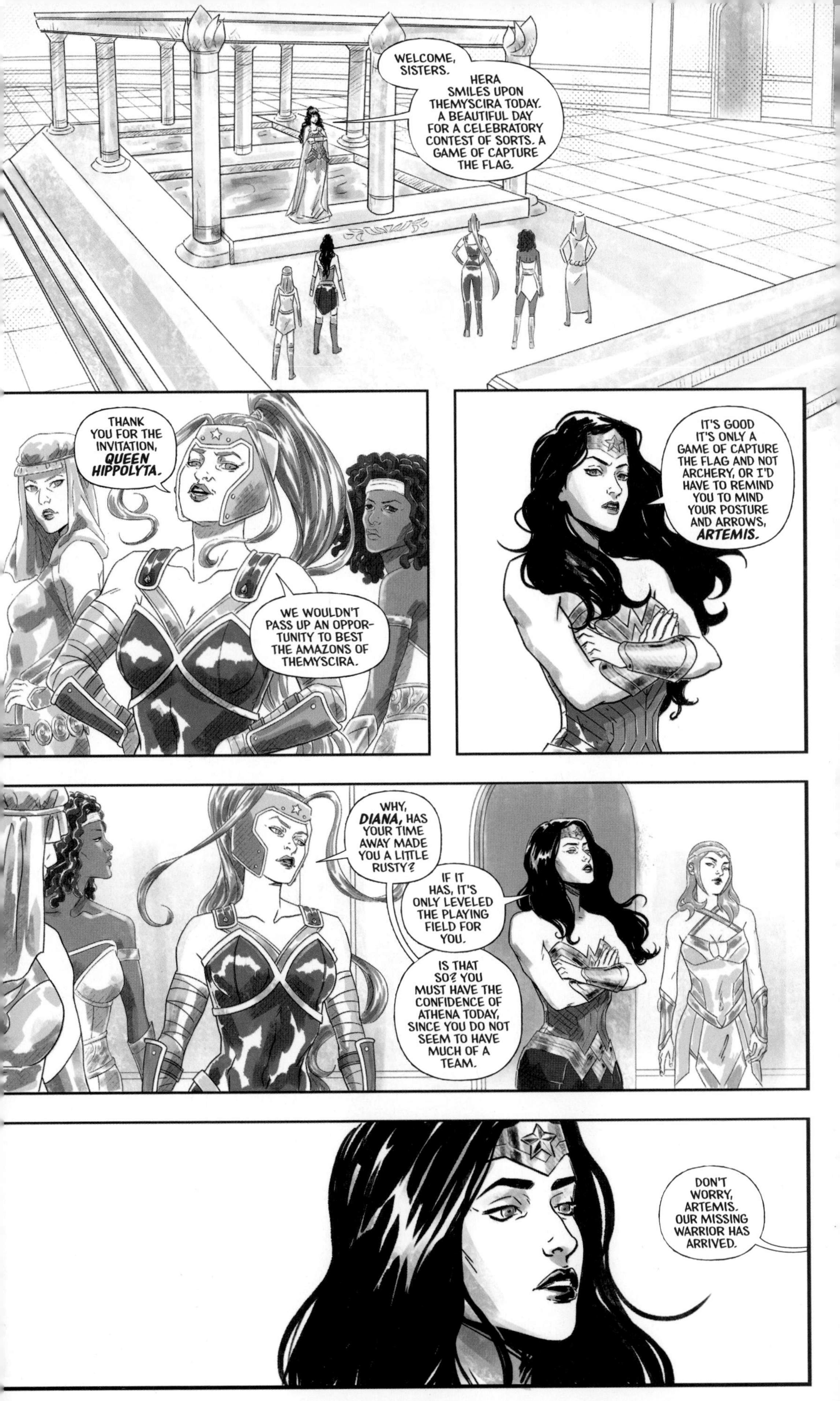
WELCOME, SISTERS.
HERA SMILES UPON THEMYSCIRA TODAY. A BEAUTIFUL DAY FOR A CELEBRATORY CONTEST OF SORTS. A GAME OF CAPTURE THE FLAG.
THANK YOU FOR THE INVITATION, QUEEN HIPPOLYTA.
WE WOULDN'T PASS UP AN OPPOR-TUNITY TO BEST THE AMAZONS OF THEMYSCIRA.
IT'S GOOD IT'S ONLY A GAME OF CAPTURE THE FLAG AND NOT ARCHERY, OR I'D HAVE TO REMIND YOU TO MIND YOUR POSTURE AND ARROWS, ARTEMIS.
WHY, DIANA, HAS YOUR TIME AWAY MADE YOU A LITTLE RUSTY?
IF IT HAS, IT'S ONLY LEVELED THE PLAYING FIELD FOR YOU.
IS THAT SO? YOU MUST HAVE THE CONFIDENCE OF ATHENA TODAY, SINCE YOU DO NOT SEEM TO HAVE MUCH OF A TEAM.
DON'T WORRY, ARTEMIS. OUR MISSING WARRIOR HAS ARRIVED.

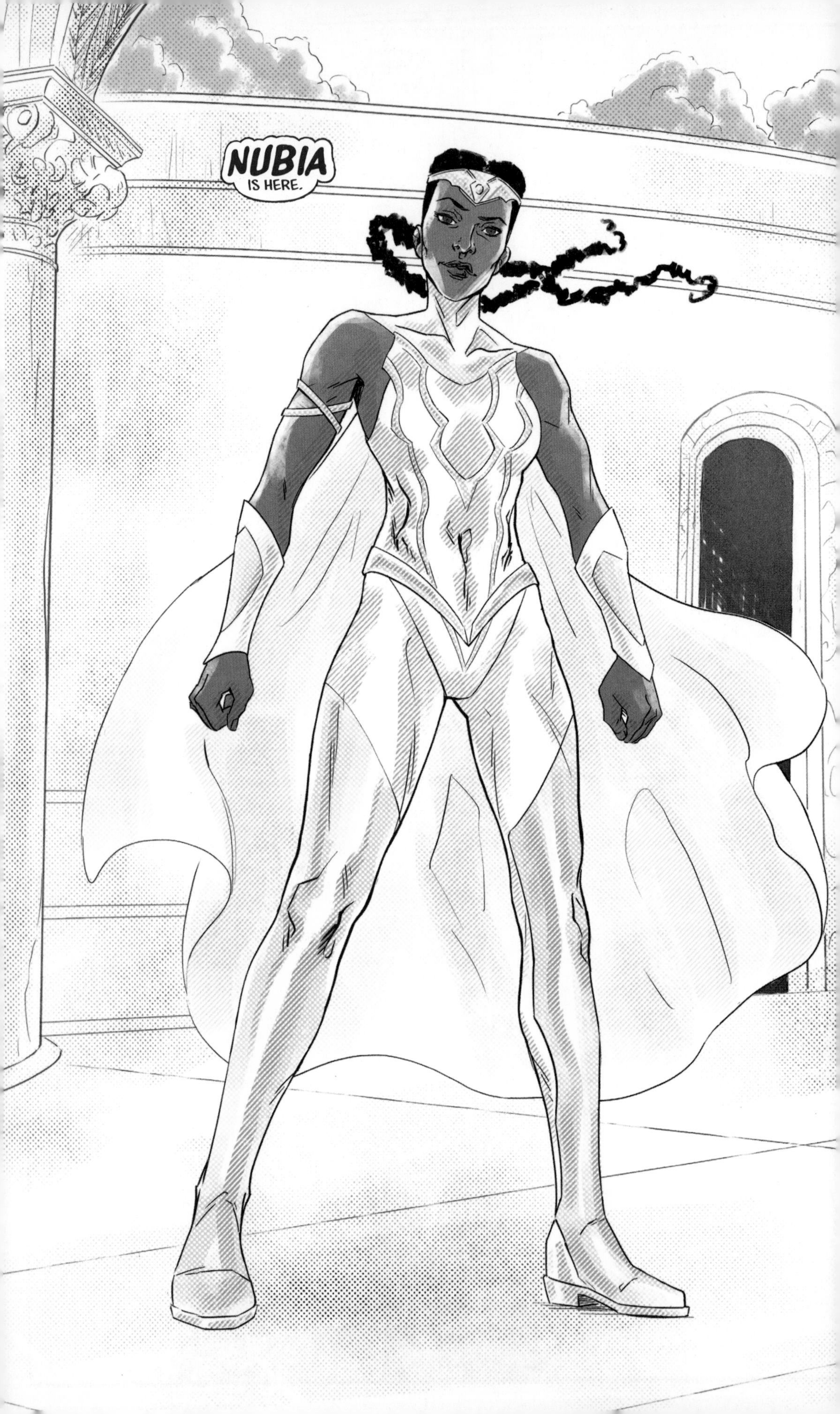
NUBIA IS HERE.

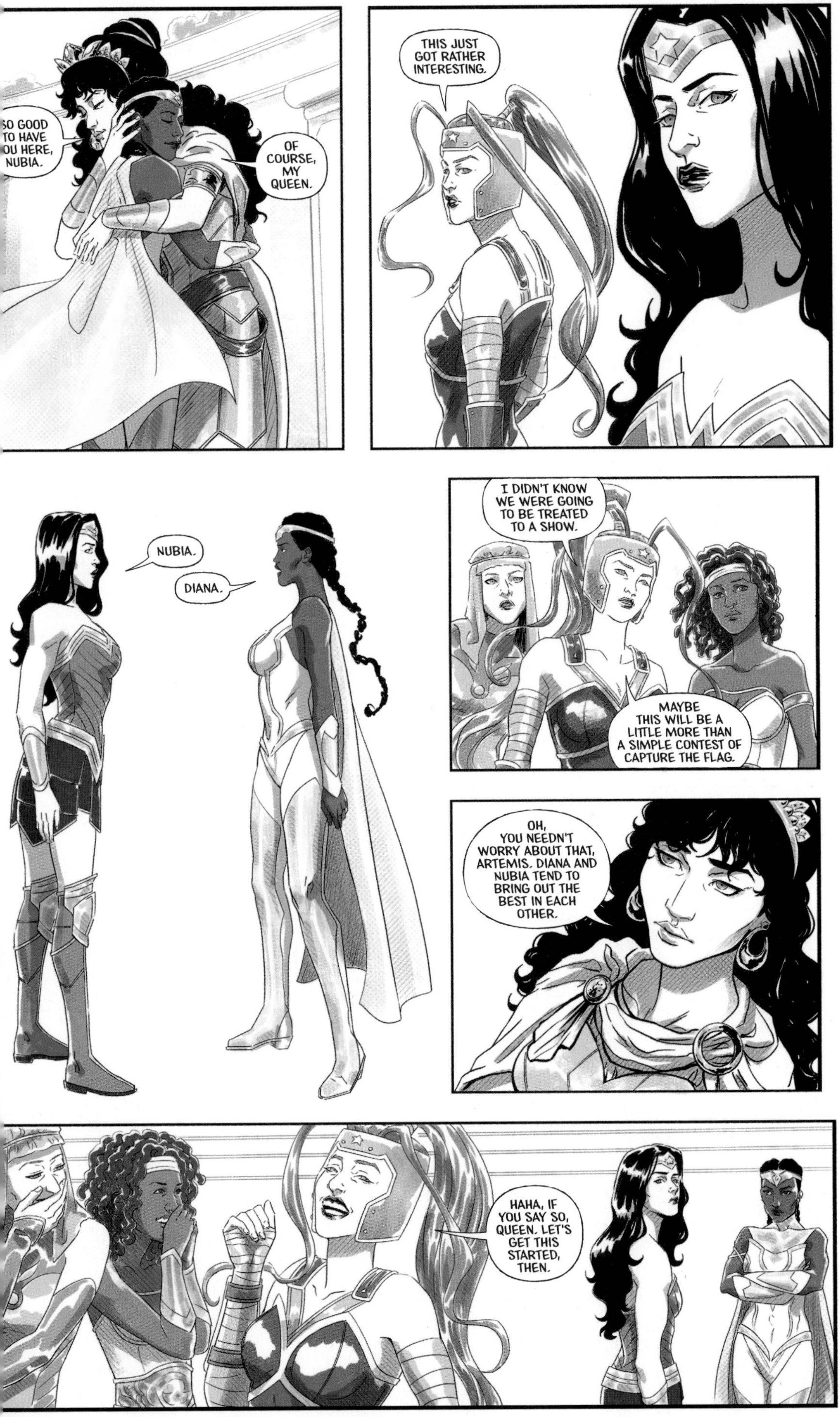
SO GOOD TO HAVE YOU HERE, NUBIA.
OF COURSE, MY QUEEN.
THIS JUST GOT RATHER INTERESTING.
NUBIA.
DIANA.
I DIDN'T KNOW WE WERE GOING TO BE TREATED TO A SHOW.
MAYBE THIS WILL BE A LITTLE MORE THAN A SIMPLE CONTEST OF CAPTURE THE FLAG.
OH, YOU NEEDN'T WORRY ABOUT THAT, ARTEMIS. DIANA AND NUBIA TEND TO BRING OUT THE BEST IN EACH OTHER.
HAHA, IF YOU SAY SO, QUEEN. LET'S GET THIS STARTED, THEN.

THE RULES ARE QUITE DIRECT. WHOEVER REACHES THE FLAG FIRST WINS.

Later.

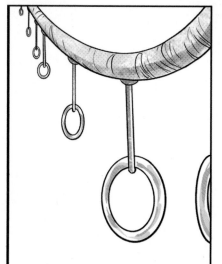

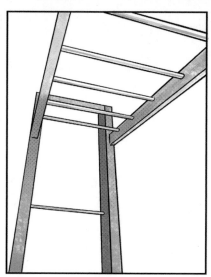

I'LL BE THE LAST LEG.

ROCK, PAPER, SCISSORS.

ARE YOU SERIOUS?

YES.

FINE.

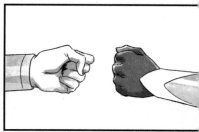

LIKE I SAID, I'LL BE THE LAST LEG.

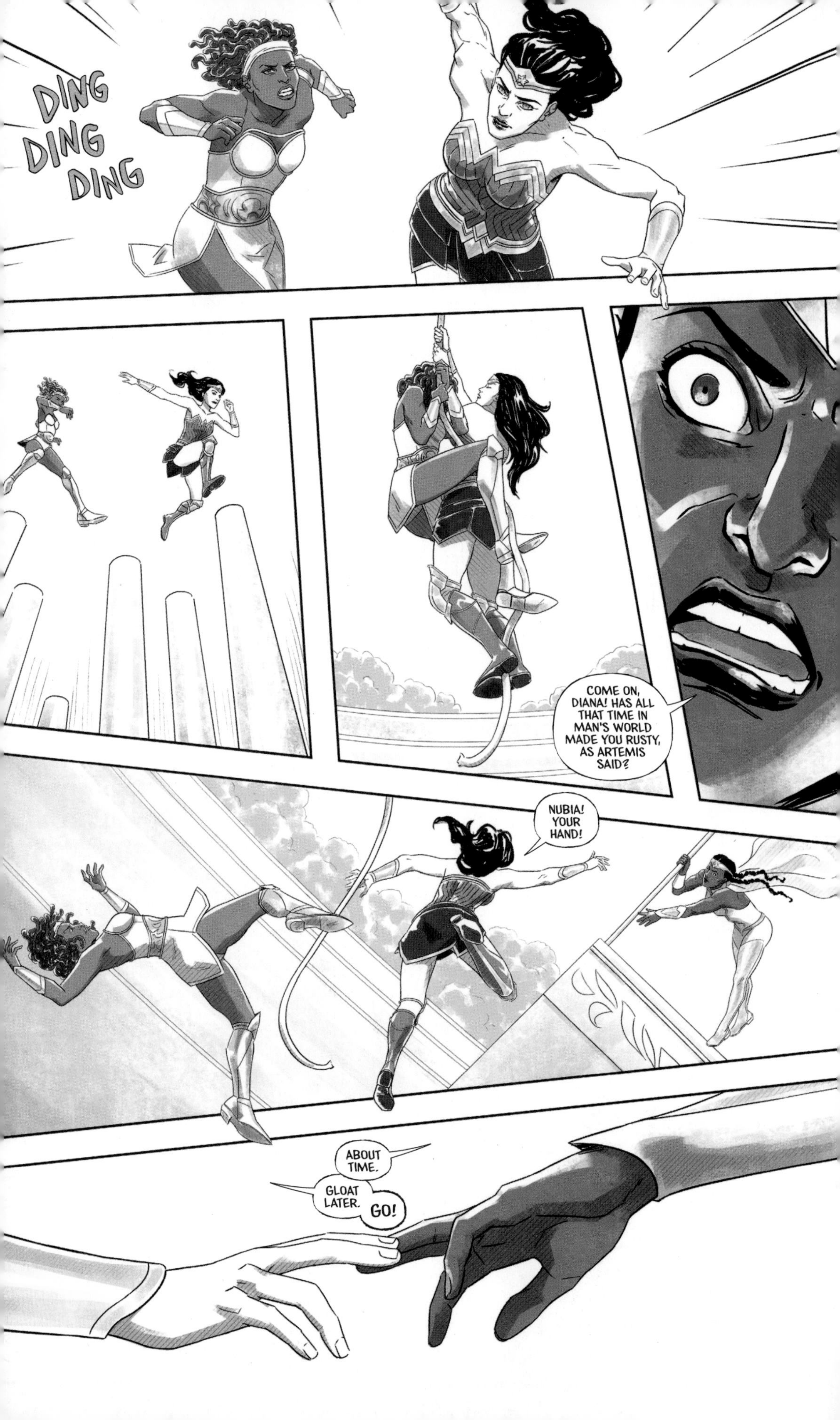
DING DING DING
COME ON, DIANA! HAS ALL THAT TIME IN MAN'S WORLD MADE YOU RUSTY, AS ARTEMIS SAID?
NUBIA! YOUR HAND!
ABOUT TIME.
GLOAT LATER.
GO!

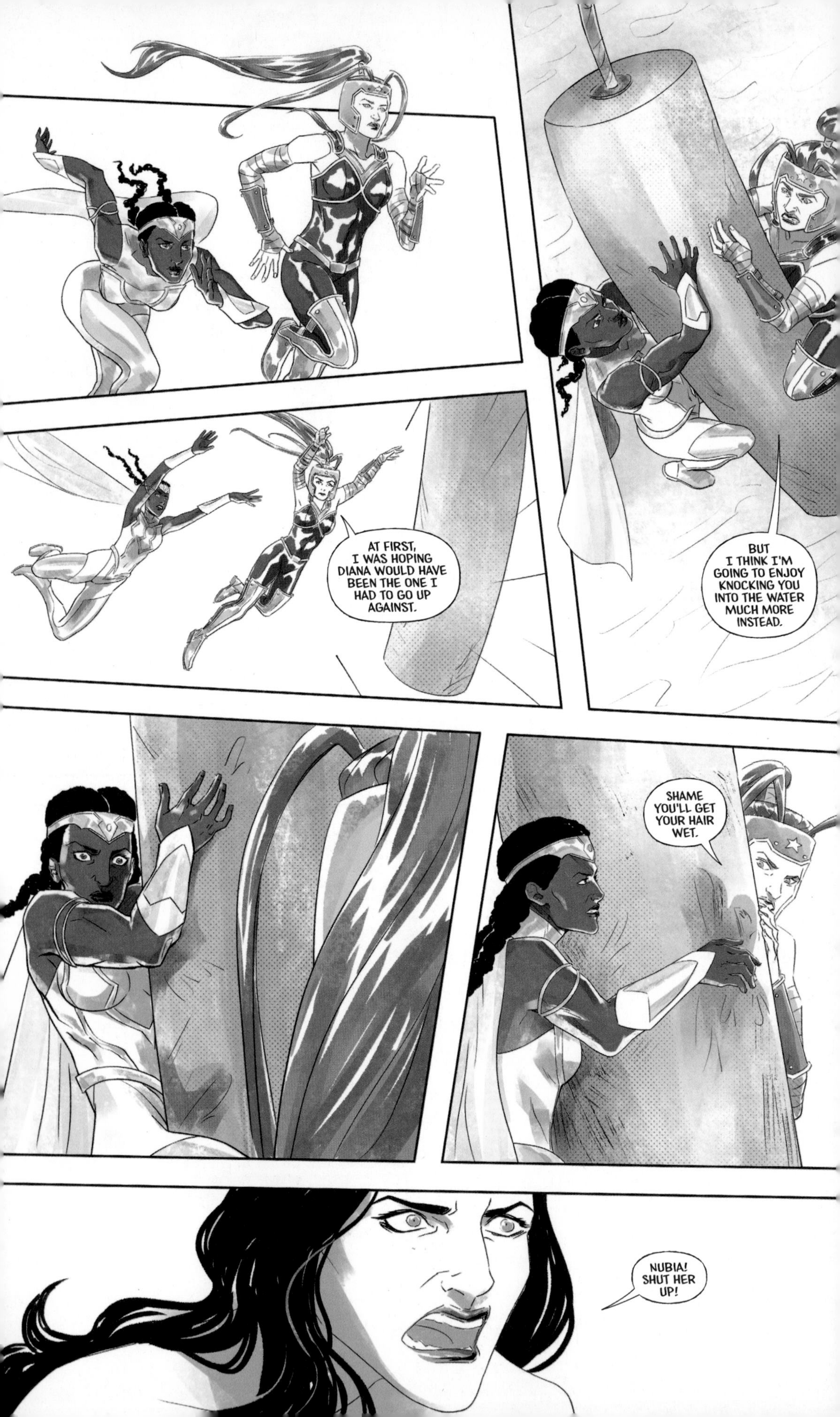

AT FIRST, I WAS HOPING DIANA WOULD HAVE BEEN THE ONE I HAD TO GO UP AGAINST.
BUT I THINK I'M GOING TO ENJOY KNOCKING YOU INTO THE WATER MUCH MORE INSTEAD.
SHAME YOU'LL GET YOUR HAIR WET.
NUBIA! SHUT HER UP!

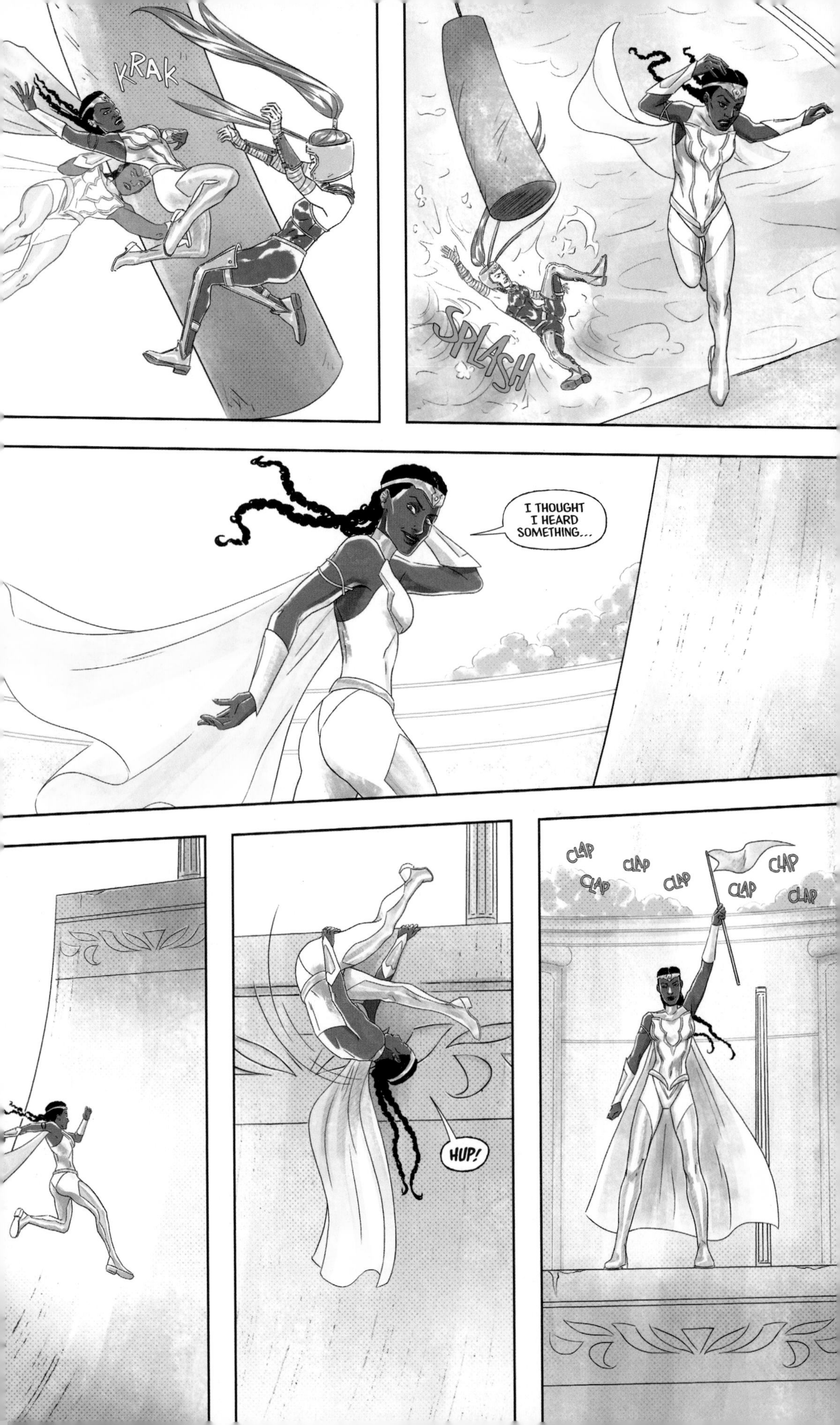
KRAK
SPLASH
I THOUGHT I HEARD SOMETHING...
HUP!
CLAP
CLAP
CLAP
CLAP
CLAP
CLAP
CLAP

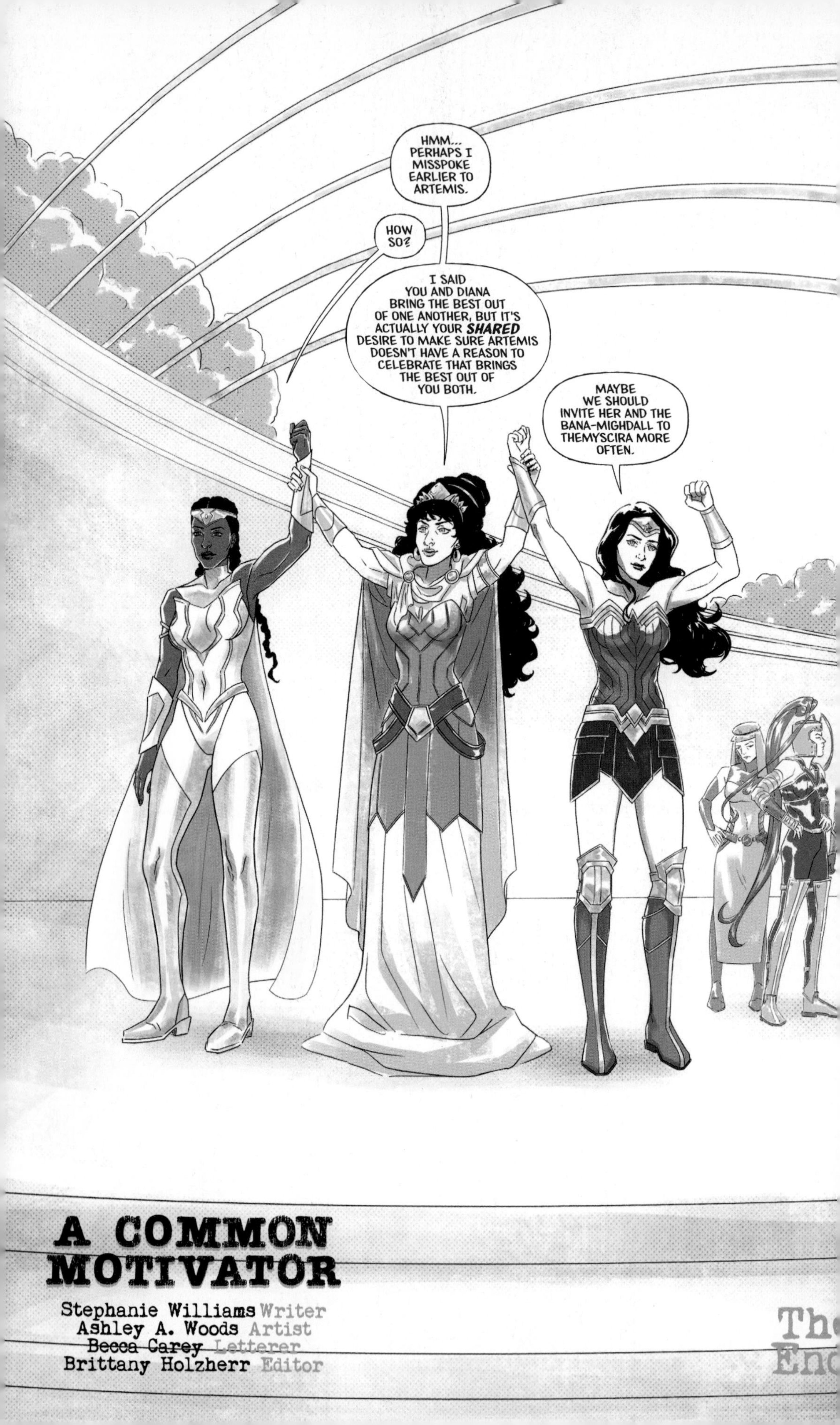
HMM... PERHAPS I MISSPOKE EARLIER TO ARTEMIS.
HOW SO?
I SAID YOU AND DIANA BRING THE BEST OUT OF ONE ANOTHER, BUT IT'S ACTUALLY YOUR ***SHARED*** DESIRE TO MAKE SURE ARTEMIS DOESN'T HAVE A REASON TO CELEBRATE THAT BRINGS THE BEST OUT OF YOU BOTH.
MAYBE WE SHOULD INVITE HER AND THE BANA-MIGHDALL TO THEMYSCIRA MORE OFTEN.
A COMMON MOTIVATOR
Stephanie Williams Writer
Ashley A. Woods Artist
Becca Carey Letterer
Brittany Holzherr Editor

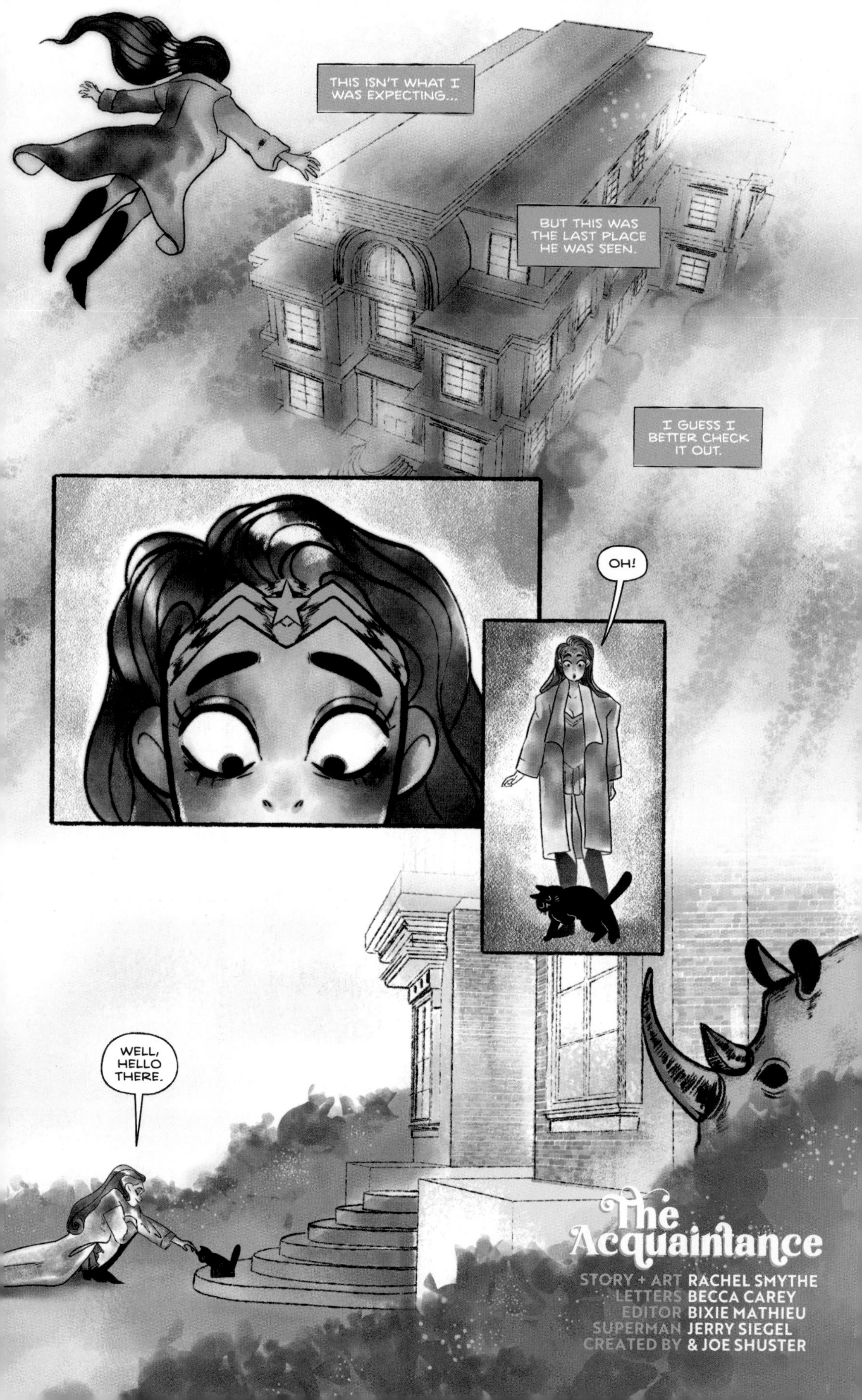
THIS ISN'T WHAT I WAS EXPECTING...
BUT THIS WAS THE LAST PLACE HE WAS SEEN.
I GUESS I BETTER CHECK IT OUT.
OH!
WELL, HELLO THERE.
The Acquaintance
STORY + ART RACHEL SMYTHE
LETTERS BECCA CAREY
EDITOR BIXIE MATHIEU
SUPERMAN CREATED BY JERRY SIEGEL & JOE SHUSTER

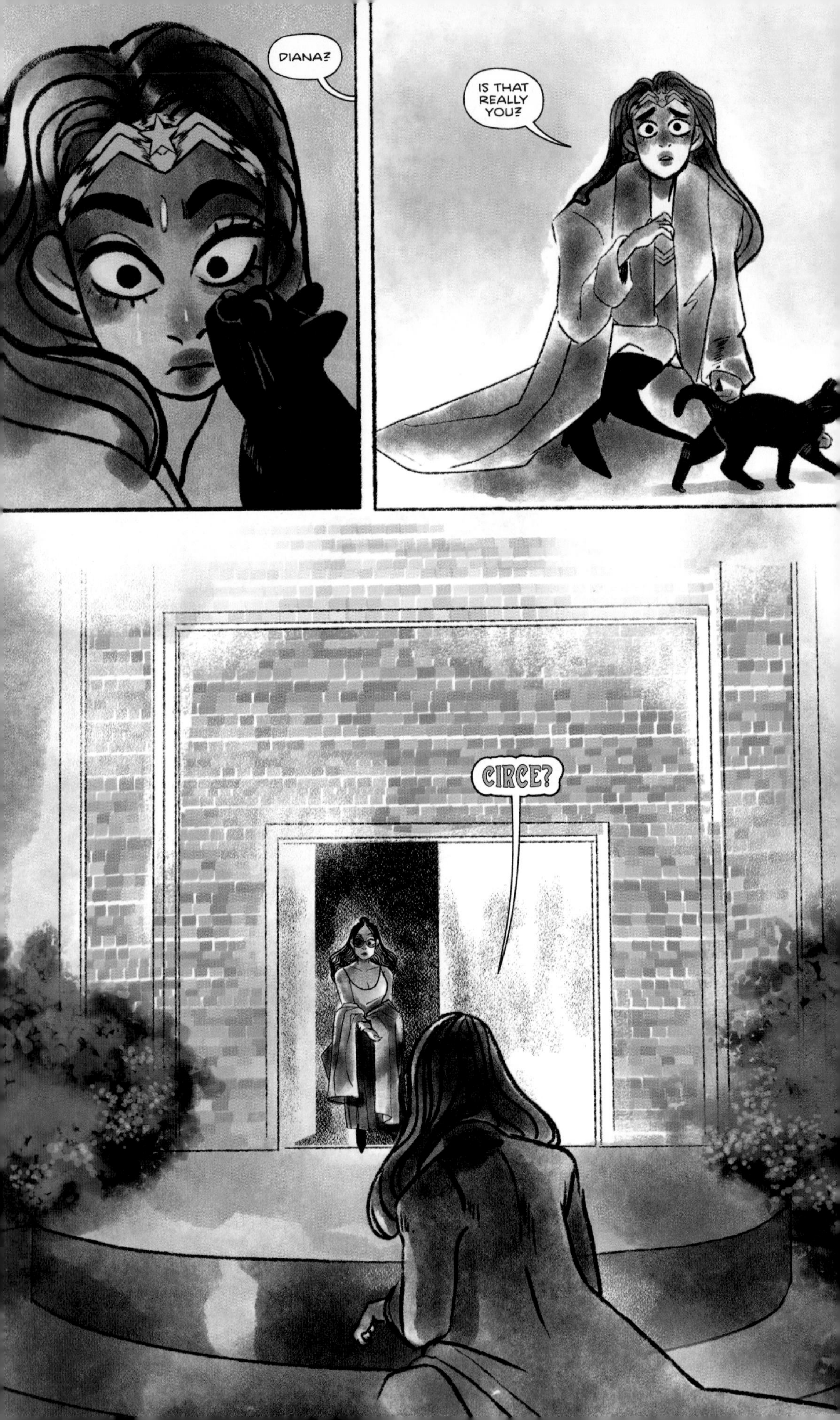
DIANA?
IS THAT REALLY YOU?
CIRCE?

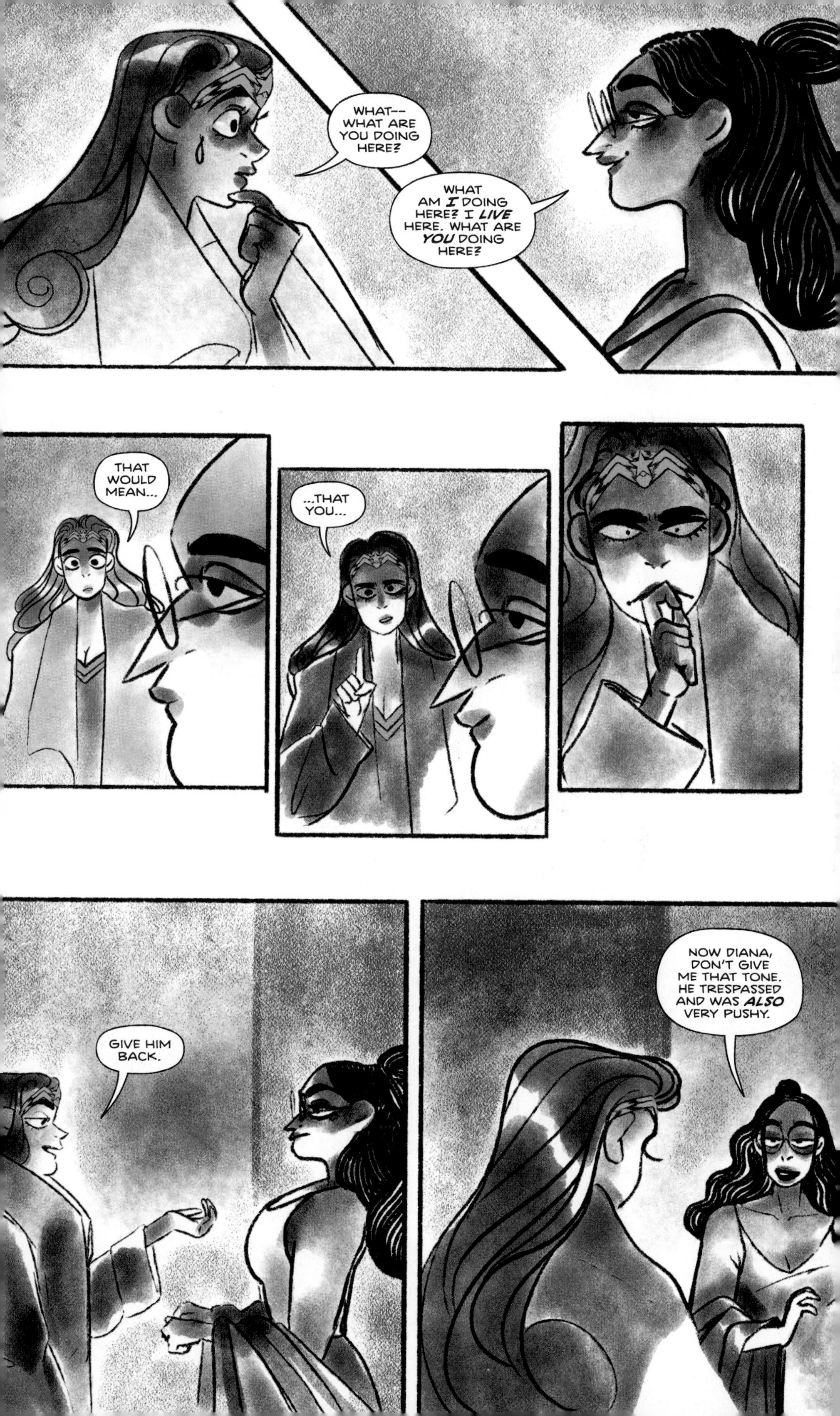

WHAT-- WHAT ARE YOU DOING HERE?
WHAT AM *I* DOING HERE? I *LIVE* HERE. WHAT ARE *YOU* DOING HERE?
THAT WOULD MEAN...
...THAT YOU...
GIVE HIM BACK.
NOW DIANA, DON'T GIVE ME THAT TONE. HE TRESPASSED AND WAS *ALSO* VERY PUSHY.

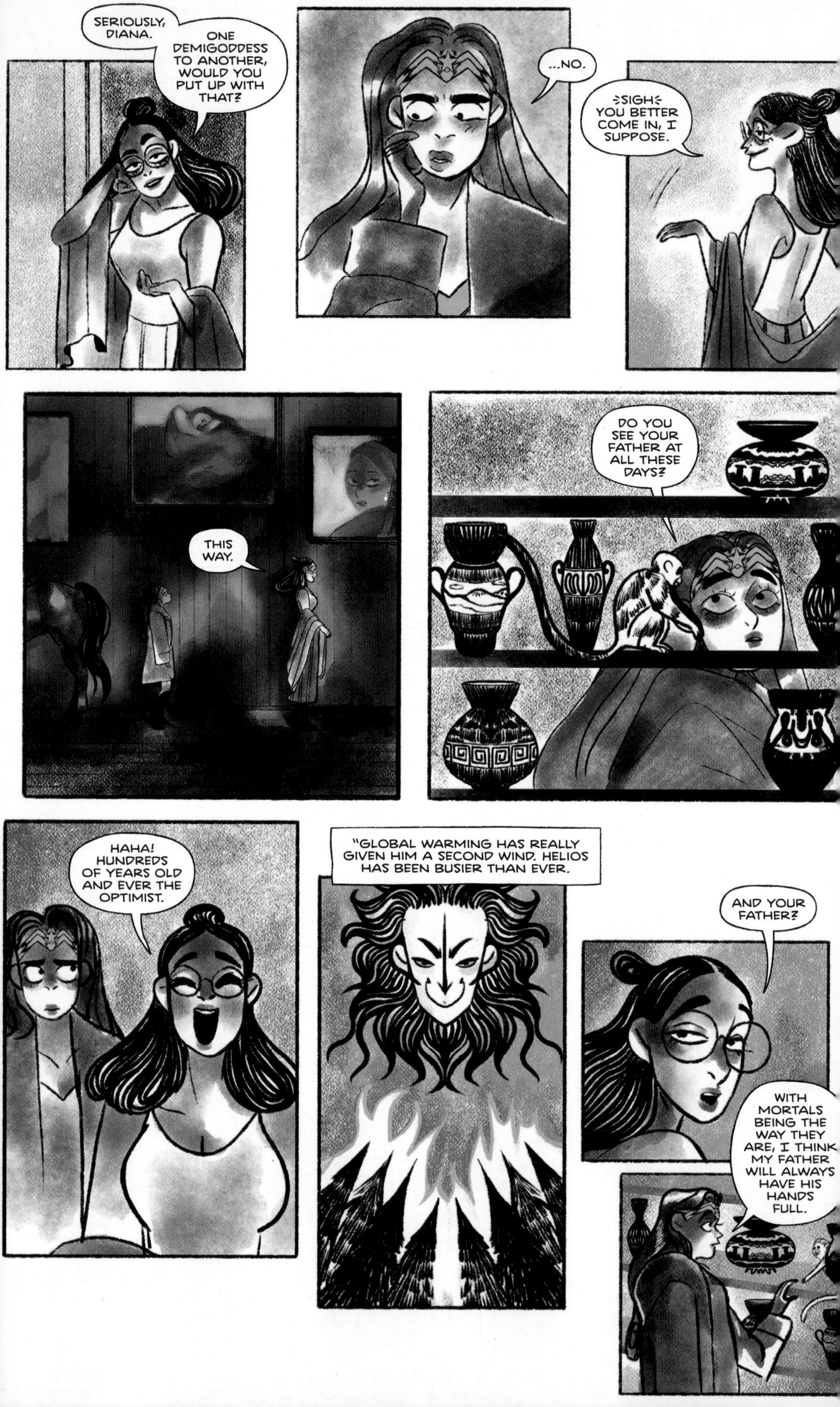
SERIOUSLY, DIANA.
ONE DEMIGODDESS TO ANOTHER, WOULD YOU PUT UP WITH THAT?
...NO.
SIGH YOU BETTER COME IN, I SUPPOSE.
THIS WAY.
DO YOU SEE YOUR FATHER AT ALL THESE DAYS?
HAHA! HUNDREDS OF YEARS OLD AND EVER THE OPTIMIST.
"GLOBAL WARMING HAS REALLY GIVEN HIM A SECOND WIND. HELIOS HAS BEEN BUSIER THAN EVER.
AND YOUR FATHER?
WITH MORTALS BEING THE WAY THEY ARE, I THINK MY FATHER WILL ALWAYS HAVE HIS HANDS FULL.

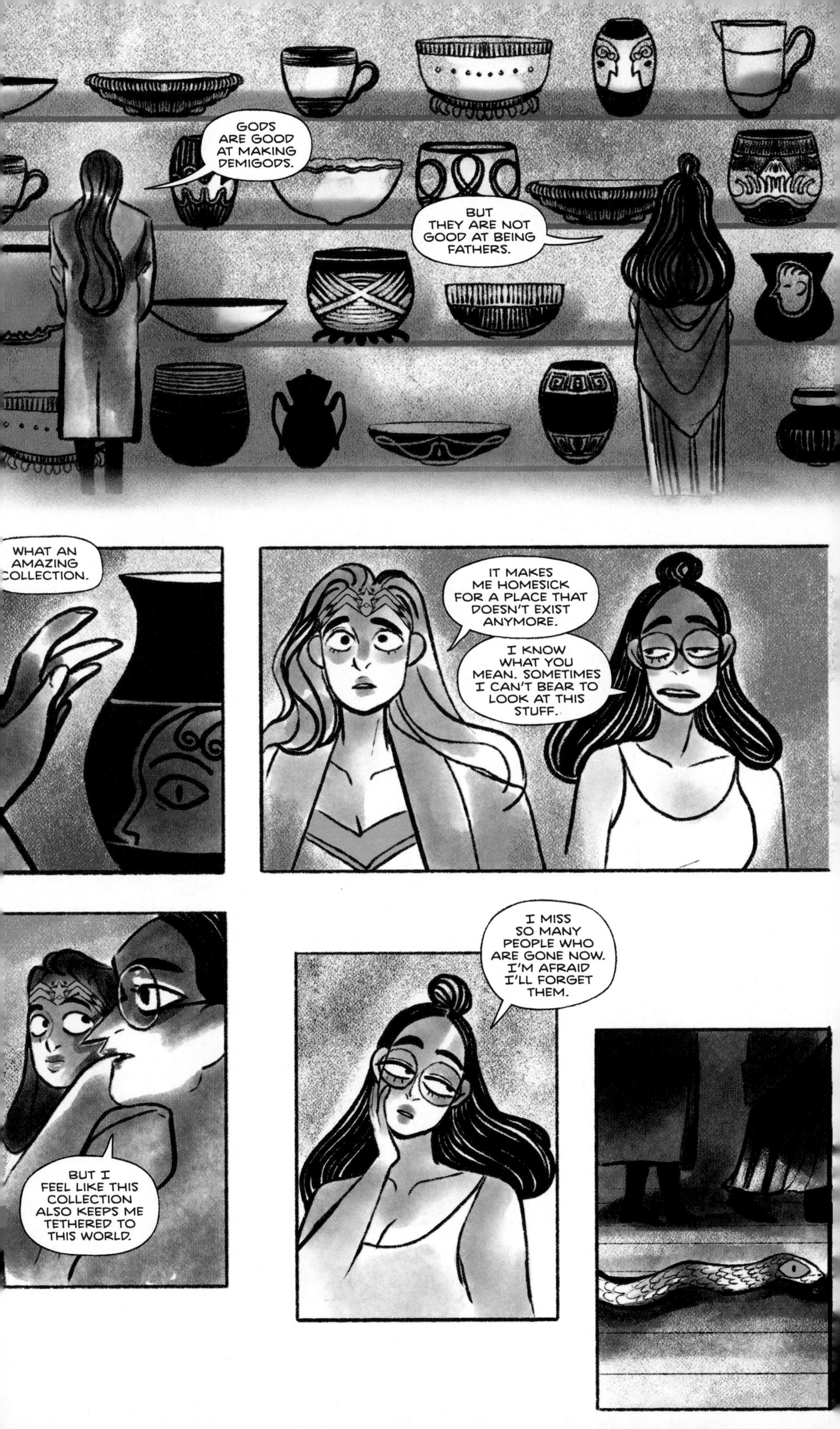
GODS ARE GOOD AT MAKING DEMIGODS.
BUT THEY ARE NOT GOOD AT BEING FATHERS.
WHAT AN AMAZING COLLECTION.
IT MAKES ME HOMESICK FOR A PLACE THAT DOESN'T EXIST ANYMORE.
I KNOW WHAT YOU MEAN. SOMETIMES I CAN'T BEAR TO LOOK AT THIS STUFF.
BUT I FEEL LIKE THIS COLLECTION ALSO KEEPS ME TETHERED TO THIS WORLD.
I MISS SO MANY PEOPLE WHO ARE GONE NOW. I'M AFRAID I'LL FORGET THEM.

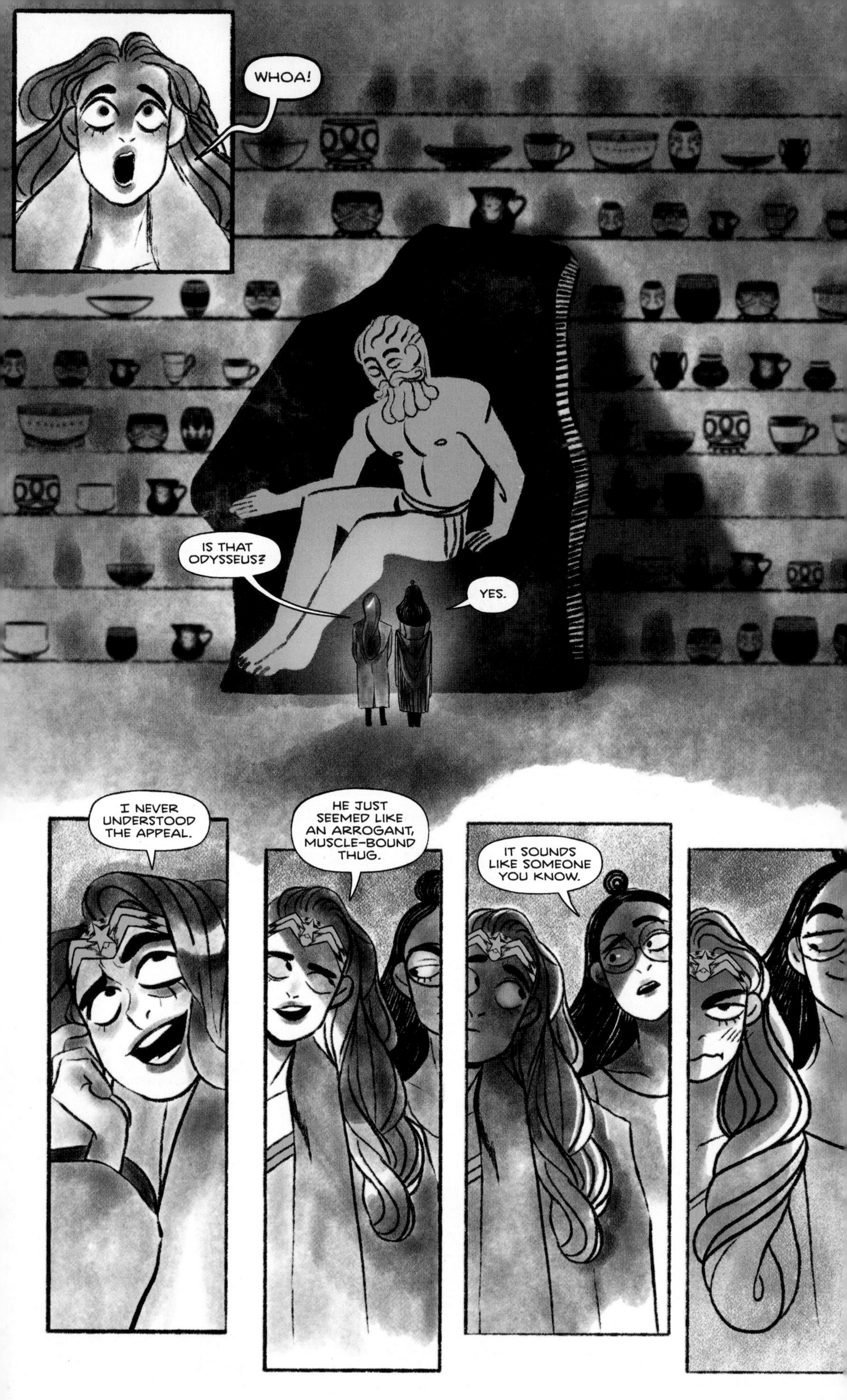
WHOA!
IS THAT ODYSSEUS?
YES.
I NEVER UNDERSTOOD THE APPEAL.
HE JUST SEEMED LIKE AN ARROGANT, MUSCLE-BOUND THUG.
IT SOUNDS LIKE SOMEONE YOU KNOW.

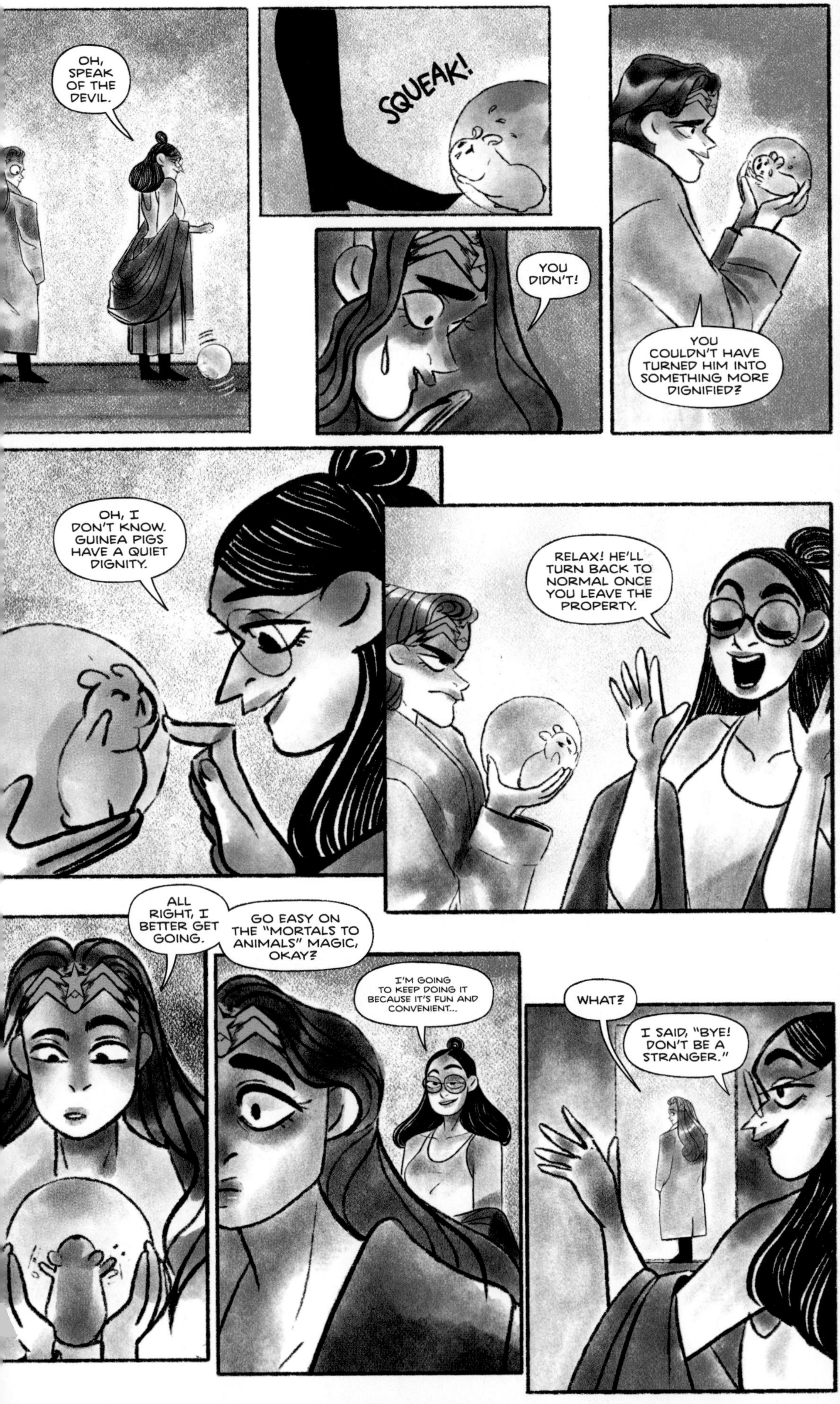

OH, SPEAK OF THE DEVIL.
SQUEAK!
YOU DIDN'T!
YOU COULDN'T HAVE TURNED HIM INTO SOMETHING MORE DIGNIFIED?
OH, I DON'T KNOW. GUINEA PIGS HAVE A QUIET DIGNITY.
RELAX! HE'LL TURN BACK TO NORMAL ONCE YOU LEAVE THE PROPERTY.
ALL RIGHT, I BETTER GET GOING.
GO EASY ON THE "MORTALS TO ANIMALS" MAGIC, OKAY?
I'M GOING TO KEEP DOING IT BECAUSE IT'S FUN AND CONVENIENT...
WHAT?
I SAID, "BYE! DON'T BE A STRANGER."

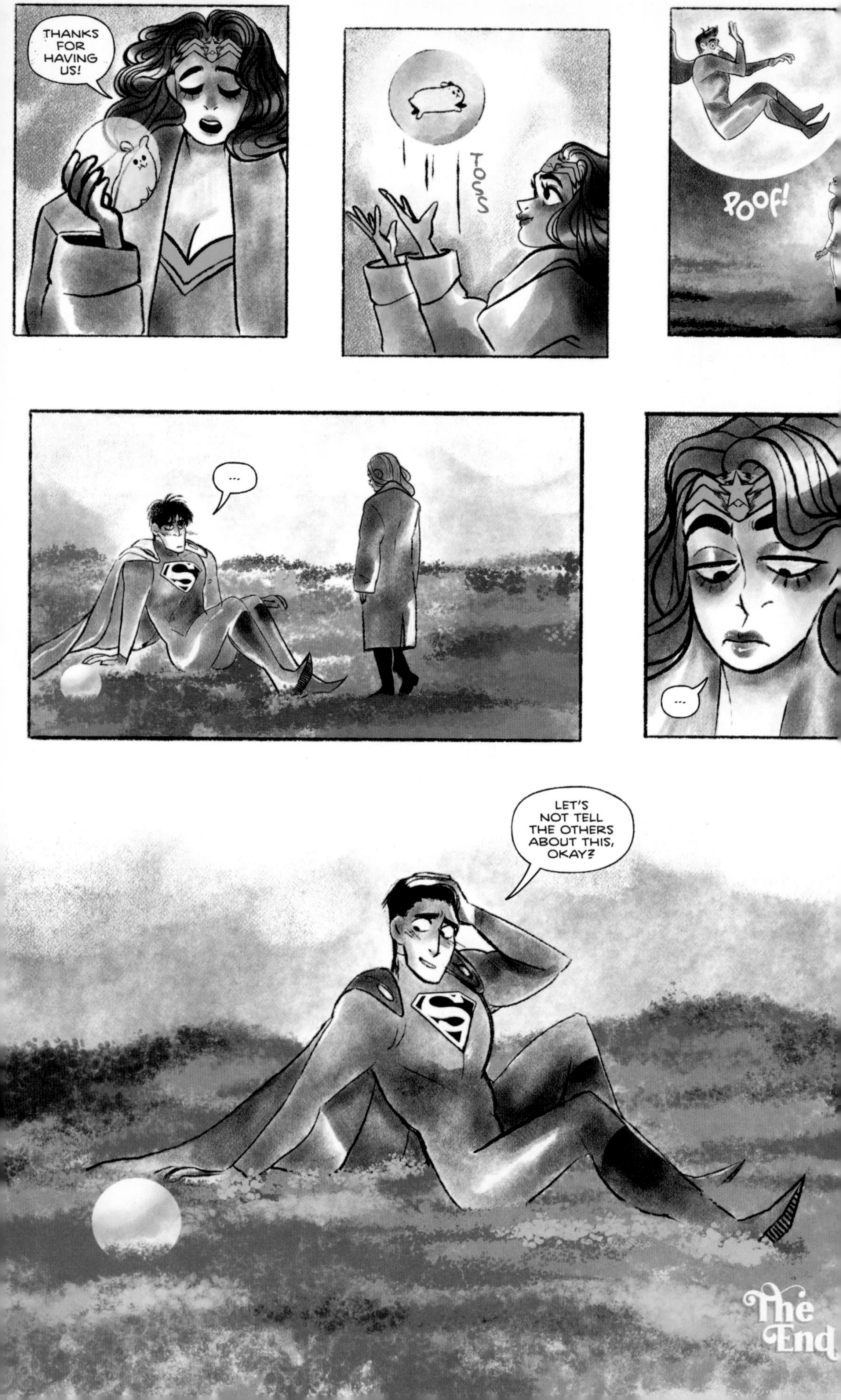

THANKS FOR HAVING US!
TOSS
POOF!
...
...
LET'S NOT TELL THE OTHERS ABOUT THIS, OKAY?
The End

Cover by Jae Lee and June Chung

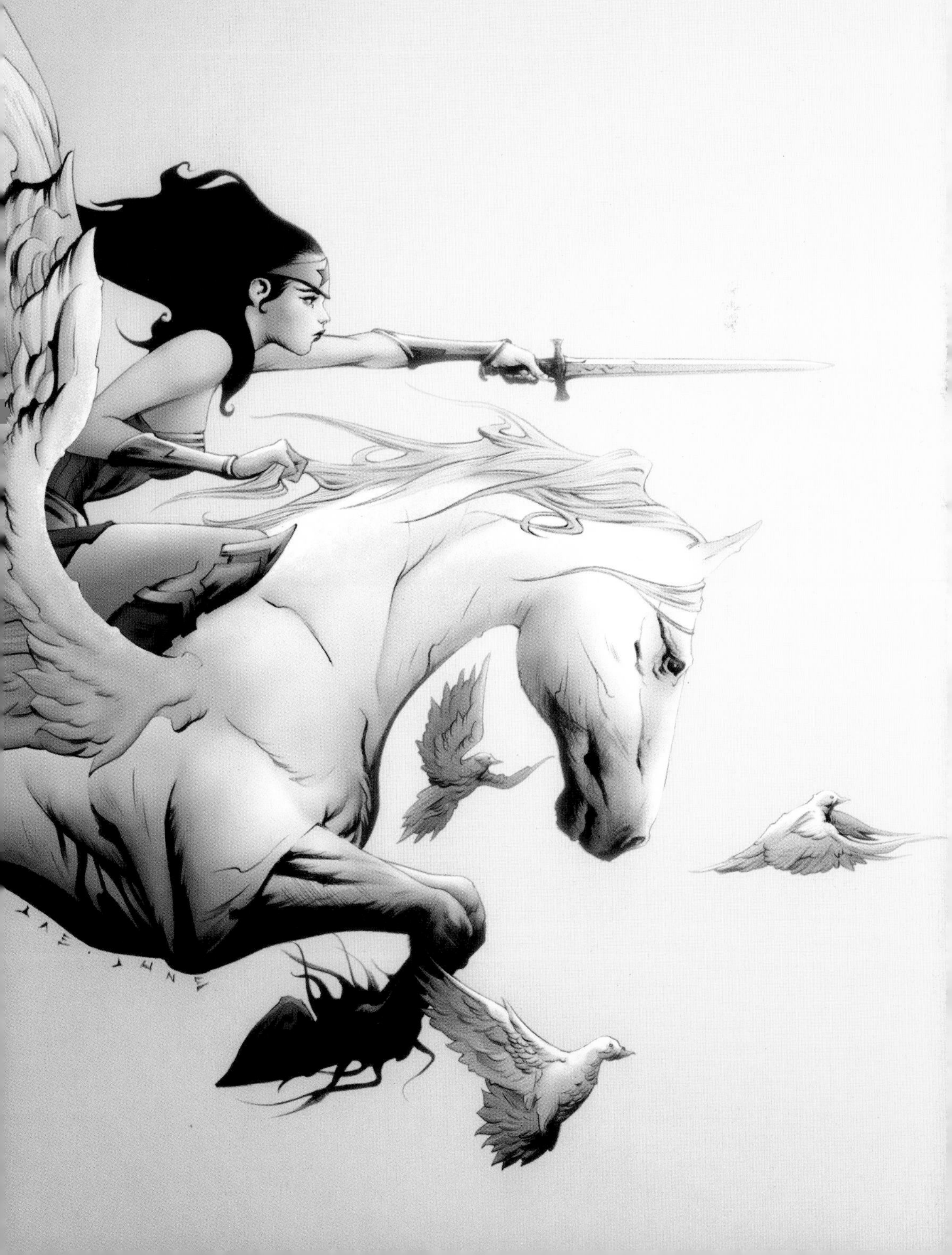

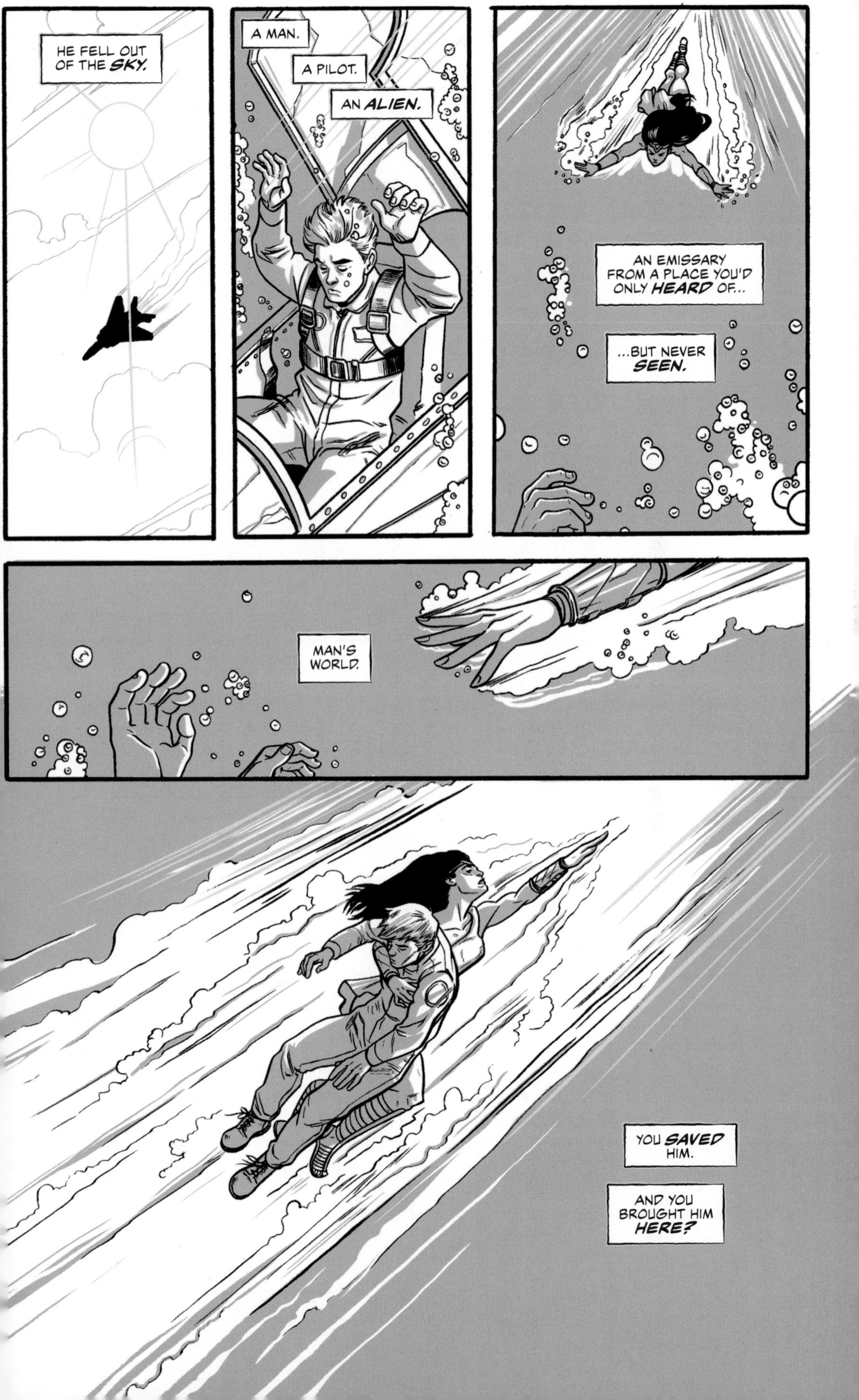
HE FELL OUT OF THE SKY.
A MAN.
A PILOT.
AN ALIEN.
AN EMISSARY FROM A PLACE YOU'D ONLY HEARD OF...
...BUT NEVER SEEN.
MAN'S WORLD.
YOU SAVED HIM.
AND YOU BROUGHT HIM HERE?

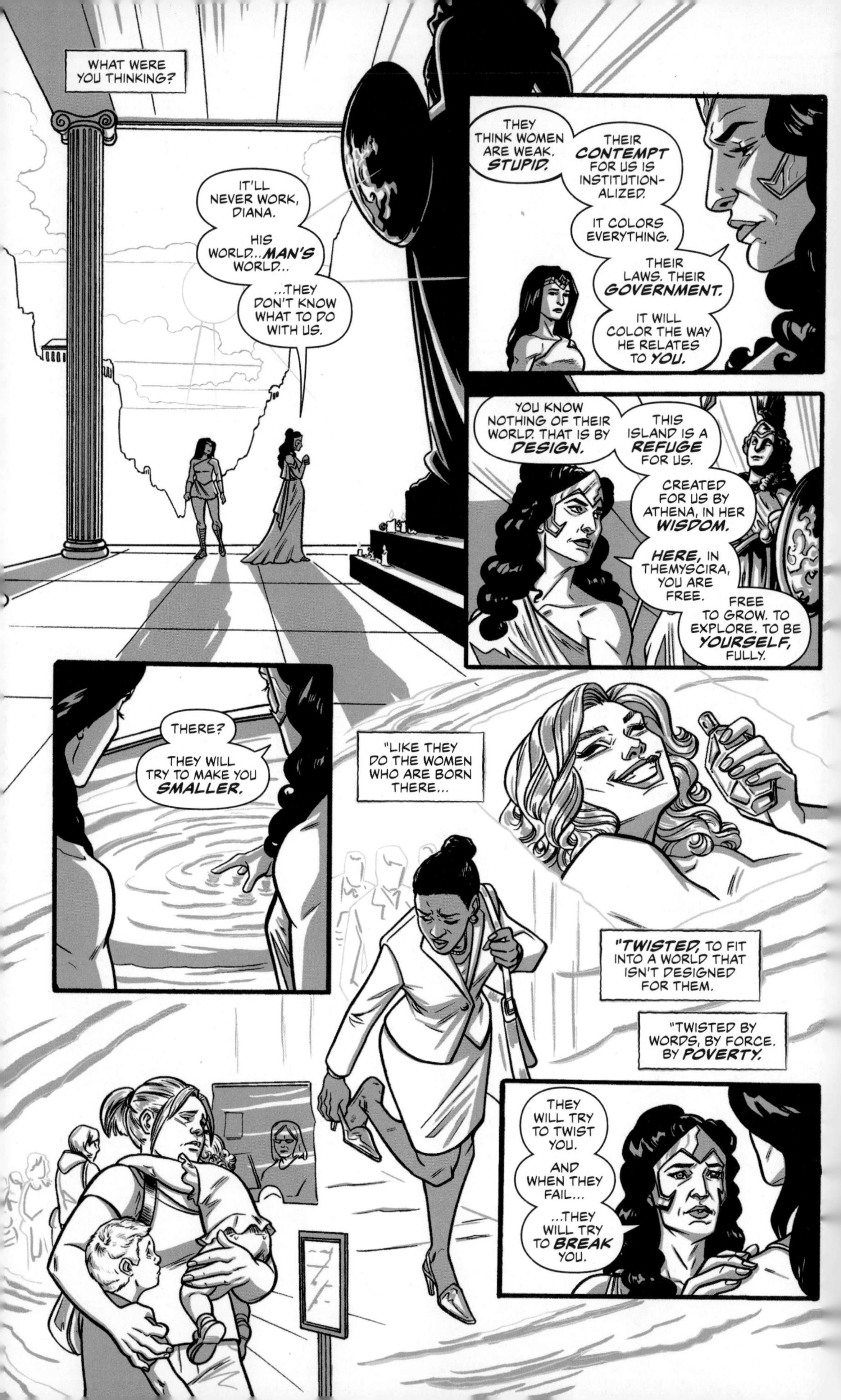

WHAT WERE YOU THINKING?
IT'LL NEVER WORK, DIANA.
HIS WORLD...MAN'S WORLD...
...THEY DON'T KNOW WHAT TO DO WITH US.
THEY THINK WOMEN ARE WEAK. STUPID.
THEIR CONTEMPT FOR US IS INSTITUTION-ALIZED.
IT COLORS EVERYTHING.
THEIR LAWS. THEIR GOVERNMENT.
IT WILL COLOR THE WAY HE RELATES TO YOU.
YOU KNOW NOTHING OF THEIR WORLD. THAT IS BY DESIGN.
THIS ISLAND IS A REFUGE FOR US.
CREATED FOR US BY ATHENA, IN HER WISDOM.
HERE, IN THEMYSCIRA, YOU ARE FREE.
FREE TO GROW. TO EXPLORE. TO BE YOURSELF, FULLY.
THERE?
THEY WILL TRY TO MAKE YOU SMALLER.
"LIKE THEY DO THE WOMEN WHO ARE BORN THERE...
"TWISTED, TO FIT INTO A WORLD THAT ISN'T DESIGNED FOR THEM.
"TWISTED BY WORDS, BY FORCE. BY POVERTY.
THEY WILL TRY TO TWIST YOU.
AND WHEN THEY FAIL...
...THEY WILL TRY TO BREAK YOU.

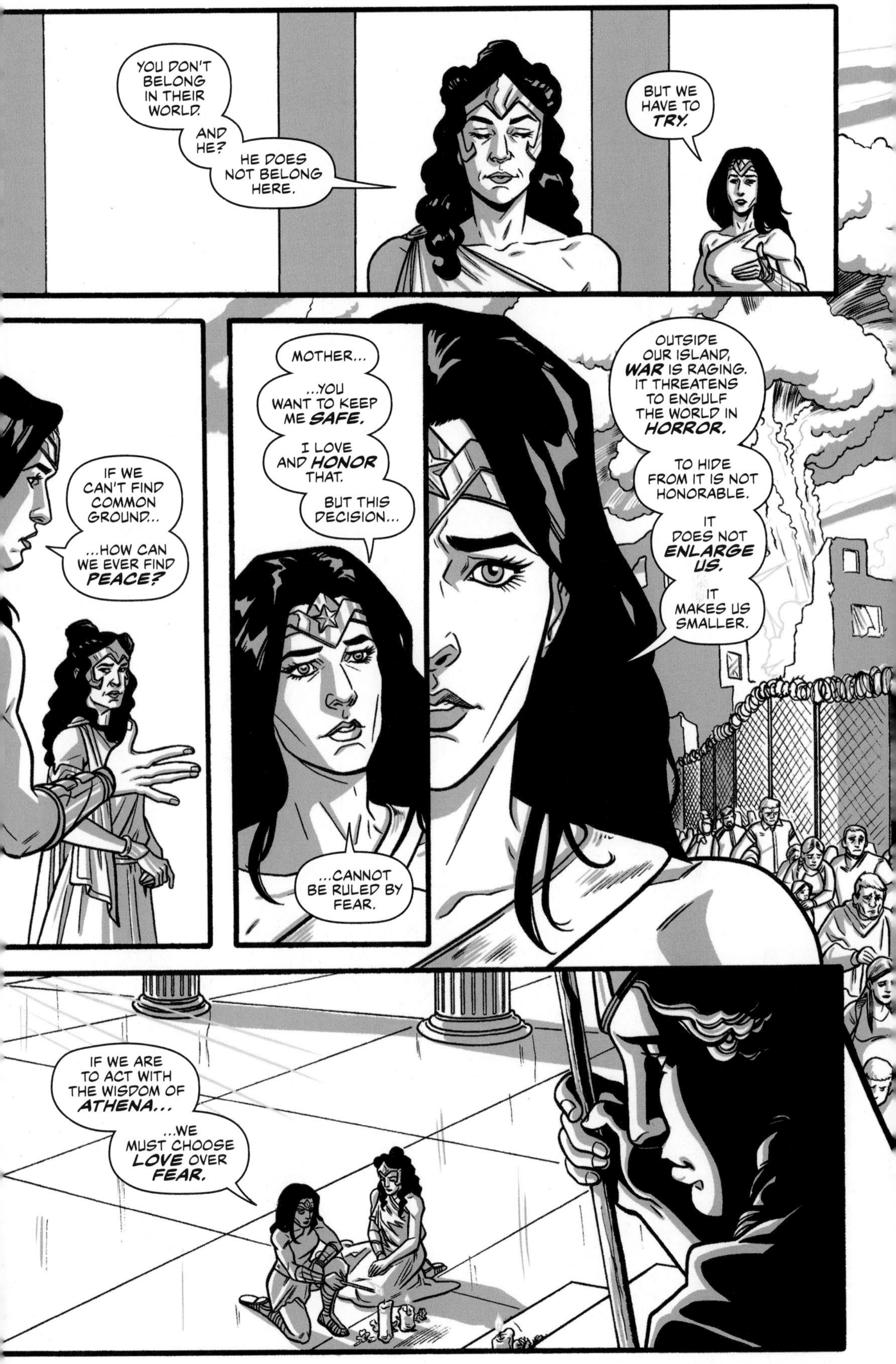
YOU DON'T BELONG IN THEIR WORLD.
AND HE?
HE DOES NOT BELONG HERE.
BUT WE HAVE TO TRY.
IF WE CAN'T FIND COMMON GROUND...
...HOW CAN WE EVER FIND PEACE?
MOTHER...
...YOU WANT TO KEEP ME SAFE.
I LOVE AND HONOR THAT.
BUT THIS DECISION...
...CANNOT BE RULED BY FEAR.
OUTSIDE OUR ISLAND, WAR IS RAGING. IT THREATENS TO ENGULF THE WORLD IN HORROR.
TO HIDE FROM IT IS NOT HONORABLE.
IT DOES NOT ENLARGE US.
IT MAKES US SMALLER.
IF WE ARE TO ACT WITH THE WISDOM OF ATHENA...
...WE MUST CHOOSE LOVE OVER FEAR.

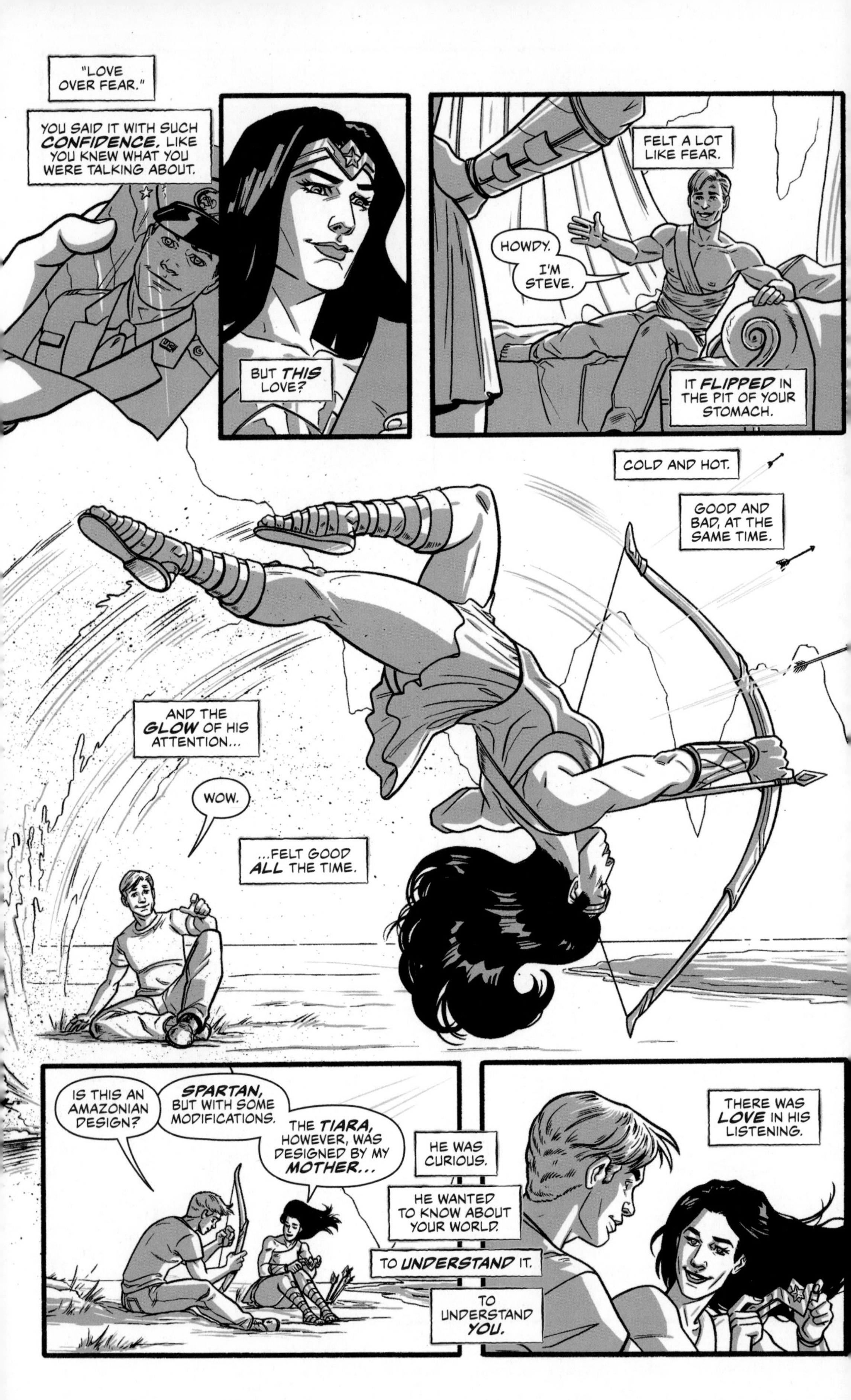
"LOVE OVER FEAR."
YOU SAID IT WITH SUCH CONFIDENCE. LIKE YOU KNEW WHAT YOU WERE TALKING ABOUT.
BUT THIS LOVE?
FELT A LOT LIKE FEAR.
HOWDY.
I'M STEVE.
IT FLIPPED IN THE PIT OF YOUR STOMACH.
COLD AND HOT.
GOOD AND BAD, AT THE SAME TIME.
AND THE GLOW OF HIS ATTENTION...
WOW.
...FELT GOOD ALL THE TIME.
IS THIS AN AMAZONIAN DESIGN?
SPARTAN, BUT WITH SOME MODIFICATIONS.
THE TIARA, HOWEVER, WAS DESIGNED BY MY MOTHER...
HE WAS CURIOUS.
HE WANTED TO KNOW ABOUT YOUR WORLD.
TO UNDERSTAND IT.
TO UNDERSTAND YOU.
THERE WAS LOVE IN HIS LISTENING.

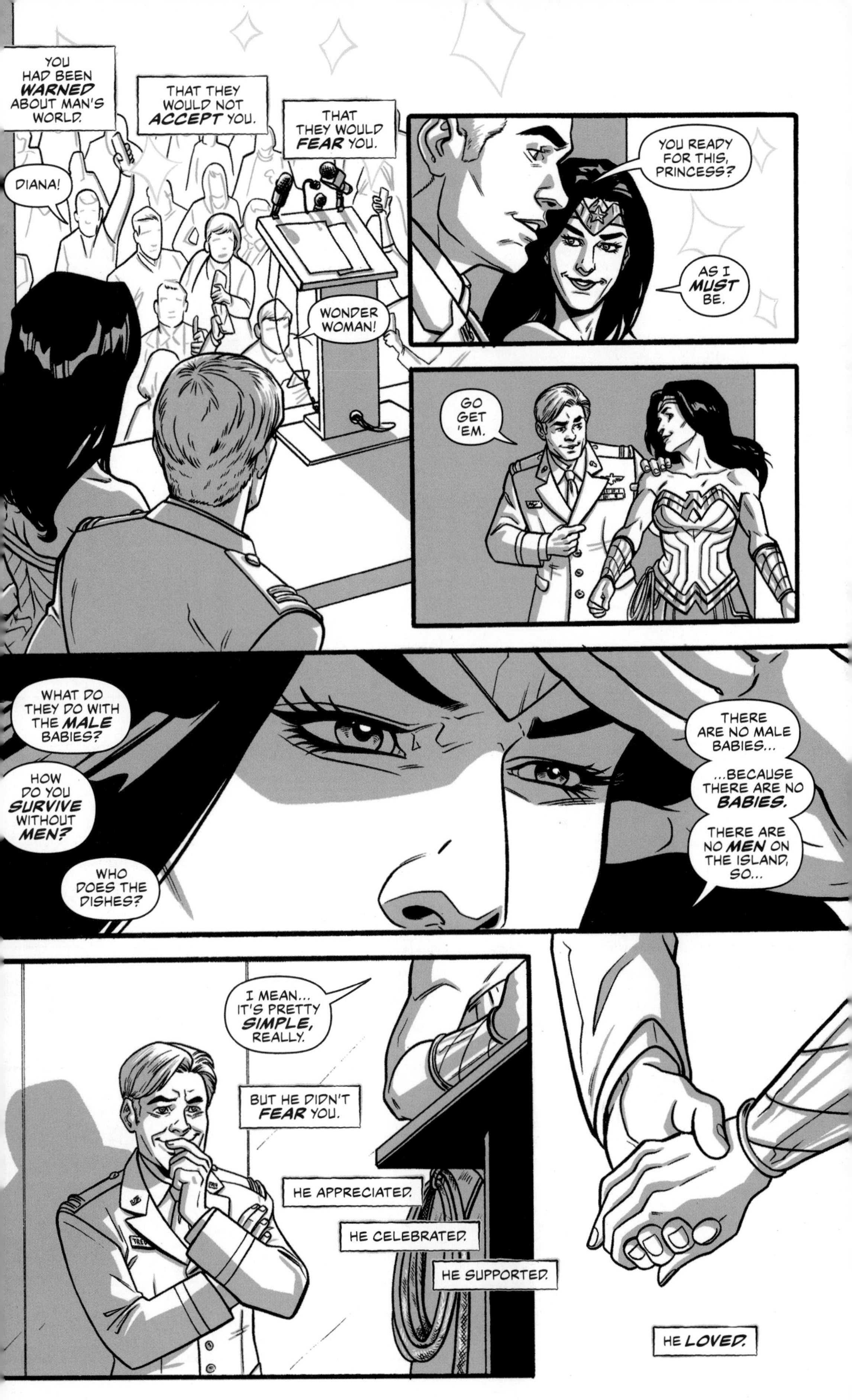
YOU HAD BEEN WARNED ABOUT MAN'S WORLD.
THAT THEY WOULD NOT ACCEPT YOU.
THAT THEY WOULD FEAR YOU.
DIANA!
WONDER WOMAN!
YOU READY FOR THIS, PRINCESS?
AS I MUST BE.
GO GET 'EM.
WHAT DO THEY DO WITH THE MALE BABIES?
HOW DO YOU SURVIVE WITHOUT MEN?
WHO DOES THE DISHES?
THERE ARE NO MALE BABIES...
...BECAUSE THERE ARE NO BABIES.
THERE ARE NO MEN ON THE ISLAND, SO...
I MEAN... IT'S PRETTY SIMPLE, REALLY.
BUT HE DIDN'T FEAR YOU.
HE APPRECIATED.
HE CELEBRATED.
HE SUPPORTED.
HE LOVED.

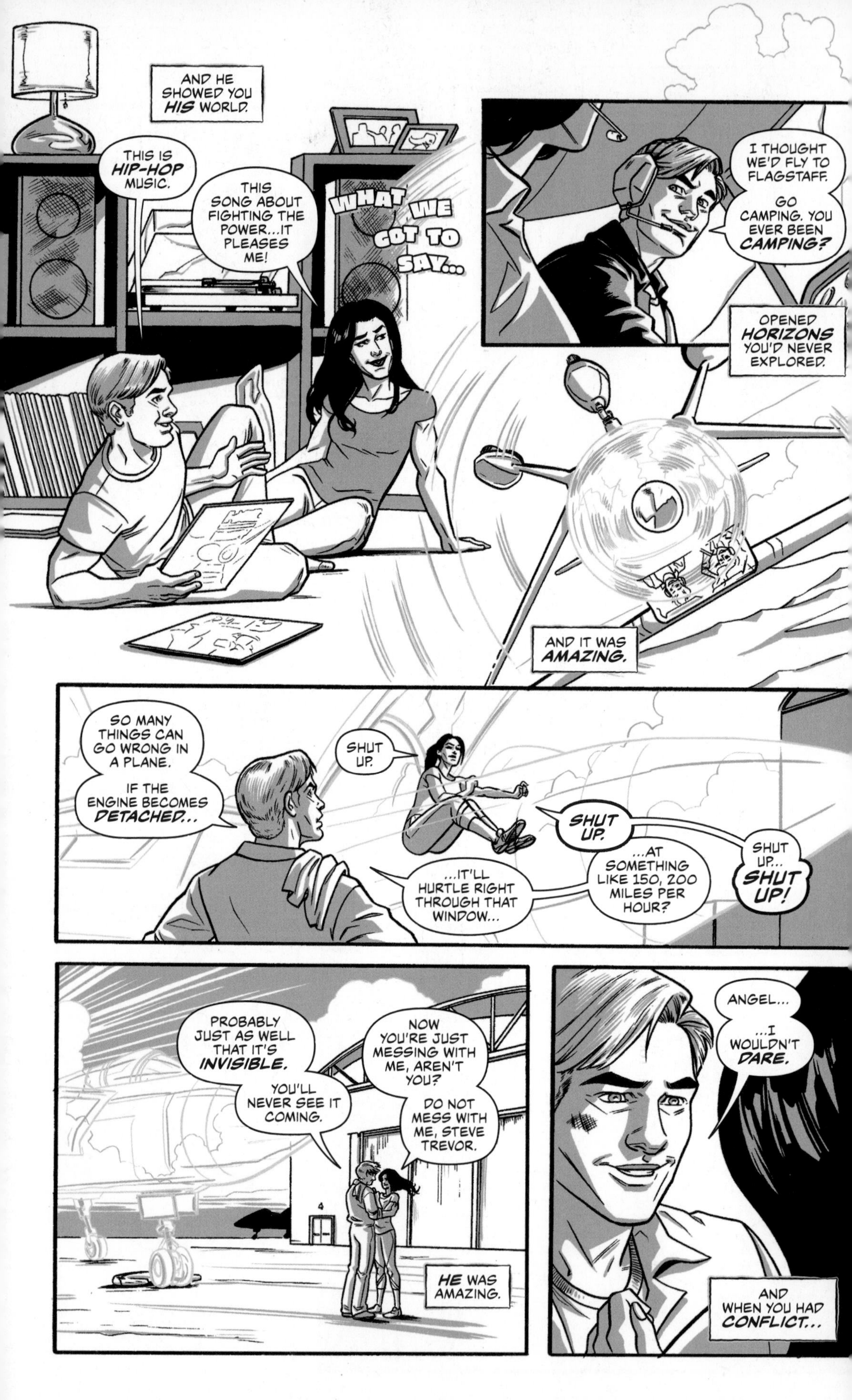
AND HE SHOWED YOU HIS WORLD.
THIS IS HIP-HOP MUSIC.
THIS SONG ABOUT FIGHTING THE POWER...IT PLEASES ME!
WHAT WE GOT TO SAY...
I THOUGHT WE'D FLY TO FLAGSTAFF.
GO CAMPING. YOU EVER BEEN CAMPING?
OPENED HORIZONS YOU'D NEVER EXPLORED.
AND IT WAS AMAZING.
SO MANY THINGS CAN GO WRONG IN A PLANE.
IF THE ENGINE BECOMES DETACHED...
SHUT UP.
...IT'LL HURTLE RIGHT THROUGH THAT WINDOW...
SHUT UP.
...AT SOMETHING LIKE 150, 200 MILES PER HOUR?
SHUT UP... SHUT UP!
PROBABLY JUST AS WELL THAT IT'S INVISIBLE.
YOU'LL NEVER SEE IT COMING.
NOW YOU'RE JUST MESSING WITH ME, AREN'T YOU?
DO NOT MESS WITH ME, STEVE TREVOR.
HE WAS AMAZING.
ANGEL...
...I WOULDN'T DARE.
AND WHEN YOU HAD CONFLICT...

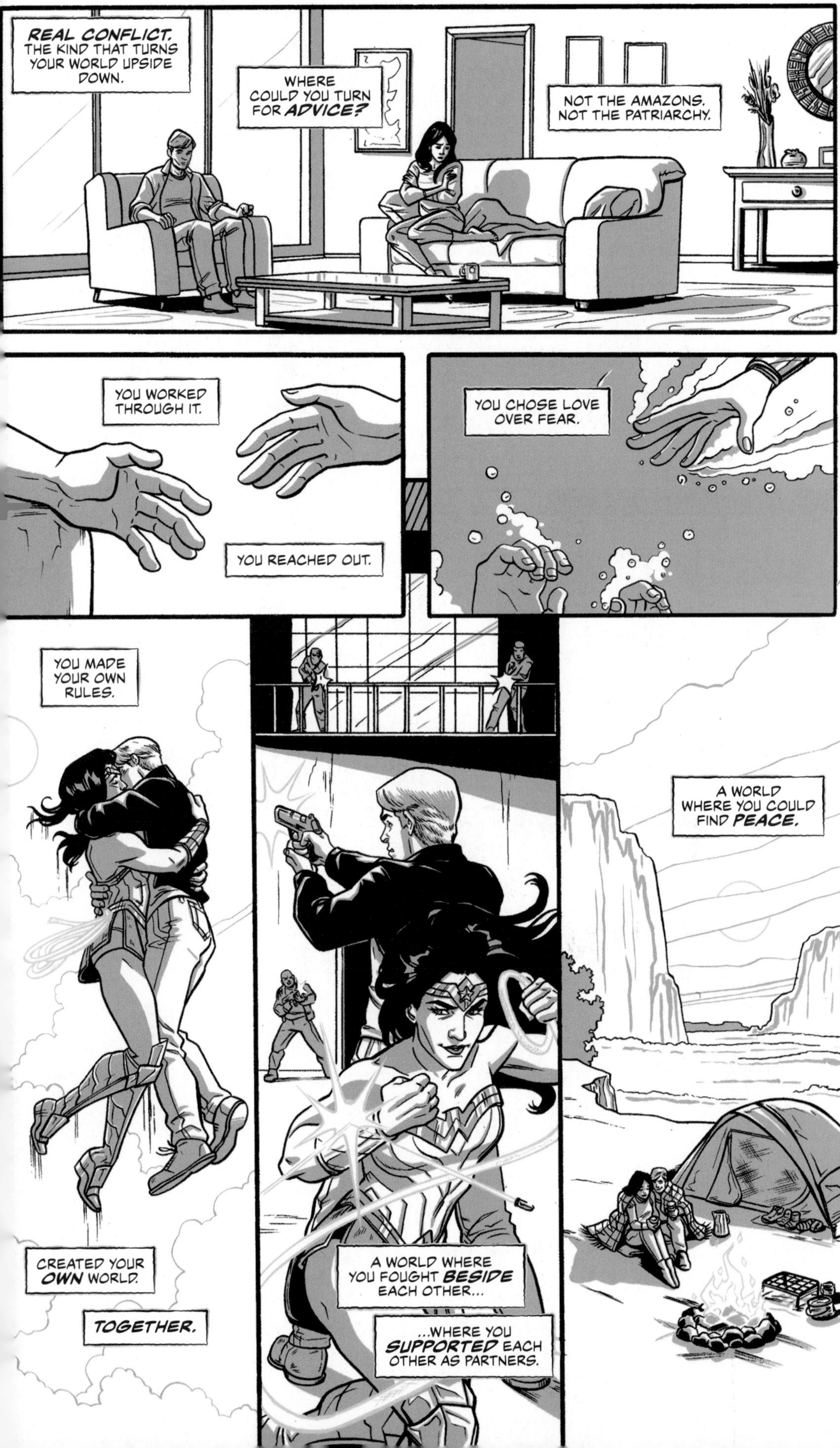
REAL CONFLICT. THE KIND THAT TURNS YOUR WORLD UPSIDE DOWN.
WHERE COULD YOU TURN FOR ADVICE?
NOT THE AMAZONS. NOT THE PATRIARCHY.
YOU WORKED THROUGH IT.
YOU REACHED OUT.
YOU CHOSE LOVE OVER FEAR.
YOU MADE YOUR OWN RULES.
CREATED YOUR OWN WORLD.
TOGETHER.
A WORLD WHERE YOU FOUGHT BESIDE EACH OTHER...
...WHERE YOU SUPPORTED EACH OTHER AS PARTNERS.
A WORLD WHERE YOU COULD FIND PEACE.

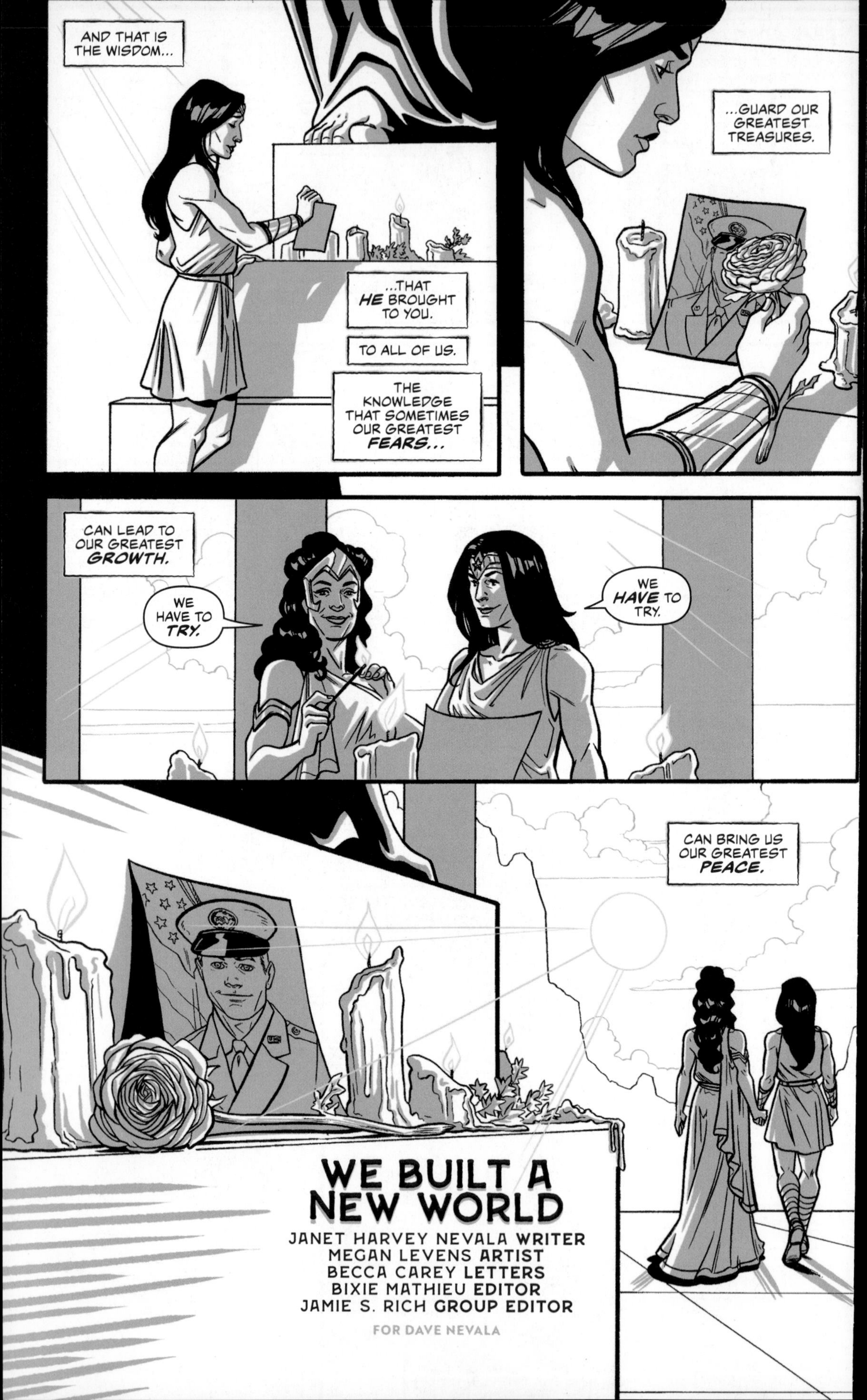
AND THAT IS THE WISDOM...
...GUARD OUR GREATEST TREASURES.
...THAT HE BROUGHT TO YOU.
TO ALL OF US.
THE KNOWLEDGE THAT SOMETIMES OUR GREATEST FEARS...
CAN LEAD TO OUR GREATEST GROWTH.
WE HAVE TO TRY.
WE HAVE TO TRY.
CAN BRING US OUR GREATEST PEACE.
WE BUILT A NEW WORLD
JANET HARVEY NEVALA WRITER
MEGAN LEVENS ARTIST
BECCA CAREY LETTERS
BIXIE MATHIEU EDITOR
JAMIE S. RICH GROUP EDITOR
FOR DAVE NEVALA

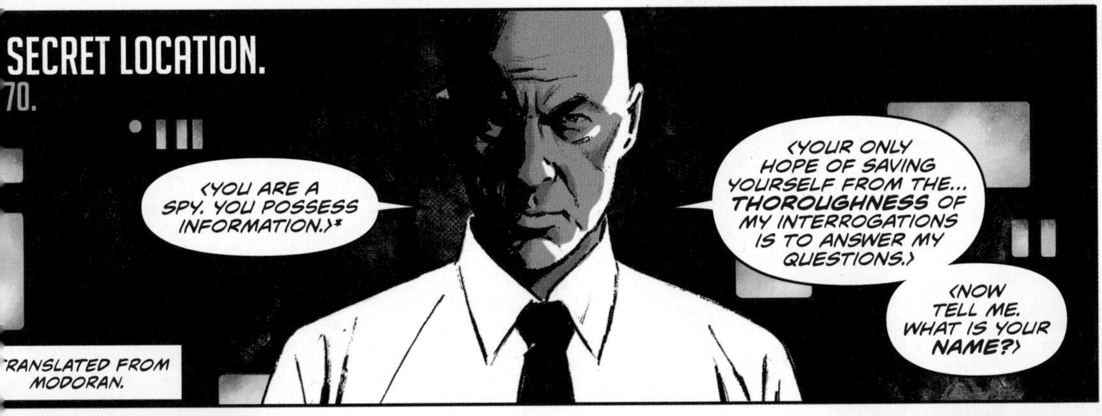
SECRET LOCATION.
70.
‹YOU ARE A SPY. YOU POSSESS INFORMATION.›*
‹YOUR ONLY HOPE OF SAVING YOURSELF FROM THE... THOROUGHNESS OF MY INTERROGATIONS IS TO ANSWER MY QUESTIONS.›
‹NOW TELL ME. WHAT IS YOUR NAME?›
RANSLATED FROM MODORAN.

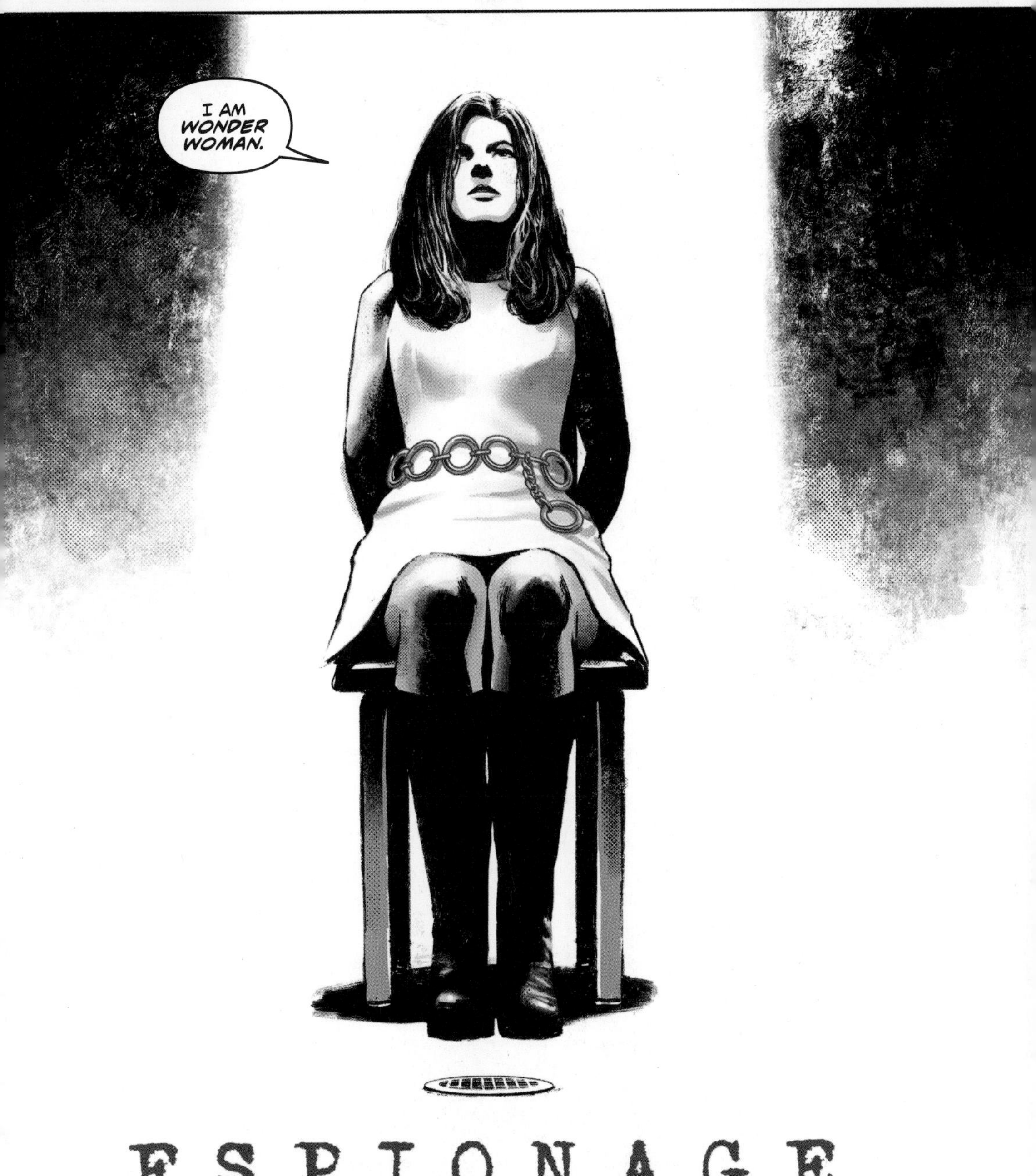
I AM WONDER WOMAN.

ESPIONAGE

WRITER: ROBERT VENDITTI ARTIST: STEVE EPTING
LETTERER: ANDWORLD DESIGN EDITOR: DIEGO LOPEZ

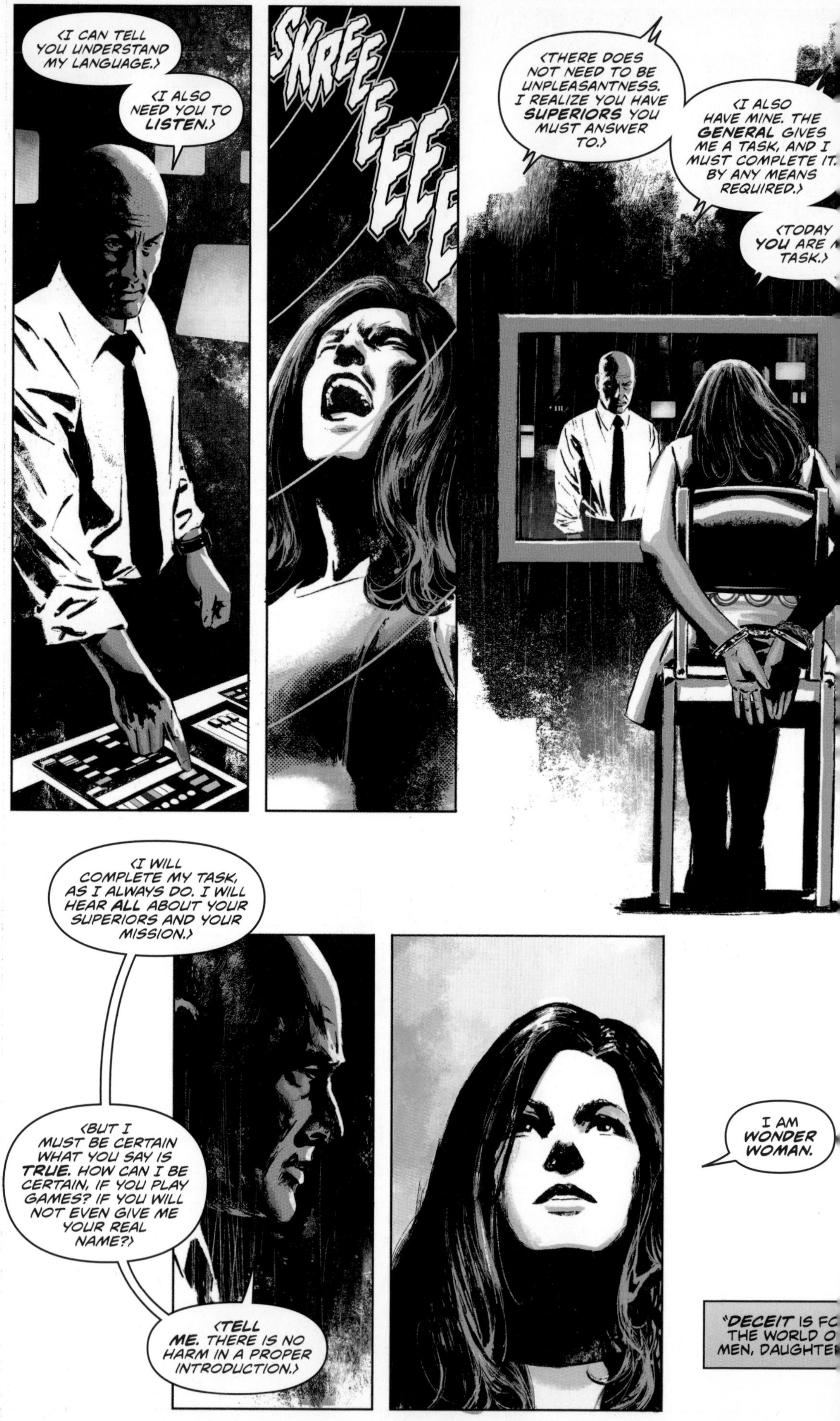
‹I CAN TELL YOU UNDERSTAND MY LANGUAGE.›
‹I ALSO NEED YOU TO LISTEN.›
SKREEEEEE
‹THERE DOES NOT NEED TO BE UNPLEASANTNESS. I REALIZE YOU HAVE SUPERIORS YOU MUST ANSWER TO.›
‹I ALSO HAVE MINE. THE GENERAL GIVES ME A TASK, AND I MUST COMPLETE IT. BY ANY MEANS REQUIRED.›
‹TODAY YOU ARE
TASK.›
‹I WILL COMPLETE MY TASK, AS I ALWAYS DO. I WILL HEAR ALL ABOUT YOUR SUPERIORS AND YOUR MISSION.›
‹BUT I MUST BE CERTAIN WHAT YOU SAY IS TRUE. HOW CAN I BE CERTAIN, IF YOU PLAY GAMES? IF YOU WILL NOT EVEN GIVE ME YOUR REAL NAME?›
‹TELL ME. THERE IS NO HARM IN A PROPER INTRODUCTION.›
I AM WONDER WOMAN.
"DECEIT IS FO
THE WORLD O
MEN, DAUGHTE

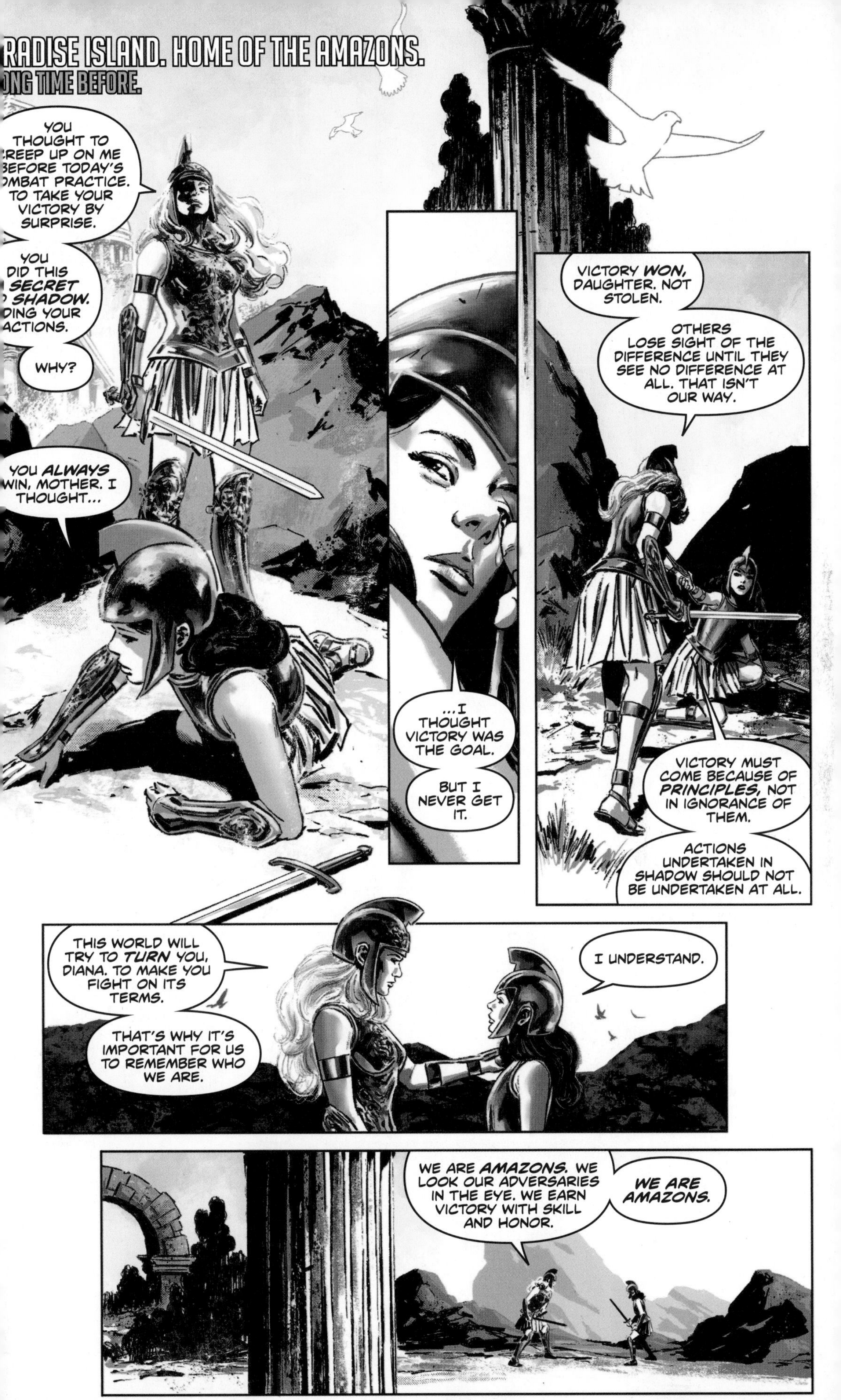

RADISE ISLAND. HOME OF THE AMAZONS.
ONG TIME BEFORE.
YOU THOUGHT TO CREEP UP ON ME BEFORE TODAY'S OMBAT PRACTICE. TO TAKE YOUR VICTORY BY SURPRISE.
YOU DID THIS SECRET SHADOW. DING YOUR ACTIONS.
WHY?
YOU ALWAYS WIN, MOTHER. I THOUGHT...
...I THOUGHT VICTORY WAS THE GOAL.
BUT I NEVER GET IT.
VICTORY WON, DAUGHTER. NOT STOLEN.
OTHERS LOSE SIGHT OF THE DIFFERENCE UNTIL THEY SEE NO DIFFERENCE AT ALL. THAT ISN'T OUR WAY.
VICTORY MUST COME BECAUSE OF PRINCIPLES, NOT IN IGNORANCE OF THEM.
ACTIONS UNDERTAKEN IN SHADOW SHOULD NOT BE UNDERTAKEN AT ALL.
THIS WORLD WILL TRY TO TURN YOU, DIANA. TO MAKE YOU FIGHT ON ITS TERMS.
THAT'S WHY IT'S IMPORTANT FOR US TO REMEMBER WHO WE ARE.
I UNDERSTAND.
WE ARE AMAZONS. WE LOOK OUR ADVERSARIES IN THE EYE. WE EARN VICTORY WITH SKILL AND HONOR.
WE ARE AMAZONS.

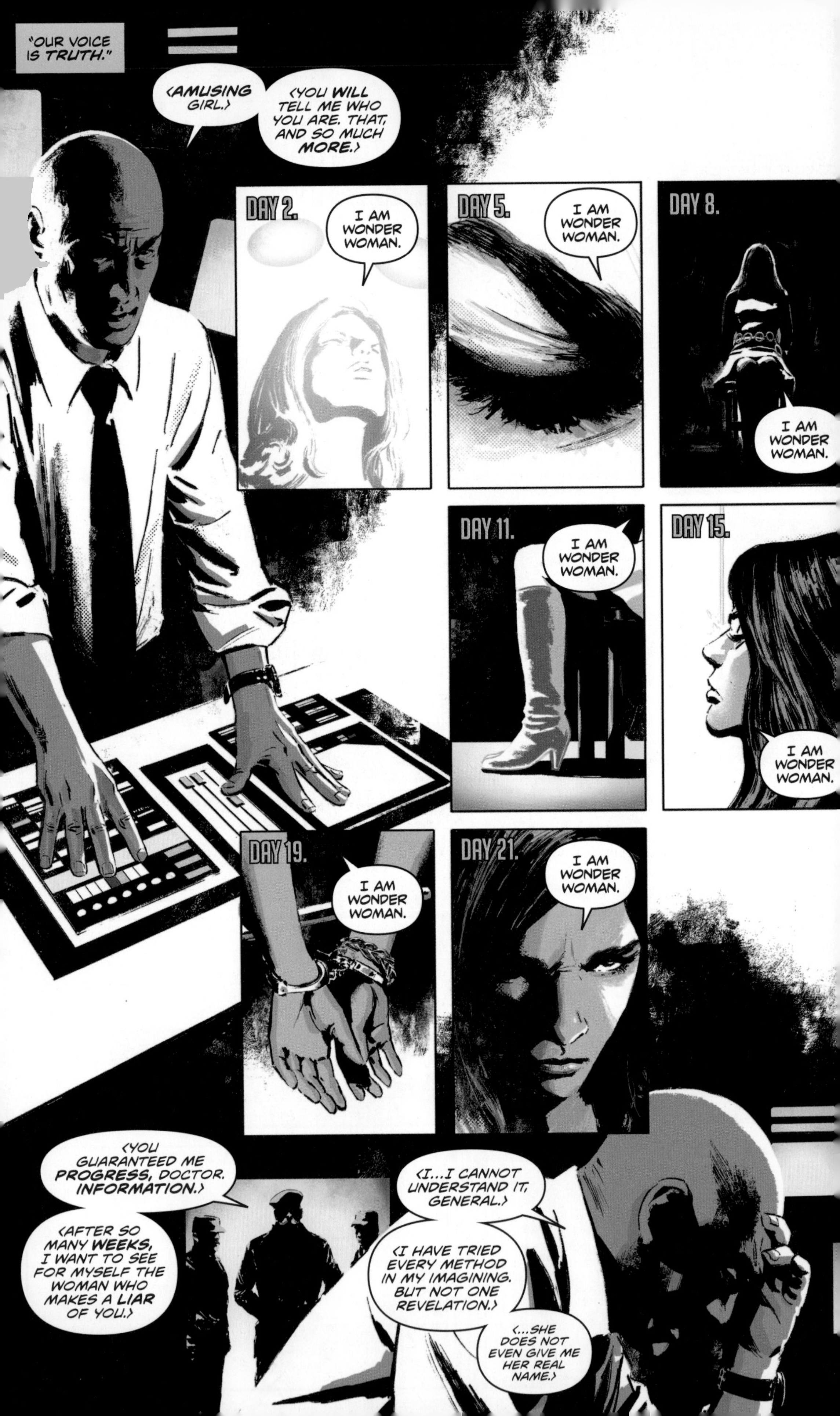
"OUR VOICE IS TRUTH."
<AMUSING GIRL.>
<YOU WILL TELL ME WHO YOU ARE. THAT, AND SO MUCH MORE.>
DAY 2.
I AM WONDER WOMAN.
DAY 5.
I AM WONDER WOMAN.
DAY 8.
I AM WONDER WOMAN.
DAY 11.
I AM WONDER WOMAN.
DAY 15.
I AM WONDER WOMAN.
DAY 19.
I AM WONDER WOMAN.
DAY 21.
I AM WONDER WOMAN.
<YOU GUARANTEED ME PROGRESS, DOCTOR. INFORMATION.>
<AFTER SO MANY WEEKS, I WANT TO SEE FOR MYSELF THE WOMAN WHO MAKES A LIAR OF YOU.>
<I...I CANNOT UNDERSTAND IT, GENERAL.>
<I HAVE TRIED EVERY METHOD IN MY IMAGINING. BUT NOT ONE REVELATION.>
<...SHE DOES NOT EVEN GIVE ME HER REAL NAME.>

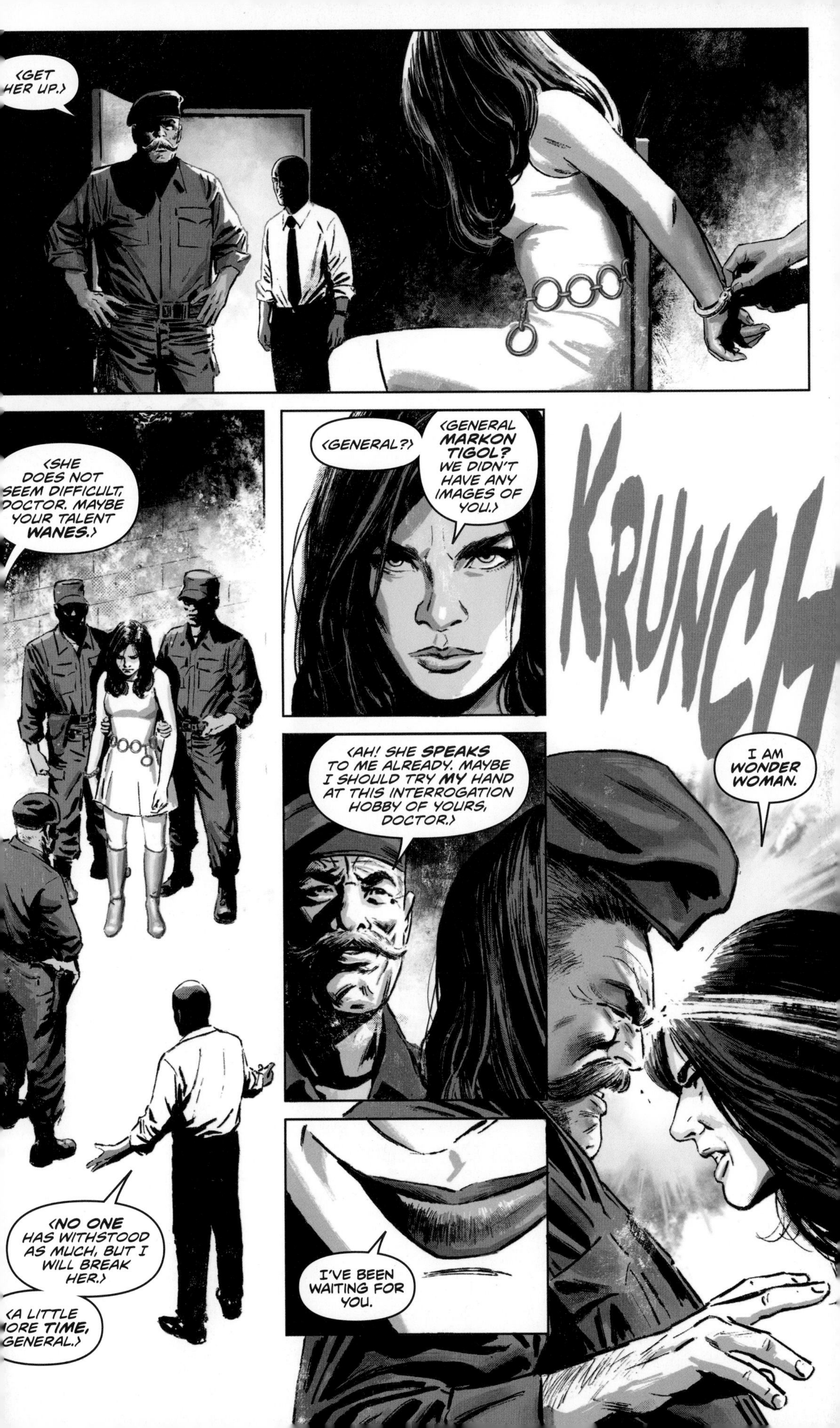

‹GET HER UP.›
‹SHE DOES NOT SEEM DIFFICULT, DOCTOR. MAYBE YOUR TALENT WANES.›
‹NO ONE HAS WITHSTOOD AS MUCH, BUT I WILL BREAK HER.›
‹A LITTLE ORE TIME, GENERAL.›
‹GENERAL?›
‹GENERAL MARKON TIGOL? WE DIDN'T HAVE ANY IMAGES OF YOU.›
‹AH! SHE SPEAKS TO ME ALREADY. MAYBE I SHOULD TRY MY HAND AT THIS INTERROGATION HOBBY OF YOURS, DOCTOR.›
I'VE BEEN WAITING FOR YOU.
KRUNCH
I AM WONDER WOMAN.

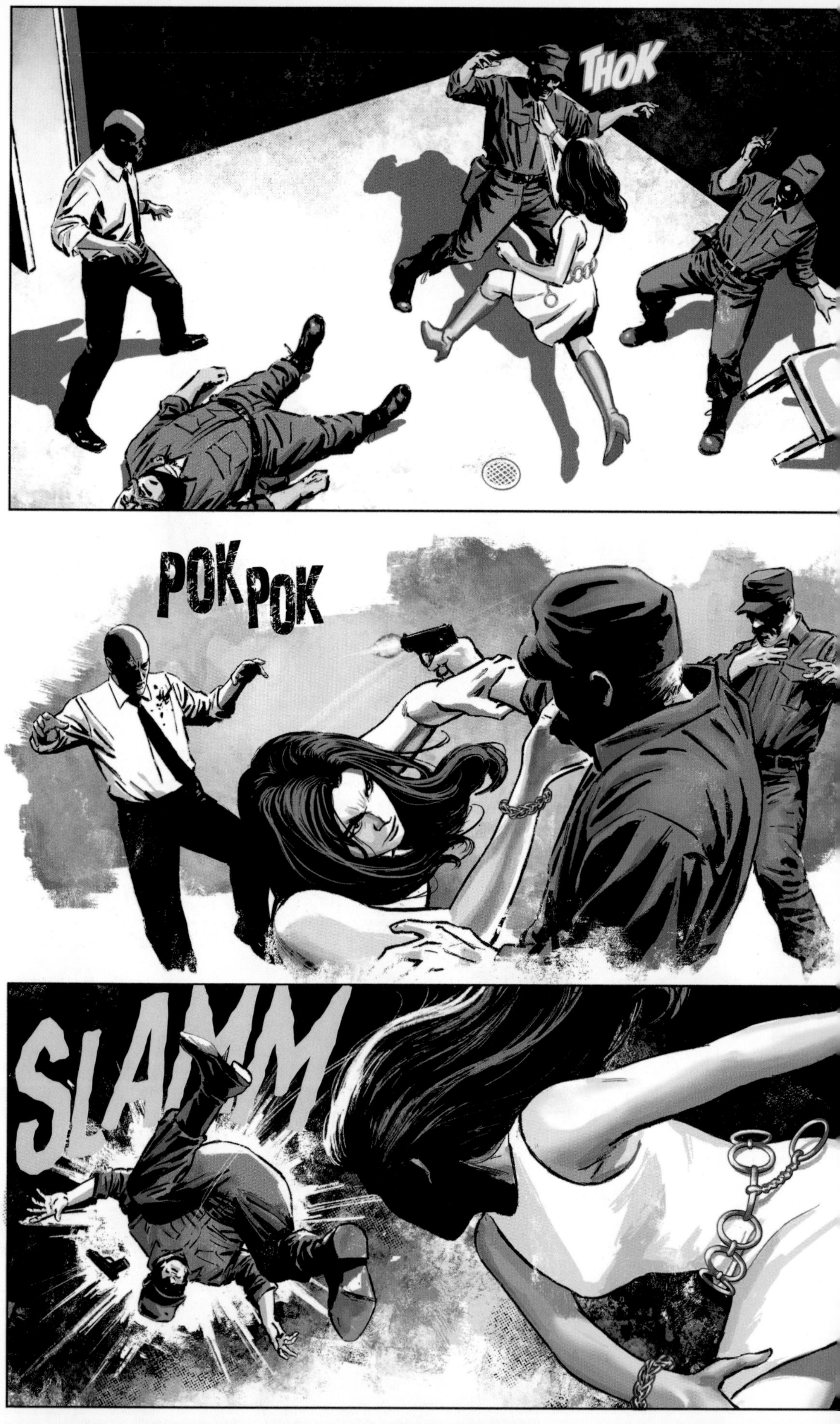
THOK
POK POK
SLAMM

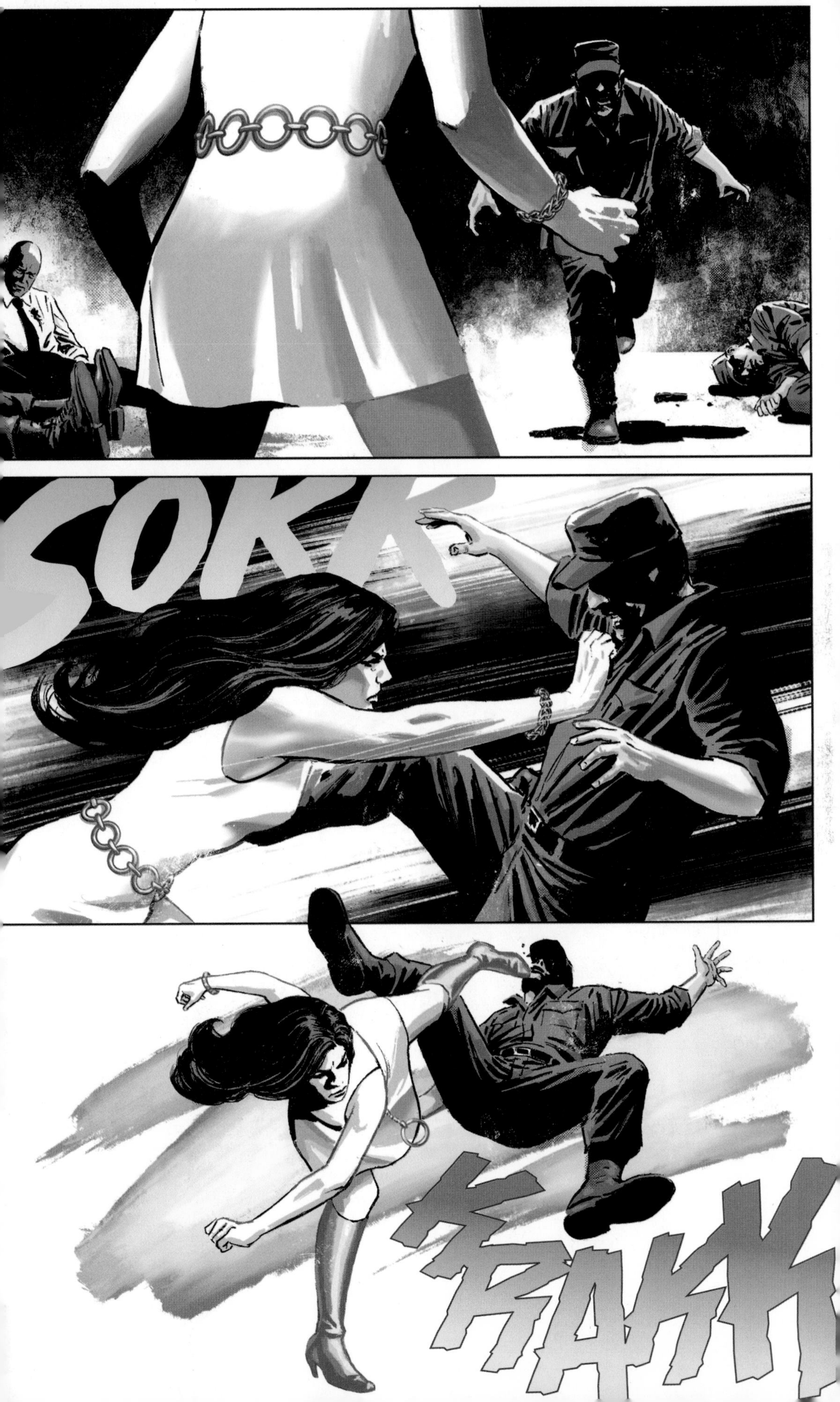
SOKK
KRAKK

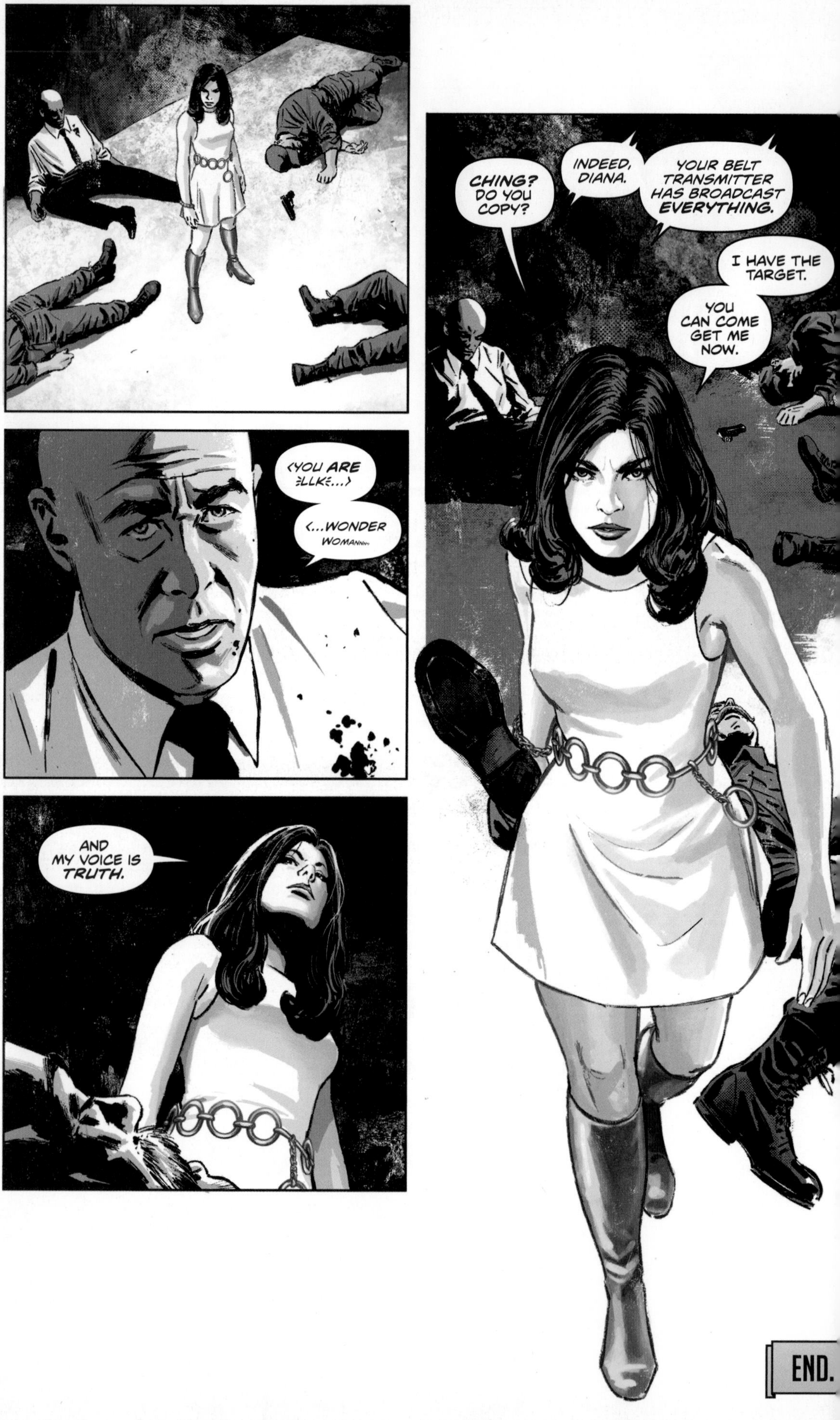
<YOU ARE ƎLLKƐ...>
<...WONDER WOMANNN
AND MY VOICE IS TRUTH.
CHING? DO YOU COPY?
INDEED, DIANA.
YOUR BELT TRANSMITTER HAS BROADCAST EVERYTHING.
I HAVE THE TARGET.
YOU CAN COME GET ME NOW.
END.

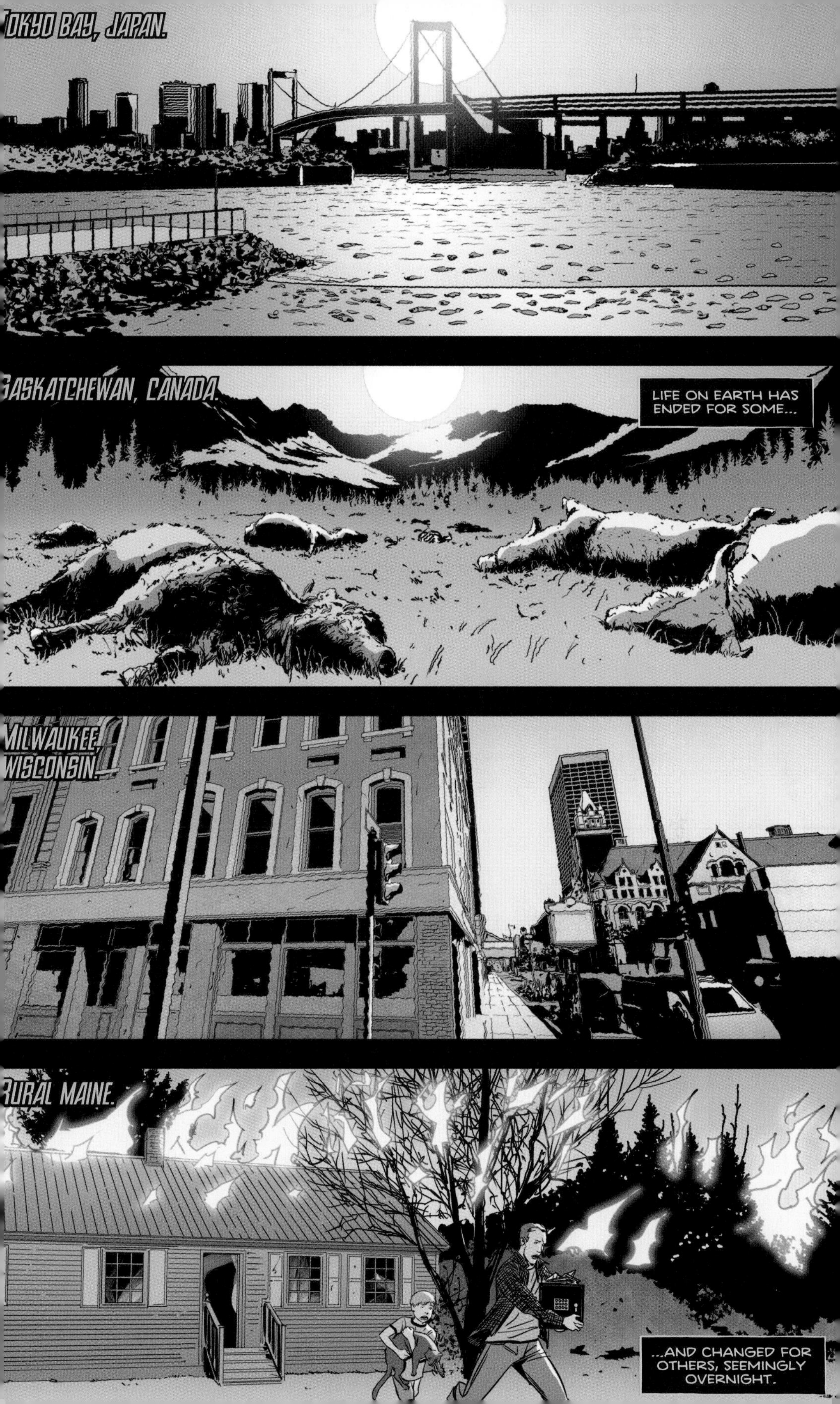
TOKYO BAY, JAPAN.
SASKATCHEWAN, CANADA.
LIFE ON EARTH HAS ENDED FOR SOME...
MILWAUKEE, WISCONSIN.
RURAL MAINE.
...AND CHANGED FOR OTHERS, SEEMINGLY OVERNIGHT.

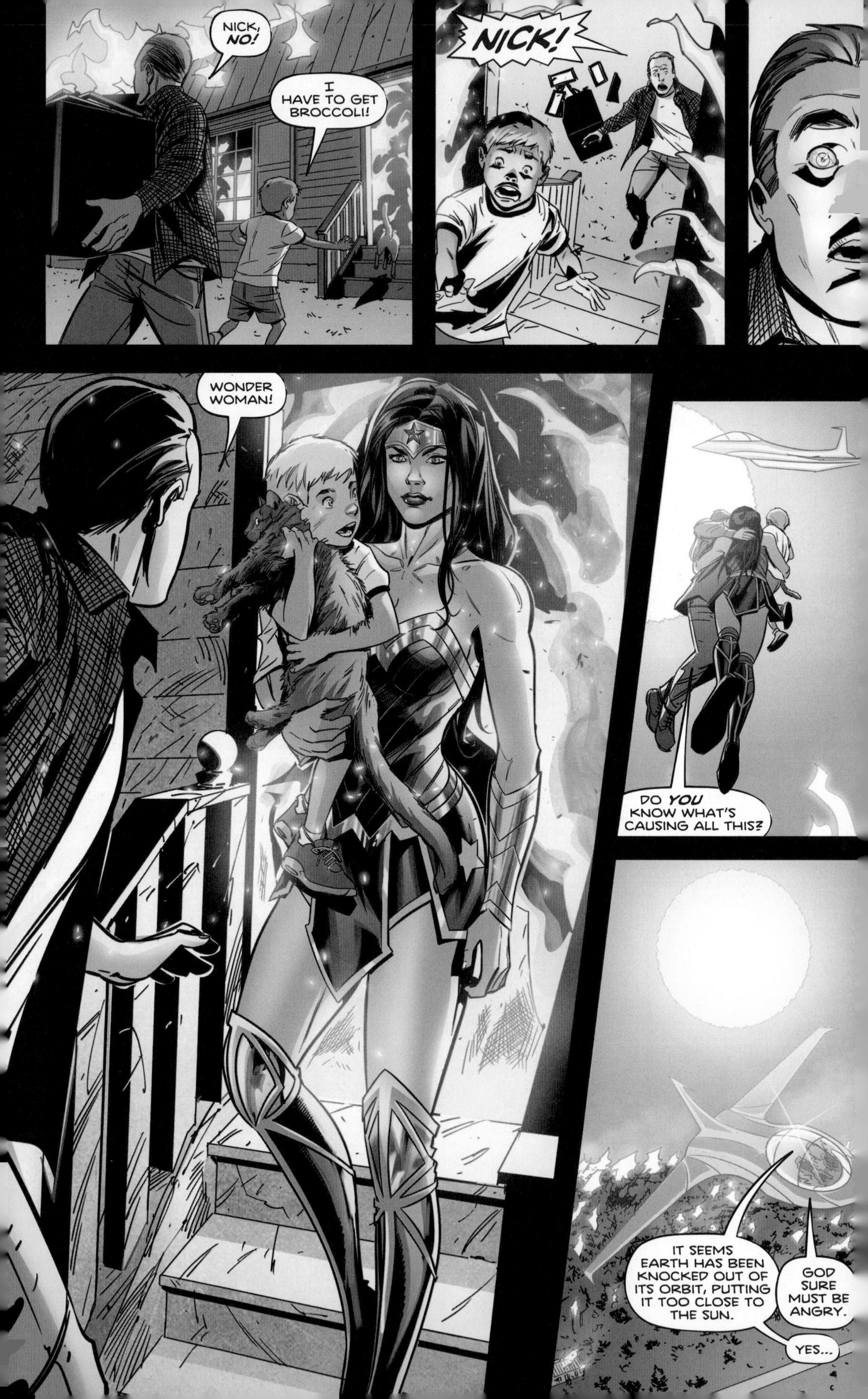
NICK, NO!
I HAVE TO GET BROCCOLI!
NICK!
WONDER WOMAN!
DO YOU KNOW WHAT'S CAUSING ALL THIS?
IT SEEMS EARTH HAS BEEN KNOCKED OUT OF ITS ORBIT, PUTTING IT TOO CLOSE TO THE SUN.
GOD SURE MUST BE ANGRY.
YES...

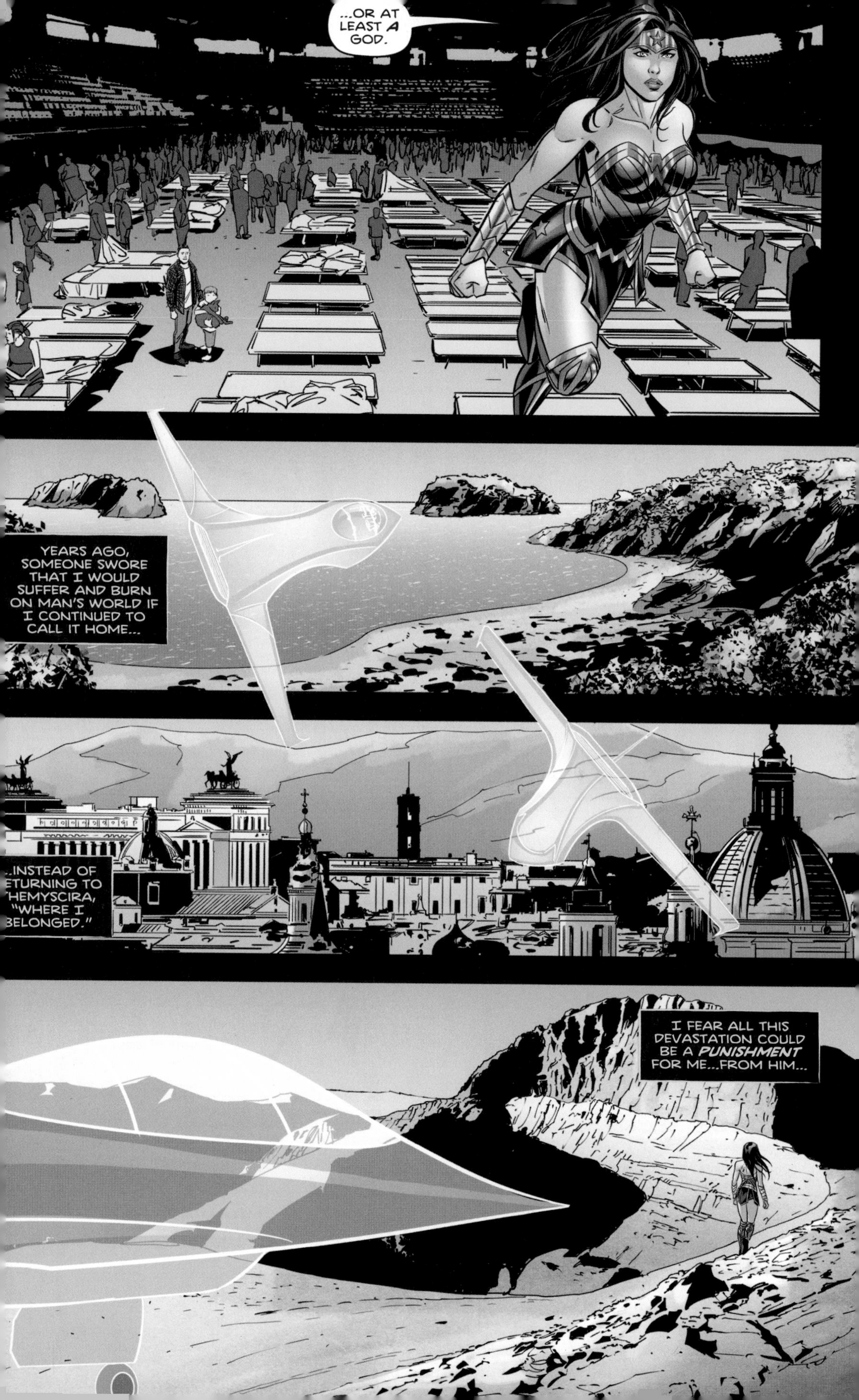
...OR AT LEAST A GOD.
YEARS AGO, SOMEONE SWORE THAT I WOULD SUFFER AND BURN ON MAN'S WORLD IF I CONTINUED TO CALL IT HOME...
..INSTEAD OF ETURNING TO HEMYSCIRA, "WHERE I BELONGED."
I FEAR ALL THIS DEVASTATION COULD BE A PUNISHMENT FOR ME...FROM HIM...

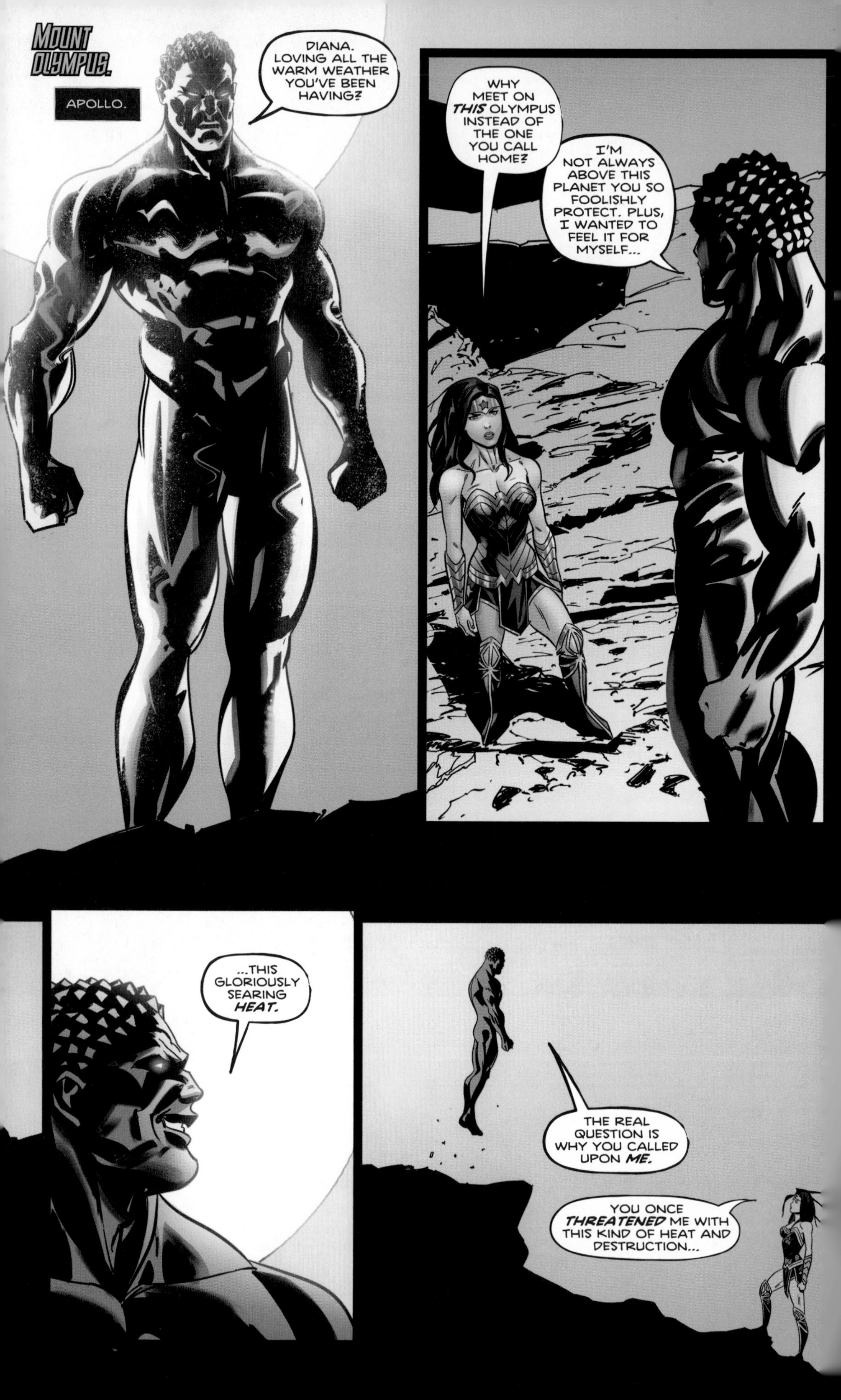
MOUNT OLYMPUS.
APOLLO.
DIANA. LOVING ALL THE WARM WEATHER YOU'VE BEEN HAVING?
WHY MEET ON THIS OLYMPUS INSTEAD OF THE ONE YOU CALL HOME?
I'M NOT ALWAYS ABOVE THIS PLANET YOU SO FOOLISHLY PROTECT. PLUS, I WANTED TO FEEL IT FOR MYSELF...
...THIS GLORIOUSLY SEARING HEAT.
THE REAL QUESTION IS WHY YOU CALLED UPON ME.
YOU ONCE THREATENED ME WITH THIS KIND OF HEAT AND DESTRUCTION...

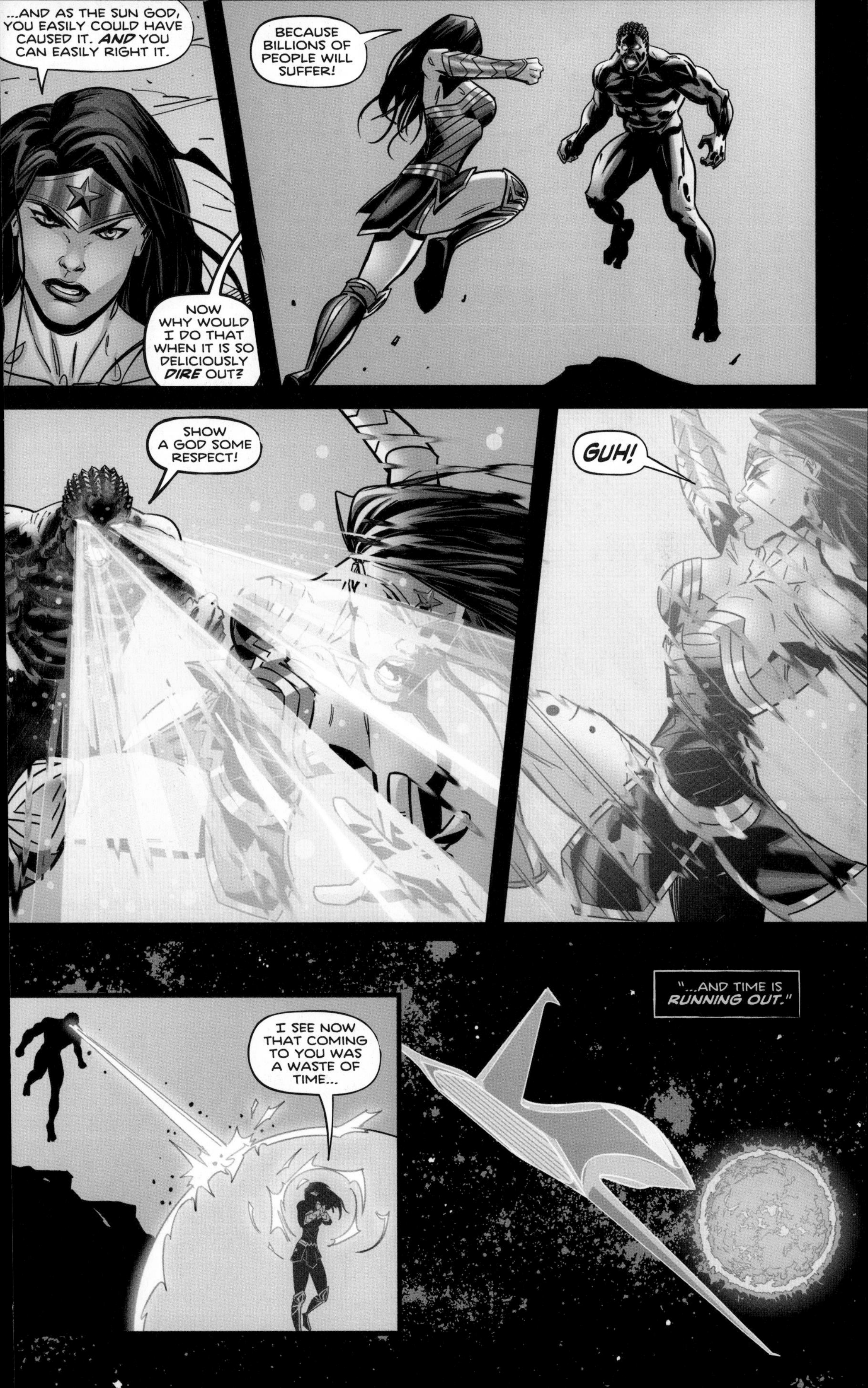
...AND AS THE SUN GOD, YOU EASILY COULD HAVE CAUSED IT. AND YOU CAN EASILY RIGHT IT.
NOW WHY WOULD I DO THAT WHEN IT IS SO DELICIOUSLY DIRE OUT?
BECAUSE BILLIONS OF PEOPLE WILL SUFFER!
SHOW A GOD SOME RESPECT!
GUH!
I SEE NOW THAT COMING TO YOU WAS A WASTE OF TIME...
"...AND TIME IS RUNNING OUT."

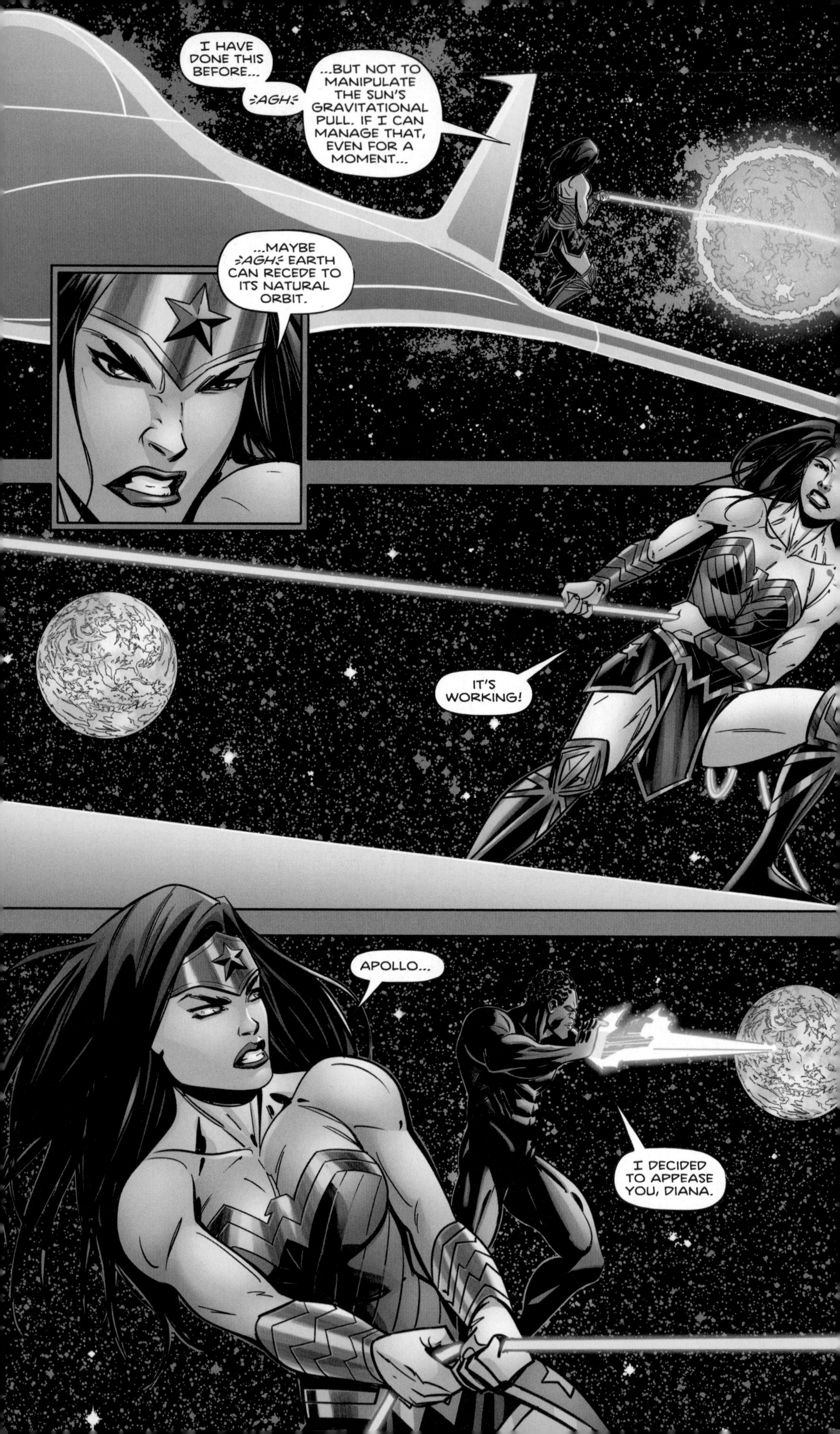
I HAVE DONE THIS BEFORE...
AGH
...BUT NOT TO MANIPULATE THE SUN'S GRAVITATIONAL PULL. IF I CAN MANAGE THAT, EVEN FOR A MOMENT...
...MAYBE AGH EARTH CAN RECEDE TO ITS NATURAL ORBIT.
IT'S WORKING!
APOLLO...
I DECIDED TO APPEASE YOU, DIANA.

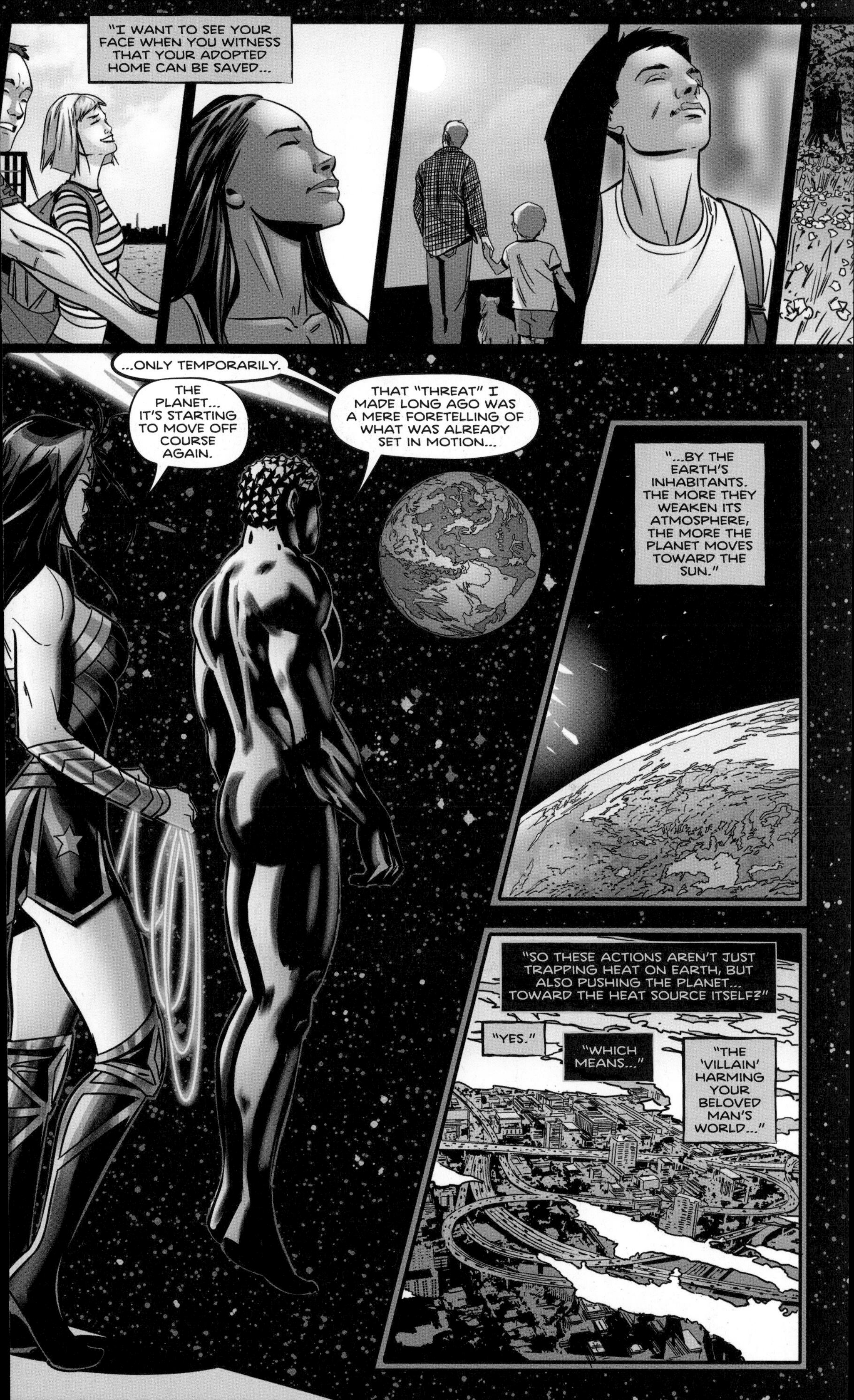
"I WANT TO SEE YOUR FACE WHEN YOU WITNESS THAT YOUR ADOPTED HOME CAN BE SAVED...
...ONLY TEMPORARILY.
THE PLANET... IT'S STARTING TO MOVE OFF COURSE AGAIN.
THAT "THREAT" I MADE LONG AGO WAS A MERE FORETELLING OF WHAT WAS ALREADY SET IN MOTION...
"...BY THE EARTH'S INHABITANTS. THE MORE THEY WEAKEN ITS ATMOSPHERE, THE MORE THE PLANET MOVES TOWARD THE SUN."
"SO THESE ACTIONS AREN'T JUST TRAPPING HEAT ON EARTH, BUT ALSO PUSHING THE PLANET... TOWARD THE HEAT SOURCE ITSELF?"
"YES."
"WHICH MEANS..."
"THE 'VILLAIN' HARMING YOUR BELOVED MAN'S WORLD..."

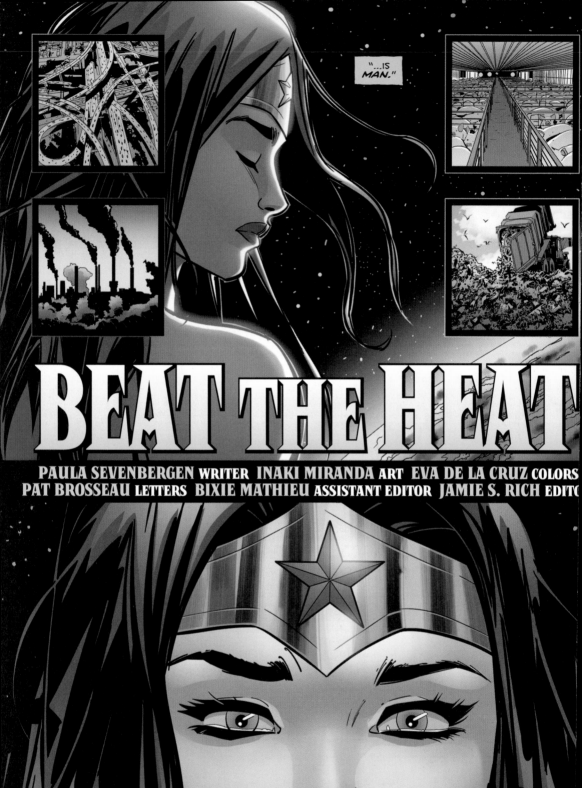

"...IS MAN."

BEAT THE HEAT

PAULA SEVENBERGEN WRITER **INAKI MIRANDA** ART **EVA DE LA CRUZ** COLORS
PAT BROSSEAU LETTERS **BIXIE MATHIEU** ASSISTANT EDITOR **JAMIE S. RICH** EDITO

ENI

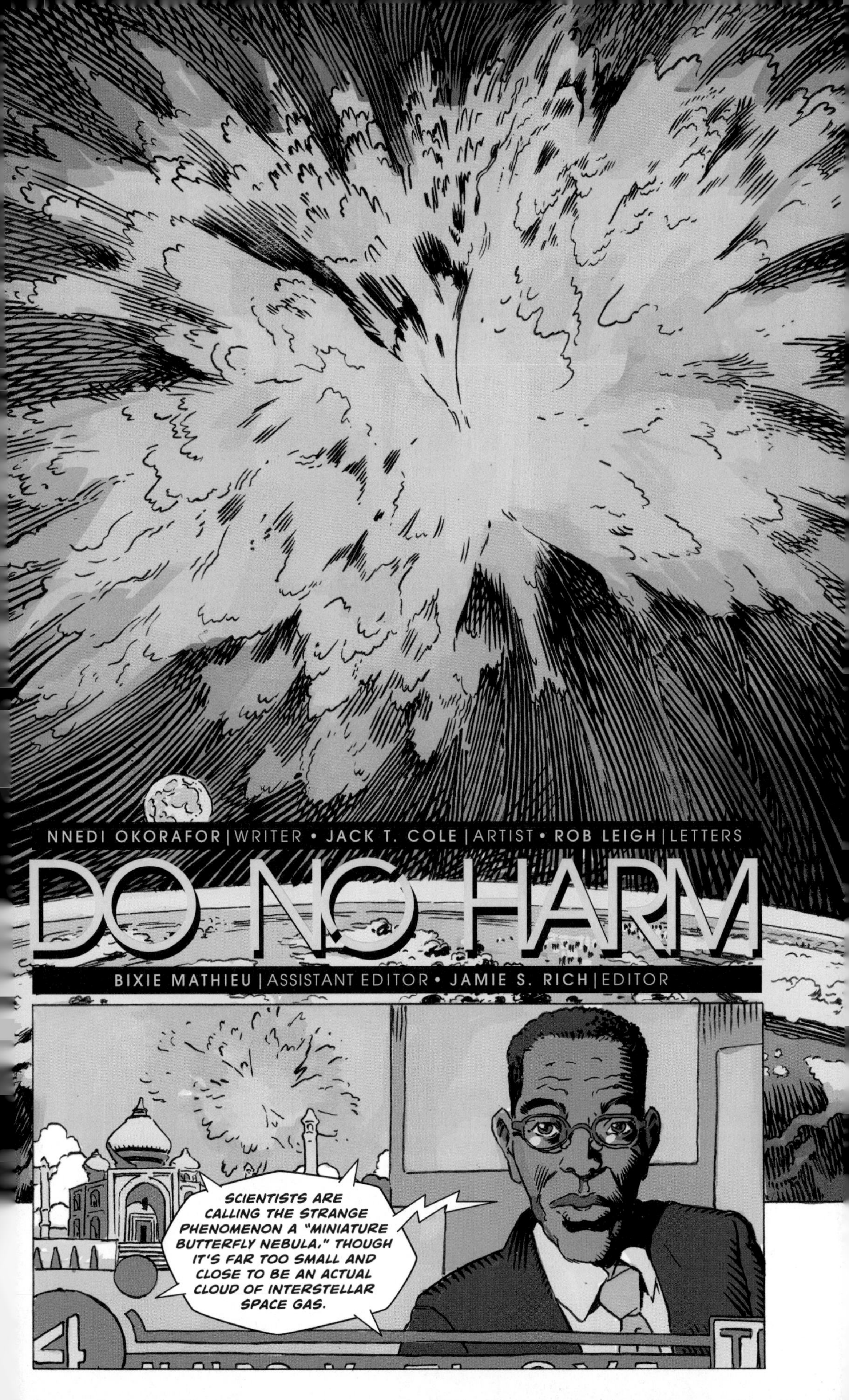
NNEDI OKORAFOR | WRITER • JACK T. COLE | ARTIST • ROB LEIGH | LETTERS
DO NO HARM
BIXIE MATHIEU | ASSISTANT EDITOR • JAMIE S. RICH | EDITOR
SCIENTISTS ARE CALLING THE STRANGE PHENOMENON A "MINIATURE BUTTERFLY NEBULA," THOUGH IT'S FAR TOO SMALL AND CLOSE TO BE AN ACTUAL CLOUD OF INTERSTELLAR SPACE GAS.

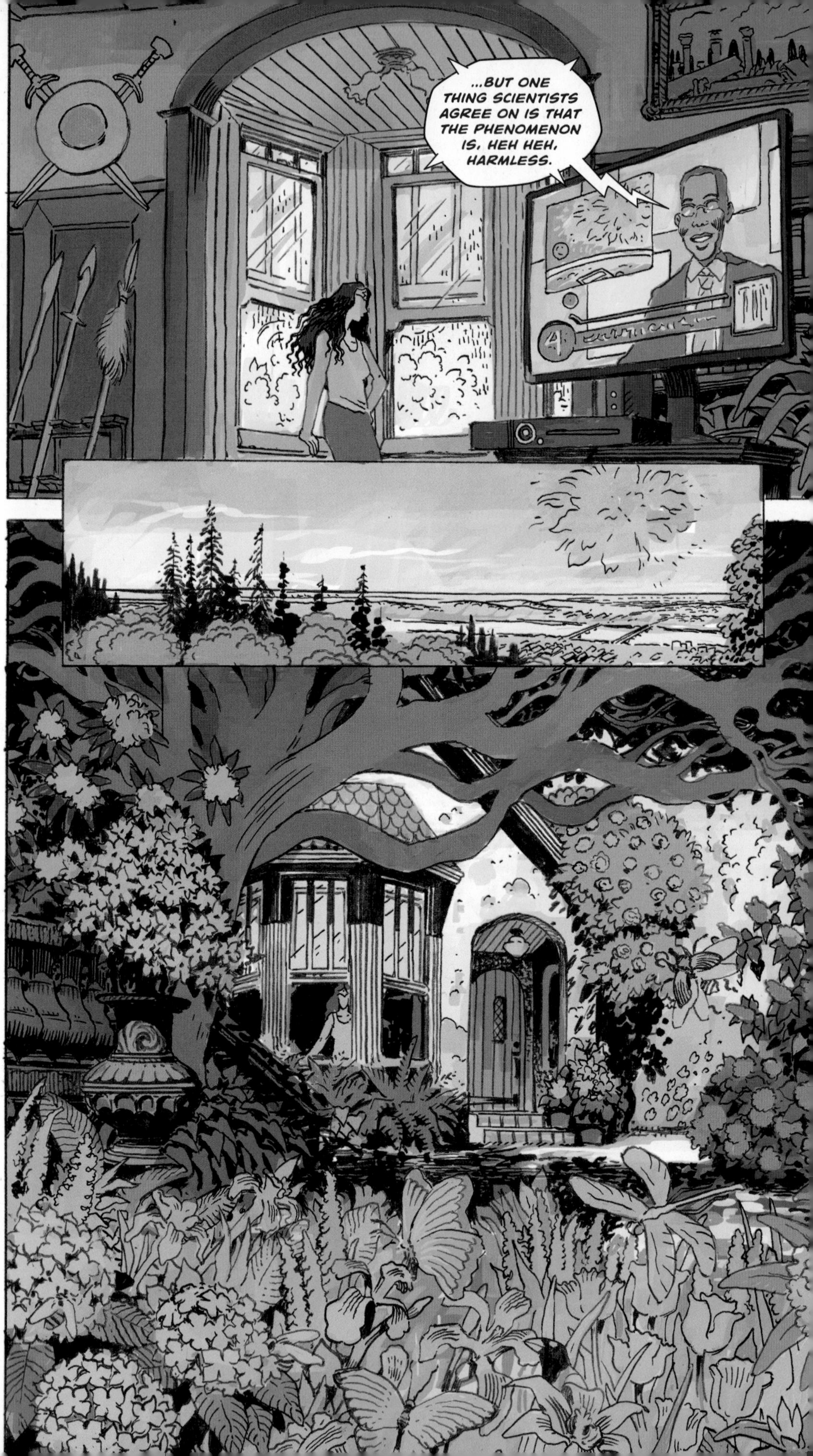
...BUT ONE THING SCIENTISTS AGREE ON IS THAT THE PHENOMENON IS, HEH HEH, HARMLESS.

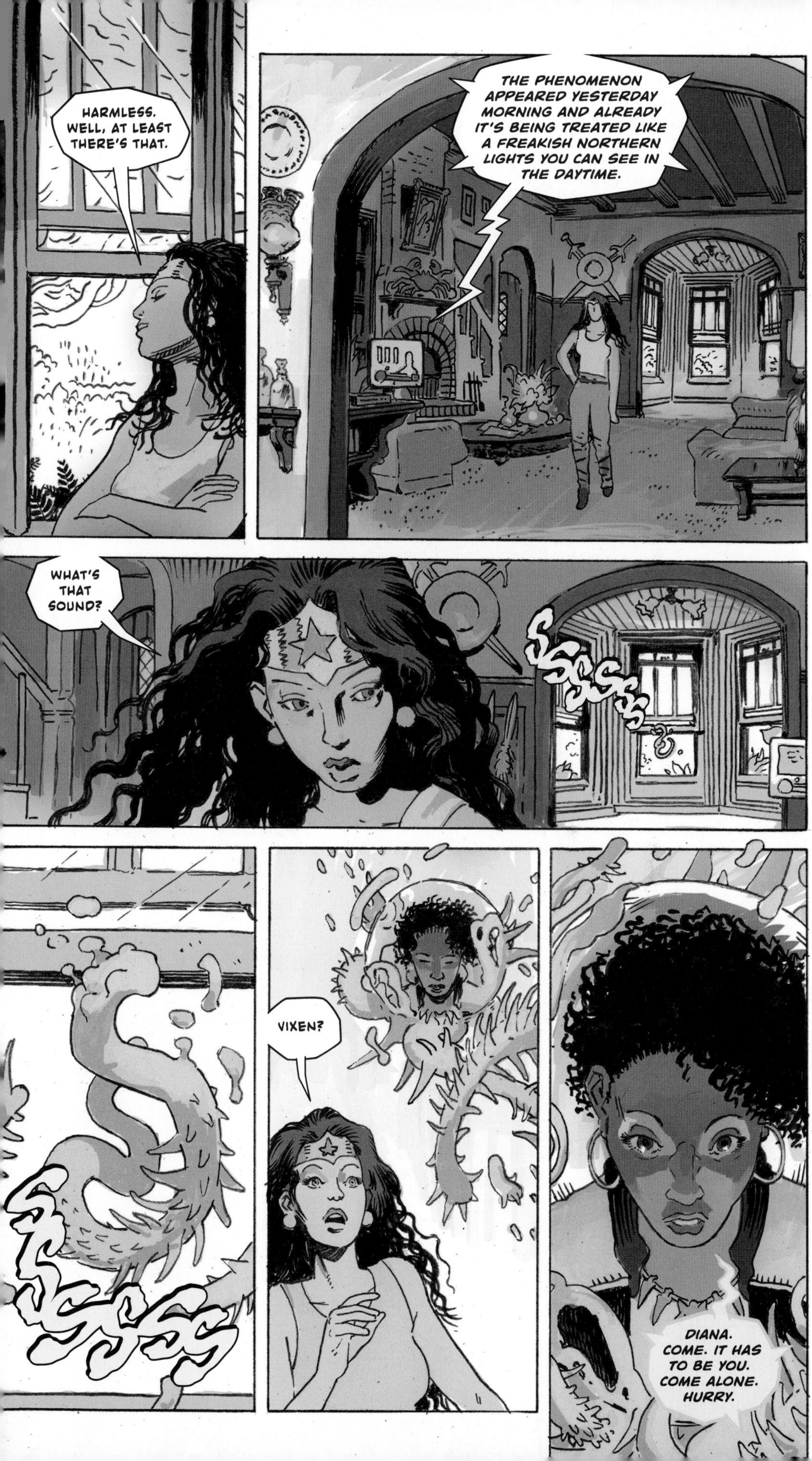
HARMLESS. WELL, AT LEAST THERE'S THAT.
THE PHENOMENON APPEARED YESTERDAY MORNING AND ALREADY IT'S BEING TREATED LIKE A FREAKISH NORTHERN LIGHTS YOU CAN SEE IN THE DAYTIME.
WHAT'S THAT SOUND?
SSSSSS
SSSSSS
VIXEN?
DIANA. COME. IT HAS TO BE YOU. COME ALONE. HURRY.

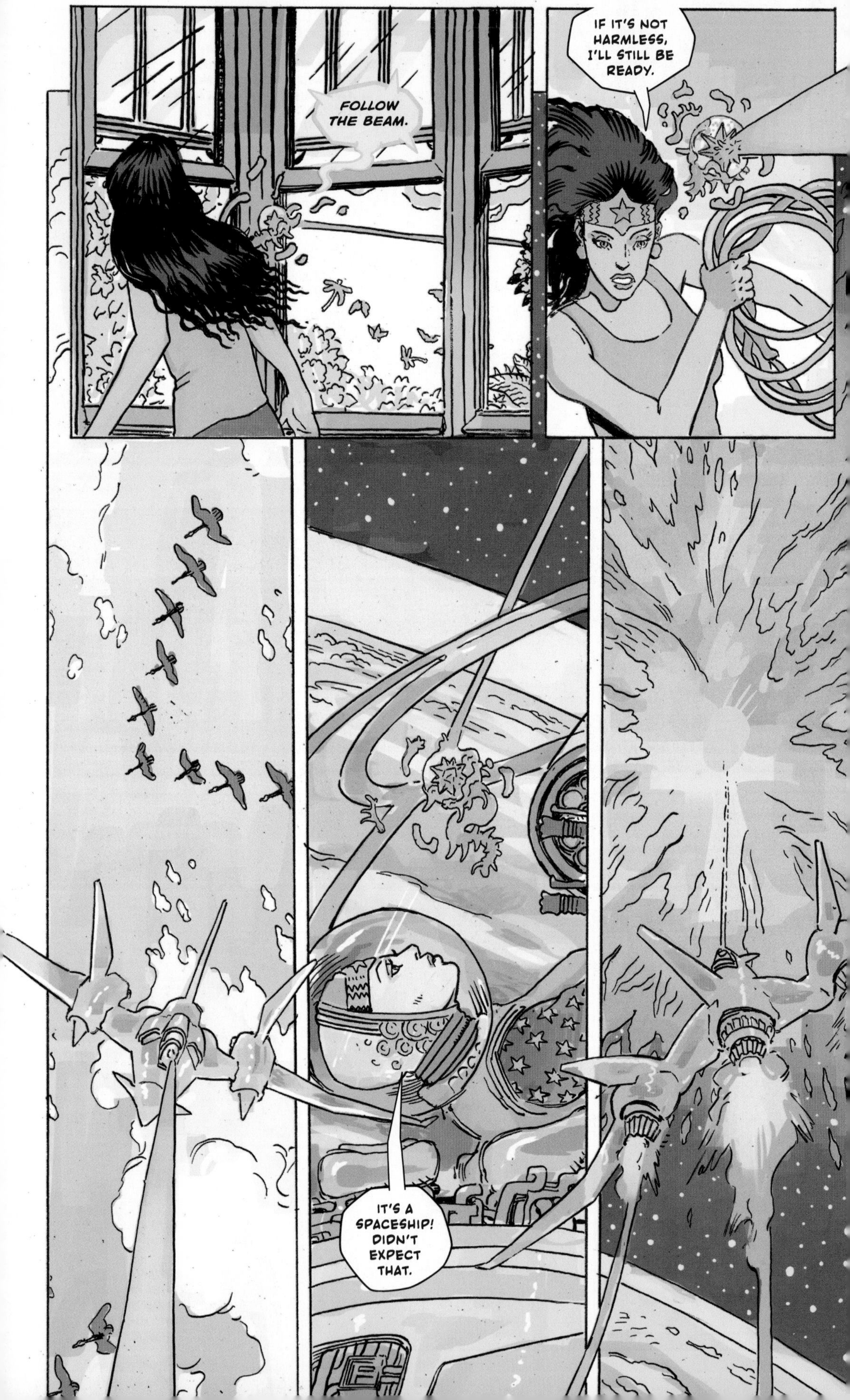
FOLLOW THE BEAM.
IF IT'S NOT HARMLESS, I'LL STILL BE READY.
IT'S A SPACESHIP! DIDN'T EXPECT THAT.

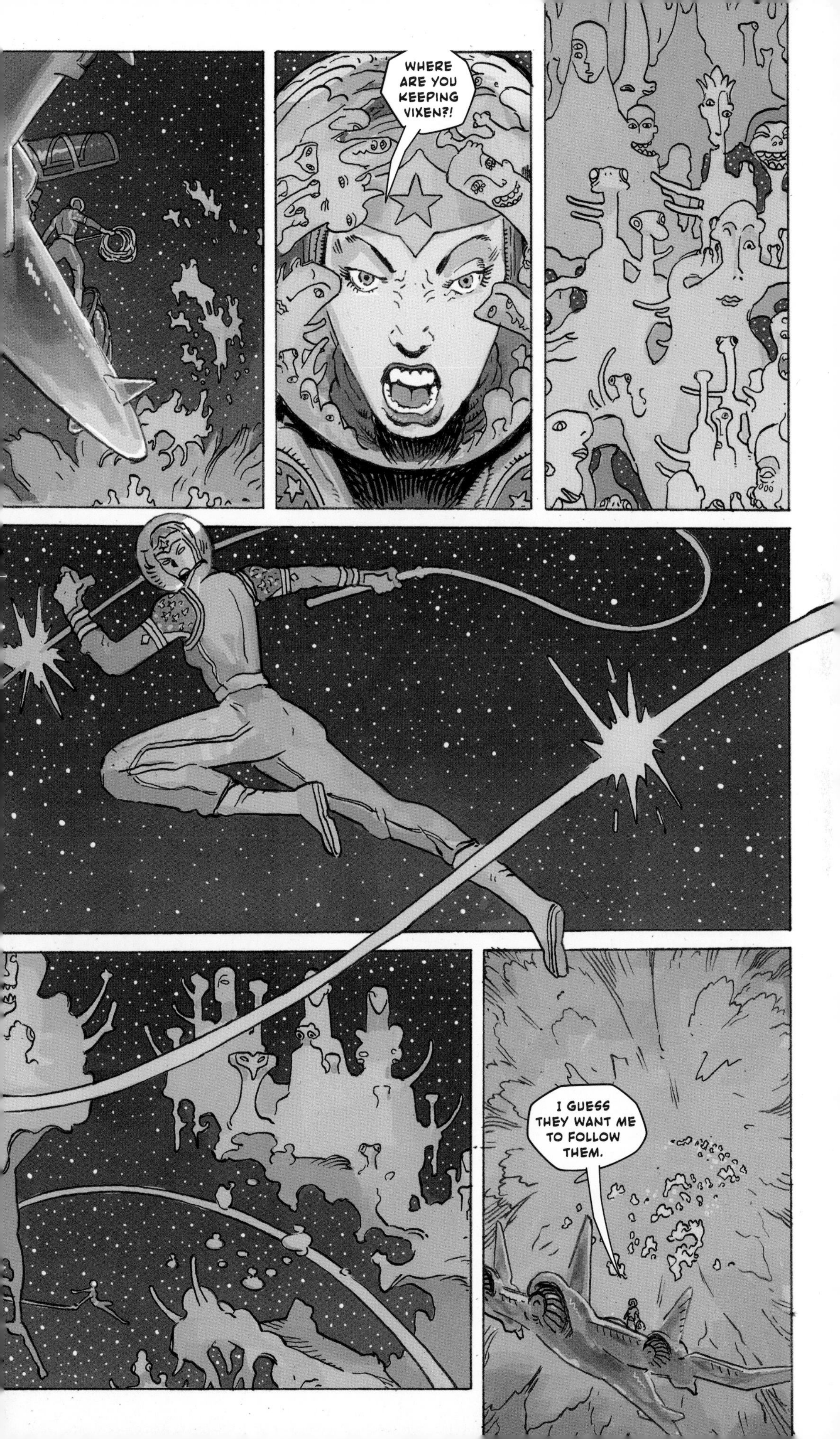
WHERE ARE YOU KEEPING VIXEN?!
I GUESS THEY WANT ME TO FOLLOW THEM.

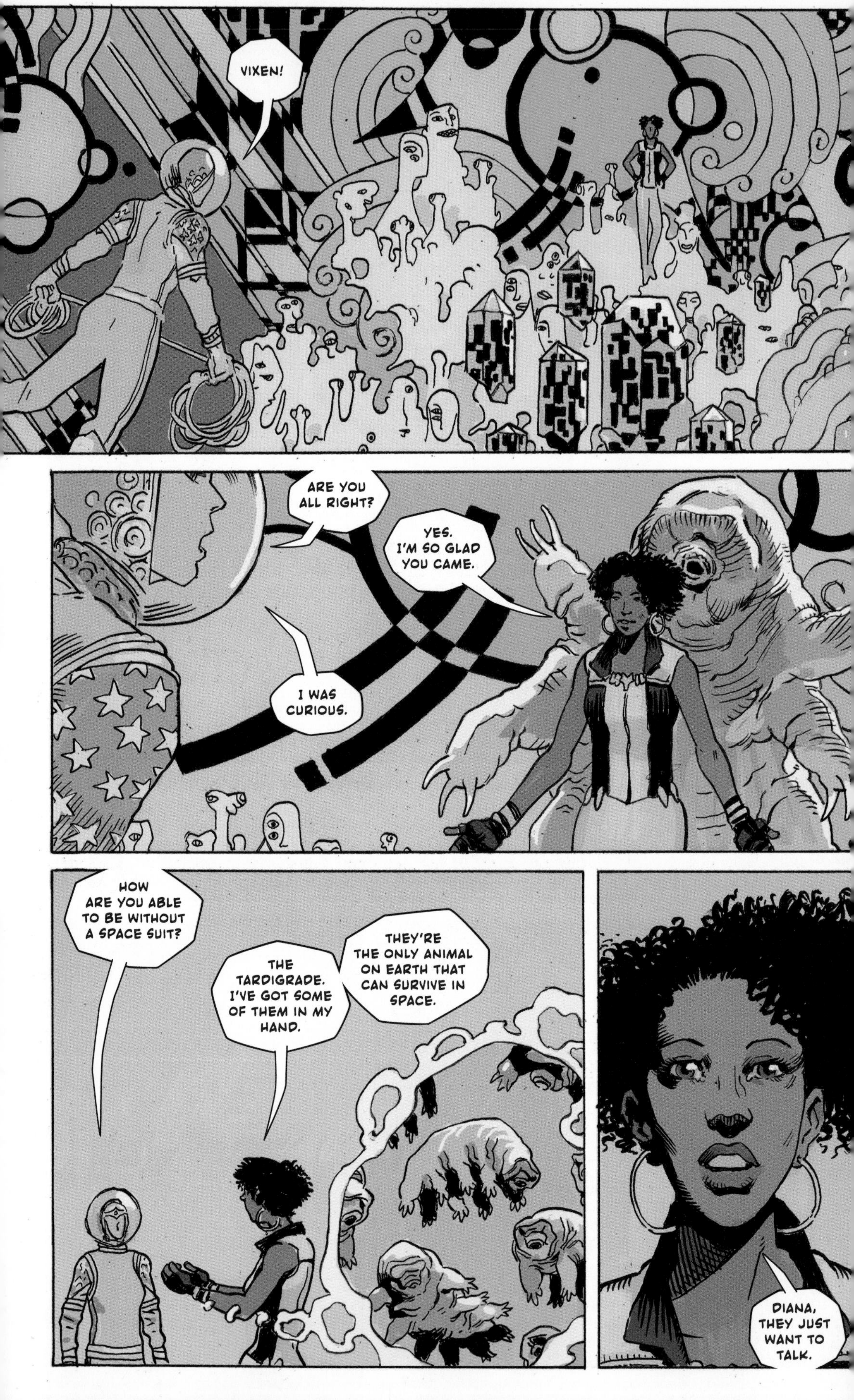
VIXEN!
ARE YOU ALL RIGHT?
YES. I'M SO GLAD YOU CAME.
I WAS CURIOUS.
HOW ARE YOU ABLE TO BE WITHOUT A SPACE SUIT?
THE TARDIGRADE. I'VE GOT SOME OF THEM IN MY HAND.
THEY'RE THE ONLY ANIMAL ON EARTH THAT CAN SURVIVE IN SPACE.
DIANA, THEY JUST WANT TO TALK.

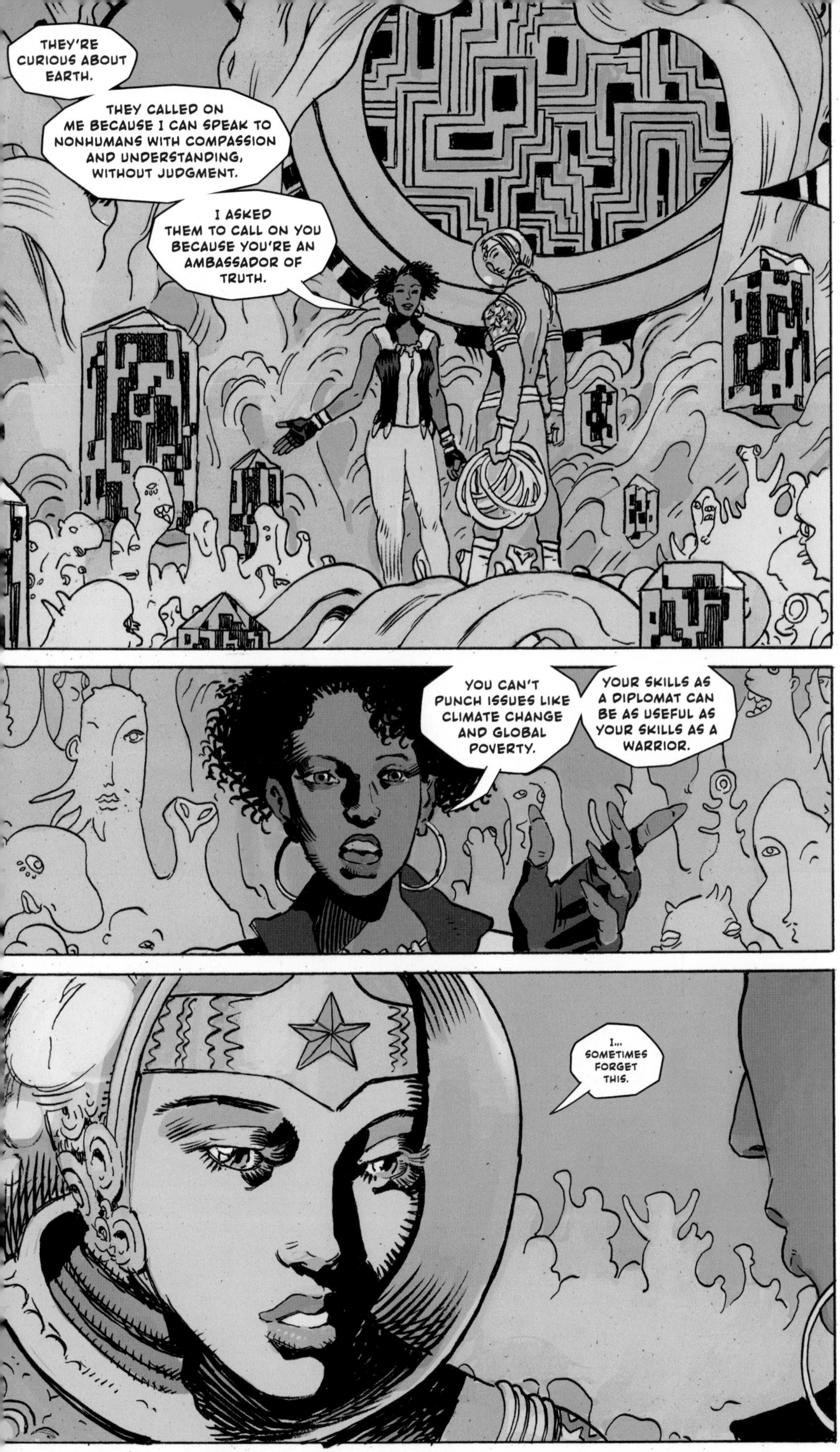
THEY'RE CURIOUS ABOUT EARTH.
THEY CALLED ON ME BECAUSE I CAN SPEAK TO NONHUMANS WITH COMPASSION AND UNDERSTANDING, WITHOUT JUDGMENT.
I ASKED THEM TO CALL ON YOU BECAUSE YOU'RE AN AMBASSADOR OF TRUTH.
YOU CAN'T PUNCH ISSUES LIKE CLIMATE CHANGE AND GLOBAL POVERTY.
YOUR SKILLS AS A DIPLOMAT CAN BE AS USEFUL AS YOUR SKILLS AS A WARRIOR.
I... SOMETIMES FORGET THIS.

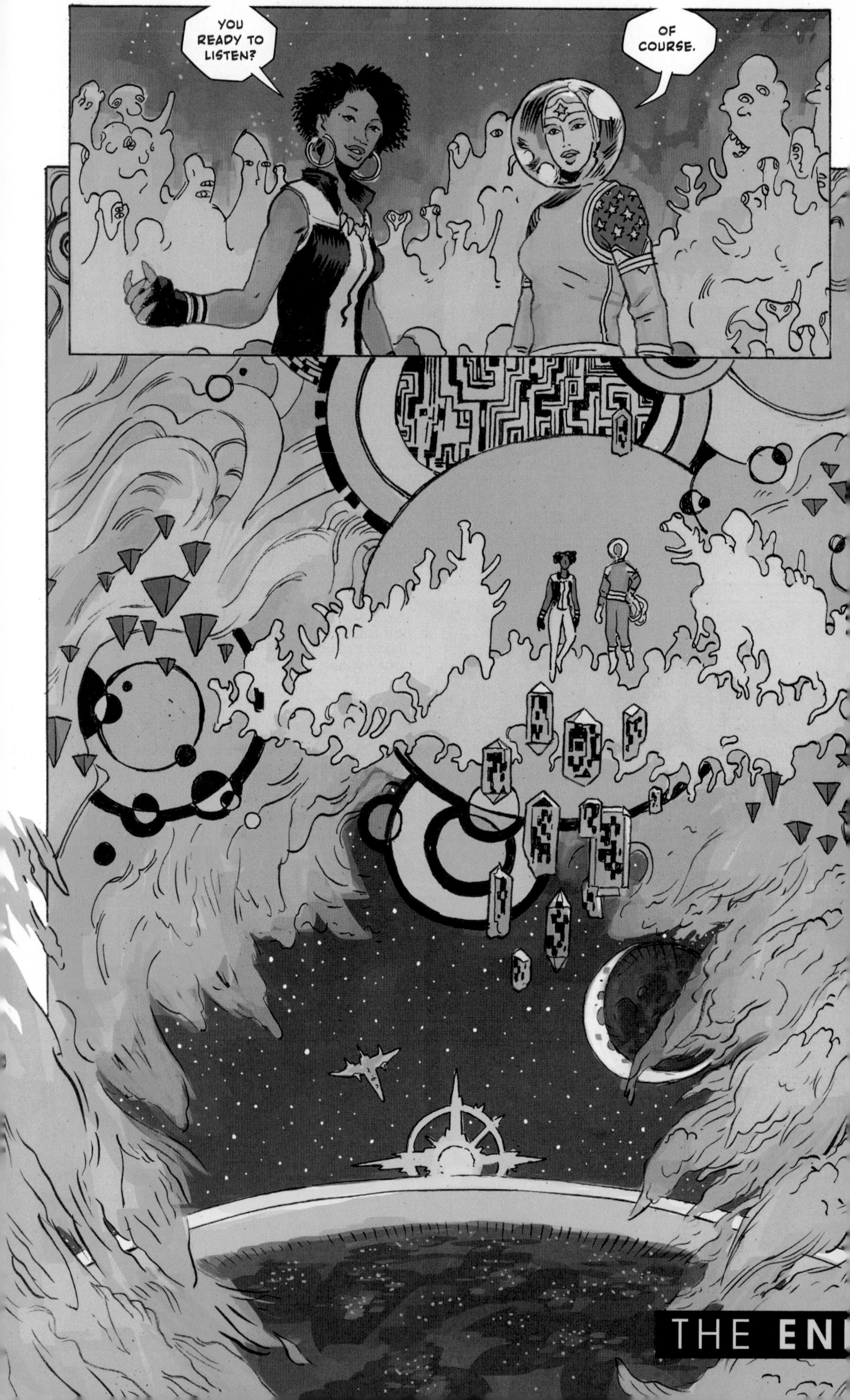
YOU READY TO LISTEN?
OF COURSE.
THE EN

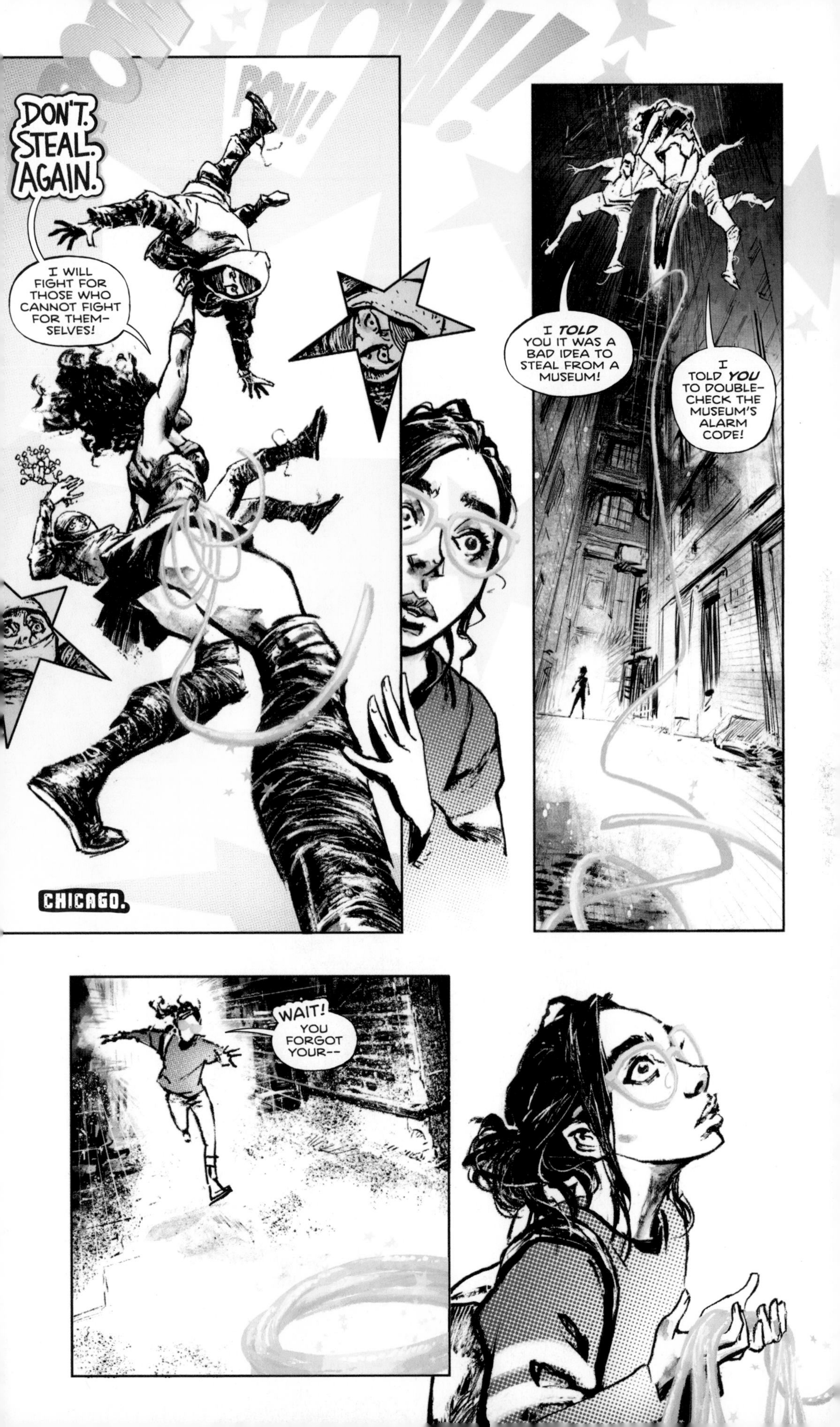
DON'T. STEAL. AGAIN.
I WILL FIGHT FOR THOSE WHO CANNOT FIGHT FOR THEM-SELVES!
CHICAGO.
I *TOLD* YOU IT WAS A BAD IDEA TO STEAL FROM A MUSEUM!
I TOLD *YOU* TO DOUBLE-CHECK THE MUSEUM'S ALARM CODE!
WAIT! YOU FORGOT YOUR--

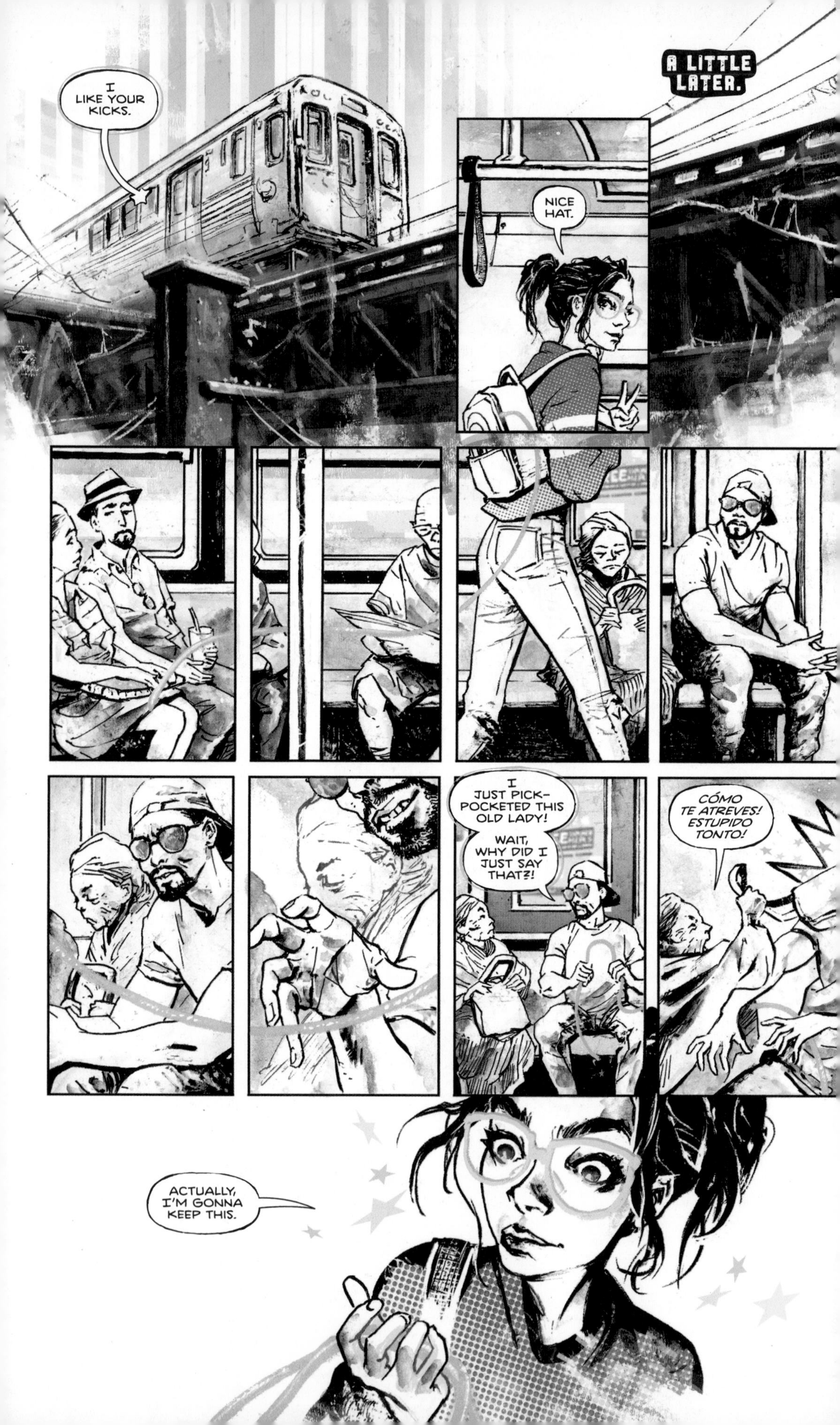
A LITTLE LATER.
I LIKE YOUR KICKS.
NICE HAT.
I JUST PICK-POCKETED THIS OLD LADY!
WAIT, WHY DID I JUST SAY THAT?!
CÓMO TE ATREVES! ESTUPIDO TONTO!
ACTUALLY, I'M GONNA KEEP THIS.

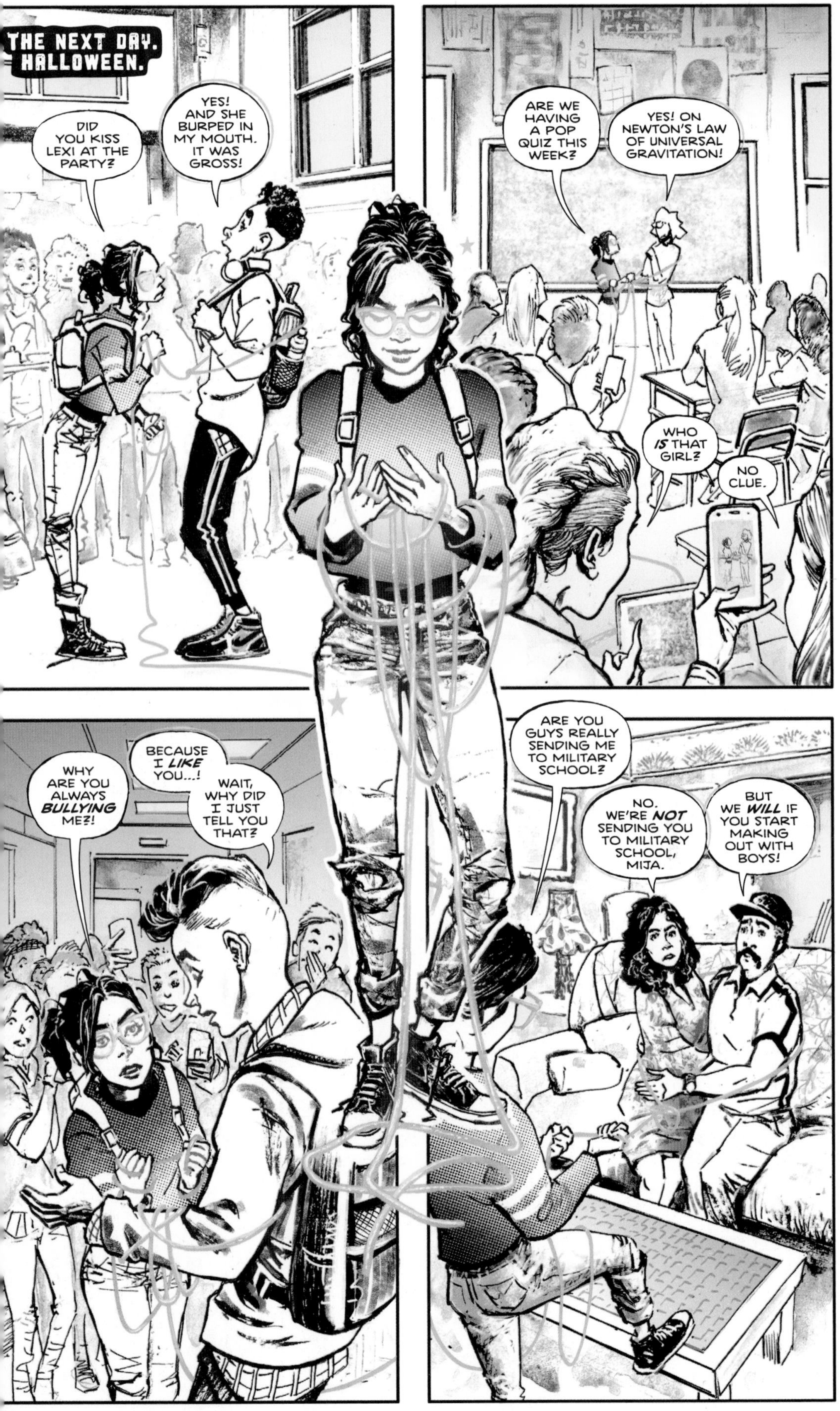
THE NEXT DAY. HALLOWEEN.
DID YOU KISS LEXI AT THE PARTY?
YES! AND SHE BURPED IN MY MOUTH. IT WAS GROSS!
ARE WE HAVING A POP QUIZ THIS WEEK?
YES! ON NEWTON'S LAW OF UNIVERSAL GRAVITATION!
WHO *IS* THAT GIRL?
NO CLUE.
WHY ARE YOU ALWAYS *BULLYING* ME?!
BECAUSE I *LIKE* YOU...!
WAIT, WHY DID I JUST TELL YOU THAT?
ARE YOU GUYS REALLY SENDING ME TO MILITARY SCHOOL?
NO. WE'RE *NOT* SENDING YOU TO MILITARY SCHOOL, MIJA.
BUT WE *WILL* IF YOU START MAKING OUT WITH BOYS!

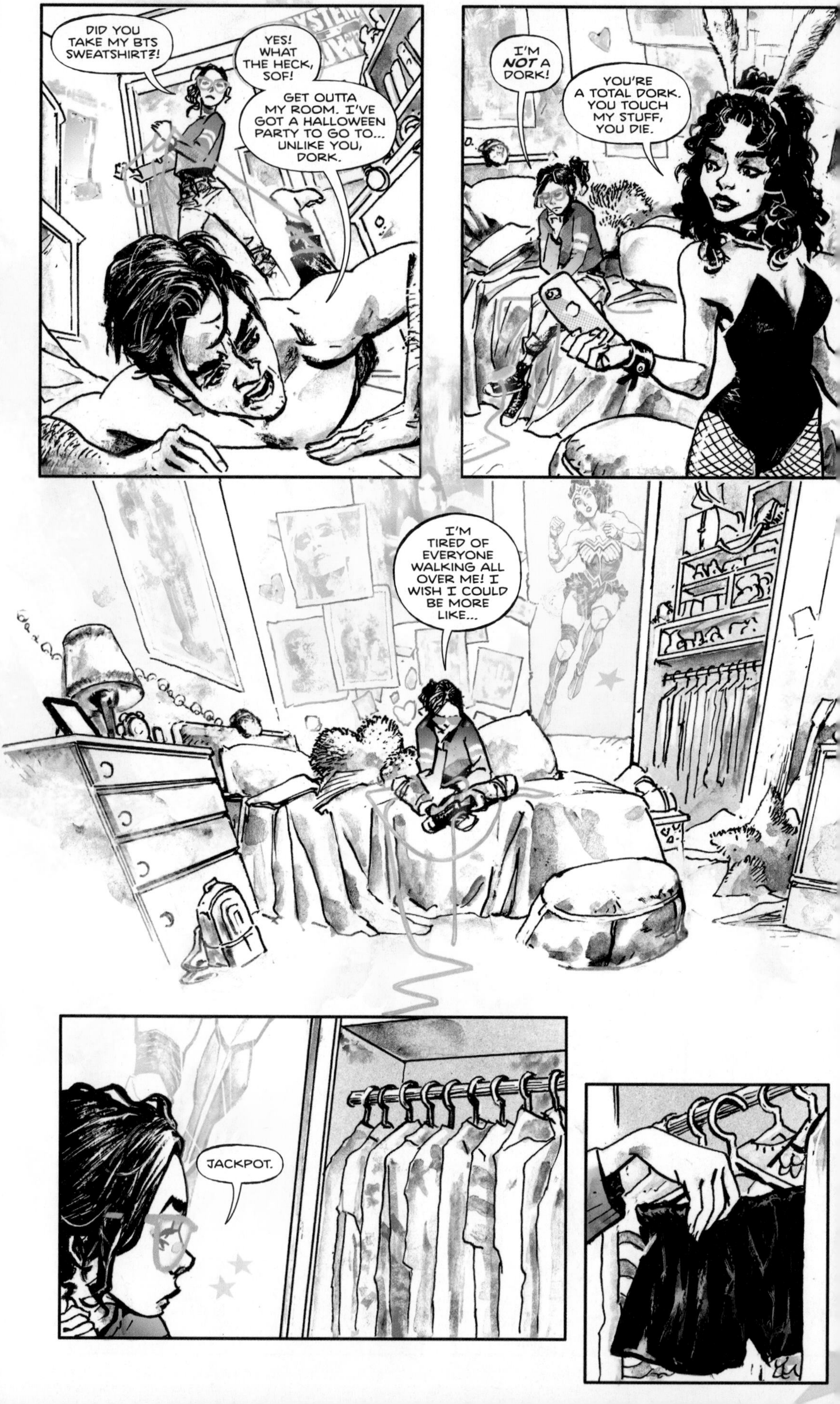
DID YOU TAKE MY BTS SWEATSHIRT?!
YES! WHAT THE HECK, SOF!
GET OUTTA MY ROOM. I'VE GOT A HALLOWEEN PARTY TO GO TO... UNLIKE YOU, DORK.
I'M *NOT* A DORK!
YOU'RE A TOTAL DORK. YOU TOUCH MY STUFF, YOU DIE.
I'M TIRED OF EVERYONE WALKING ALL OVER ME! I WISH I COULD BE MORE LIKE...
JACKPOT.

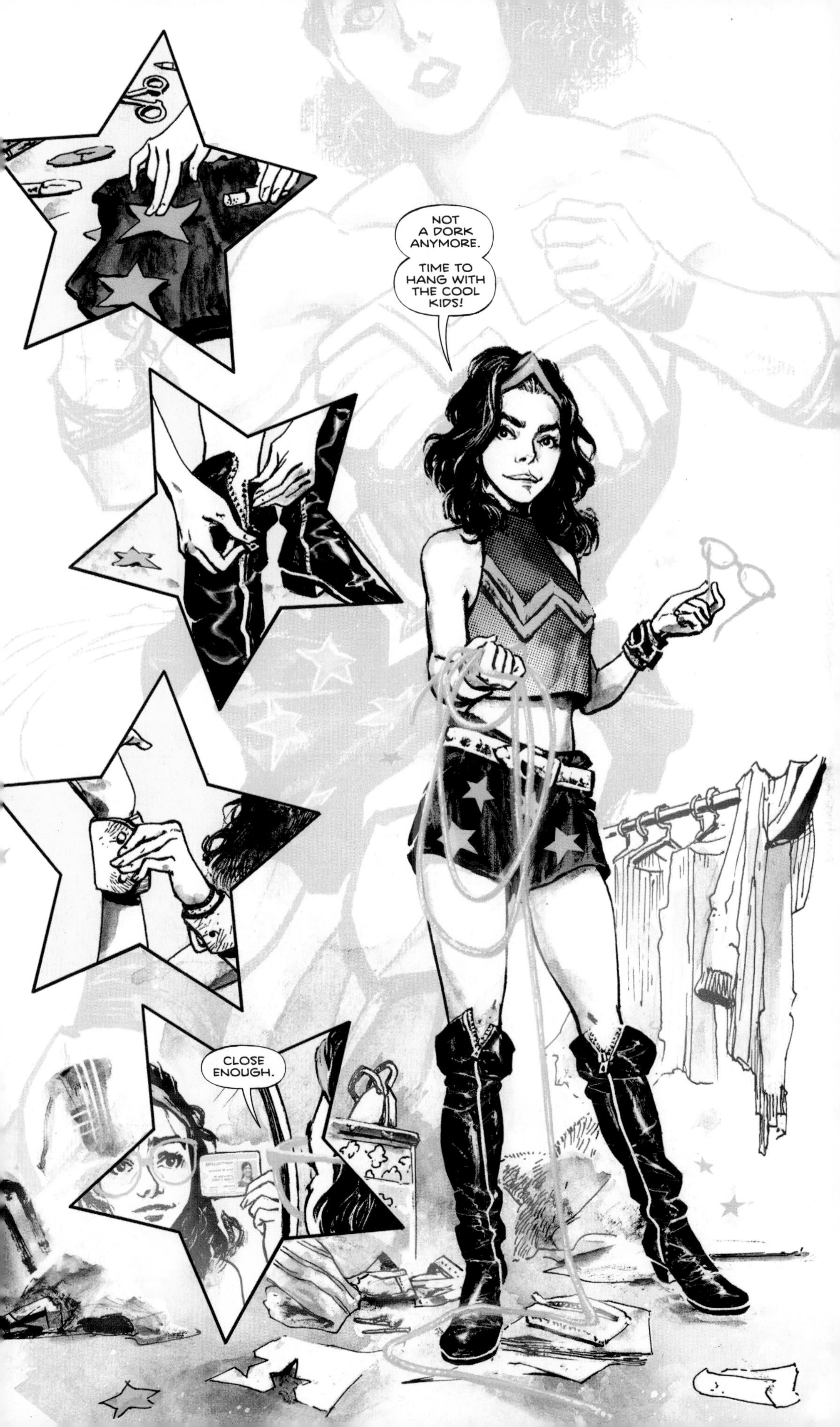
NOT A DORK ANYMORE.
TIME TO HANG WITH THE COOL KIDS!
CLOSE ENOUGH.

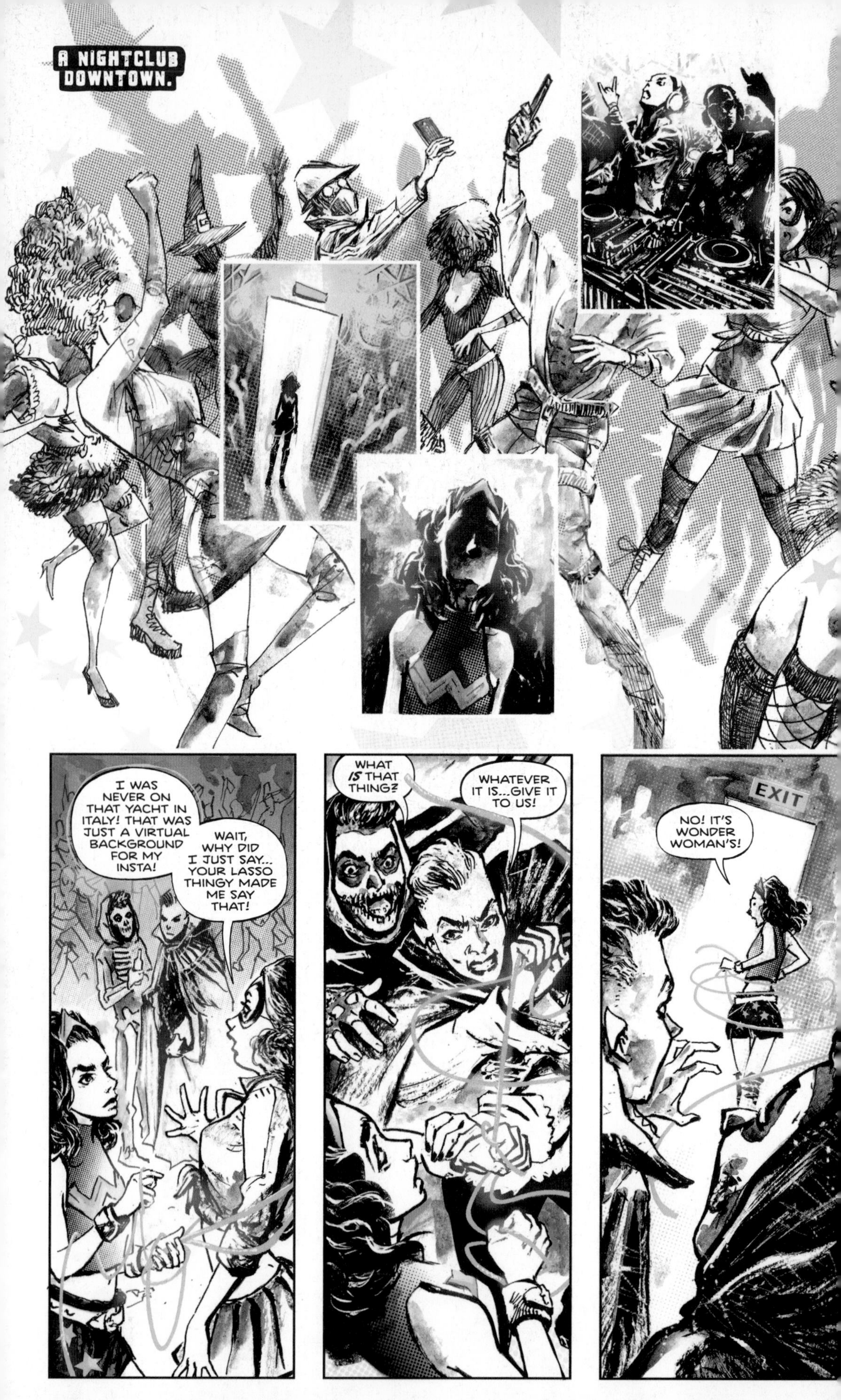
A NIGHTCLUB DOWNTOWN.
I WAS NEVER ON THAT YACHT IN ITALY! THAT WAS JUST A VIRTUAL BACKGROUND FOR MY INSTA!
WAIT, WHY DID I JUST SAY... YOUR LASSO THINGY MADE ME SAY THAT!
WHAT IS THAT THING?
WHATEVER IT IS...GIVE IT TO US!
EXIT
NO! IT'S WONDER WOMAN'S!

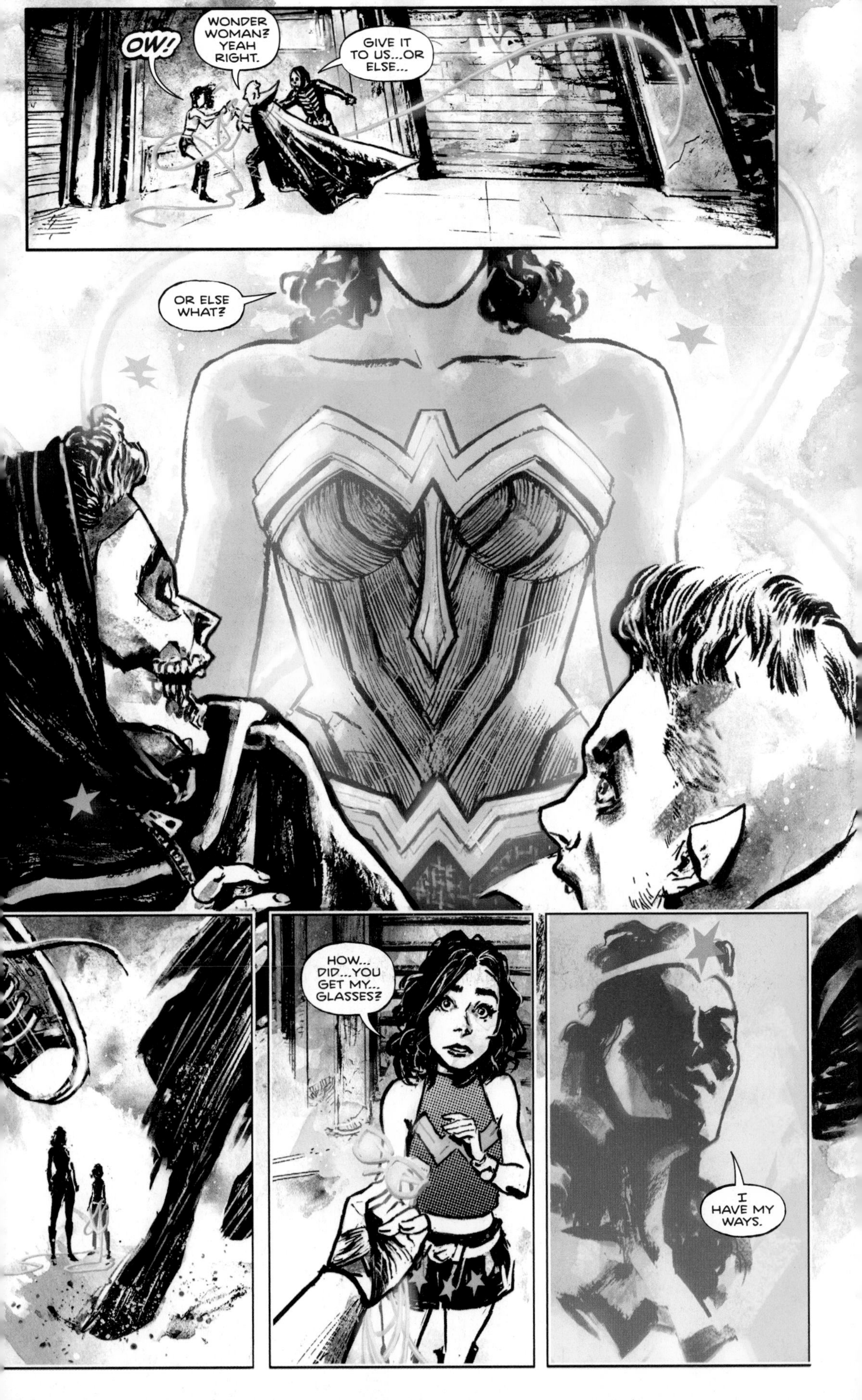
OW!
WONDER WOMAN? YEAH RIGHT.
GIVE IT TO US...OR ELSE...
OR ELSE WHAT?
HOW... DID...YOU GET MY... GLASSES?
I HAVE MY WAYS.

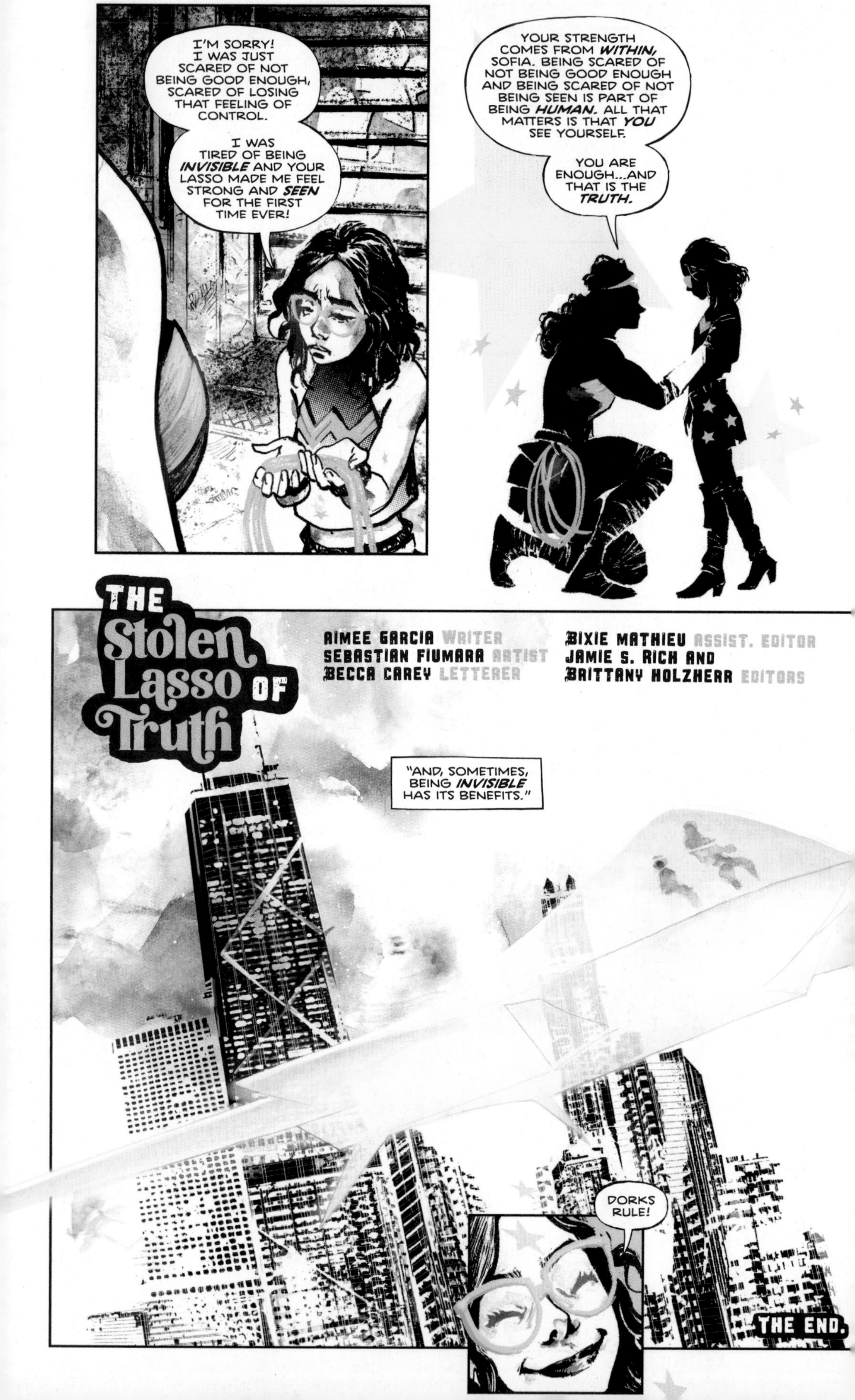
I'M SORRY! I WAS JUST SCARED OF NOT BEING GOOD ENOUGH, SCARED OF LOSING THAT FEELING OF CONTROL.
I WAS TIRED OF BEING INVISIBLE AND YOUR LASSO MADE ME FEEL STRONG AND SEEN FOR THE FIRST TIME EVER!
YOUR STRENGTH COMES FROM WITHIN, SOFIA. BEING SCARED OF NOT BEING GOOD ENOUGH AND BEING SCARED OF NOT BEING SEEN IS PART OF BEING HUMAN. ALL THAT MATTERS IS THAT YOU SEE YOURSELF.
YOU ARE ENOUGH...AND THAT IS THE TRUTH.
THE Stolen Lasso OF Truth
AIMEE GARCIA WRITER
SEBASTIAN FIUMARA ARTIST
BECCA CAREY LETTERER
BIXIE MATHIEU ASSIST. EDITOR
JAMIE S. RICH AND
BRITTANY HOLZHERR EDITORS
"AND, SOMETIMES, BEING INVISIBLE HAS ITS BENEFITS."
DORKS RULE!
THE END.

Cover by Tula Lotay

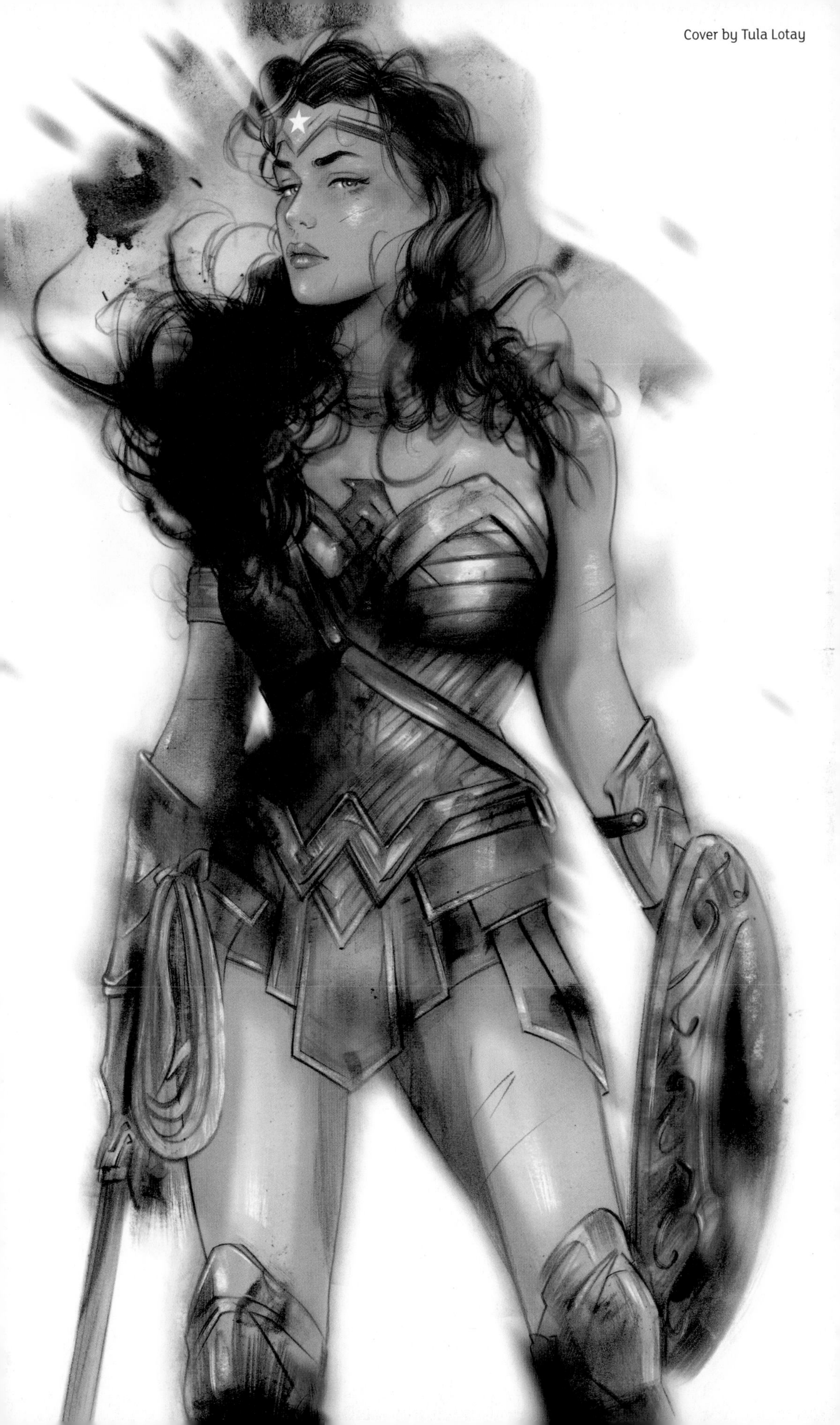

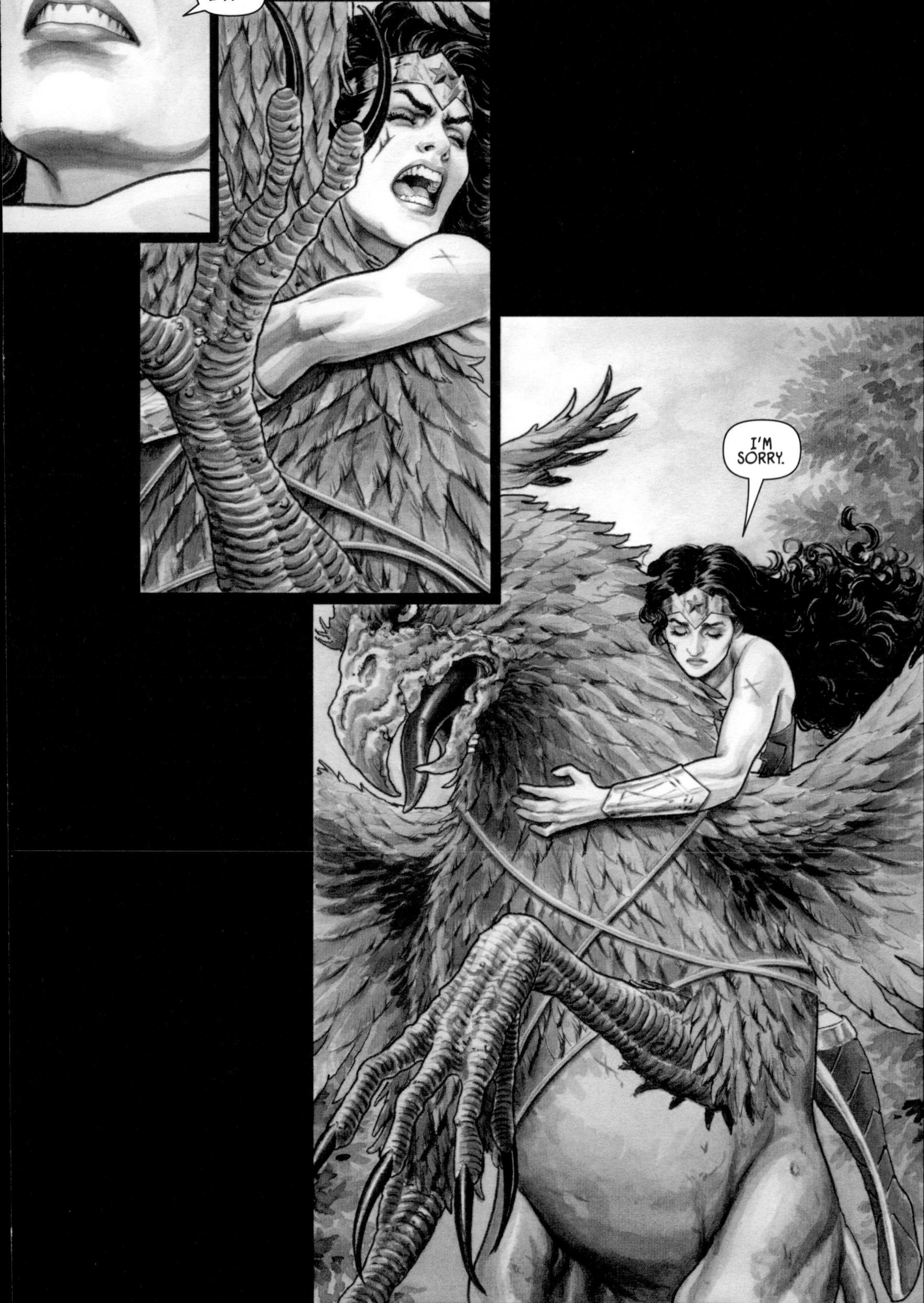
I'M SORRY.

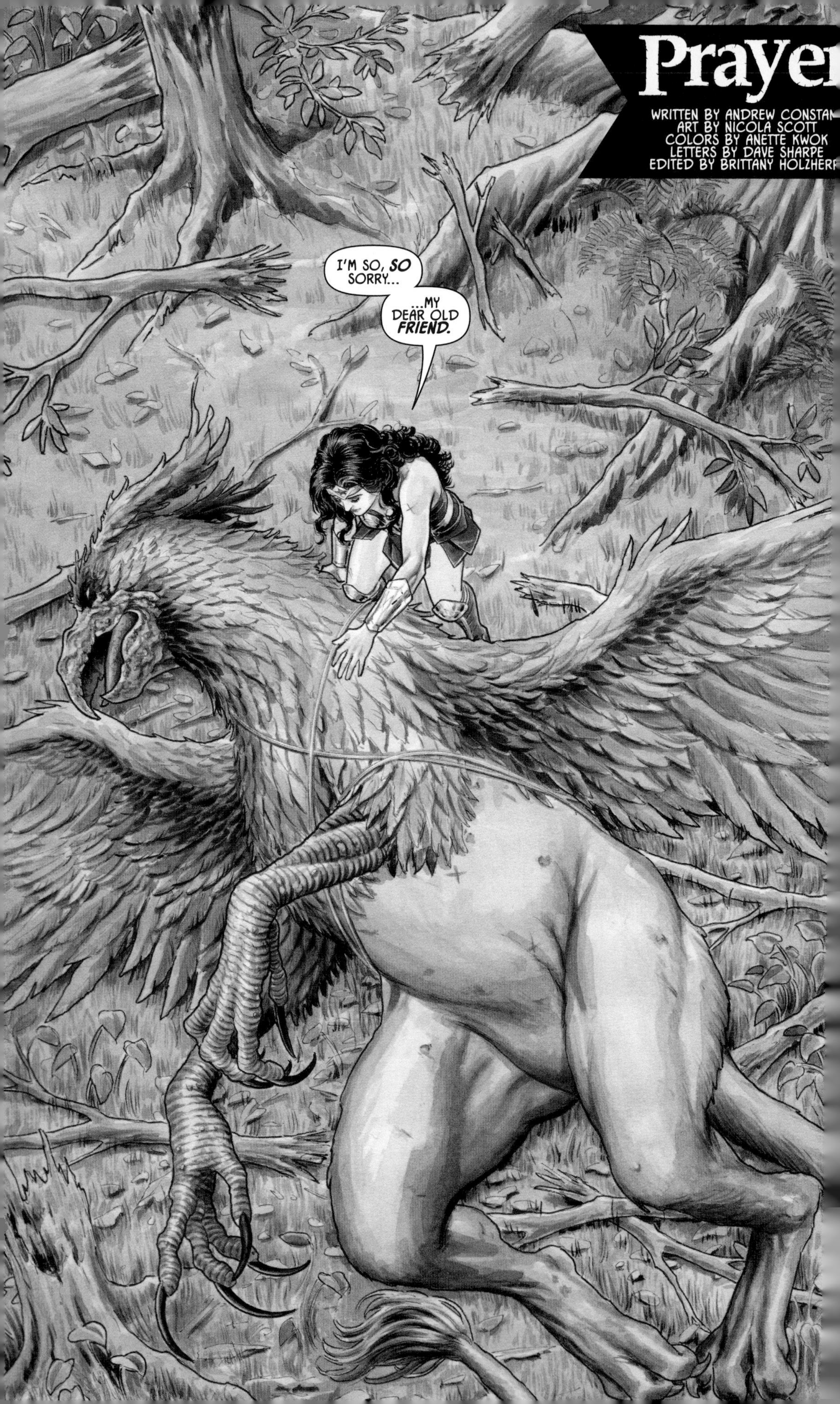
Prayer
WRITTEN BY ANDREW CONSTAN
ART BY NICOLA SCOTT
COLORS BY ANETTE KWOK
LETTERS BY DAVE SHARPE
EDITED BY BRITTANY HOLZHERR
I'M SO, SO SORRY...
...MY DEAR OLD FRIEND.

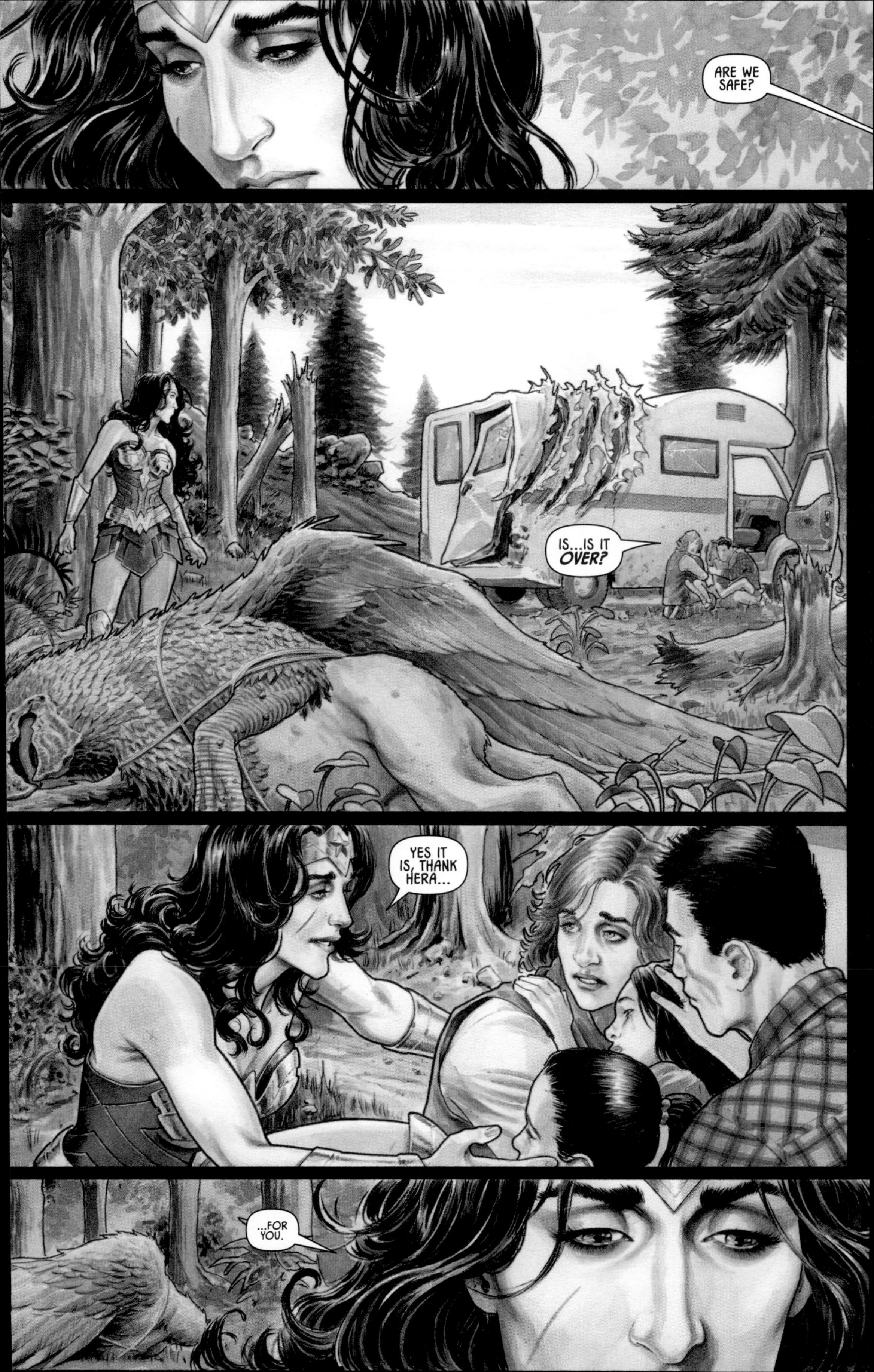
ARE WE SAFE?
IS...IS IT OVER?
YES IT IS, THANK HERA...
...FOR YOU.

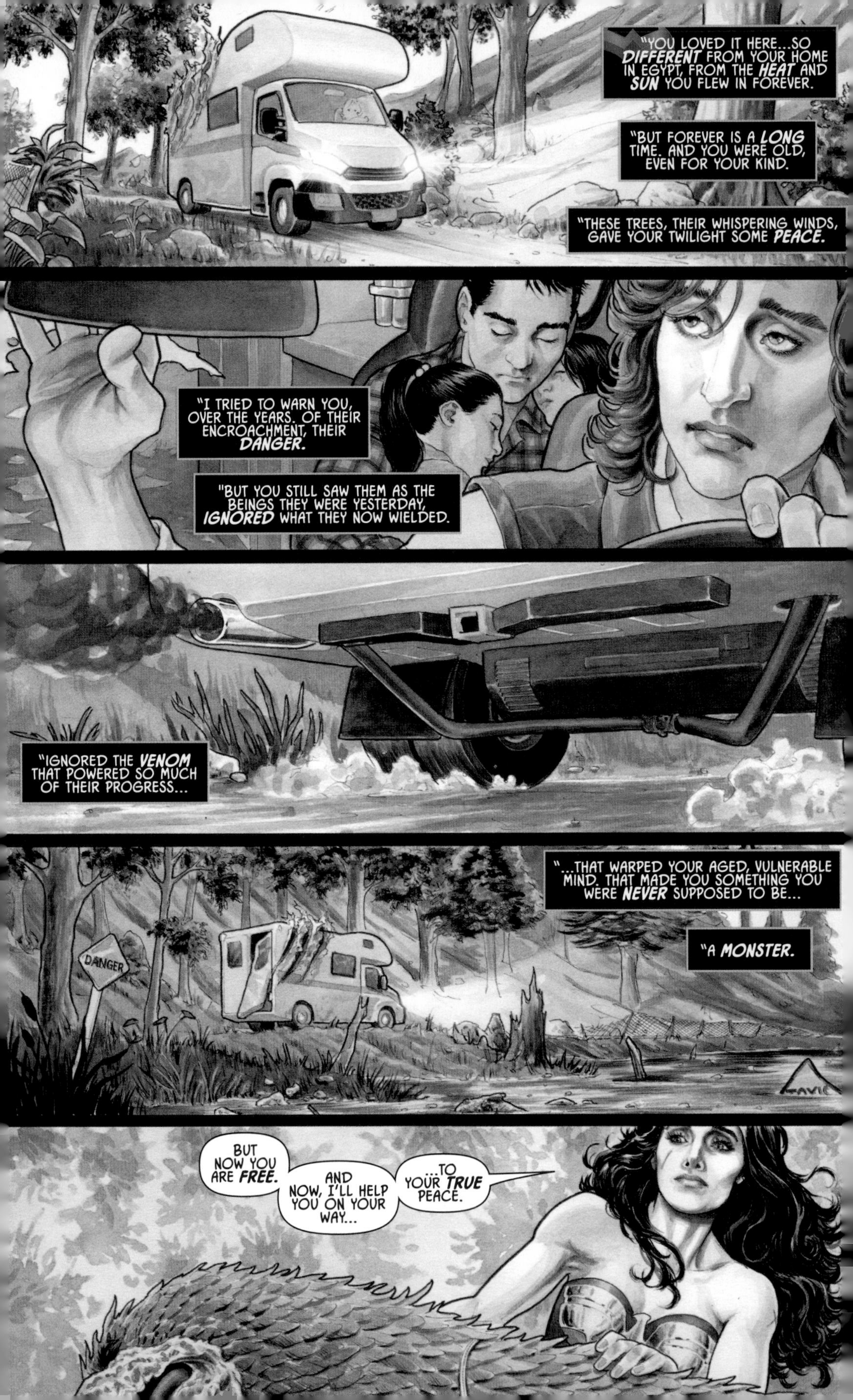
"YOU LOVED IT HERE...SO DIFFERENT FROM YOUR HOME IN EGYPT, FROM THE HEAT AND SUN YOU FLEW IN FOREVER.
"BUT FOREVER IS A LONG TIME. AND YOU WERE OLD, EVEN FOR YOUR KIND.
"THESE TREES, THEIR WHISPERING WINDS, GAVE YOUR TWILIGHT SOME PEACE.
"I TRIED TO WARN YOU, OVER THE YEARS. OF THEIR ENCROACHMENT, THEIR DANGER.
"BUT YOU STILL SAW THEM AS THE BEINGS THEY WERE YESTERDAY, IGNORED WHAT THEY NOW WIELDED.
"IGNORED THE VENOM THAT POWERED SO MUCH OF THEIR PROGRESS...
"...THAT WARPED YOUR AGED, VULNERABLE MIND. THAT MADE YOU SOMETHING YOU WERE NEVER SUPPOSED TO BE...
"A MONSTER.
DANGER
BUT NOW YOU ARE FREE.
AND NOW, I'LL HELP YOU ON YOUR WAY...
...TO YOUR TRUE PEACE.

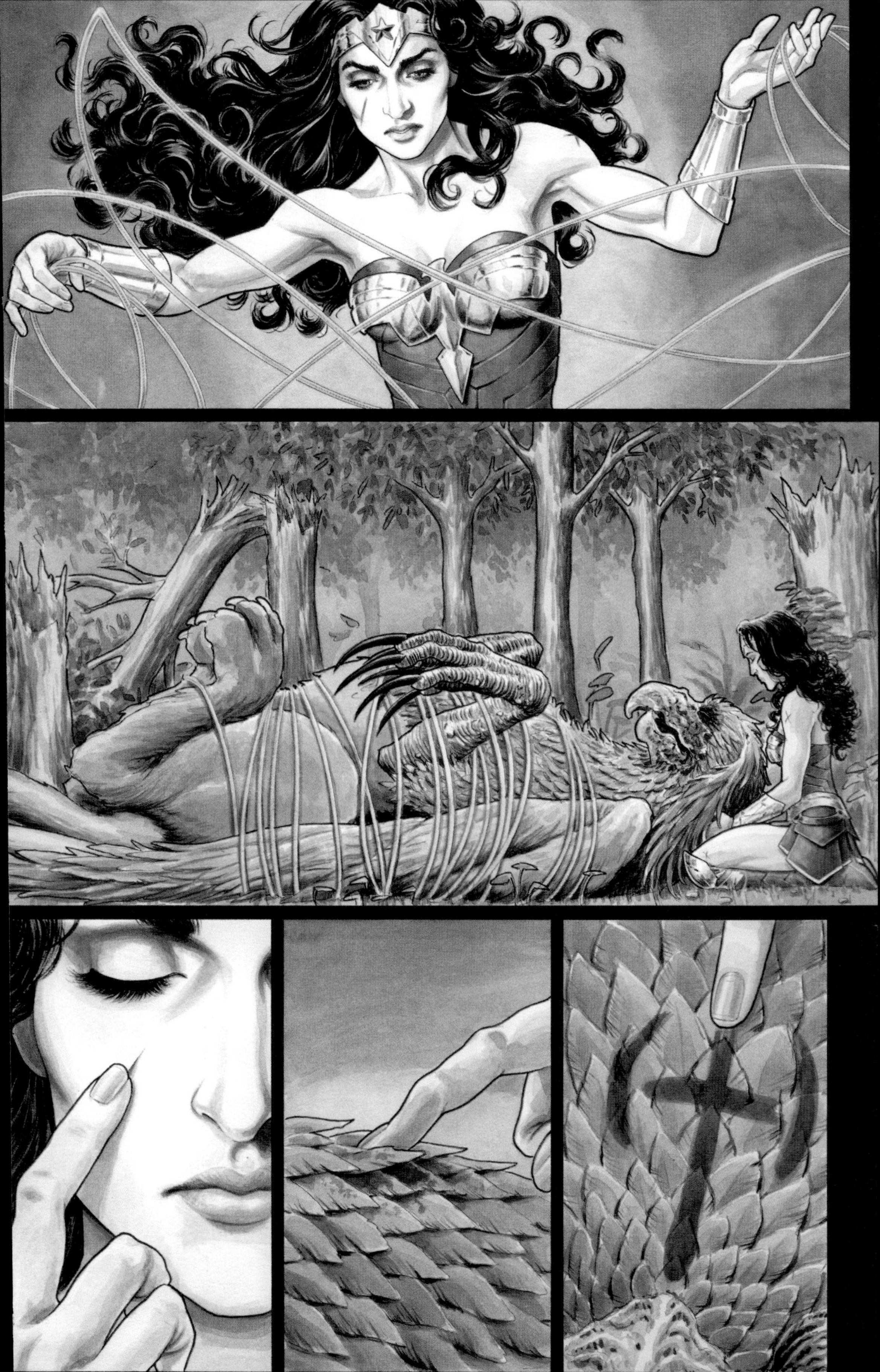

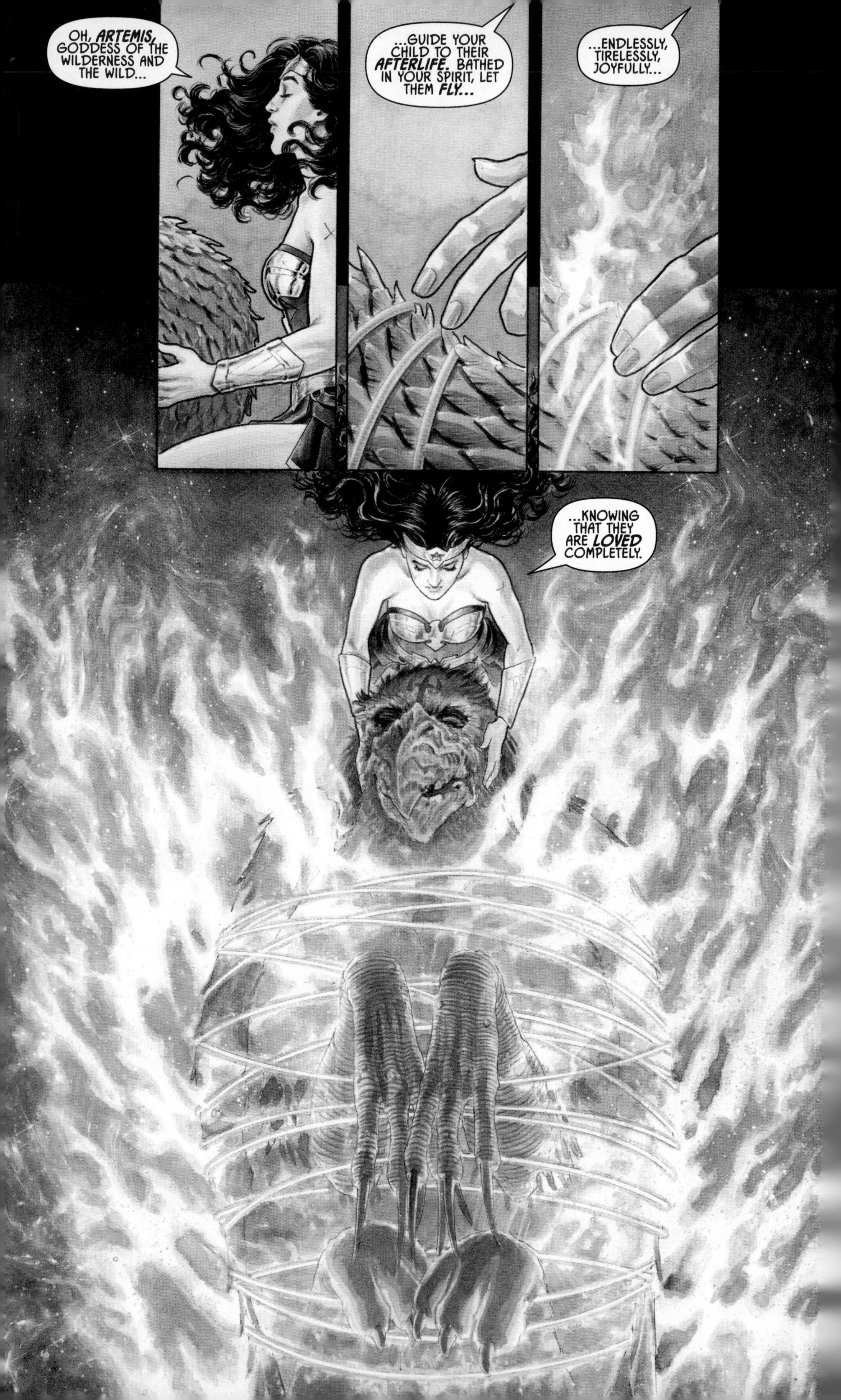
OH, ARTEMIS, GODDESS OF THE WILDERNESS AND THE WILD...
...GUIDE YOUR CHILD TO THEIR AFTERLIFE. BATHED IN YOUR SPIRIT, LET THEM FLY...
...ENDLESSLY, TIRELESSLY, JOYFULLY...
...KNOWING THAT THEY ARE LOVED COMPLETELY.

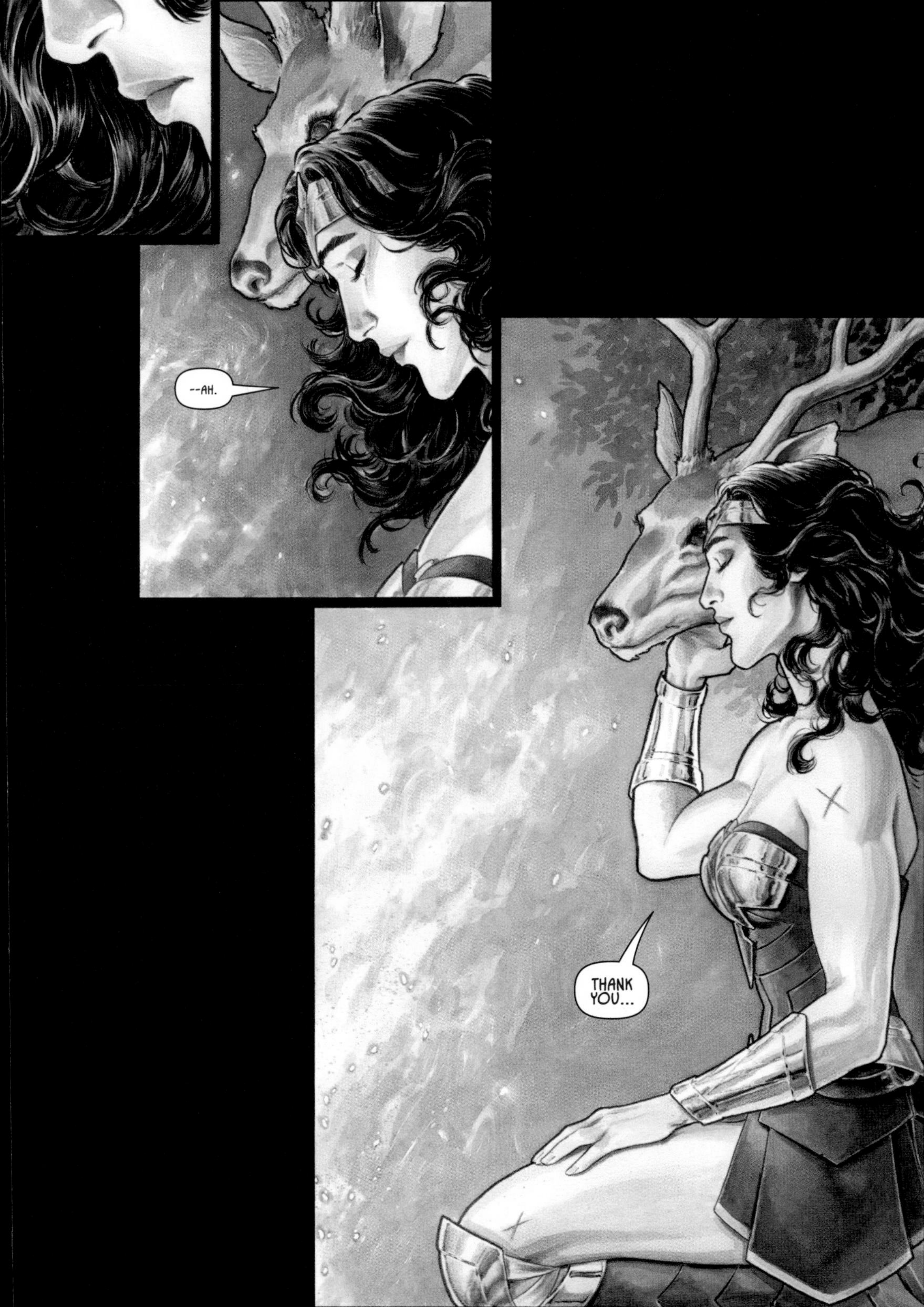
--AH.
THANK YOU...

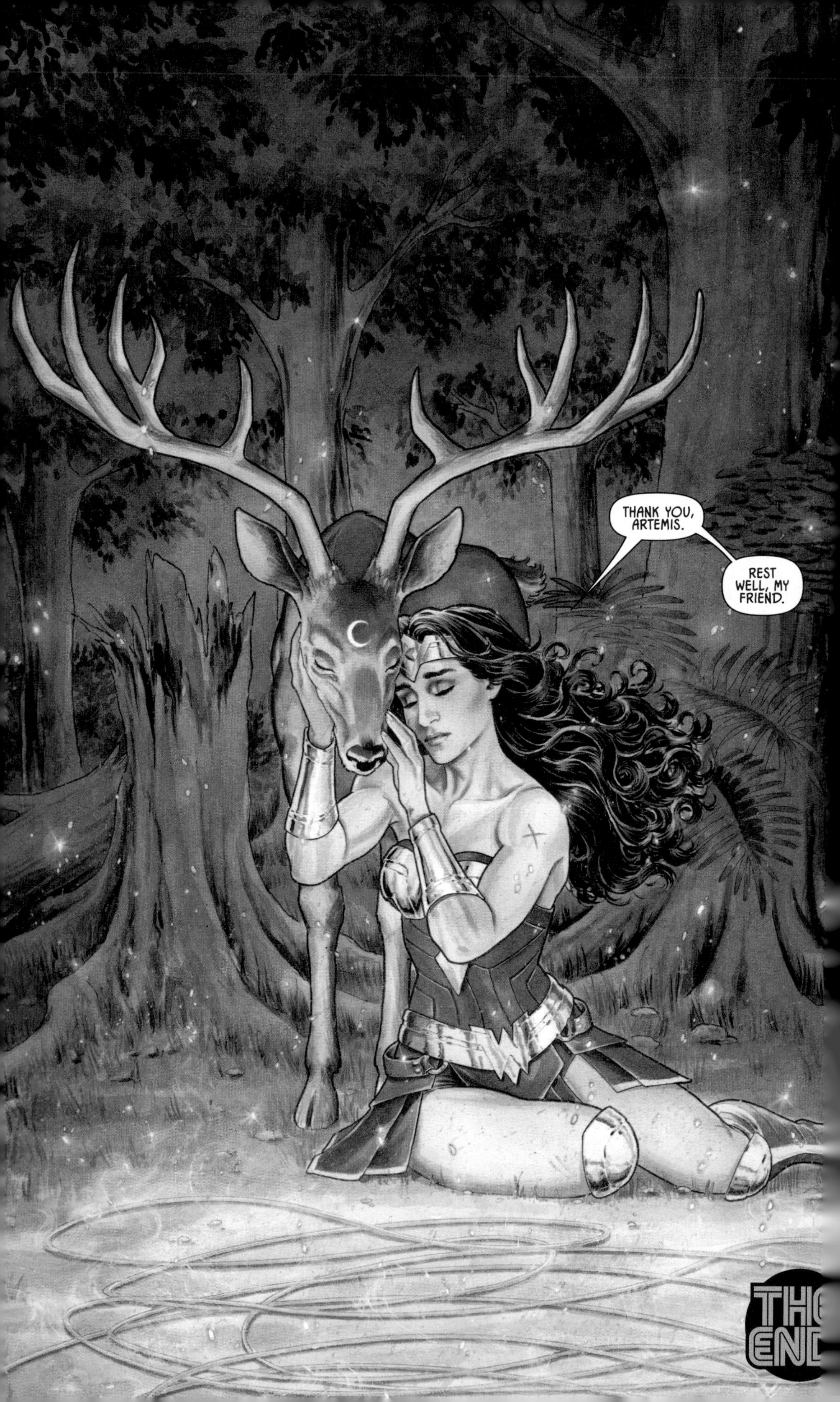

THANK YOU, ARTEMIS.
REST WELL, MY FRIEND.

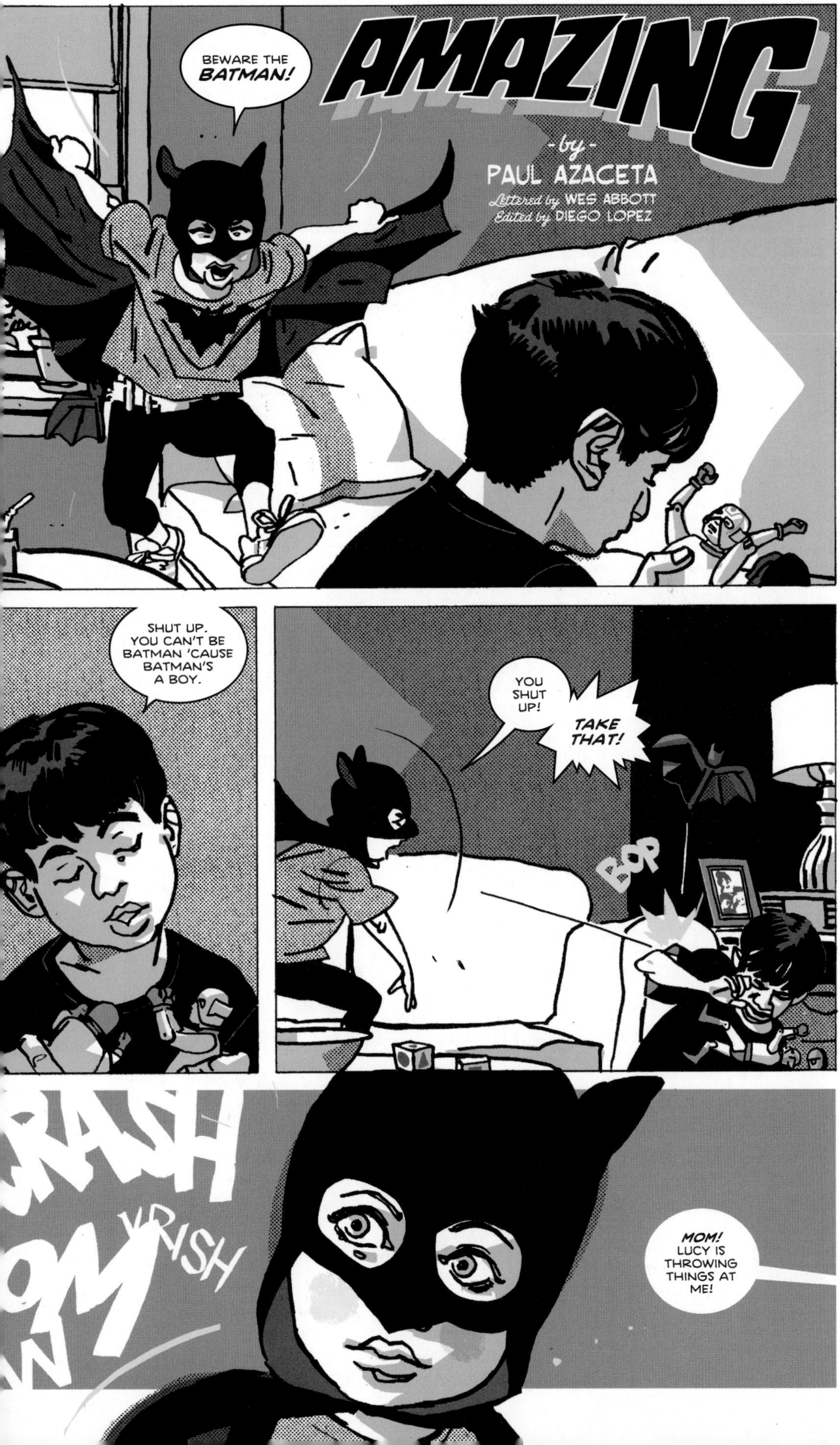

AMAZING
-by-
PAUL AZACETA
Lettered by WES ABBOTT
Edited by DIEGO LOPEZ
BEWARE THE BATMAN!
SHUT UP. YOU CAN'T BE BATMAN 'CAUSE BATMAN'S A BOY.
YOU SHUT UP!
TAKE THAT!
BOP
MOM! LUCY IS THROWING THINGS AT ME!

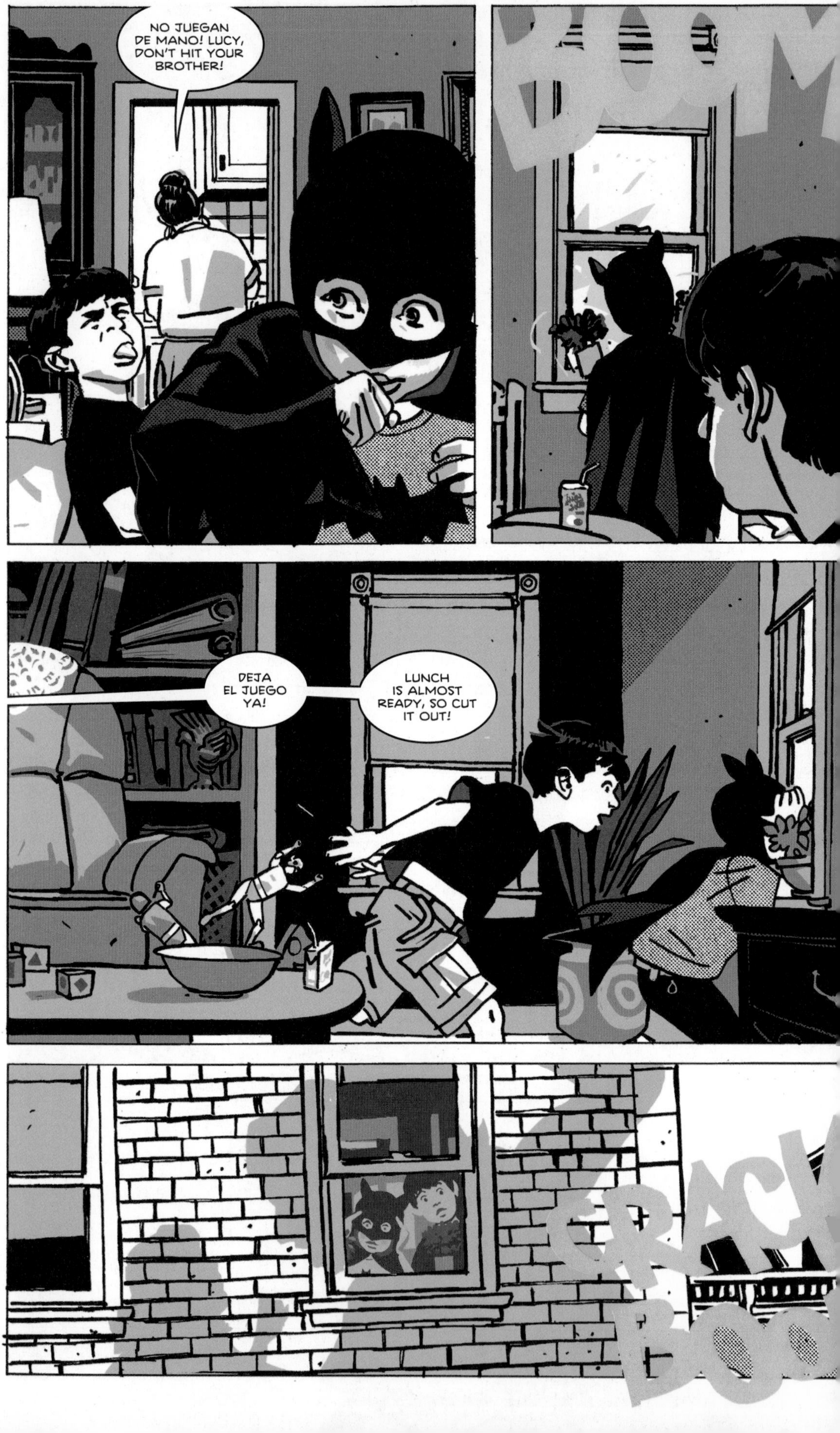
NO JUEGAN DE MANO! LUCY, DON'T HIT YOUR BROTHER!
BOOM
DEJA EL JUEGO YA!
LUNCH IS ALMOST READY, SO CUT IT OUT!

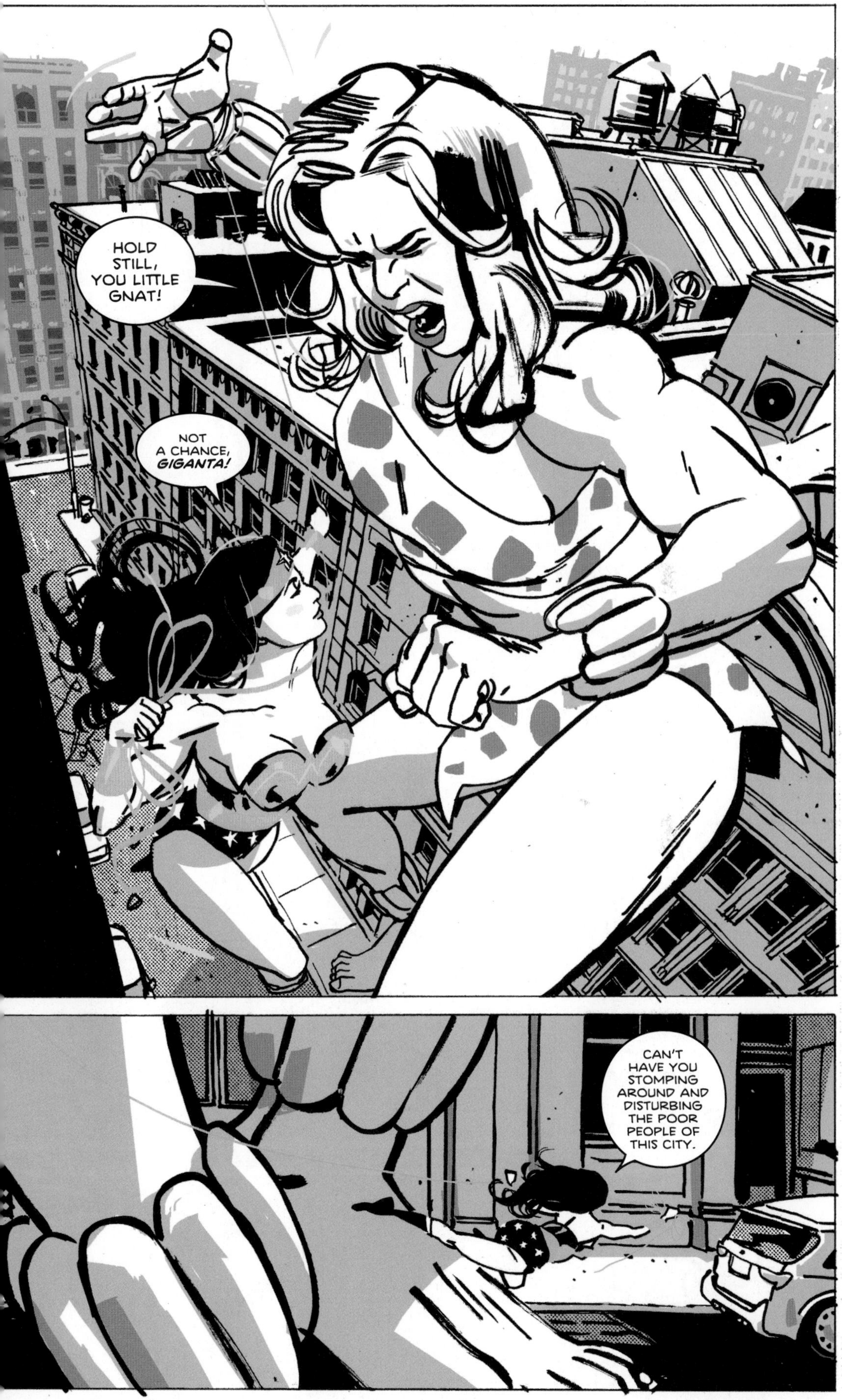
HOLD STILL, YOU LITTLE GNAT!
NOT A CHANCE, *GIGANTA!*
CAN'T HAVE YOU STOMPING AROUND AND DISTURBING THE POOR PEOPLE OF THIS CITY.

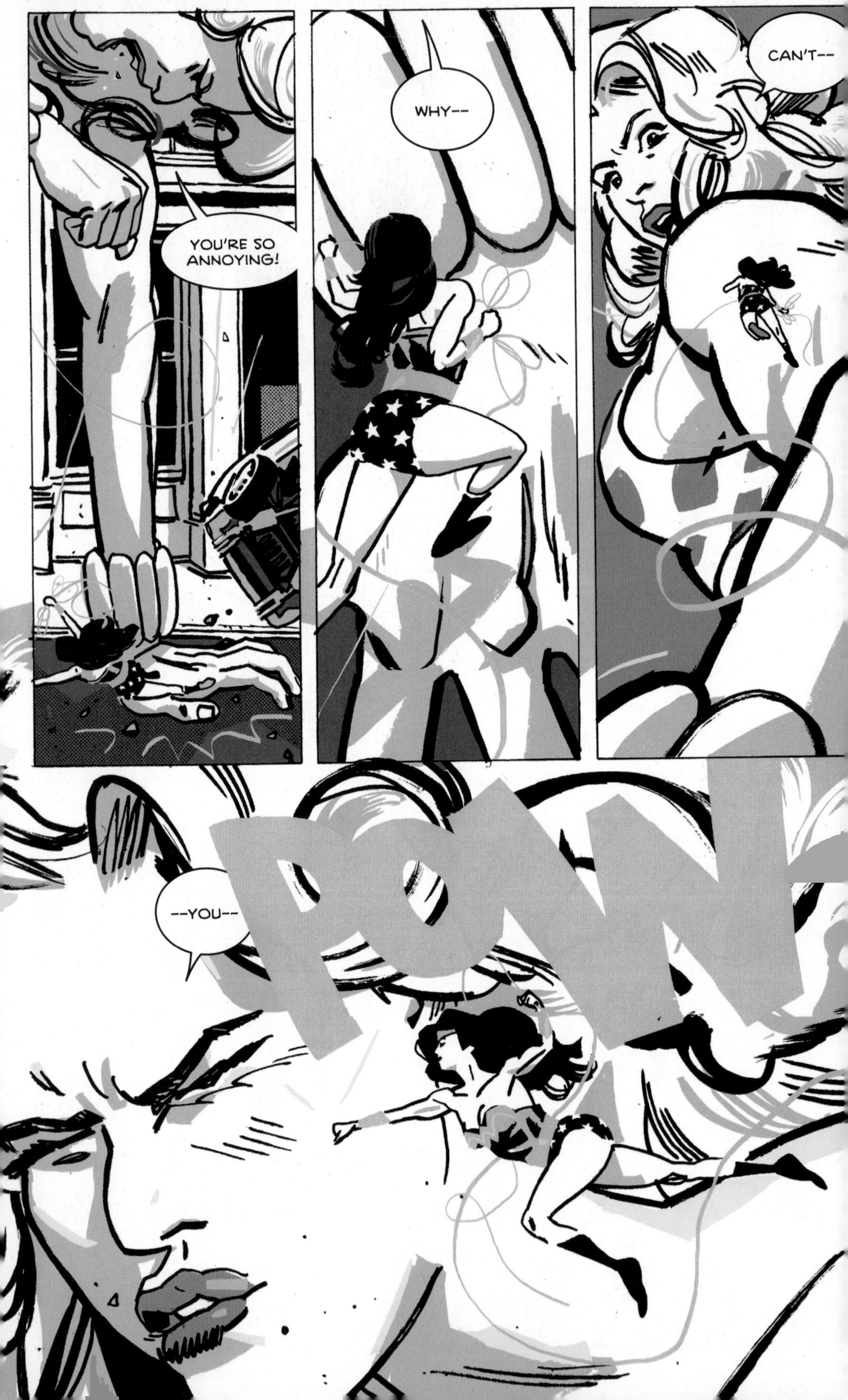
YOU'RE SO ANNOYING!
WHY--
CAN'T--
--YOU--
POW

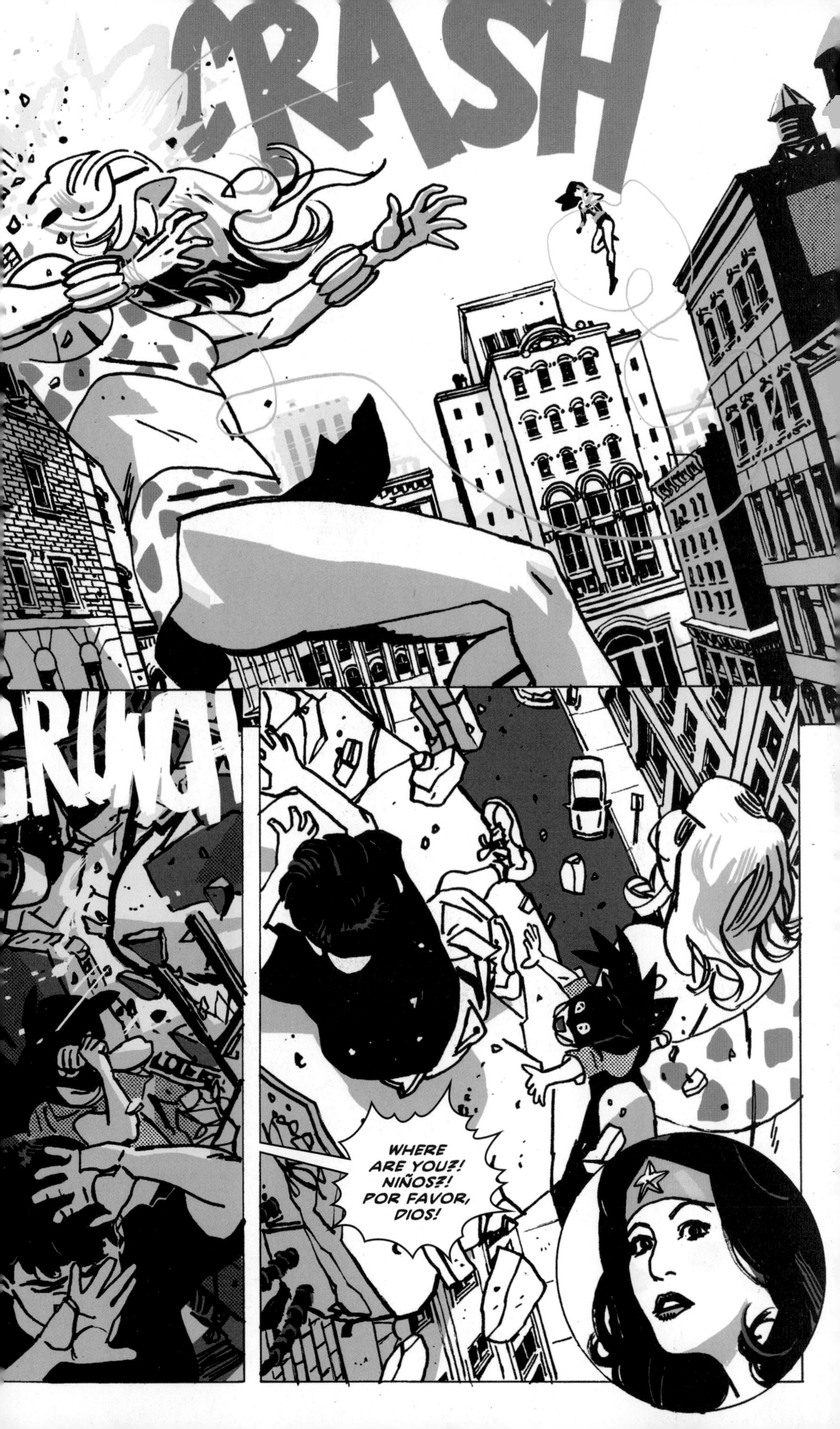
CRASH
CRUNCH
WHERE ARE YOU?! NIÑOS?! POR FAVOR, DIOS!

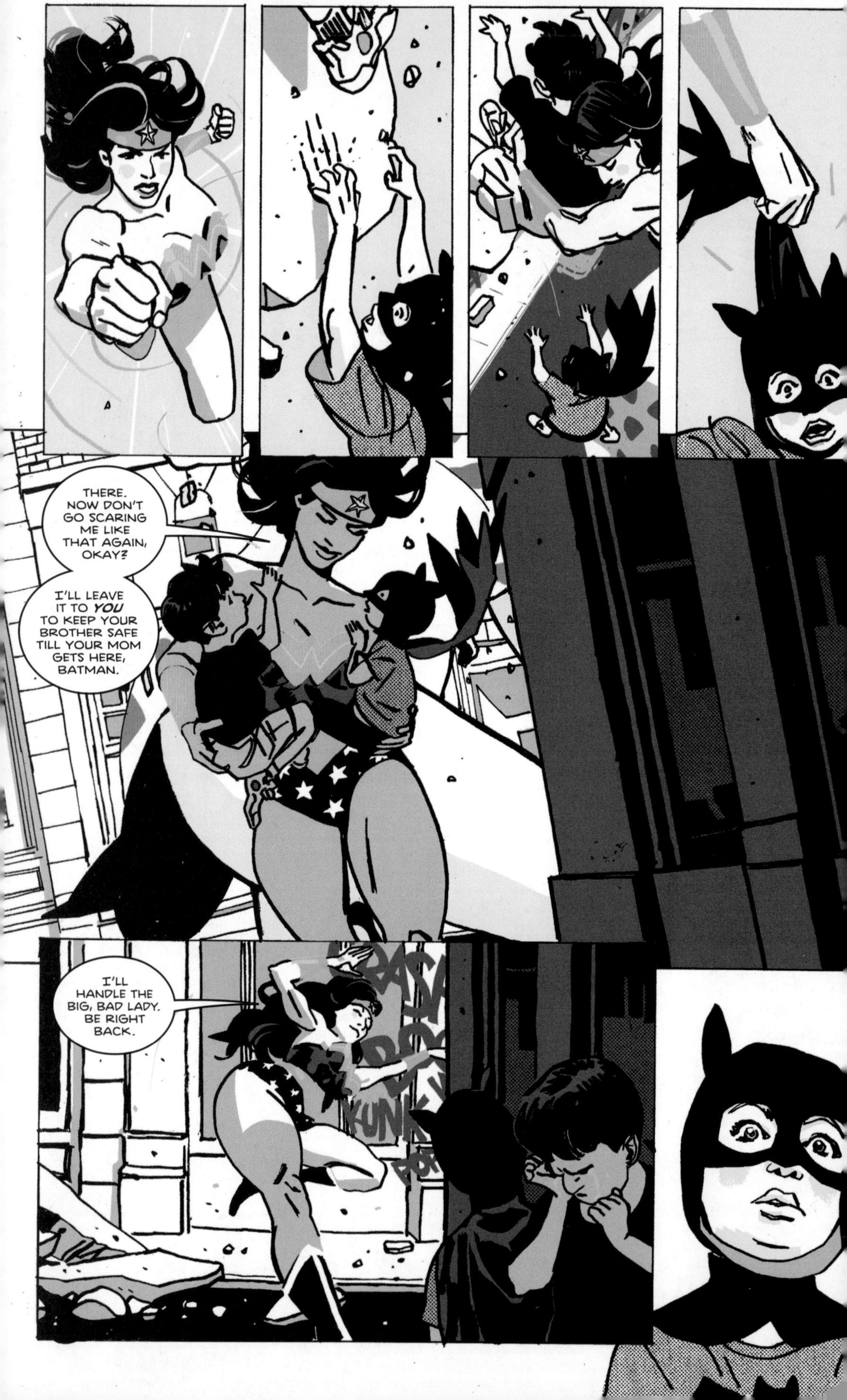
THERE. NOW DON'T GO SCARING ME LIKE THAT AGAIN, OKAY?
I'LL LEAVE IT TO *YOU* TO KEEP YOUR BROTHER SAFE TILL YOUR MOM GETS HERE, BATMAN.
I'LL HANDLE THE BIG, BAD LADY. BE RIGHT BACK.

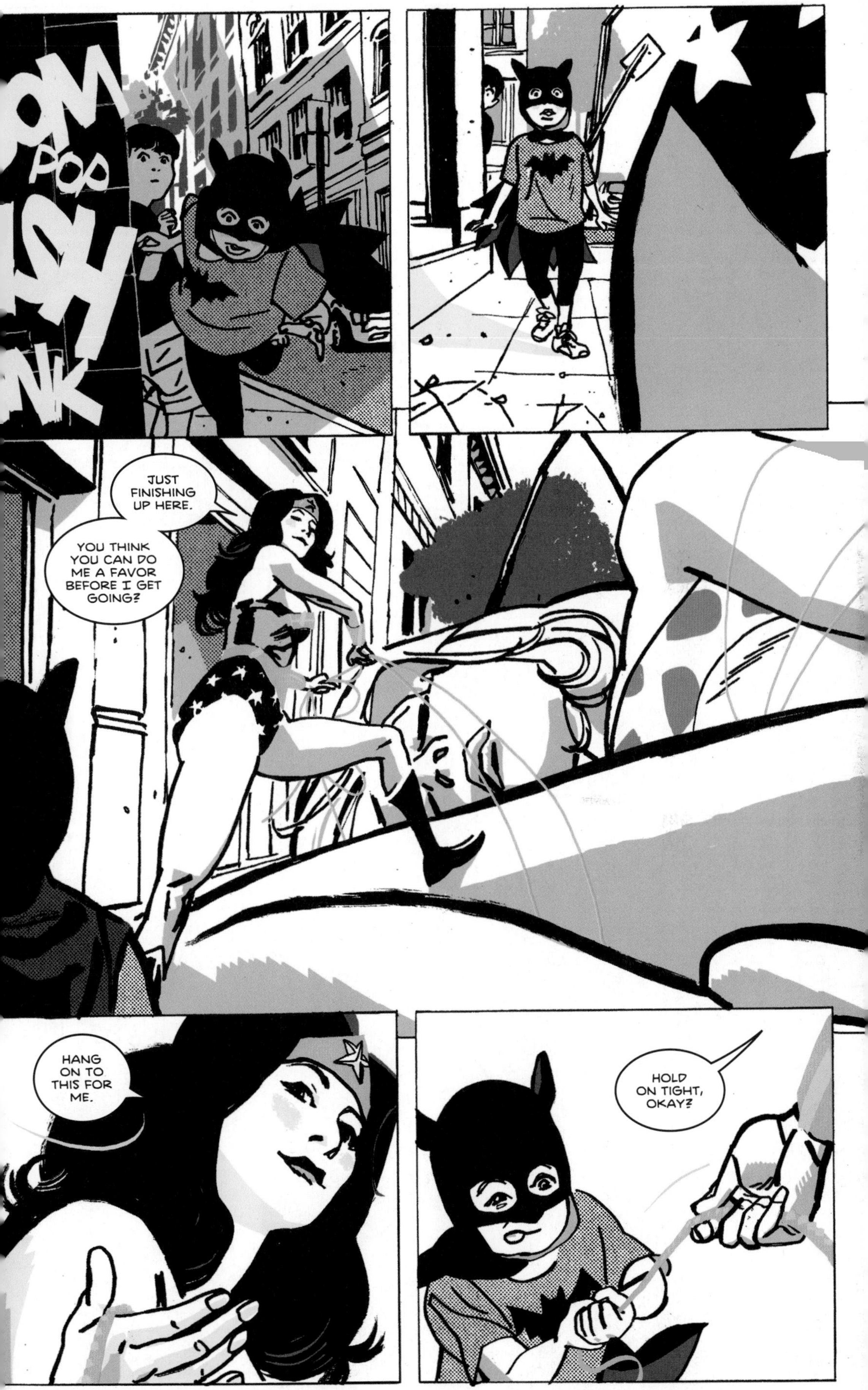
OM
POP
NK
JUST FINISHING UP HERE.
YOU THINK YOU CAN DO ME A FAVOR BEFORE I GET GOING?
HANG ON TO THIS FOR ME.
HOLD ON TIGHT, OKAY?

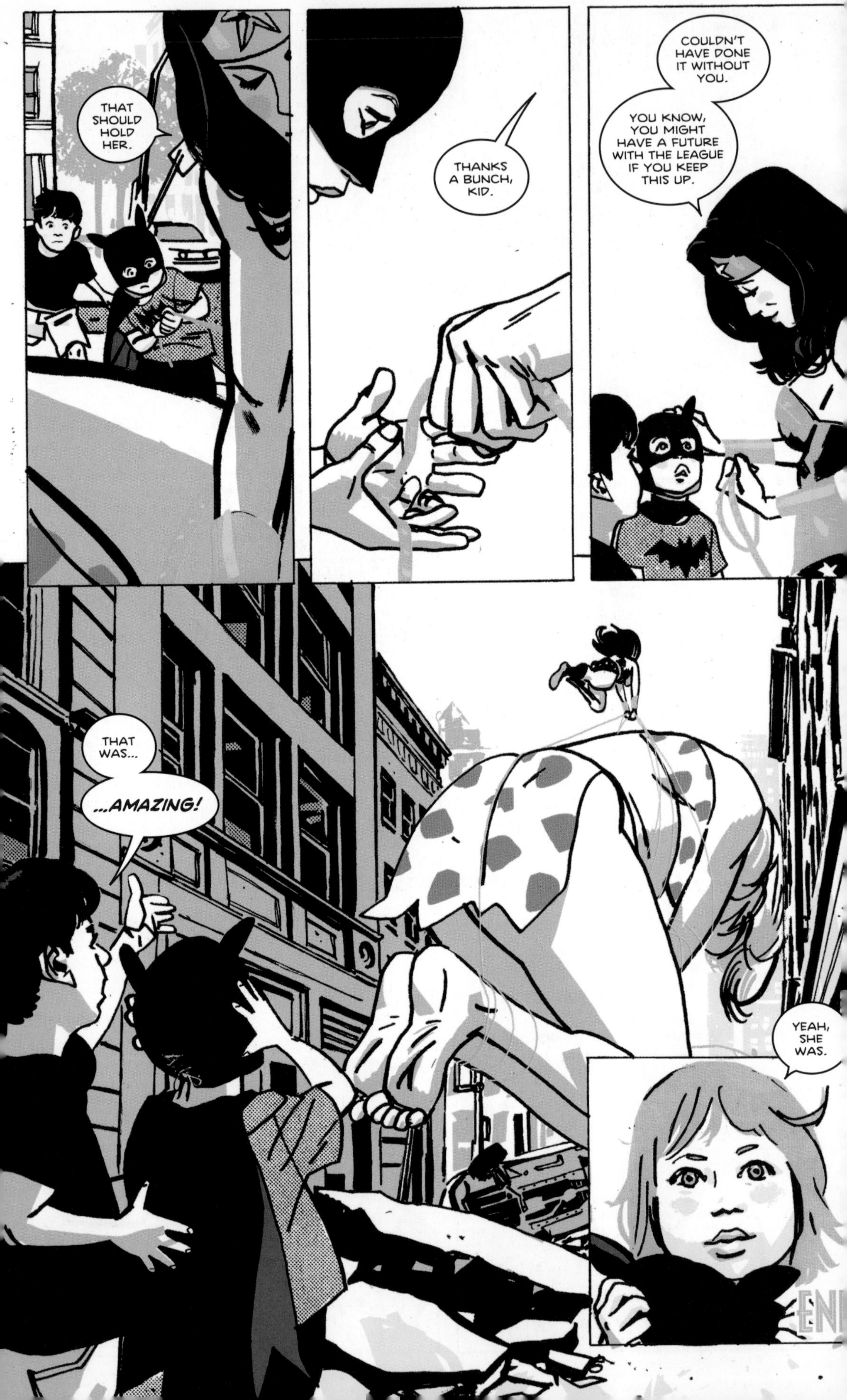
THAT SHOULD HOLD HER.
THANKS A BUNCH, KID.
COULDN'T HAVE DONE IT WITHOUT YOU.
YOU KNOW, YOU MIGHT HAVE A FUTURE WITH THE LEAGUE IF YOU KEEP THIS UP.
THAT WAS...
...AMAZING!
YEAH, SHE WAS.

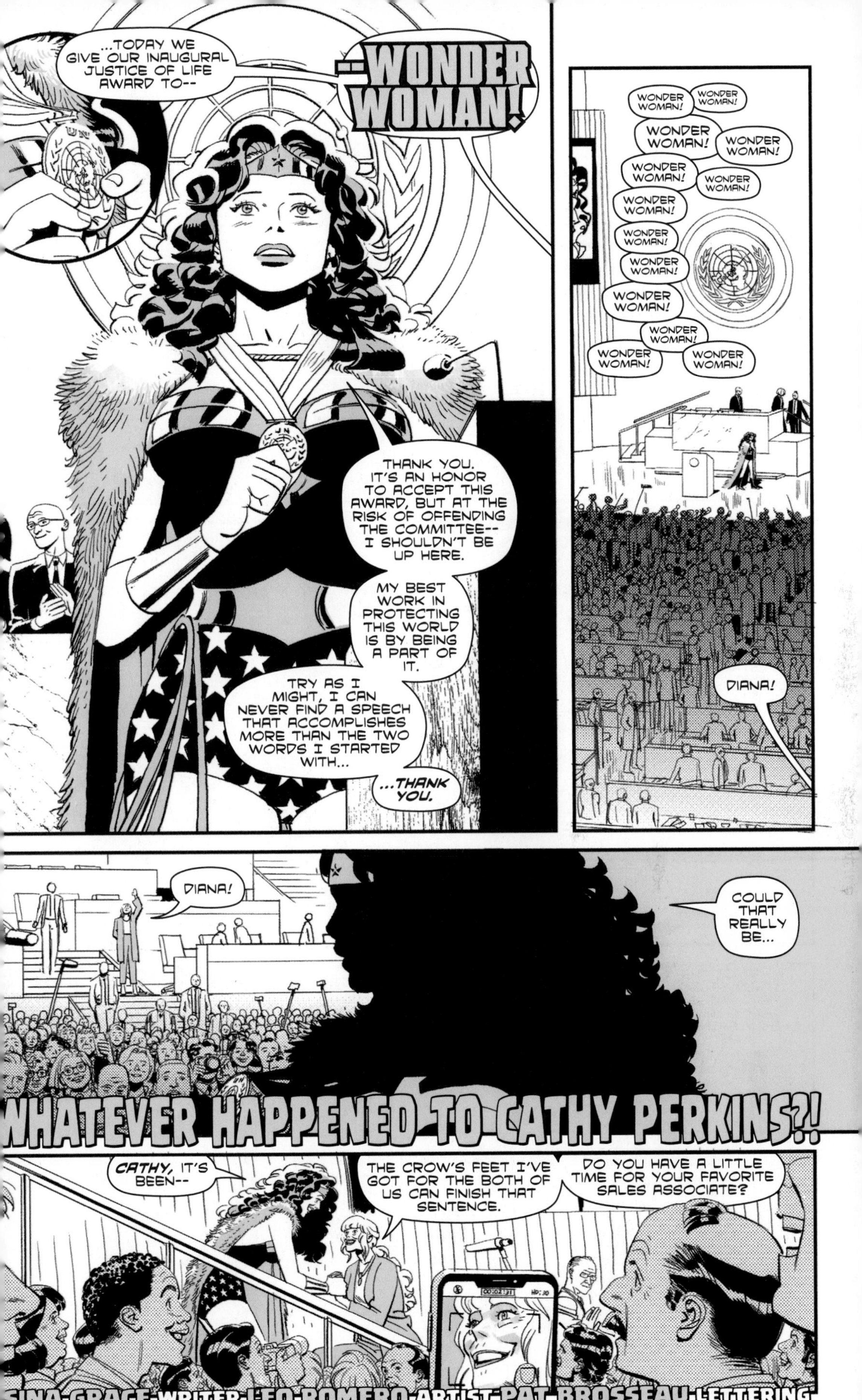
...TODAY WE GIVE OUR INAUGURAL JUSTICE OF LIFE AWARD TO--
--WONDER WOMAN!
WONDER WOMAN!
WONDER WOMAN!
WONDER WOMAN!
WONDER WOMAN!
WONDER WOMAN!
WONDER WOMAN!
WONDER WOMAN!
WONDER WOMAN!
WONDER WOMAN!
WONDER WOMAN!
WONDER WOMAN!
WONDER WOMAN!
WONDER WOMAN!
THANK YOU. IT'S AN HONOR TO ACCEPT THIS AWARD, BUT AT THE RISK OF OFFENDING THE COMMITTEE-- I SHOULDN'T BE UP HERE.
MY BEST WORK IN PROTECTING THIS WORLD IS BY BEING A PART OF IT.
TRY AS I MIGHT, I CAN NEVER FIND A SPEECH THAT ACCOMPLISHES MORE THAN THE TWO WORDS I STARTED WITH...
...THANK YOU.
DIANA!
DIANA!
COULD THAT REALLY BE...
WHATEVER HAPPENED TO CATHY PERKINS?!
CATHY, IT'S BEEN--
THE CROW'S FEET I'VE GOT FOR THE BOTH OF US CAN FINISH THAT SENTENCE.
DO YOU HAVE A LITTLE TIME FOR YOUR FAVORITE SALES ASSOCIATE?
SINA GRACE WRITER LEO ROMERO ARTIST PAT BROSSEAU LETTERING
BIXIE MATHIEU EDITOR JAMIE S. RICH GROUP EDITOR

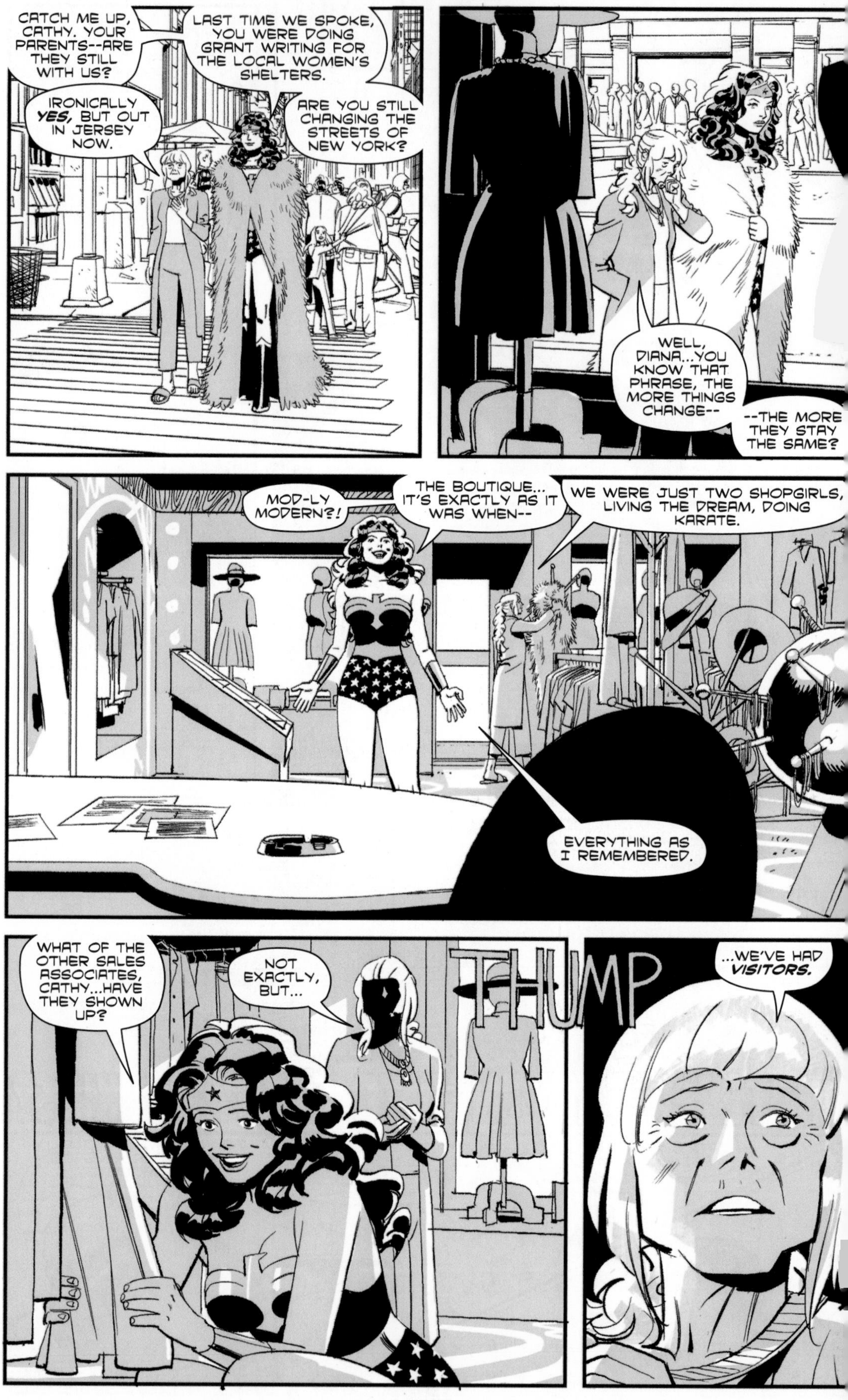
CATCH ME UP, CATHY. YOUR PARENTS--ARE THEY STILL WITH US?
LAST TIME WE SPOKE, YOU WERE DOING GRANT WRITING FOR THE LOCAL WOMEN'S SHELTERS.
IRONICALLY **YES,** BUT OUT IN JERSEY NOW.
ARE YOU STILL CHANGING THE STREETS OF NEW YORK?
WELL, DIANA...YOU KNOW THAT PHRASE, THE MORE THINGS CHANGE--
--THE MORE THEY STAY THE SAME?
MOD-LY MODERN?!
THE BOUTIQUE... IT'S EXACTLY AS IT WAS WHEN--
WE WERE JUST TWO SHOPGIRLS, LIVING THE DREAM, DOING KARATE.
EVERYTHING AS I REMEMBERED.
WHAT OF THE OTHER SALES ASSOCIATES, CATHY...HAVE THEY SHOWN UP?
NOT EXACTLY, BUT...
THUMP
...WE'VE HAD ***VISITORS.***

FINALLY-- NOW WHERE WERE WE?!

DON'T LET THESE BROADS GET THE BEST OF YA, KOLMAR!

BLAM

KI-YA!

SWISH!

GLAD YOU HAVEN'T FORGOTTEN YOUR TRAINING--

KRAK

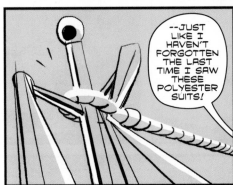

--JUST LIKE I HAVEN'T FORGOTTEN THE LAST TIME I SAW THESE POLYESTER SUITS!

THUNK

THEY ATTACKED THE BOUTIQUE DECADES AGO...ONLY WEEKS AFTER I BROUGHT YOU IN.

WHAT ARE THE ODDS?!

ODD IS APT.

I WAS JUST WALKING DOWN THE STREET, SAW MOD-LY MODERN, AND I KNEW IT WAS TOO GOOD TO BE--

OH NO.

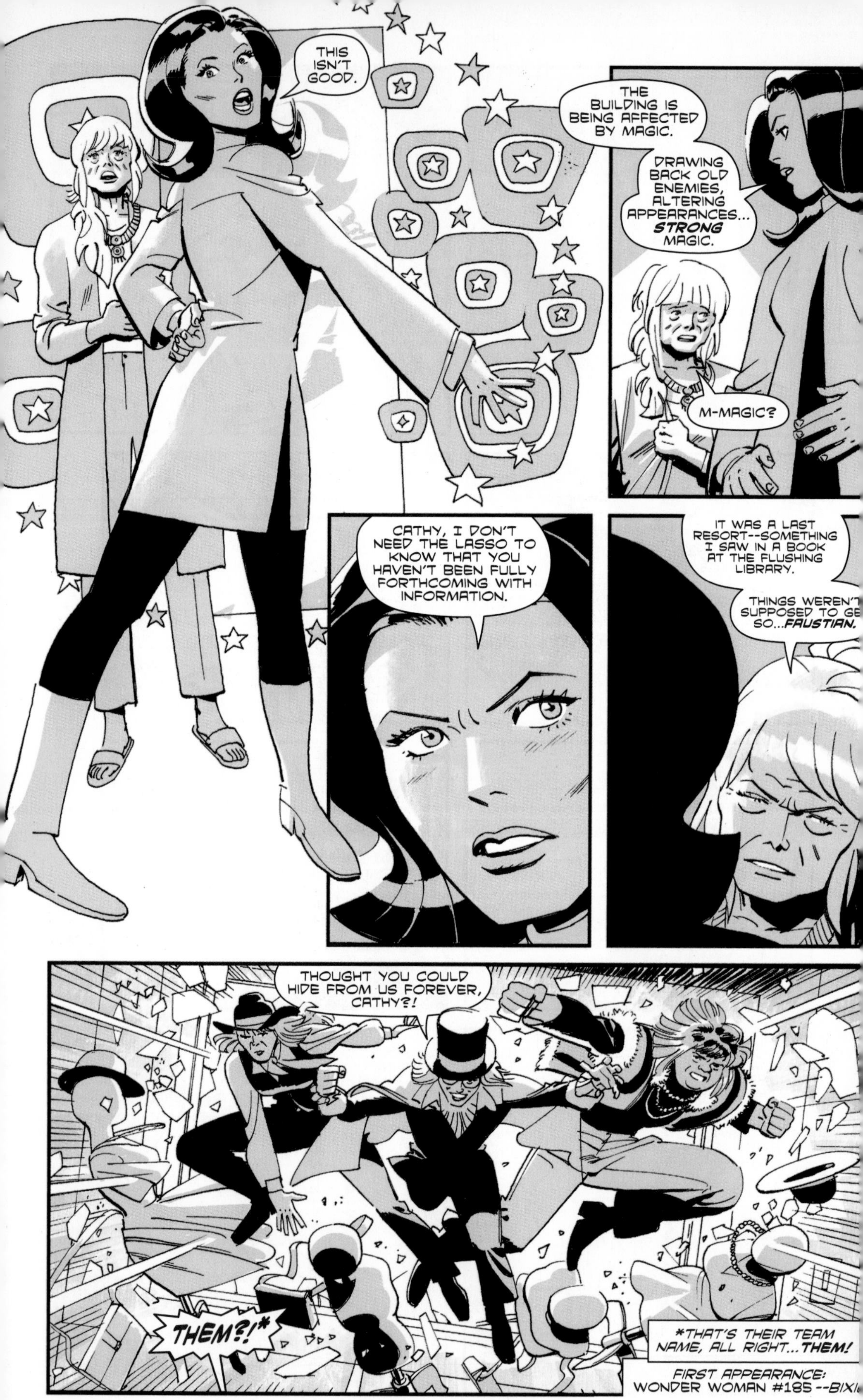
THIS ISN'T GOOD.
THE BUILDING IS BEING AFFECTED BY MAGIC.
DRAWING BACK OLD ENEMIES, ALTERING APPEARANCES... **STRONG** MAGIC.
M-MAGIC?
CATHY, I DON'T NEED THE LASSO TO KNOW THAT YOU HAVEN'T BEEN FULLY FORTHCOMING WITH INFORMATION.
IT WAS A LAST RESORT--SOMETHING I SAW IN A BOOK AT THE FLUSHING LIBRARY.
THINGS WEREN'T SUPPOSED TO GE SO...**FAUSTIAN.**
THOUGHT YOU COULD HIDE FROM US FOREVER, CATHY?!
THEM?!*
*THAT'S THEIR TEAM NAME, ALL RIGHT...**THEM!**
FIRST APPEARANCE: WONDER WOMAN #185 --BIXI

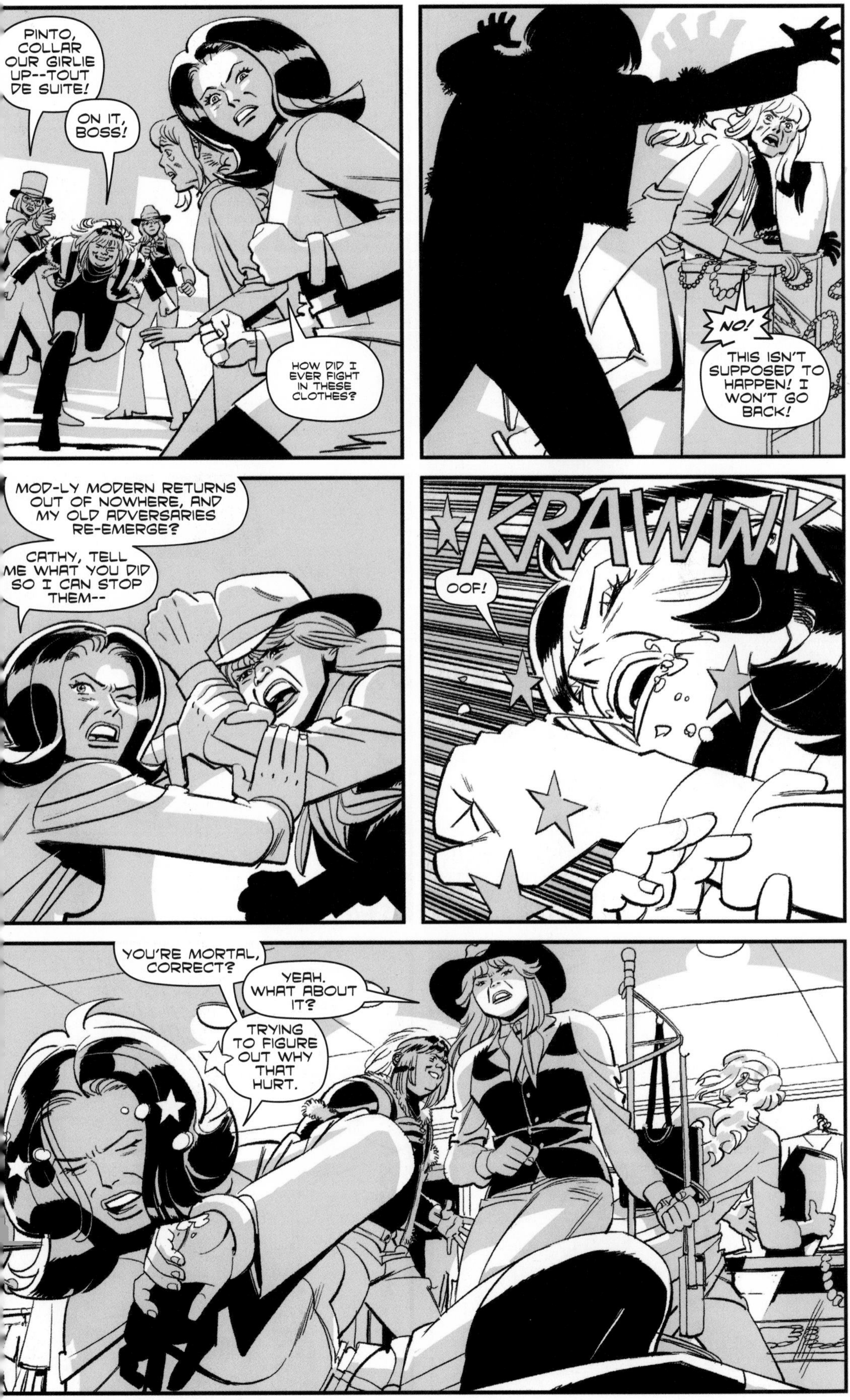
PINTO, COLLAR OUR GIRLIE UP--TOUT DE SUITE!
ON IT, BOSS!
HOW DID I EVER FIGHT IN THESE CLOTHES?
NO!
THIS ISN'T SUPPOSED TO HAPPEN! I WON'T GO BACK!
MOD-LY MODERN RETURNS OUT OF NOWHERE, AND MY OLD ADVERSARIES RE-EMERGE?
CATHY, TELL ME WHAT YOU DID SO I CAN STOP THEM--
KRAWWK
OOF!
YOU'RE MORTAL, CORRECT?
YEAH. WHAT ABOUT IT?
TRYING TO FIGURE OUT WHY THAT HURT.

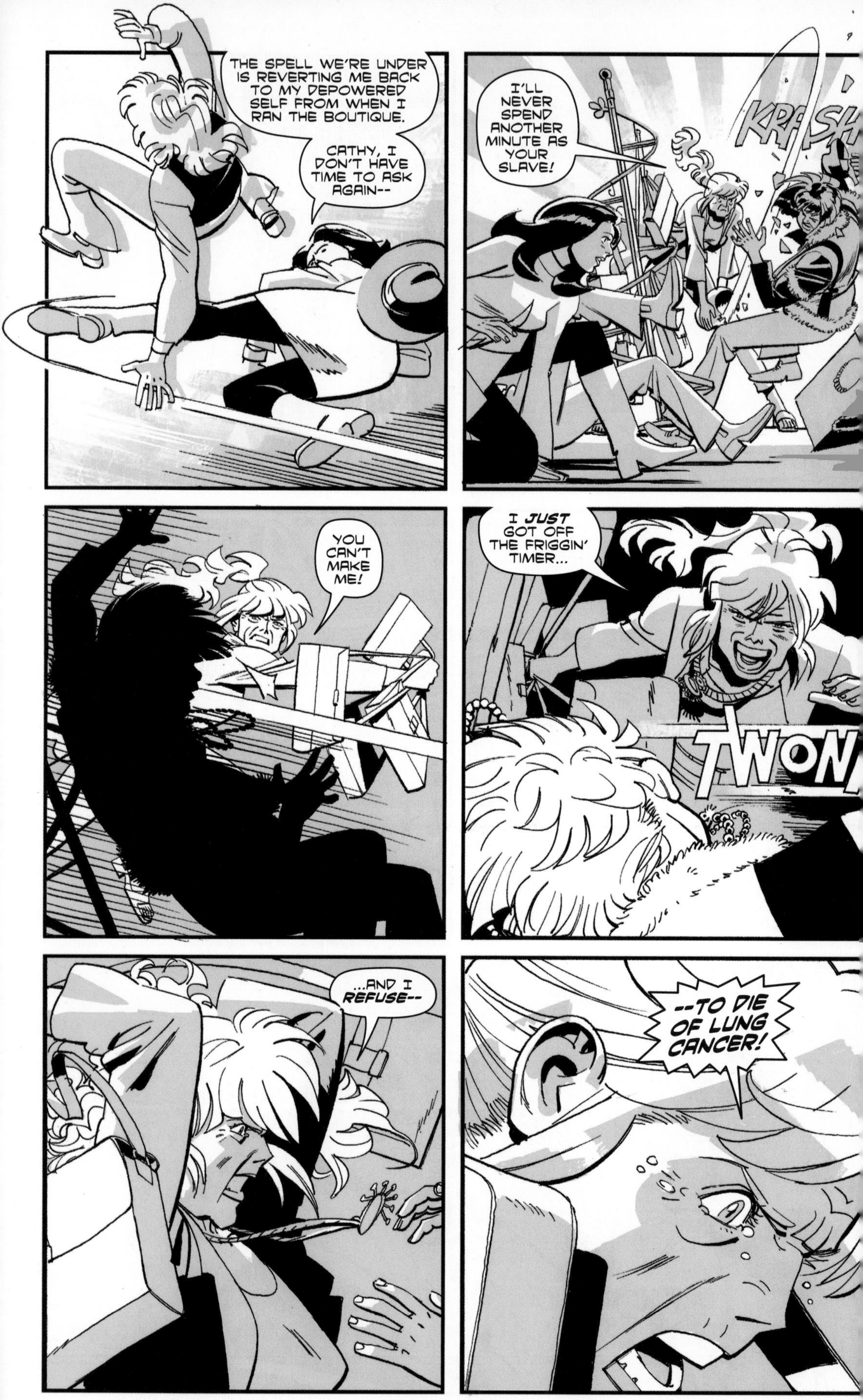
9
THE SPELL WE'RE UNDER IS REVERTING ME BACK TO MY DEPOWERED SELF FROM WHEN I RAN THE BOUTIQUE.
CATHY, I DON'T HAVE TIME TO ASK AGAIN--
I'LL NEVER SPEND ANOTHER MINUTE AS YOUR SLAVE!
KRASH
YOU CAN'T MAKE ME!
I JUST GOT OFF THE FRIGGIN' TIMER...
TWON
...AND I REFUSE--
--TO DIE OF LUNG CANCER!

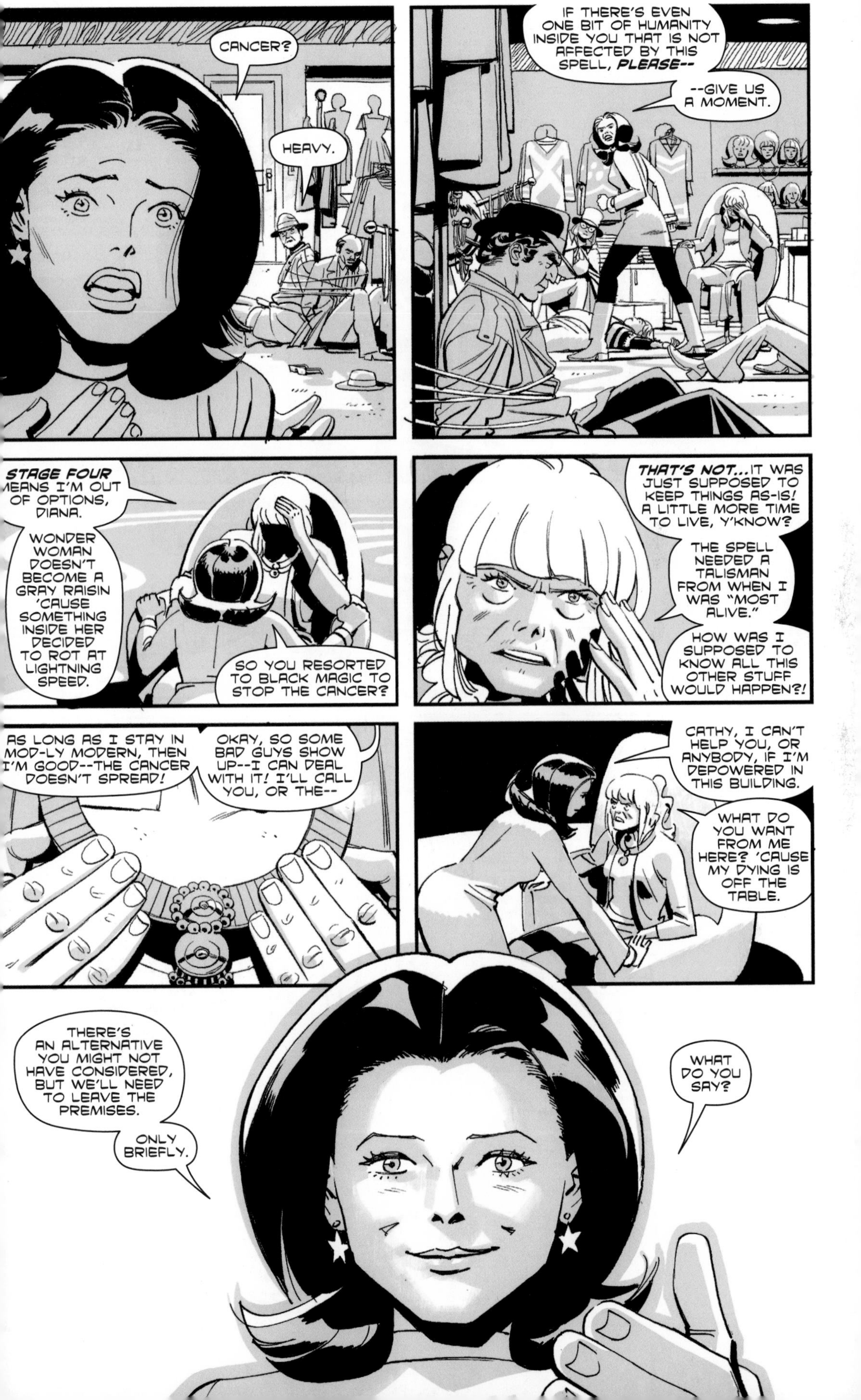
CANCER?
HEAVY.
IF THERE'S EVEN ONE BIT OF HUMANITY INSIDE YOU THAT IS NOT AFFECTED BY THIS SPELL, PLEASE--
--GIVE US A MOMENT.
STAGE FOUR MEANS I'M OUT OF OPTIONS, DIANA.
WONDER WOMAN DOESN'T BECOME A GRAY RAISIN 'CAUSE SOMETHING INSIDE HER DECIDED TO ROT AT LIGHTNING SPEED.
SO YOU RESORTED TO BLACK MAGIC TO STOP THE CANCER?
THAT'S NOT... IT WAS JUST SUPPOSED TO KEEP THINGS AS-IS! A LITTLE MORE TIME TO LIVE, Y'KNOW?
THE SPELL NEEDED A TALISMAN FROM WHEN I WAS "MOST ALIVE."
HOW WAS I SUPPOSED TO KNOW ALL THIS OTHER STUFF WOULD HAPPEN?!
AS LONG AS I STAY IN MOD-LY MODERN, THEN I'M GOOD--THE CANCER DOESN'T SPREAD!
OKAY, SO SOME BAD GUYS SHOW UP--I CAN DEAL WITH IT! I'LL CALL YOU, OR THE--
CATHY, I CAN'T HELP YOU, OR ANYBODY, IF I'M DEPOWERED IN THIS BUILDING.
WHAT DO YOU WANT FROM ME HERE? 'CAUSE MY DYING IS OFF THE TABLE.
THERE'S AN ALTERNATIVE YOU MIGHT NOT HAVE CONSIDERED, BUT WE'LL NEED TO LEAVE THE PREMISES.
ONLY BRIEFLY.
WHAT DO YOU SAY?

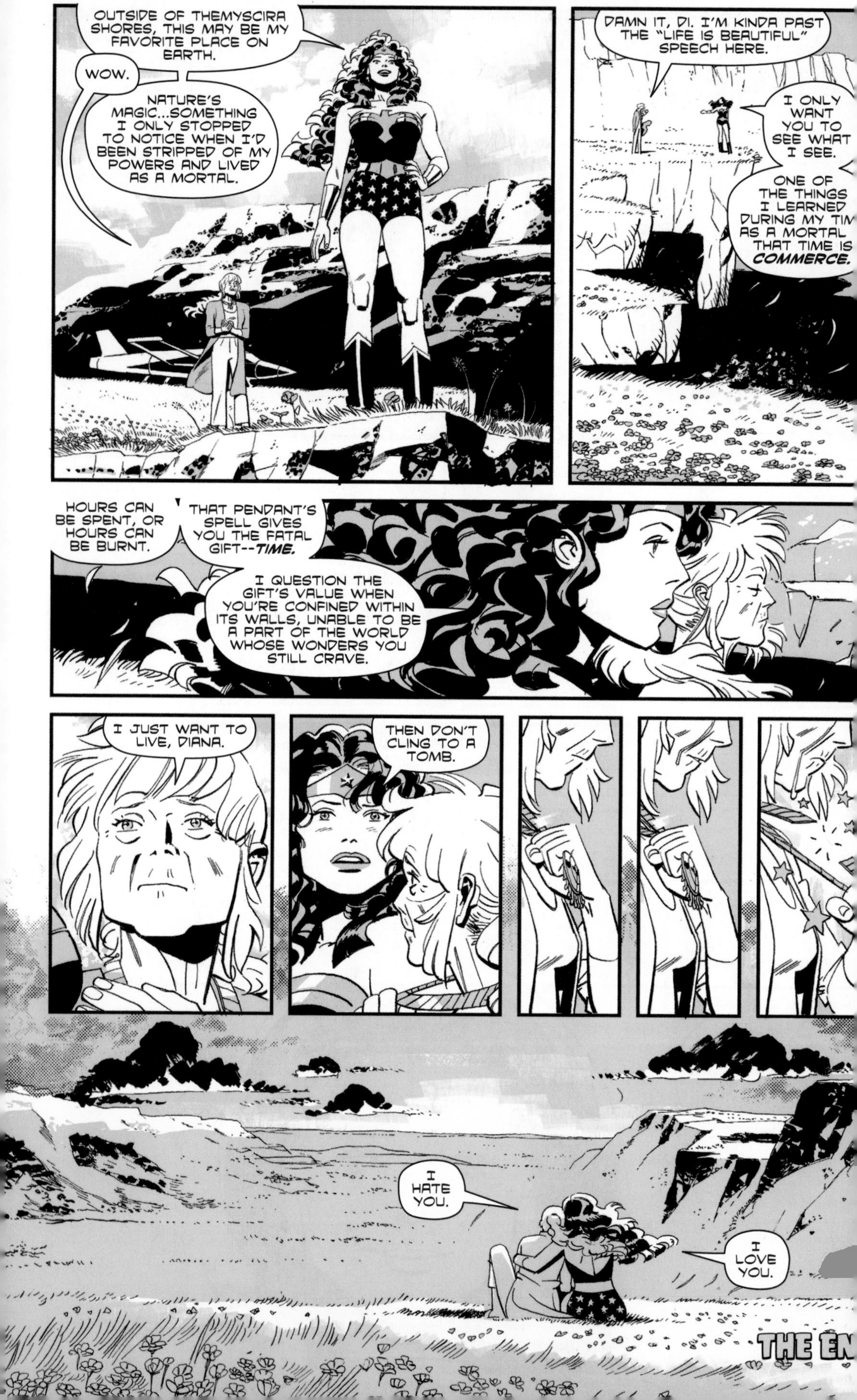

OUTSIDE OF THEMYSCIRA SHORES, THIS MAY BE MY FAVORITE PLACE ON EARTH.
WOW.
NATURE'S MAGIC...SOMETHING I ONLY STOPPED TO NOTICE WHEN I'D BEEN STRIPPED OF MY POWERS AND LIVED AS A MORTAL.
DAMN IT, DI. I'M KINDA PAST THE "LIFE IS BEAUTIFUL" SPEECH HERE.
I ONLY WANT YOU TO SEE WHAT I SEE.
ONE OF THE THINGS I LEARNED DURING MY TIM AS A MORTAL THAT TIME IS *COMMERCE.*
HOURS CAN BE SPENT, OR HOURS CAN BE BURNT.
THAT PENDANT'S SPELL GIVES YOU THE FATAL GIFT--*TIME.*
I QUESTION THE GIFT'S VALUE WHEN YOU'RE CONFINED WITHIN ITS WALLS, UNABLE TO BE A PART OF THE WORLD WHOSE WONDERS YOU STILL CRAVE.
I JUST WANT TO LIVE, DIANA.
THEN DON'T CLING TO A TOMB.
I HATE YOU.
I LOVE YOU.
THE EN

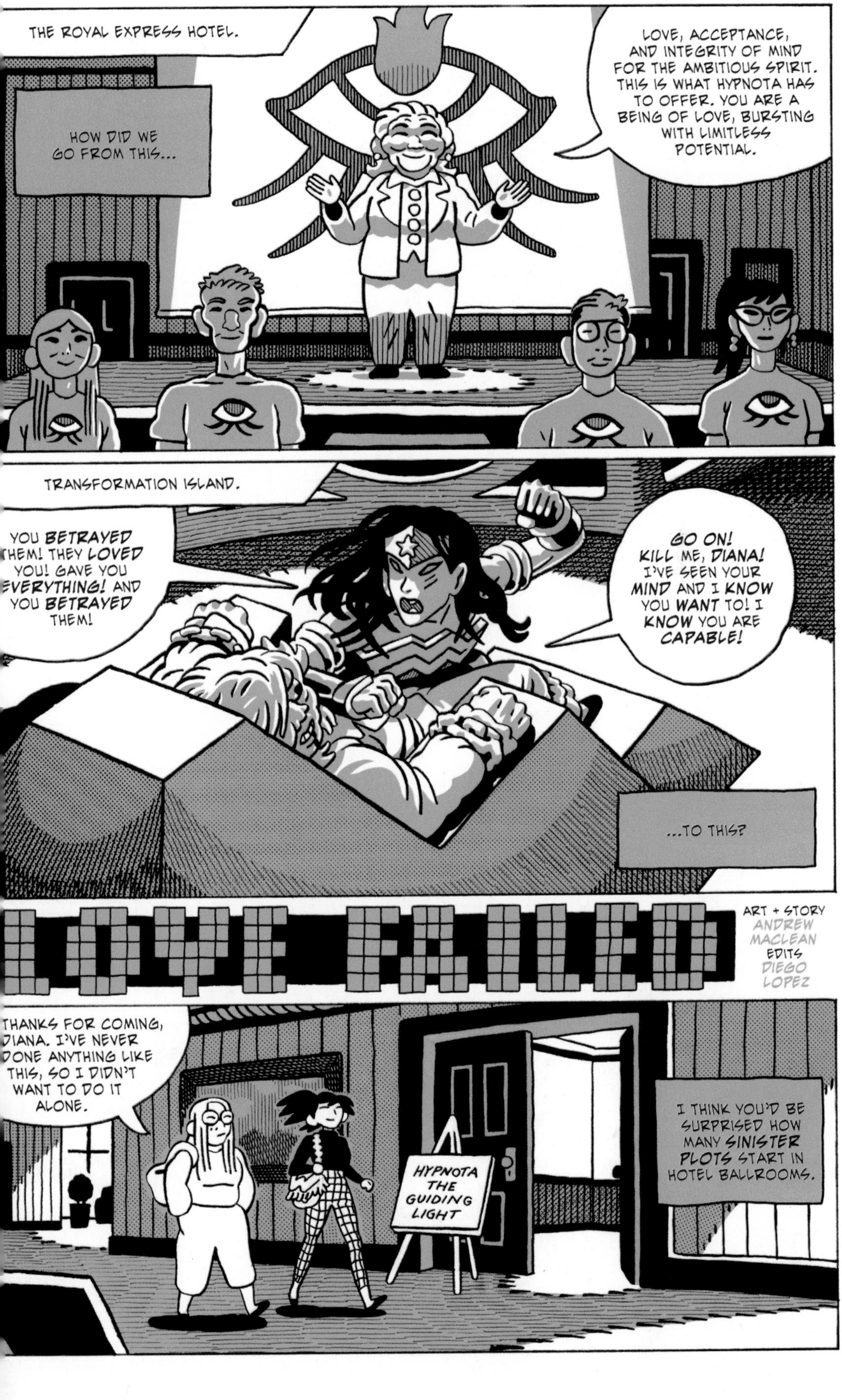

THE ROYAL EXPRESS HOTEL.
HOW DID WE GO FROM THIS...
LOVE, ACCEPTANCE, AND INTEGRITY OF MIND FOR THE AMBITIOUS SPIRIT. THIS IS WHAT HYPNOTA HAS TO OFFER. YOU ARE A BEING OF LOVE, BURSTING WITH LIMITLESS POTENTIAL.
TRANSFORMATION ISLAND.
YOU BETRAYED HEM! THEY LOVED YOU! GAVE YOU VERYTHING! AND YOU BETRAYED THEM!
GO ON! KILL ME, DIANA! I'VE SEEN YOUR MIND AND I KNOW YOU WANT TO! I KNOW YOU ARE CAPABLE!
...TO THIS?
LOVE FAILED
ART + STORY ANDREW MACLEAN
EDITS DIEGO LOPEZ
THANKS FOR COMING, IANA. I'VE NEVER ONE ANYTHING LIKE THIS, SO I DIDN'T WANT TO DO IT ALONE.
HYPNOTA THE GUIDING LIGHT
I THINK YOU'D BE SURPRISED HOW MANY SINISTER PLOTS START IN HOTEL BALLROOMS.

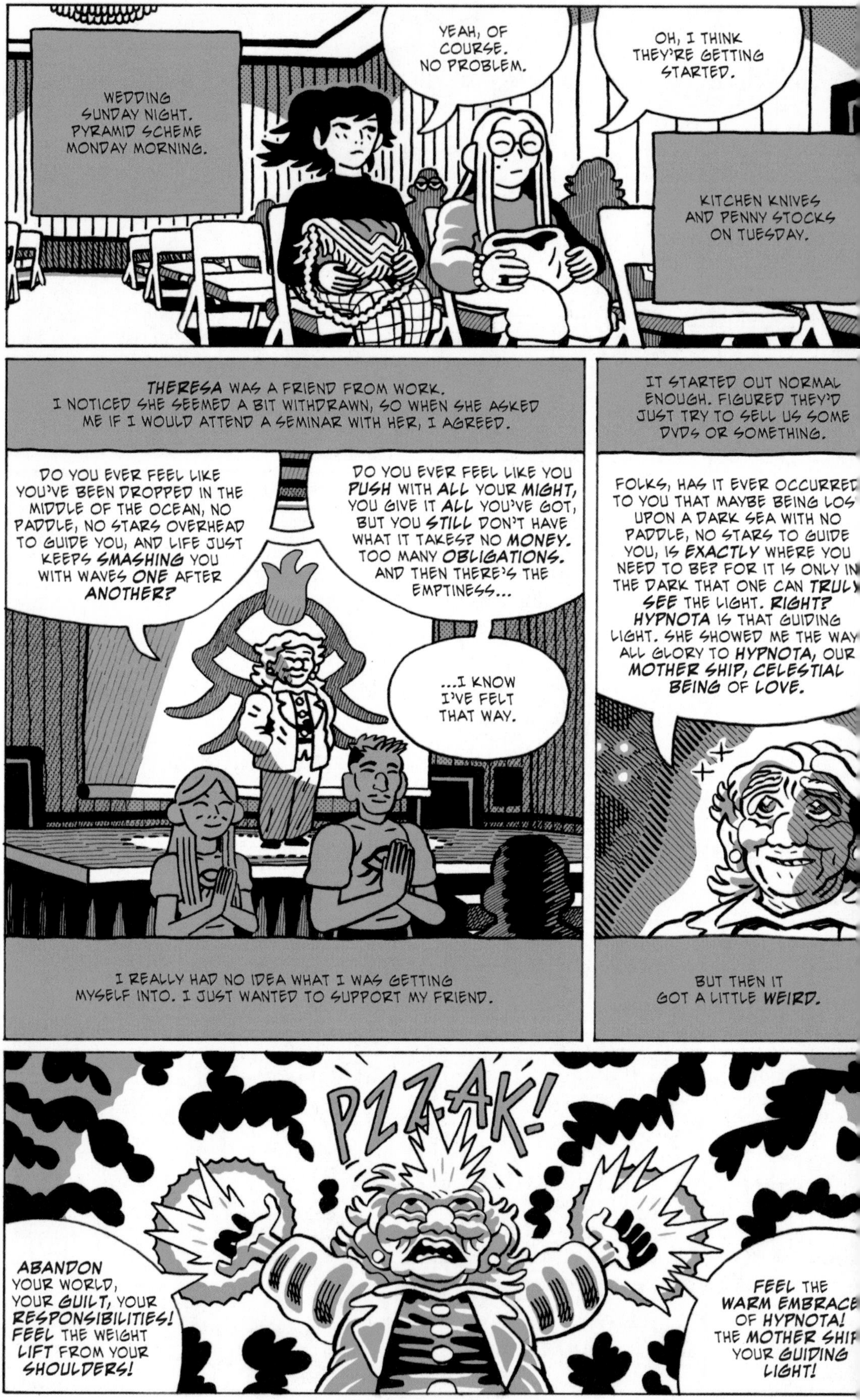
WEDDING SUNDAY NIGHT. PYRAMID SCHEME MONDAY MORNING.
YEAH, OF COURSE. NO PROBLEM.
OH, I THINK THEY'RE GETTING STARTED.
KITCHEN KNIVES AND PENNY STOCKS ON TUESDAY.
THERESA WAS A FRIEND FROM WORK. I NOTICED SHE SEEMED A BIT WITHDRAWN, SO WHEN SHE ASKED ME IF I WOULD ATTEND A SEMINAR WITH HER, I AGREED.
DO YOU EVER FEEL LIKE YOU'VE BEEN DROPPED IN THE MIDDLE OF THE OCEAN, NO PADDLE, NO STARS OVERHEAD TO GUIDE YOU, AND LIFE JUST KEEPS SMASHING YOU WITH WAVES ONE AFTER ANOTHER?
DO YOU EVER FEEL LIKE YOU PUSH WITH ALL YOUR MIGHT, YOU GIVE IT ALL YOU'VE GOT, BUT YOU STILL DON'T HAVE WHAT IT TAKES? NO MONEY. TOO MANY OBLIGATIONS. AND THEN THERE'S THE EMPTINESS...
...I KNOW I'VE FELT THAT WAY.
I REALLY HAD NO IDEA WHAT I WAS GETTING MYSELF INTO. I JUST WANTED TO SUPPORT MY FRIEND.
IT STARTED OUT NORMAL ENOUGH. FIGURED THEY'D JUST TRY TO SELL US SOME DVDS OR SOMETHING.
FOLKS, HAS IT EVER OCCURRED TO YOU THAT MAYBE BEING LOST UPON A DARK SEA WITH NO PADDLE, NO STARS TO GUIDE YOU, IS EXACTLY WHERE YOU NEED TO BE? FOR IT IS ONLY IN THE DARK THAT ONE CAN TRULY SEE THE LIGHT. RIGHT? HYPNOTA IS THAT GUIDING LIGHT. SHE SHOWED ME THE WAY. ALL GLORY TO HYPNOTA, OUR MOTHER SHIP, CELESTIAL BEING OF LOVE.
BUT THEN IT GOT A LITTLE WEIRD.
PZZZAK!
ABANDON YOUR WORLD, YOUR GUILT, YOUR RESPONSIBILITIES! FEEL THE WEIGHT LIFT FROM YOUR SHOULDERS!
FEEL THE WARM EMBRACE OF HYPNOTA! THE MOTHER SHIP! YOUR GUIDING LIGHT!

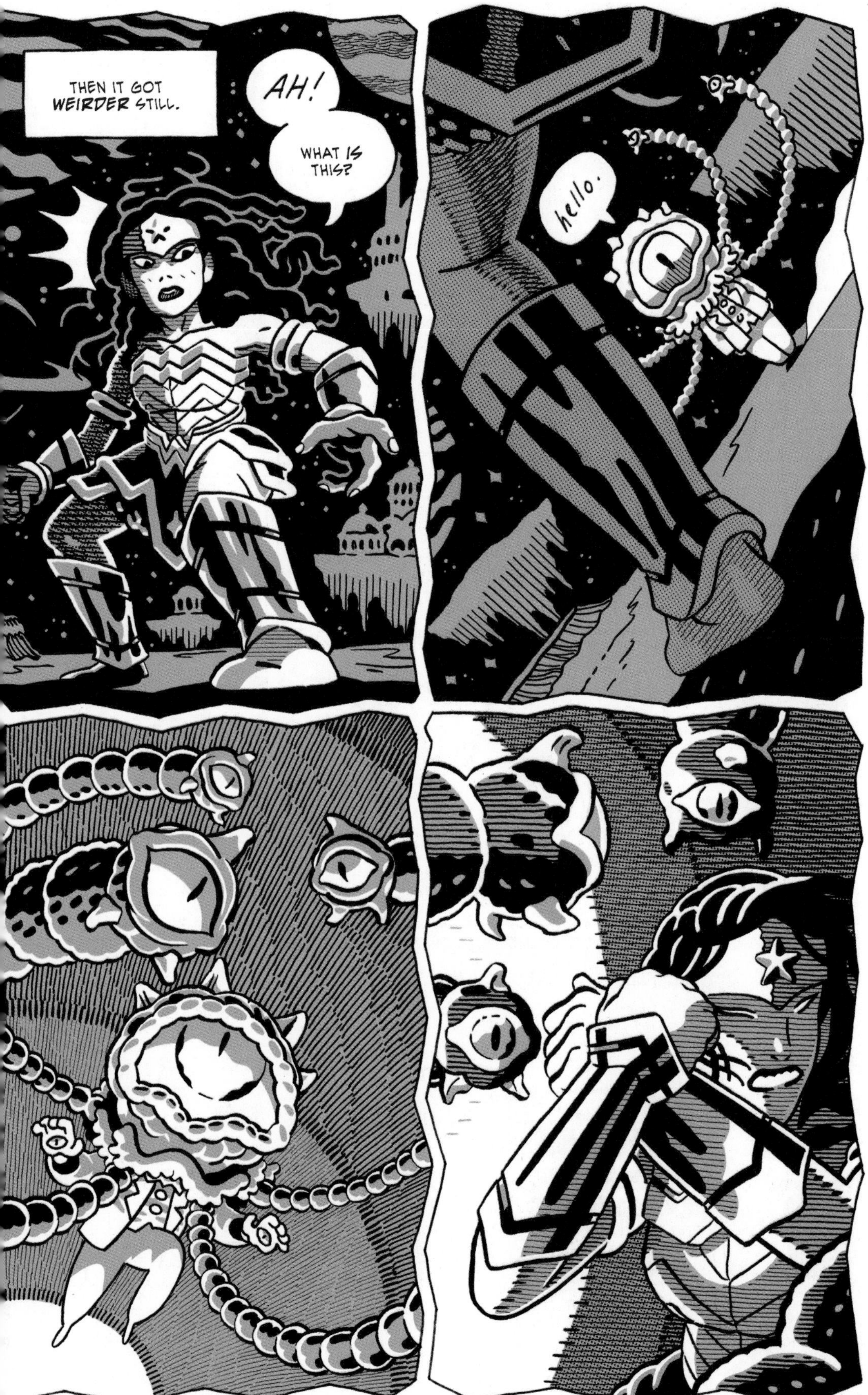
THEN IT GOT WEIRDER STILL.
AH!
WHAT IS THIS?
hello.

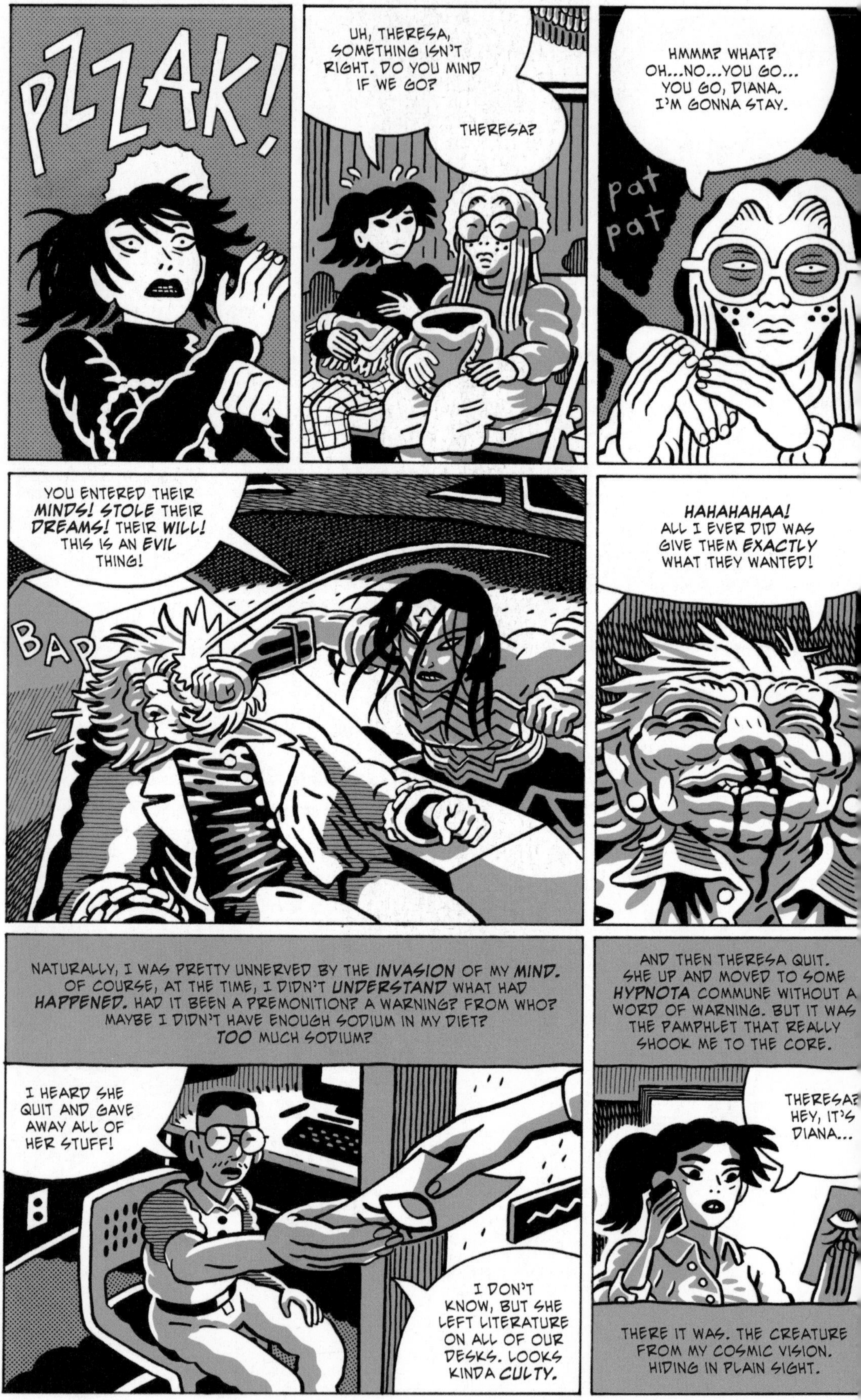
PZZAK!
UH, THERESA, SOMETHING ISN'T RIGHT. DO YOU MIND IF WE GO?
THERESA?
HMMM? WHAT? OH...NO...YOU GO... YOU GO, DIANA. I'M GONNA STAY.
pat pat
YOU ENTERED THEIR MINDS! STOLE THEIR DREAMS! THEIR WILL! THIS IS AN EVIL THING!
BAP
HAHAHAHAA! ALL I EVER DID WAS GIVE THEM EXACTLY WHAT THEY WANTED!
NATURALLY, I WAS PRETTY UNNERVED BY THE INVASION OF MY MIND. OF COURSE, AT THE TIME, I DIDN'T UNDERSTAND WHAT HAD HAPPENED. HAD IT BEEN A PREMONITION? A WARNING? FROM WHO? MAYBE I DIDN'T HAVE ENOUGH SODIUM IN MY DIET? TOO MUCH SODIUM?
AND THEN THERESA QUIT. SHE UP AND MOVED TO SOME HYPNOTA COMMUNE WITHOUT A WORD OF WARNING. BUT IT WAS THE PAMPHLET THAT REALLY SHOOK ME TO THE CORE.
I HEARD SHE QUIT AND GAVE AWAY ALL OF HER STUFF!
I DON'T KNOW, BUT SHE LEFT LITERATURE ON ALL OF OUR DESKS. LOOKS KINDA CULTY.
THERESA? HEY, IT'S DIANA...
THERE IT WAS. THE CREATURE FROM MY COSMIC VISION. HIDING IN PLAIN SIGHT.

I MET UP WITH THERESA AT SOMETHING SHE CALLED AN *INDUCTION*. I DIDN'T KNOW WHAT THAT WAS, BUT IT WAS *SURPRISINGLY EXPENSIVE*.

IT'S SO GOOD TO SEE YOU. HOW HAVE YOU BEEN?

AMAZING! EVERYONE HERE HAS BEEN SO WONDERFUL. I LOVE THE COMMUNITY. AND GUESS WHAT...

...TODAY WE FINALLY GET TO SEE HYPNOTA, THE MOTHER SHIP, MY GUIDING LIGHT.

YOU ARE SO *LUCKY*, DIANA. USUALLY ONLY *SECOND-LEVEL CENTURIONS* ARE ALLOWED TO *GAZE* UPON HER. FOR SHE IS *LOVE*, AND MANY ARE *UNCLEAN*.

I WAS GETTING REALLY WORRIED ABOUT THERESA.

FRIENDS!

WELCOME!

ENTER INTO HYPNOTA!

!

OKAY. I'D SEEN ENOUGH.

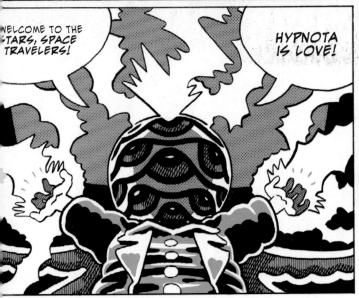

WELCOME TO THE STARS, SPACE TRAVELERS!

HYPNOTA IS LOVE!

PZZAK

AH!

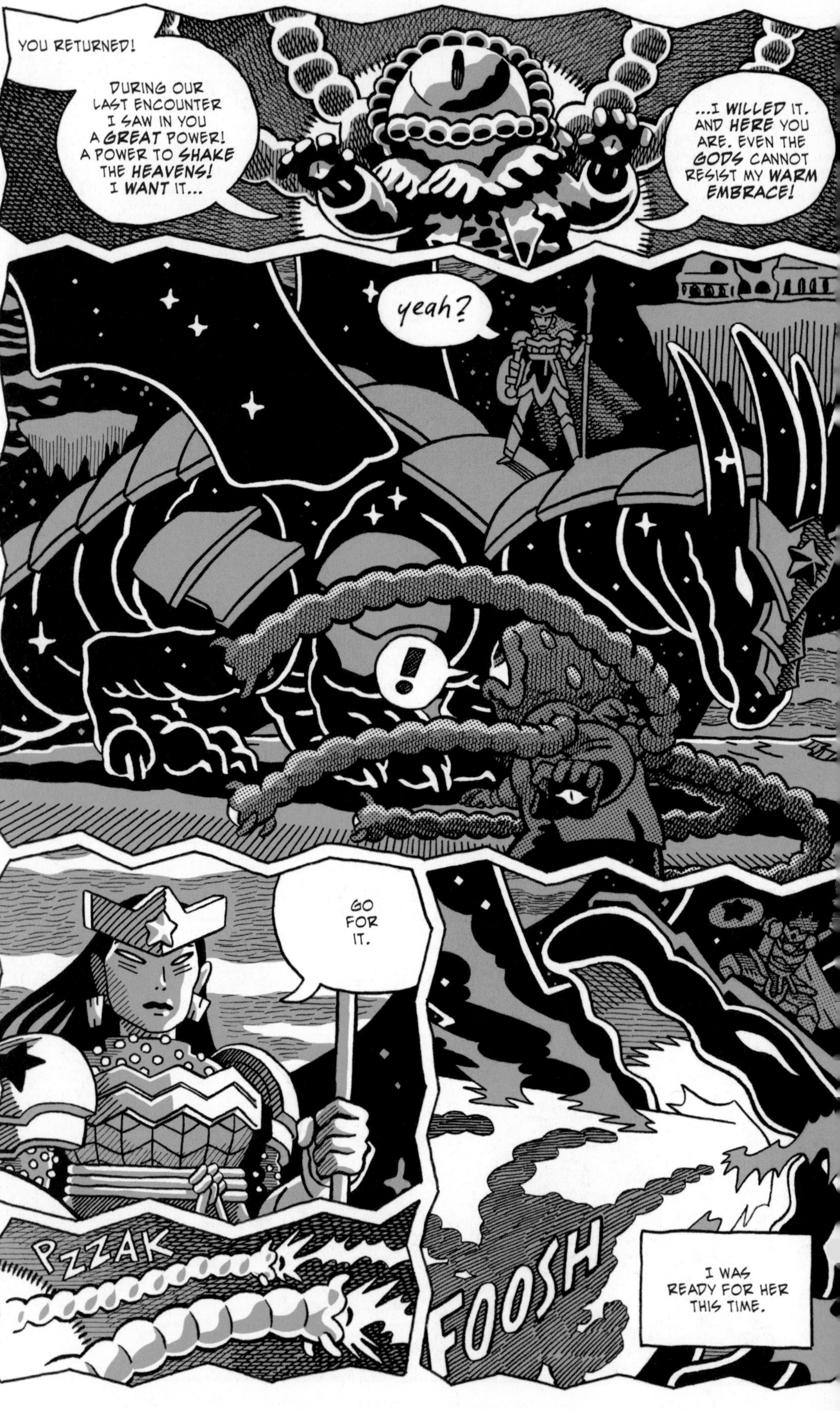
YOU RETURNED!
DURING OUR LAST ENCOUNTER I SAW IN YOU A GREAT POWER! A POWER TO SHAKE THE HEAVENS! I WANT IT...
...I WILLED IT. AND HERE YOU ARE. EVEN THE GODS CANNOT RESIST MY WARM EMBRACE!
yeah?
!
GO FOR IT.
PZZAK
FOOSH
I WAS READY FOR HER THIS TIME.

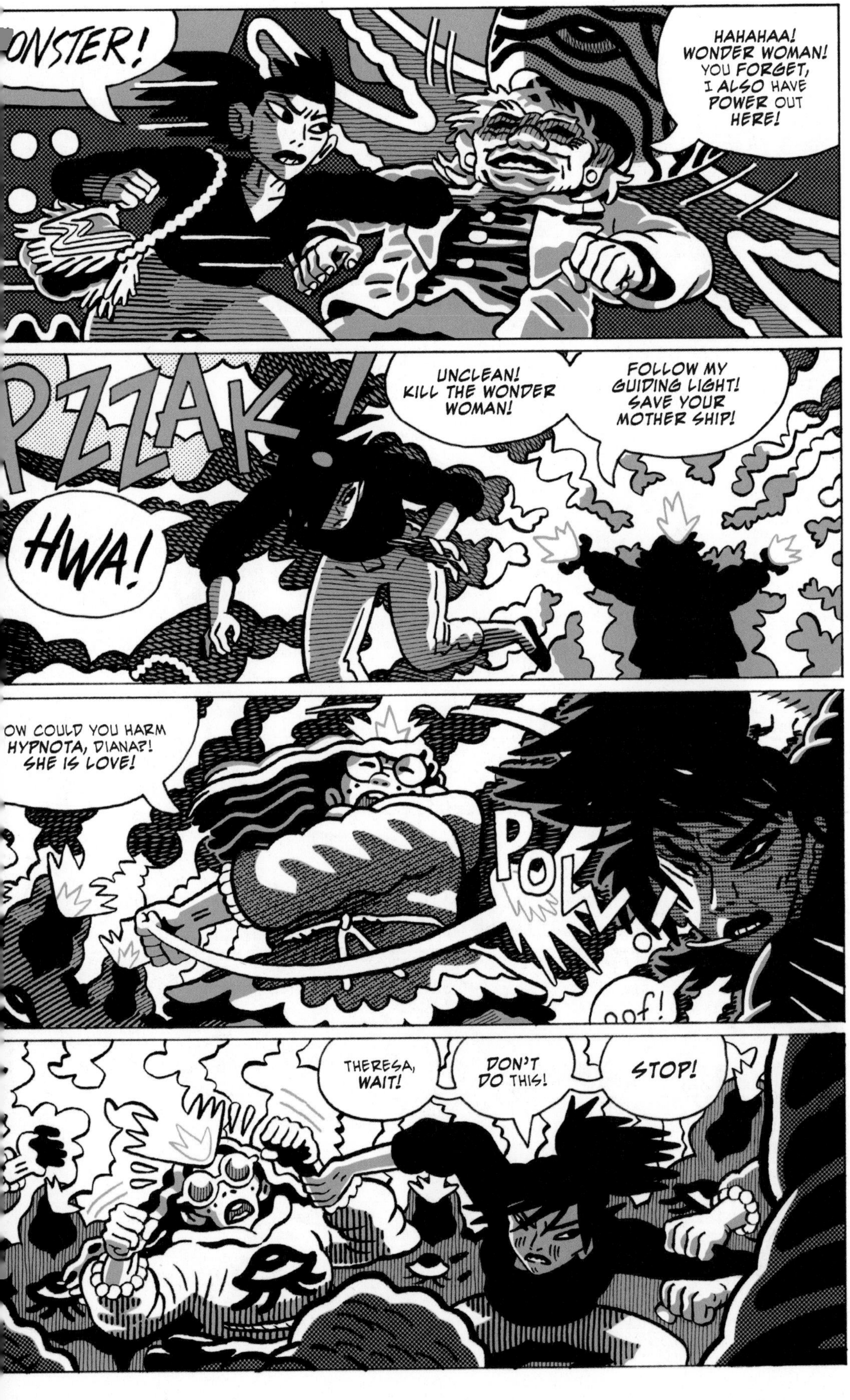
ONSTER!
HAHAHAA! WONDER WOMAN! YOU FORGET, I ALSO HAVE POWER OUT HERE!
PZZZAK!
UNCLEAN! KILL THE WONDER WOMAN!
FOLLOW MY GUIDING LIGHT! SAVE YOUR MOTHER SHIP!
HWA!
OW COULD YOU HARM HYPNOTA, DIANA?! SHE IS LOVE!
POW!
oof!
THERESA, WAIT!
DON'T DO THIS!
STOP!

STOP!

PLEASE! STOP!

PLEASE!

YOU **FORCED** ME TO HURT **INNOCENT** PEOPLE.

YOU'RE A PARASITE **CLINGING** TO OTHERS, FEEDING ON THEIR **ESSENCE**, THEIR **ADORATION**.

AND YET YOU KNOW NOT WHAT LOVE IS. YOUR LOVE IS **TOXIC**. A MEANS TO AN **END**. A **BID** FOR **POWER**.

YOU **BEG** FOR **DEATH** BUT I WILL **NOT** GRANT IT. AND THOUGH YOU CANNOT SEE IT, **THIS** IS AN **ACT** OF **LOVE**.

koff! koff!

I'M LEAVING YOU HERE UNTIL YOUR MIND **ROTS** WITH **LONELINESS**. FOR IT IS NOT LOVE THAT **FAILED**...BUT **YOU**, HYPNOTA.

YOU'LL VISIT, DIANA! I'M YOUR **GUIDING LIGHT!** YOUR **WARM EMBRACE!** RIGHT?

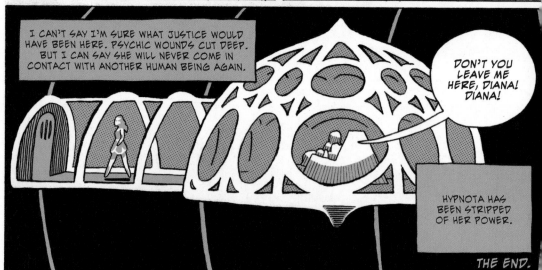

I CAN'T SAY I'M SURE WHAT JUSTICE WOULD HAVE BEEN HERE. PSYCHIC WOUNDS CUT DEEP. BUT I CAN SAY SHE WILL NEVER COME IN CONTACT WITH ANOTHER HUMAN BEING AGAIN.

DON'T YOU LEAVE ME HERE, DIANA! DIANA!

HYPNOTA HAS BEEN STRIPPED OF HER POWER.

THE END.

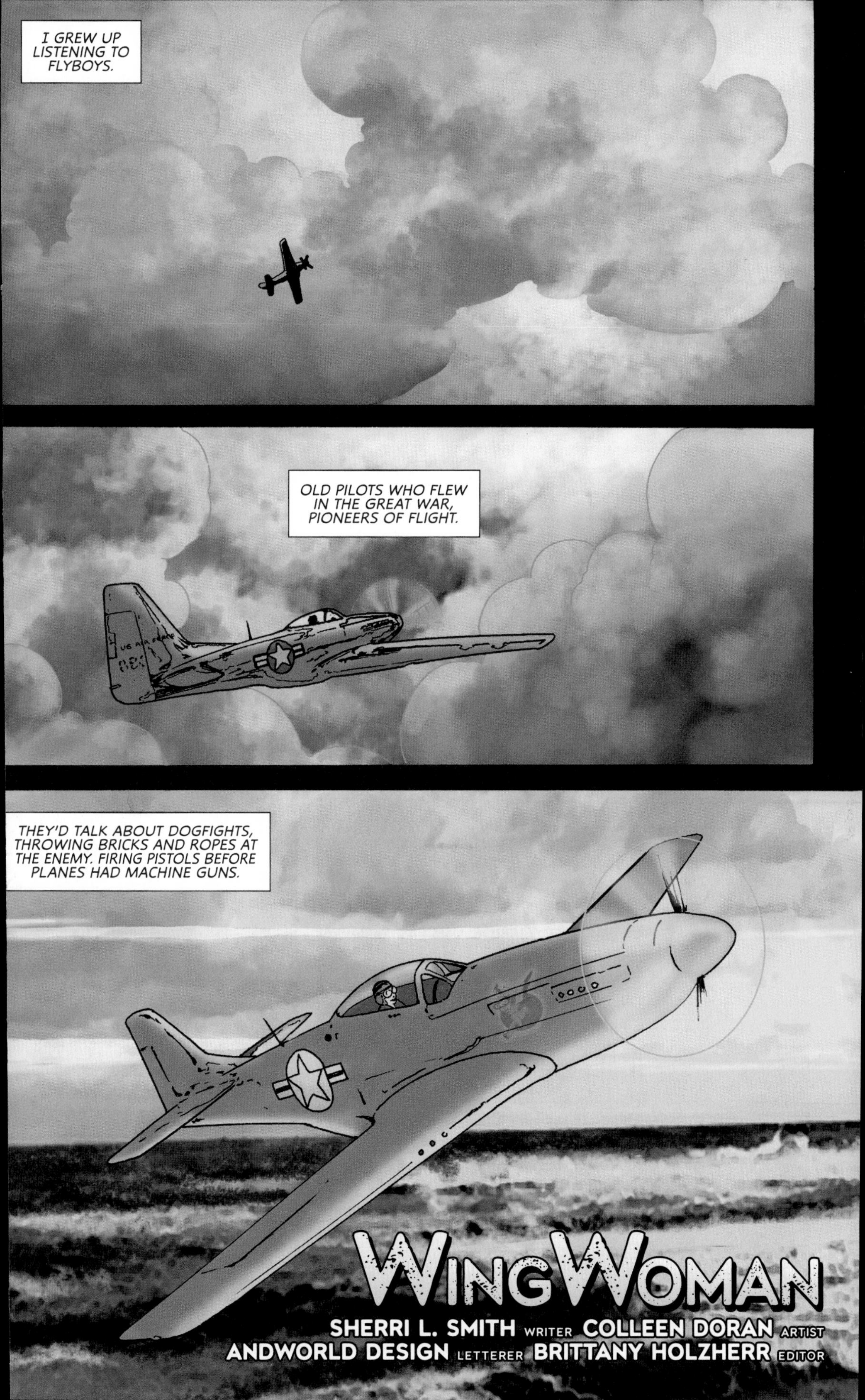
I GREW UP LISTENING TO FLYBOYS.
OLD PILOTS WHO FLEW IN THE GREAT WAR, PIONEERS OF FLIGHT.
THEY'D TALK ABOUT DOGFIGHTS, THROWING BRICKS AND ROPES AT THE ENEMY. FIRING PISTOLS BEFORE PLANES HAD MACHINE GUNS.
WINGWOMAN
SHERRI L. SMITH WRITER COLLEEN DORAN ARTIST
ANDWORLD DESIGN LETTERER BRITTANY HOLZHERR EDITOR

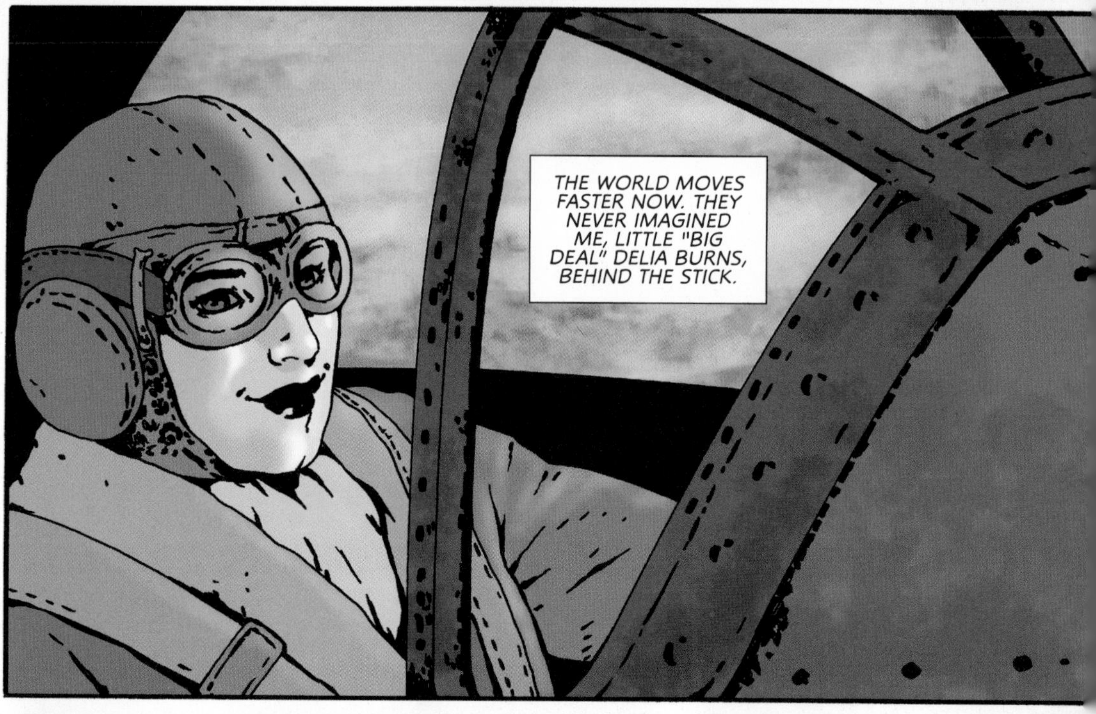
THE WORLD MOVES FASTER NOW. THEY NEVER IMAGINED ME, LITTLE "BIG DEAL" DELIA BURNS, BEHIND THE STICK.
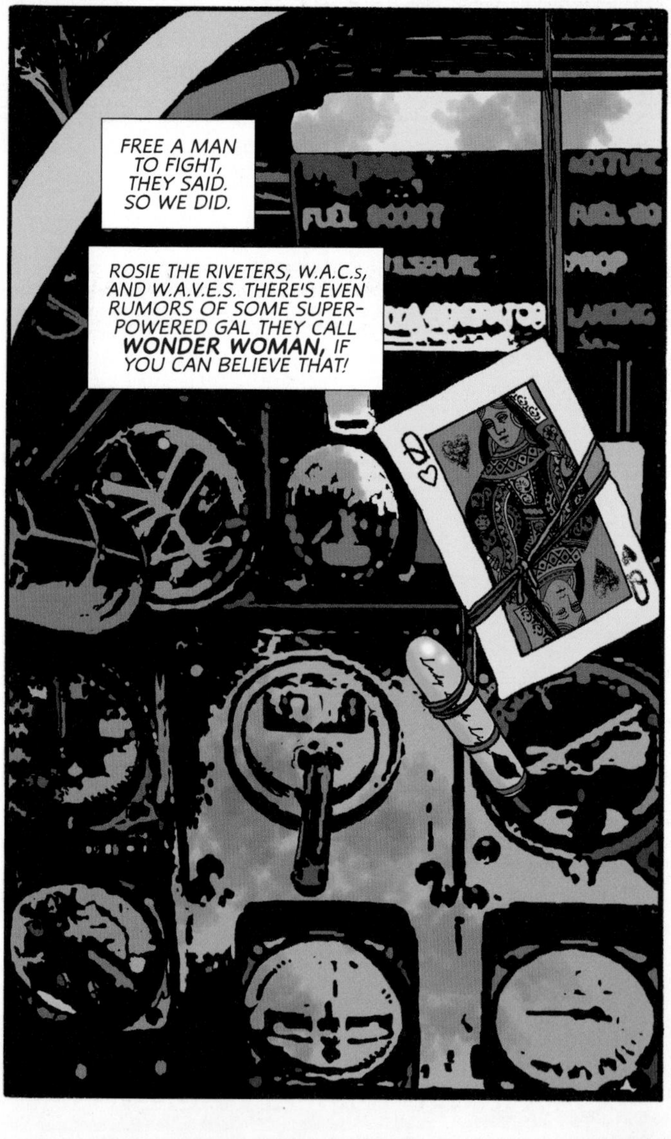
FREE A MAN TO FIGHT, THEY SAID. SO WE DID.
ROSIE THE RIVETERS, W.A.C.s, AND W.A.V.E.S. THERE'S EVEN RUMORS OF SOME SUPER-POWERED GAL THEY CALL **WONDER WOMAN,** IF YOU CAN BELIEVE THAT!
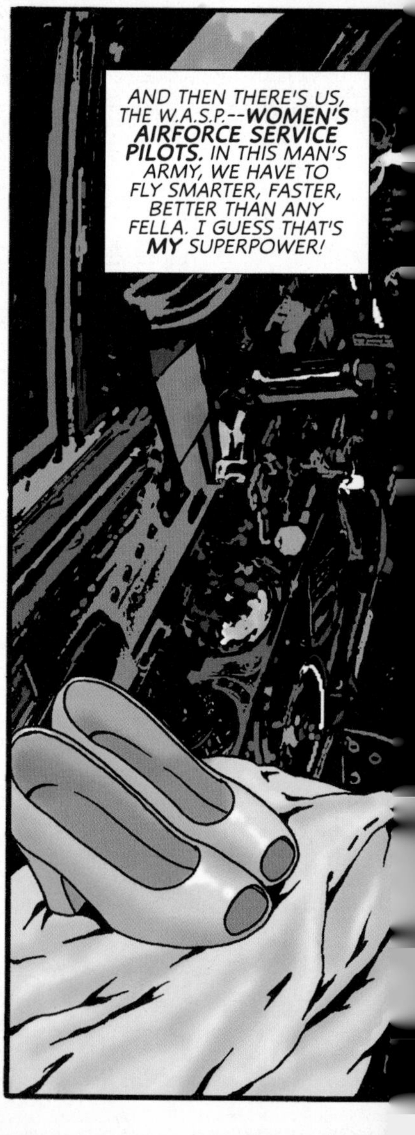
AND THEN THERE'S US, THE W.A.S.P.--**WOMEN'S AIRFORCE SERVICE PILOTS.** IN THIS MAN'S ARMY, WE HAVE TO FLY SMARTER, FASTER, BETTER THAN ANY FELLA. I GUESS THAT'S **MY** SUPERPOWER!

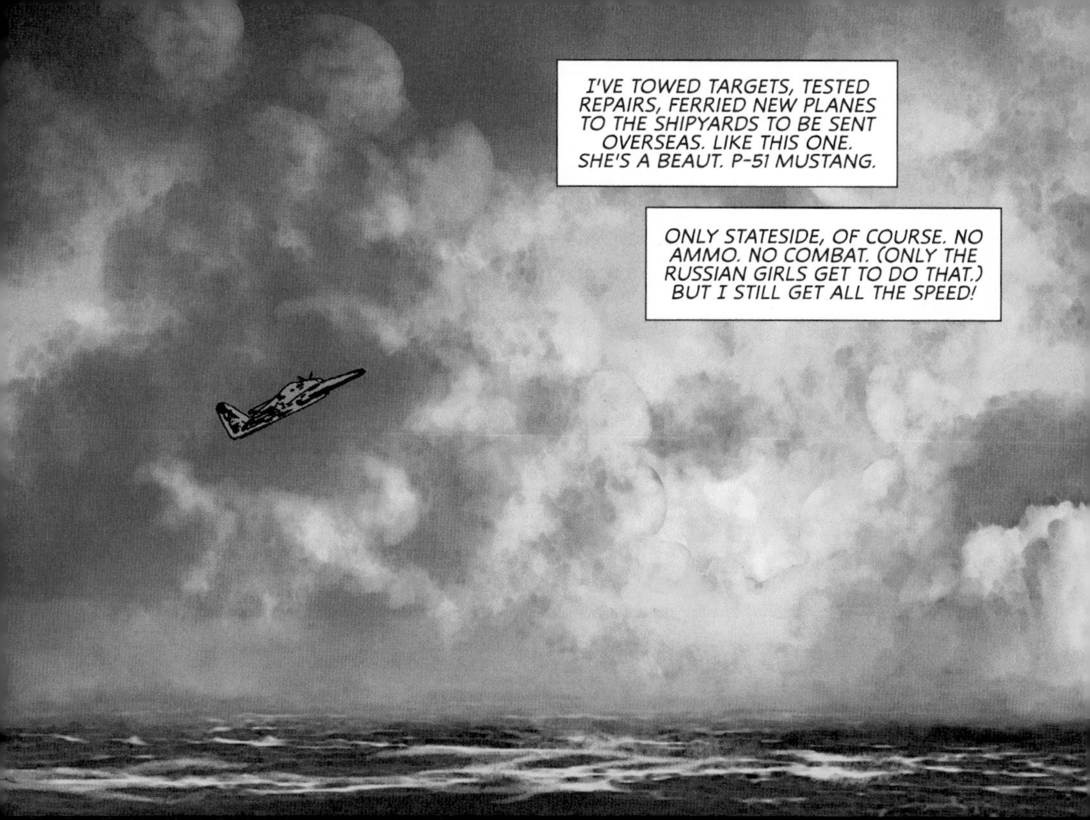
I'VE TOWED TARGETS, TESTED REPAIRS, FERRIED NEW PLANES TO THE SHIPYARDS TO BE SENT OVERSEAS. LIKE THIS ONE. SHE'S A BEAUT. P-51 MUSTANG.
ONLY STATESIDE, OF COURSE. NO AMMO. NO COMBAT. (ONLY THE RUSSIAN GIRLS GET TO DO THAT.) BUT I STILL GET ALL THE SPEED!

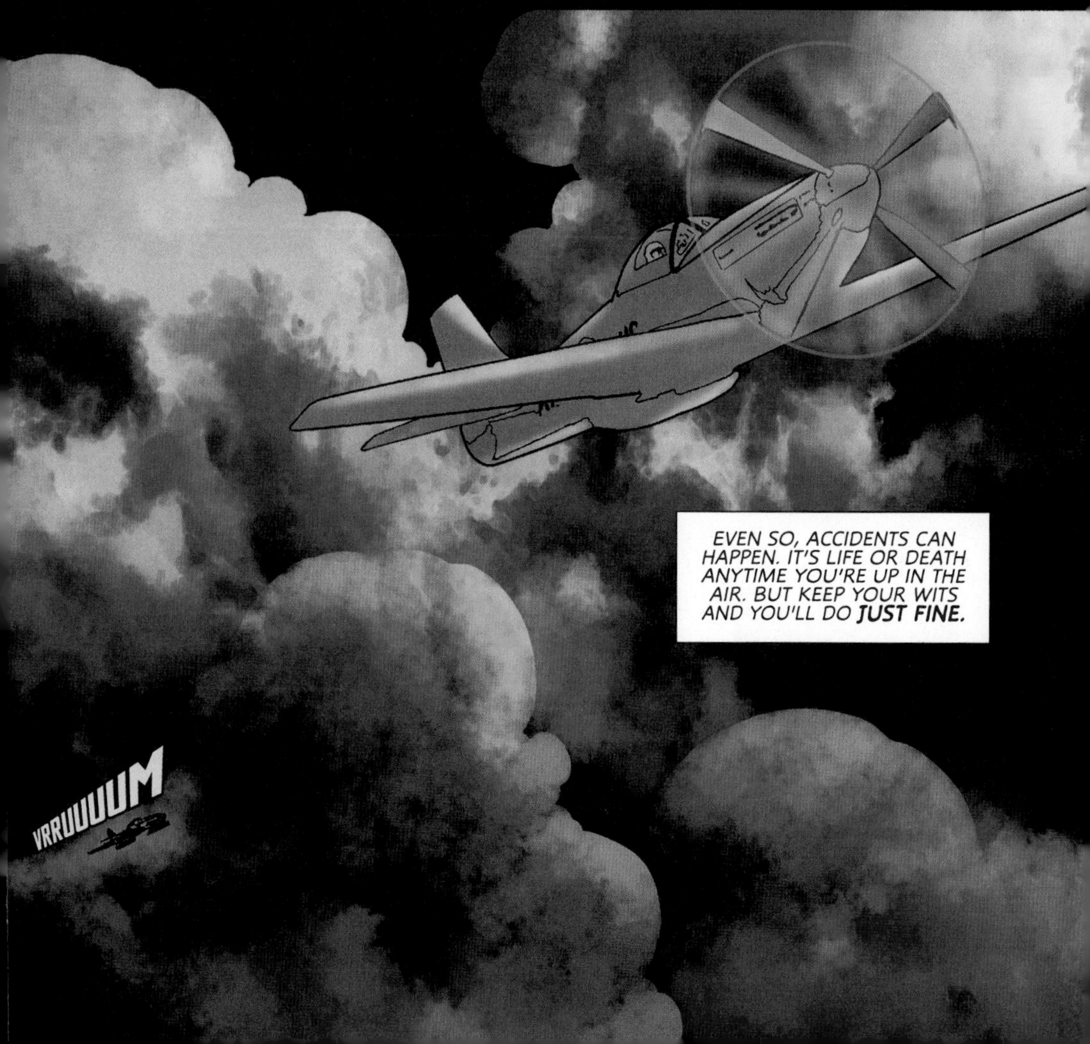
EVEN SO, ACCIDENTS CAN HAPPEN. IT'S LIFE OR DEATH ANYTIME YOU'RE UP IN THE AIR. BUT KEEP YOUR WITS AND YOU'LL DO **JUST FINE.**
VRRUUUUM

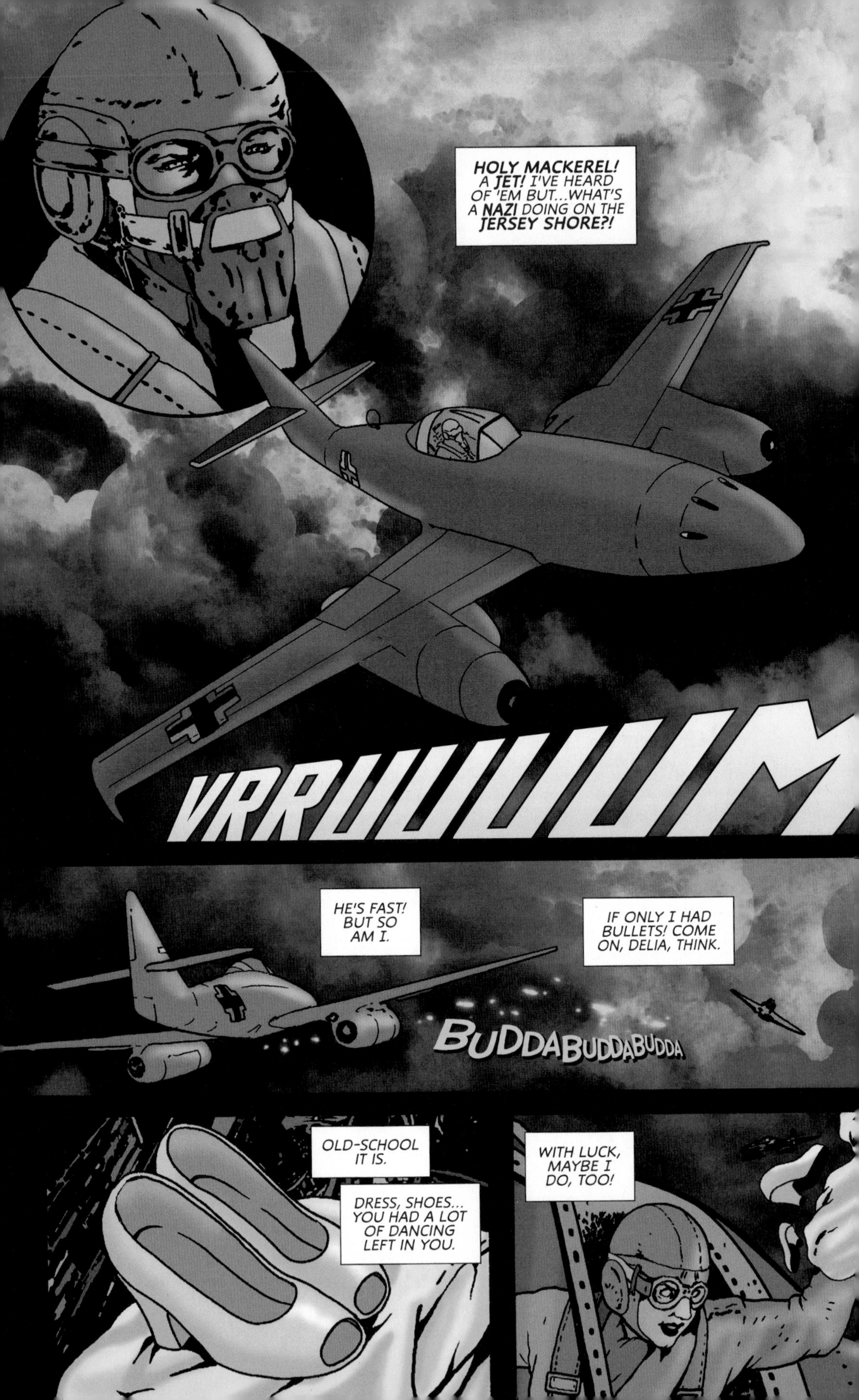
HOLY MACKEREL! A JET! I'VE HEARD OF 'EM BUT...WHAT'S A NAZI DOING ON THE JERSEY SHORE?!
VRRUUUUM
HE'S FAST! BUT SO AM I.
IF ONLY I HAD BULLETS! COME ON, DELIA, THINK.
BUDDABUDDABUDDA
OLD-SCHOOL IT IS.
DRESS, SHOES... YOU HAD A LOT OF DANCING LEFT IN YOU.
WITH LUCK, MAYBE I DO, TOO!

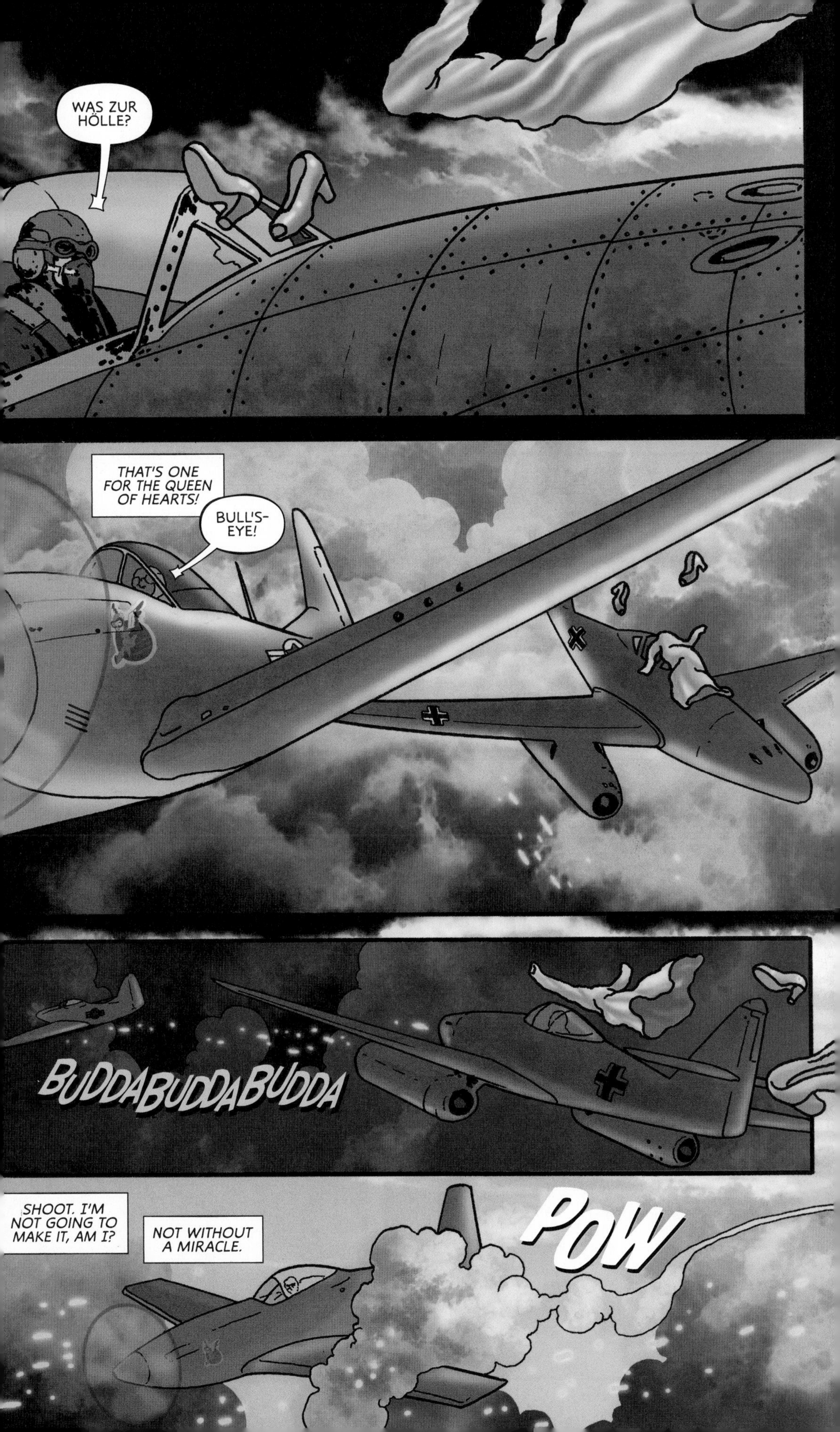
WAS ZUR HÖLLE?
THAT'S ONE FOR THE QUEEN OF HEARTS!
BULL'S-EYE!
BUDDABUDDABUDDA
SHOOT. I'M NOT GOING TO MAKE IT, AM I?
NOT WITHOUT A MIRACLE.
POW

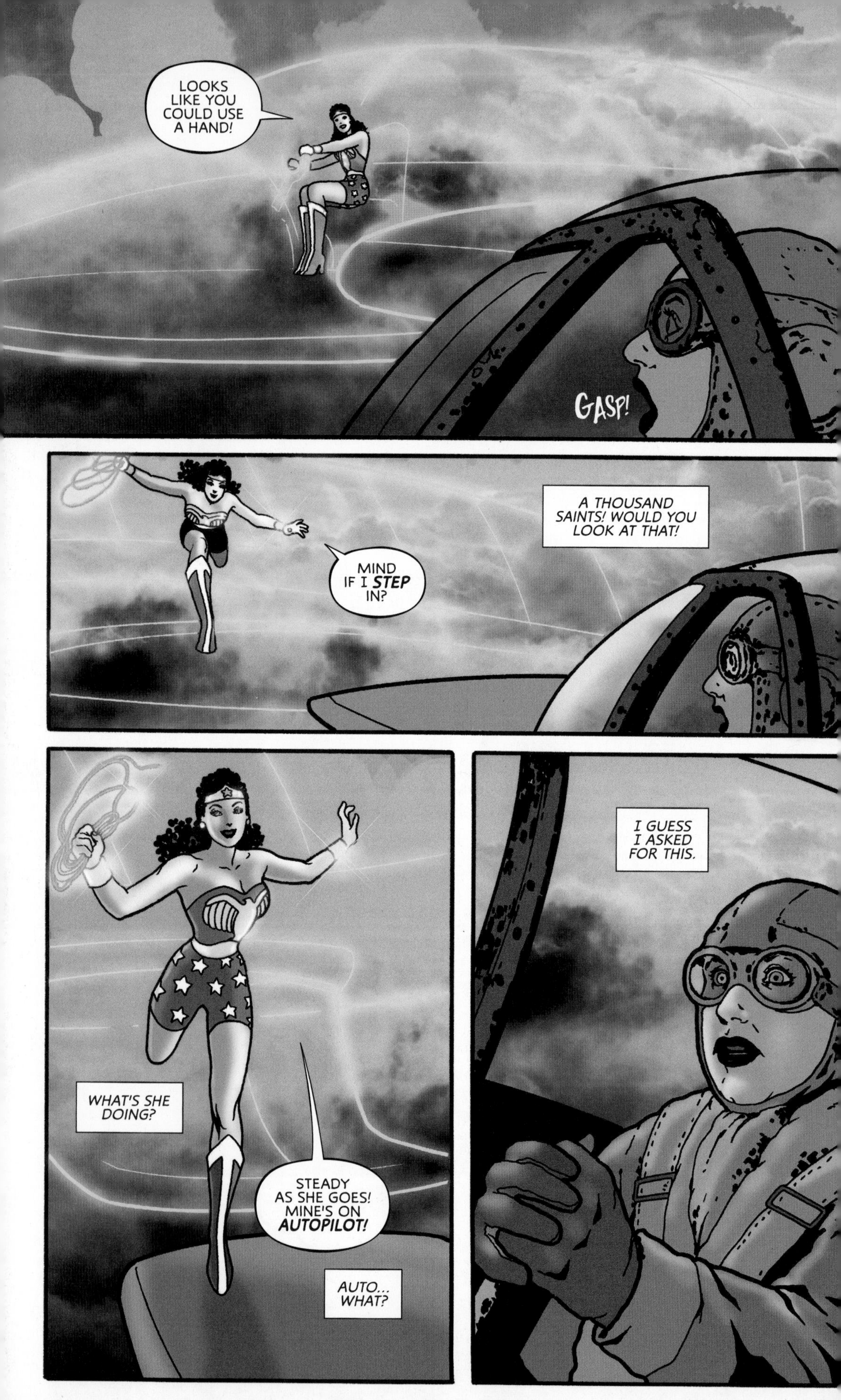
LOOKS LIKE YOU COULD USE A HAND!
GASP!
A THOUSAND SAINTS! WOULD YOU LOOK AT THAT!
MIND IF I STEP IN?
WHAT'S SHE DOING?
STEADY AS SHE GOES! MINE'S ON AUTOPILOT!
AUTO... WHAT?
I GUESS I ASKED FOR THIS.

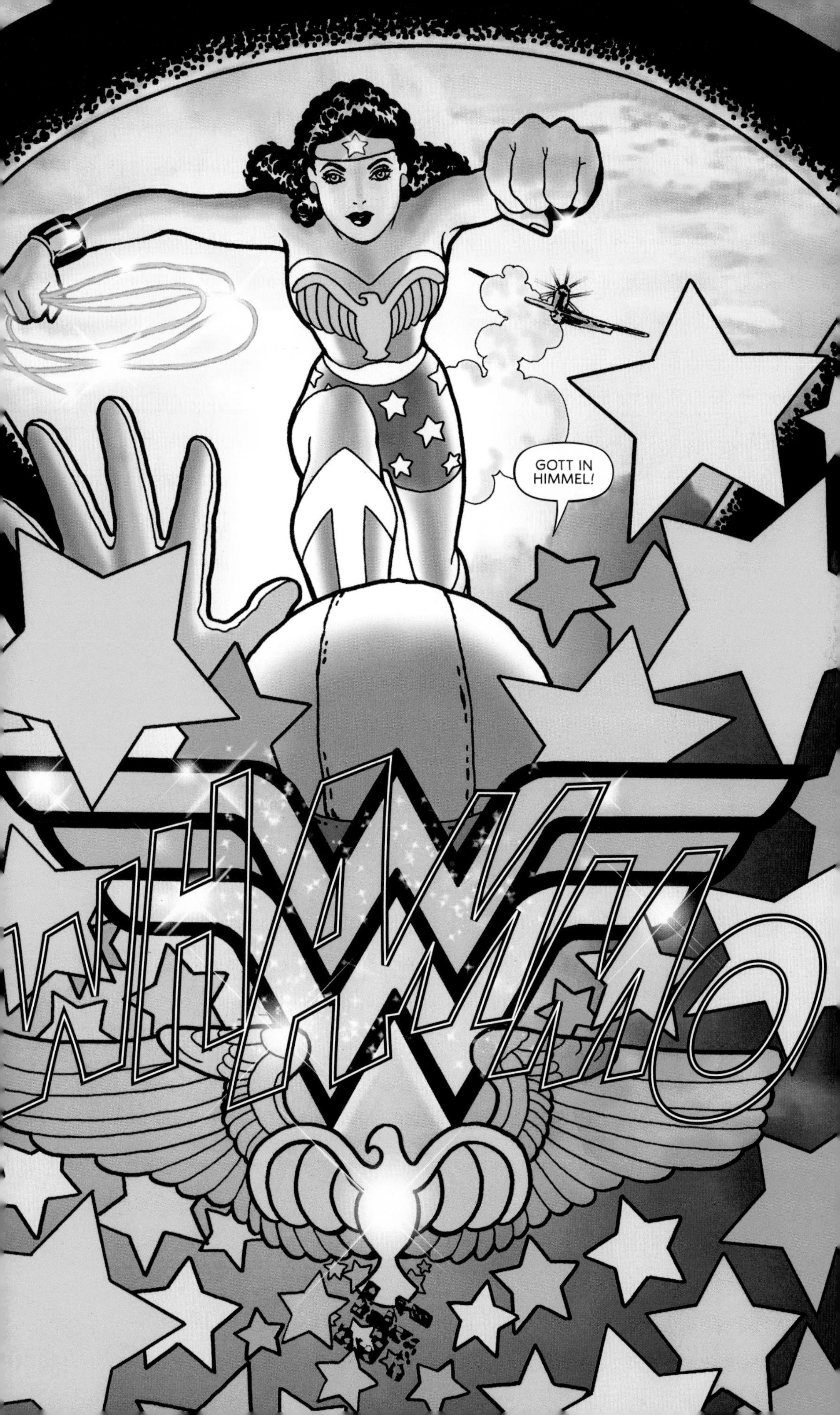
GOTT IN HIMMEL!

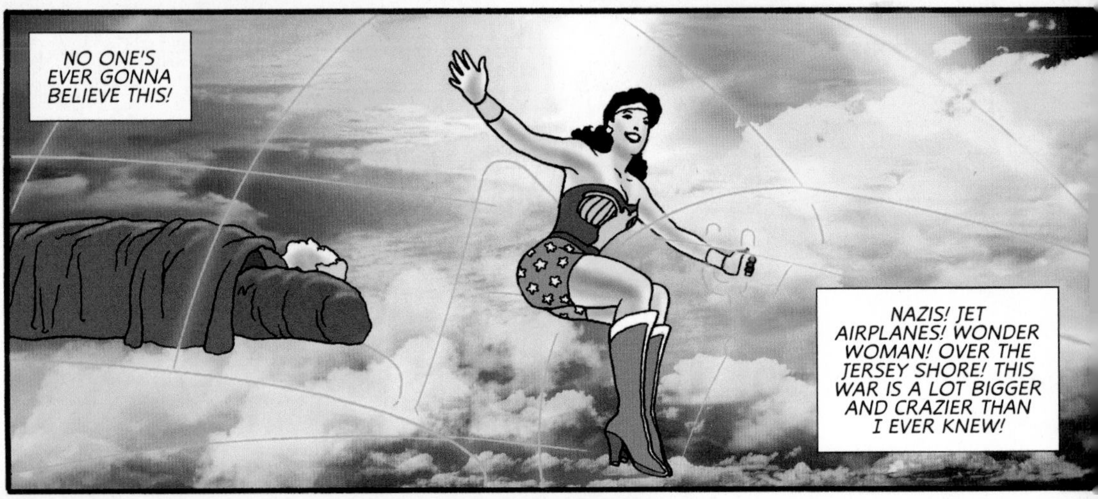
NO ONE'S EVER GONNA BELIEVE THIS!
NAZIS! JET AIRPLANES! WONDER WOMAN! OVER THE JERSEY SHORE! THIS WAR IS A LOT BIGGER AND CRAZIER THAN I EVER KNEW!

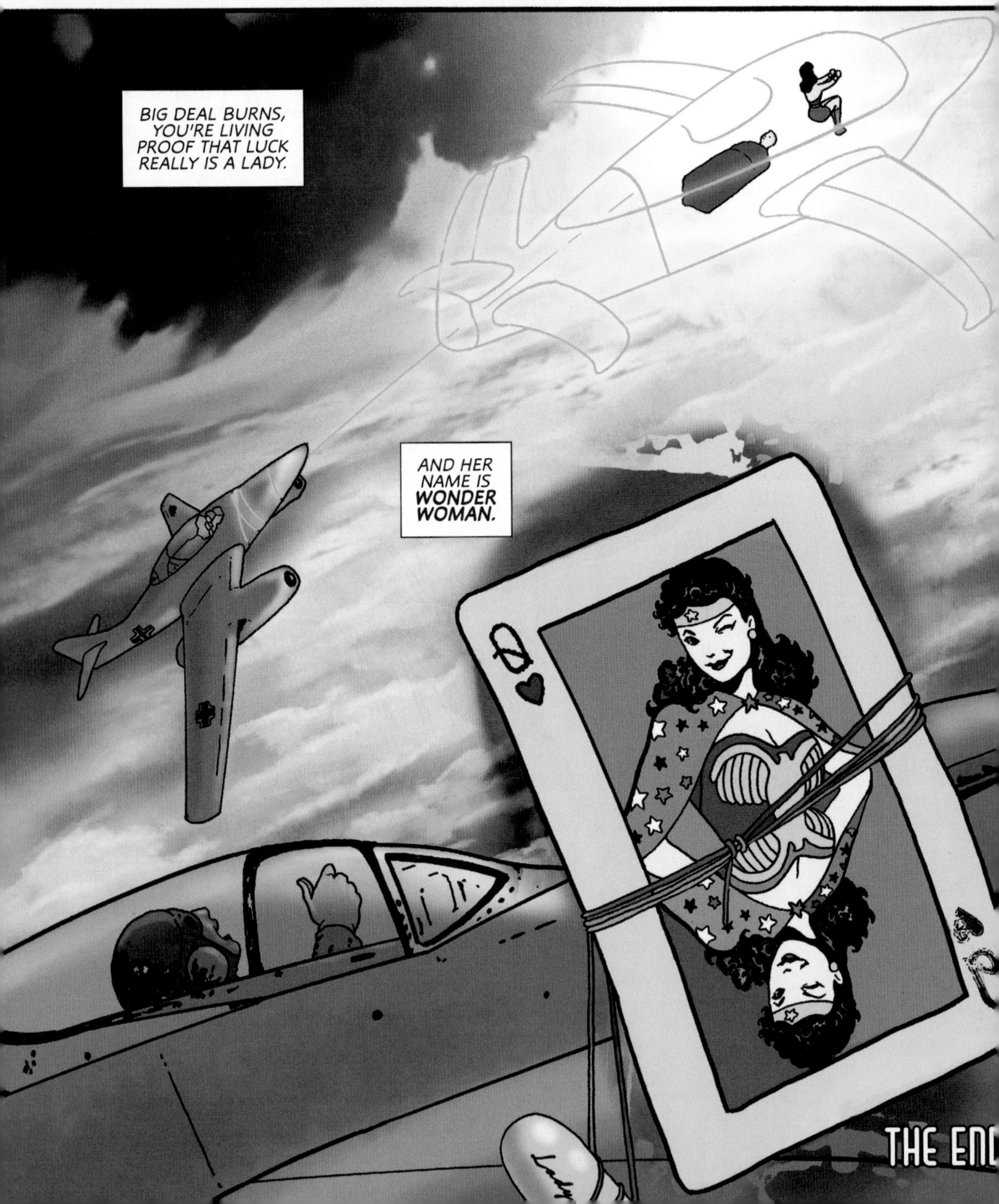
BIG DEAL BURNS, YOU'RE LIVING PROOF THAT LUCK REALLY IS A LADY.
AND HER NAME IS **WONDER WOMAN.**
THE END

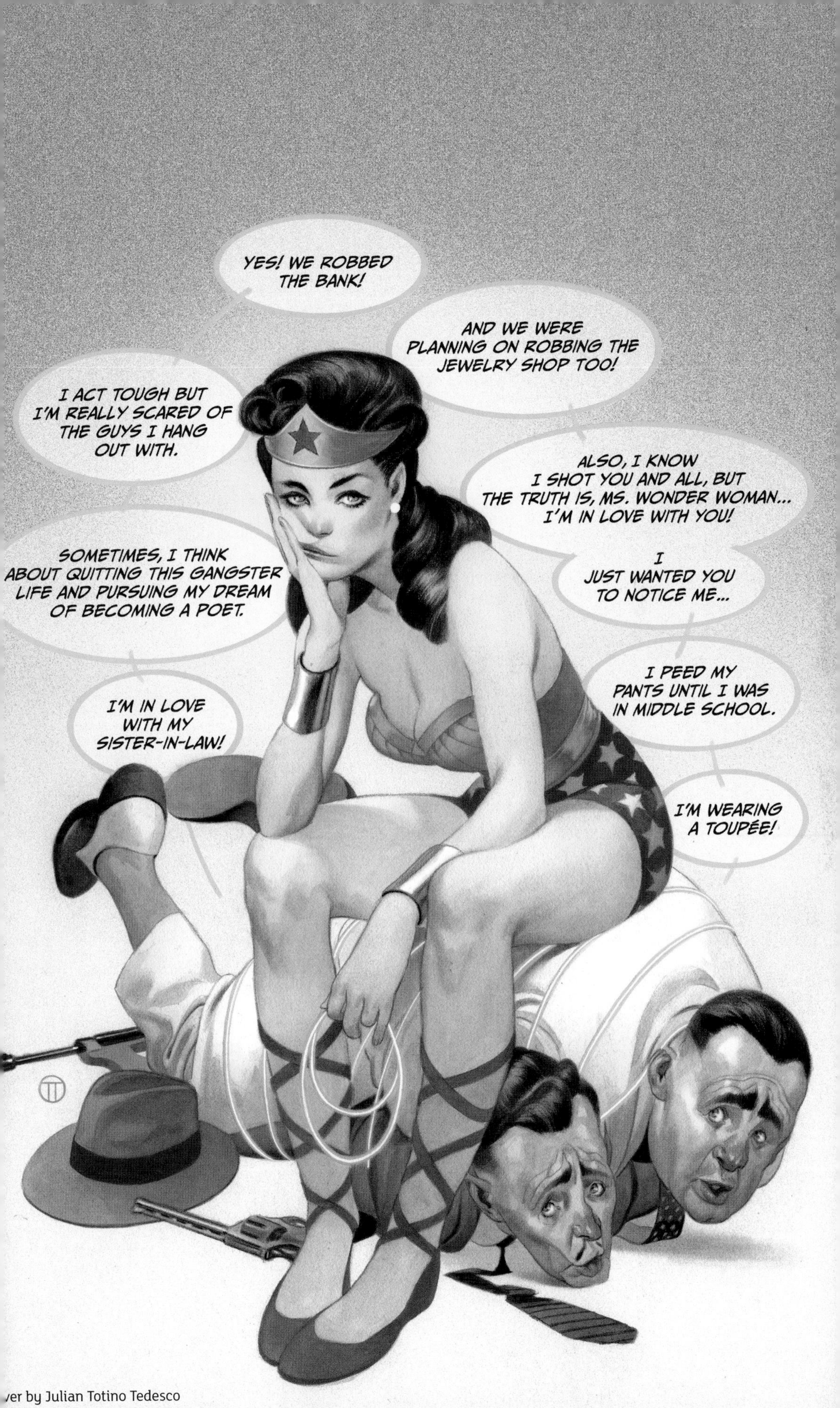
YES! WE ROBBED THE BANK!
AND WE WERE PLANNING ON ROBBING THE JEWELRY SHOP TOO!
I ACT TOUGH BUT I'M REALLY SCARED OF THE GUYS I HANG OUT WITH.
ALSO, I KNOW I SHOT YOU AND ALL, BUT THE TRUTH IS, MS. WONDER WOMAN... I'M IN LOVE WITH YOU!
SOMETIMES, I THINK ABOUT QUITTING THIS GANGSTER LIFE AND PURSUING MY DREAM OF BECOMING A POET.
I JUST WANTED YOU TO NOTICE ME...
I'M IN LOVE WITH MY SISTER-IN-LAW!
I PEED MY PANTS UNTIL I WAS IN MIDDLE SCHOOL.
I'M WEARING A TOUPÉE!

ver by Julian Totino Tedesco

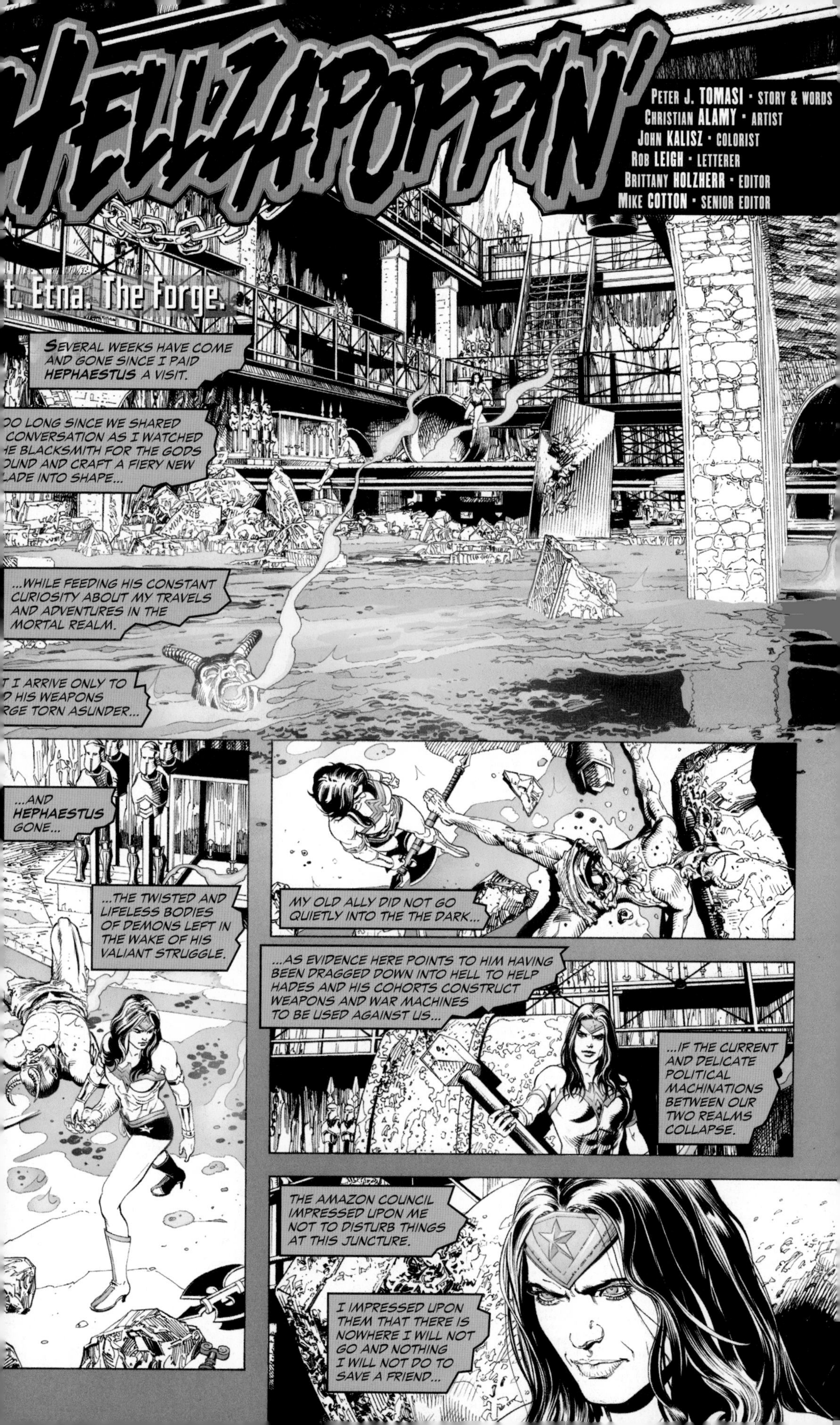
HELLZAPOPPIN'
PETER J. TOMASI · STORY & WORDS
CHRISTIAN ALAMY · ARTIST
JOHN KALISZ · COLORIST
ROB LEIGH · LETTERER
BRITTANY HOLZHERR · EDITOR
MIKE COTTON · SENIOR EDITOR
t. Etna. The Forge.
SEVERAL WEEKS HAVE COME AND GONE SINCE I PAID HEPHAESTUS A VISIT.
OO LONG SINCE WE SHARED CONVERSATION AS I WATCHED HE BLACKSMITH FOR THE GODS OUND AND CRAFT A FIERY NEW LADE INTO SHAPE...
...WHILE FEEDING HIS CONSTANT CURIOSITY ABOUT MY TRAVELS AND ADVENTURES IN THE MORTAL REALM.
T I ARRIVE ONLY TO D HIS WEAPONS RGE TORN ASUNDER...
...AND HEPHAESTUS GONE...
...THE TWISTED AND LIFELESS BODIES OF DEMONS LEFT IN THE WAKE OF HIS VALIANT STRUGGLE.
MY OLD ALLY DID NOT GO QUIETLY INTO THE THE DARK...
...AS EVIDENCE HERE POINTS TO HIM HAVING BEEN DRAGGED DOWN INTO HELL TO HELP HADES AND HIS COHORTS CONSTRUCT WEAPONS AND WAR MACHINES TO BE USED AGAINST US...
...IF THE CURRENT AND DELICATE POLITICAL MACHINATIONS BETWEEN OUR TWO REALMS COLLAPSE.
THE AMAZON COUNCIL IMPRESSED UPON ME NOT TO DISTURB THINGS AT THIS JUNCTURE.
I IMPRESSED UPON THEM THAT THERE IS NOWHERE I WILL NOT GO AND NOTHING I WILL NOT DO TO SAVE A FRIEND...

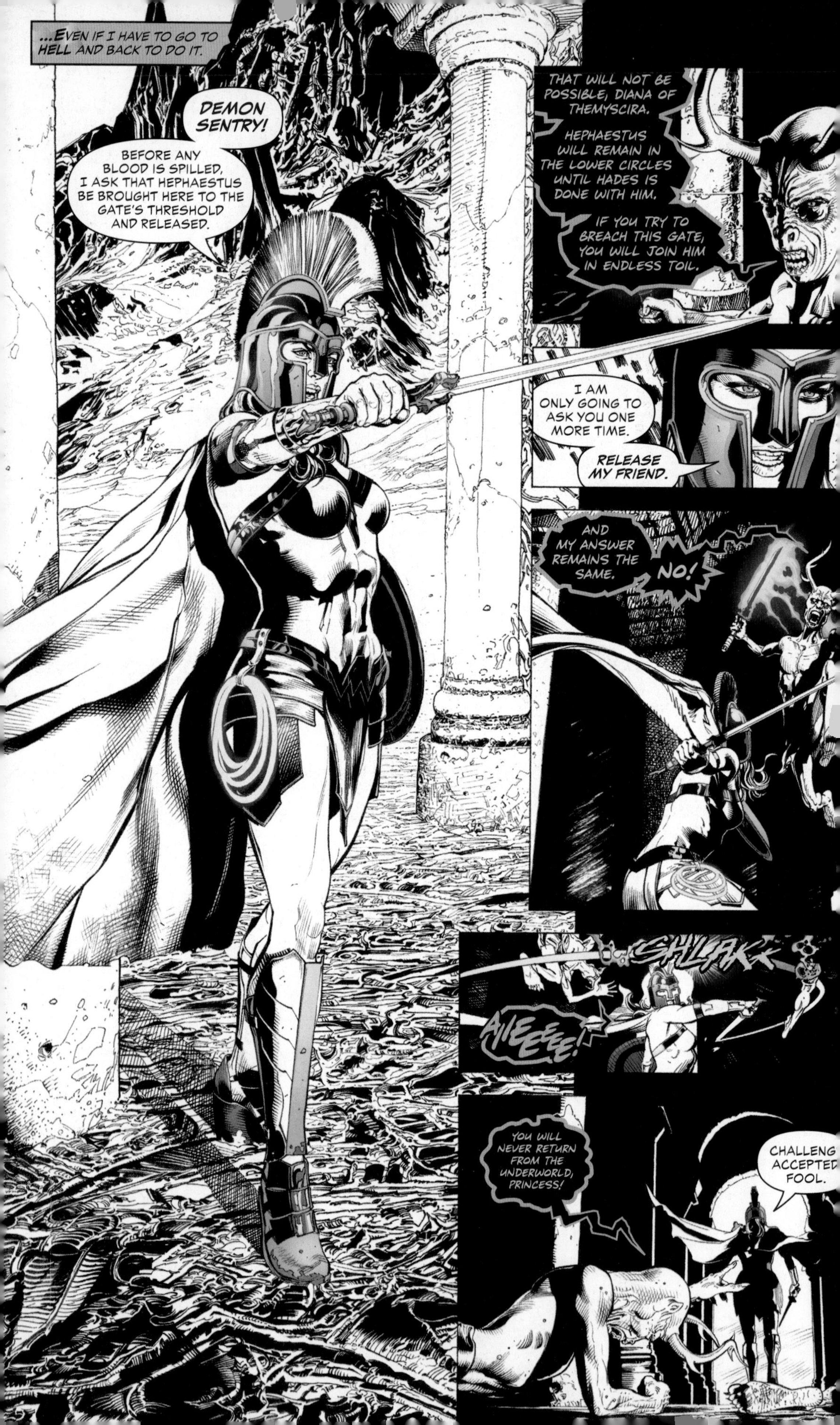
...EVEN IF I HAVE TO GO TO HELL AND BACK TO DO IT.
DEMON SENTRY!
BEFORE ANY BLOOD IS SPILLED, I ASK THAT HEPHAESTUS BE BROUGHT HERE TO THE GATE'S THRESHOLD AND RELEASED.
THAT WILL NOT BE POSSIBLE, DIANA OF THEMYSCIRA.
HEPHAESTUS WILL REMAIN IN THE LOWER CIRCLES UNTIL HADES IS DONE WITH HIM.
IF YOU TRY TO BREACH THIS GATE, YOU WILL JOIN HIM IN ENDLESS TOIL.
I AM ONLY GOING TO ASK YOU ONE MORE TIME.
RELEASE MY FRIEND.
AND MY ANSWER REMAINS THE SAME.
NO!
SHLAKK
AIIEEEEE!
YOU WILL NEVER RETURN FROM THE UNDERWORLD, PRINCESS!
CHALLENG ACCEPTED FOOL.

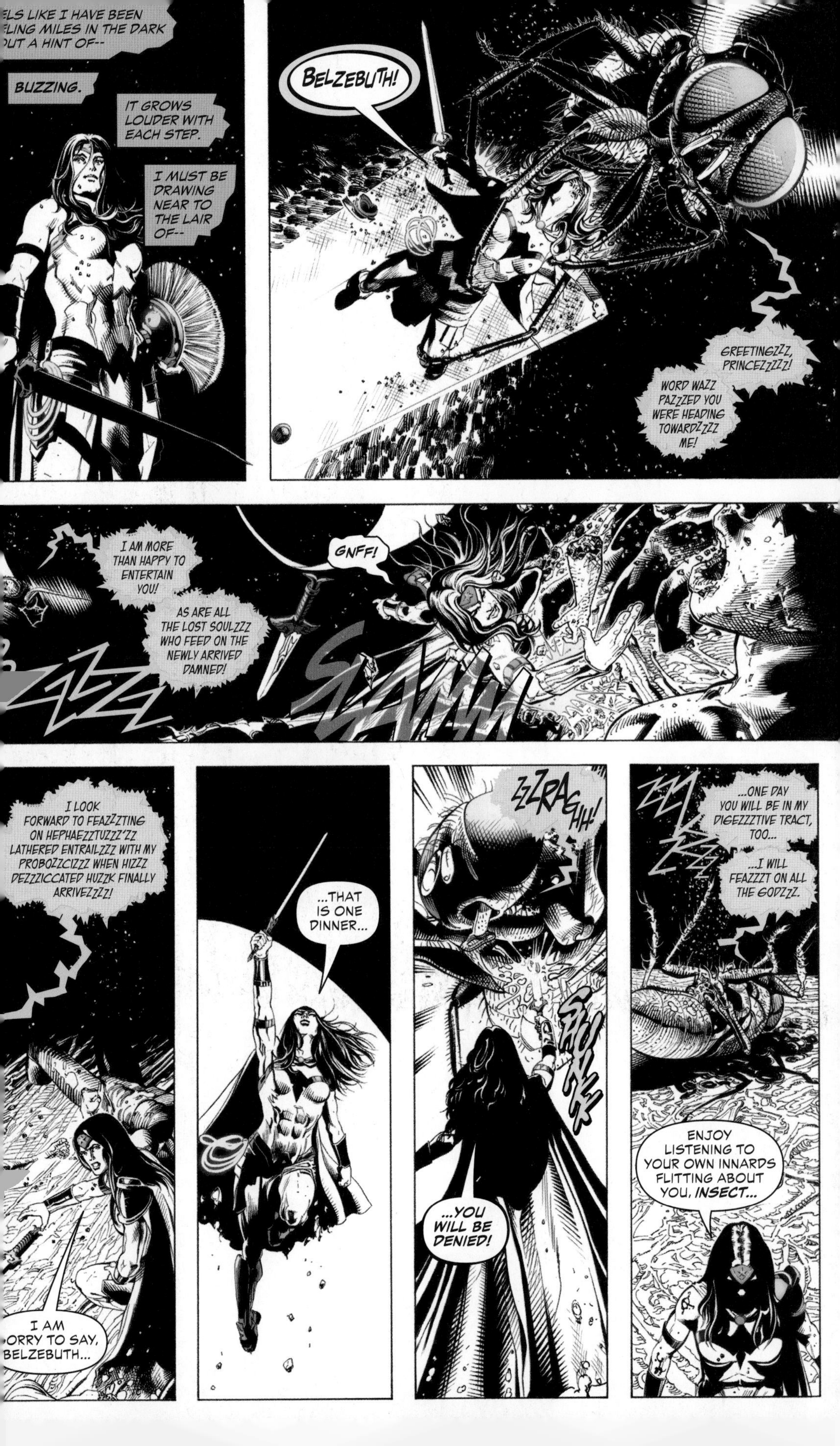

ELS LIKE I HAVE BEEN
ELING MILES IN THE DARK
OUT A HINT OF--
BUZZING.
IT GROWS LOUDER WITH EACH STEP.
I MUST BE DRAWING NEAR TO THE LAIR OF--
BELZEBUTH!
GREETINGZZZ, PRINCEZZZZZ!
WORD WAZZ PAZZZED YOU WERE HEADING TOWARDZZZZ ME!
I AM MORE THAN HAPPY TO ENTERTAIN YOU!
AS ARE ALL THE LOST SOULZZZ WHO FEED ON THE NEWLY ARRIVED DAMNED!
GNFF!
ZZZZZ
SLAMM
I LOOK FORWARD TO FEAZZZTING ON HEPHAEZZTUZZZ'ZZ LATHERED ENTRAILZZZ WITH MY PROBOZZCIZZZ WHEN HIZZZ DEZZZICCATED HUZZK FINALLY ARRIVEZZZZ!
I AM
ORRY TO SAY,
BELZEBUTH...
...THAT IS ONE DINNER...
ZZZRAGHH!
...YOU WILL BE DENIED!
SHUNK
...ONE DAY YOU WILL BE IN MY DIGEZZZTIVE TRACT, TOO...
...I WILL FEAZZZT ON ALL THE GODZZZ.
ENJOY LISTENING TO YOUR OWN INNARDS FLITTING ABOUT YOU, INSECT...

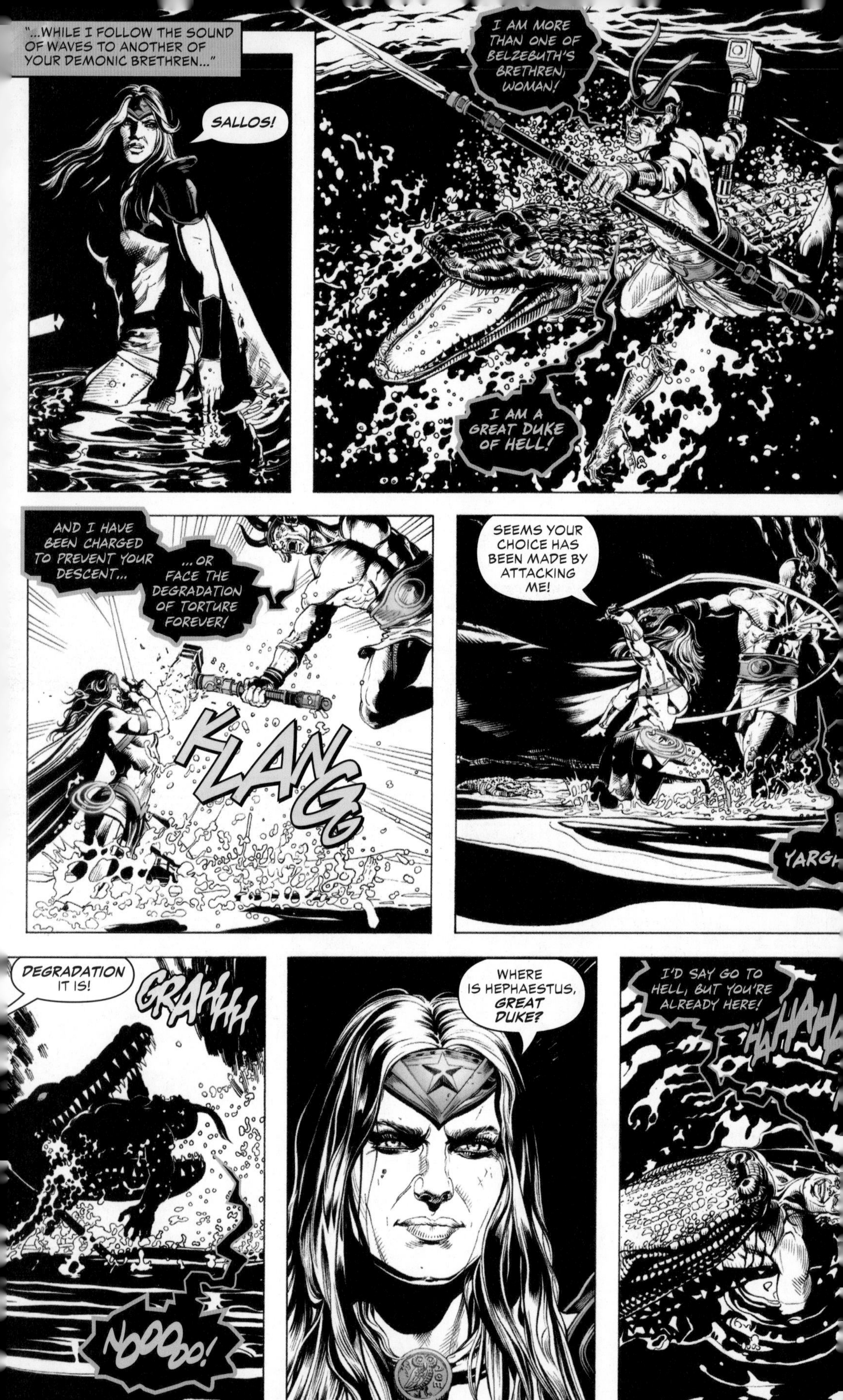
"...WHILE I FOLLOW THE SOUND OF WAVES TO ANOTHER OF YOUR DEMONIC BRETHREN..."
SALLOS!
I AM MORE THAN ONE OF BELZEBUTH'S BRETHREN, WOMAN!
I AM A GREAT DUKE OF HELL!
AND I HAVE BEEN CHARGED TO PREVENT YOUR DESCENT...
...OR FACE THE DEGRADATION OF TORTURE FOREVER!
KLANGG
SEEMS YOUR CHOICE HAS BEEN MADE BY ATTACKING ME!
YARGH
DEGRADATION IT IS!
GRAHHH
NOOOoo!
WHERE IS HEPHAESTUS, GREAT DUKE?
I'D SAY GO TO HELL, BUT YOU'RE ALREADY HERE!
HAHAHA

...RIES AND SCREAMS FOR ...LP BURN MY EARS AS ...MAKE MY WAY THROUGH ...E DARK DEN OF ...RBORYM.

THESE PITIFUL SOULS ASK ME TO SAVE THEM, BUT ALL I CAN DO IS REMIND THEM THAT THEIR DECISIONS IN LIFE LED THEM TO THIS HOPELESS PLACE...

SHRAKK!

...AND THAT THEY ARE CURSED AND FOREVER DEAD.

SO SORRY YOU DON'T DELIGHT IN THE MUSIC OF PAIN YET, DIANA!

BUT ONCE YOU AND HEPHAESTUS JOIN ME...

...EVEN HADES WILL REJOICE IN LISTENING TO OUR CHOIR OF CACOPHONY!

HOW DARE YOU WRAP ME IN YOUR VILE TOUCH!

THE ONLY SONGS YOU WILL BE SINGING, HARBORYM...

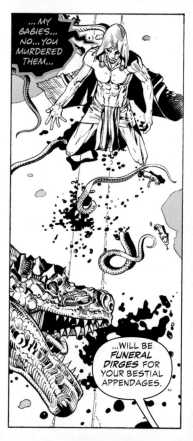

...MY BABIES... NO...YOU MURDERED THEM...

...WILL BE FUNERAL DIRGES FOR YOUR BESTIAL APPENDAGES.

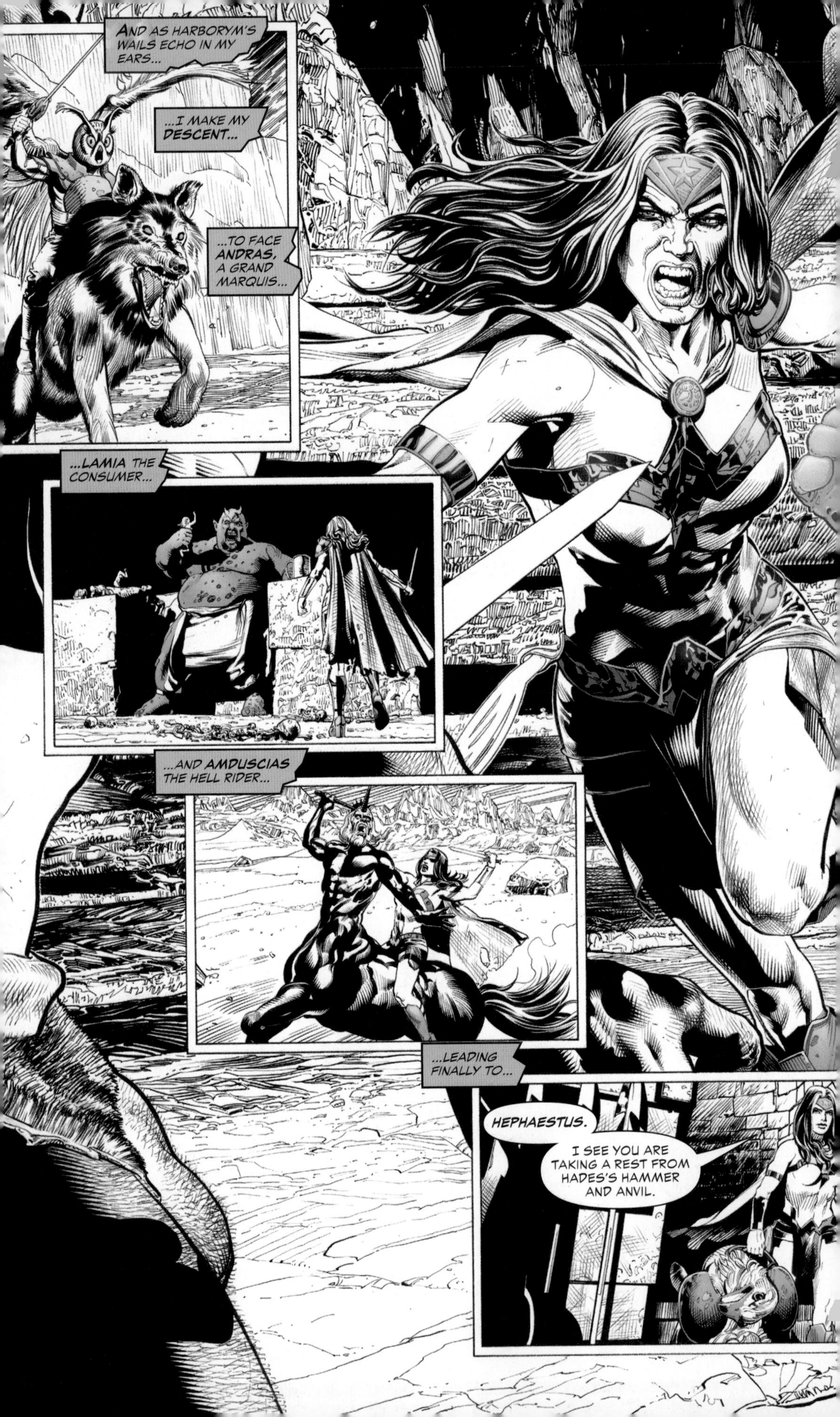
AND AS HARBORYM'S WAILS ECHO IN MY EARS...
...I MAKE MY DESCENT...
...TO FACE ANDRAS, A GRAND MARQUIS...
...LAMIA THE CONSUMER...
...AND AMDUSCIAS THE HELL RIDER...
...LEADING FINALLY TO...
HEPHAESTUS.
I SEE YOU ARE TAKING A REST FROM HADES'S HAMMER AND ANVIL.

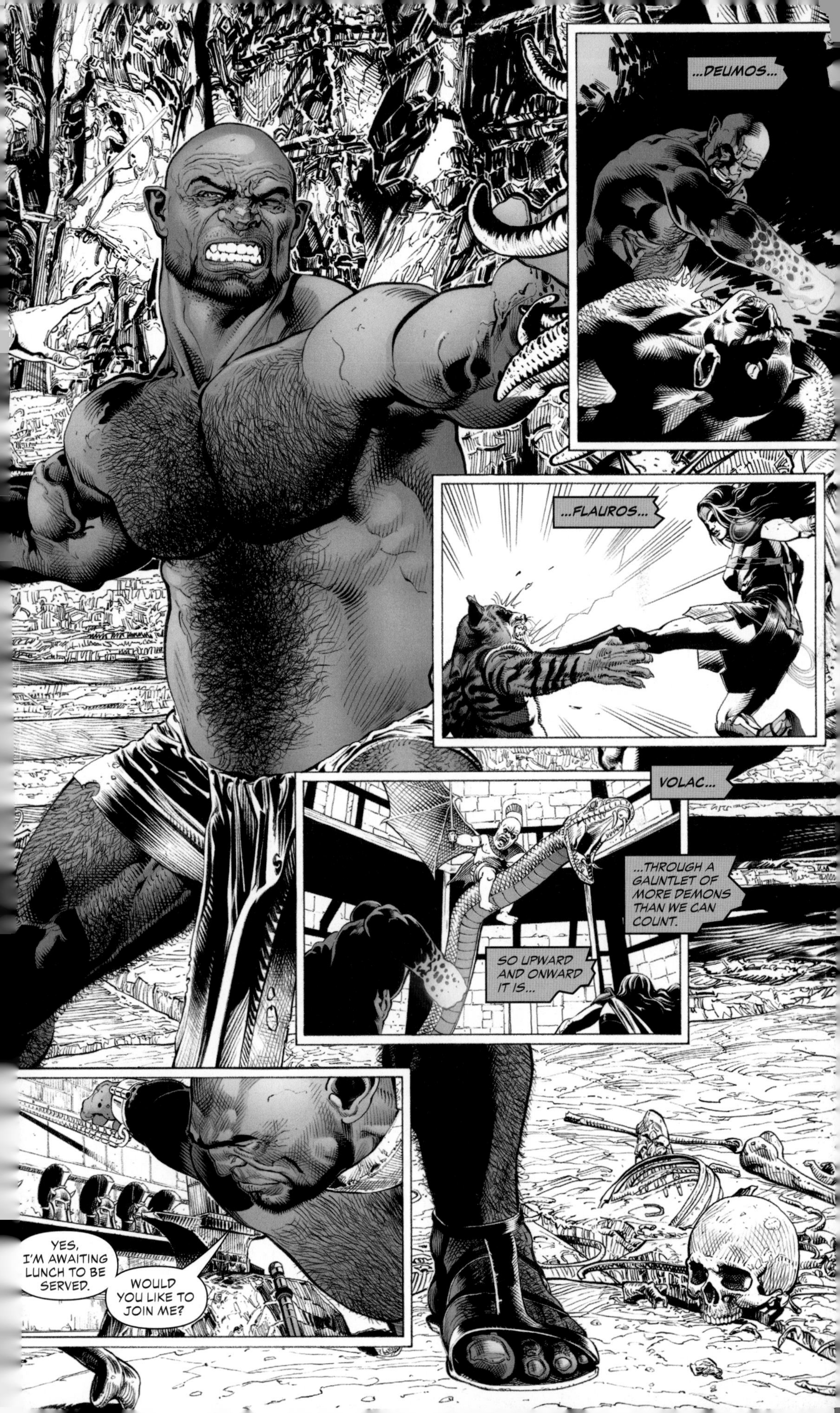
...DEUMOS...
...FLAUROS...
VOLAC...
...THROUGH A GAUNTLET OF MORE DEMONS THAN WE CAN COUNT.
SO UPWARD AND ONWARD IT IS...
YES, I'M AWAITING LUNCH TO BE SERVED.
WOULD YOU LIKE TO JOIN ME?

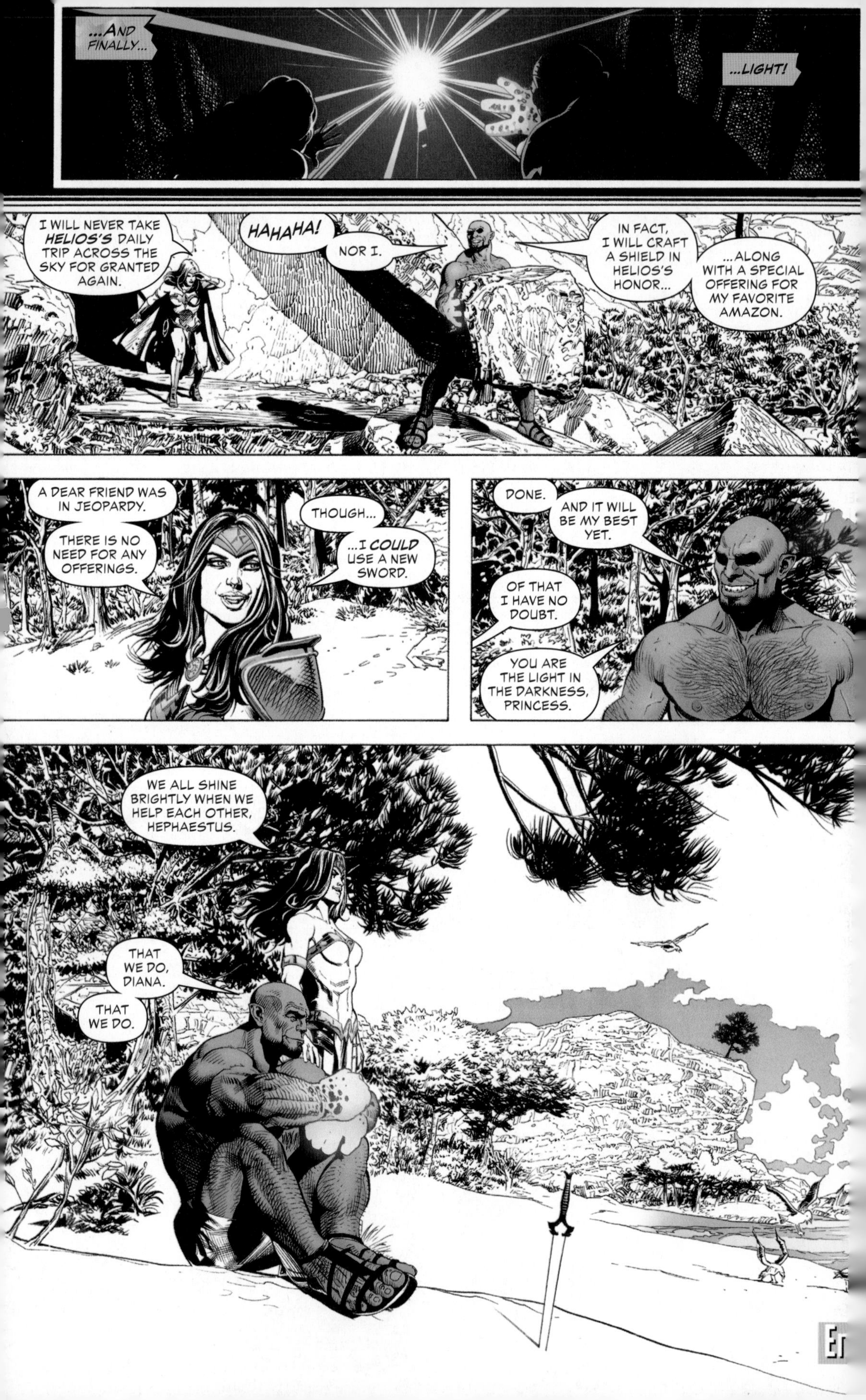
...AND FINALLY...
...LIGHT!
I WILL NEVER TAKE HELIOS'S DAILY TRIP ACROSS THE SKY FOR GRANTED AGAIN.
HAHAHA!
NOR I.
IN FACT, I WILL CRAFT A SHIELD IN HELIOS'S HONOR...
...ALONG WITH A SPECIAL OFFERING FOR MY FAVORITE AMAZON.
A DEAR FRIEND WAS IN JEOPARDY.
THERE IS NO NEED FOR ANY OFFERINGS.
THOUGH...
...I COULD USE A NEW SWORD.
DONE.
AND IT WILL BE MY BEST YET.
OF THAT I HAVE NO DOUBT.
YOU ARE THE LIGHT IN THE DARKNESS, PRINCESS.
WE ALL SHINE BRIGHTLY WHEN WE HELP EACH OTHER, HEPHAESTUS.
THAT WE DO, DIANA.
THAT WE DO.

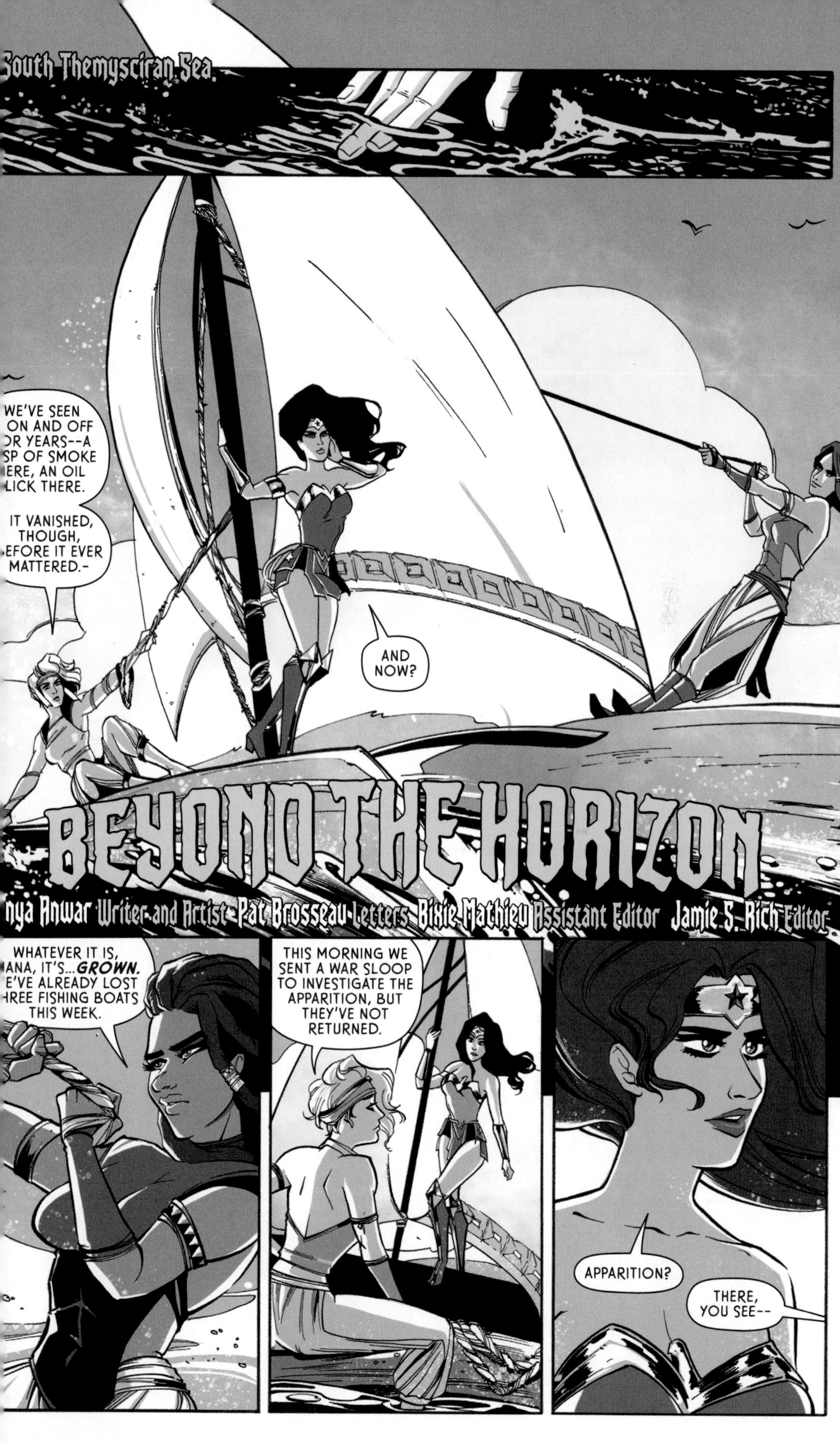
South Themysciran Sea.
WE'VE SEEN ON AND OFF OR YEARS--A SP OF SMOKE ERE, AN OIL LICK THERE.
IT VANISHED, THOUGH, EFORE IT EVER MATTERED.-
AND NOW?
BEYOND THE HORIZON
nya Anwar Writer and Artist Pat Brosseau Letters Bixie Mathieu Assistant Editor Jamie S. Rich Editor
WHATEVER IT IS, ANA, IT'S...GROWN. E'VE ALREADY LOST HREE FISHING BOATS THIS WEEK.
THIS MORNING WE SENT A WAR SLOOP TO INVESTIGATE THE APPARITION, BUT THEY'VE NOT RETURNED.
APPARITION?
THERE, YOU SEE--

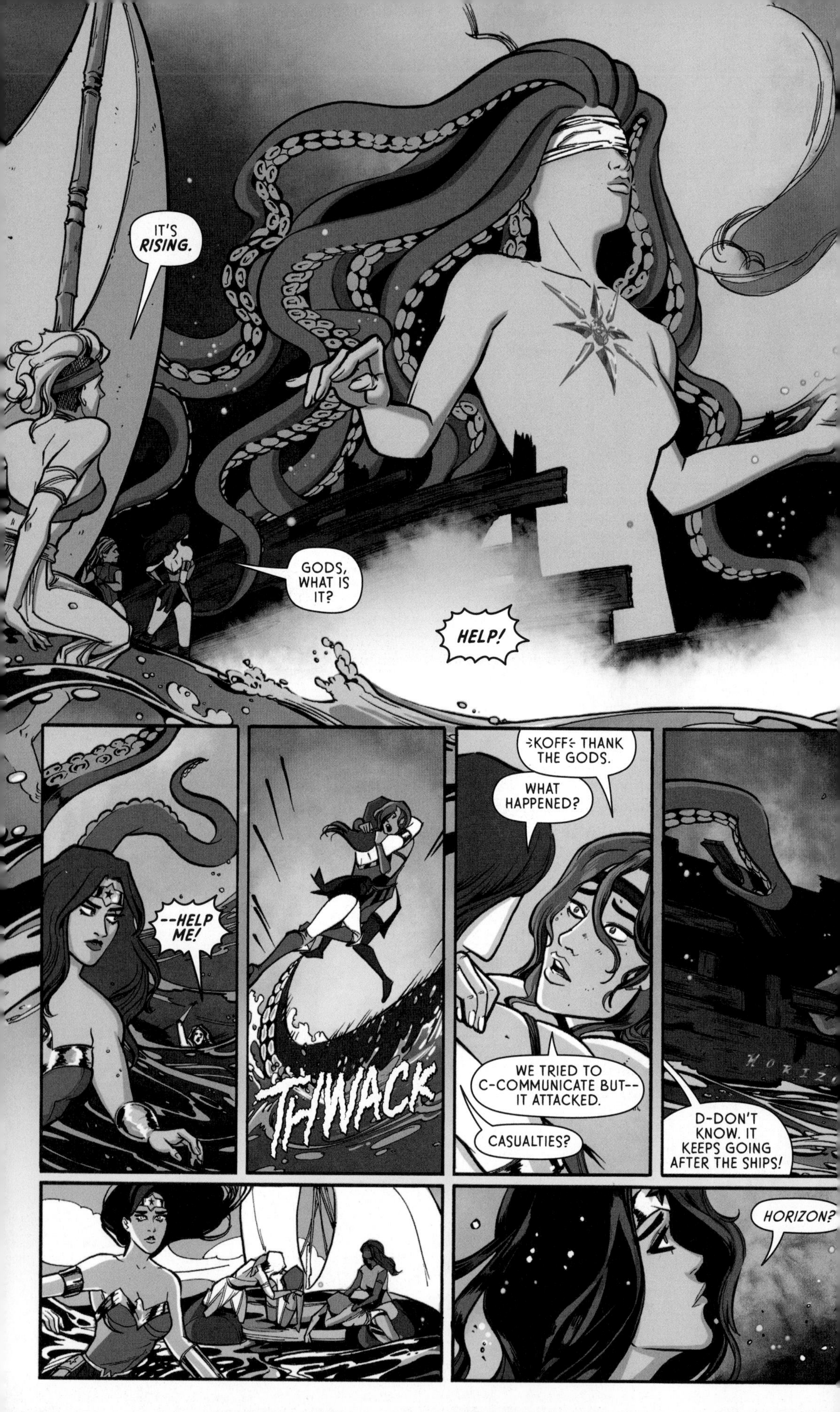

IT'S *RISING.*
GODS, WHAT IS IT?
HELP!
--HELP ME!
THWACK
-KOFF- THANK THE GODS.
WHAT HAPPENED?
WE TRIED TO C-COMMUNICATE BUT-- IT ATTACKED.
CASUALTIES?
D-DON'T KNOW. IT KEEPS GOING AFTER THE SHIPS!
HORIZON?

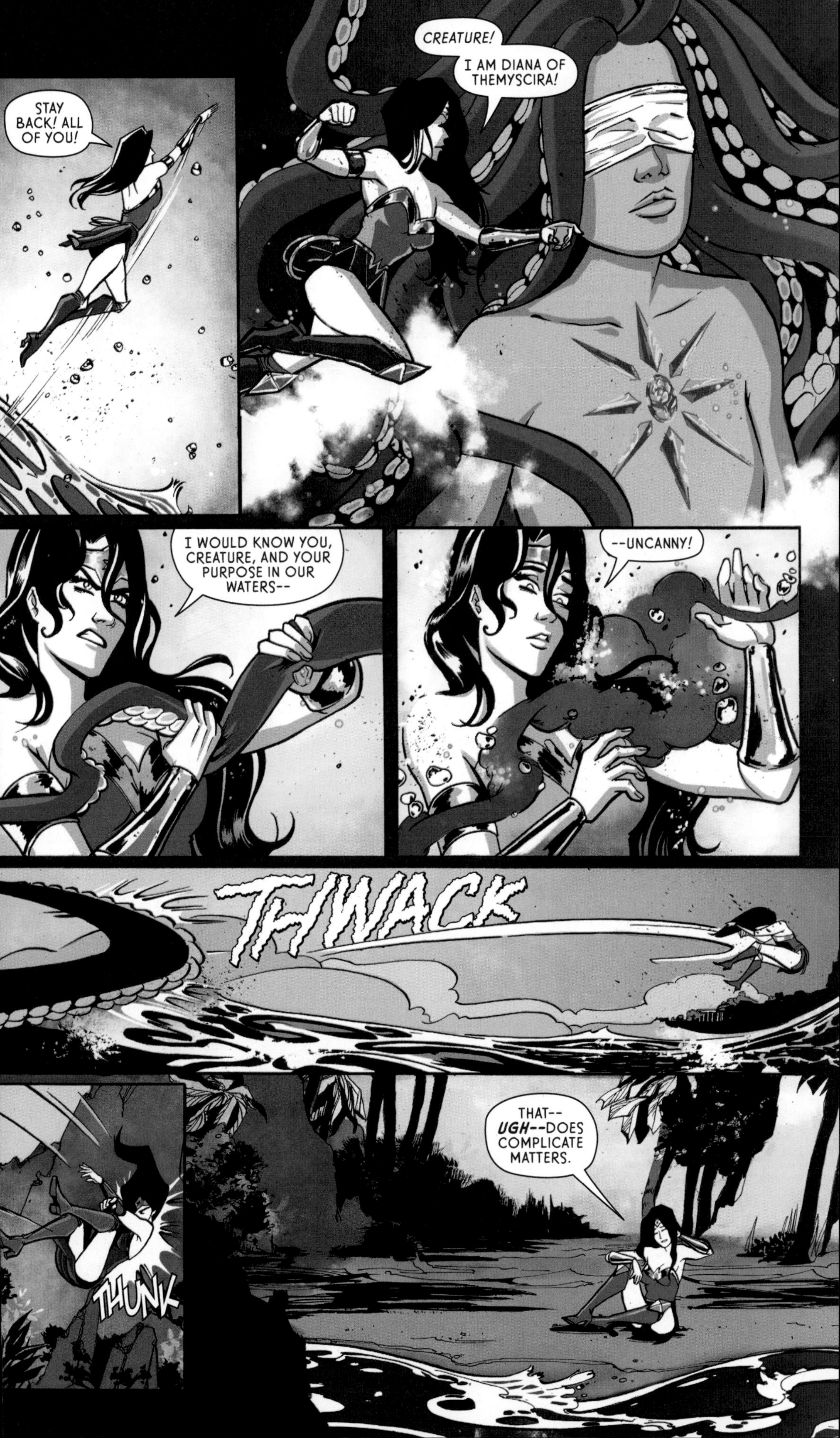
STAY BACK! ALL OF YOU!
CREATURE!
I AM DIANA OF THEMYSCIRA!
I WOULD KNOW YOU, CREATURE, AND YOUR PURPOSE IN OUR WATERS--
--UNCANNY!
THWACK
THUNK
THAT-- *UGH*--DOES COMPLICATE MATTERS.

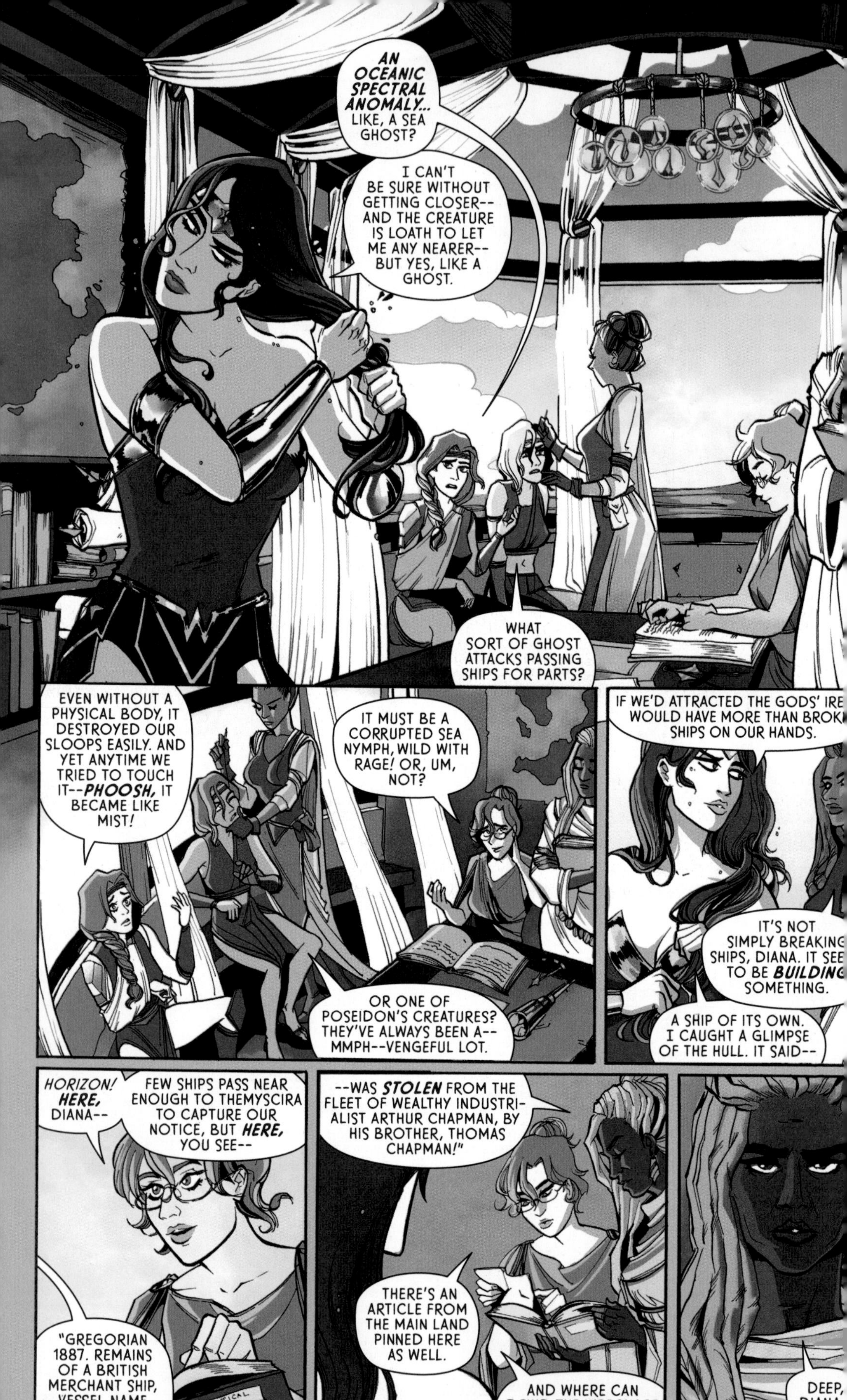
AN OCEANIC SPECTRAL ANOMALY... LIKE, A SEA GHOST?
I CAN'T BE SURE WITHOUT GETTING CLOSER-- AND THE CREATURE IS LOATH TO LET ME ANY NEARER-- BUT YES, LIKE A GHOST.
WHAT SORT OF GHOST ATTACKS PASSING SHIPS FOR PARTS?
EVEN WITHOUT A PHYSICAL BODY, IT DESTROYED OUR SLOOPS EASILY. AND YET ANYTIME WE TRIED TO TOUCH IT--PHOOSH, IT BECAME LIKE MIST!
IT MUST BE A CORRUPTED SEA NYMPH, WILD WITH RAGE! OR, UM, NOT?
OR ONE OF POSEIDON'S CREATURES? THEY'VE ALWAYS BEEN A-- MMPH--VENGEFUL LOT.
IF WE'D ATTRACTED THE GODS' IRE WOULD HAVE MORE THAN BROK SHIPS ON OUR HANDS.
IT'S NOT SIMPLY BREAKING SHIPS, DIANA. IT SEE TO BE BUILDING SOMETHING.
A SHIP OF ITS OWN. I CAUGHT A GLIMPSE OF THE HULL. IT SAID--
HORIZON! HERE, DIANA--
FEW SHIPS PASS NEAR ENOUGH TO THEMYSCIRA TO CAPTURE OUR NOTICE, BUT HERE, YOU SEE--
"GREGORIAN 1887. REMAINS OF A BRITISH MERCHANT SHIP, VESSEL NAME HORIZON, THAT--
NAUTICAL RECORD
--WAS STOLEN FROM THE FLEET OF WEALTHY INDUSTRIALIST ARTHUR CHAPMAN, BY HIS BROTHER, THOMAS CHAPMAN!"
THERE'S AN ARTICLE FROM THE MAIN LAND PINNED HERE AS WELL.
AND WHERE CAN I FIND THE WRECKAGE OF THIS STOLEN SHIP?
DEEP, DIANA.

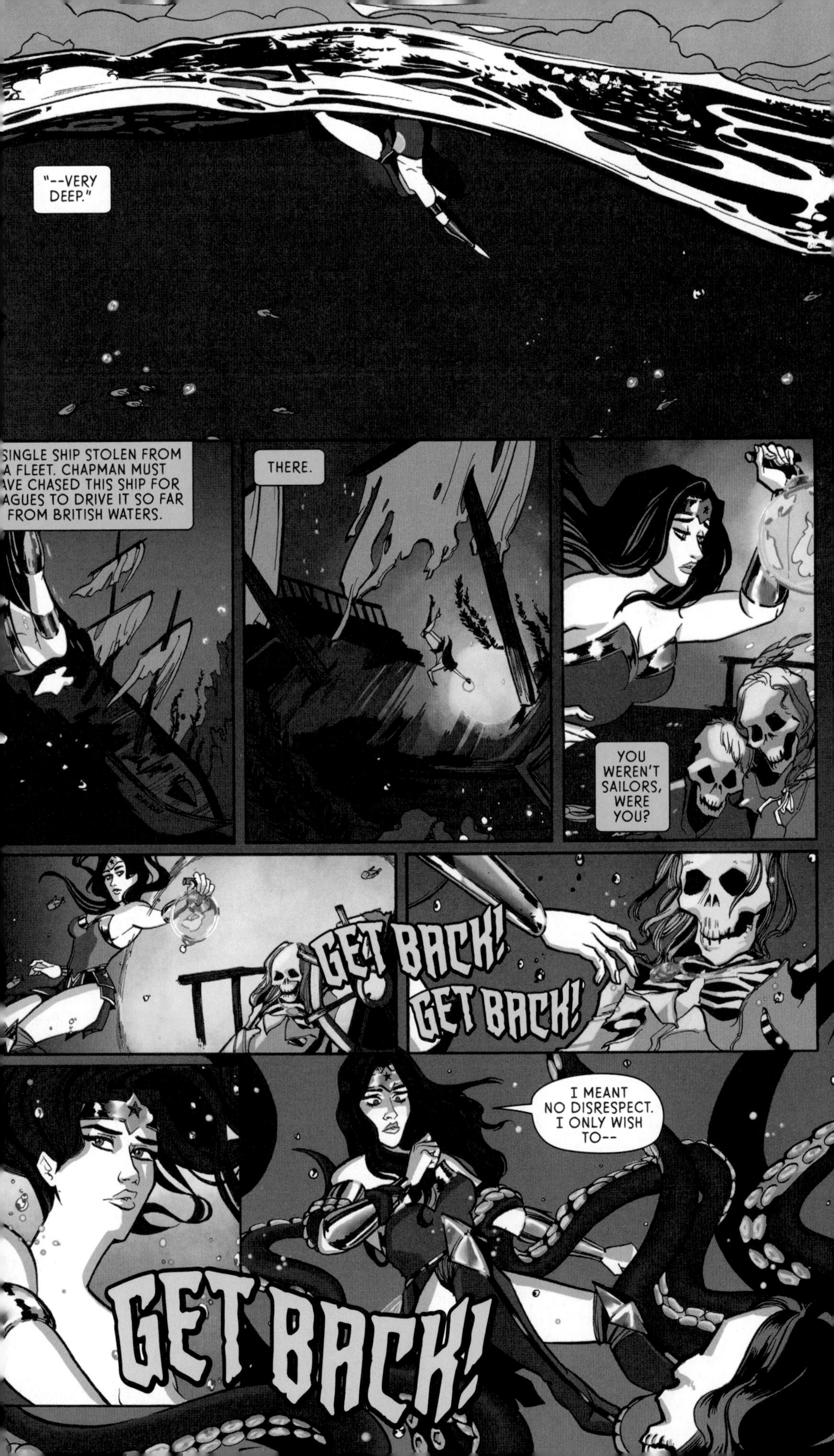
"--VERY DEEP."
SINGLE SHIP STOLEN FROM A FLEET. CHAPMAN MUST AVE CHASED THIS SHIP FOR AGUES TO DRIVE IT SO FAR FROM BRITISH WATERS.
THERE.
YOU WEREN'T SAILORS, WERE YOU?
GET BACK!
GET BACK!
I MEANT NO DISRESPECT. I ONLY WISH TO--
GET BACK!

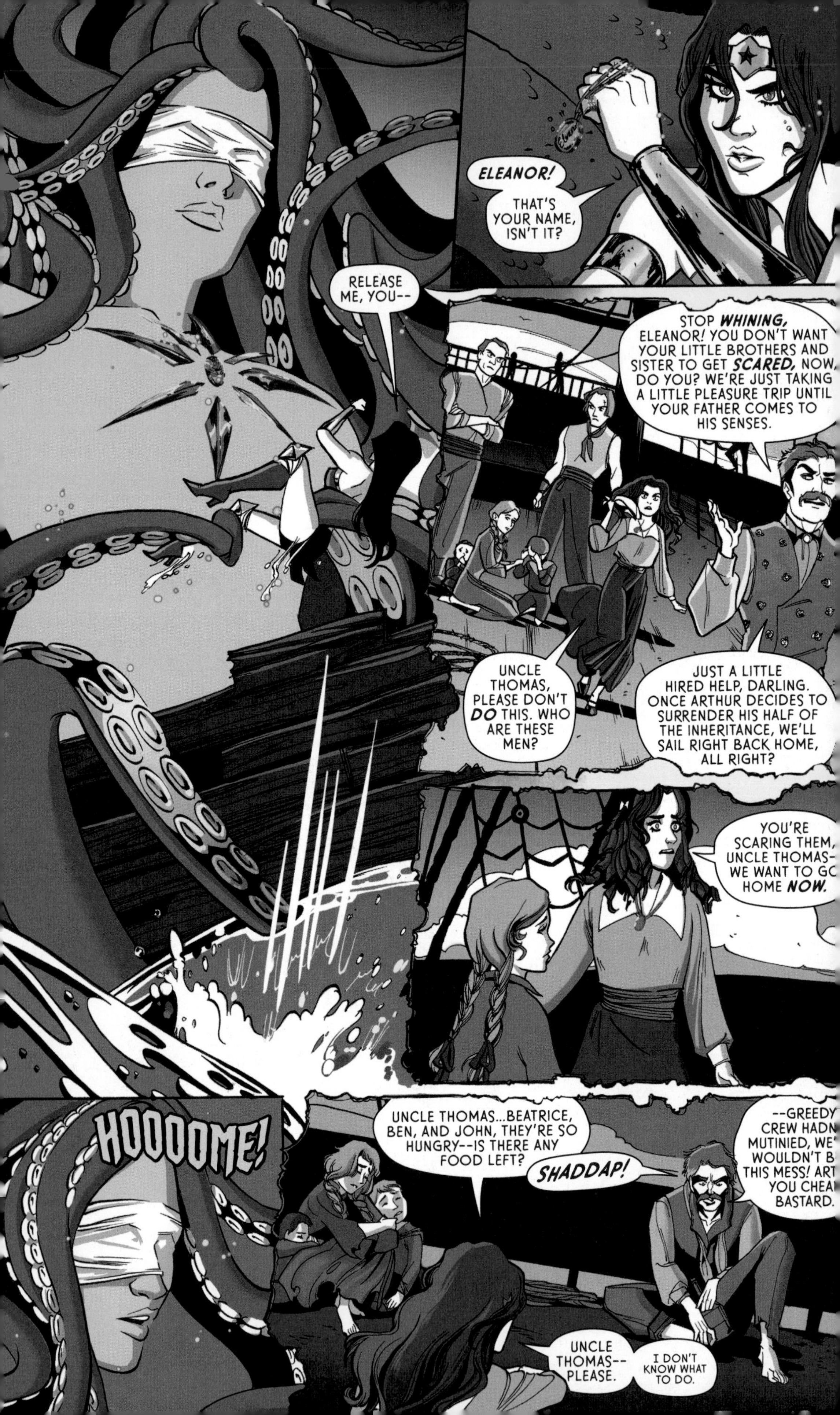
ELEANOR!
THAT'S YOUR NAME, ISN'T IT?
RELEASE ME, YOU--
STOP WHINING, ELEANOR! YOU DON'T WANT YOUR LITTLE BROTHERS AND SISTER TO GET SCARED, NOW, DO YOU? WE'RE JUST TAKING A LITTLE PLEASURE TRIP UNTIL YOUR FATHER COMES TO HIS SENSES.
UNCLE THOMAS, PLEASE DON'T DO THIS. WHO ARE THESE MEN?
JUST A LITTLE HIRED HELP, DARLING. ONCE ARTHUR DECIDES TO SURRENDER HIS HALF OF THE INHERITANCE, WE'LL SAIL RIGHT BACK HOME, ALL RIGHT?
YOU'RE SCARING THEM, UNCLE THOMAS-
WE WANT TO GO HOME NOW.
HOOOOME!
UNCLE THOMAS...BEATRICE, BEN, AND JOHN, THEY'RE SO HUNGRY--IS THERE ANY FOOD LEFT?
SHADDAP!
--GREEDY CREW HADN MUTINIED, WE WOULDN'T B THIS MESS! ART YOU CHEA BASTARD.
UNCLE THOMAS-- PLEASE.
I DON'T KNOW WHAT TO DO.

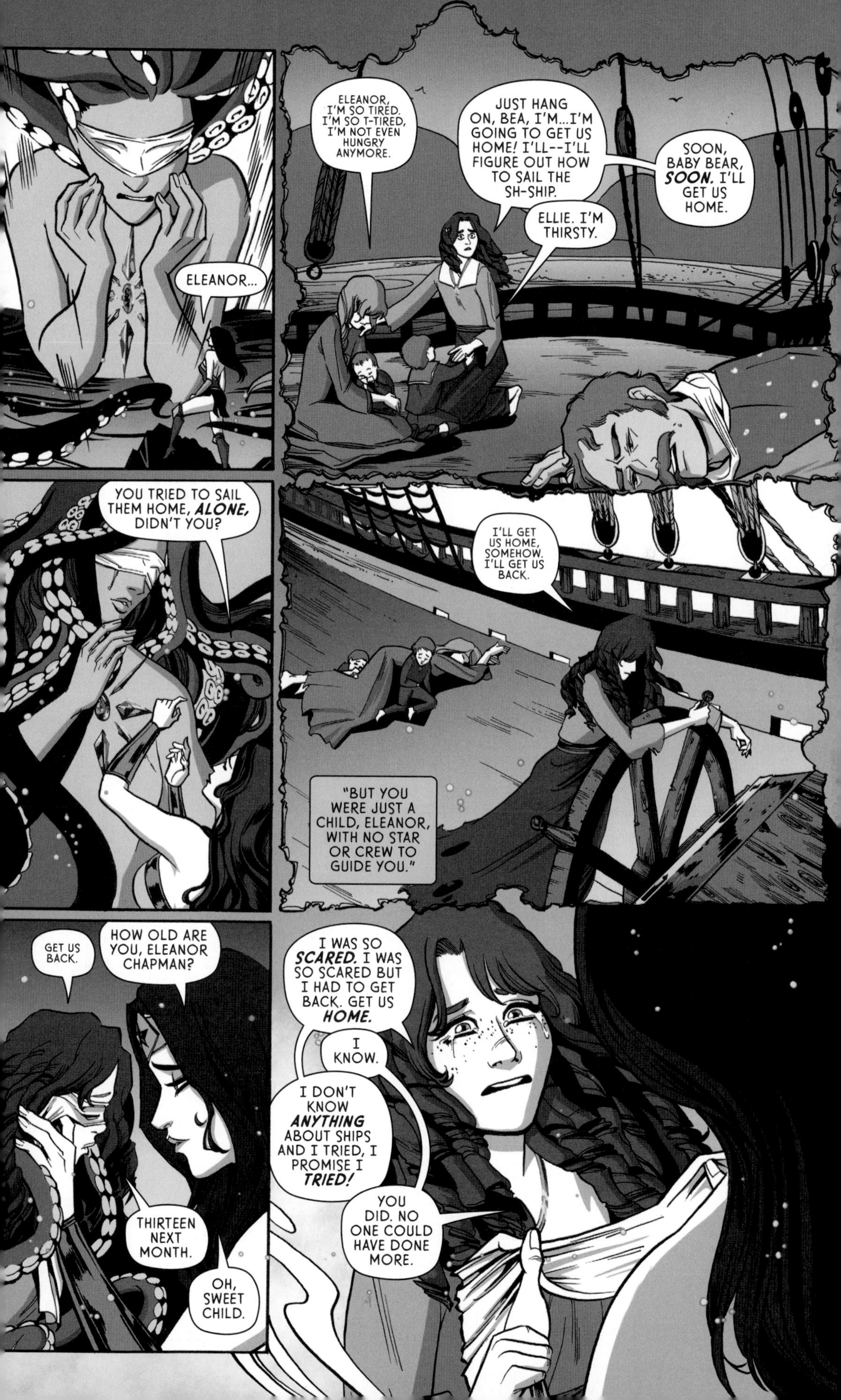

ELEANOR...
ELEANOR, I'M SO TIRED. I'M SO T-TIRED, I'M NOT EVEN HUNGRY ANYMORE.
JUST HANG ON, BEA, I'M...I'M GOING TO GET US HOME! I'LL--I'LL FIGURE OUT HOW TO SAIL THE SH-SHIP.
ELLIE. I'M THIRSTY.
SOON, BABY BEAR, SOON. I'LL GET US HOME.
YOU TRIED TO SAIL THEM HOME, ALONE, DIDN'T YOU?
I'LL GET US HOME, SOMEHOW. I'LL GET US BACK.
"BUT YOU WERE JUST A CHILD, ELEANOR, WITH NO STAR OR CREW TO GUIDE YOU."
GET US BACK.
HOW OLD ARE YOU, ELEANOR CHAPMAN?
THIRTEEN NEXT MONTH.
OH, SWEET CHILD.
I WAS SO SCARED. I WAS SO SCARED BUT I HAD TO GET BACK. GET US HOME.
I KNOW.
I DON'T KNOW ANYTHING ABOUT SHIPS AND I TRIED, I PROMISE I TRIED!
YOU DID. NO ONE COULD HAVE DONE MORE.

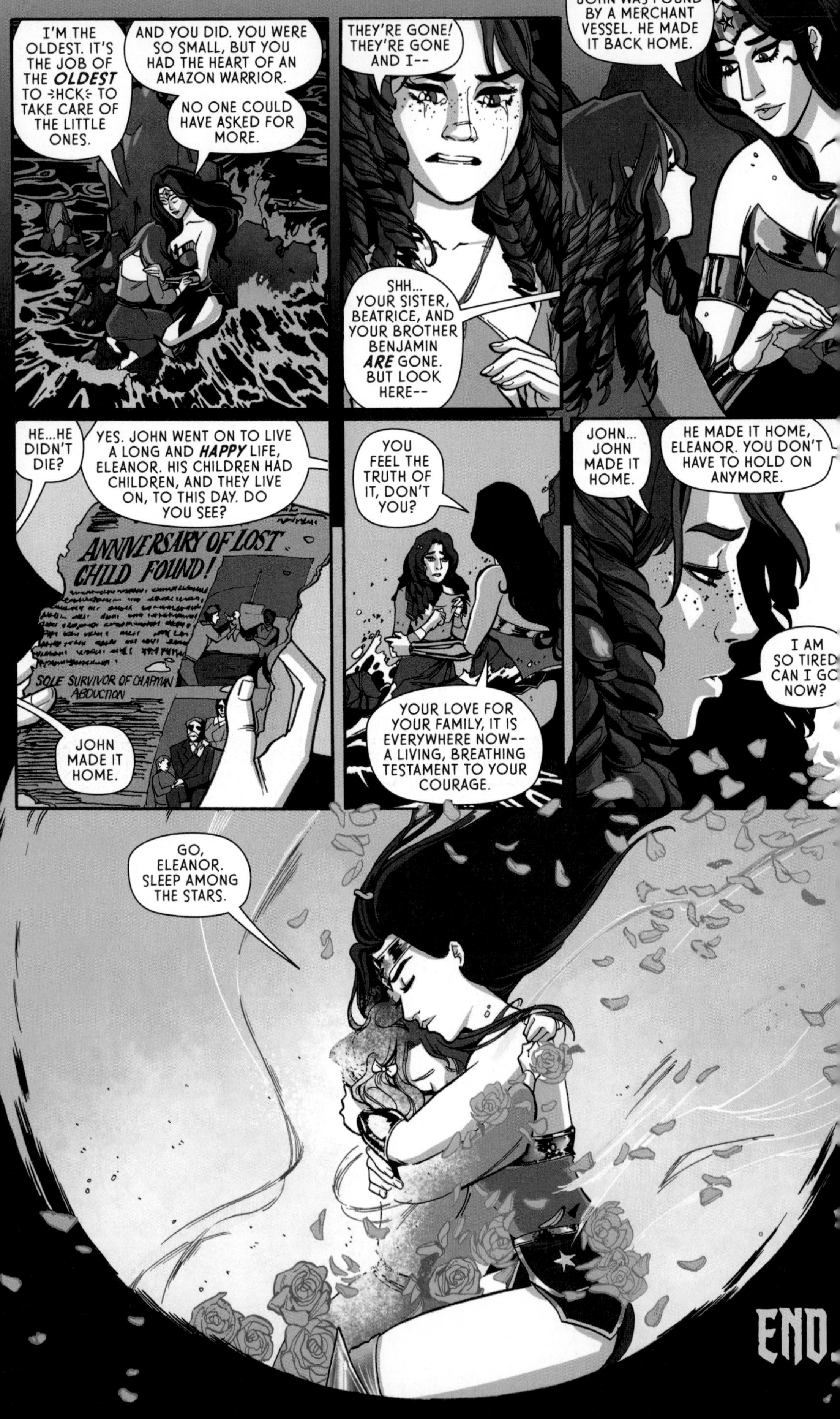

I'M THE OLDEST. IT'S THE JOB OF THE *OLDEST* TO =HCK= TO TAKE CARE OF THE LITTLE ONES.
AND YOU DID. YOU WERE SO SMALL, BUT YOU HAD THE HEART OF AN AMAZON WARRIOR.
NO ONE COULD HAVE ASKED FOR MORE.
THEY'RE GONE! THEY'RE GONE AND I--
SHH... YOUR SISTER, BEATRICE, AND YOUR BROTHER BENJAMIN *ARE* GONE. BUT LOOK HERE--
YOUR BROTHER JOHN WAS FOUND BY A MERCHANT VESSEL. HE MADE IT BACK HOME.
HE...HE DIDN'T DIE?
YES. JOHN WENT ON TO LIVE A LONG AND *HAPPY* LIFE, ELEANOR. HIS CHILDREN HAD CHILDREN, AND THEY LIVE ON, TO THIS DAY. DO YOU SEE?
ANNIVERSARY OF LOST CHILD FOUND!
SOLE SURVIVOR OF CHAPMAN ABDUCTION
JOHN MADE IT HOME.
YOU FEEL THE TRUTH OF IT, DON'T YOU?
YOUR LOVE FOR YOUR FAMILY, IT IS EVERYWHERE NOW-- A LIVING, BREATHING TESTAMENT TO YOUR COURAGE.
JOHN... JOHN MADE IT HOME.
HE MADE IT HOME, ELEANOR. YOU DON'T HAVE TO HOLD ON ANYMORE.
I AM SO TIRED CAN I GO NOW?
GO, ELEANOR. SLEEP AMONG THE STARS.
END.

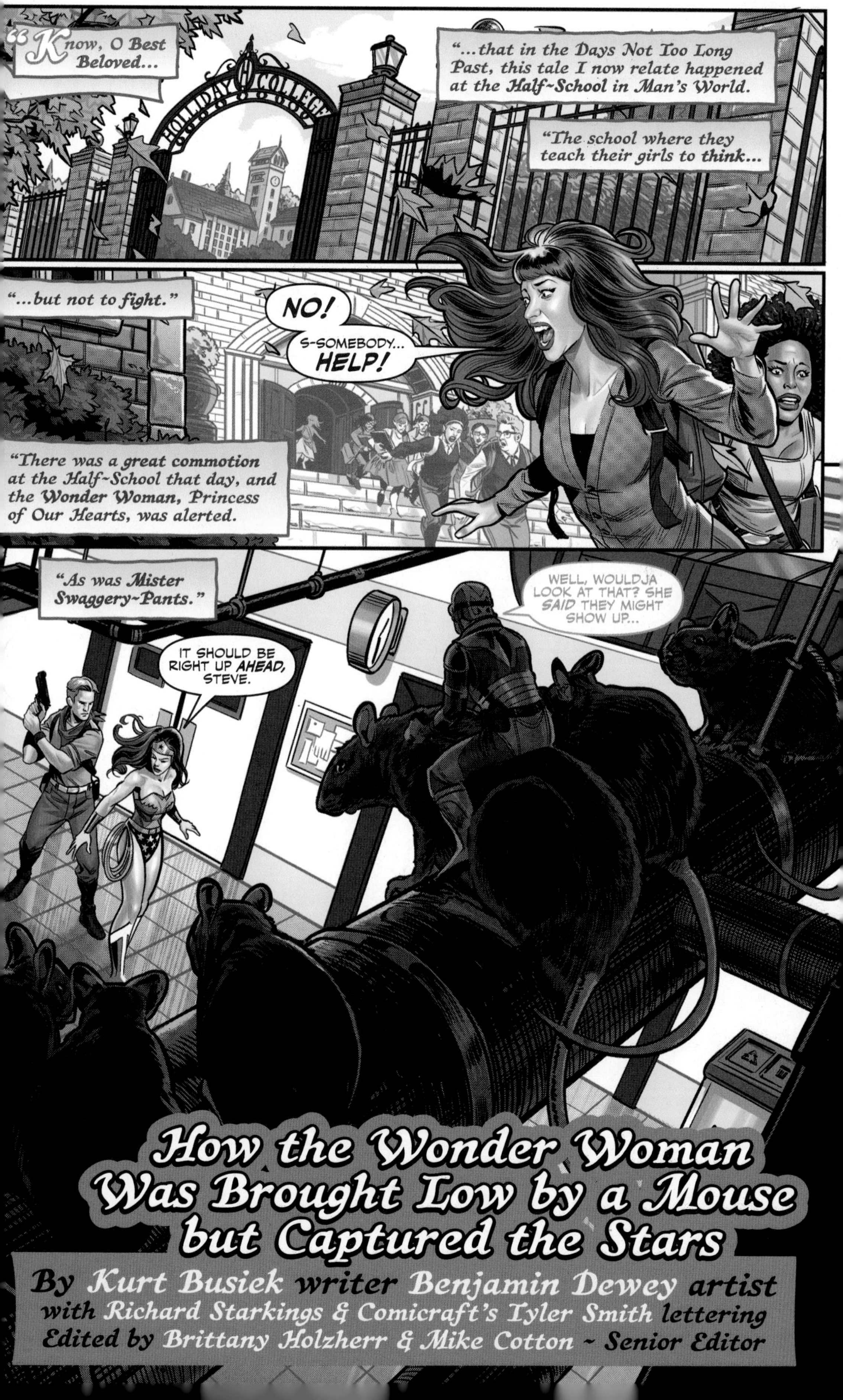
"Know, O Best Beloved...
"...that in the Days Not Too Long Past, this tale I now relate happened at the Half~School in Man's World.
HOLLIDAY COLLEGE
"The school where they teach their girls to think...
"...but not to fight."
NO!
S-SOMEBODY... HELP!
"There was a great commotion at the Half~School that day, and the Wonder Woman, Princess of Our Hearts, was alerted.
"As was Mister Swaggery~Pants."
WELL, WOULDJA LOOK AT THAT? SHE SAID THEY MIGHT SHOW UP...
IT SHOULD BE RIGHT UP AHEAD, STEVE.
How the Wonder Woman Was Brought Low by a Mouse but Captured the Stars
By Kurt Busiek writer Benjamin Dewey artist
with Richard Starkings & Comicraft's Tyler Smith lettering
Edited by Brittany Holzherr & Mike Cotton ~ Senior Editor

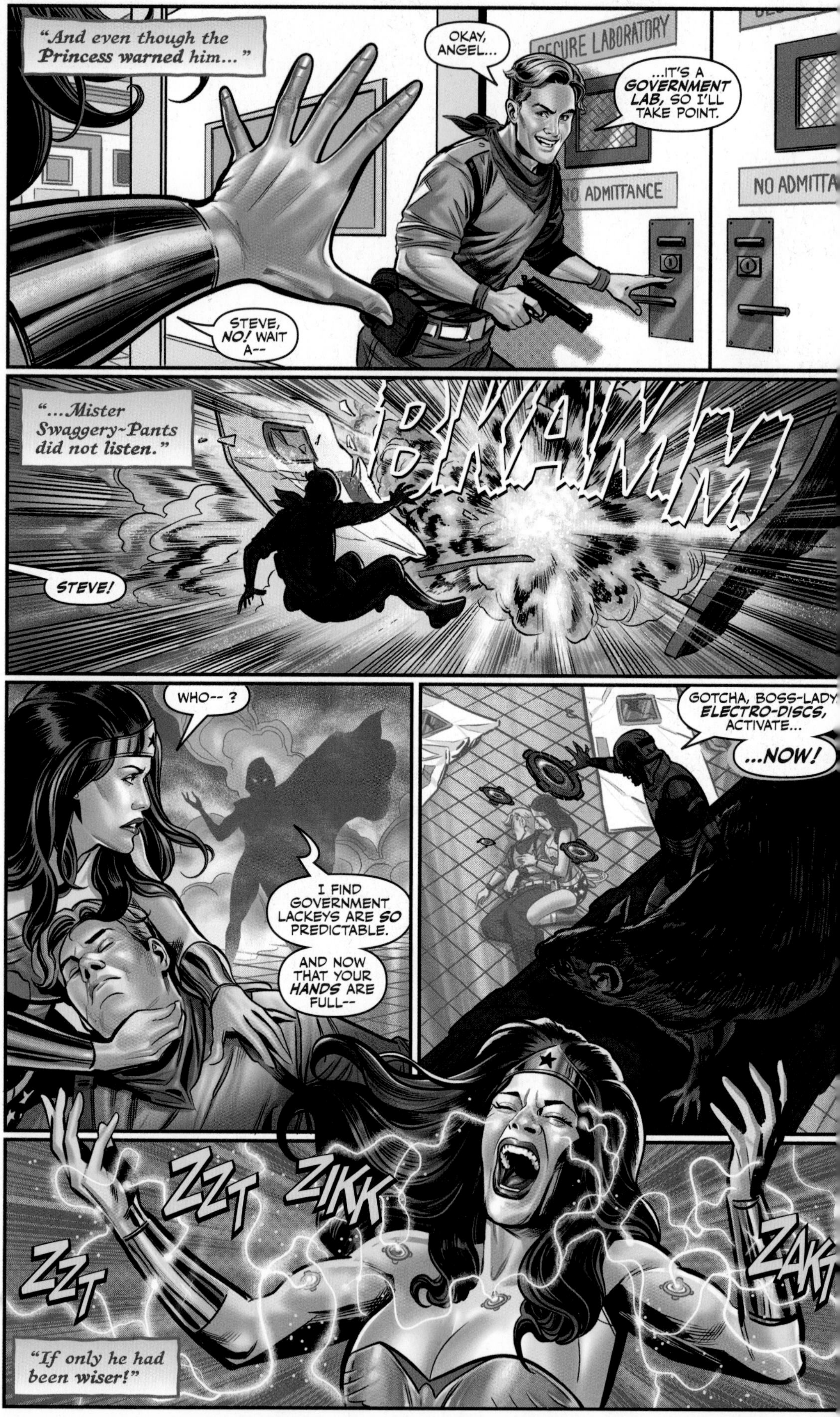
"And even though the Princess warned him..."
OKAY, ANGEL...
SECURE LABORATORY
...IT'S A GOVERNMENT LAB, SO I'LL TAKE POINT.
NO ADMITTANCE
STEVE, NO! WAIT A--
"...Mister Swaggery-Pants did not listen."
BKAMM
STEVE!
WHO-- ?
I FIND GOVERNMENT LACKEYS ARE SO PREDICTABLE.
AND NOW THAT YOUR HANDS ARE FULL--
GOTCHA, BOSS-LADY. ELECTRO-DISCS, ACTIVATE...
...NOW!
ZZT
ZIKK
ZZT
"If only he had been wiser!"

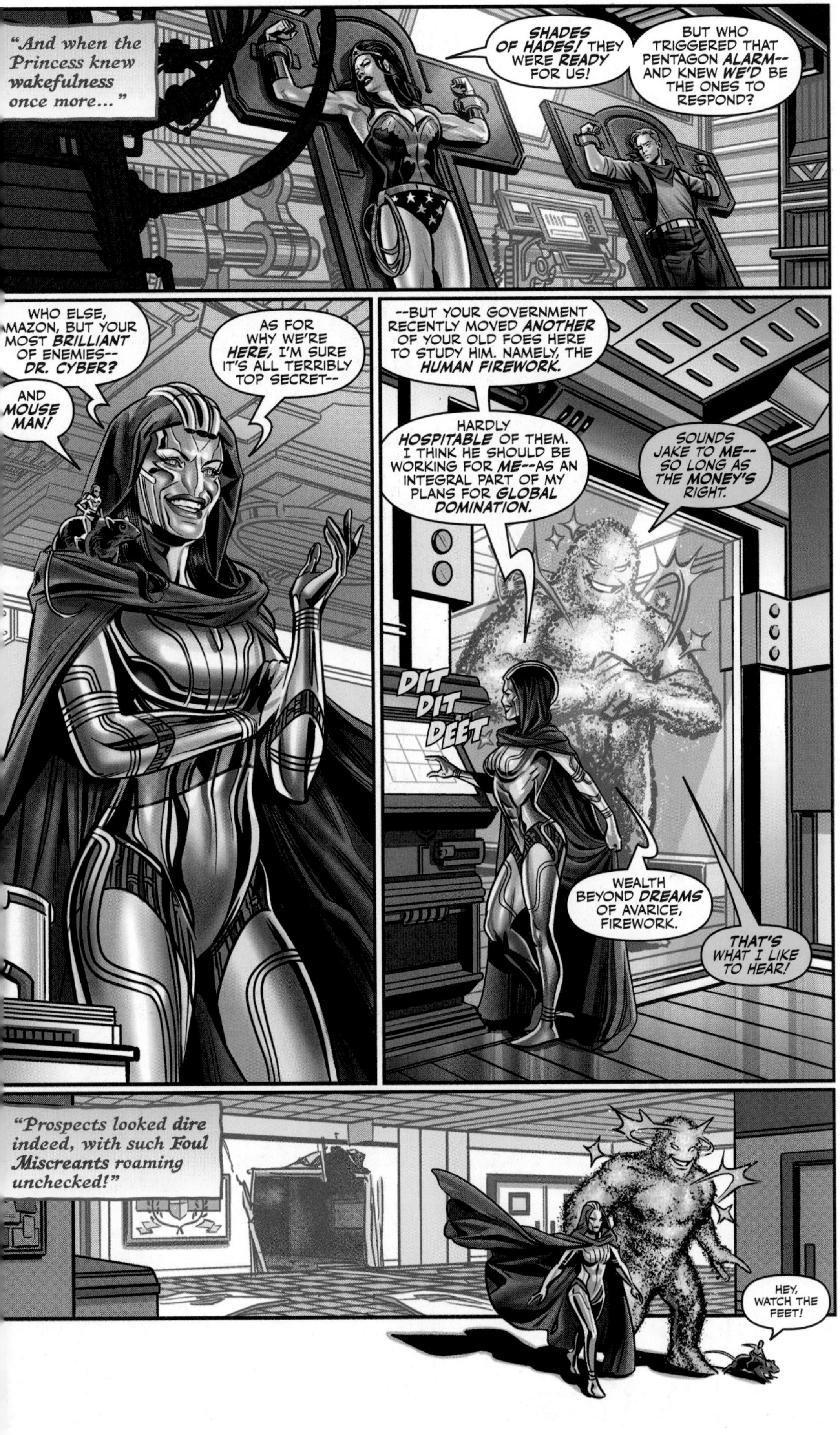
"And when the Princess knew wakefulness once more..."
SHADES OF HADES! THEY WERE READY FOR US!
BUT WHO TRIGGERED THAT PENTAGON ALARM-- AND KNEW WE'D BE THE ONES TO RESPOND?
WHO ELSE, AMAZON, BUT YOUR MOST BRILLIANT OF ENEMIES-- DR. CYBER?
AND MOUSE MAN!
AS FOR WHY WE'RE HERE, I'M SURE IT'S ALL TERRIBLY TOP SECRET--
--BUT YOUR GOVERNMENT RECENTLY MOVED ANOTHER OF YOUR OLD FOES HERE TO STUDY HIM. NAMELY, THE HUMAN FIREWORK.
HARDLY HOSPITABLE OF THEM. I THINK HE SHOULD BE WORKING FOR ME--AS AN INTEGRAL PART OF MY PLANS FOR GLOBAL DOMINATION.
SOUNDS JAKE TO ME-- SO LONG AS THE MONEY'S RIGHT.
DIT DIT DEET
WEALTH BEYOND DREAMS OF AVARICE, FIREWORK.
THAT'S WHAT I LIKE TO HEAR!
"Prospects looked dire indeed, with such Foul Miscreants roaming unchecked!"
HEY, WATCH THE FEET!

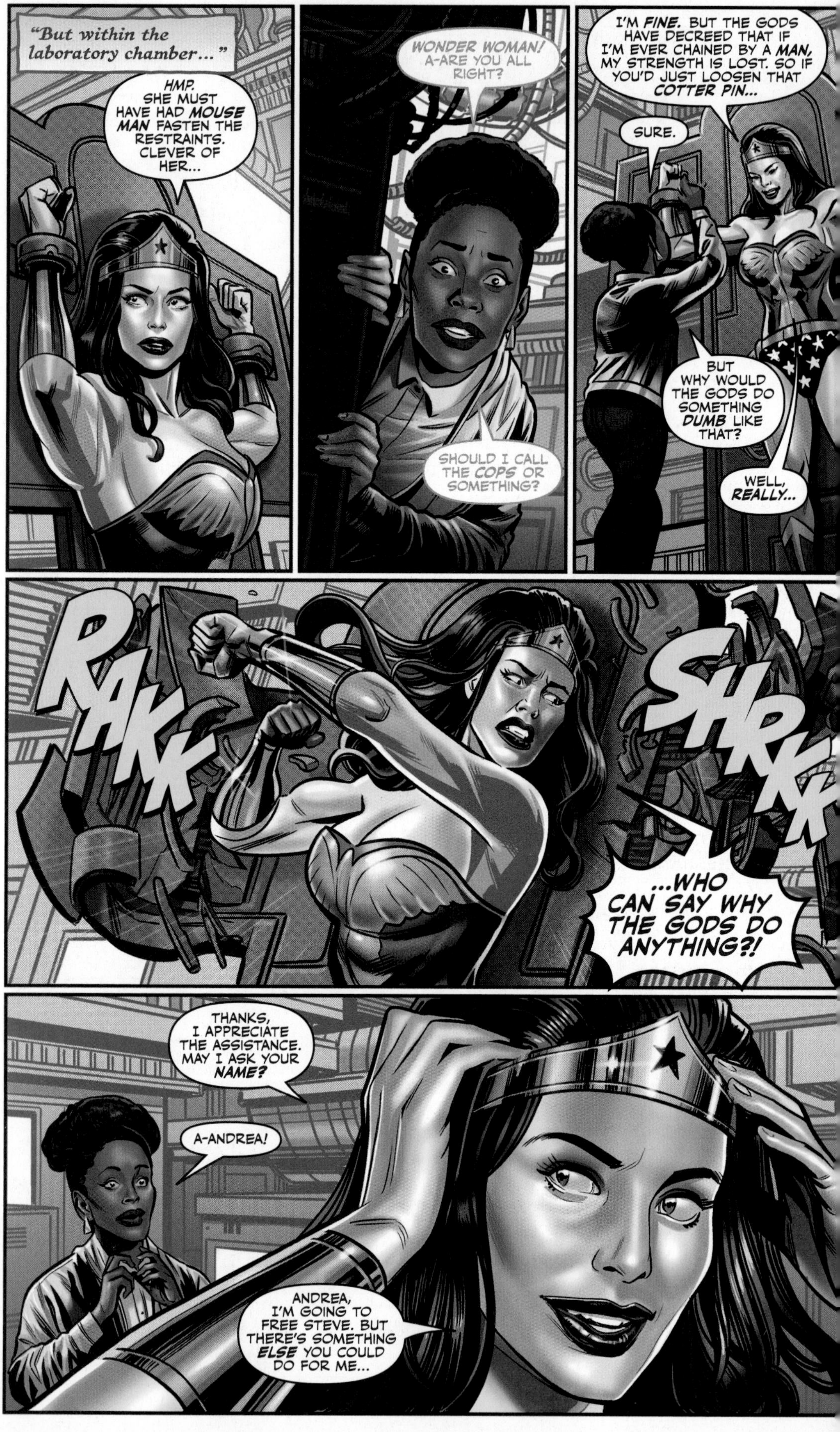
"But within the laboratory chamber..."
HMP. SHE MUST HAVE HAD MOUSE MAN FASTEN THE RESTRAINTS. CLEVER OF HER...
WONDER WOMAN! A-ARE YOU ALL RIGHT?
SHOULD I CALL THE COPS OR SOMETHING?
I'M FINE. BUT THE GODS HAVE DECREED THAT IF I'M EVER CHAINED BY A MAN, MY STRENGTH IS LOST. SO IF YOU'D JUST LOOSEN THAT COTTER PIN...
SURE.
BUT WHY WOULD THE GODS DO SOMETHING DUMB LIKE THAT?
WELL, REALLY...
RAKK
SHRKK
...WHO CAN SAY WHY THE GODS DO ANYTHING?!
THANKS, I APPRECIATE THE ASSISTANCE. MAY I ASK YOUR NAME?
A-ANDREA!
ANDREA, I'M GOING TO FREE STEVE. BUT THERE'S SOMETHING ELSE YOU COULD DO FOR ME...

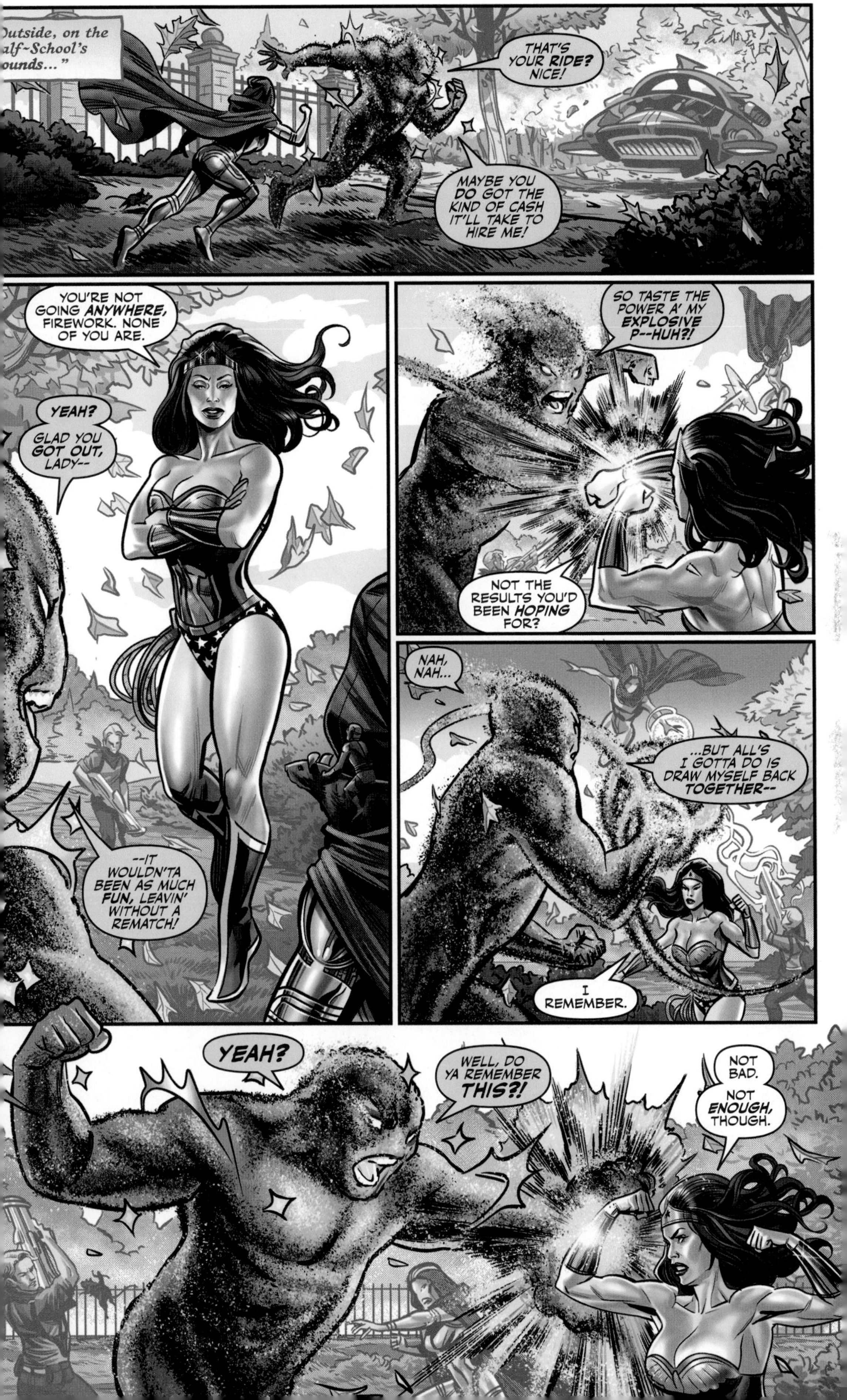

Outside, on the alf-School's ounds..."
THAT'S YOUR RIDE? NICE!
MAYBE YOU DO GOT THE KIND OF CASH IT'LL TAKE TO HIRE ME!
YOU'RE NOT GOING ANYWHERE, FIREWORK. NONE OF YOU ARE.
YEAH?
GLAD YOU GOT OUT, LADY--
--IT WOULDN'TA BEEN AS MUCH FUN, LEAVIN' WITHOUT A REMATCH!
SO TASTE THE POWER A' MY EXPLOSIVE P--HUH?!
NOT THE RESULTS YOU'D BEEN HOPING FOR?
NAH, NAH...
...BUT ALL'S I GOTTA DO IS DRAW MYSELF BACK TOGETHER--
I REMEMBER.
YEAH?
WELL, DO YA REMEMBER THIS?!
NOT BAD.
NOT ENOUGH, THOUGH.

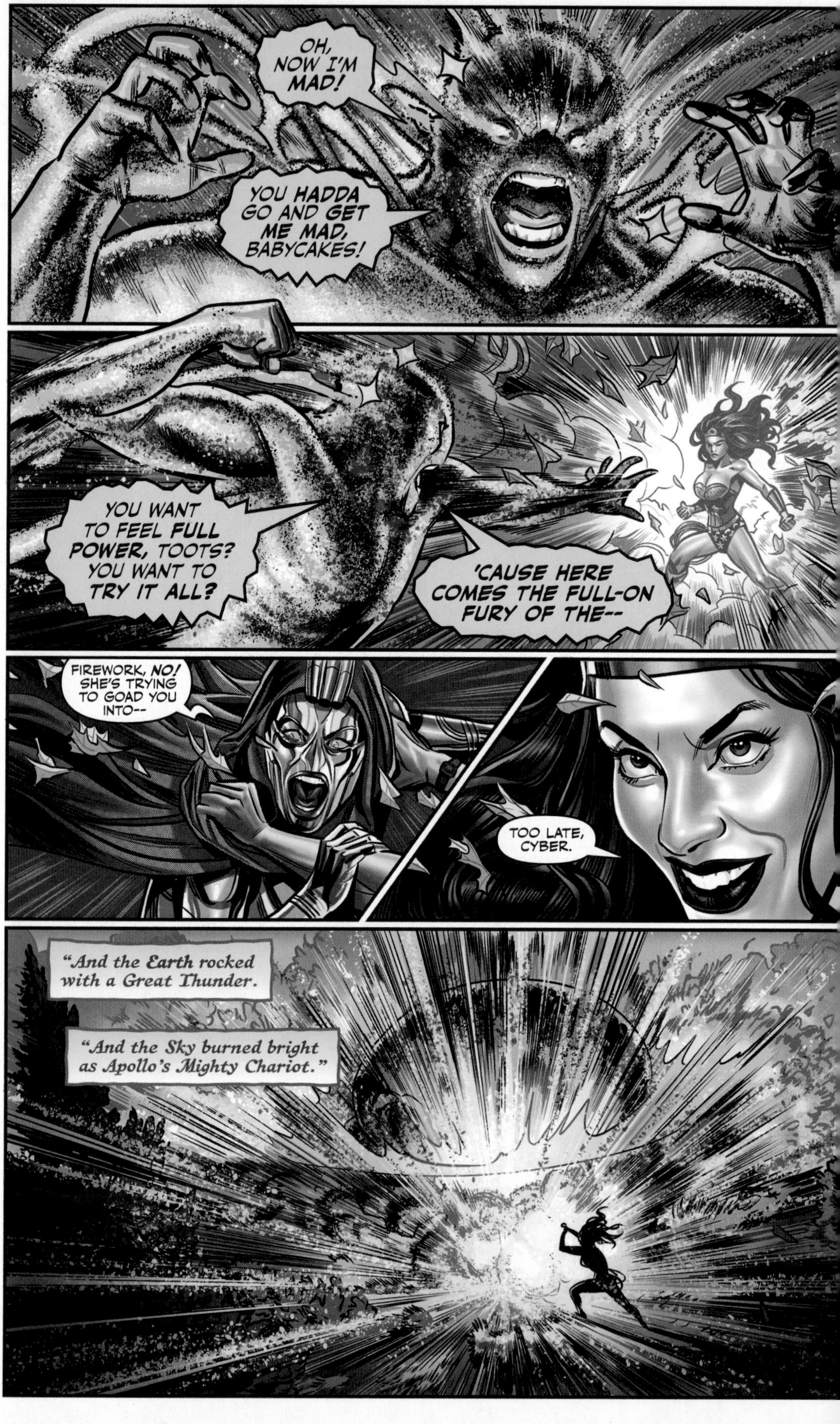
OH, NOW I'M MAD!
YOU HADDA GO AND GET ME MAD, BABYCAKES!
YOU WANT TO FEEL FULL POWER, TOOTS? YOU WANT TO TRY IT ALL?
'CAUSE HERE COMES THE FULL-ON FURY OF THE--
FIREWORK, NO! SHE'S TRYING TO GOAD YOU INTO--
TOO LATE, CYBER.
"And the Earth rocked with a Great Thunder.
"And the Sky burned bright as Apollo's Mighty Chariot."

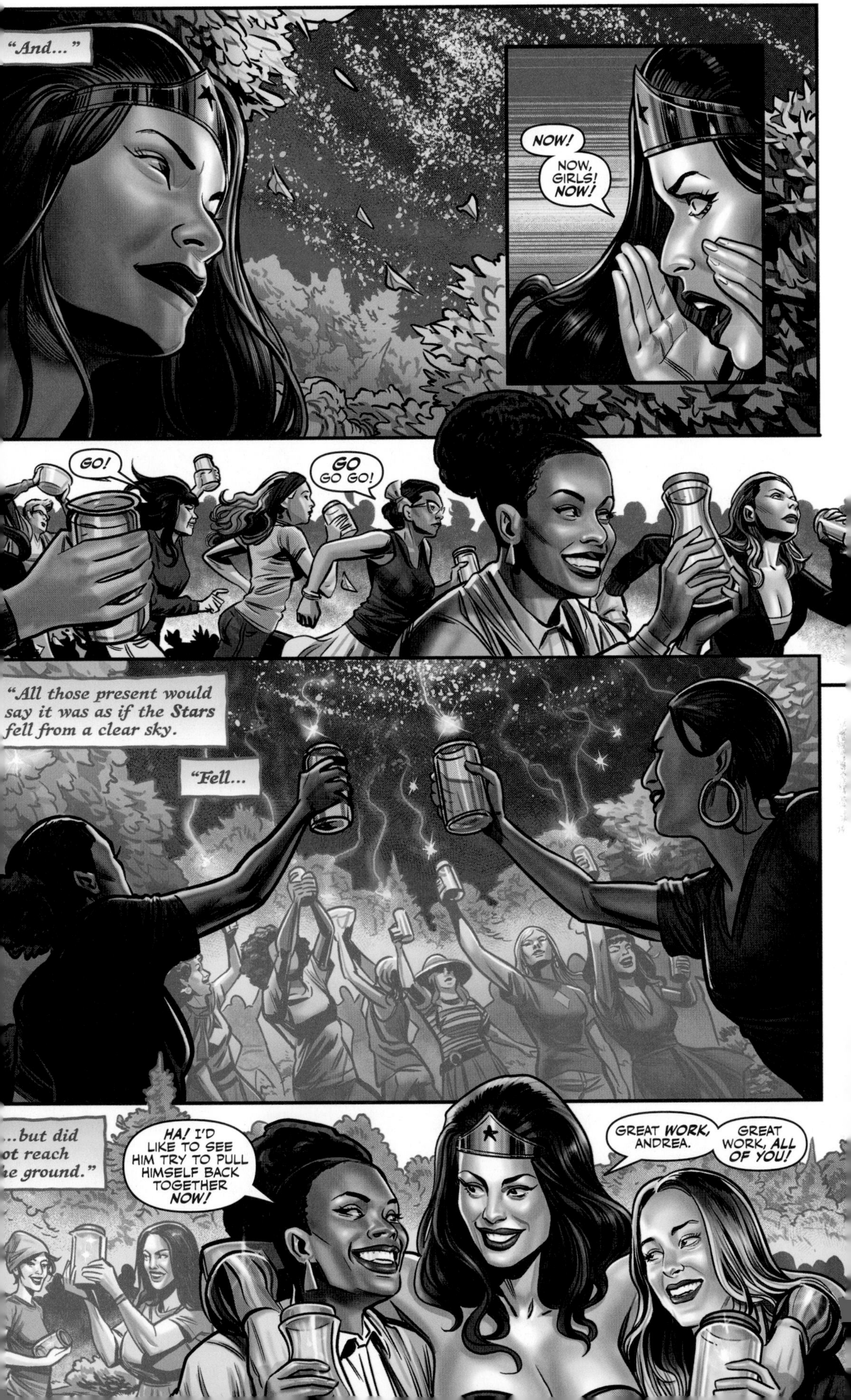
"And..."
NOW!
NOW, GIRLS! NOW!
GO!
GO GO GO!
"All those present would say it was as if the Stars fell from a clear sky.
"Fell...
...but did ot reach he ground."
HA! I'D LIKE TO SEE HIM TRY TO PULL HIMSELF BACK TOGETHER NOW!
GREAT WORK, ANDREA.
GREAT WORK, ALL OF YOU!

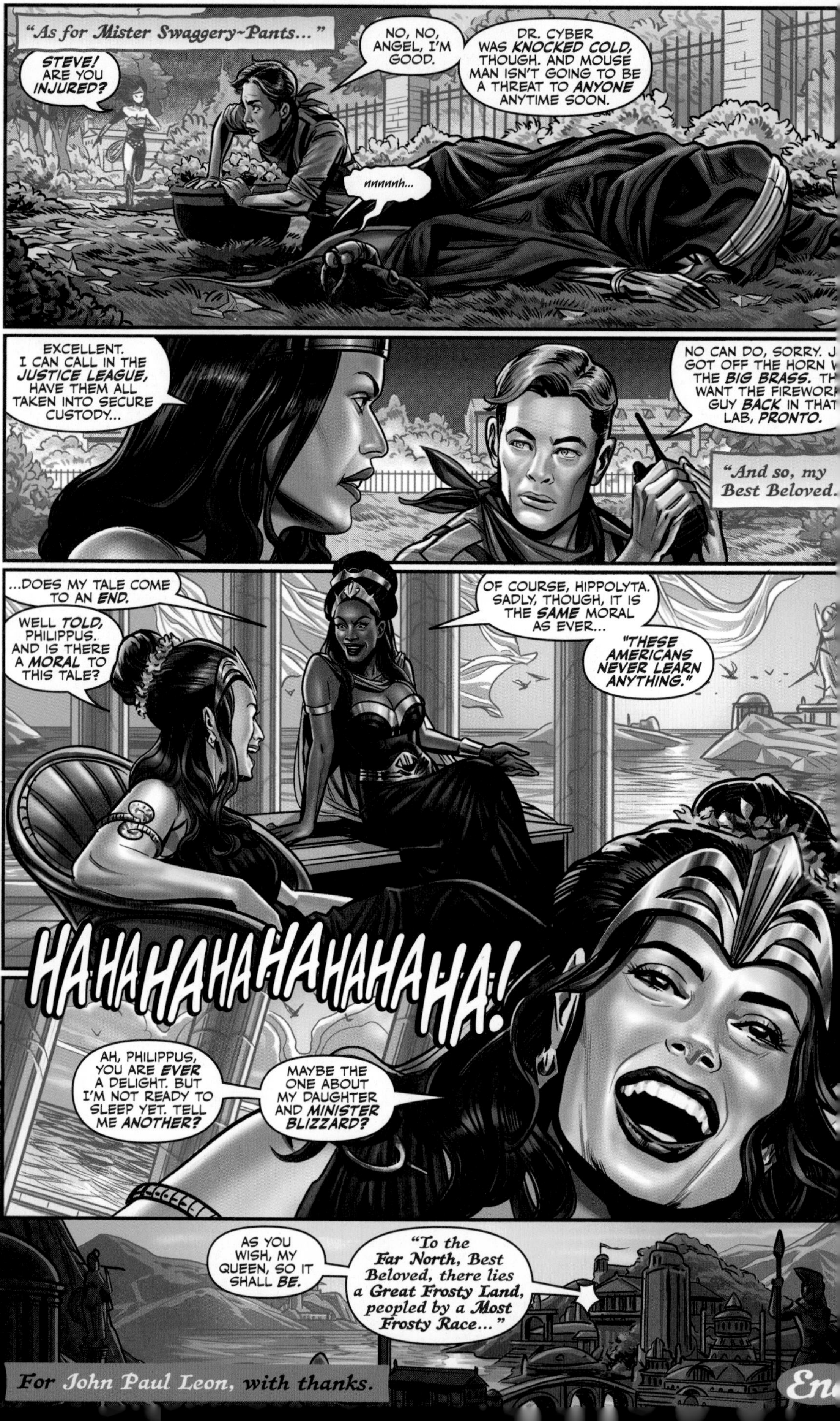
"As for Mister Swaggery-Pants..."
STEVE! ARE YOU INJURED?
NO, NO, ANGEL, I'M GOOD.
DR. CYBER WAS KNOCKED COLD, THOUGH. AND MOUSE MAN ISN'T GOING TO BE A THREAT TO ANYONE ANYTIME SOON.
nnnnnh...
EXCELLENT. I CAN CALL IN THE JUSTICE LEAGUE, HAVE THEM ALL TAKEN INTO SECURE CUSTODY...
NO CAN DO, SORRY. J
GOT OFF THE HORN W
THE BIG BRASS. TH
WANT THE FIREWORK
GUY BACK IN THAT
LAB, PRONTO.
"And so, my Best Beloved...
...DOES MY TALE COME TO AN END.
WELL TOLD, PHILIPPUS. AND IS THERE A MORAL TO THIS TALE?
OF COURSE, HIPPOLYTA. SADLY, THOUGH, IT IS THE SAME MORAL AS EVER...
"THESE AMERICANS NEVER LEARN ANYTHING."
HAHAHAHAHAHAHAHAHAHA!
AH, PHILIPPUS, YOU ARE EVER A DELIGHT. BUT I'M NOT READY TO SLEEP YET. TELL ME ANOTHER?
MAYBE THE ONE ABOUT MY DAUGHTER AND MINISTER BLIZZARD?
AS YOU WISH, MY QUEEN, SO IT SHALL BE.
"To the Far North, Best Beloved, there lies a Great Frosty Land, peopled by a Most Frosty Race..."
For John Paul Leon, with thanks.
En

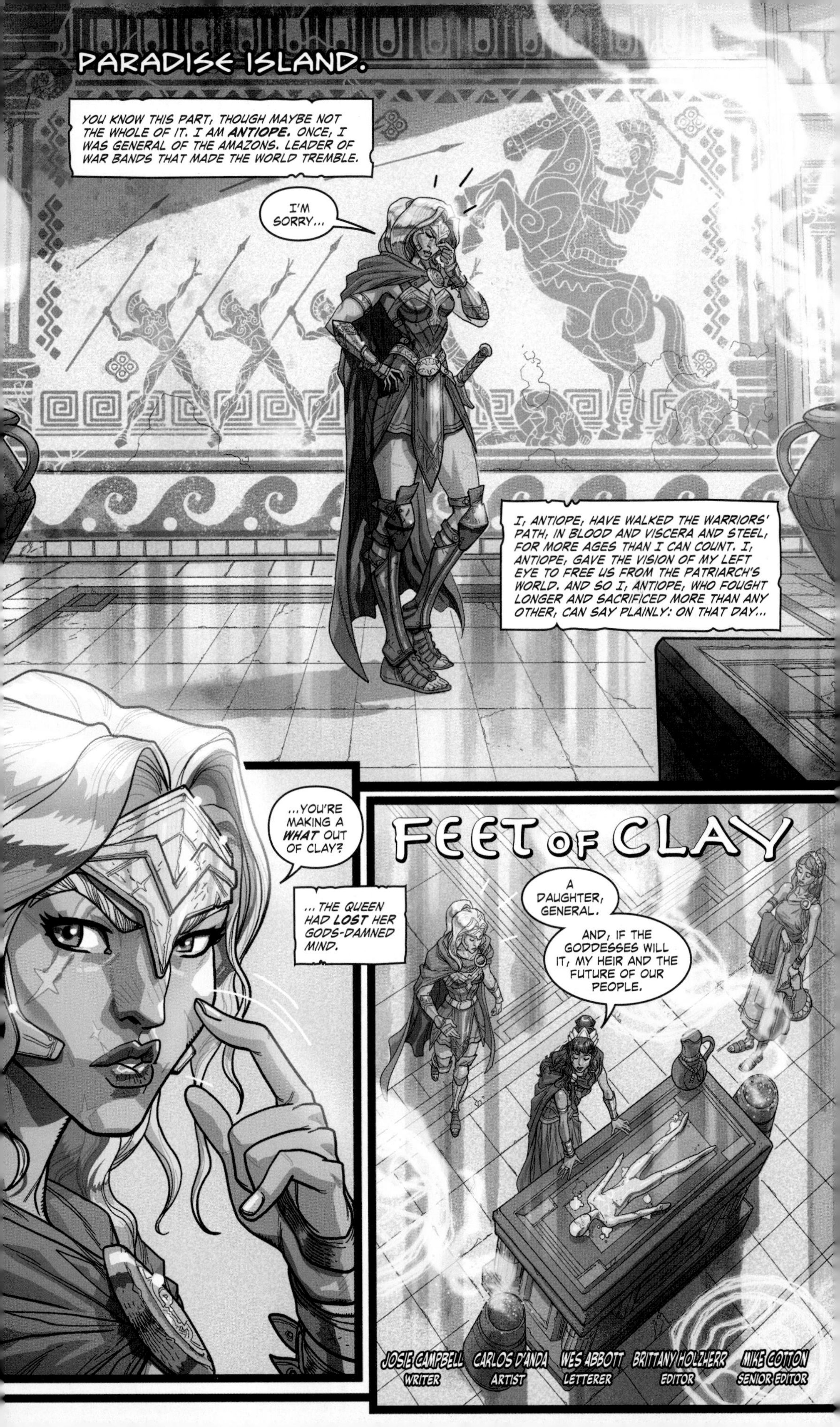
PARADISE ISLAND.
YOU KNOW THIS PART, THOUGH MAYBE NOT THE WHOLE OF IT. I AM ANTIOPE. ONCE, I WAS GENERAL OF THE AMAZONS. LEADER OF WAR BANDS THAT MADE THE WORLD TREMBLE.
I'M SORRY...
I, ANTIOPE, HAVE WALKED THE WARRIORS' PATH, IN BLOOD AND VISCERA AND STEEL, FOR MORE AGES THAN I CAN COUNT. I, ANTIOPE, GAVE THE VISION OF MY LEFT EYE TO FREE US FROM THE PATRIARCH'S WORLD. AND SO I, ANTIOPE, WHO FOUGHT LONGER AND SACRIFICED MORE THAN ANY OTHER, CAN SAY PLAINLY: ON THAT DAY...
...THE QUEEN HAD LOST HER GODS-DAMNED MIND.
...YOU'RE MAKING A WHAT OUT OF CLAY?
FEET OF CLAY
A DAUGHTER, GENERAL.
AND, IF THE GODDESSES WILL IT, MY HEIR AND THE FUTURE OF OUR PEOPLE.
JOSIE CAMPBELL WRITER
CARLOS D'ANDA ARTIST
WES ABBOTT LETTERER
BRITTANY HOLZHERR EDITOR
MIKE COTTON SENIOR EDITOR

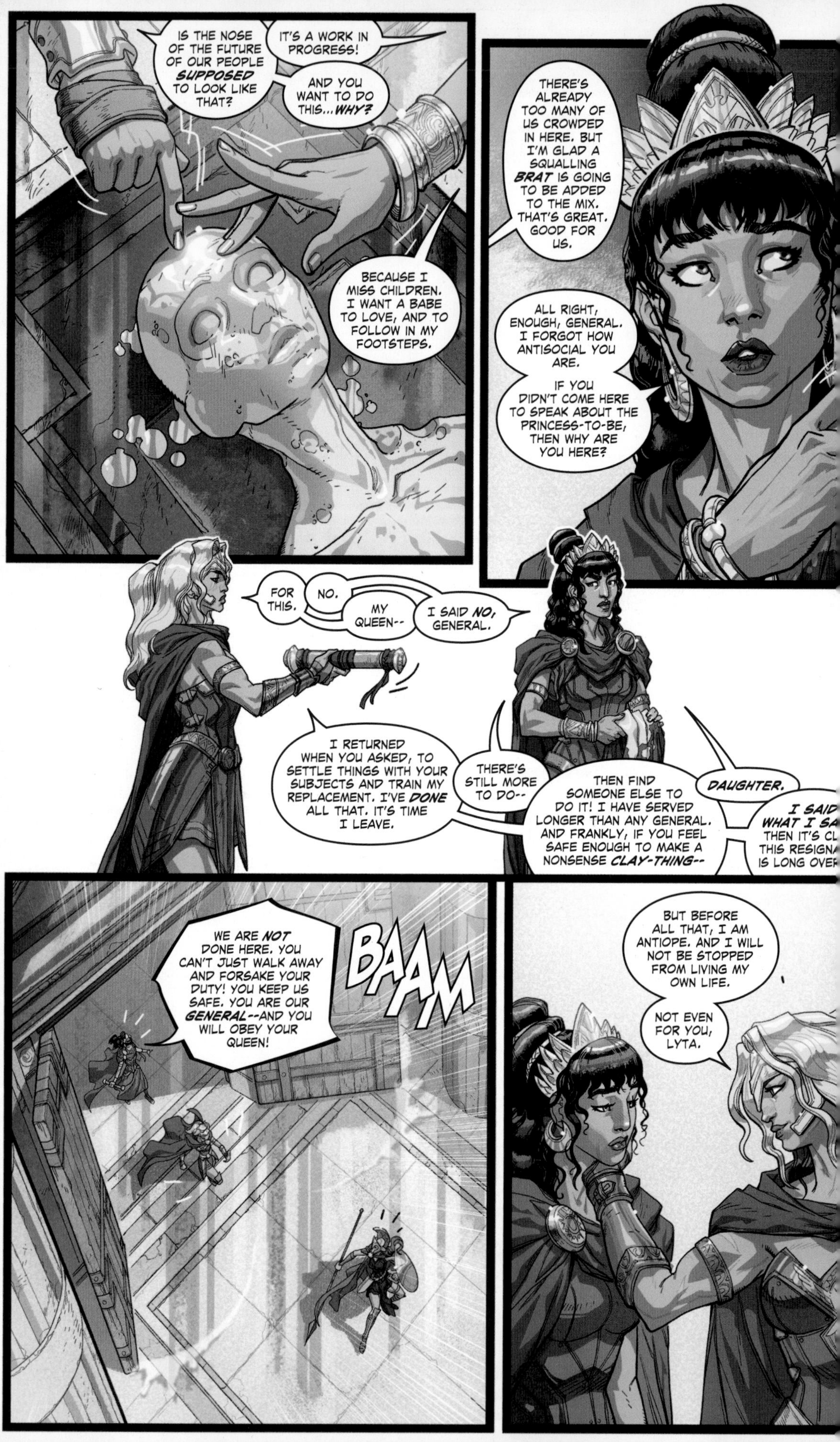
IS THE NOSE OF THE FUTURE OF OUR PEOPLE *SUPPOSED* TO LOOK LIKE THAT?
IT'S A WORK IN PROGRESS!
AND YOU WANT TO DO THIS...*WHY?*
BECAUSE I MISS CHILDREN. I WANT A BABE TO LOVE, AND TO FOLLOW IN MY FOOTSTEPS.
THERE'S ALREADY TOO MANY OF US CROWDED IN HERE. BUT I'M GLAD A SQUALLING *BRAT* IS GOING TO BE ADDED TO THE MIX. THAT'S GREAT. GOOD FOR US.
ALL RIGHT, ENOUGH, GENERAL. I FORGOT HOW ANTISOCIAL YOU ARE.
IF YOU DIDN'T COME HERE TO SPEAK ABOUT THE PRINCESS-TO-BE, THEN WHY ARE YOU HERE?
FOR THIS.
NO.
MY QUEEN--
I SAID *NO,* GENERAL.
I RETURNED WHEN YOU ASKED, TO SETTLE THINGS WITH YOUR SUBJECTS AND TRAIN MY REPLACEMENT. I'VE *DONE* ALL THAT. IT'S TIME I LEAVE.
THERE'S STILL MORE TO DO--
THEN FIND SOMEONE ELSE TO DO IT! I HAVE SERVED LONGER THAN ANY GENERAL. AND FRANKLY, IF YOU FEEL SAFE ENOUGH TO MAKE A NONSENSE *CLAY-THING--*
DAUGHTER.
I SAID WHAT I SA THEN IT'S CL THIS RESIGNA IS LONG OVER
WE ARE *NOT* DONE HERE. YOU CAN'T JUST WALK AWAY AND FORSAKE YOUR DUTY! YOU KEEP US SAFE. YOU ARE OUR *GENERAL--*AND YOU WILL OBEY YOUR QUEEN!
BAAM
BUT BEFORE ALL THAT, I AM ANTIOPE. AND I WILL NOT BE STOPPED FROM LIVING MY OWN LIFE.
NOT EVEN FOR YOU, LYTA.

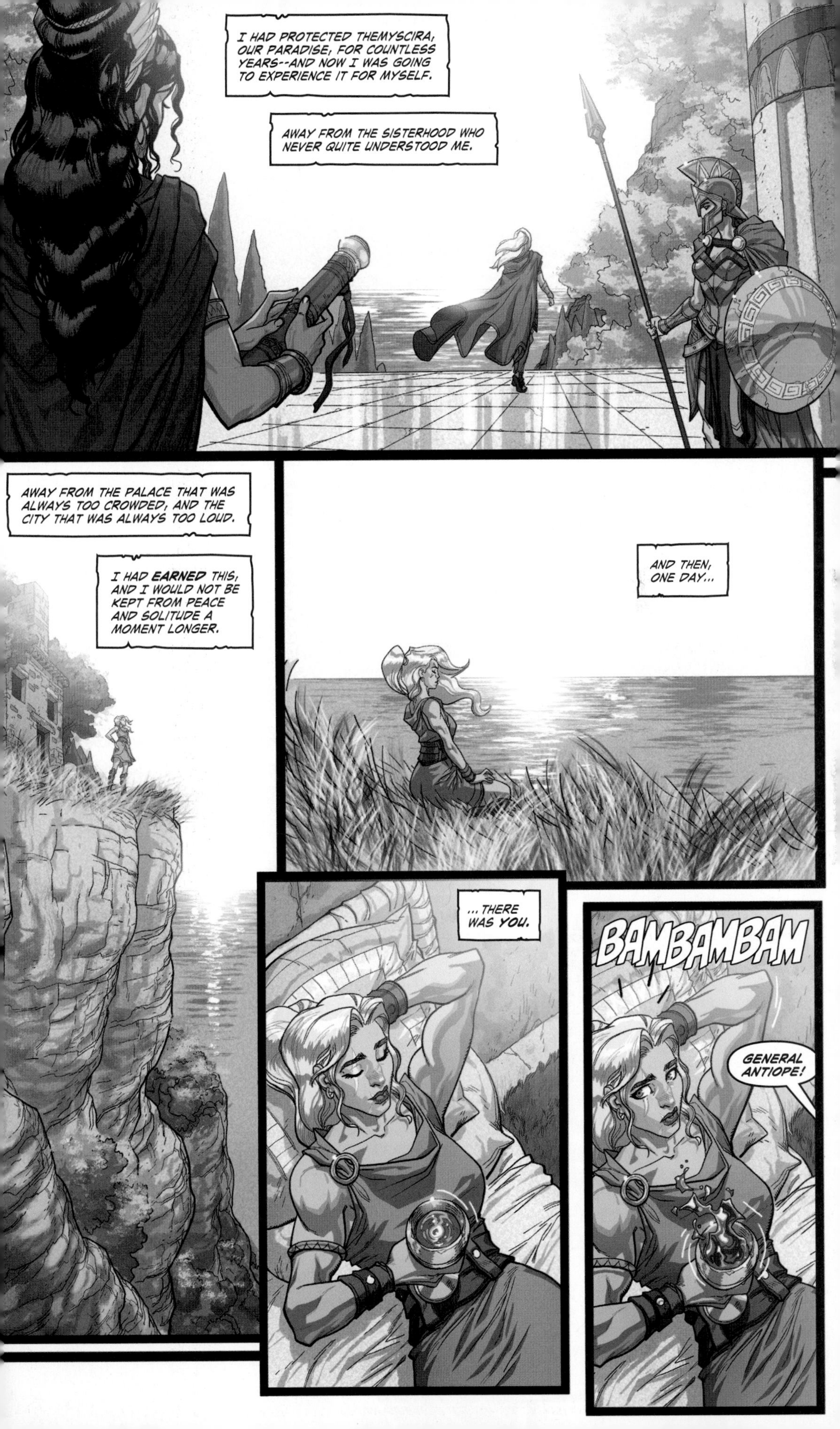
I HAD PROTECTED THEMYSCIRA, OUR PARADISE, FOR COUNTLESS YEARS--AND NOW I WAS GOING TO EXPERIENCE IT FOR MYSELF.
AWAY FROM THE SISTERHOOD WHO NEVER QUITE UNDERSTOOD ME.
AWAY FROM THE PALACE THAT WAS ALWAYS TOO CROWDED, AND THE CITY THAT WAS ALWAYS TOO LOUD.
I HAD EARNED THIS, AND I WOULD NOT BE KEPT FROM PEACE AND SOLITUDE A MOMENT LONGER.
AND THEN, ONE DAY...
...THERE WAS YOU.
BAMBAMBAM
GENERAL ANTIOPE!

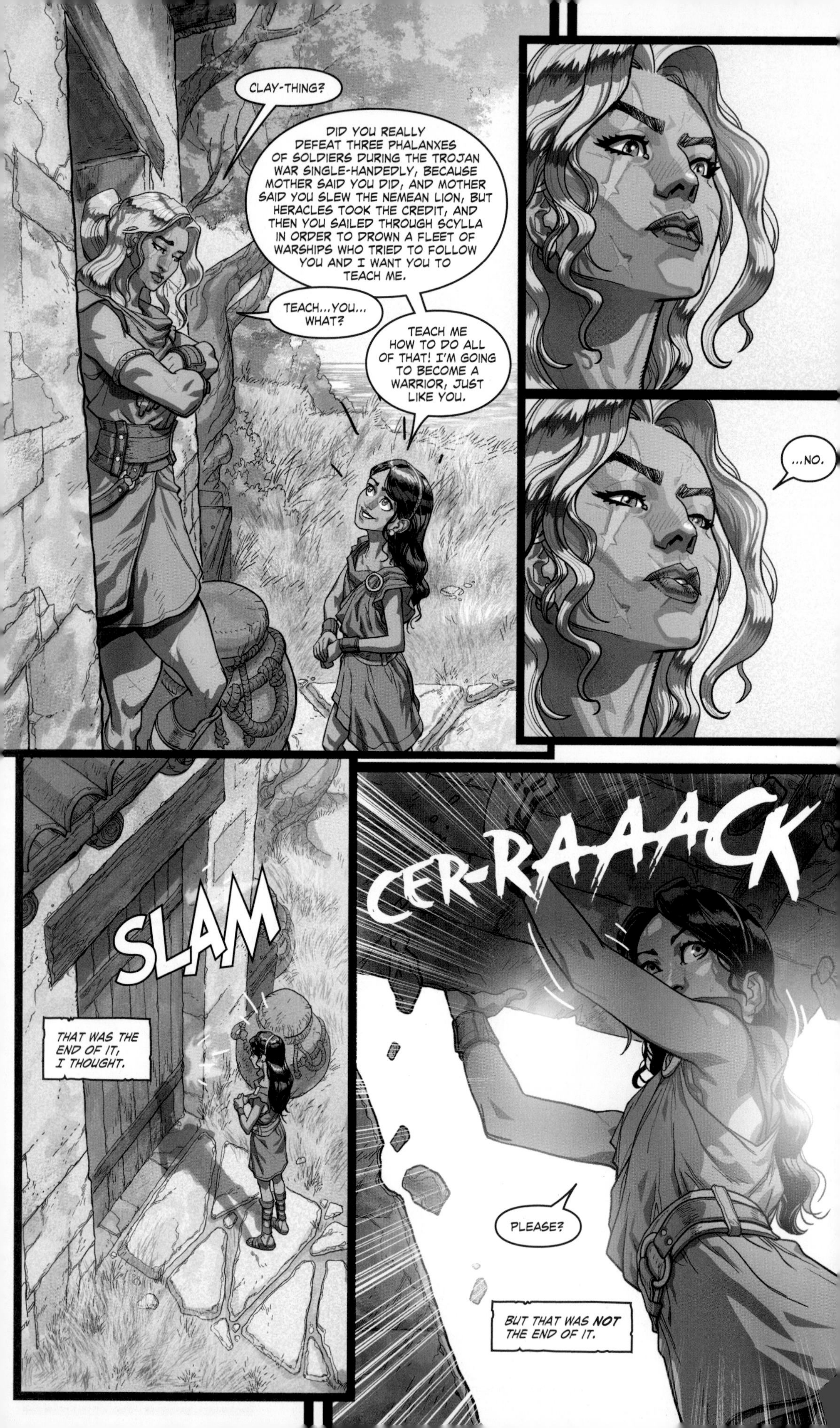
CLAY-THING?
DID YOU REALLY DEFEAT THREE PHALANXES OF SOLDIERS DURING THE TROJAN WAR SINGLE-HANDEDLY, BECAUSE MOTHER SAID YOU DID, AND MOTHER SAID YOU SLEW THE NEMEAN LION, BUT HERACLES TOOK THE CREDIT, AND THEN YOU SAILED THROUGH SCYLLA IN ORDER TO DROWN A FLEET OF WARSHIPS WHO TRIED TO FOLLOW YOU AND I WANT YOU TO TEACH ME.
TEACH...YOU... WHAT?
TEACH ME HOW TO DO ALL OF THAT! I'M GOING TO BECOME A WARRIOR, JUST LIKE YOU.
...NO.
SLAM
THAT WAS THE END OF IT, I THOUGHT.
CER-RAAACK
PLEASE?
BUT THAT WAS NOT THE END OF IT.

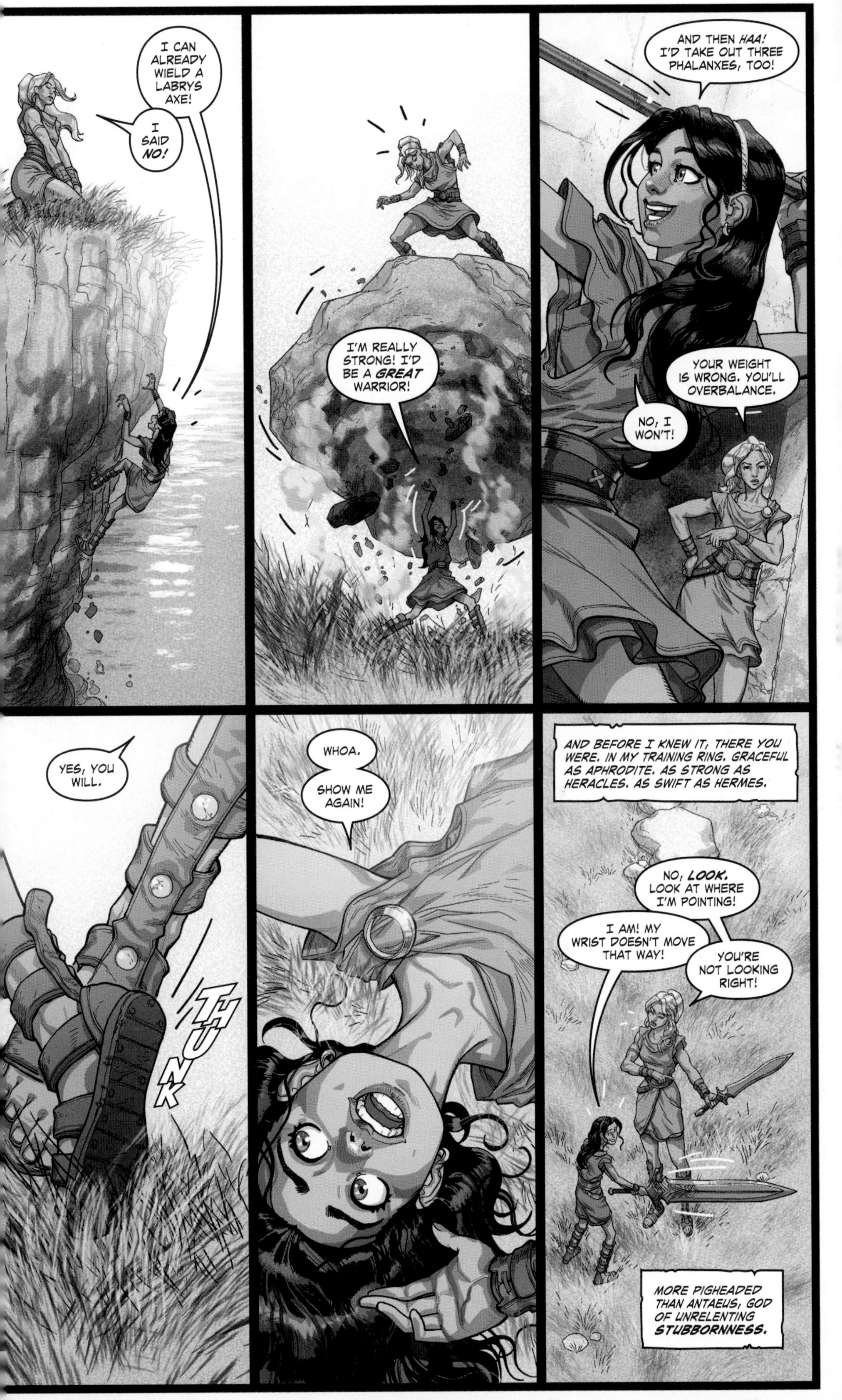
I CAN ALREADY WIELD A LABRYS AXE!
I SAID NO!
I'M REALLY STRONG! I'D BE A GREAT WARRIOR!
AND THEN HAA! I'D TAKE OUT THREE PHALANXES, TOO!
YOUR WEIGHT IS WRONG. YOU'LL OVERBALANCE.
NO, I WON'T!
YES, YOU WILL.
THUNK
WHOA.
SHOW ME AGAIN!
AND BEFORE I KNEW IT, THERE YOU WERE. IN MY TRAINING RING. GRACEFUL AS APHRODITE. AS STRONG AS HERACLES. AS SWIFT AS HERMES.
NO, LOOK. LOOK AT WHERE I'M POINTING!
I AM! MY WRIST DOESN'T MOVE THAT WAY!
YOU'RE NOT LOOKING RIGHT!
MORE PIGHEADED THAN ANTAEUS, GOD OF UNRELENTING STUBBORNNESS.

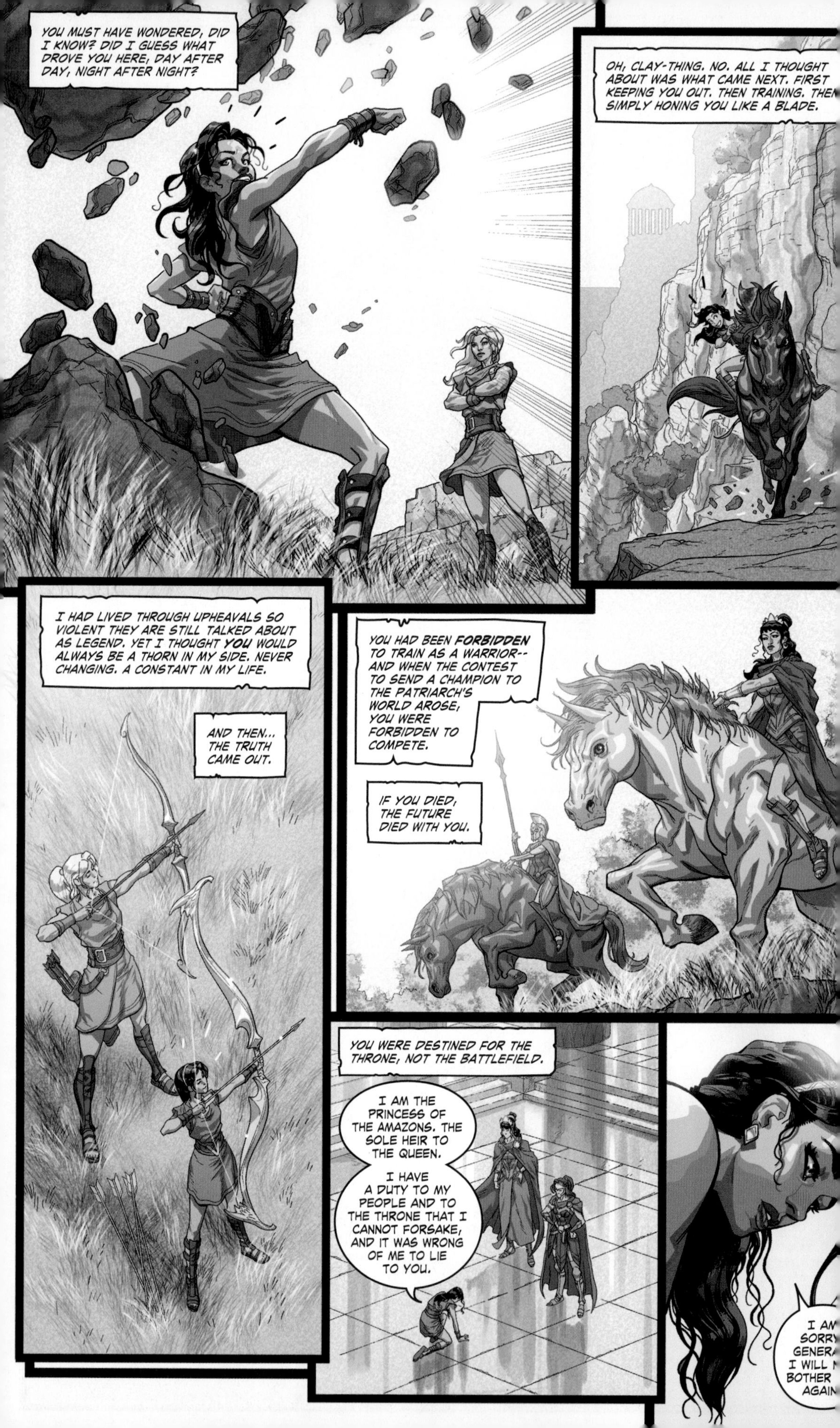

YOU MUST HAVE WONDERED, DID I KNOW? DID I GUESS WHAT DROVE YOU HERE, DAY AFTER DAY, NIGHT AFTER NIGHT?
OH, CLAY-THING. NO. ALL I THOUGHT ABOUT WAS WHAT CAME NEXT. FIRST KEEPING YOU OUT. THEN TRAINING. THE
SIMPLY HONING YOU LIKE A BLADE.
I HAD LIVED THROUGH UPHEAVALS SO VIOLENT THEY ARE STILL TALKED ABOUT AS LEGEND. YET I THOUGHT **YOU** WOULD ALWAYS BE A THORN IN MY SIDE. NEVER CHANGING. A CONSTANT IN MY LIFE.
AND THEN... THE TRUTH CAME OUT.
YOU HAD BEEN **FORBIDDEN** TO TRAIN AS A WARRIOR--AND WHEN THE CONTEST TO SEND A CHAMPION TO THE PATRIARCH'S WORLD AROSE, YOU WERE FORBIDDEN TO COMPETE.
IF YOU DIED, THE FUTURE DIED WITH YOU.
YOU WERE DESTINED FOR THE THRONE, NOT THE BATTLEFIELD.
I AM THE PRINCESS OF THE AMAZONS. THE SOLE HEIR TO THE QUEEN.
I HAVE A DUTY TO MY PEOPLE AND TO THE THRONE THAT I CANNOT FORSAKE, AND IT WAS WRONG OF ME TO LIE TO YOU.
I AM SORRY GENERA I WILL BOTHER AGAIN

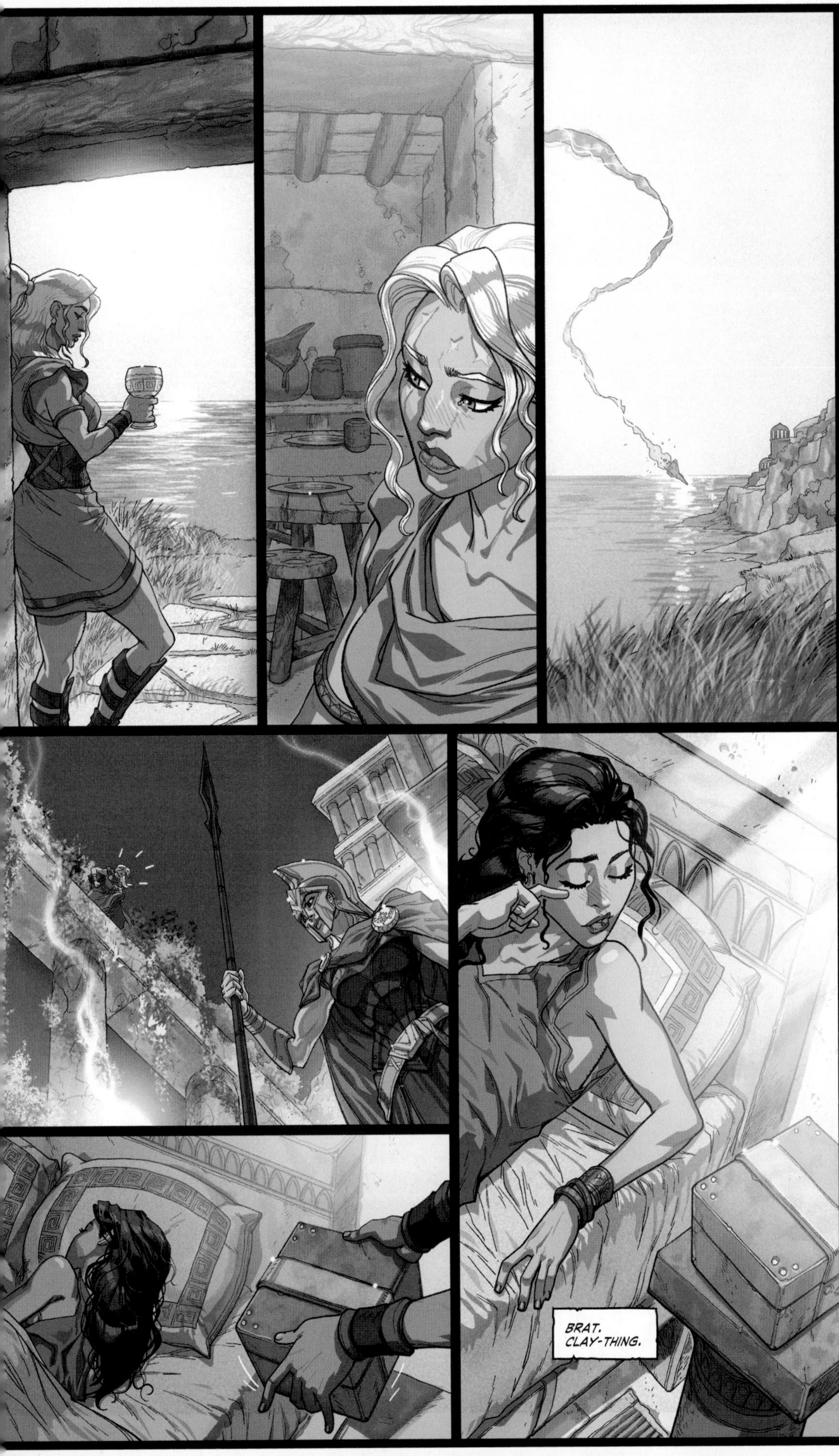
BRAT.
CLAY-THING.

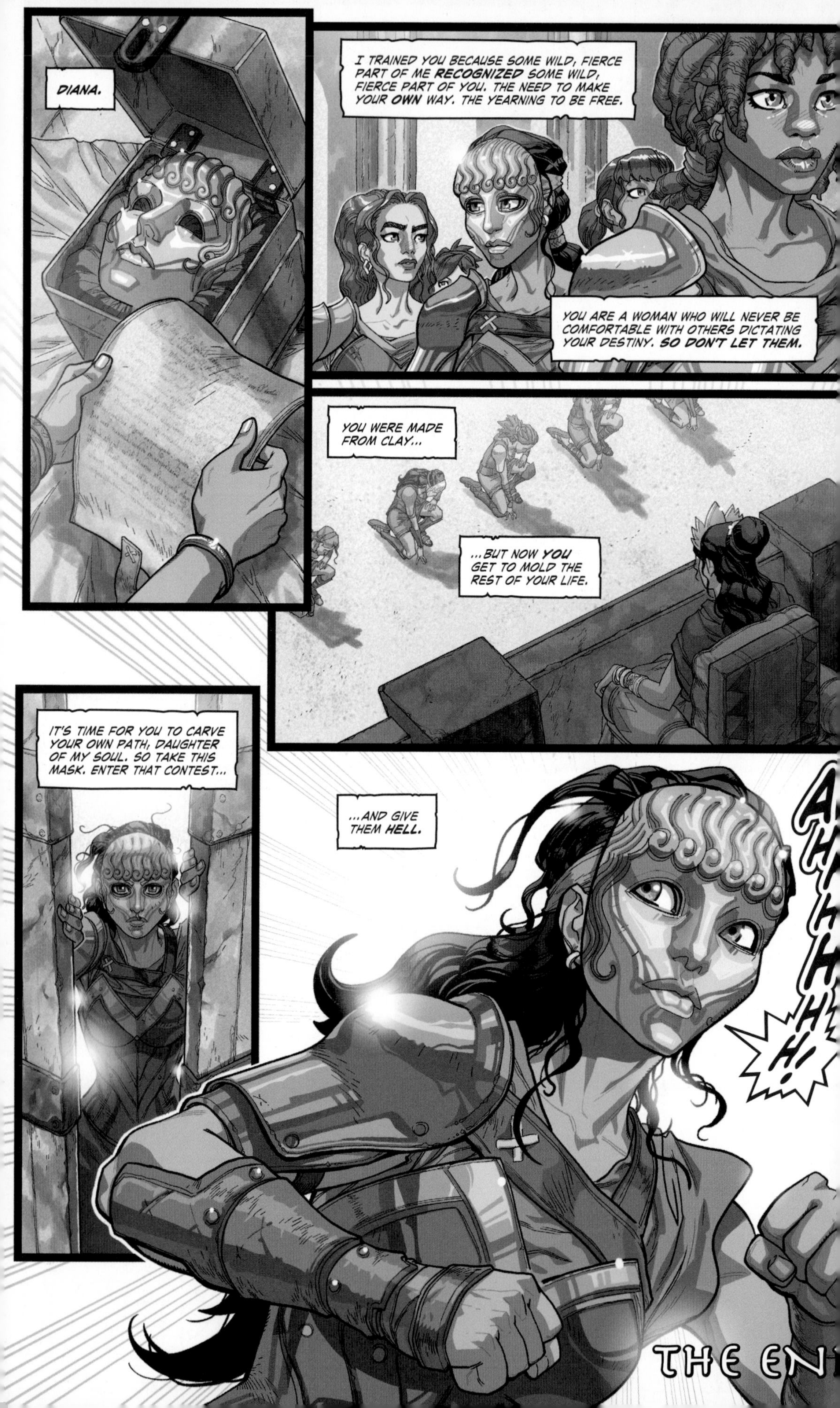
DIANA.
I TRAINED YOU BECAUSE SOME WILD, FIERCE PART OF ME RECOGNIZED SOME WILD, FIERCE PART OF YOU. THE NEED TO MAKE YOUR OWN WAY. THE YEARNING TO BE FREE.
YOU ARE A WOMAN WHO WILL NEVER BE COMFORTABLE WITH OTHERS DICTATING YOUR DESTINY. SO DON'T LET THEM.
YOU WERE MADE FROM CLAY...
...BUT NOW YOU GET TO MOLD THE REST OF YOUR LIFE.
IT'S TIME FOR YOU TO CARVE YOUR OWN PATH, DAUGHTER OF MY SOUL. SO TAKE THIS MASK. ENTER THAT CONTEST...
...AND GIVE THEM HELL.
AHHHHHHH!
THE EN

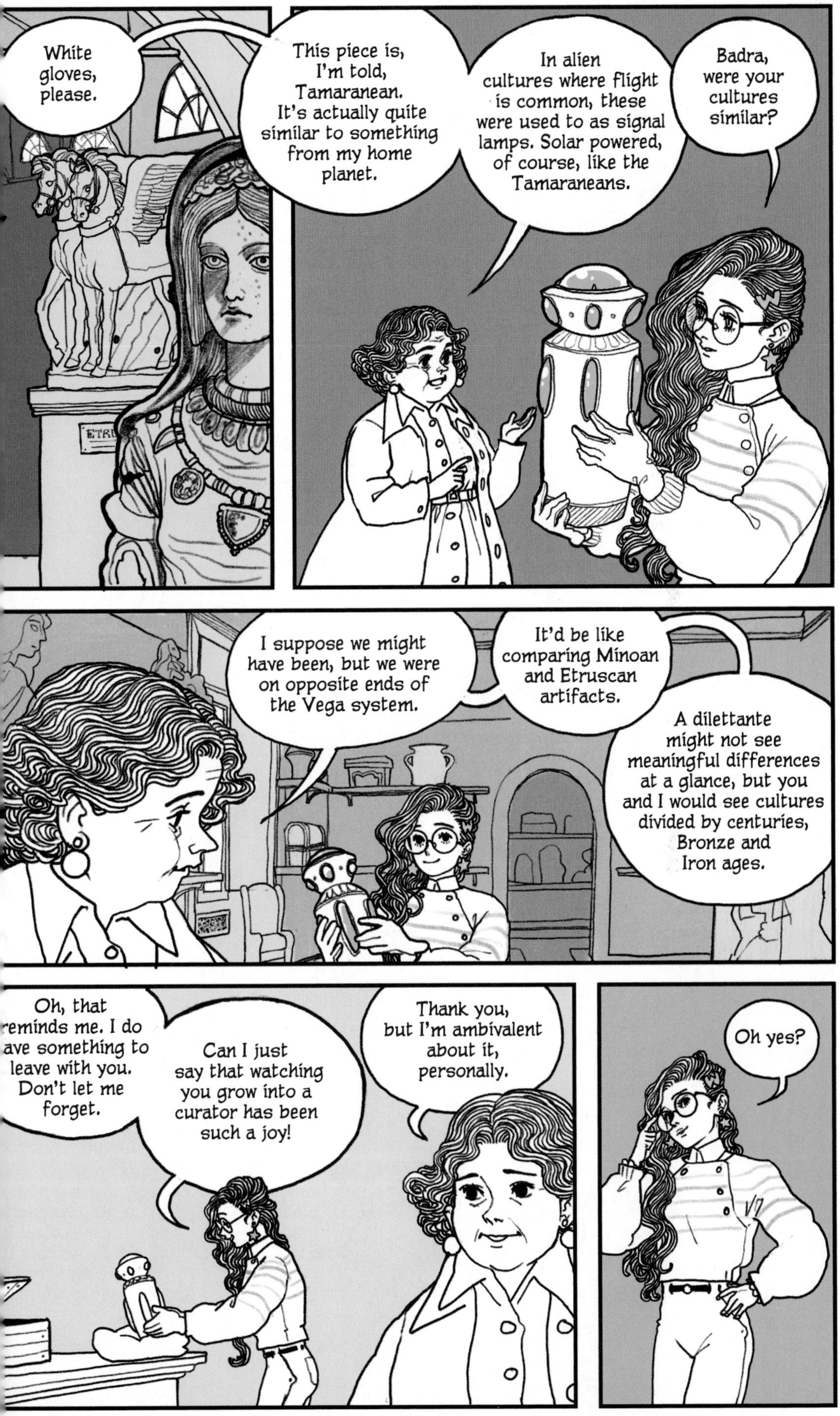
White gloves, please.
This piece is, I'm told, Tamaranean. It's actually quite similar to something from my home planet.
In alien cultures where flight is common, these were used to as signal lamps. Solar powered, of course, like the Tamaraneans.
Badra, were your cultures similar?
I suppose we might have been, but we were on opposite ends of the Vega system.
It'd be like comparing Minoan and Etruscan artifacts.
A dilettante might not see meaningful differences at a glance, but you and I would see cultures divided by centuries, Bronze and Iron ages.
Oh, that reminds me. I do have something to leave with you. Don't let me forget.
Can I just say that watching you grow into a curator has been such a joy!
Thank you, but I'm ambivalent about it, personally.
Oh yes?

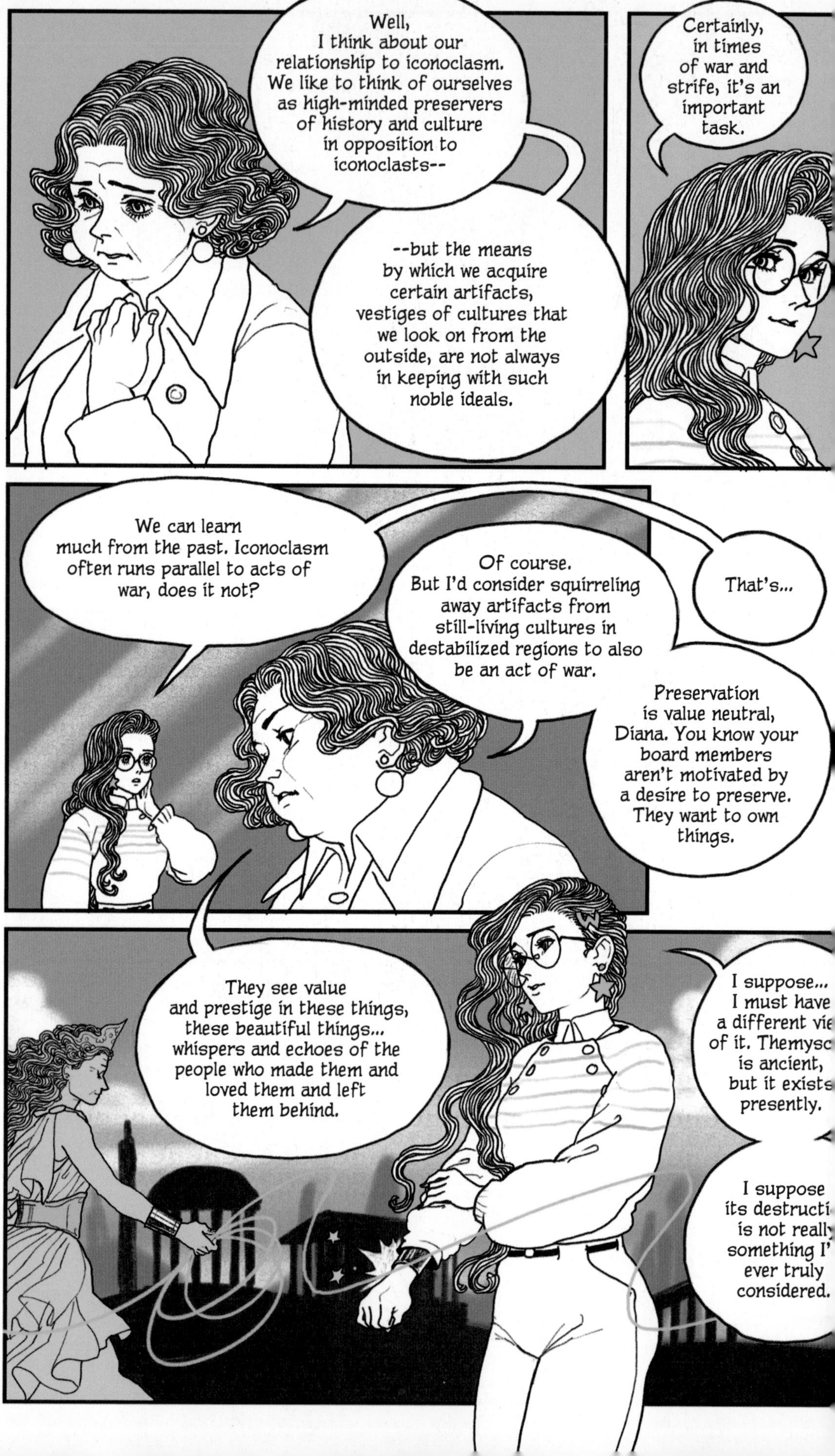

Well, I think about our relationship to iconoclasm. We like to think of ourselves as high-minded preservers of history and culture in opposition to iconoclasts--
--but the means by which we acquire certain artifacts, vestiges of cultures that we look on from the outside, are not always in keeping with such noble ideals.
Certainly, in times of war and strife, it's an important task.
We can learn much from the past. Iconoclasm often runs parallel to acts of war, does it not?
That's...
Of course. But I'd consider squirreling away artifacts from still-living cultures in destabilized regions to also be an act of war.
Preservation is value neutral, Diana. You know your board members aren't motivated by a desire to preserve. They want to own things.
They see value and prestige in these things, these beautiful things... whispers and echoes of the people who made them and loved them and left them behind.
I suppose... I must have a different vie of it. Themysc is ancient, but it exists presently.
I suppose its destructi is not reall something I' ever truly considered.

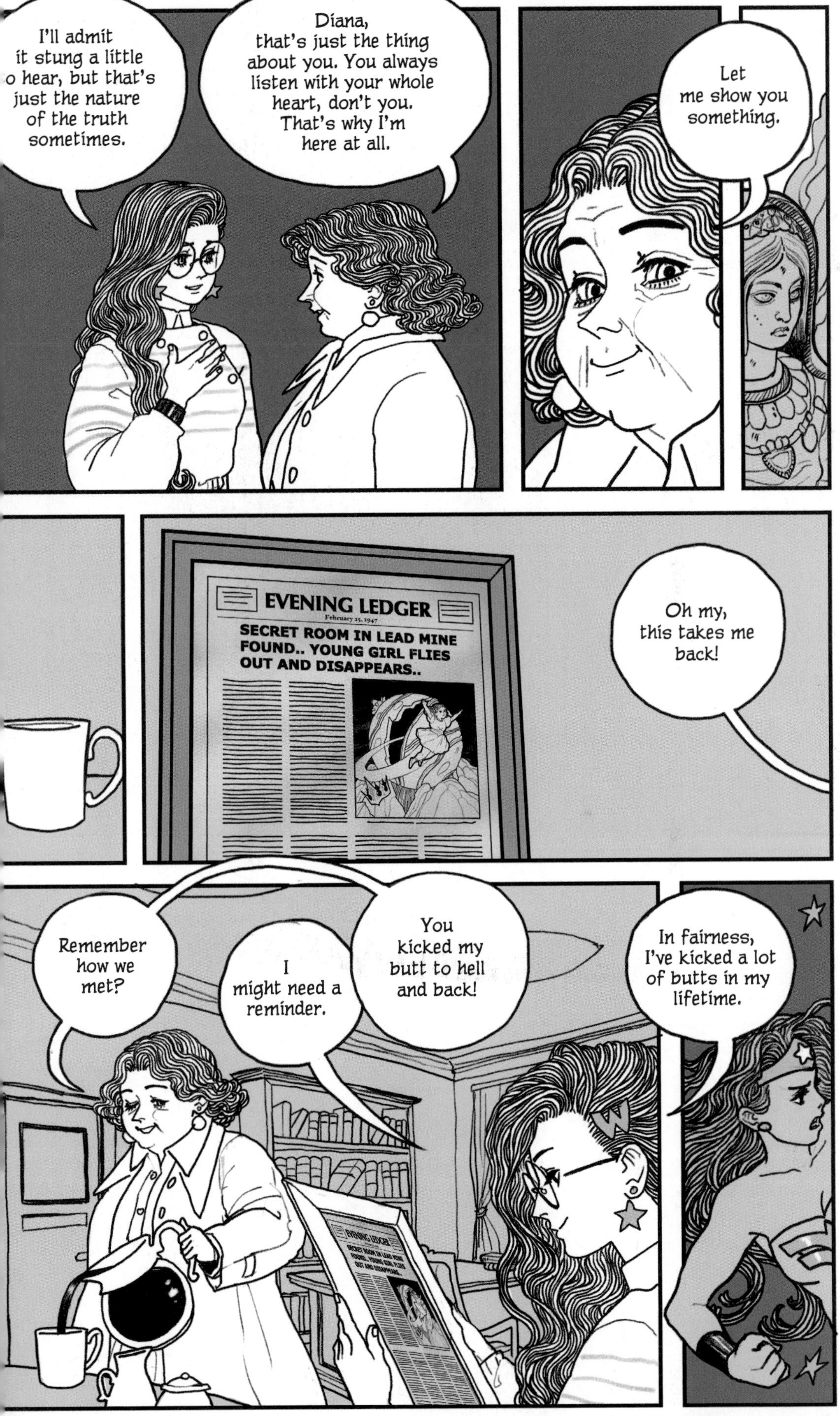
I'll admit it stung a little o hear, but that's just the nature of the truth sometimes.
Diana, that's just the thing about you. You always listen with your whole heart, don't you. That's why I'm here at all.
Let me show you something.
EVENING LEDGER
February 25, 1947
SECRET ROOM IN LEAD MINE FOUND.. YOUNG GIRL FLIES OUT AND DISAPPEARS..
Oh my, this takes me back!
Remember how we met?
I might need a reminder.
You kicked my butt to hell and back!
In fairness, I've kicked a lot of butts in my lifetime.

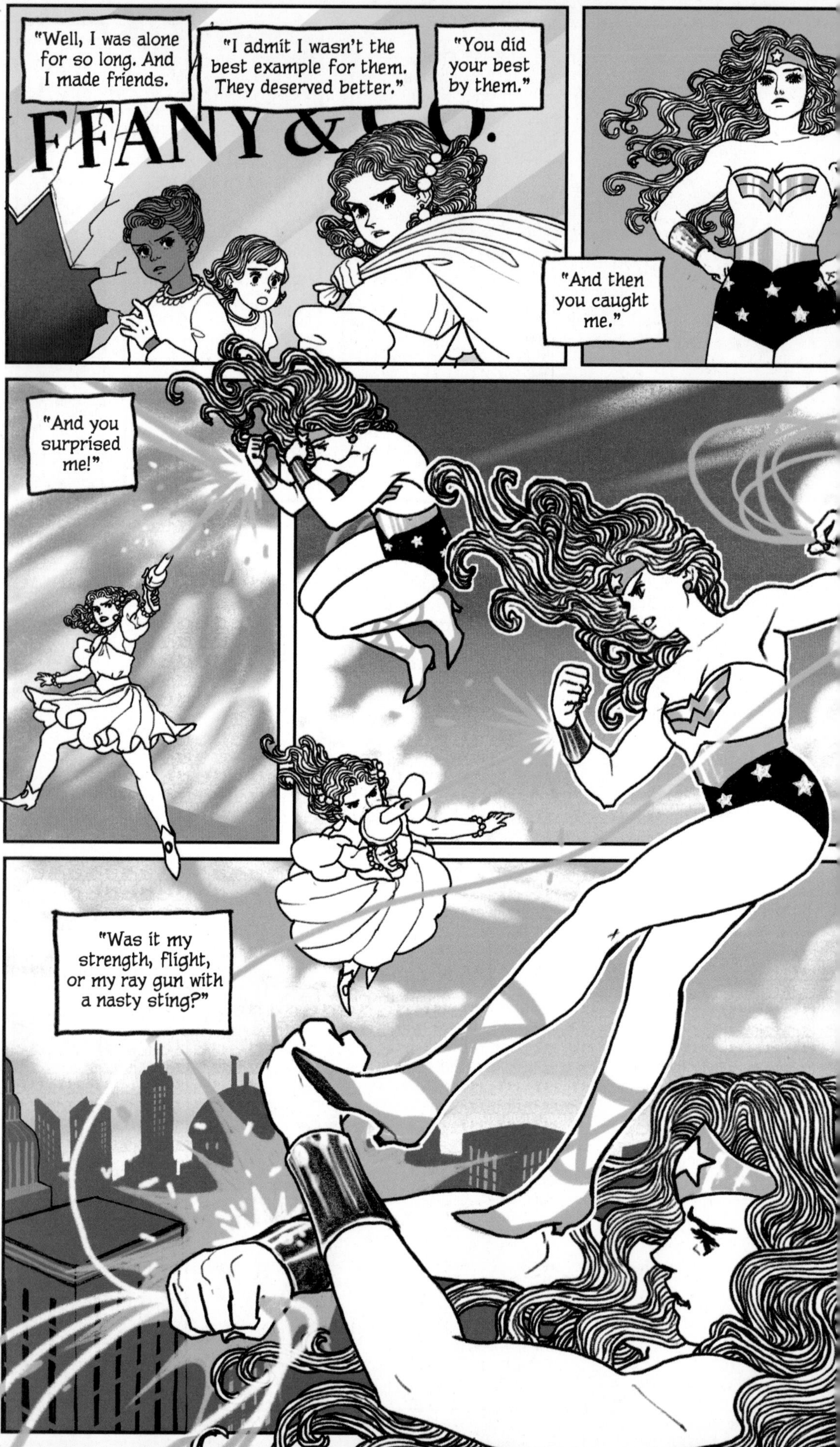
"Well, I was alone for so long. And I made friends.
"I admit I wasn't the best example for them. They deserved better."
"You did your best by them."
FFANY&CO.
"And then you caught me."
"And you surprised me!"
"Was it my strength, flight, or my ray gun with a nasty sting?"

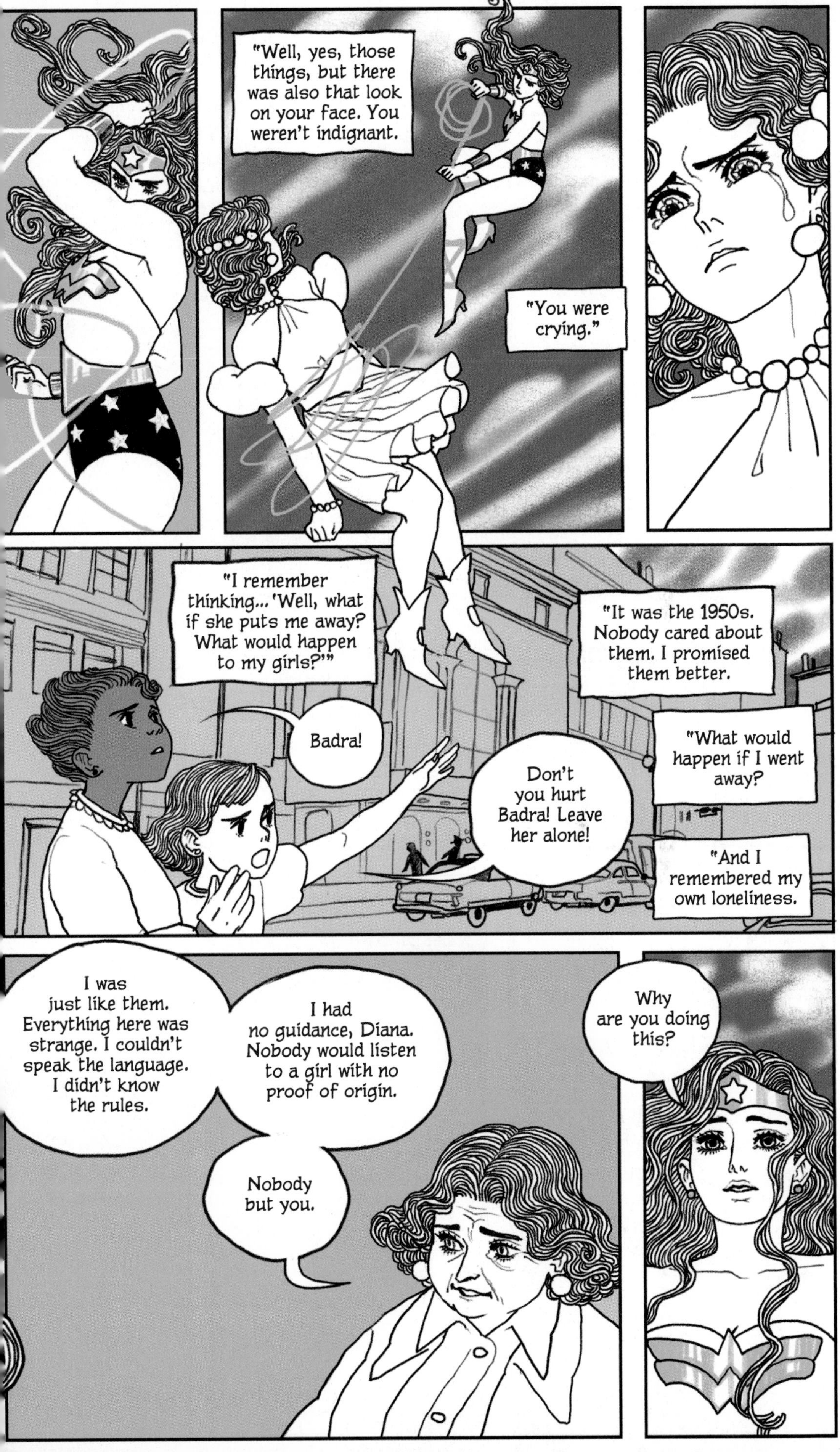
"Well, yes, those things, but there was also that look on your face. You weren't indignant.
"You were crying."
"I remember thinking... 'Well, what if she puts me away? What would happen to my girls?'"
"It was the 1950s. Nobody cared about them. I promised them better.
Badra!
Don't you hurt Badra! Leave her alone!
"What would happen if I went away?
"And I remembered my own loneliness.
I was just like them. Everything here was strange. I couldn't speak the language. I didn't know the rules.
I had no guidance, Diana. Nobody would listen to a girl with no proof of origin.
Nobody but you.
Why are you doing this?

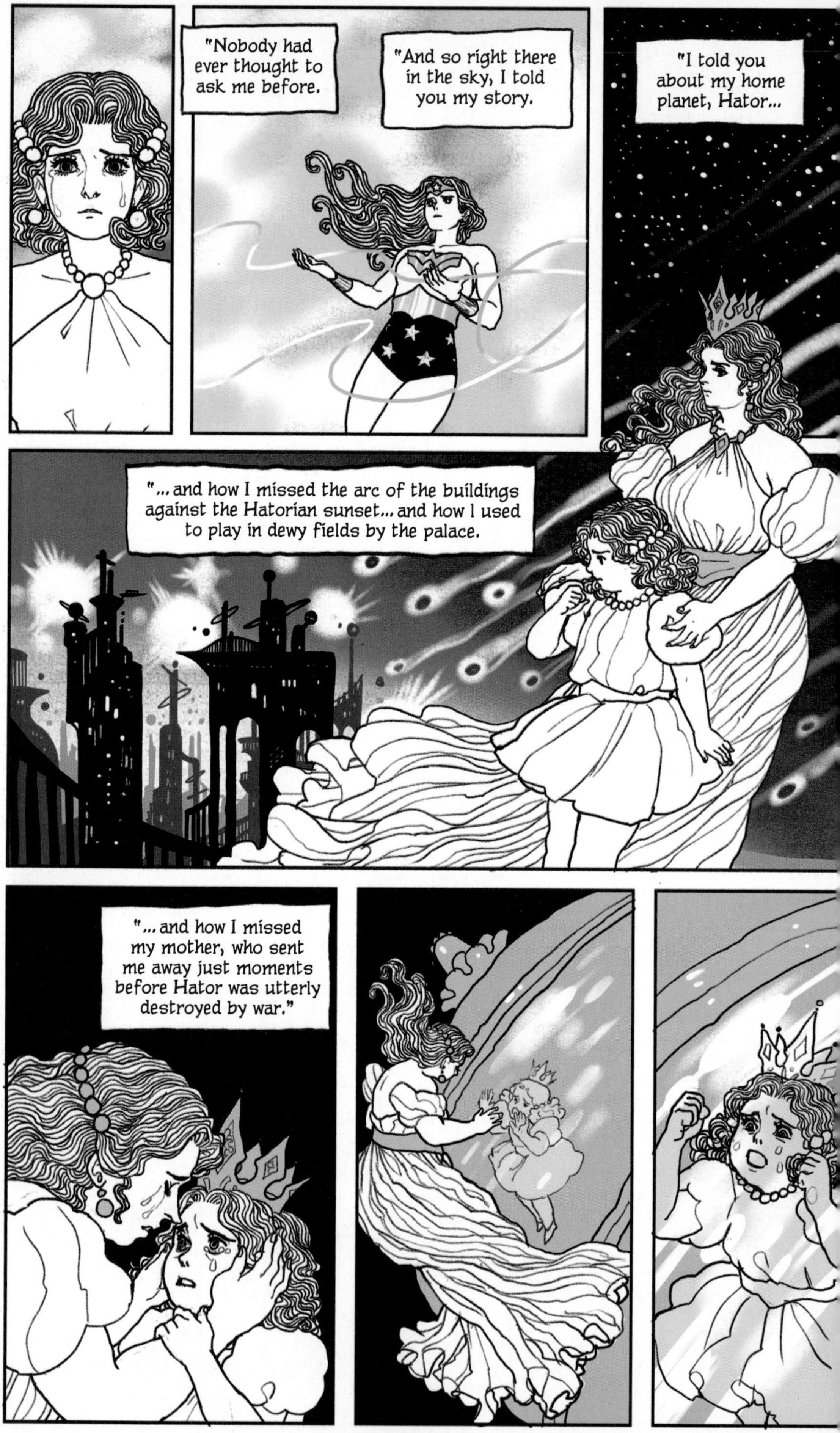
"Nobody had ever thought to ask me before.
"And so right there in the sky, I told you my story.
"I told you about my home planet, Hator...
"... and how I missed the arc of the buildings against the Hatorian sunset... and how I used to play in dewy fields by the palace.
"... and how I missed my mother, who sent me away just moments before Hator was utterly destroyed by war."

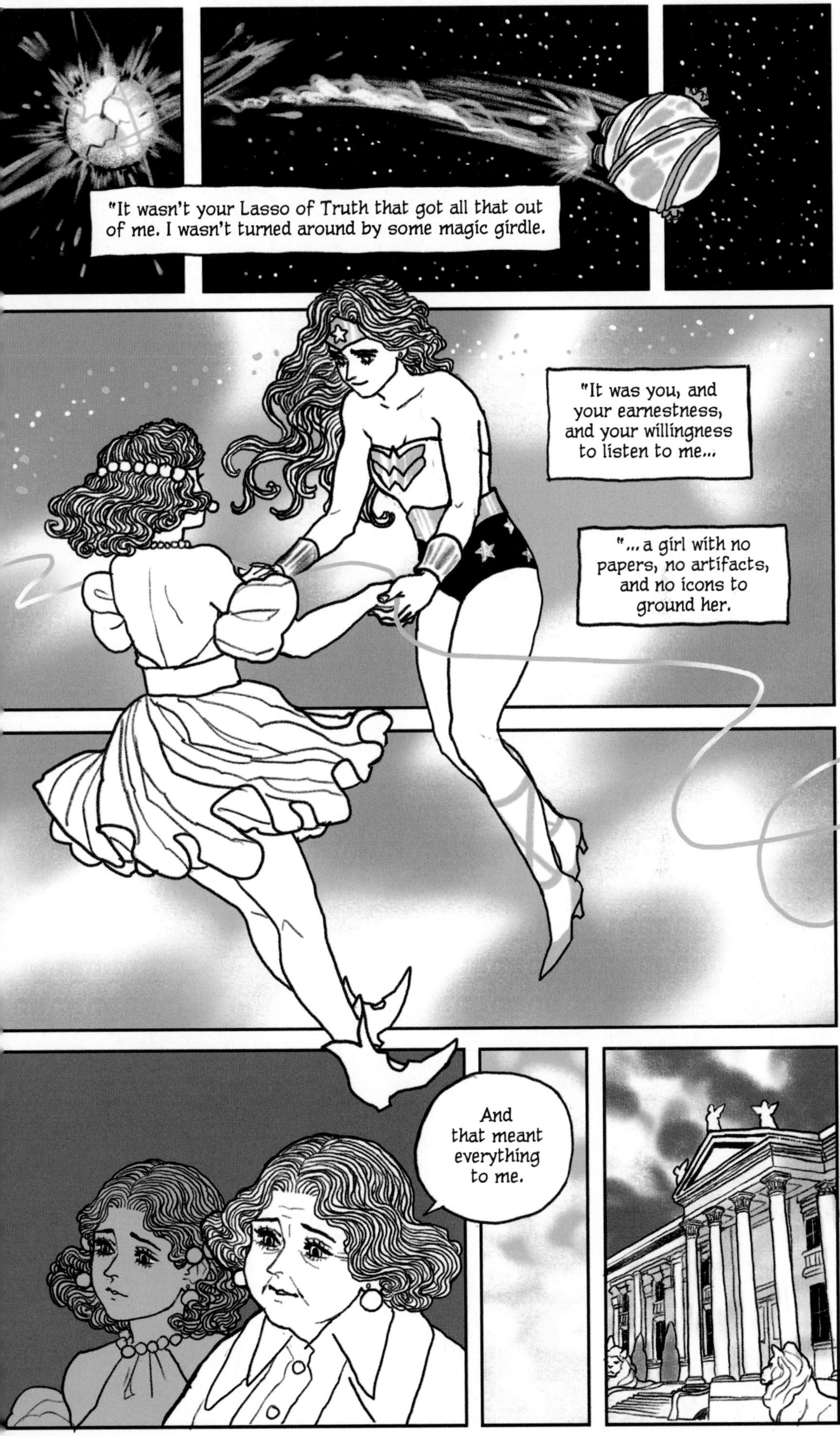
"It wasn't your Lasso of Truth that got all that out of me. I wasn't turned around by some magic girdle.
"It was you, and your earnestness, and your willingness to listen to me...
"...a girl with no papers, no artifacts, and no icons to ground her.
And that meant everything to me.

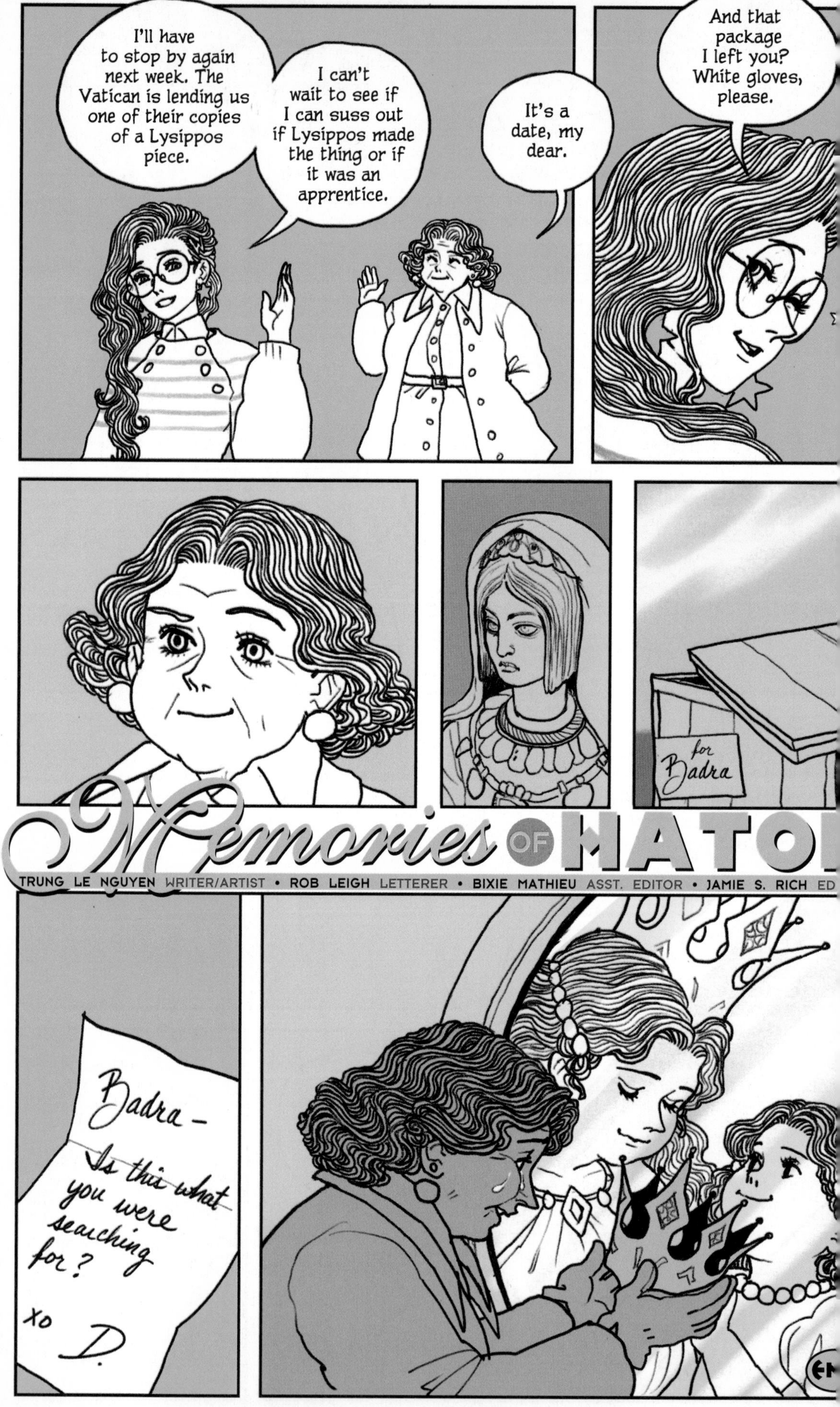
I'll have to stop by again next week. The Vatican is lending us one of their copies of a Lysippos piece.
I can't wait to see if I can suss out if Lysippos made the thing or if it was an apprentice.
It's a date, my dear.
And that package I left you? White gloves, please.
for Badra
Memories OF HATO
TRUNG LE NGUYEN WRITER/ARTIST • ROB LEIGH LETTERER • BIXIE MATHIEU ASST. EDITOR • JAMIE S. RICH ED
Badra — Is this what you were searching for?
xo D.

Cover by Lee Bermejo

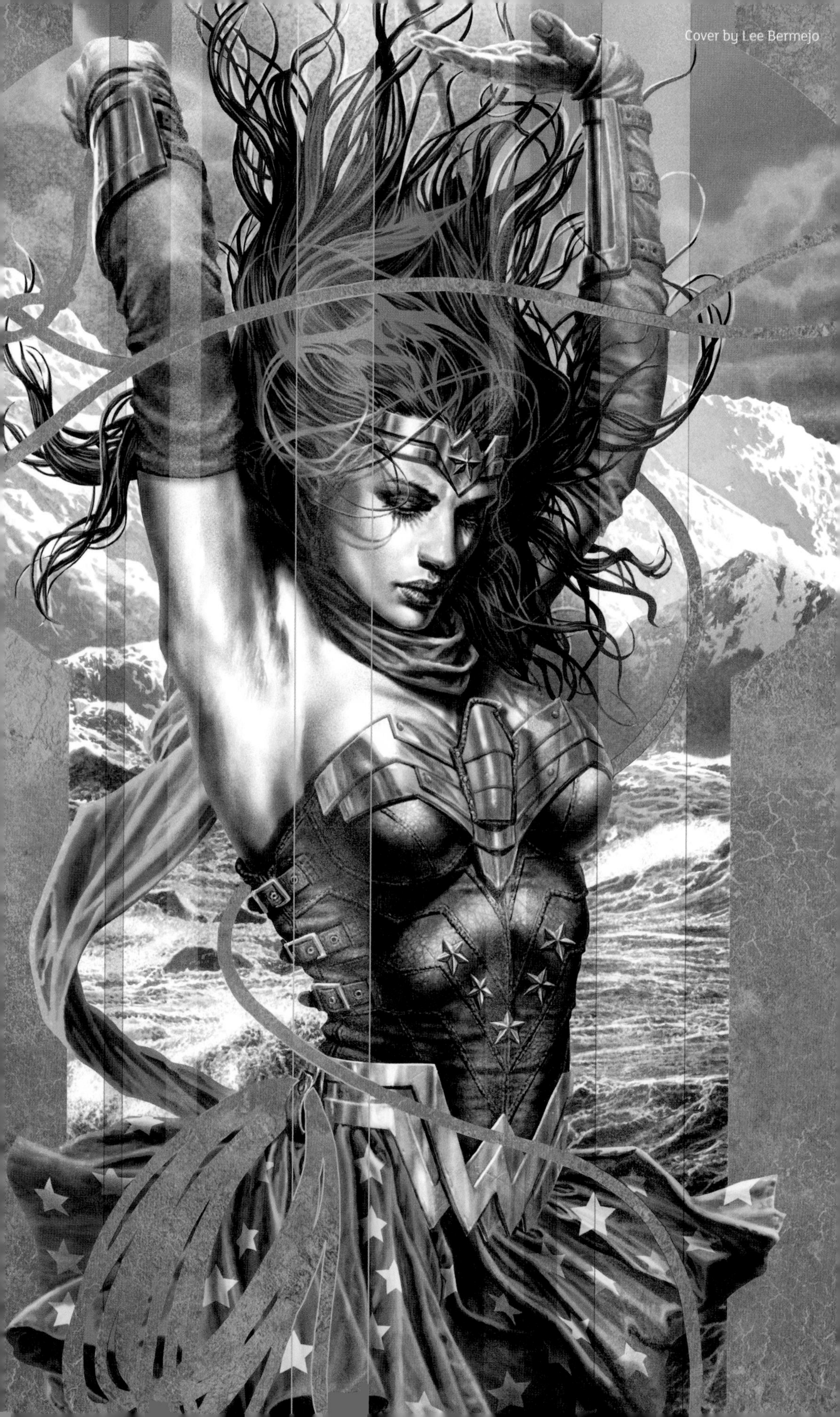

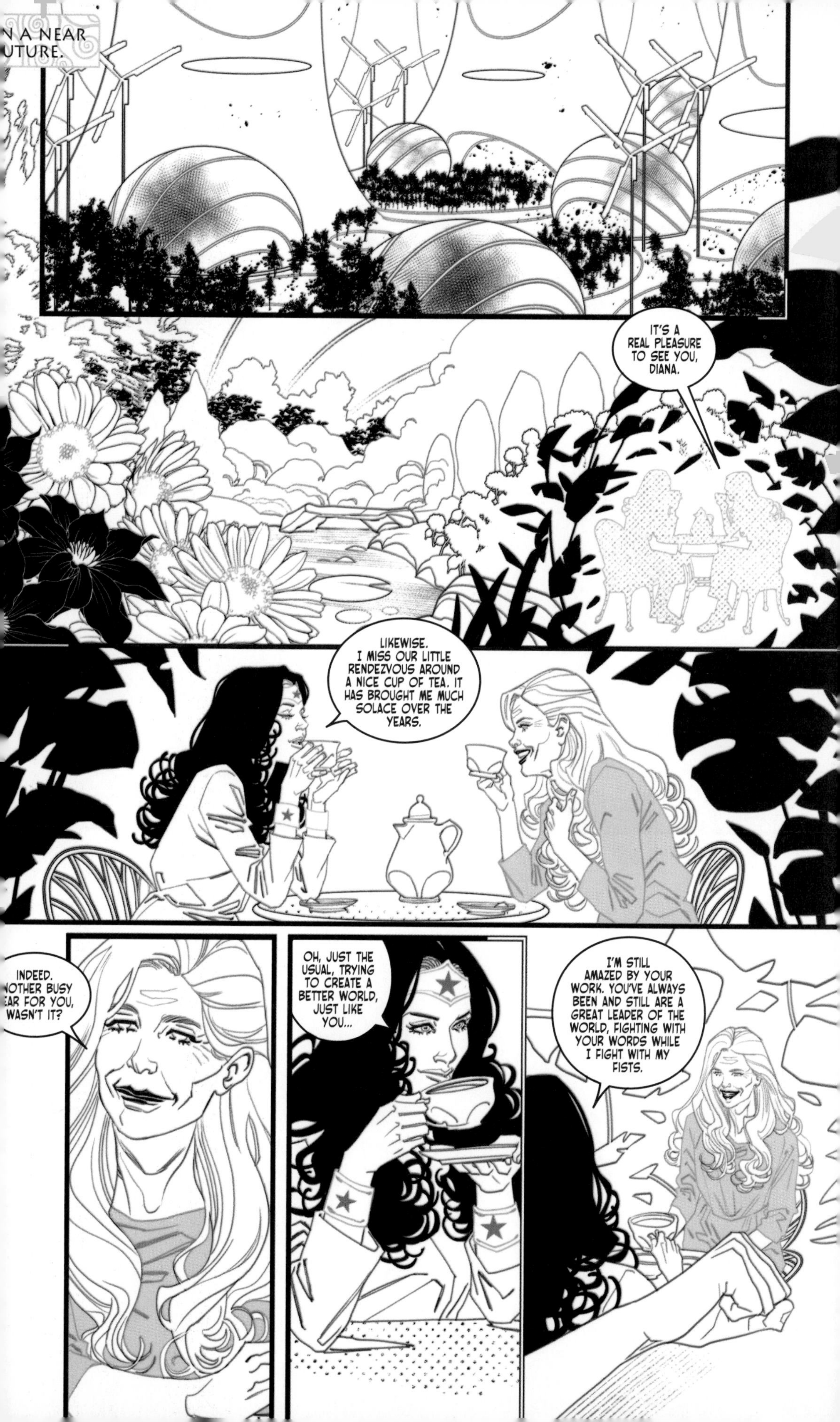
N A NEAR
UTURE.
IT'S A REAL PLEASURE TO SEE YOU, DIANA.
LIKEWISE. I MISS OUR LITTLE RENDEZVOUS AROUND A NICE CUP OF TEA. IT HAS BROUGHT ME MUCH SOLACE OVER THE YEARS.
INDEED. NOTHER BUSY EAR FOR YOU, WASN'T IT?
OH, JUST THE USUAL, TRYING TO CREATE A BETTER WORLD, JUST LIKE YOU...
I'M STILL AMAZED BY YOUR WORK. YOU'VE ALWAYS BEEN AND STILL ARE A GREAT LEADER OF THE WORLD, FIGHTING WITH YOUR WORDS WHILE I FIGHT WITH MY FISTS.

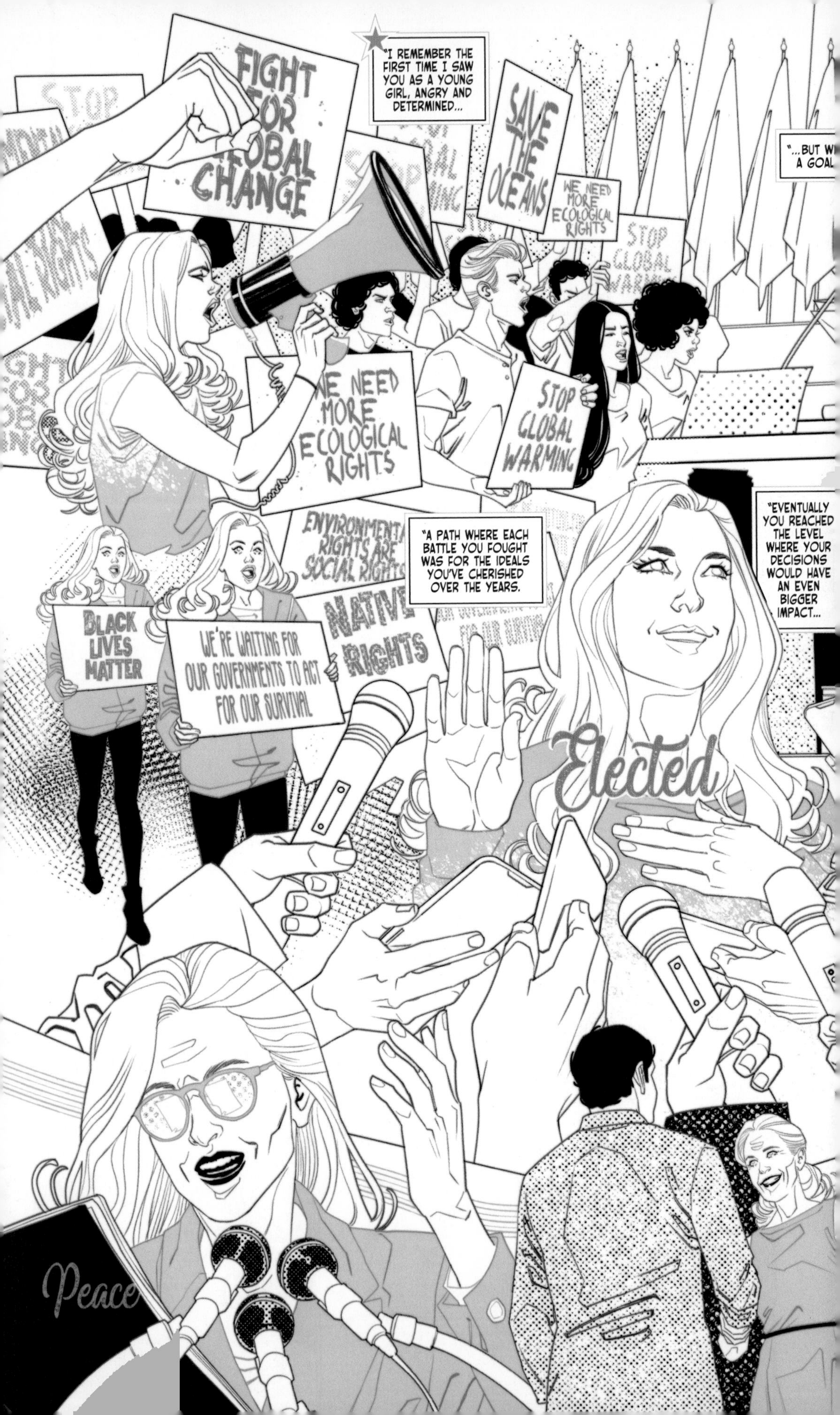

"I REMEMBER THE FIRST TIME I SAW YOU AS A YOUNG GIRL, ANGRY AND DETERMINED...
"...BUT W
A GOAL
FIGHT FOR GLOBAL CHANGE
STOP
SAVE THE OCEANS
WE NEED MORE ECOLOGICAL RIGHTS
STOP GLOBAL WARMING
WE NEED MORE ECOLOGICAL RIGHTS
STOP GLOBAL WARMING
ENVIRONMENTAL RIGHTS ARE SOCIAL RIGHTS
"A PATH WHERE EACH BATTLE YOU FOUGHT WAS FOR THE IDEALS YOU'VE CHERISHED OVER THE YEARS.
"EVENTUALLY YOU REACHED THE LEVEL WHERE YOUR DECISIONS WOULD HAVE AN EVEN BIGGER IMPACT...
BLACK LIVES MATTER
WE'RE WAITING FOR OUR GOVERNMENTS TO ACT FOR OUR SURVIVAL
NATIVE RIGHTS
Elected
Peace

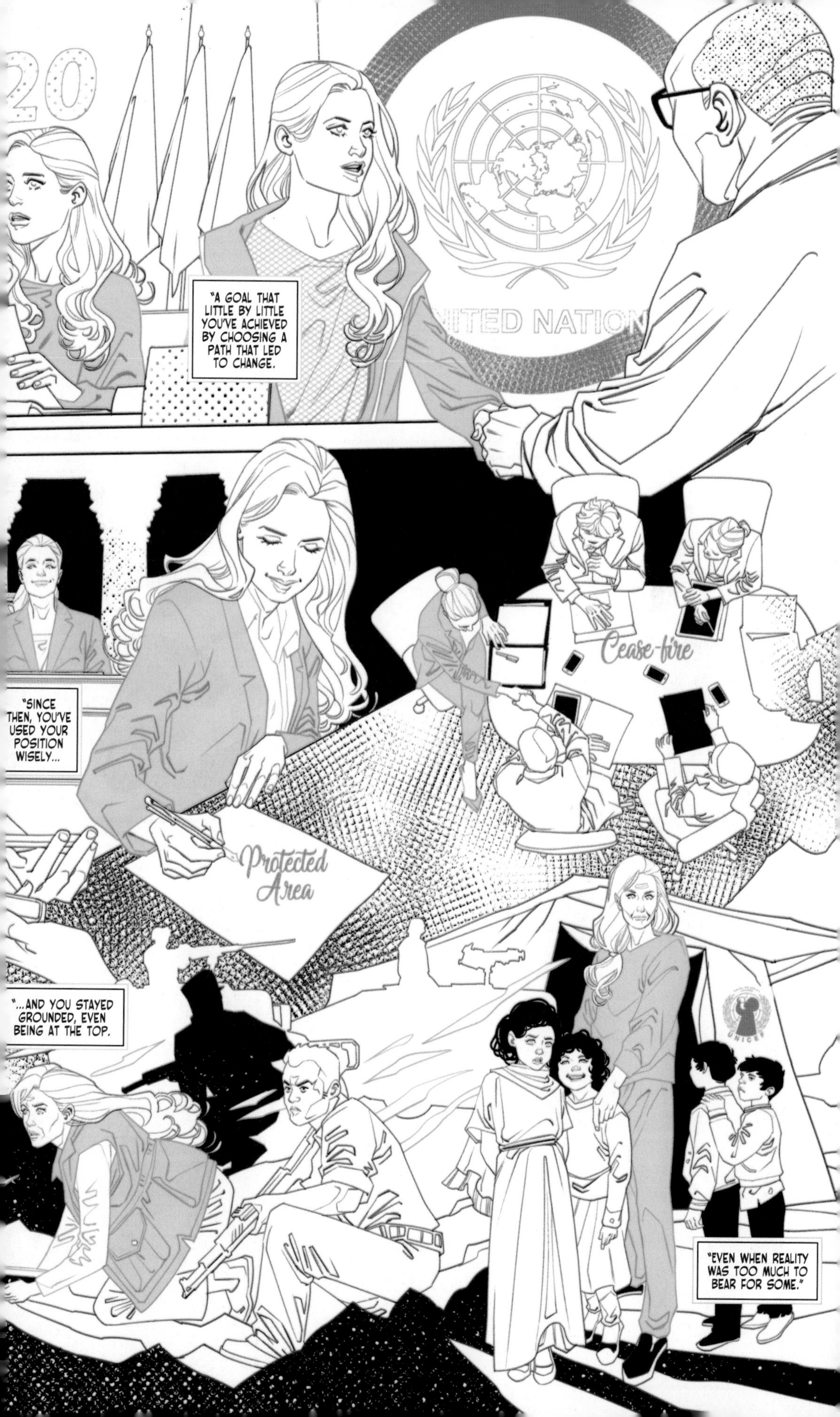
20
"A GOAL THAT LITTLE BY LITTLE YOU'VE ACHIEVED BY CHOOSING A PATH THAT LED TO CHANGE.
UNITED NATIONS
Cease-fire
"SINCE THEN, YOU'VE USED YOUR POSITION WISELY...
Protected Area
"...AND YOU STAYED GROUNDED, EVEN BEING AT THE TOP.
UNICEF
"EVEN WHEN REALITY WAS TOO MUCH TO BEAR FOR SOME."

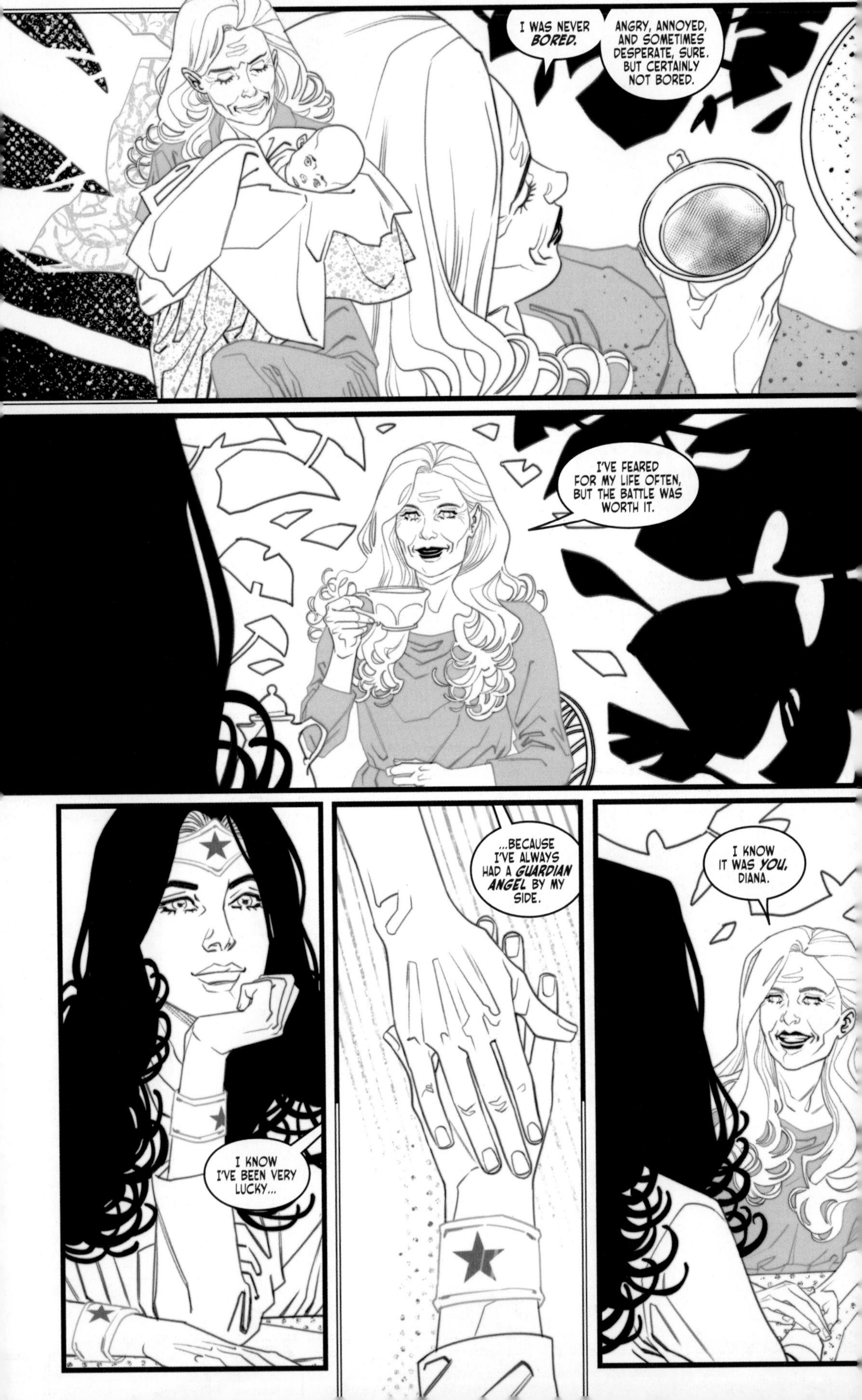
I WAS NEVER *BORED.*
ANGRY, ANNOYED, AND SOMETIMES DESPERATE, SURE. BUT CERTAINLY NOT BORED.
I'VE FEARED FOR MY LIFE OFTEN, BUT THE BATTLE WAS WORTH IT.
I KNOW I'VE BEEN VERY LUCKY...
...BECAUSE I'VE ALWAYS HAD A *GUARDIAN ANGEL* BY MY SIDE.
I KNOW IT WAS *YOU,* DIANA.

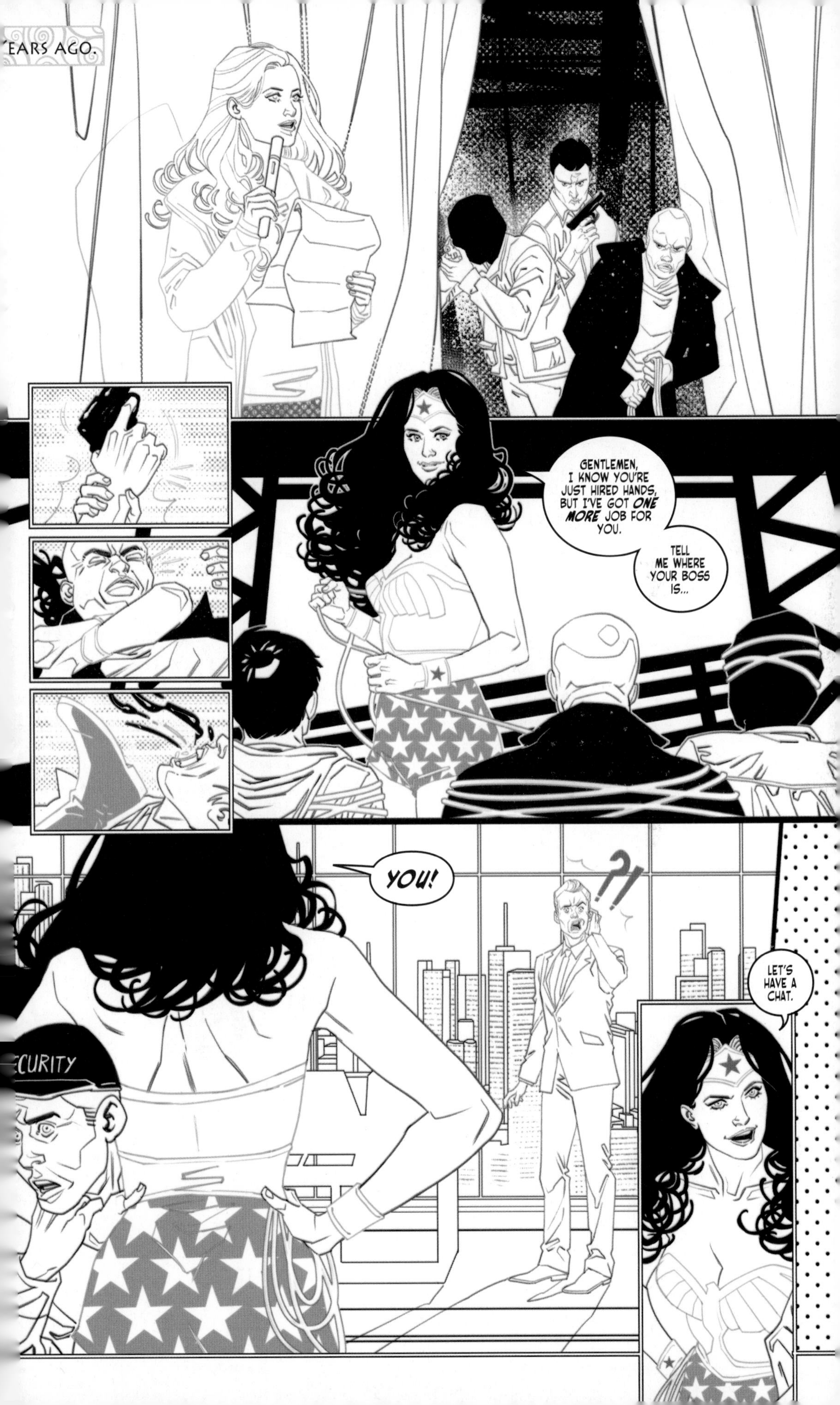

ʼEARS AGO.
GENTLEMEN, I KNOW YOU'RE JUST HIRED HANDS, BUT I'VE GOT *ONE MORE* JOB FOR YOU.
TELL ME WHERE YOUR BOSS IS...
YOU!
?!
CURITY
LET'S HAVE A CHAT.

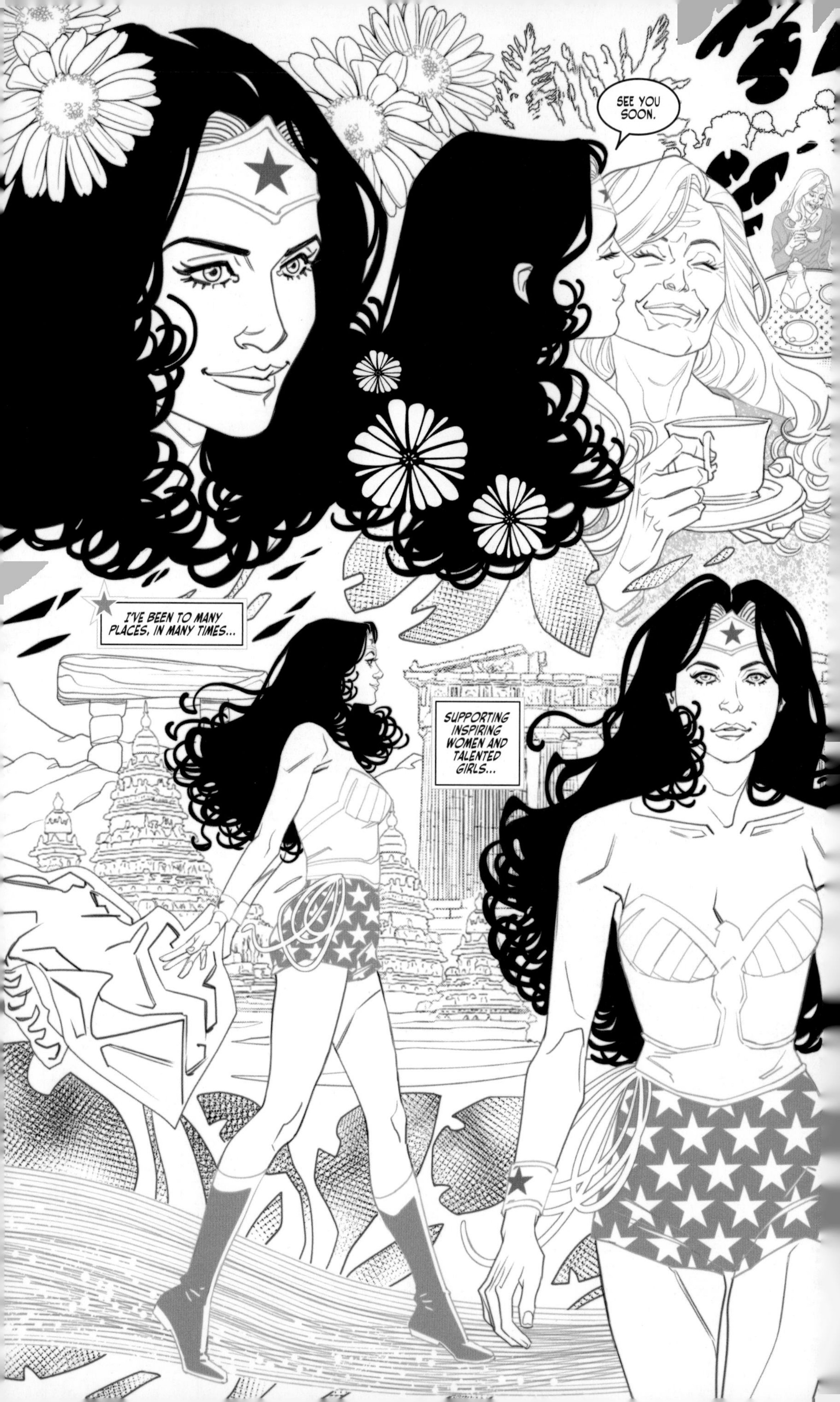
SEE YOU SOON.
I'VE BEEN TO MANY PLACES, IN MANY TIMES...
SUPPORTING INSPIRING WOMEN AND TALENTED GIRLS...

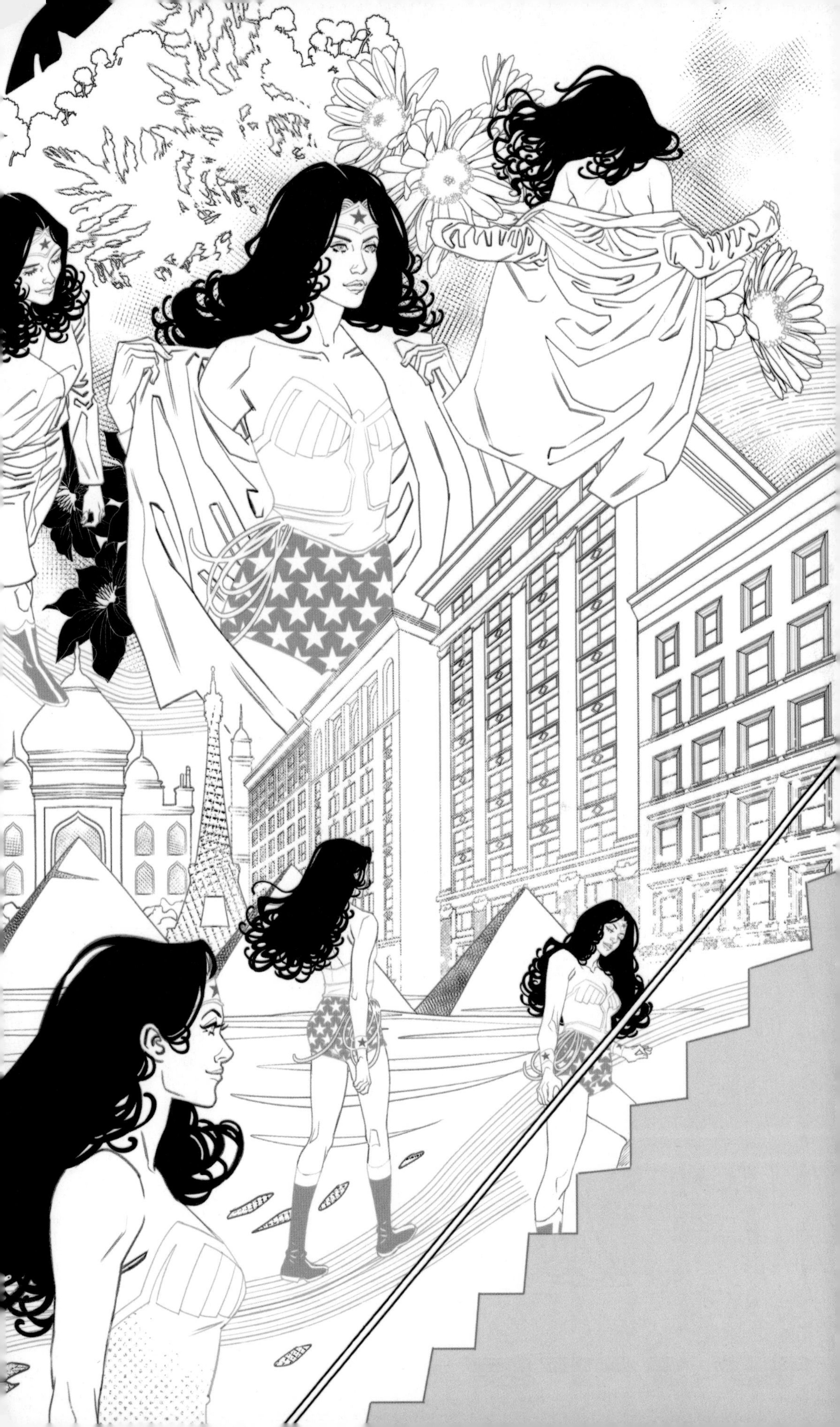

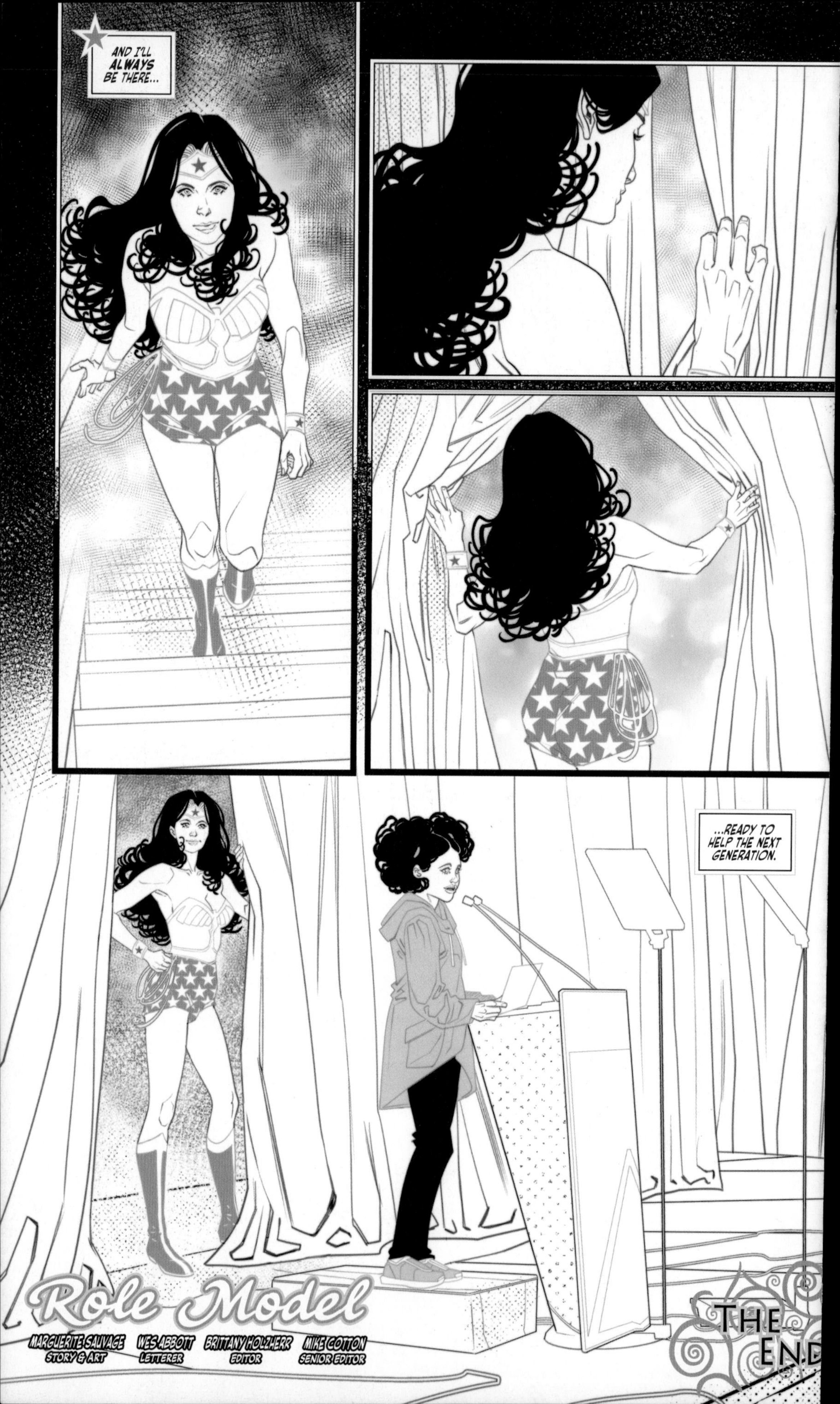

AND I'LL ALWAYS BE THERE...
...READY TO HELP THE NEXT GENERATION.
Role Model
MARGUERITE SAUVAGE STORY & ART
WES ABBOTT LETTERER
BRITTANY HOLZHERR EDITOR
MIKE COTTON SENIOR EDITOR
THE END

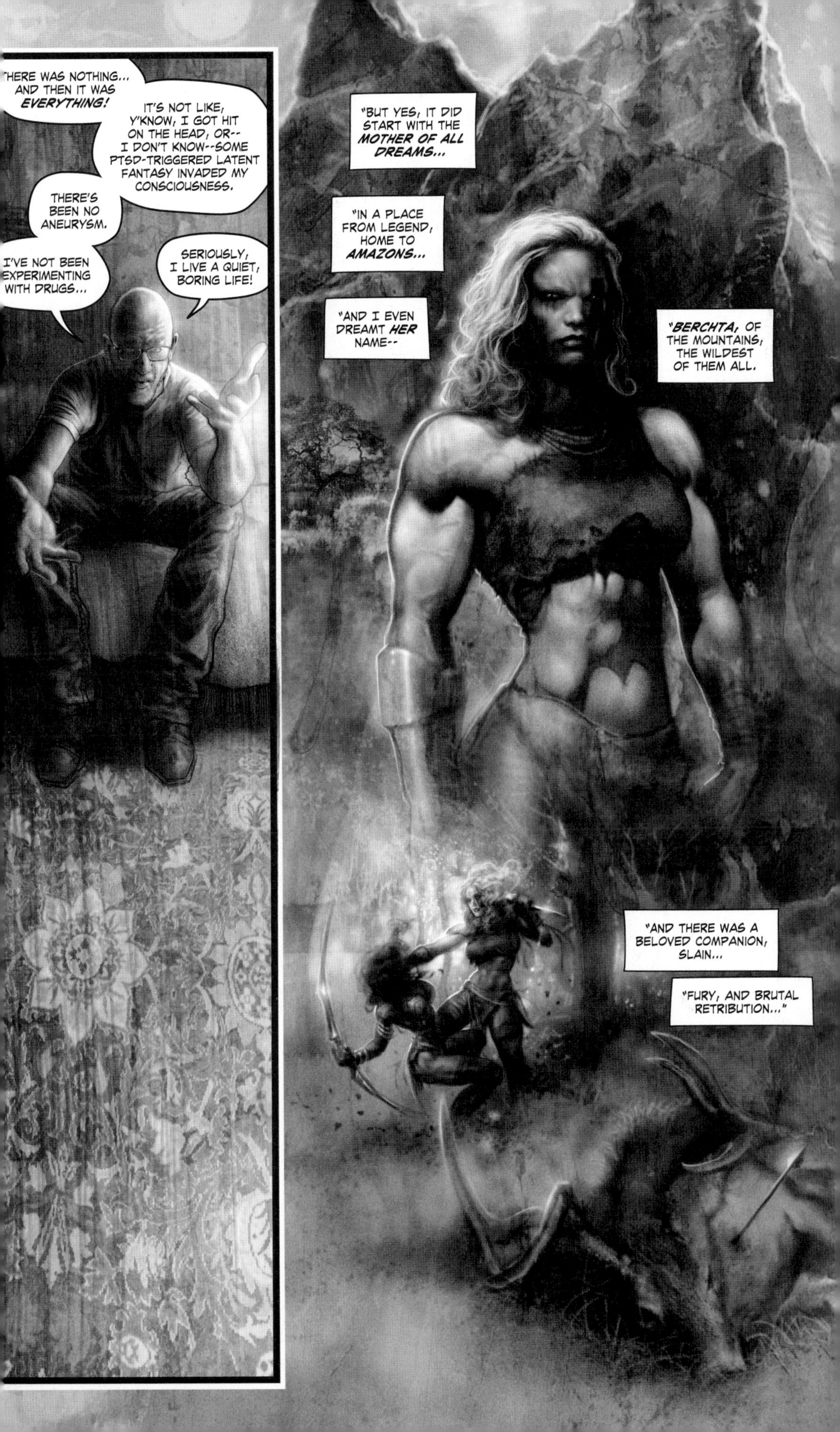

THERE WAS NOTHING... AND THEN IT WAS EVERYTHING!
IT'S NOT LIKE, Y'KNOW, I GOT HIT ON THE HEAD, OR-- I DON'T KNOW--SOME PTSD-TRIGGERED LATENT FANTASY INVADED MY CONSCIOUSNESS.
THERE'S BEEN NO ANEURYSM.
I'VE NOT BEEN EXPERIMENTING WITH DRUGS...
SERIOUSLY, I LIVE A QUIET, BORING LIFE!
"BUT YES, IT DID START WITH THE MOTHER OF ALL DREAMS...
"IN A PLACE FROM LEGEND, HOME TO AMAZONS...
"AND I EVEN DREAMT HER NAME--
"BERCHTA, OF THE MOUNTAINS, THE WILDEST OF THEM ALL.
"AND THERE WAS A BELOVED COMPANION, SLAIN...
"FURY, AND BRUTAL RETRIBUTION..."

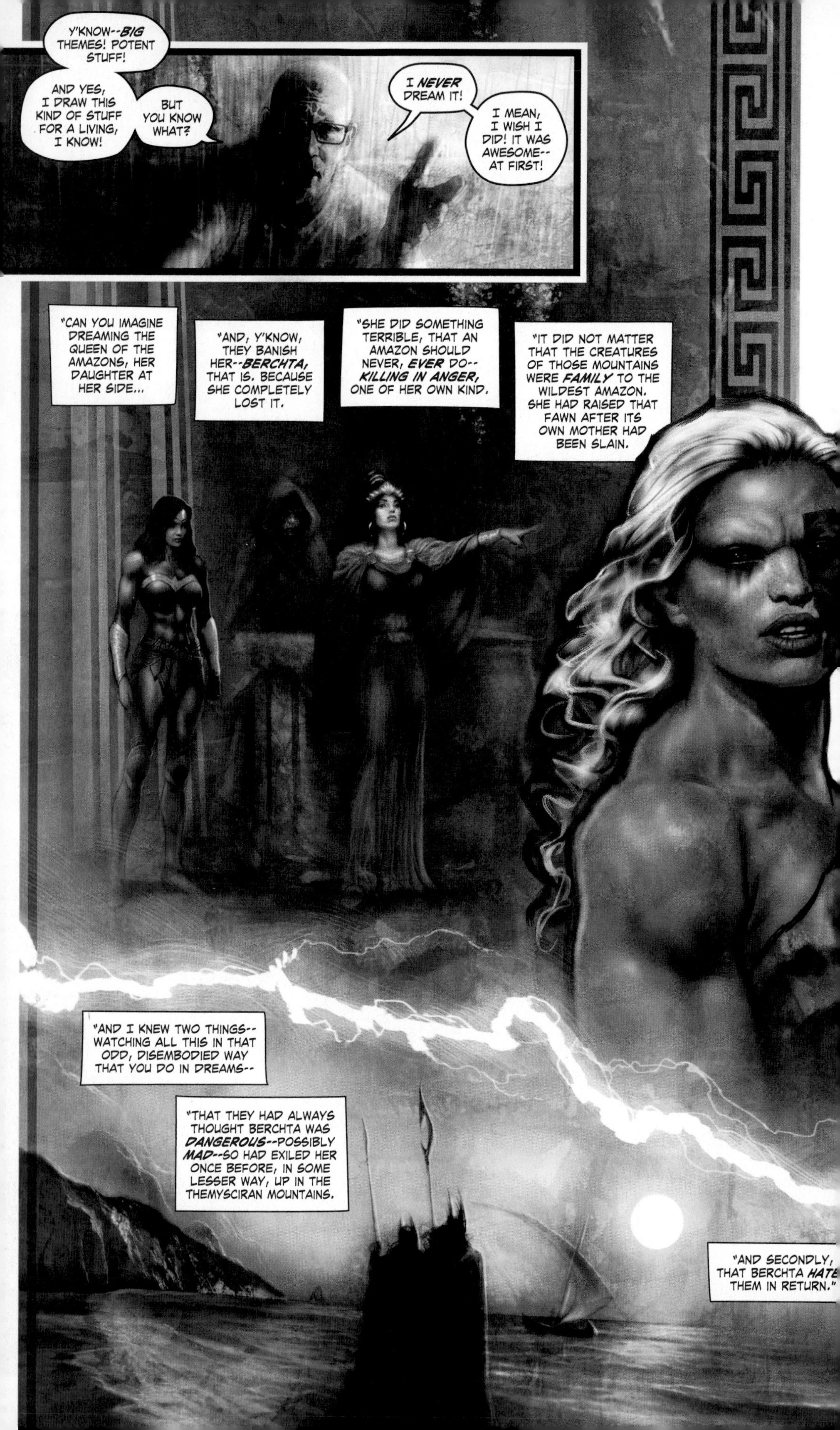

Y'KNOW--BIG THEMES! POTENT STUFF!
AND YES, I DRAW THIS KIND OF STUFF FOR A LIVING, I KNOW!
BUT YOU KNOW WHAT?
I NEVER DREAM IT!
I MEAN, I WISH I DID! IT WAS AWESOME--AT FIRST!
"CAN YOU IMAGINE DREAMING THE QUEEN OF THE AMAZONS, HER DAUGHTER AT HER SIDE...
"AND, Y'KNOW, THEY BANISH HER--BERCHTA, THAT IS. BECAUSE SHE COMPLETELY LOST IT.
"SHE DID SOMETHING TERRIBLE, THAT AN AMAZON SHOULD NEVER, EVER DO--KILLING IN ANGER, ONE OF HER OWN KIND.
"IT DID NOT MATTER THAT THE CREATURES OF THOSE MOUNTAINS WERE FAMILY TO THE WILDEST AMAZON. SHE HAD RAISED THAT FAWN AFTER ITS OWN MOTHER HAD BEEN SLAIN.
"AND I KNEW TWO THINGS--WATCHING ALL THIS IN THAT ODD, DISEMBODIED WAY THAT YOU DO IN DREAMS--
"THAT THEY HAD ALWAYS THOUGHT BERCHTA WAS DANGEROUS--POSSIBLY MAD--SO HAD EXILED HER ONCE BEFORE, IN SOME LESSER WAY, UP IN THE THEMYSCIRAN MOUNTAINS.
"AND SECONDLY, THAT BERCHTA HATE THEM IN RETURN."

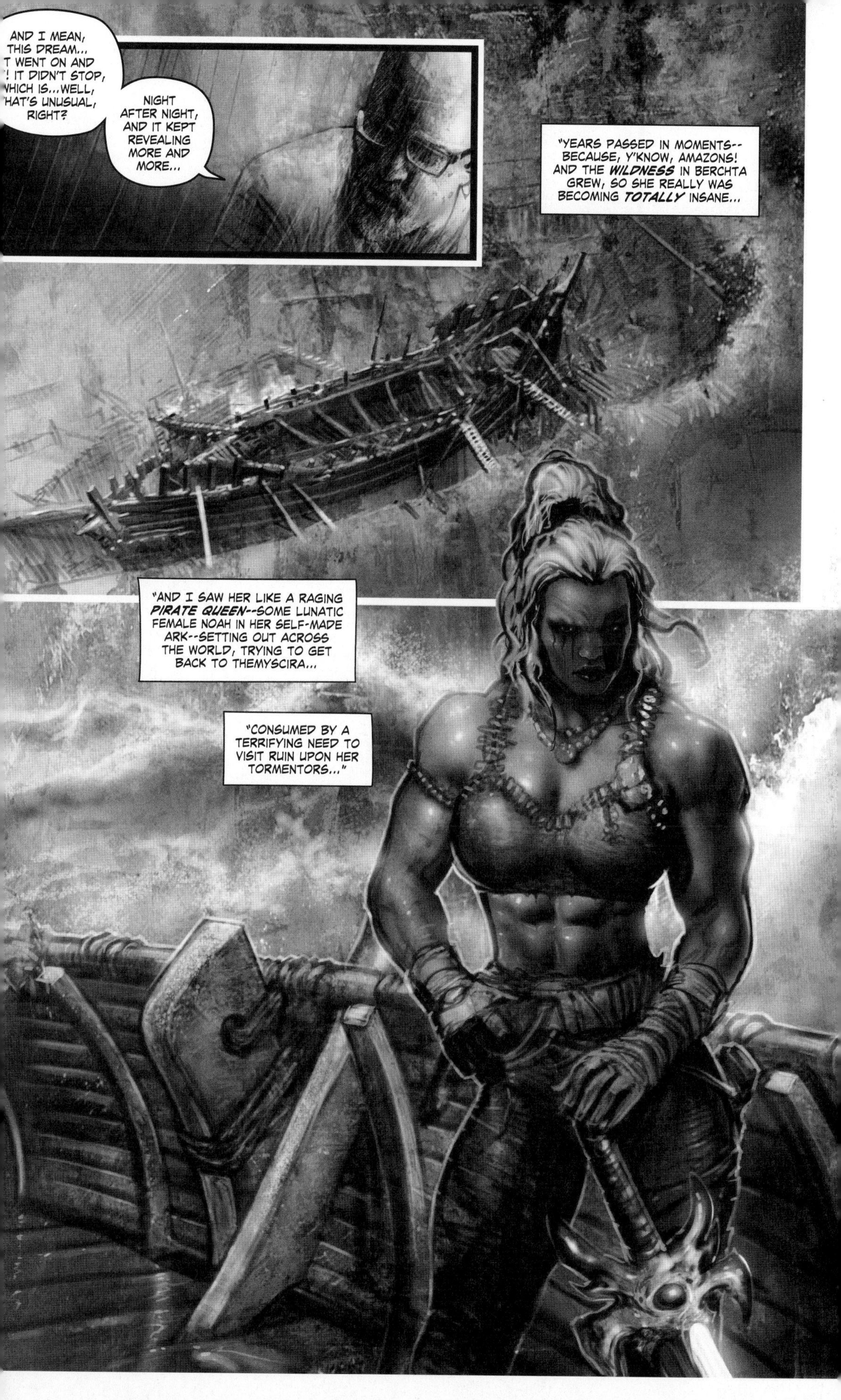
AND I MEAN, THIS DREAM... T WENT ON AND ! IT DIDN'T STOP, WHICH IS...WELL, HAT'S UNUSUAL, RIGHT?
NIGHT AFTER NIGHT, AND IT KEPT REVEALING MORE AND MORE...
"YEARS PASSED IN MOMENTS-- BECAUSE, Y'KNOW, AMAZONS! AND THE *WILDNESS* IN BERCHTA GREW, SO SHE REALLY WAS BECOMING *TOTALLY* INSANE...
"AND I SAW HER LIKE A RAGING *PIRATE QUEEN*--SOME LUNATIC FEMALE NOAH IN HER SELF-MADE ARK--SETTING OUT ACROSS THE WORLD, TRYING TO GET BACK TO THEMYSCIRA...
"CONSUMED BY A TERRIFYING NEED TO VISIT RUIN UPON HER TORMENTORS..."

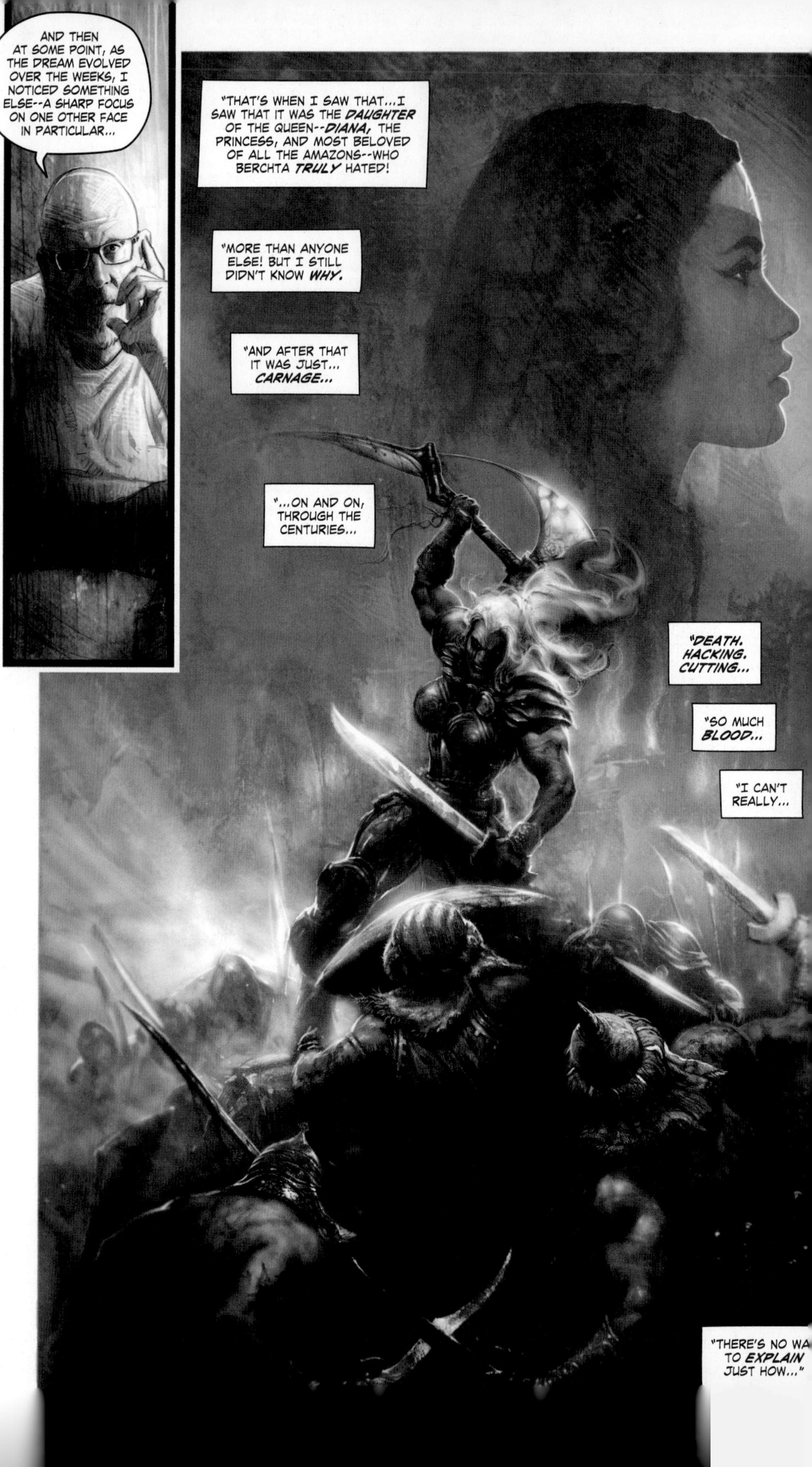
AND THEN AT SOME POINT, AS THE DREAM EVOLVED OVER THE WEEKS, I NOTICED SOMETHING ELSE--A SHARP FOCUS ON ONE OTHER FACE IN PARTICULAR...
"THAT'S WHEN I SAW THAT...I SAW THAT IT WAS THE DAUGHTER OF THE QUEEN--DIANA, THE PRINCESS, AND MOST BELOVED OF ALL THE AMAZONS--WHO BERCHTA TRULY HATED!
"MORE THAN ANYONE ELSE! BUT I STILL DIDN'T KNOW WHY.
"AND AFTER THAT IT WAS JUST... CARNAGE...
"...ON AND ON, THROUGH THE CENTURIES...
"DEATH. HACKING. CUTTING...
"SO MUCH BLOOD...
"I CAN'T REALLY...
"THERE'S NO WA
TO EXPLAIN JUST HOW..."

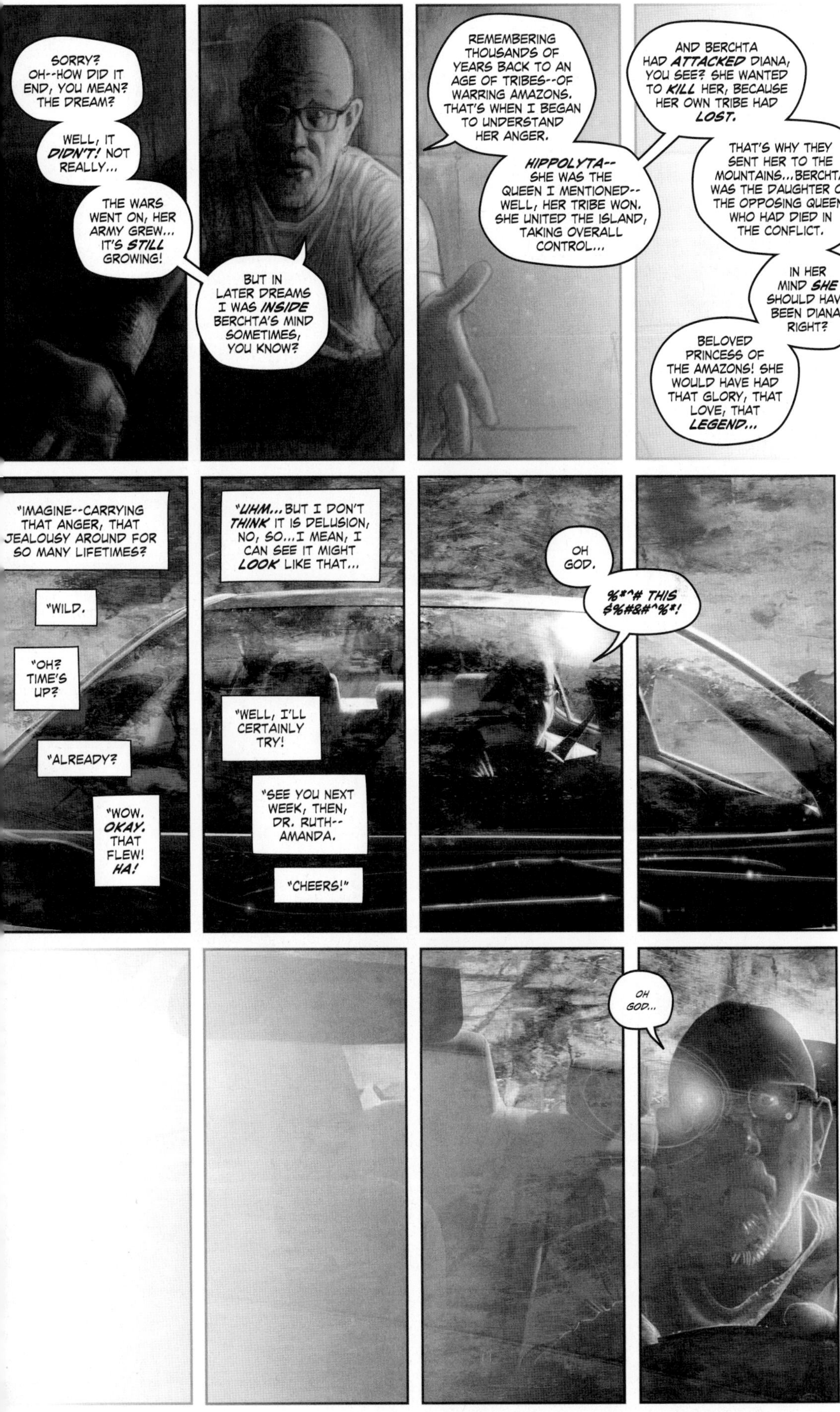
SORRY? OH--HOW DID IT END, YOU MEAN? THE DREAM?
WELL, IT DIDN'T! NOT REALLY...
THE WARS WENT ON, HER ARMY GREW... IT'S STILL GROWING!
BUT IN LATER DREAMS I WAS INSIDE BERCHTA'S MIND SOMETIMES, YOU KNOW?
REMEMBERING THOUSANDS OF YEARS BACK TO AN AGE OF TRIBES--OF WARRING AMAZONS. THAT'S WHEN I BEGAN TO UNDERSTAND HER ANGER.
HIPPOLYTA-- SHE WAS THE QUEEN I MENTIONED-- WELL, HER TRIBE WON. SHE UNITED THE ISLAND, TAKING OVERALL CONTROL...
AND BERCHTA HAD ATTACKED DIANA, YOU SEE? SHE WANTED TO KILL HER, BECAUSE HER OWN TRIBE HAD LOST.
THAT'S WHY THEY SENT HER TO THE MOUNTAINS...BERCHTA WAS THE DAUGHTER OF THE OPPOSING QUEEN, WHO HAD DIED IN THE CONFLICT.
IN HER MIND SHE SHOULD HAVE BEEN DIANA, RIGHT?
BELOVED PRINCESS OF THE AMAZONS! SHE WOULD HAVE HAD THAT GLORY, THAT LOVE, THAT LEGEND...
"IMAGINE--CARRYING THAT ANGER, THAT JEALOUSY AROUND FOR SO MANY LIFETIMES?
"WILD.
"OH? TIME'S UP?
"ALREADY?
"WOW. OKAY. THAT FLEW! HA!
"UHM...BUT I DON'T THINK IT IS DELUSION, NO, SO...I MEAN, I CAN SEE IT MIGHT LOOK LIKE THAT...
"WELL, I'LL CERTAINLY TRY!
"SEE YOU NEXT WEEK, THEN, DR. RUTH-- AMANDA.
"CHEERS!"
OH GOD.
%*^# THIS $%#&#^%*!
OH GOD...

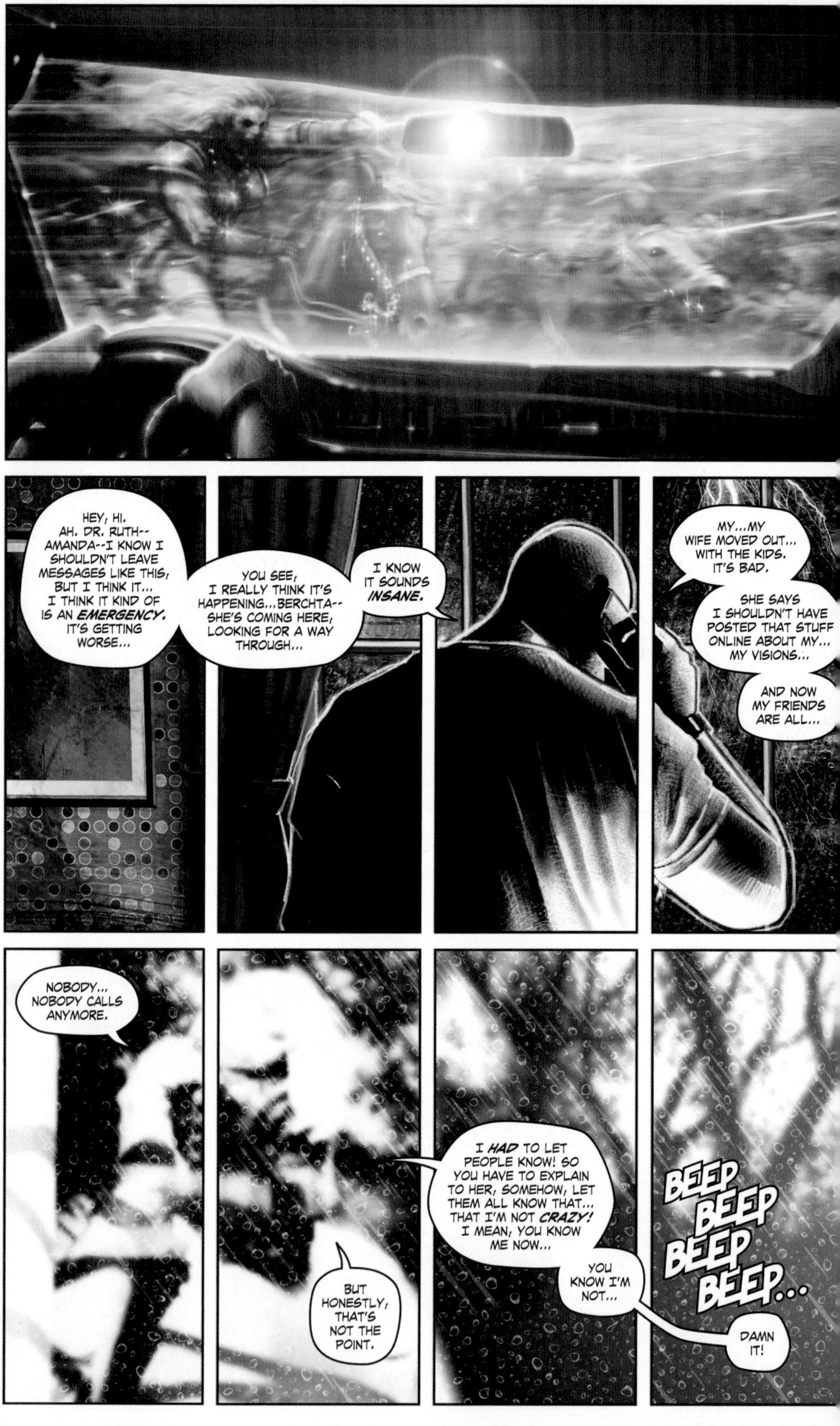
HEY, HI.
AH. DR. RUTH--
AMANDA--I KNOW I SHOULDN'T LEAVE MESSAGES LIKE THIS, BUT I THINK IT... I THINK IT KIND OF IS AN *EMERGENCY.* IT'S GETTING WORSE...
YOU SEE, I REALLY THINK IT'S HAPPENING...BERCHTA--SHE'S COMING HERE, LOOKING FOR A WAY THROUGH...
I KNOW IT SOUNDS *INSANE.*
MY...MY WIFE MOVED OUT... WITH THE KIDS. IT'S BAD.
SHE SAYS I SHOULDN'T HAVE POSTED THAT STUFF ONLINE ABOUT MY... MY VISIONS...
AND NOW MY FRIENDS ARE ALL...
NOBODY... NOBODY CALLS ANYMORE.
BUT HONESTLY, THAT'S NOT THE POINT.
I *HAD* TO LET PEOPLE KNOW! SO YOU HAVE TO EXPLAIN TO HER, SOMEHOW, LET THEM ALL KNOW THAT... THAT I'M NOT *CRAZY!* I MEAN, YOU KNOW ME NOW...
YOU KNOW I'M NOT...
BEEP BEEP BEEP BEEP...
DAMN IT!

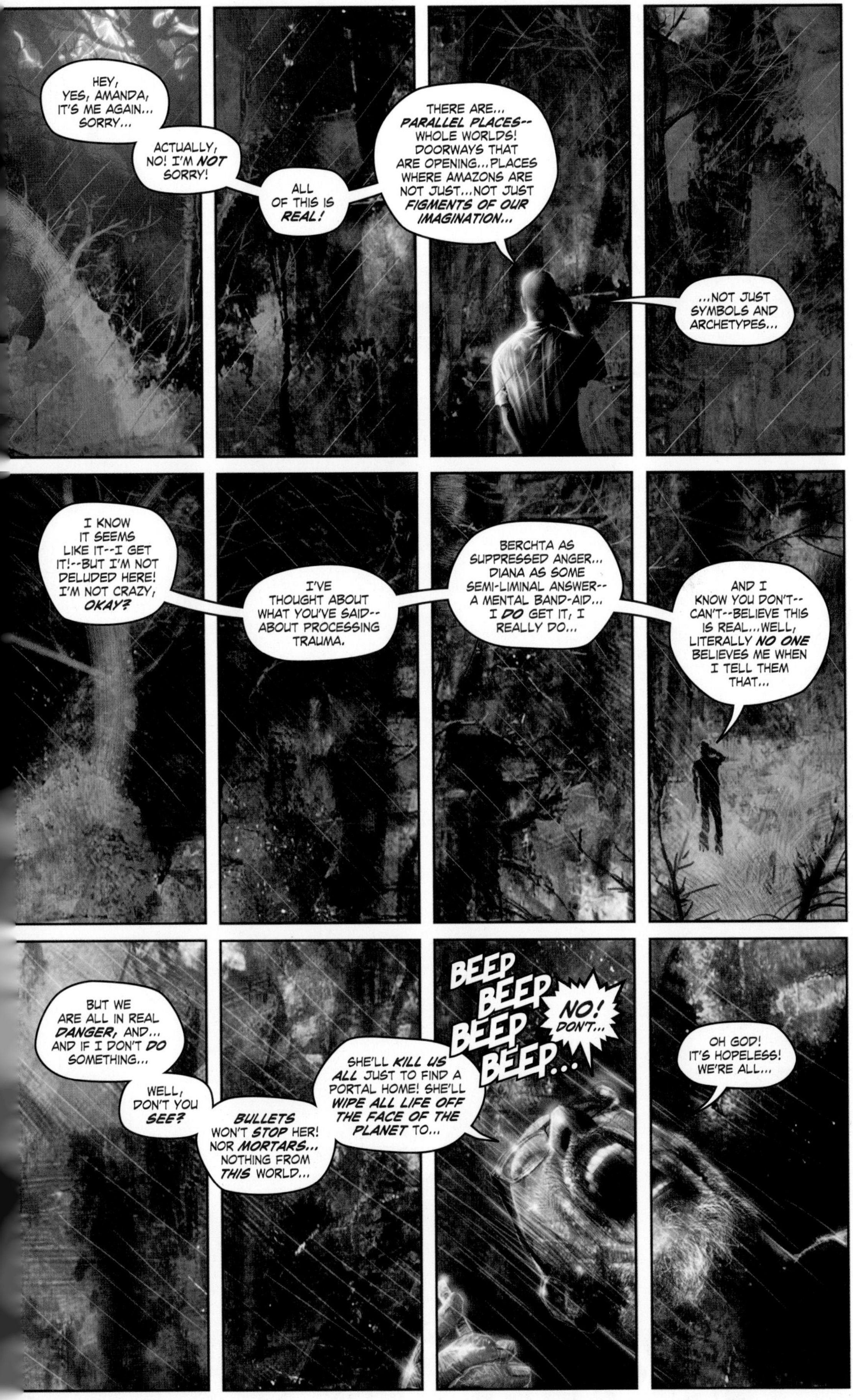
HEY, YES, AMANDA, IT'S ME AGAIN... SORRY...
ACTUALLY, NO! I'M NOT SORRY!
ALL OF THIS IS REAL!
THERE ARE... PARALLEL PLACES-- WHOLE WORLDS! DOORWAYS THAT ARE OPENING...PLACES WHERE AMAZONS ARE NOT JUST...NOT JUST FIGMENTS OF OUR IMAGINATION...
...NOT JUST SYMBOLS AND ARCHETYPES...
I KNOW IT SEEMS LIKE IT--I GET IT!--BUT I'M NOT DELUDED HERE! I'M NOT CRAZY, OKAY?
I'VE THOUGHT ABOUT WHAT YOU'VE SAID-- ABOUT PROCESSING TRAUMA.
BERCHTA AS SUPPRESSED ANGER... DIANA AS SOME SEMI-LIMINAL ANSWER-- A MENTAL BAND-AID... I DO GET IT, I REALLY DO...
AND I KNOW YOU DON'T-- CAN'T--BELIEVE THIS IS REAL...WELL, LITERALLY NO ONE BELIEVES ME WHEN I TELL THEM THAT...
BUT WE ARE ALL IN REAL DANGER, AND... AND IF I DON'T DO SOMETHING...
WELL, DON'T YOU SEE?
BULLETS WON'T STOP HER! NOR MORTARS... NOTHING FROM THIS WORLD...
SHE'LL KILL US ALL JUST TO FIND A PORTAL HOME! SHE'LL WIPE ALL LIFE OFF THE FACE OF THE PLANET TO...
BEEP BEEP BEEP BEEP...
NO! DON'T...
OH GOD! IT'S HOPELESS! WE'RE ALL...

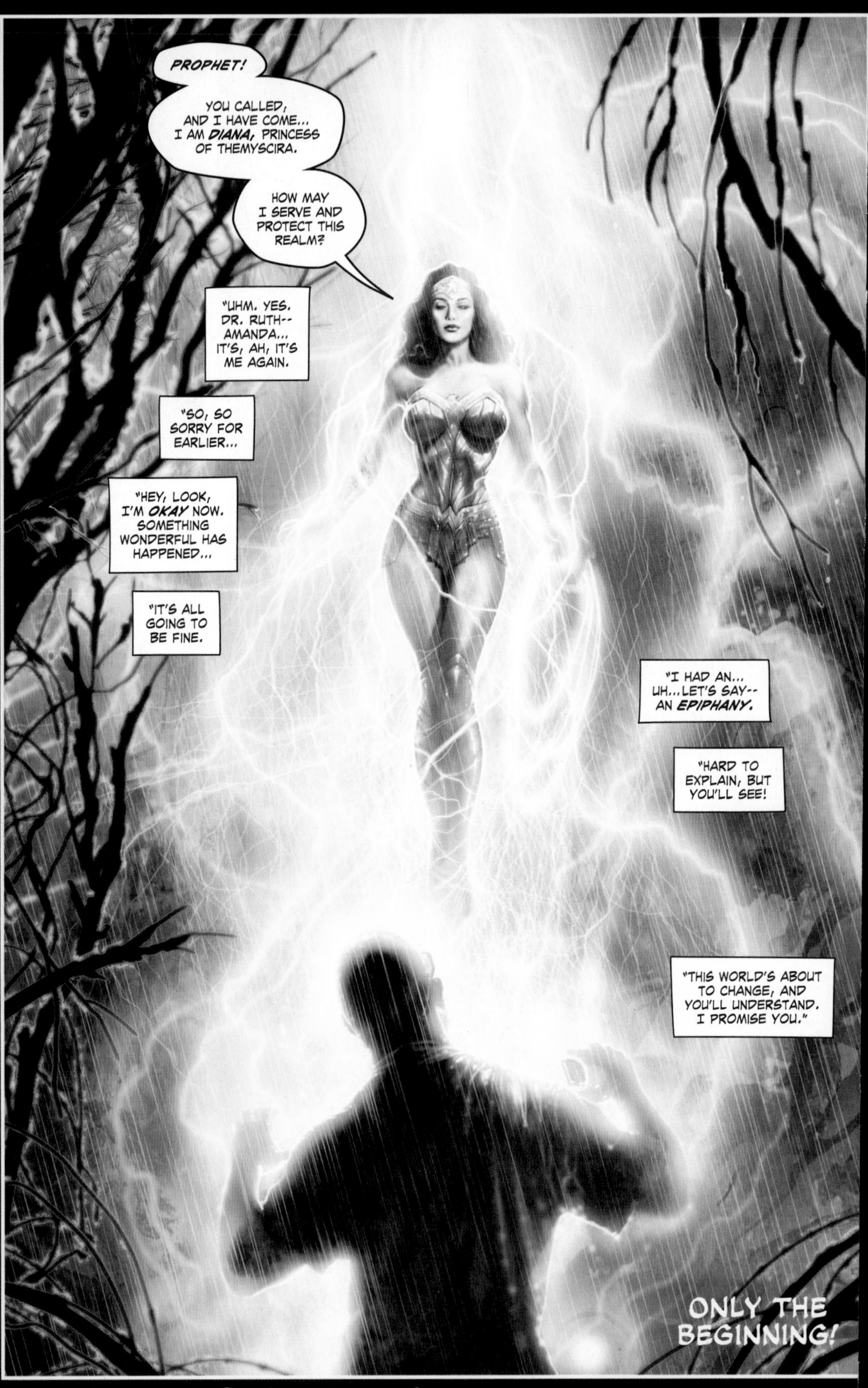
PROPHET!
YOU CALLED, AND I HAVE COME... I AM *DIANA,* PRINCESS OF THEMYSCIRA.
HOW MAY I SERVE AND PROTECT THIS REALM?
"UHM. YES. DR. RUTH-- AMANDA... IT'S, AH, IT'S ME AGAIN.
"SO, SO SORRY FOR EARLIER...
"HEY, LOOK, I'M *OKAY* NOW. SOMETHING WONDERFUL HAS HAPPENED...
"IT'S ALL GOING TO BE FINE.
"I HAD AN... UH...LET'S SAY-- AN *EPIPHANY.*
"HARD TO EXPLAIN, BUT YOU'LL SEE!
"THIS WORLD'S ABOUT TO CHANGE, AND YOU'LL UNDERSTAND. I PROMISE YOU."
ONLY THE BEGINNING!

THE PROPHET

Words and art by LIAM SHAR
based on the mother of all dreams.
Letters by Wes Abbott, Edits by Diego Lopez and Brittany Holzherr. Mike Cotton, Senior Ed

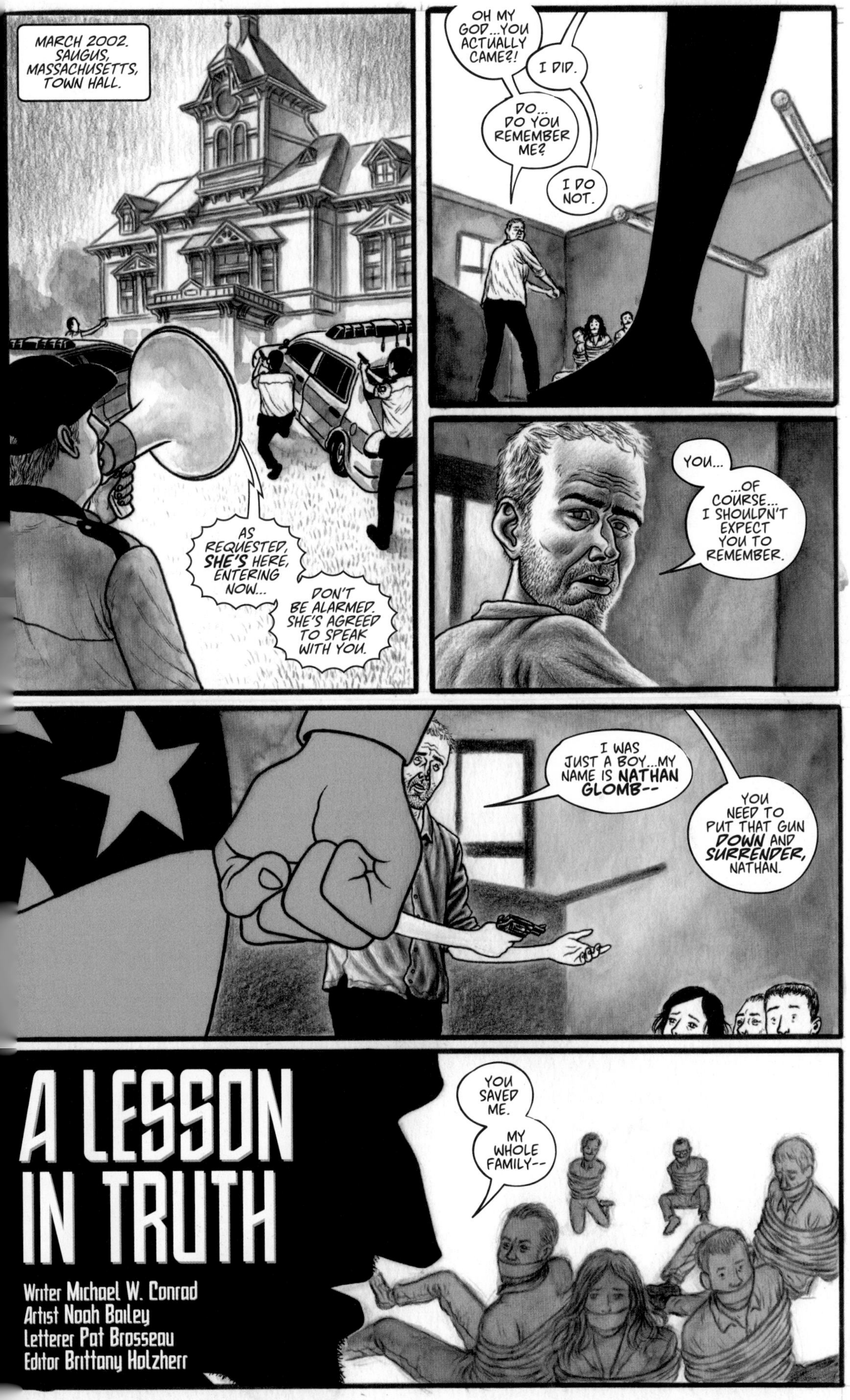
MARCH 2002. SAUGUS, MASSACHUSETTS, TOWN HALL.
AS REQUESTED, SHE'S HERE, ENTERING NOW...
DON'T BE ALARMED. SHE'S AGREED TO SPEAK WITH YOU.
OH MY GOD...YOU ACTUALLY CAME?!
I DID.
DO... DO YOU REMEMBER ME?
I DO NOT.
YOU...
...OF COURSE... I SHOULDN'T EXPECT YOU TO REMEMBER.
I WAS JUST A BOY...MY NAME IS NATHAN GLOMB--
YOU NEED TO PUT THAT GUN DOWN AND SURRENDER, NATHAN.
A LESSON IN TRUTH
Writer Michael W. Conrad
Artist Noah Bailey
Letterer Pat Brosseau
Editor Brittany Holzherr
YOU SAVED ME.
MY WHOLE FAMILY--

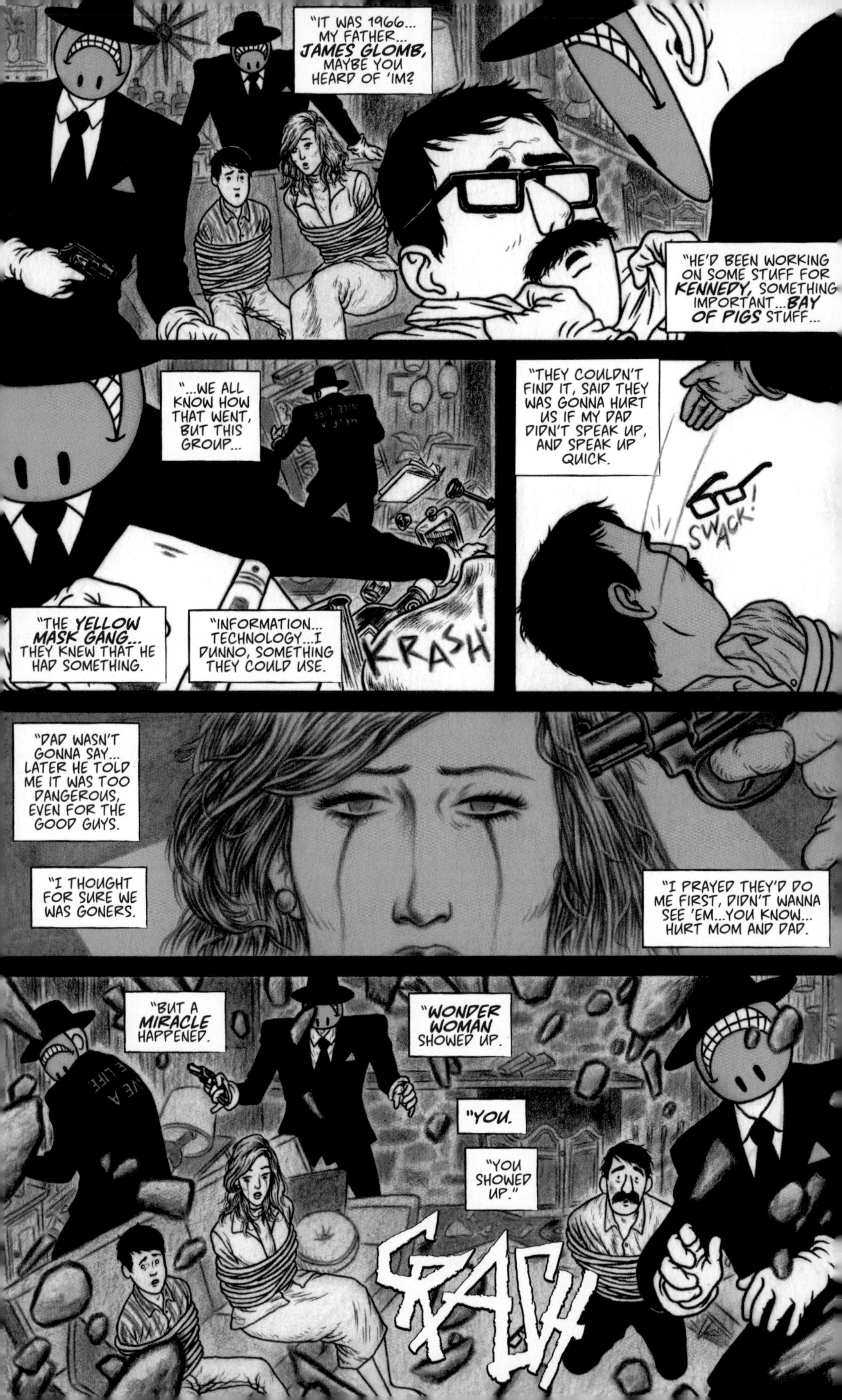
"IT WAS 1966... MY FATHER... JAMES GLOMB, MAYBE YOU HEARD OF 'IM?
"HE'D BEEN WORKING ON SOME STUFF FOR KENNEDY, SOMETHING IMPORTANT...BAY OF PIGS STUFF...
"...WE ALL KNOW HOW THAT WENT, BUT THIS GROUP...
"THE YELLOW MASK GANG... THEY KNEW THAT HE HAD SOMETHING.
"INFORMATION... TECHNOLOGY...I DUNNO, SOMETHING THEY COULD USE.
KRASH!
"THEY COULDN'T FIND IT, SAID THEY WAS GONNA HURT US IF MY DAD DIDN'T SPEAK UP, AND SPEAK UP QUICK.
SWACK!
"DAD WASN'T GONNA SAY... LATER HE TOLD ME IT WAS TOO DANGEROUS, EVEN FOR THE GOOD GUYS.
"I THOUGHT FOR SURE WE WAS GONERS.
"I PRAYED THEY'D DO ME FIRST, DIDN'T WANNA SEE 'EM...YOU KNOW... HURT MOM AND DAD.
"BUT A MIRACLE HAPPENED.
"WONDER WOMAN SHOWED UP.
"YOU.
"YOU SHOWED UP."
CRASH

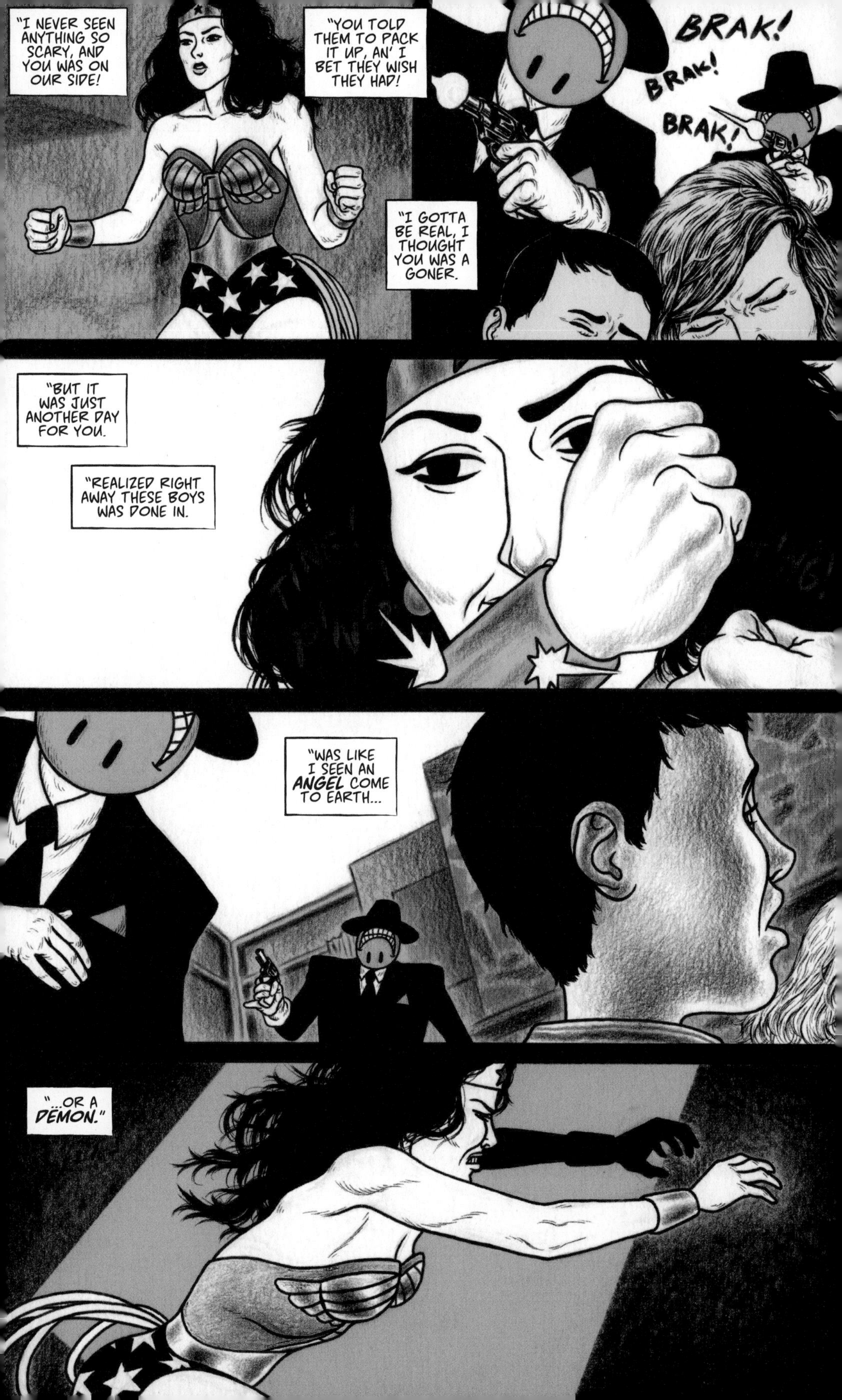
"I NEVER SEEN ANYTHING SO SCARY, AND YOU WAS ON OUR SIDE!
"YOU TOLD THEM TO PACK IT UP, AN' I BET THEY WISH THEY HAD!
BRAK!
BRAK!
BRAK!
"I GOTTA BE REAL, I THOUGHT YOU WAS A GONER.
"BUT IT WAS JUST ANOTHER DAY FOR YOU.
"REALIZED RIGHT AWAY THESE BOYS WAS DONE IN.
"WAS LIKE I SEEN AN ANGEL COME TO EARTH...
"...OR A DEMON."

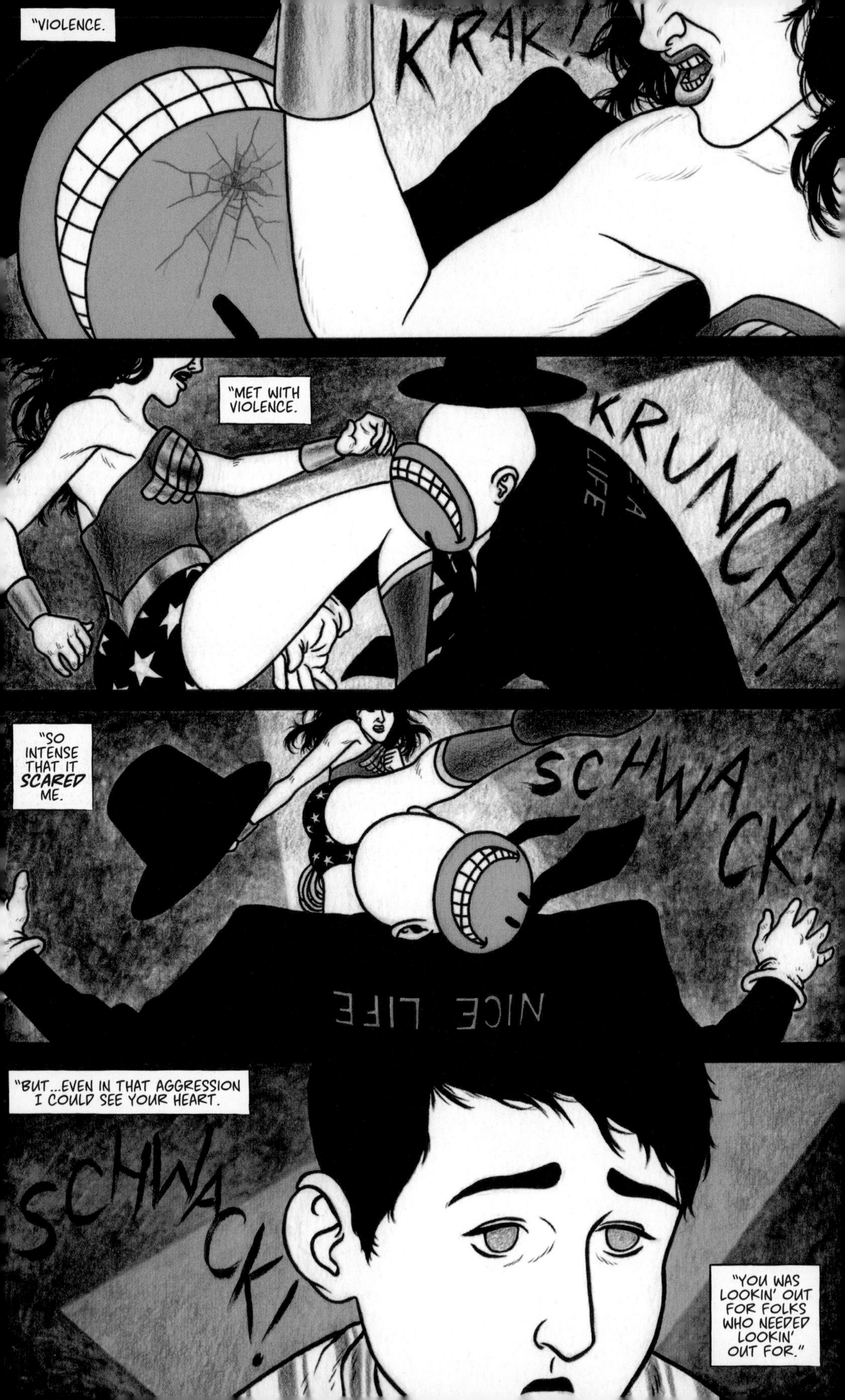
"VIOLENCE.
KRAK!
"MET WITH VIOLENCE.
KRUNCH!!
"SO INTENSE THAT IT *SCARED* ME.
SCHWACK!
NICE LIFE
"BUT...EVEN IN THAT AGGRESSION I COULD SEE YOUR HEART.
SCHWACK!
"YOU WAS LOOKIN' OUT FOR FOLKS WHO NEEDED LOOKIN' OUT FOR."

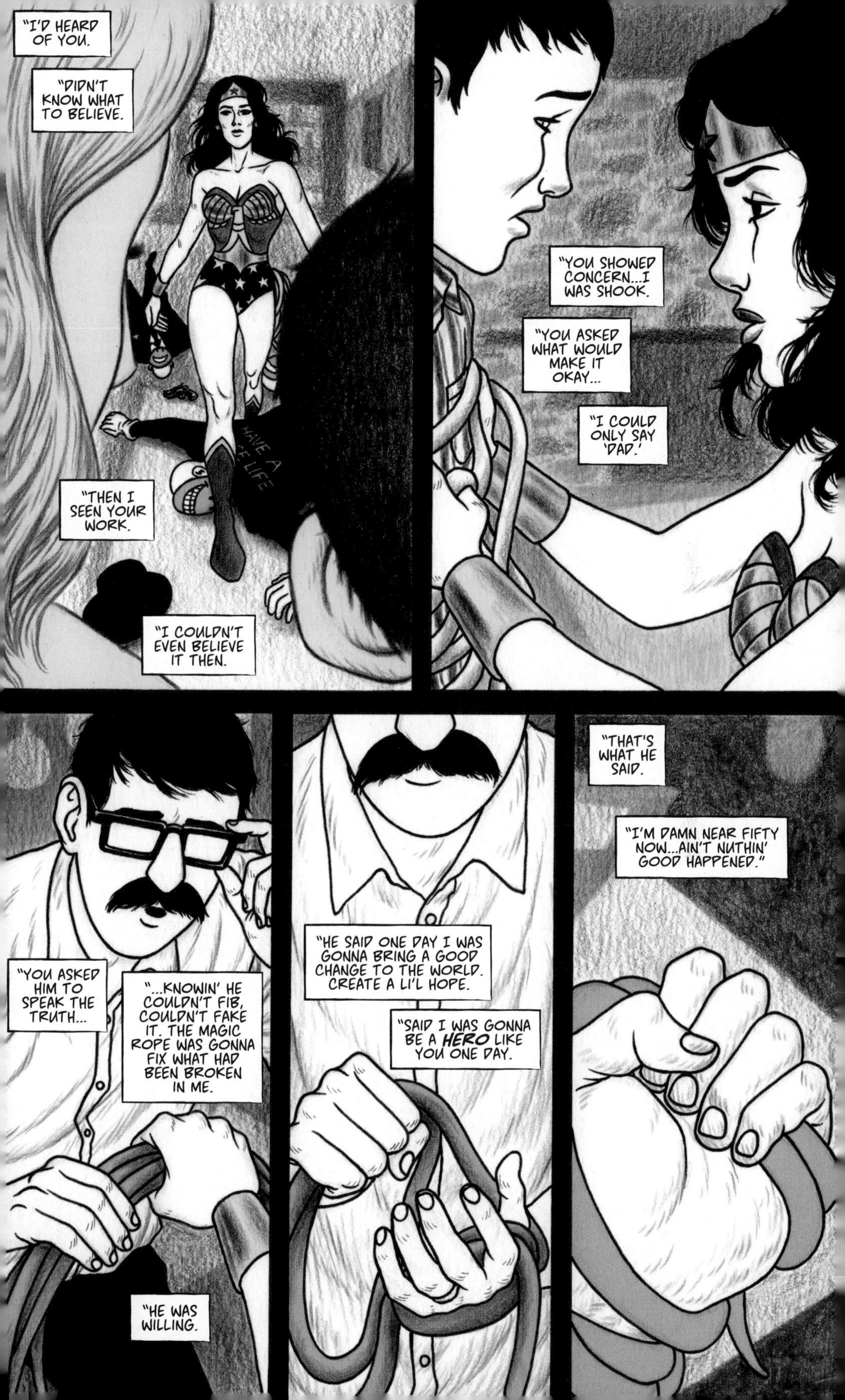
"I'D HEARD OF YOU.
"DIDN'T KNOW WHAT TO BELIEVE.
HAVE A ... LIFE
"THEN I SEEN YOUR WORK.
"I COULDN'T EVEN BELIEVE IT THEN.
"YOU SHOWED CONCERN...I WAS SHOOK.
"YOU ASKED WHAT WOULD MAKE IT OKAY...
"I COULD ONLY SAY 'DAD.'
"YOU ASKED HIM TO SPEAK THE TRUTH...
"...KNOWIN' HE COULDN'T FIB, COULDN'T FAKE IT. THE MAGIC ROPE WAS GONNA FIX WHAT HAD BEEN BROKEN IN ME.
"HE WAS WILLING.
"HE SAID ONE DAY I WAS GONNA BRING A GOOD CHANGE TO THE WORLD. CREATE A LI'L HOPE.
"SAID I WAS GONNA BE A HERO LIKE YOU ONE DAY.
"THAT'S WHAT HE SAID.
"I'M DAMN NEAR FIFTY NOW...AIN'T NUTHIN' GOOD HAPPENED."

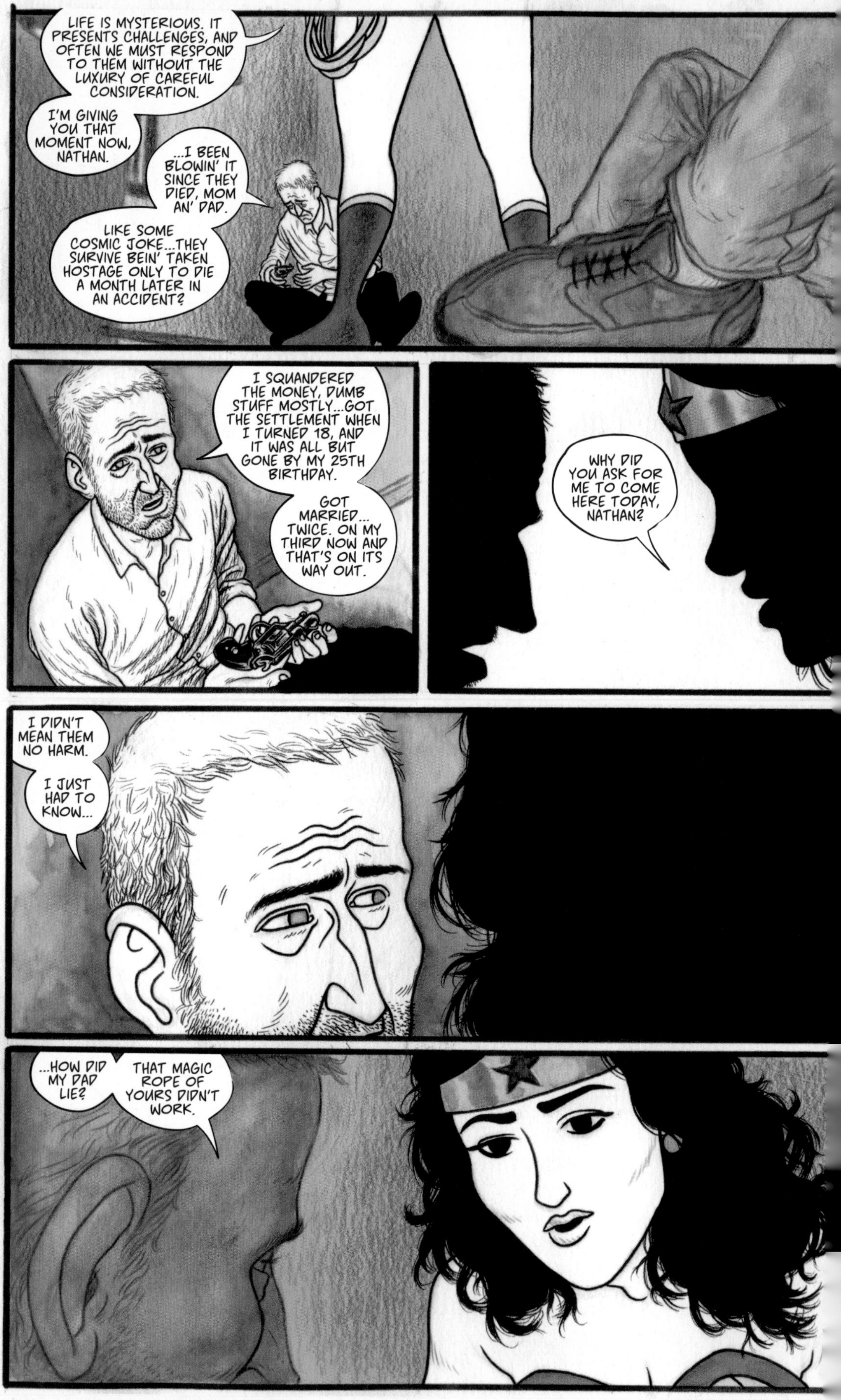
LIFE IS MYSTERIOUS. IT PRESENTS CHALLENGES, AND OFTEN WE MUST RESPOND TO THEM WITHOUT THE LUXURY OF CAREFUL CONSIDERATION.
I'M GIVING YOU THAT MOMENT NOW, NATHAN.
...I BEEN BLOWIN' IT SINCE THEY DIED, MOM AN' DAD.
LIKE SOME COSMIC JOKE...THEY SURVIVE BEIN' TAKEN HOSTAGE ONLY TO DIE A MONTH LATER IN AN ACCIDENT?
I SQUANDERED THE MONEY, DUMB STUFF MOSTLY...GOT THE SETTLEMENT WHEN I TURNED 18, AND IT WAS ALL BUT GONE BY MY 25TH BIRTHDAY.
GOT MARRIED... TWICE. ON MY THIRD NOW AND THAT'S ON ITS WAY OUT.
WHY DID YOU ASK FOR ME TO COME HERE TODAY, NATHAN?
I DIDN'T MEAN THEM NO HARM.
I JUST HAD TO KNOW...
...HOW DID MY DAD LIE?
THAT MAGIC ROPE OF YOURS DIDN'T WORK.

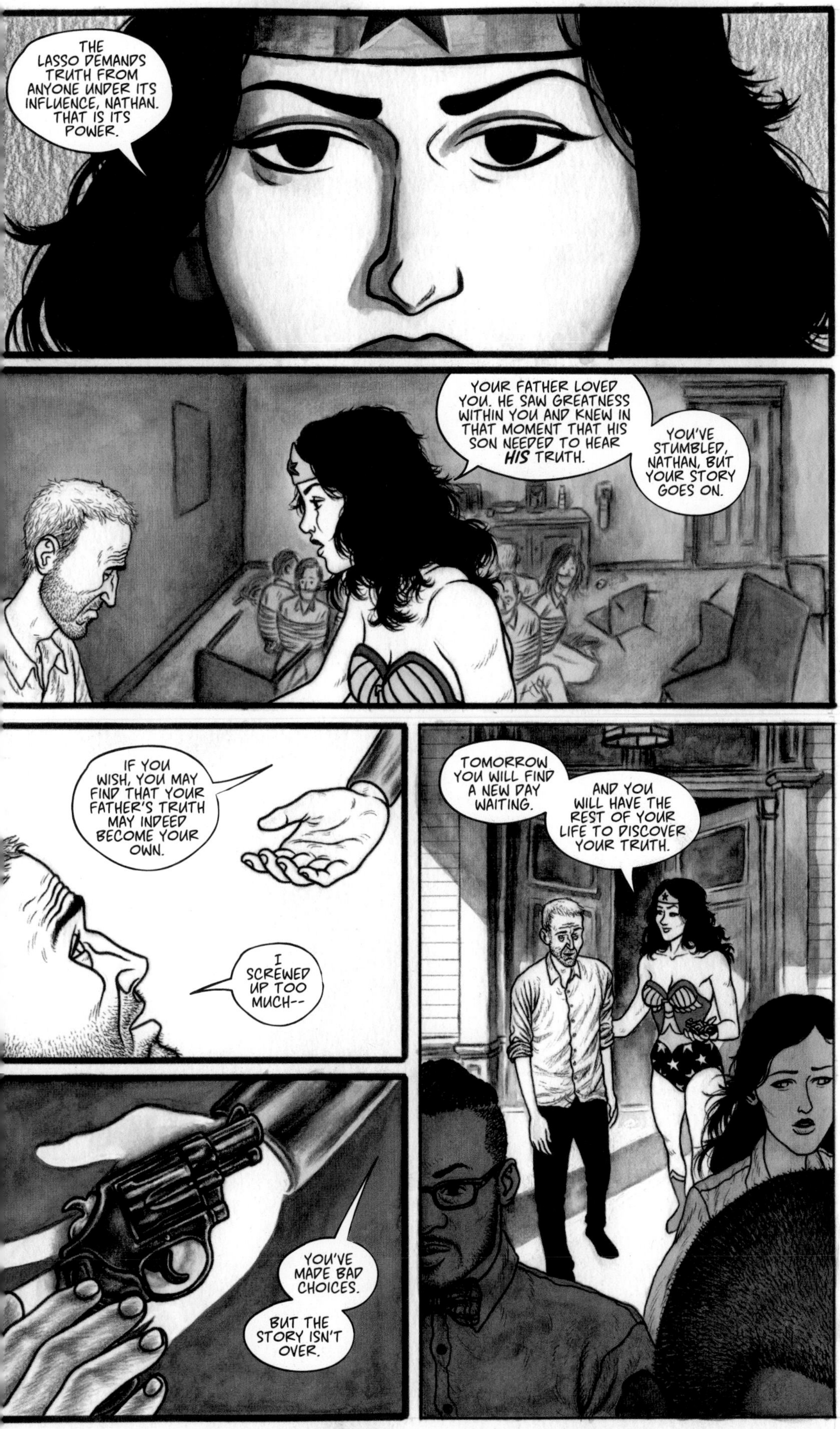
THE LASSO DEMANDS TRUTH FROM ANYONE UNDER ITS INFLUENCE, NATHAN. THAT IS ITS POWER.
YOUR FATHER LOVED YOU. HE SAW GREATNESS WITHIN YOU AND KNEW IN THAT MOMENT THAT HIS SON NEEDED TO HEAR ***HIS*** TRUTH.
YOU'VE STUMBLED, NATHAN, BUT YOUR STORY GOES ON.
IF YOU WISH, YOU MAY FIND THAT YOUR FATHER'S TRUTH MAY INDEED BECOME YOUR OWN.
I SCREWED UP TOO MUCH--
YOU'VE MADE BAD CHOICES.
BUT THE STORY ISN'T OVER.
TOMORROW YOU WILL FIND A NEW DAY WAITING.
AND YOU WILL HAVE THE REST OF YOUR LIFE TO DISCOVER YOUR TRUTH.

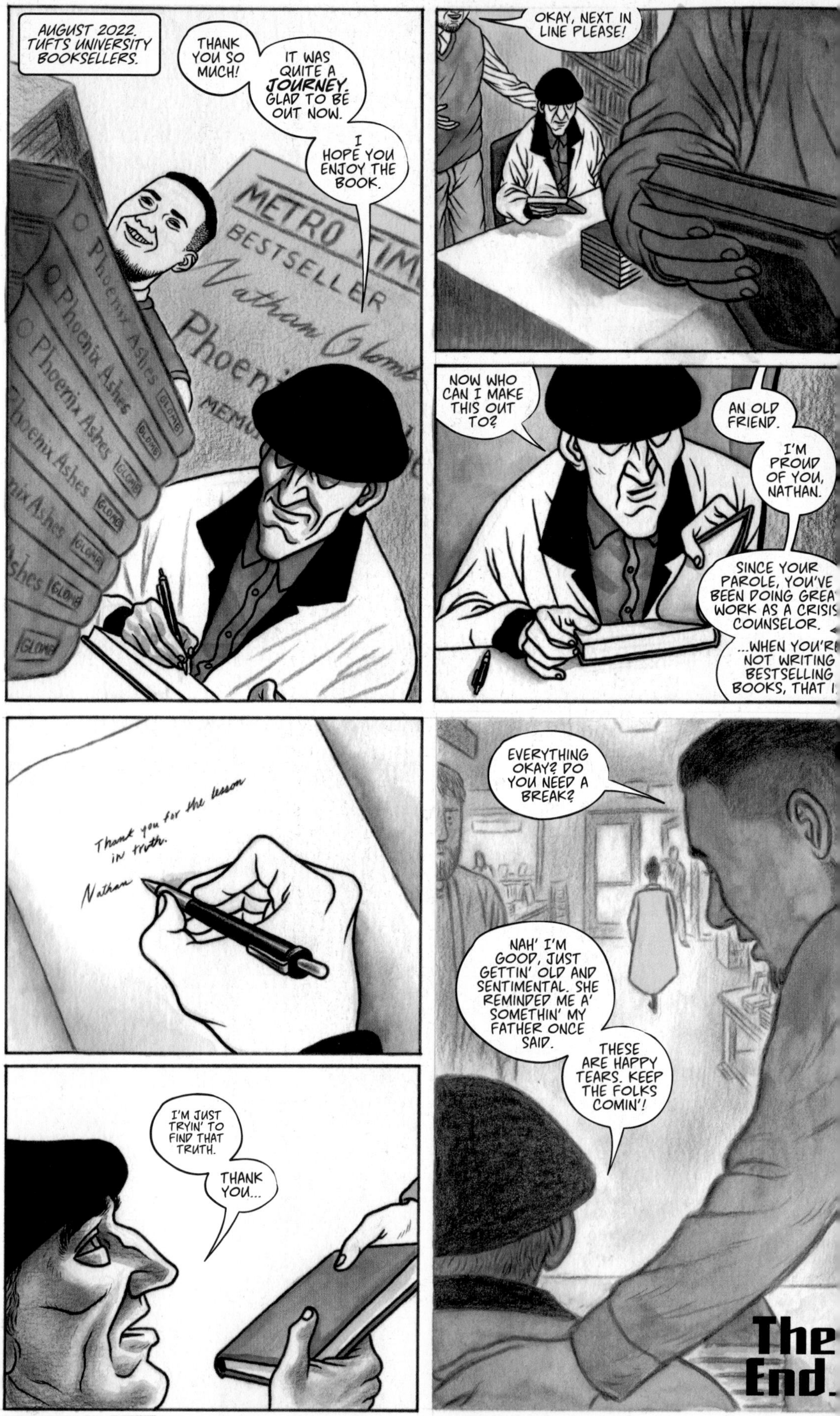
AUGUST 2022. TUFTS UNIVERSITY BOOKSELLERS.
THANK YOU SO MUCH!
IT WAS QUITE A JOURNEY. GLAD TO BE OUT NOW.
I HOPE YOU ENJOY THE BOOK.
METRO TIM
BESTSELLER
Nathan Glomb
Phoeni
MEMO
Phoenix Ashes GLOMB
OKAY, NEXT IN LINE PLEASE!
NOW WHO CAN I MAKE THIS OUT TO?
AN OLD FRIEND.
I'M PROUD OF YOU, NATHAN.
SINCE YOUR PAROLE, YOU'VE BEEN DOING GREA WORK AS A CRISIS COUNSELOR.
...WHEN YOU'R NOT WRITING BESTSELLING BOOKS, THAT I
Thank you for the lesson in truth.
Nathan
I'M JUST TRYIN' TO FIND THAT TRUTH.
THANK YOU...
EVERYTHING OKAY? DO YOU NEED A BREAK?
NAH' I'M GOOD, JUST GETTIN' OLD AND SENTIMENTAL. SHE REMINDED ME A' SOMETHIN' MY FATHER ONCE SAID.
THESE ARE HAPPY TEARS. KEEP THE FOLKS COMIN'!
The End.

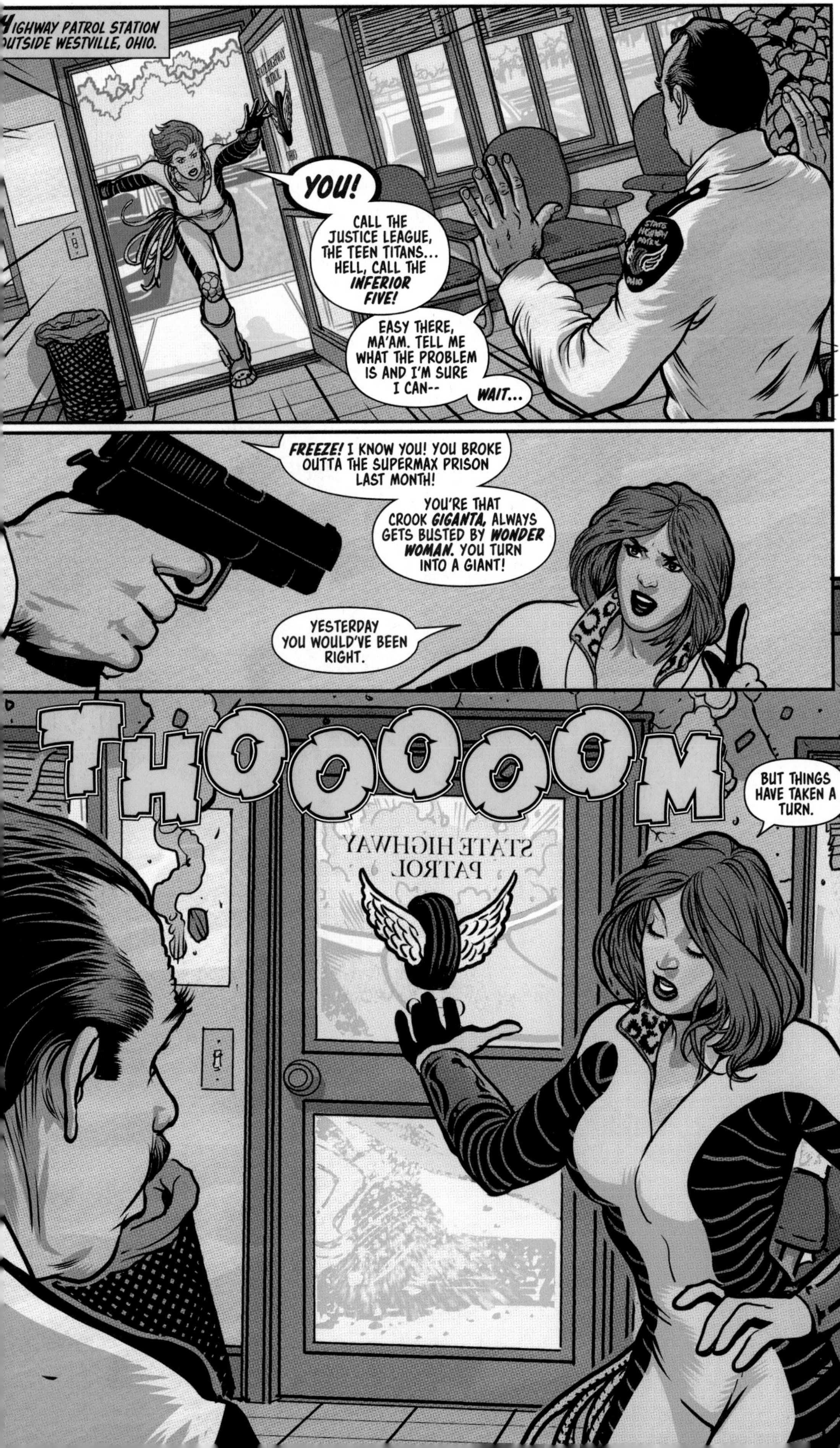
HIGHWAY PATROL STATION
OUTSIDE WESTVILLE, OHIO.
YOU!
CALL THE JUSTICE LEAGUE, THE TEEN TITANS... HELL, CALL THE INFERIOR FIVE!
EASY THERE, MA'AM. TELL ME WHAT THE PROBLEM IS AND I'M SURE I CAN--
WAIT...
FREEZE! I KNOW YOU! YOU BROKE OUTTA THE SUPERMAX PRISON LAST MONTH!
YOU'RE THAT CROOK GIGANTA, ALWAYS GETS BUSTED BY WONDER WOMAN. YOU TURN INTO A GIANT!
YESTERDAY YOU WOULD'VE BEEN RIGHT.
THOOOOOM
BUT THINGS HAVE TAKEN A TURN.
STATE HIGHWAY PATROL

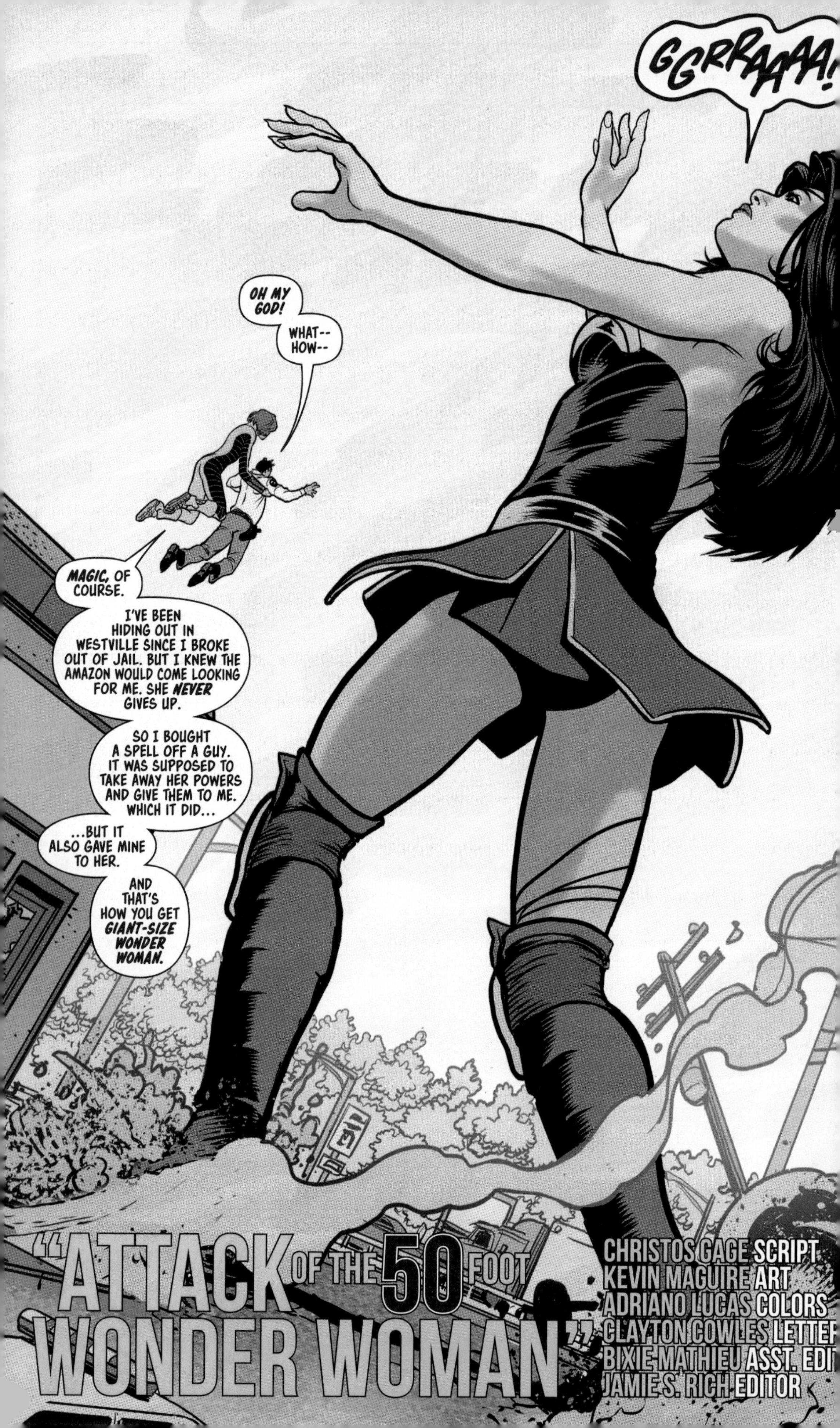
GGRRAAAA!
OH MY GOD!
WHAT-- HOW--
MAGIC, OF COURSE.
I'VE BEEN HIDING OUT IN WESTVILLE SINCE I BROKE OUT OF JAIL. BUT I KNEW THE AMAZON WOULD COME LOOKING FOR ME. SHE NEVER GIVES UP.
SO I BOUGHT A SPELL OFF A GUY. IT WAS SUPPOSED TO TAKE AWAY HER POWERS AND GIVE THEM TO ME. WHICH IT DID...
...BUT IT ALSO GAVE MINE TO HER.
AND THAT'S HOW YOU GET GIANT-SIZE WONDER WOMAN.
"ATTACK OF THE 50 FOOT WONDER WOMAN"
CHRISTOS GAGE SCRIPT
KEVIN MAGUIRE ART
ADRIANO LUCAS COLORS
CLAYTON COWLES LETTER
BIXIE MATHIEU ASST. EDI
JAMIE S. RICH EDITOR

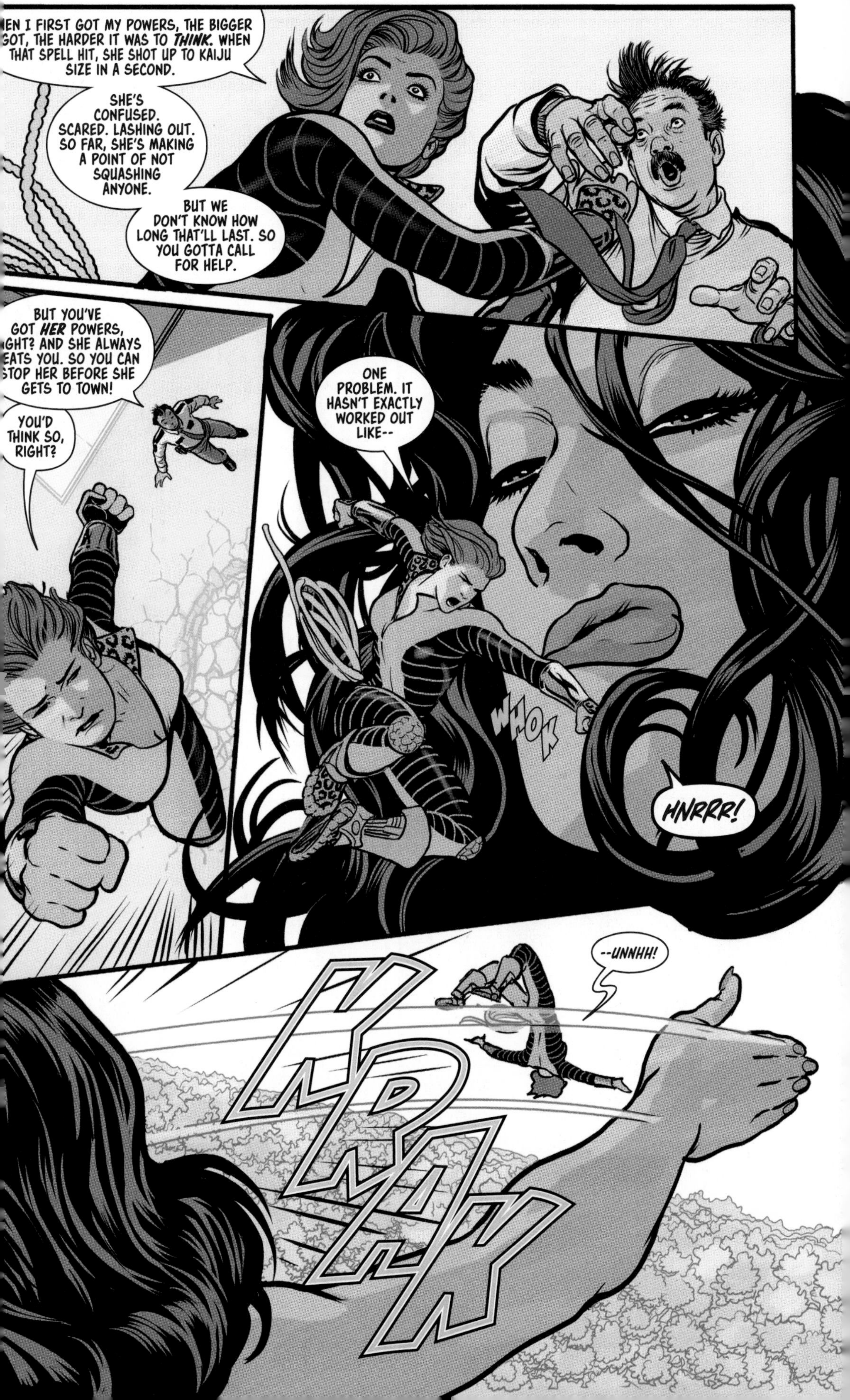

EN I FIRST GOT MY POWERS, THE BIGGER GOT, THE HARDER IT WAS TO *THINK*. WHEN THAT SPELL HIT, SHE SHOT UP TO KAIJU SIZE IN A SECOND.
SHE'S CONFUSED. SCARED. LASHING OUT. SO FAR, SHE'S MAKING A POINT OF NOT SQUASHING ANYONE.
BUT WE DON'T KNOW HOW LONG THAT'LL LAST. SO YOU GOTTA CALL FOR HELP.
BUT YOU'VE GOT *HER* POWERS, GHT? AND SHE ALWAYS EATS YOU. SO YOU CAN STOP HER BEFORE SHE GETS TO TOWN!
YOU'D THINK SO, RIGHT?
ONE PROBLEM. IT HASN'T EXACTLY WORKED OUT LIKE--
WHOK
HNRRR!
--UNNHH!
KRAK

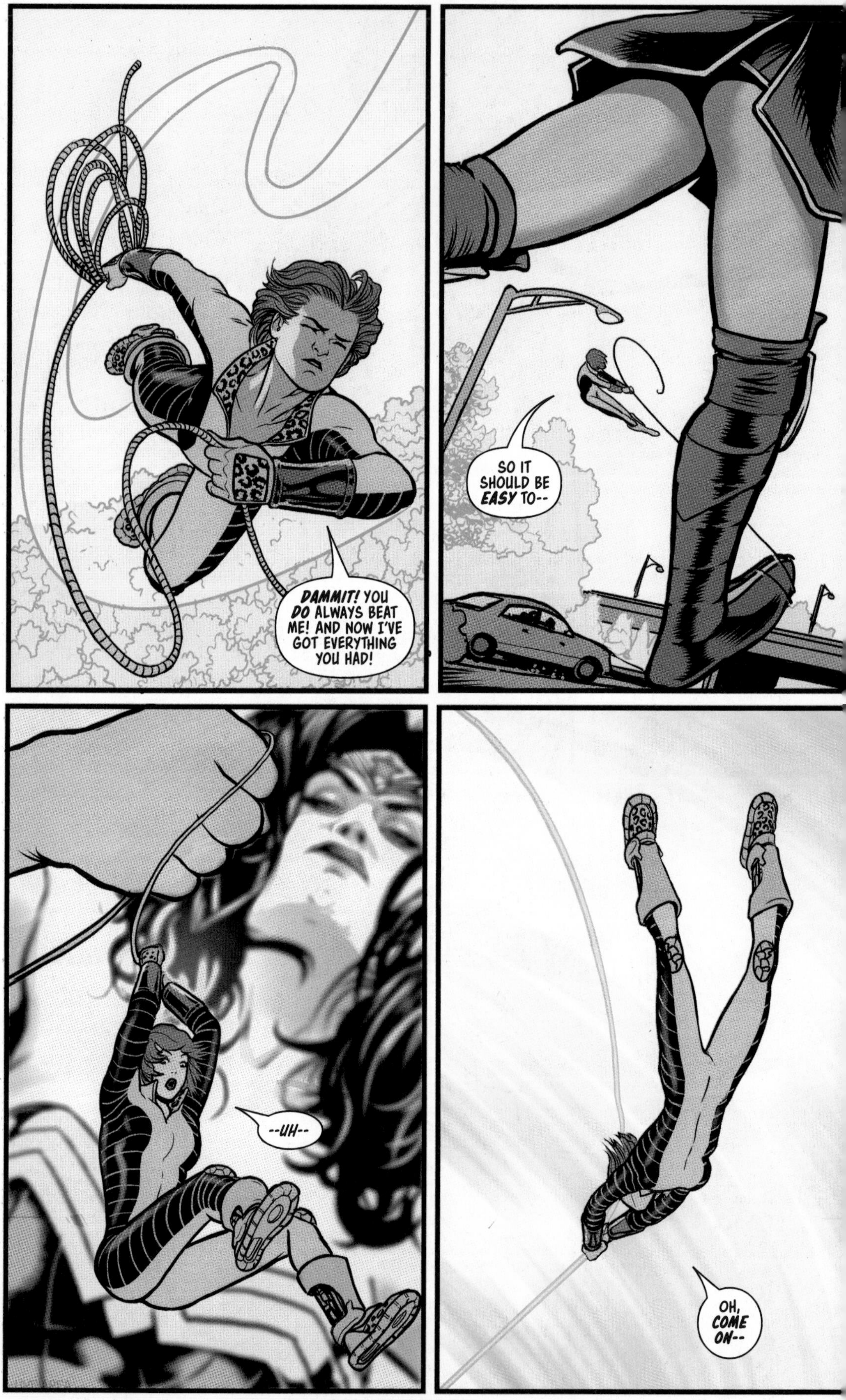
DAMMIT! YOU DO ALWAYS BEAT ME! AND NOW I'VE GOT EVERYTHING YOU HAD!
SO IT SHOULD BE EASY TO--
--UH--
OH, COME ON--

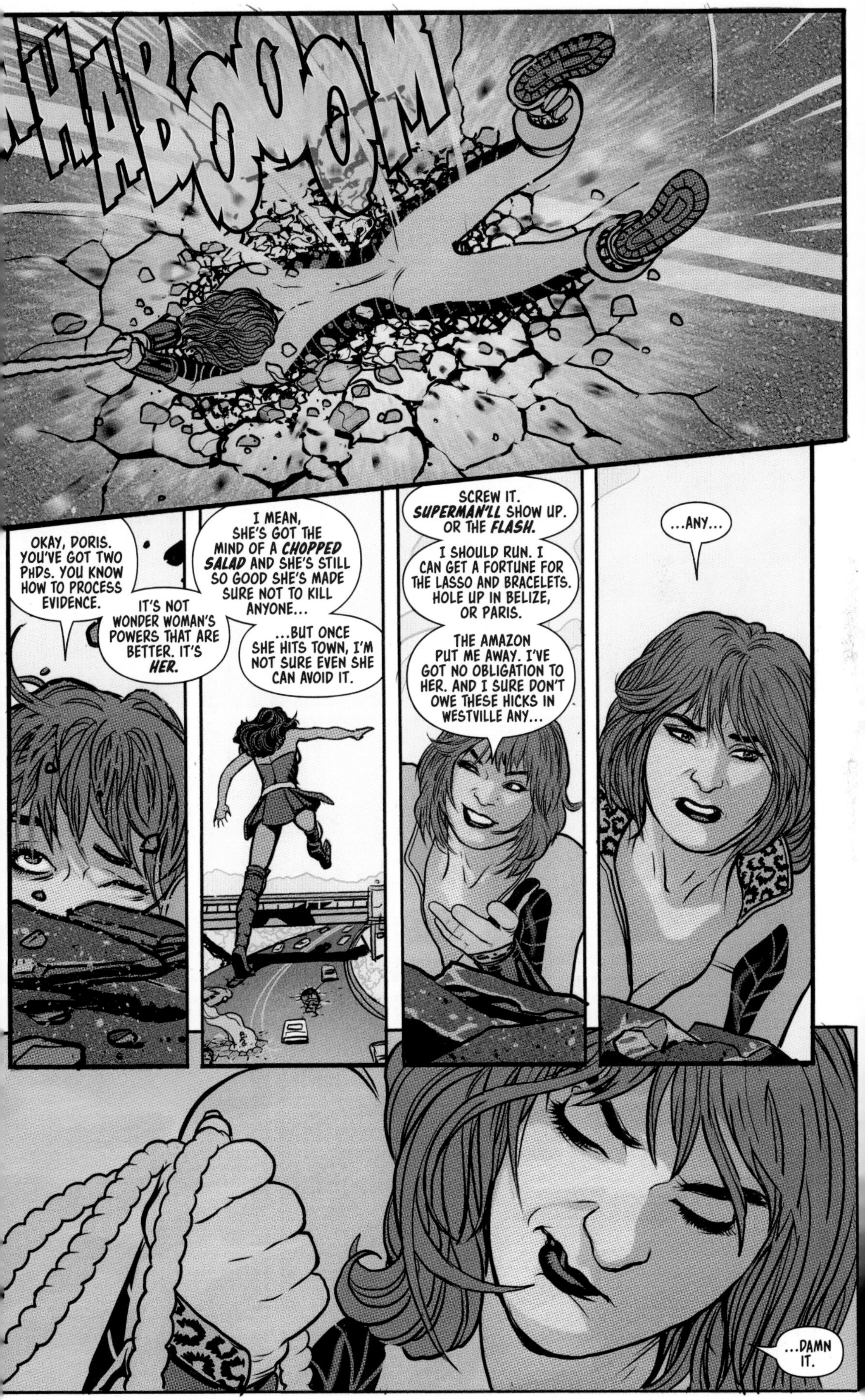
KHABOOOM
OKAY, DORIS. YOU'VE GOT TWO PhDs. YOU KNOW HOW TO PROCESS EVIDENCE.
IT'S NOT WONDER WOMAN'S POWERS THAT ARE BETTER. IT'S HER.
I MEAN, SHE'S GOT THE MIND OF A CHOPPED SALAD AND SHE'S STILL SO GOOD SHE'S MADE SURE NOT TO KILL ANYONE...
...BUT ONCE SHE HITS TOWN, I'M NOT SURE EVEN SHE CAN AVOID IT.
SCREW IT. SUPERMAN'LL SHOW UP. OR THE FLASH.
I SHOULD RUN. I CAN GET A FORTUNE FOR THE LASSO AND BRACELETS. HOLE UP IN BELIZE, OR PARIS.
THE AMAZON PUT ME AWAY. I'VE GOT NO OBLIGATION TO HER. AND I SURE DON'T OWE THESE HICKS IN WESTVILLE ANY...
...ANY...
...DAMN IT.

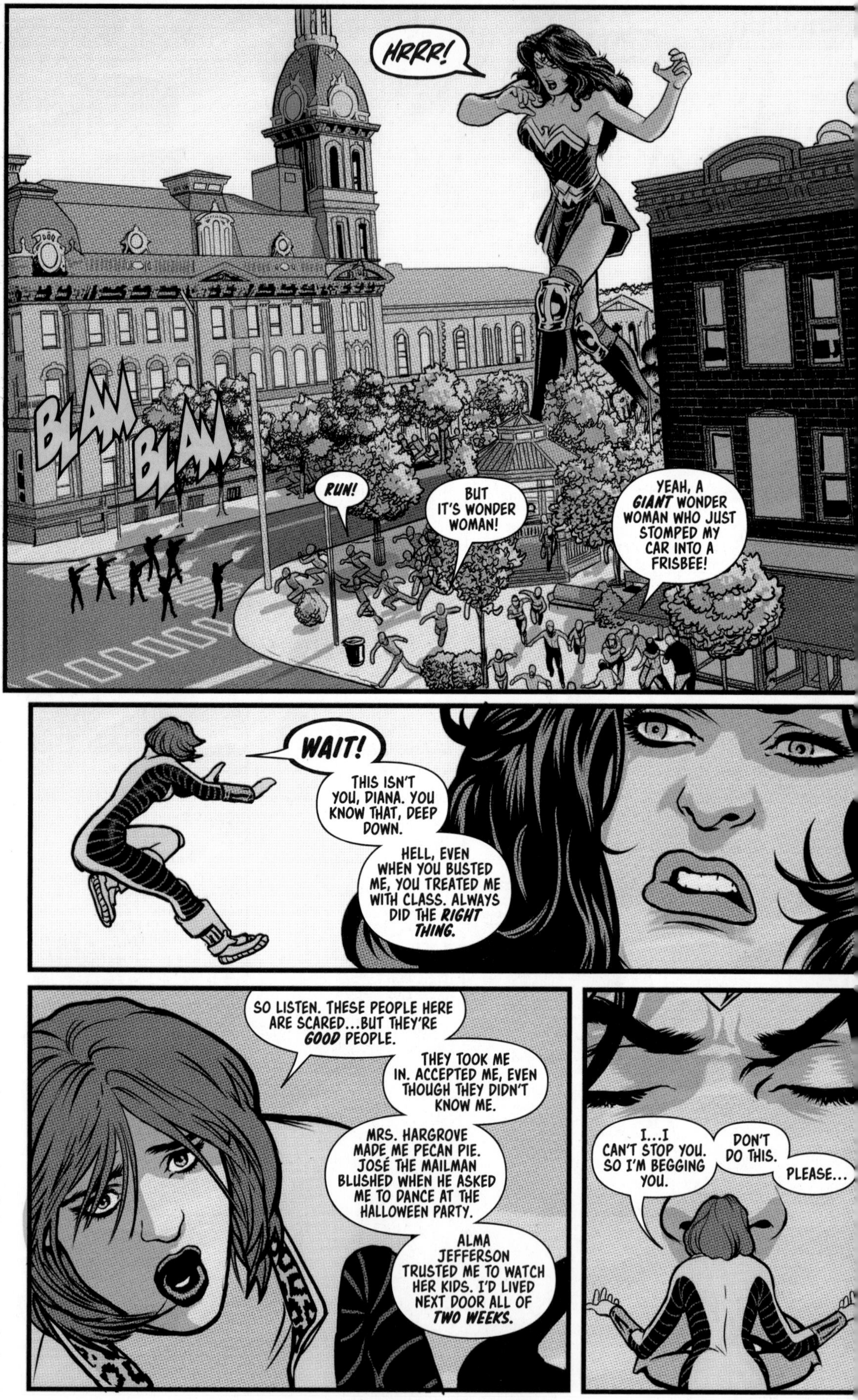
HRRR!
BLAM BLAM
RUN!
BUT IT'S WONDER WOMAN!
YEAH, A GIANT WONDER WOMAN WHO JUST STOMPED MY CAR INTO A FRISBEE!
WAIT!
THIS ISN'T YOU, DIANA. YOU KNOW THAT, DEEP DOWN.
HELL, EVEN WHEN YOU BUSTED ME, YOU TREATED ME WITH CLASS. ALWAYS DID THE RIGHT THING.
SO LISTEN. THESE PEOPLE HERE ARE SCARED...BUT THEY'RE GOOD PEOPLE.
THEY TOOK ME IN. ACCEPTED ME, EVEN THOUGH THEY DIDN'T KNOW ME.
MRS. HARGROVE MADE ME PECAN PIE. JOSÉ THE MAILMAN BLUSHED WHEN HE ASKED ME TO DANCE AT THE HALLOWEEN PARTY.
ALMA JEFFERSON TRUSTED ME TO WATCH HER KIDS. I'D LIVED NEXT DOOR ALL OF TWO WEEKS.
I...I CAN'T STOP YOU. SO I'M BEGGING YOU.
DON'T DO THIS.
PLEASE...

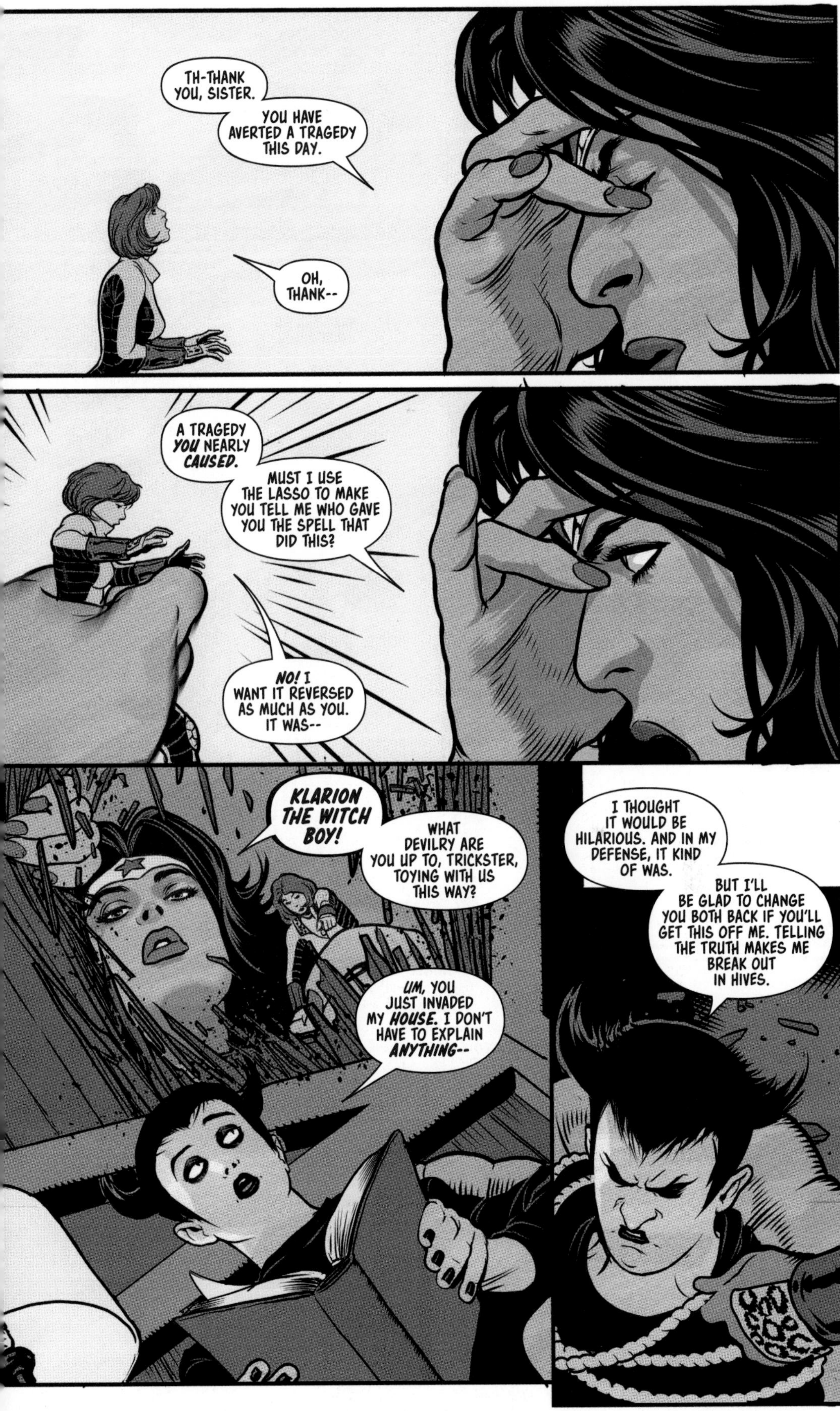

TH-THANK YOU, SISTER.
YOU HAVE AVERTED A TRAGEDY THIS DAY.
OH, THANK--
A TRAGEDY *YOU* NEARLY *CAUSED.*
MUST I USE THE LASSO TO MAKE YOU TELL ME WHO GAVE YOU THE SPELL THAT DID THIS?
NO! I WANT IT REVERSED AS MUCH AS YOU. IT WAS--
KLARION THE WITCH BOY!
WHAT DEVILRY ARE YOU UP TO, TRICKSTER, TOYING WITH US THIS WAY?
UM, YOU JUST INVADED MY *HOUSE.* I DON'T HAVE TO EXPLAIN *ANYTHING--*
I THOUGHT IT WOULD BE HILARIOUS. AND IN MY DEFENSE, IT KIND OF WAS.
BUT I'LL BE GLAD TO CHANGE YOU BOTH BACK IF YOU'LL GET THIS OFF ME. TELLING THE TRUTH MAKES ME BREAK OUT IN HIVES.

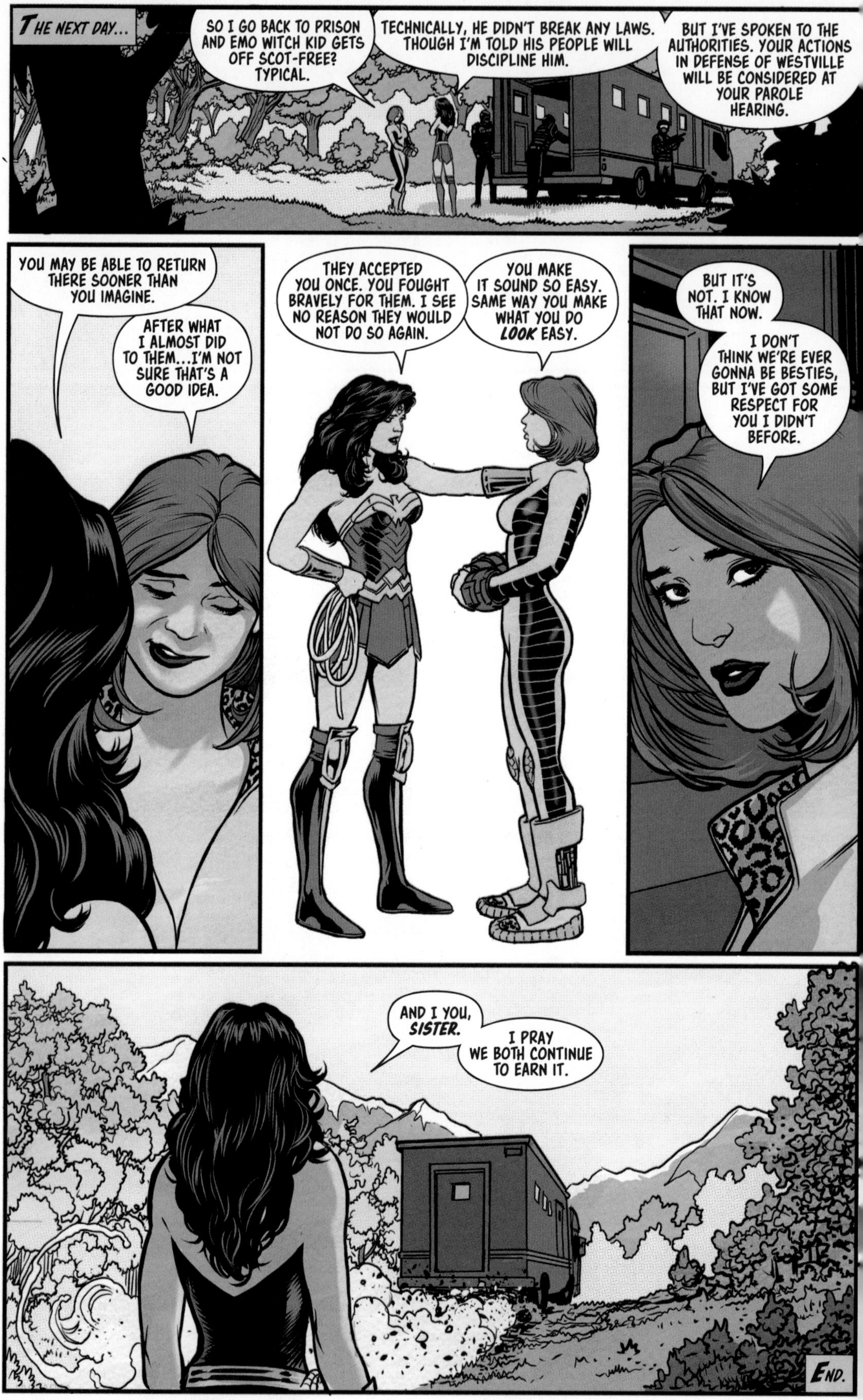
THE NEXT DAY...
SO I GO BACK TO PRISON AND EMO WITCH KID GETS OFF SCOT-FREE? TYPICAL.
TECHNICALLY, HE DIDN'T BREAK ANY LAWS. THOUGH I'M TOLD HIS PEOPLE WILL DISCIPLINE HIM.
BUT I'VE SPOKEN TO THE AUTHORITIES. YOUR ACTIONS IN DEFENSE OF WESTVILLE WILL BE CONSIDERED AT YOUR PAROLE HEARING.
YOU MAY BE ABLE TO RETURN THERE SOONER THAN YOU IMAGINE.
AFTER WHAT I ALMOST DID TO THEM...I'M NOT SURE THAT'S A GOOD IDEA.
THEY ACCEPTED YOU ONCE. YOU FOUGHT BRAVELY FOR THEM. I SEE NO REASON THEY WOULD NOT DO SO AGAIN.
YOU MAKE IT SOUND SO EASY. SAME WAY YOU MAKE WHAT YOU DO LOOK EASY.
BUT IT'S NOT. I KNOW THAT NOW.
I DON'T THINK WE'RE EVER GONNA BE BESTIES, BUT I'VE GOT SOME RESPECT FOR YOU I DIDN'T BEFORE.
AND I YOU, SISTER.
I PRAY WE BOTH CONTINUE TO EARN IT.
END.

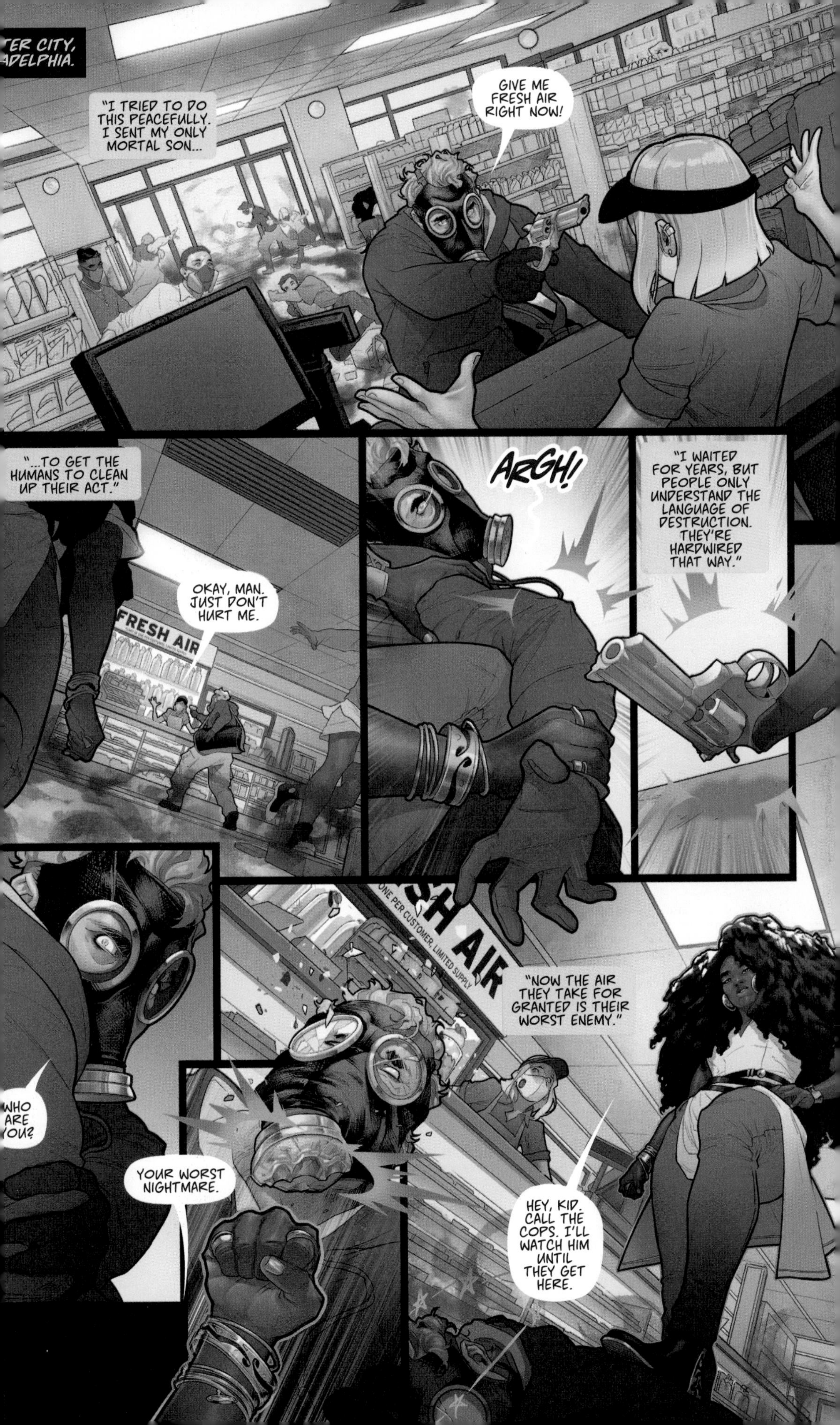
...TER CITY, ...ADELPHIA.
"I TRIED TO DO THIS PEACEFULLY. I SENT MY ONLY MORTAL SON...
GIVE ME FRESH AIR RIGHT NOW!
"...TO GET THE HUMANS TO CLEAN UP THEIR ACT."
OKAY, MAN. JUST DON'T HURT ME.
FRESH AIR
ARGH!
"I WAITED FOR YEARS, BUT PEOPLE ONLY UNDERSTAND THE LANGUAGE OF DESTRUCTION. THEY'RE HARDWIRED THAT WAY."
WHO ARE YOU?
YOUR WORST NIGHTMARE.
SH AIR
ONE PER CUSTOMER, LIMITED SUPPLY
"NOW THE AIR THEY TAKE FOR GRANTED IS THEIR WORST ENEMY."
HEY, KID. CALL THE COPS. I'LL WATCH HIM UNTIL THEY GET HERE.

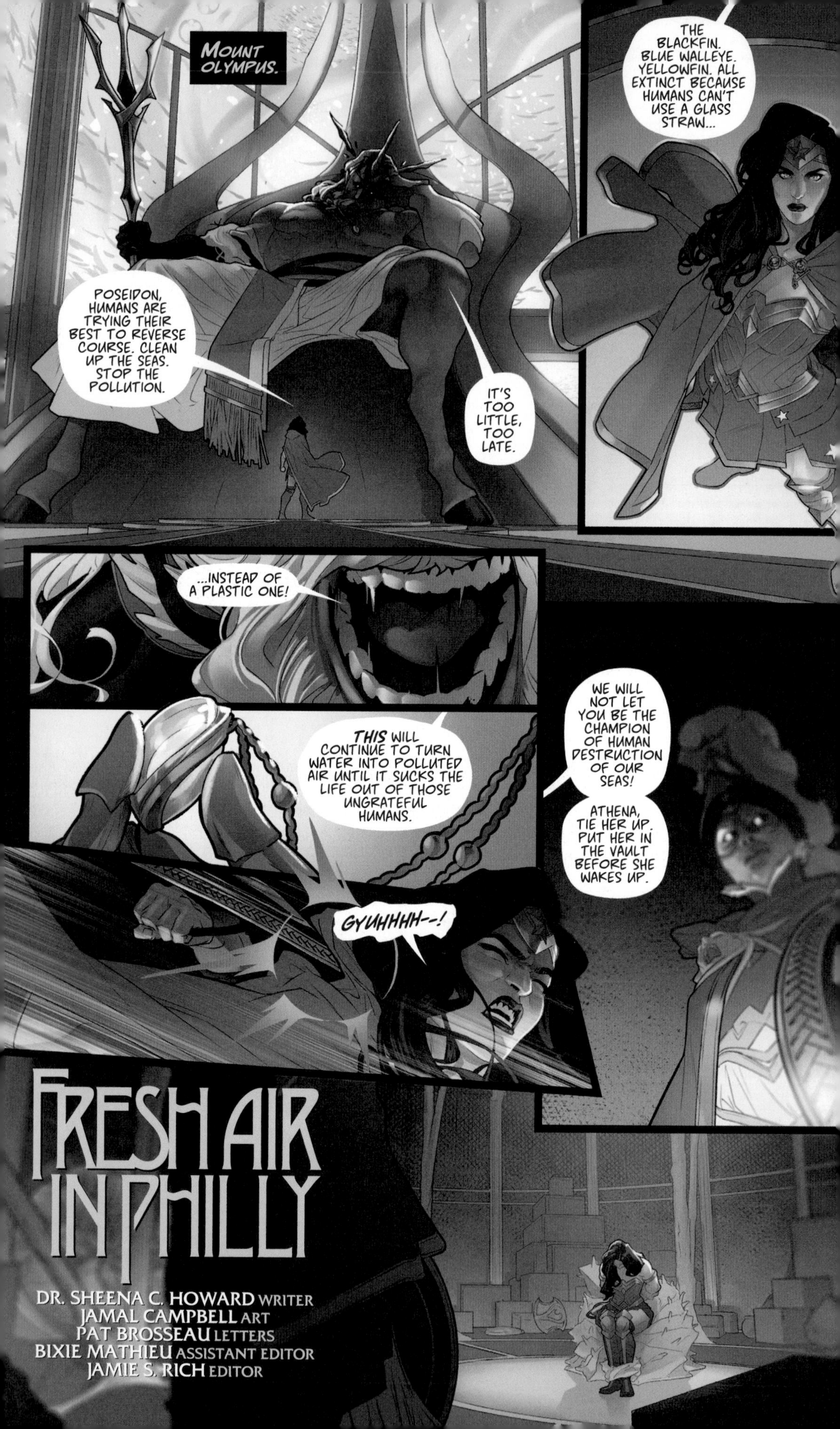
MOUNT OLYMPUS.
POSEIDON, HUMANS ARE TRYING THEIR BEST TO REVERSE COURSE. CLEAN UP THE SEAS. STOP THE POLLUTION.
IT'S TOO LITTLE, TOO LATE.
THE BLACKFIN. BLUE WALLEYE. YELLOWFIN. ALL EXTINCT BECAUSE HUMANS CAN'T USE A GLASS STRAW...
...INSTEAD OF A PLASTIC ONE!
THIS WILL CONTINUE TO TURN WATER INTO POLLUTED AIR UNTIL IT SUCKS THE LIFE OUT OF THOSE UNGRATEFUL HUMANS.
WE WILL NOT LET YOU BE THE CHAMPION OF HUMAN DESTRUCTION OF OUR SEAS!
GYUHHHH--!
ATHENA, TIE HER UP. PUT HER IN THE VAULT BEFORE SHE WAKES UP.
FRESH AIR IN PHILLY
DR. SHEENA C. HOWARD WRITER
JAMAL CAMPBELL ART
PAT BROSSEAU LETTERS
BIXIE MATHIEU ASSISTANT EDITOR
JAMIE S. RICH EDITOR

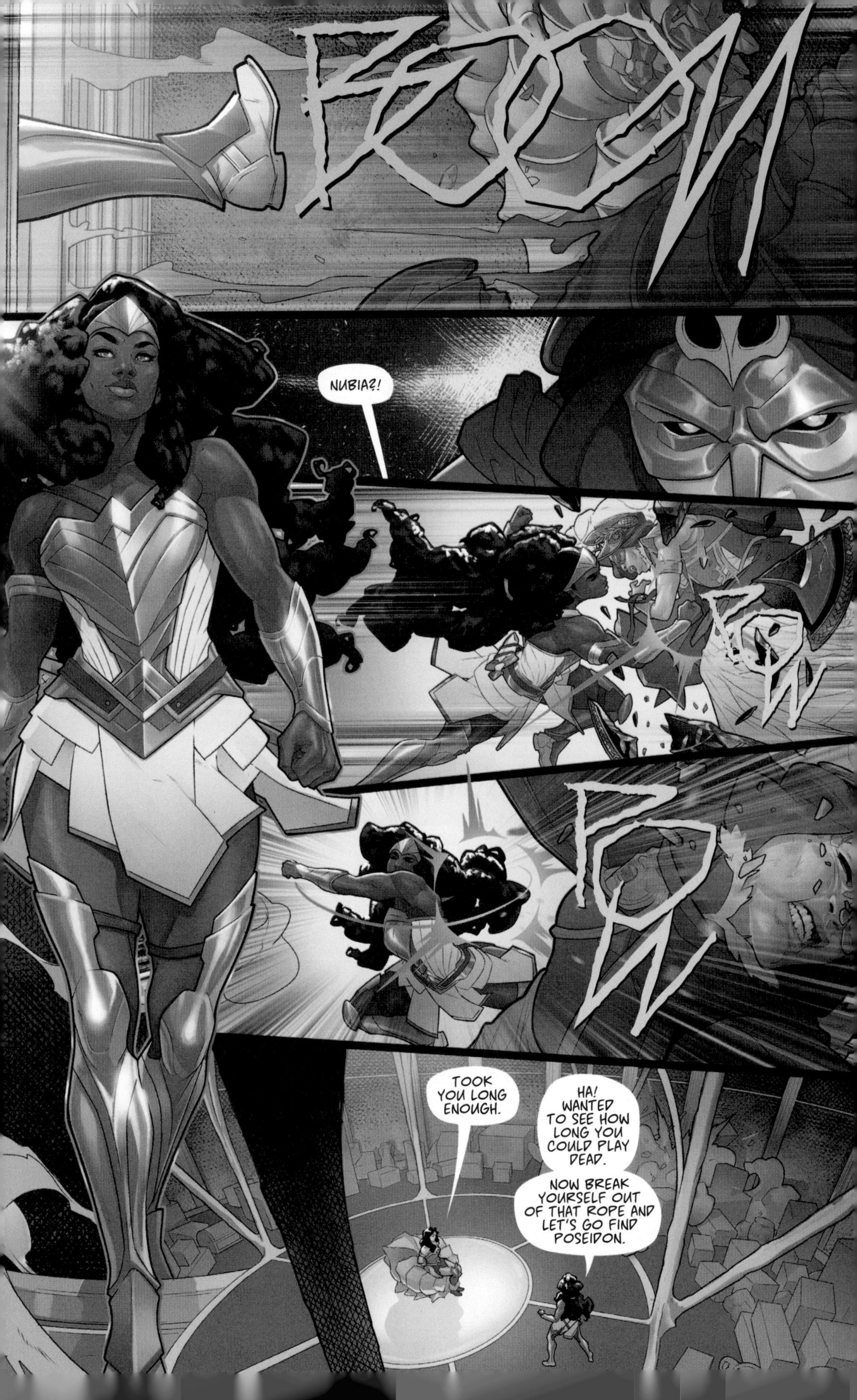
BOOM
NUBIA?!
POW
POW
TOOK YOU LONG ENOUGH.
HA! WANTED TO SEE HOW LONG YOU COULD PLAY DEAD.
NOW BREAK YOURSELF OUT OF THAT ROPE AND LET'S GO FIND POSEIDON.

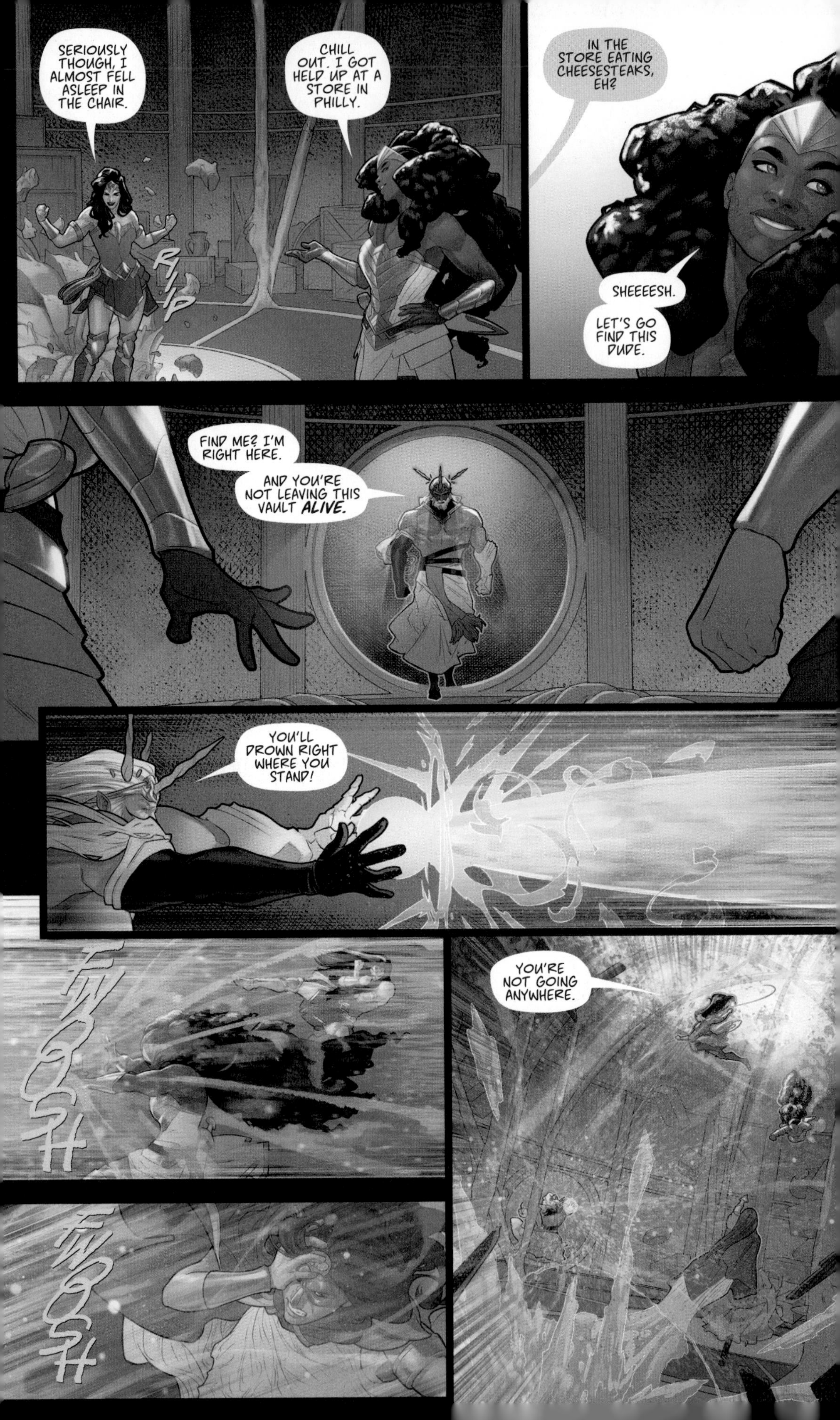
SERIOUSLY THOUGH, I ALMOST FELL ASLEEP IN THE CHAIR.
RIP
CHILL OUT. I GOT HELD UP AT A STORE IN PHILLY.
IN THE STORE EATING CHEESESTEAKS, EH?
SHEEEESH.
LET'S GO FIND THIS DUDE.
FIND ME? I'M RIGHT HERE.
AND YOU'RE NOT LEAVING THIS VAULT ALIVE.
YOU'LL DROWN RIGHT WHERE YOU STAND!
FWOOSH
YOU'RE NOT GOING ANYWHERE.
FWOOSH

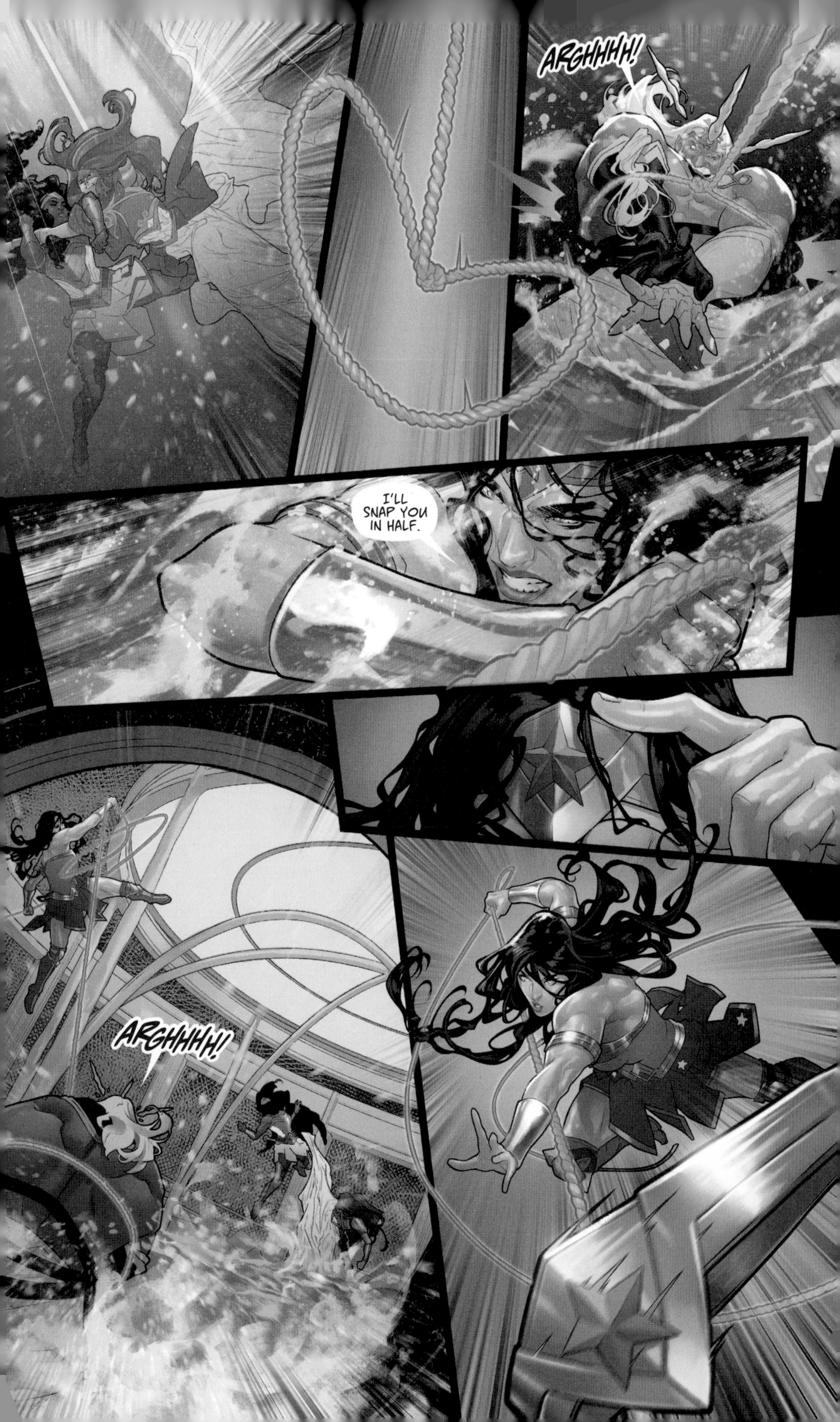
ARGHHHH!
I'LL SNAP YOU IN HALF.
ARGHHHH!

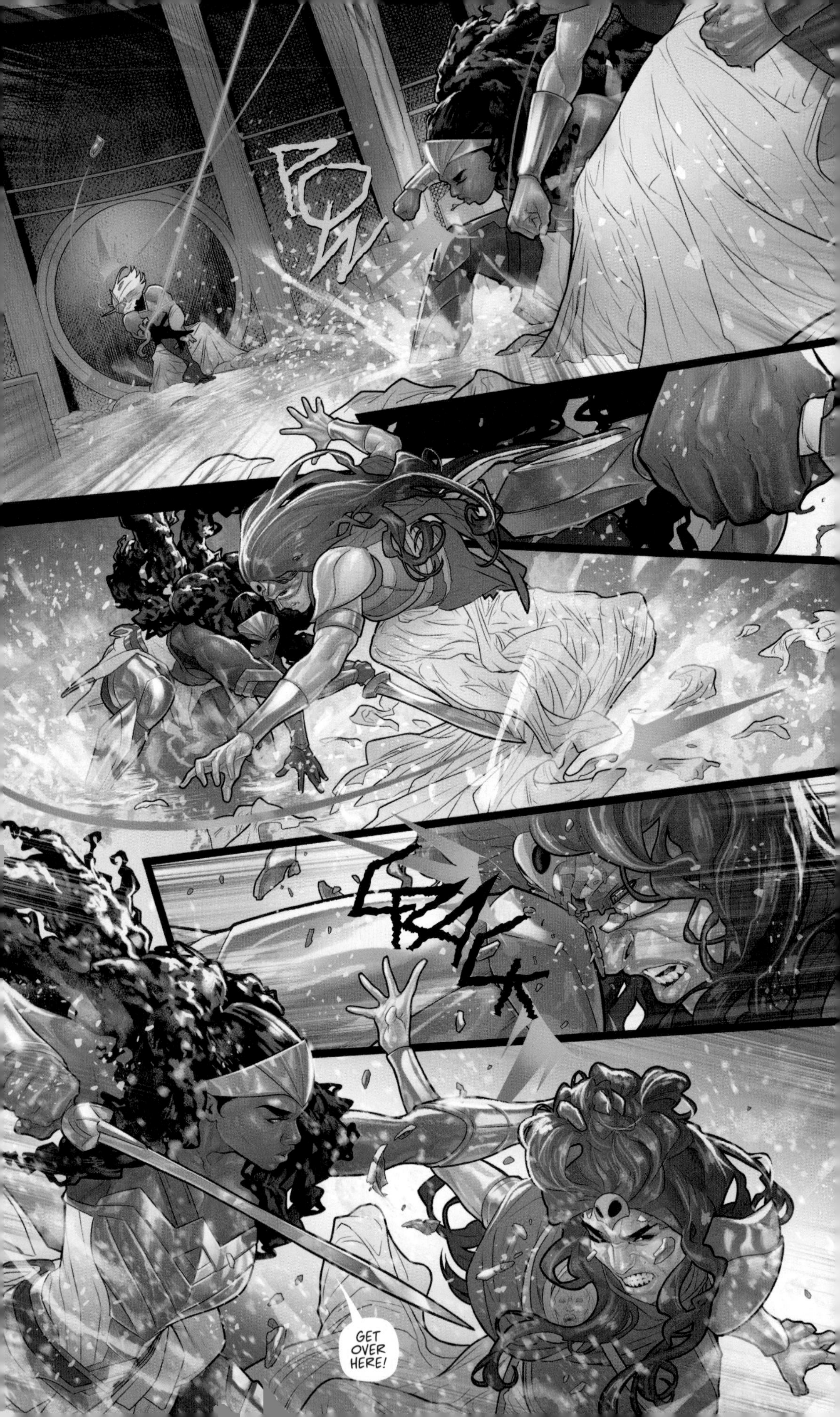
POW
CRACK
GET OVER HERE!

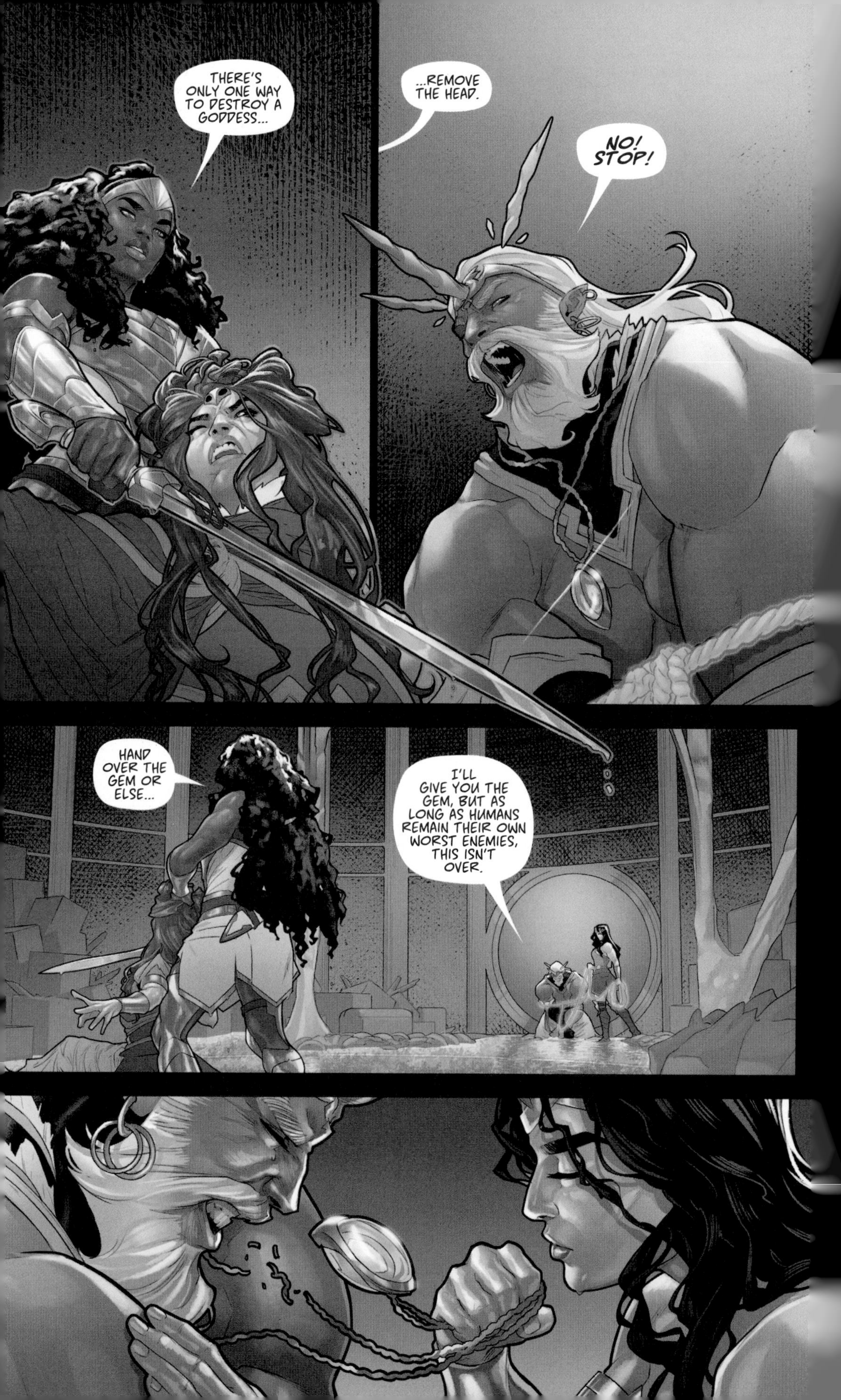

THERE'S ONLY ONE WAY TO DESTROY A GODDESS...
...REMOVE THE HEAD.
NO! STOP!
HAND OVER THE GEM OR ELSE...
I'LL GIVE YOU THE GEM, BUT AS LONG AS HUMANS REMAIN THEIR OWN WORST ENEMIES, THIS ISN'T OVER.

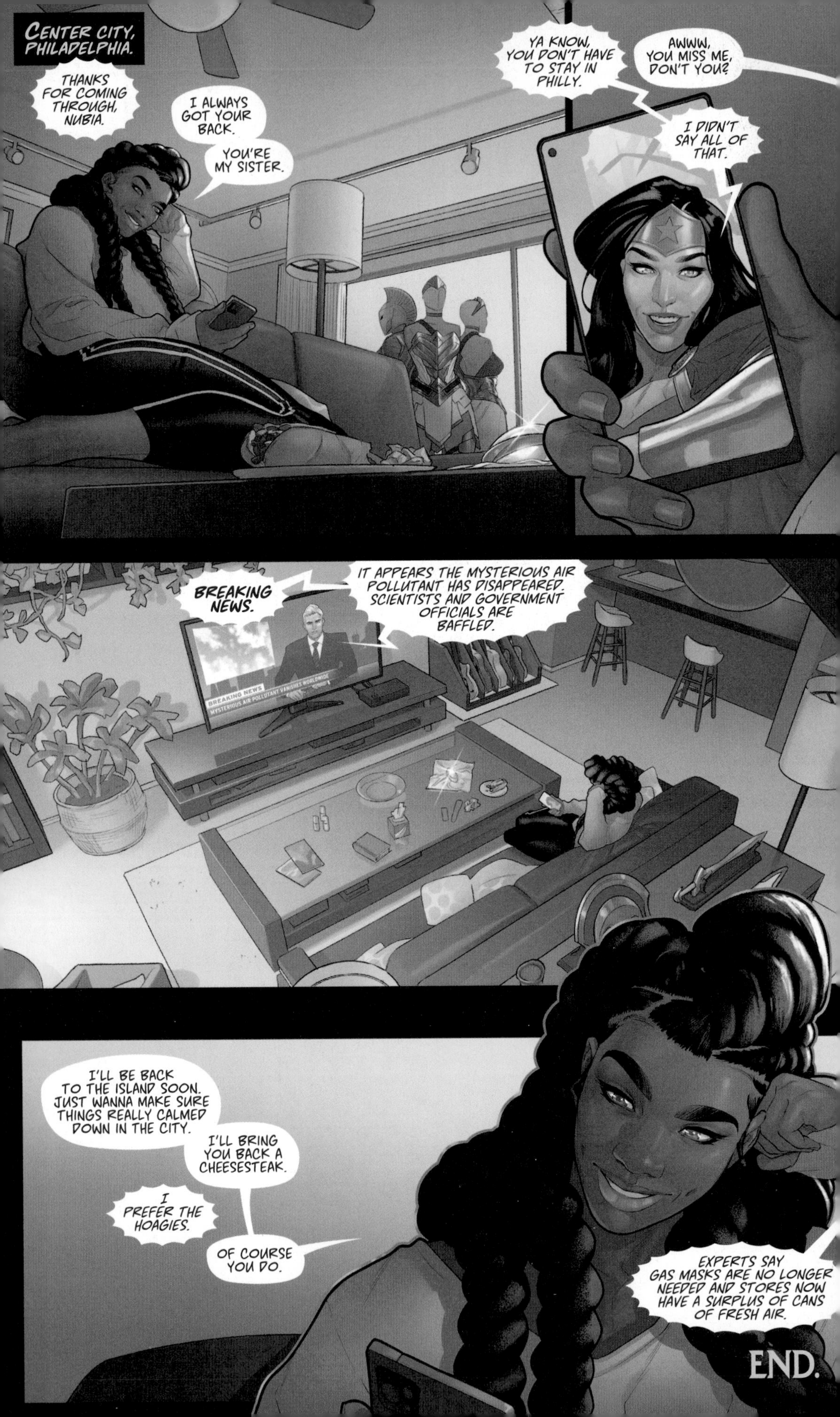
CENTER CITY, PHILADELPHIA.
THANKS FOR COMING THROUGH, NUBIA.
I ALWAYS GOT YOUR BACK.
YOU'RE MY SISTER.
YA KNOW, YOU DON'T HAVE TO STAY IN PHILLY.
AWWW, YOU MISS ME, DON'T YOU?
I DIDN'T SAY ALL OF THAT.
BREAKING NEWS.
IT APPEARS THE MYSTERIOUS AIR POLLUTANT HAS DISAPPEARED. SCIENTISTS AND GOVERNMENT OFFICIALS ARE BAFFLED.
BREAKING NEWS
MYSTERIOUS AIR POLLUTANT VANISHES WORLDWIDE
I'LL BE BACK TO THE ISLAND SOON. JUST WANNA MAKE SURE THINGS REALLY CALMED DOWN IN THE CITY.
I'LL BRING YOU BACK A CHEESESTEAK.
I PREFER THE HOAGIES.
OF COURSE YOU DO.
EXPERTS SAY GAS MASKS ARE NO LONGER NEEDED AND STORES NOW HAVE A SURPLUS OF CANS OF FRESH AIR.
END.

Wonder Woman Black & Gold #1
variant cover art by Frank Cho

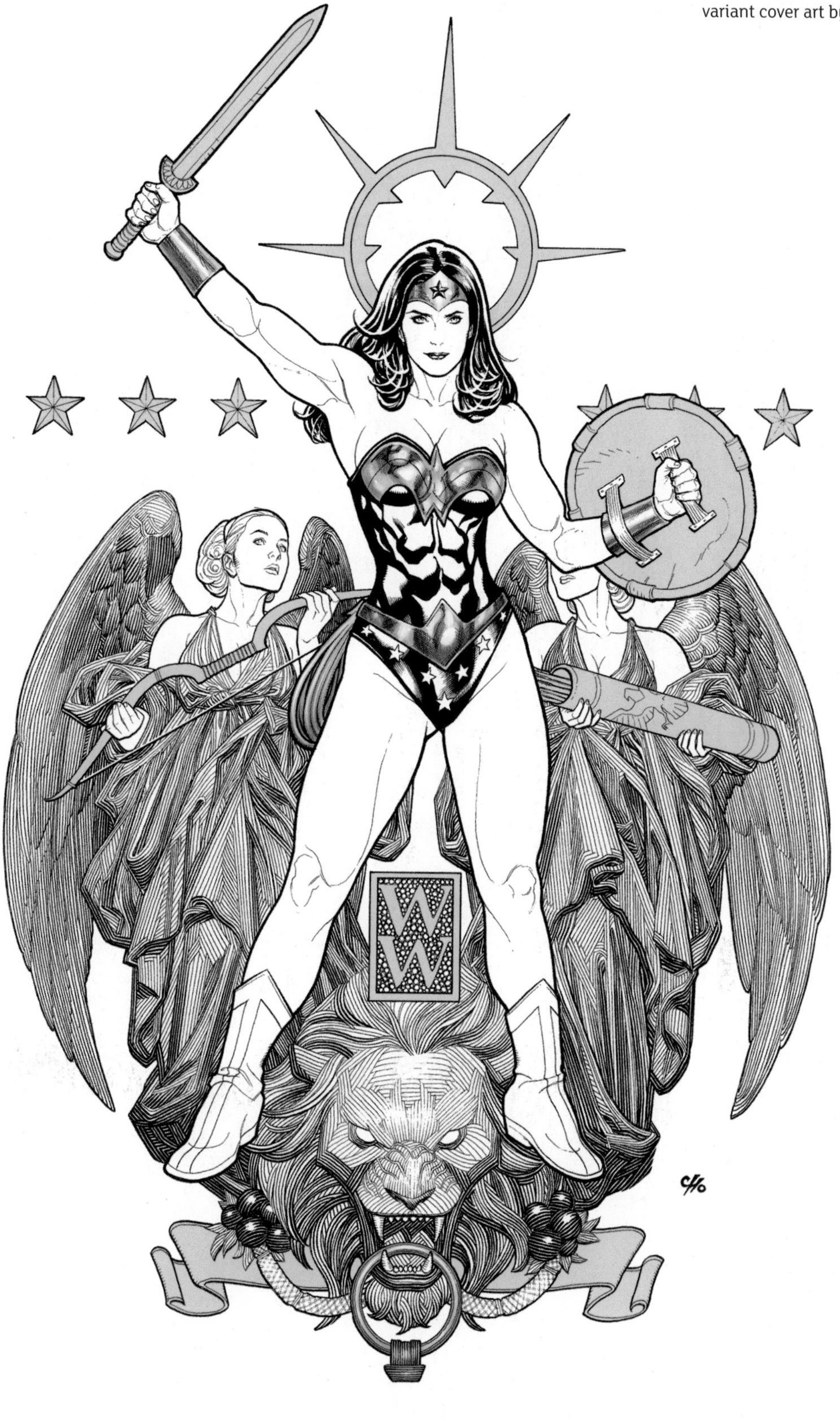

VARIANT COVER GALLERY

Wonder Woman Black & Gold #1
variant cover art by Yanick Paquette

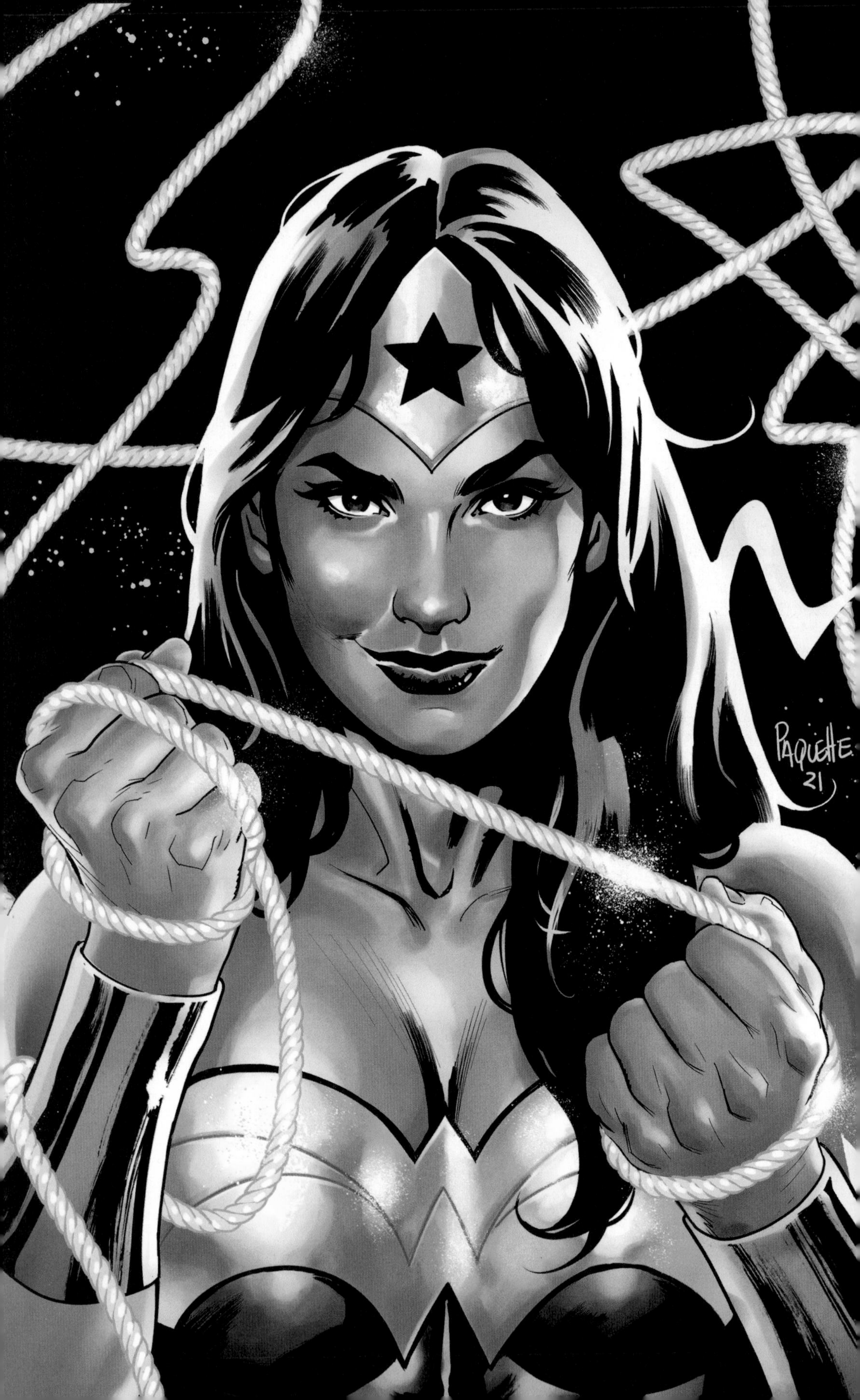
PAQUETTE
21

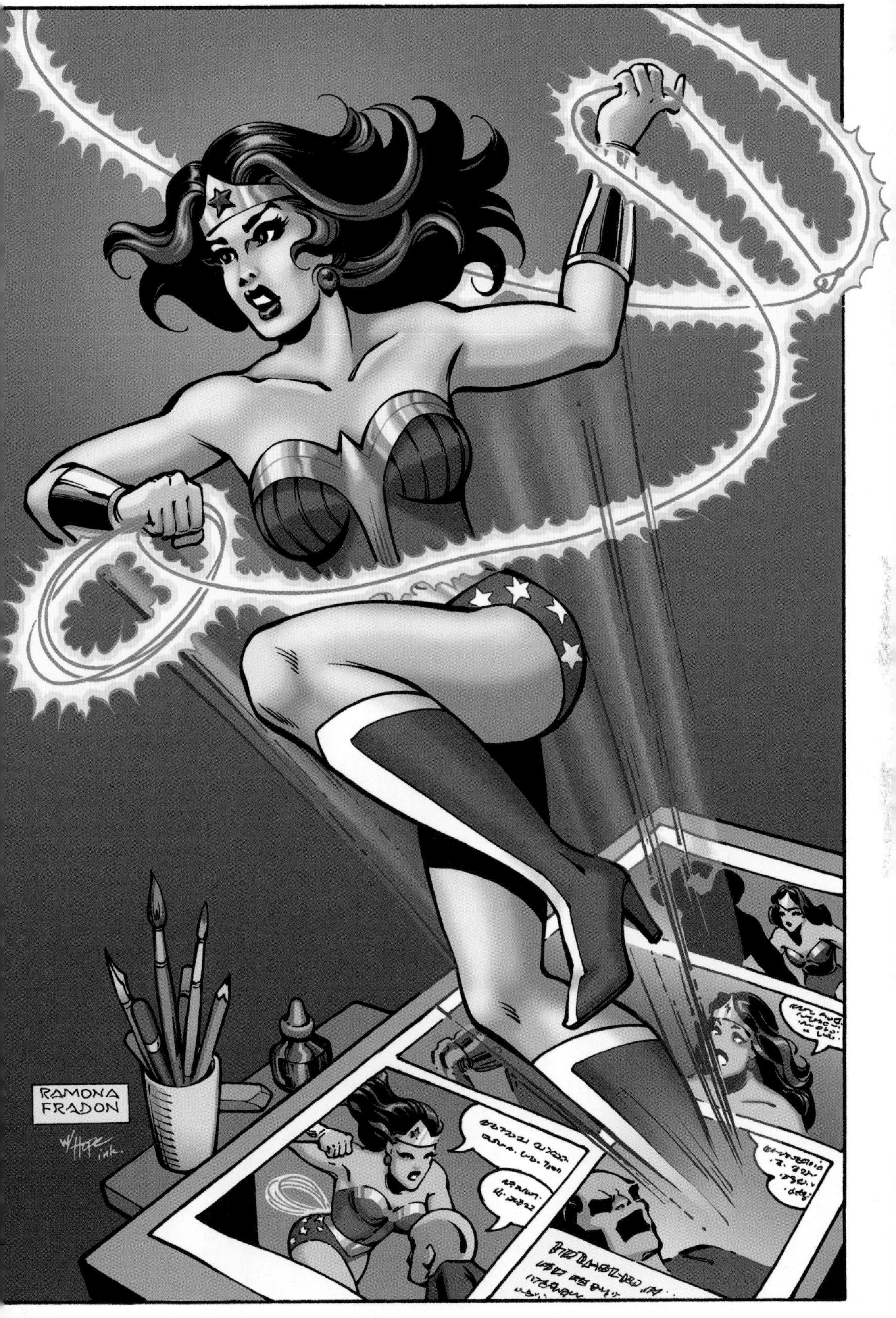
RAMONA FRADON
w/Hope ink.

Wonder Woman Black & Gold #1
variant cover art by Ramona Fradon,
Sandra Hope, and Trish Mulvihill

Wonder Woman Black & Gold #1
variant cover art by Joshua Middleton

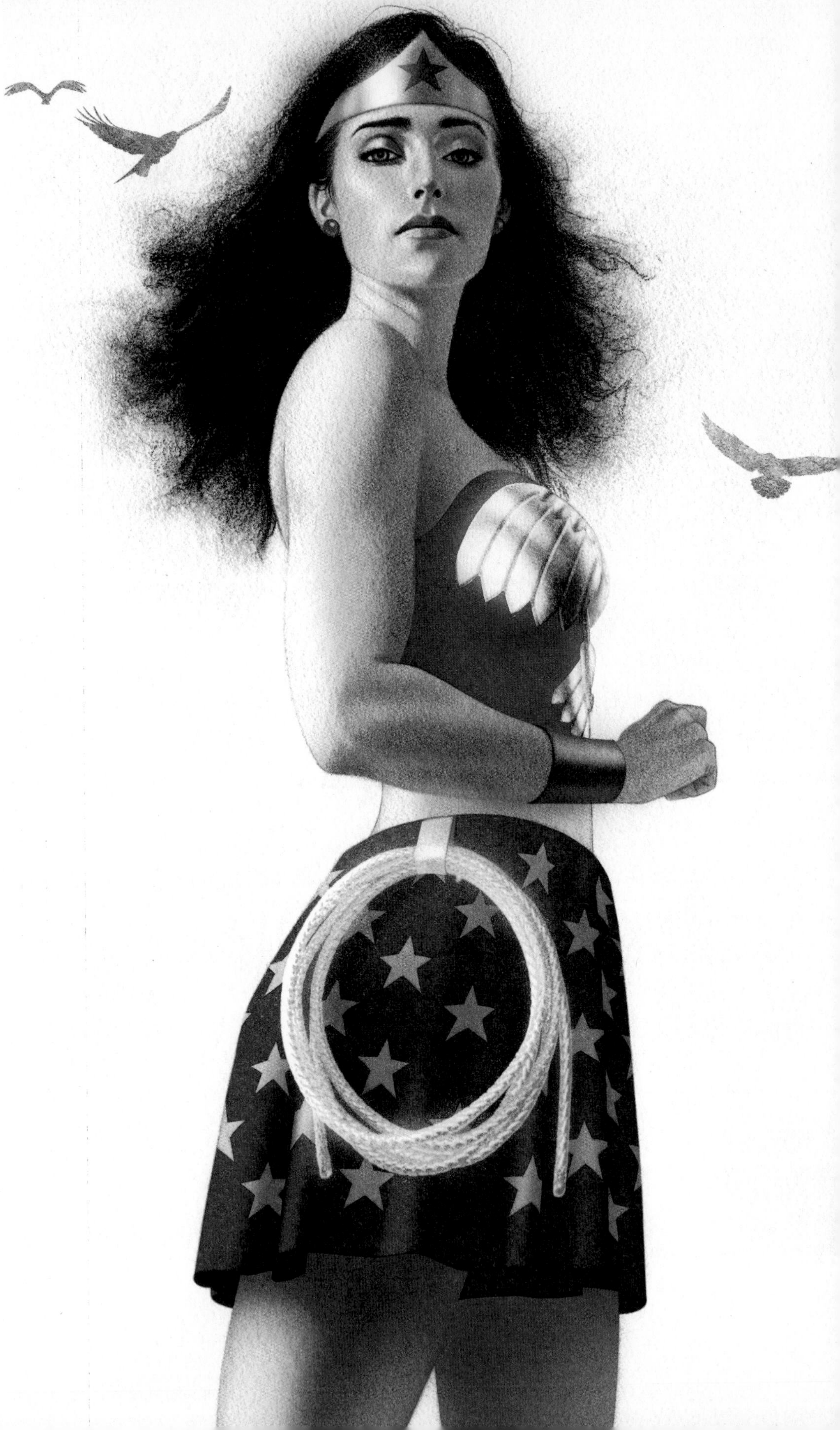

Wonder Woman Black & Gold #1
variant cover art by Carla Cohen

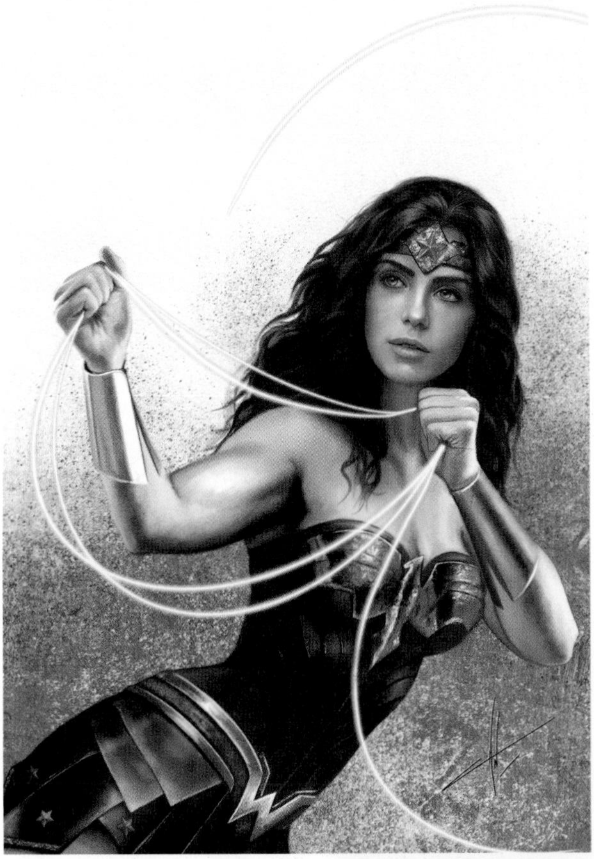

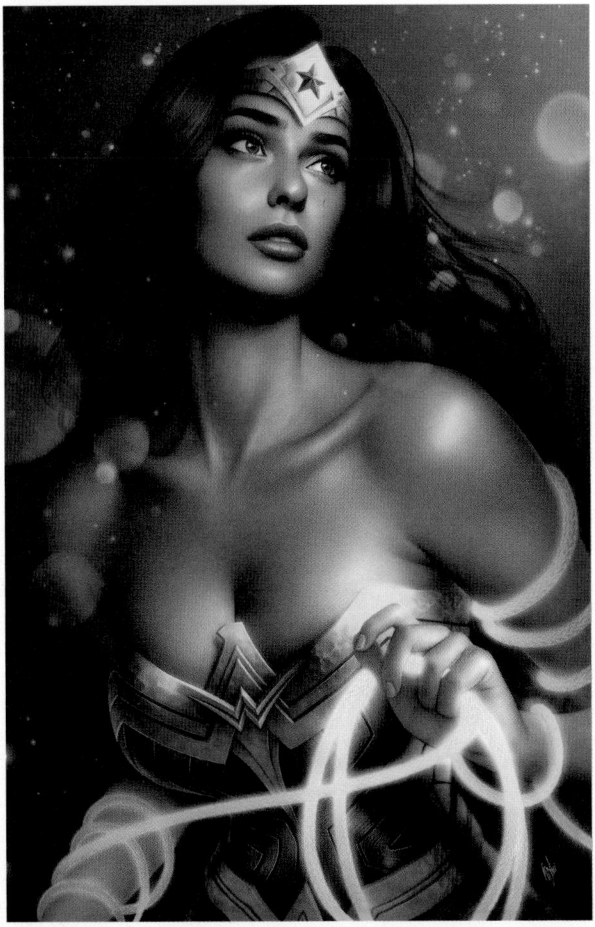

Wonder Woman Black & Gold #1
variant cover art by Warren Louw

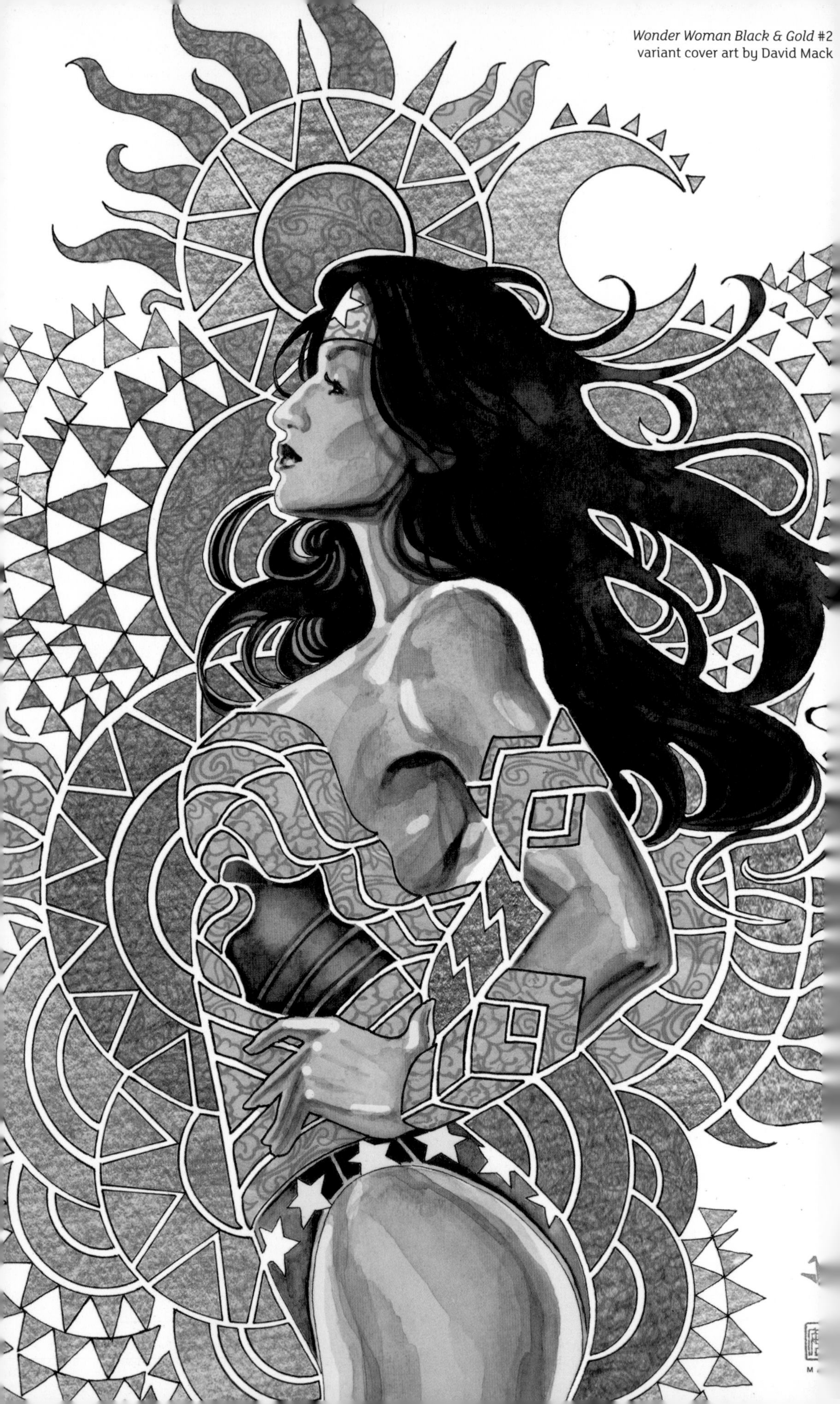

Wonder Woman Black & Gold #2
variant cover art by David Mack

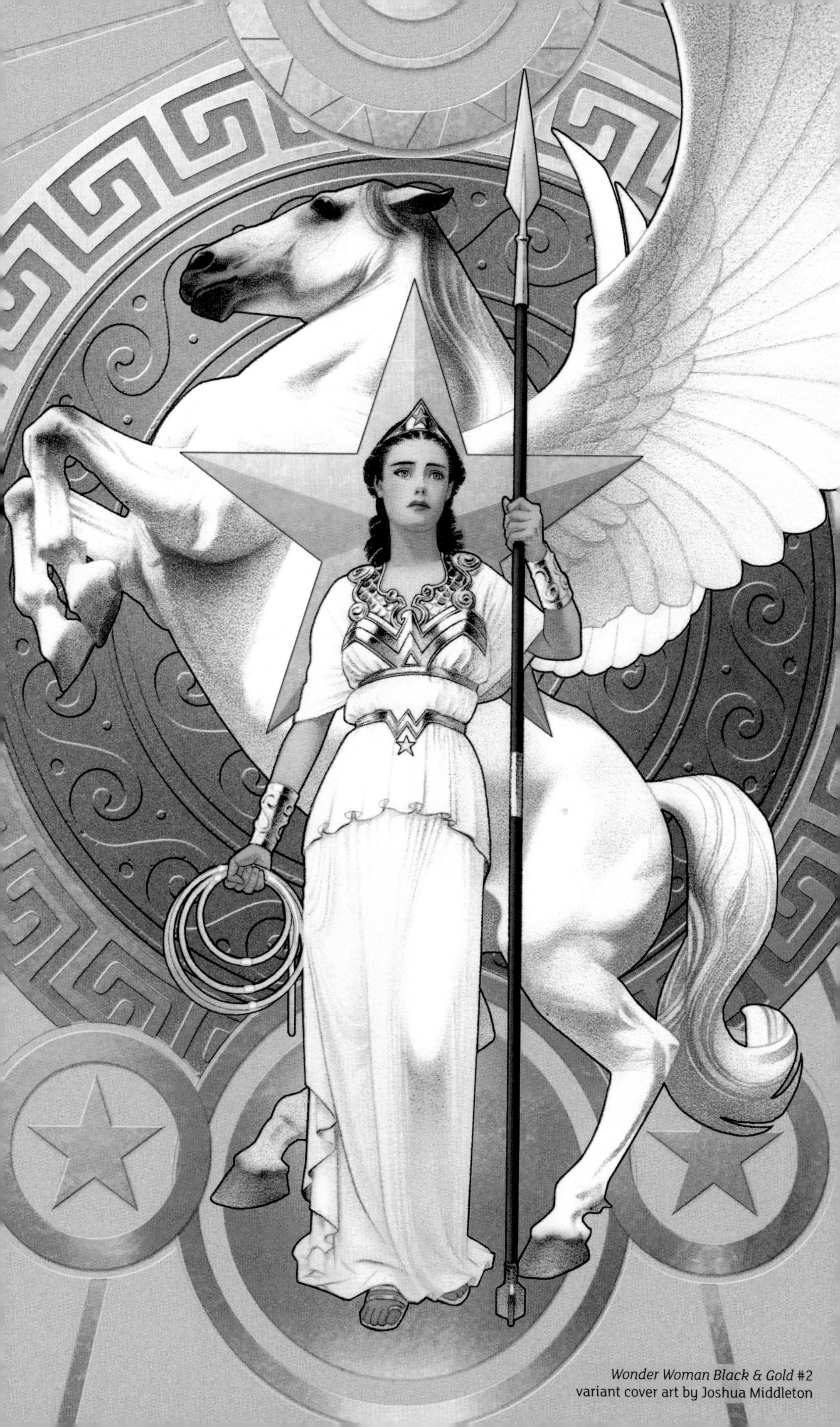

Wonder Woman Black & Gold #2
variant cover art by Joshua Middleton

Wonder Woman Black & Gold #3
variant cover art by Janaina Medeiros

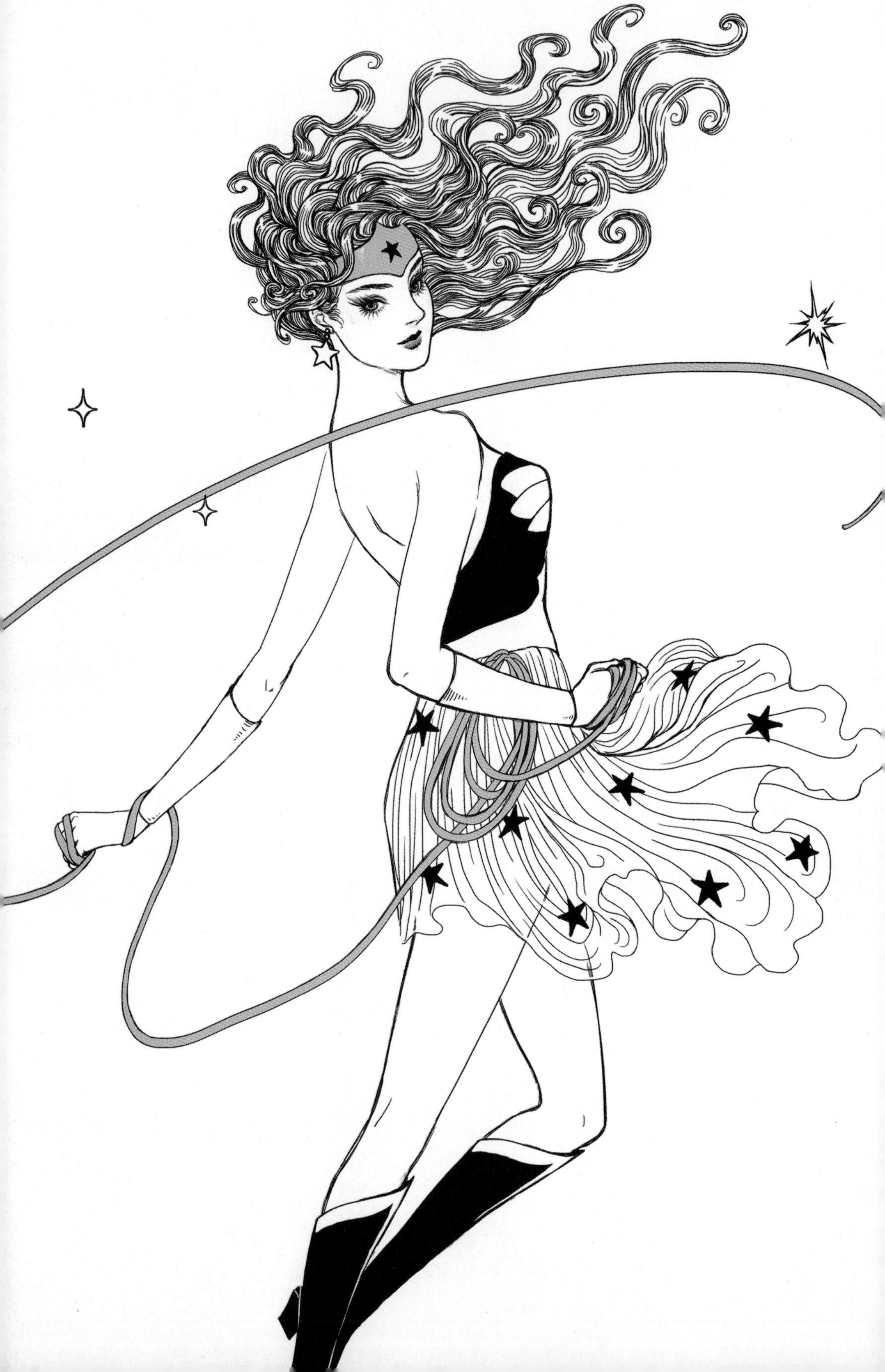

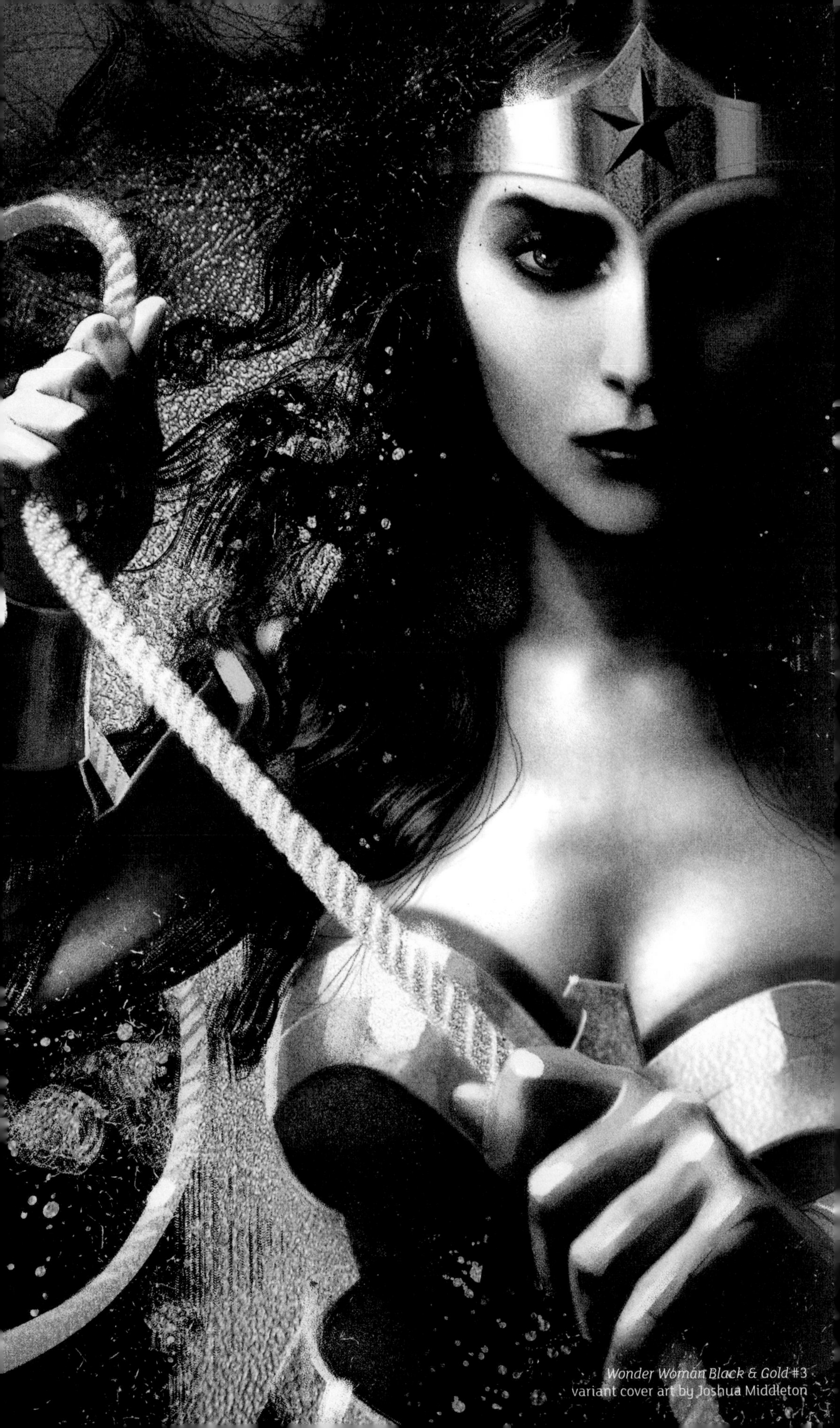

Wonder Woman Black & Gold #3
variant cover art by Joshua Middleton

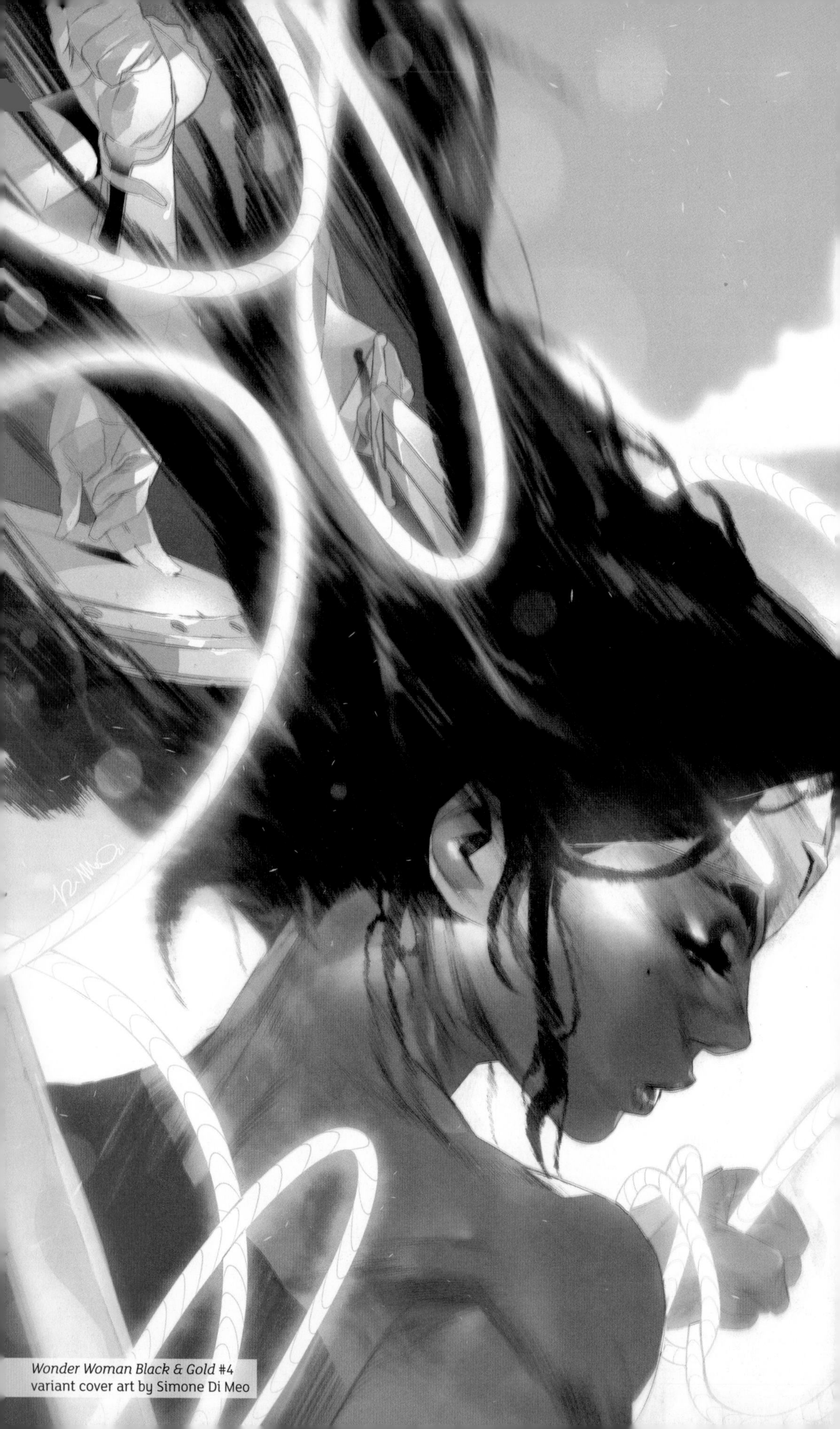

Wonder Woman Black & Gold #4
variant cover art by Simone Di Meo

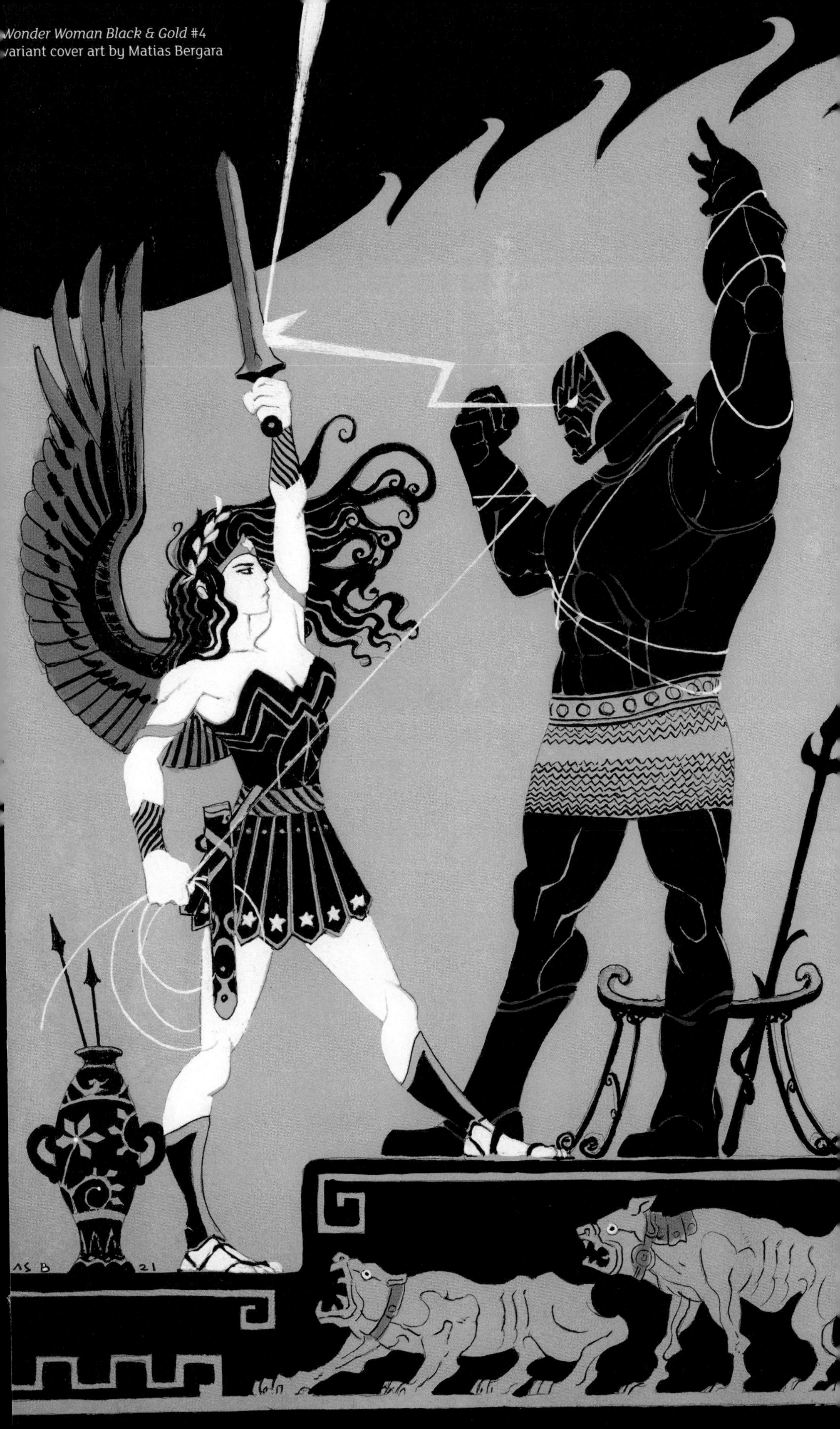

Wonder Woman Black & Gold #4
variant cover art by Matias Bergara

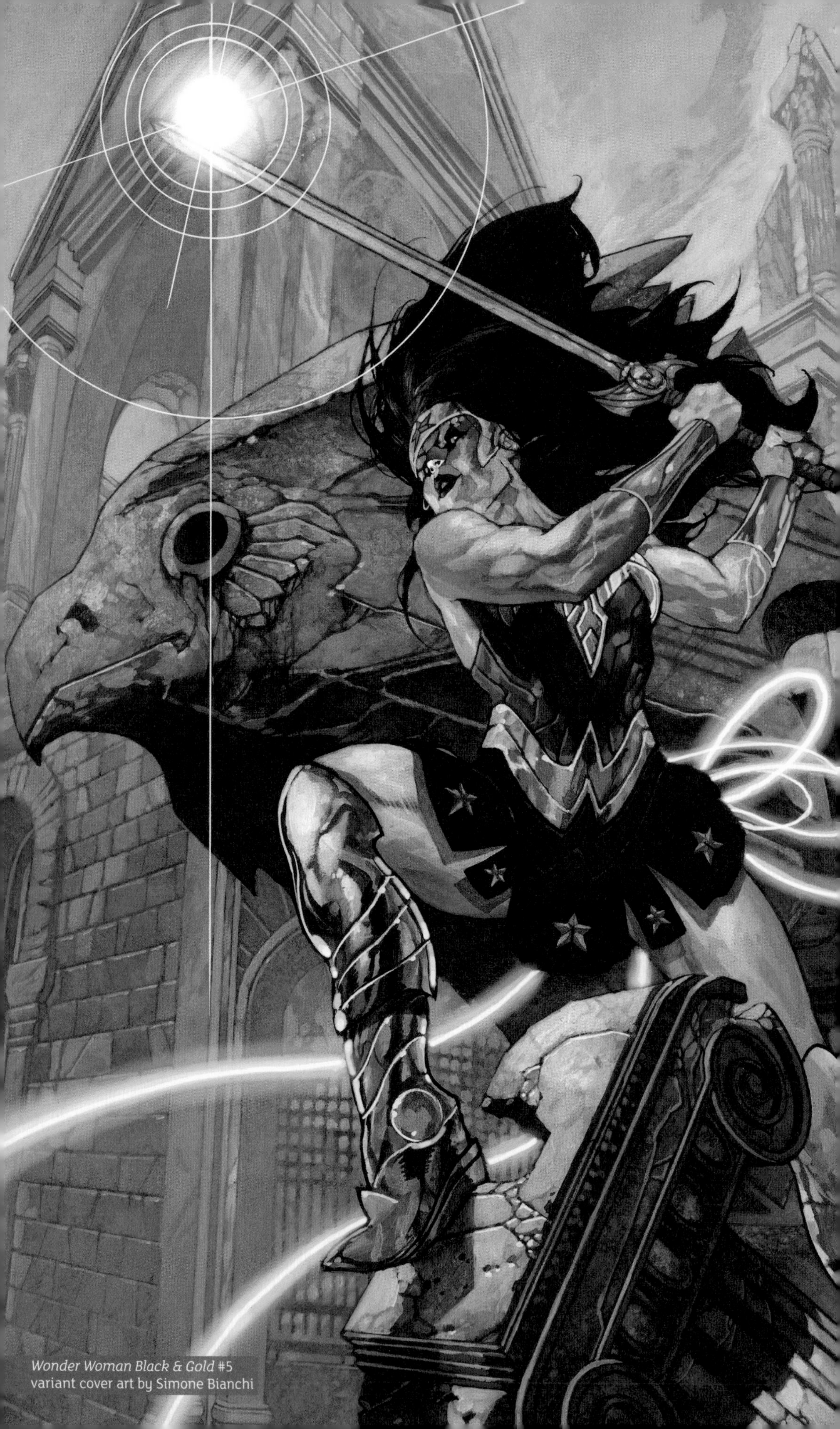

Wonder Woman Black & Gold #5
variant cover art by Simone Bianchi

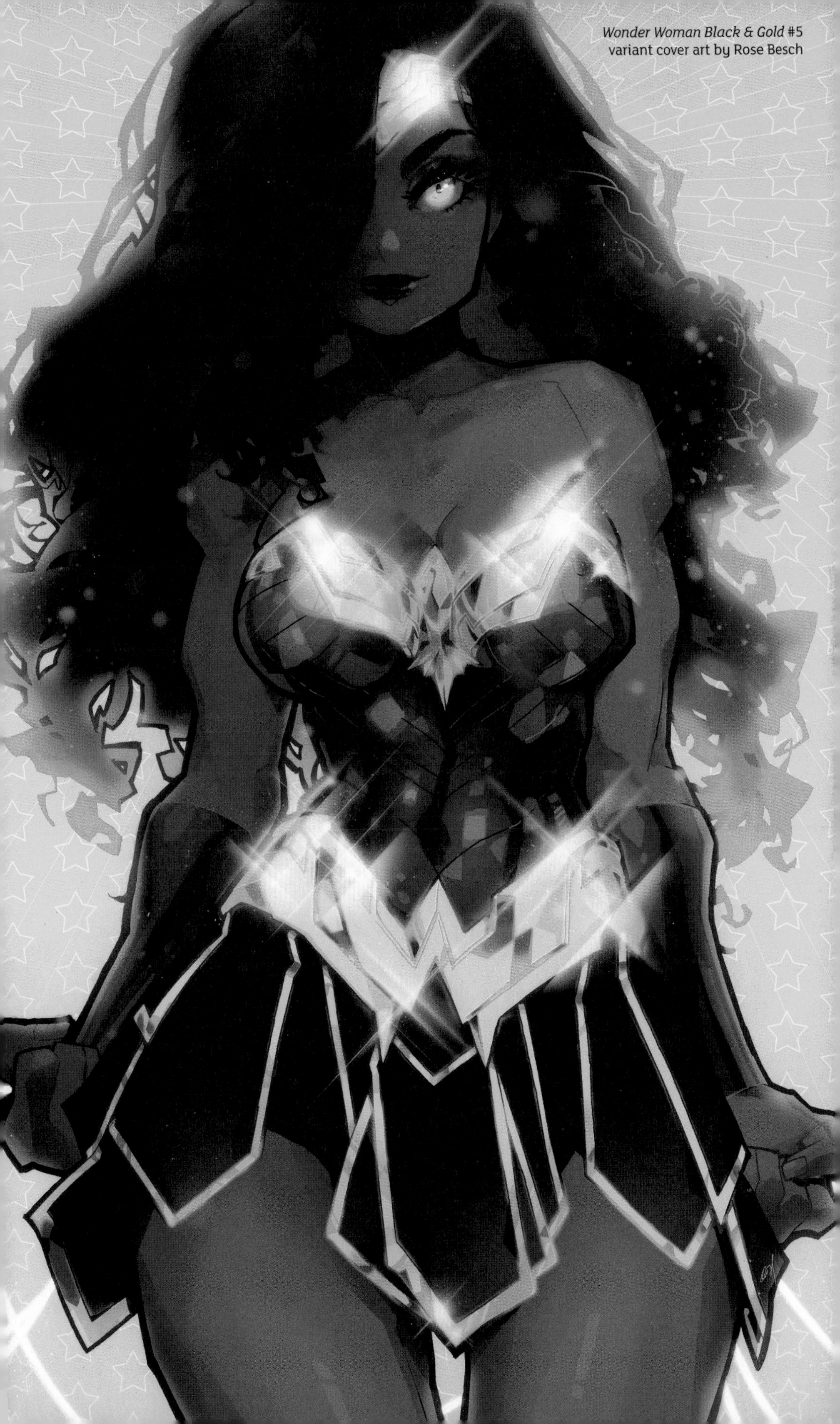

Wonder Woman Black & Gold #5
variant cover art by Rose Besch

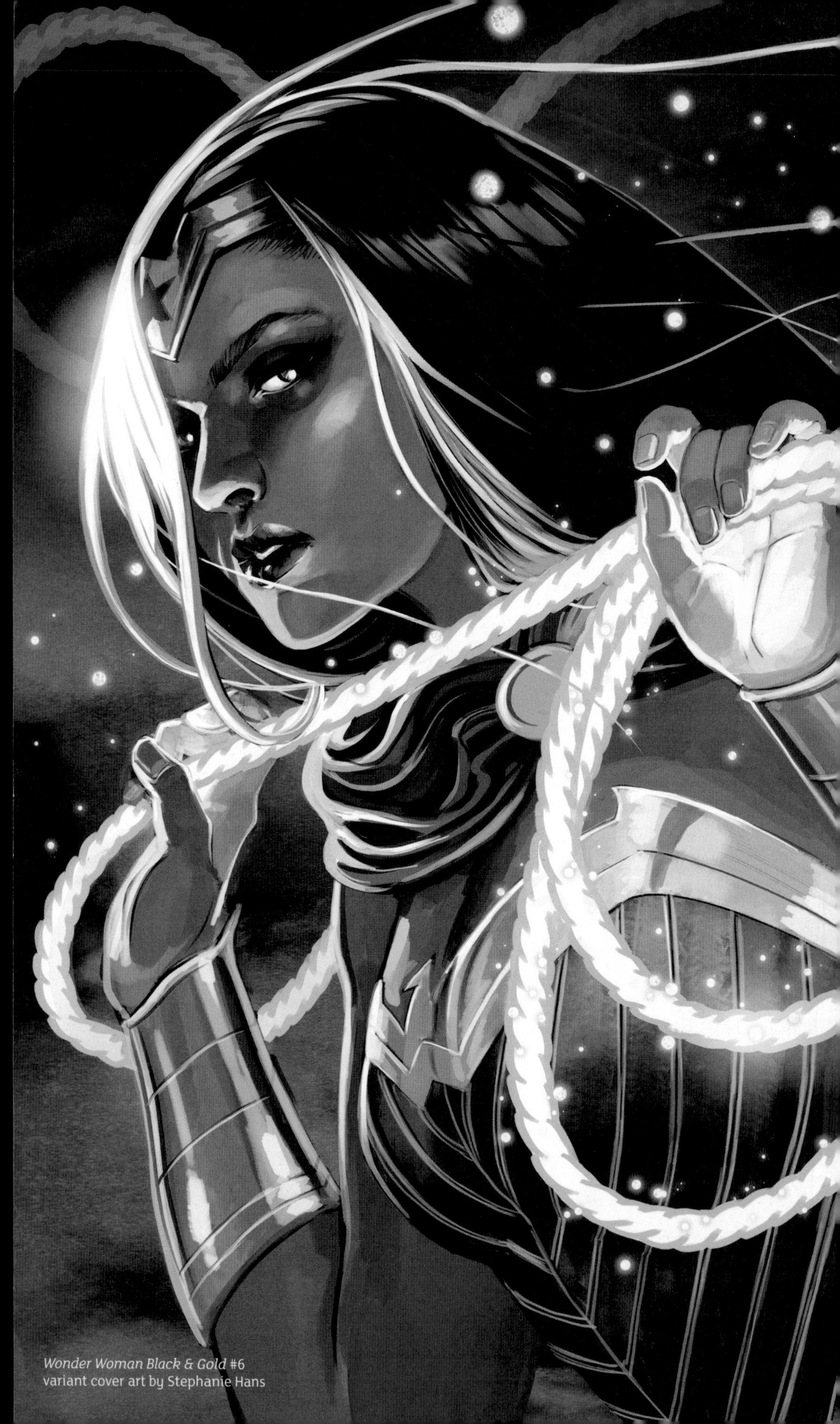

Wonder Woman Black & Gold #6
variant cover art by Stephanie Hans

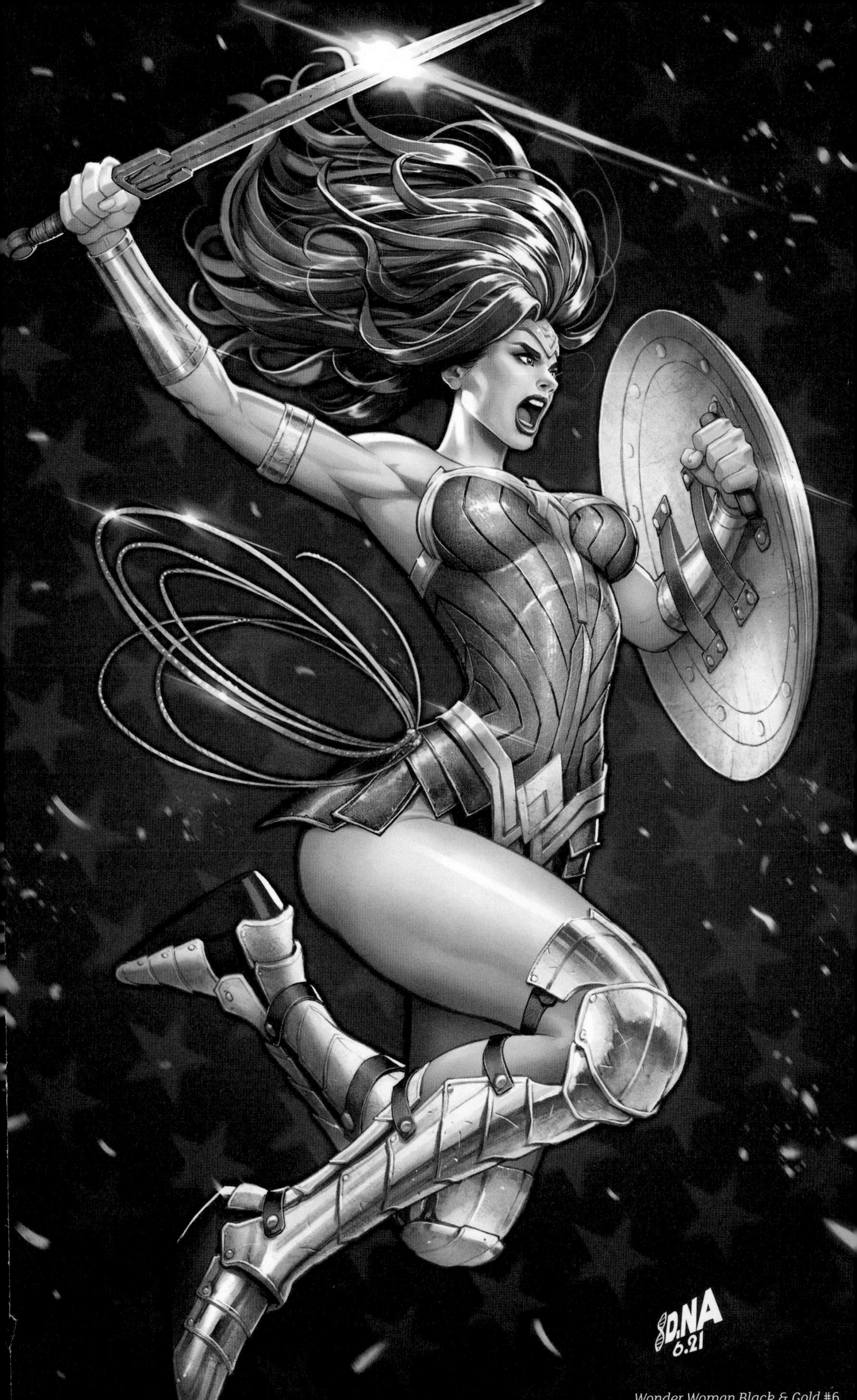
D.NA
6.21

Wonder Woman Black & Gold #6
variant cover art by David Nakayama

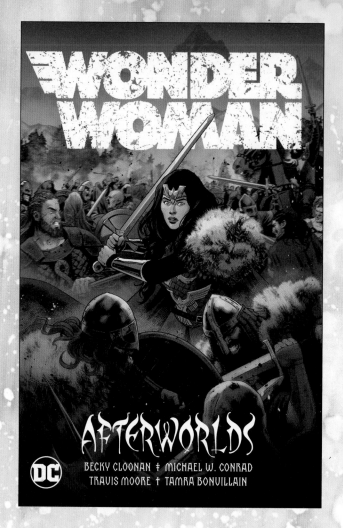